CURRICULUM IMPROVEMENT

NINTH EDITION

CURRICULUM IMPROVEMENT

Decision Making and Process

Ronald C. Doll
Professor Emeritus
The City University of New York
Professor-at-Large
Georgian Court College

Allyn and Bacon
Boston • London • Toronto • Sydney • Tokyo • Singapore

Series Editor: Virginia Lanigan
Editorial Assistant: Nihad Farooq
Marketing Manager: Kathy Hunter
Production Administrator: Susan Brown
Production Coordinator: Jeanne Yost
Editorial-Production Service: Lifland et al., Bookmakers
Cover Administrator: Suzanne Harbison
Composition Buyer: Linda Cox
Manufacturing Buyer: Megan Cochran

Copyright © 1996, 1992, 1989, 1986, 1982, 1978, 1974, 1970, 1964 by Allyn & Bacon
A Simon & Schuster Company
Needham Heights, MA 02194

Library of Congress Cataloging-in-Publication Data
Doll, Ronald C.
    Curriculum improvement :   decision making and process   /   Ronald C.
Doll. — 9th ed.
    p.   cm.
    Includes bibliographical references and indexes.
    ISBN 0–205–16457–9:
    1. Curriculum planning—United States.   2.   Education—United
States—Curricula.   3.   Curriculum change—United States.   I.   Title.
LB2806.15.D65 1995
375′.001′0973—dc20   94–48644
                                                                                                          CIP

Printed in the United States of America
10 9 8 7 6 5 4 3 2 1   99 98 97 96 95

For Ruth, whose faith in God, love for people, basic wisdom about human relationships, and realistic sense of the feasible have undergirded five decades of her husband's writing for publication.

CONTENTS

PREFACE

Since 1964, *Curriculum Improvement: Decision Making and Process* has been both a standard text and a practitioner's handbook on the essential elements of curriculum planning. So much has happened in the curriculum field, particularly during the last three decades, that continuing revision of the book has been necessary. Because the fundamental issues, problems, and concerns in curriculum planning have remained constant, however, the chapter themes, in general, have been preserved.

Beginning in the early 1960s with my polling of curriculum leaders about their major concerns, I have tried to keep in contact with both theoreticians and grassroots practitioners. The Ninth Edition continues to mirror the interests of people in the field. It provides basic understanding of new developments without neglecting older, tested principles and practices of intelligent planning.

The Eighth Edition was published in 1992. The present edition is appearing now because the rapid changes occurring in the curriculum field seem to demand prompt review and consideration.

Following the style of earlier editions, the Ninth Edition is divided into two parts. The first part deals with bases for deciding what the curriculum should be, and the second part pertains to the process of improving the curriculum. The distinction is between deciding on the nature of curriculum content and taking specific and practical steps to implement curriculum decisions. Interspersed throughout the chapters are descriptions of curriculum planning situations that call for careful analysis. Few of these situations were invented; the great majority originated in suggestions and anecdotes submitted by experienced practitioners. Several come from my own experience during numerous pleasant and satisfying years of service as teacher, department chairperson, principal, guidance director, curriculum coordinator, central office administrator, and consultant. Most of the situations, in addition to adding spice to classroom discussions, should provide opportunities to simulate solving the kinds of problems that occur commonly in the process of improving curricu-

lum. The situations yield to some of the familiar methods of case analysis. Instructors may wish to use the following questions to guide the analysis:

- What are the issues or problems in this situation?
- What pertinent facts do you know?
- What seems to have been left unsaid or obscure?
- What solutions or ameliorations can you suggest?
- What related issues or problems are involved in putting these solutions or
  ameliorations into effect?

Students need to be taught that in educational decision making, the facts are
never complete, else there would be no issue or problem.

The situations in the text are sometimes supplemented by student activities that call for thinking, observing, reading, and writing. I have included
these learning exercises because they are valuable in teaching certain subject
matter.

In each of the several revisions of this text, my position on curriculum
planning in the schools of a democratic society has been that curriculum plans
are most effective when they are made and applied from the bottom up rather
than from the top down. In the Ninth Edition, new discussions of the following topics emphasize this point of view:

- The importance of treating children and youth humanely, even affection-
  ately, without being suspected of pedophilic behavior
- The significance of achieving equity *with* excellence
- The need to control disruption and violence in the schools
- The need for both pupils and teachers to try harder to increase and im-
  prove learning
- The continuing need to improve the teaching of basic subject matter and
  academic content
- The need to redefine and enhance the roles of administrators and coordi-
  nators in improving teaching and learning
- The importance of limiting top-down control, especially by state educa-
  tion agencies and by federal authorities
- The mandate to deal with curriculum problems on the local front
- The trend toward increased empowerment of teachers and wider participa-
  tion by parents
- The call for restructuring local schools to meet local needs
- The need to deal appropriately with the morals/manners/ethics crisis
  among pupils

More specifically, the Ninth Edition emphasizes new ways of defining intelligence and achievement; the challenge that exists in educating increasingly diverse populations of pupils; the pressures on schools occasioned by social
and cultural shortcomings; the changes being made in evaluation schemata;

the need for collaboration among planners; the applications of technology; the effects of information and communication explosions; and the new challenges to educational leaders and their leadership. A totally new element of the Ninth Edition is a prologue that points to the need for curriculum planning in our era.

Curriculum Improvement: Decision Making and Process is used by thousands of college and university professors and their students in courses, seminars, and workshops in curriculum development and in educational supervision and administration. Practitioners of the helping professions have used the text as a handbook in schools, colleges, and elsewhere. Though the thrust of the book's discussion is directed toward improving elementary and secondary schools, many college and university faculties are finding it helpful in determining and monitoring the process of curriculum improvement at the post–high school level.

Sexist and other prejudicial expressions can easily find their way into a manuscript. I have tried to eliminate from my writing these and other marks of discrimination against any group or category of people. At the same time I have emphasized the importance of identifying and meeting the special needs of pupils with particular physical, mental, emotional, cultural, and environmental handicaps.

I wish to recognize the contributions of the following persons: my former students at New York University, Hunter College, Richmond College, and Georgian Court College, who have helped me find errors and overstatements in previous editions of the book; Virginia Lanigan, Education Editor, Allyn and Bacon; William C. Hedge, specialist in the technology of communication; Mary Meola, Reference Librarian, Georgian Court College, Lakewood, New Jersey; Nicole DePalma, former Editorial Assistant for Education, Allyn and Bacon; and the many reviewers who have critiqued the content of the various editions. Of this group, I extend special thanks to those reviewers who provided counsel during the preparation of the Ninth Edition: Dr. Noel T. Framer, Hood College; Dr. Larry Stuber, Purdue University; and William C. Thomas, California State University, Northridge.

R. C. D.

PROLOGUE

If Ever We Needed . . .

If ever we needed curriculum improvement in its fullest sense, it's now.

In April 1983, in its vaunted publication entitled *A Nation at Risk,* the bipartisan Commission on Excellence in Education warned that American schools were endangering the United States in a "tide of mediocrity."[1] The commission recommended that the high school curriculum include additional emphasis on the so-called new basics—English, mathematics, science, social studies, and computer science—and that novel programs highlight pupils' personal, educational, and occupational goals, as in the fine and performing arts and vocational education.

The commission said that pupils in the first eight grades should gain useful background in English language development and writing, as well as in computation and mathematical problem solving. Other elementary school subject matter should include experiences in science, social studies, and the arts. Pupils should begin foreign language study in elementary school and continue it for a minimum total of four to six years.

The commission, like a number of its contemporaries, touched on other matters relating to the operation of schools: graduation requirements, allocation of time to productive learning, textbook adoption, study skills, homework assignments, pupil behavior, lengths of the school year and the school day, special education, teacher effectiveness, educational leadership, fiscal support, and the federal government's role in education.

Publication of the report caused a flurry of discussion, and activity focused on what could be done to increase and improve pupil achievement. The term *school reform* (a term reminiscent of *prison reform* and, more recently, *health reform)* came into vogue. When considered item by item, few of the new proposals had anything direct and promising to do with improvement of school curriculum. Almost none of the proposals dealt with the malaise that schools

1

had been experiencing as a consequence of flaws in American social structure, which included a breakdown in the traditional values held by many American citizens, and the varied and sometimes unusual cultures that were crowding the American social scene.

Meanwhile, the American public at large had little understanding of what governors, state legislators, and federal officials were advocating. In many American homes, the term *curriculum* had little meaning. What parents knew, or thought they knew, about schools was whether the family's young pride and joy expressed at least some liking for school, could endure the mannerisms and behaviors of teachers, and seemed otherwise to be getting along. Actually, parents' knowledge of the curriculum was scarcely less limited than that of reformers who avoided facing curriculum issues by concentrating on electronic teaching aids, increasing the time pupils spent in school, discussing our losing competition with foreign business firms, urging school leaders to compete with one another for pupils, and advocating other modes of reform external to curriculum study. The failure of would-be reformers to confront curriculum problems is reminiscent of the title of a 1993 article: "School Reform: Big Pain, Little Gain."[2]

The actual "owner" of the curriculum is the child or youth who attends school. Adults sometimes pause long enough to wonder what influences, pleasures, and pressures youngsters feel. For generations, pupils have felt the effects of the experiences they have had in their schools. For generations, too, they have brought to school with them the support and encouragement—and also the deficiencies, injuries, troubles, and worries—that have originated in their home and community environments. As we near the end of this century, many school-related factors affecting youngsters remain similar to the factors that affected their grandparents and great-grandparents during the period between 1910 and 1940. This comment is less true of out-of-school factors. Children and youth of today have encountered and are now encountering more numerous and frequently different inhibitors of wholesome development. Many of these inhibitors damage directly what youngsters are able to accomplish.

In the chapters of this book, affirmative, encouraging comments will be made about the supportive contributions to pupils' learning made by homes, communities, and schools. However, inasmuch as the book deals with curriculum *improvement,* we must look immediately at some of the things that need improving: situations and conditions that impede learning and school achievement.

Some blocks to learning and achievement are readily identifiable. A survey of literature in psychology and education, together with reports by teachers and guidance counselors, confirms the fact that some impediments develop in homes and communities and others originate in schools. Sometimes, pupils are the best judges of what blocks their progress.

In their own language, pupils have discussed a variety of impediments that have their basis in homes, on the streets, and in communities generally. They speak for themselves:

"My mother shoots dope. Some nights she's so wild, my sister and I can't sleep."

"One or two nights a week, Mom and Pop start drinking. When they're drunk, no homework, no rest."

"I'm sad when my father's lost another good job."

"My folks never ask me about school. Of course they don't help me with my studies."

"We've been in this country five years. The people who got here first seem to let us alone."

"I watch television about 35 hours a week. I can find kids who watch more hours than that."

"The older kids in our neighborhood don't like school. They criticize me for going."

"My father and mother beat me up once or twice a week."

"I let myself into our house nearly every afternoon because my dad and mother are working."

"I haven't seen my mother since she left us. Home isn't the same these days."

"When it gets dark, people in the street start yelling, fighting, and selling crack."

"We never speak English at home."

"My gang makes me plan heists and look out for other gangs."

"My family and I have moved four times in the last five years."

"My folks are pushovers. They'll write fake excuses to keep me out of school anytime."

"I'm tired all the time."

"You know about the oldest profession. My mother's in it, right in our house."

"Both my father and my mother are away from home most of the time, trying to make big money."

"I'd like to have a father around. Mine isn't."

From these comments, one can infer immediately the kinds of problems these and other youngsters face in their personal lives, ranging from drug abuse to absentee fathers.

More blocks to pupil achievement originate in schools than teachers and administrators commonly realize. The following comments by learners suggest needs for real curriculum reform:

About misplaced emphasis: "I'm worn out. It's football, the school play, and clubs on top of the heavy studying my parents want me to do. Something has to give."

About uninterested teachers: "This year I have teachers who seem to care less than the teachers I used to know. Somehow the spirit is out of them."

About harassment: "My mind is too much on what happens in hallways and the cafeteria. If it isn't mean remarks, it's hands that get where they shouldn't be."

About bedlam in classrooms: "I think some teachers can't discipline anyone. How can you learn anything when kids are acting like animals?"

About closer counseling: "I wish I had someone to talk with about things other than marks, SATs, and so on. How about what we're afraid of and what we have to decide?"

About time for thinking: "I don't believe I know how to think. How can I learn about this?"

About violence: "I've learned a lot here in intermediate school. What I remember best is seeing kids with knives, teachers being pushed on the stairs, and visiting in the hospital the girl who was stabbed here in Room 205."

About the basics: "When I get my papers back in math and English, I don't feel so bad with D or F because other kids do worse in a whole marking period than I do."

About discouraging high achievers: "It really doesn't pay to succeed in school. Those who don't succeed are always trying to cut you down one way or another."

About prejudice: "I guess schools are filled with little groups. My group won't have anything to do with Orientals, Afro-Americans, Hispanics, Jews, or even strict Christians. I wonder if I ought to barge into another group."

About interruptions: "When during a school day can we ever be free of interruptions? You can't concentrate on anything very long."

About holding back: "Our classes are supposed to have a lot of bright students in them. The truth is we don't do any more than we absolutely have to."

About worthwhile knowledge: "Is it real? Is it a good backup for something we should learn later? Will we ever use it? I'd like to ask these questions about some of the things we have to learn."

About values and valuing: "No one helps us with what we ought to believe or do. We have nothing to guide us when we're up against a personal problem."

About newcomers: "Some of us are new to our school. Helping newcomers— wouldn't that make a good project?"

About boredom: "If someone should ask you what school is like, just say, 'Bring your workbook, fill the blanks, memorize these ten points, just get bored'."

About incoordination: "Every kid in my classrooms seems to be doing something different. Why can't we get together to do worthwhile things?"

Naturally, lists of complaints like these bear the marks of the amateur observer. Nonetheless, they suggest the breadth of the need for curriculum improvement in our time.

We need not be surprised that the number of complaints about home and community equals or surpasses the number of complaints about schooling itself. In homes and communities, we see widespread use of illegal drugs, alcoholism among youth, overuse of television, child abuse, a high incidence of divorce, turmoil in city streets, an increase in crime, prevalence of two-career households, changing populations, dysfunctional home life, lack of community interest and support, and migrant families. At the same time, schools have been giving confused signals about what is worth learning and have other shortcomings that will be discussed subsequently in this book.

The complaints about home and community do not reveal the circumstances and conditions that underlie them; for example, increased incidence of sexual abuse, deprecation of hard work, absence of common agreement about sets of virtues and values, a disposition toward violence, and a lack of love. Meanwhile, the complaints about schools and schooling frequently reflect complaints about home and community life. Clearly, malaise that damages American society and culture has come into the schools. If laypeople in our communities exhibit don't-care attitudes about the school achievements of their children and if careless teachers, themselves sometimes reared in home environments that bespeak neglect, are assigned to teach youngsters who are unwilling to learn, tragic results are assured. Pupils refuse to work, conscientious teachers become discouraged with non-learners, and parents don't bother to cooperate with teachers and schools.

The two lists, considered together, raise a pressing question: Will our schools be more readily improved by actions taken by people of power who operate outside school systems or by actions taken by people who work inside these systems? The former group of actors includes governors, commissioners of education and their staffs, and business leaders. In the latter group are teachers, local school administrators, parents, pupils, and a miscellany of interested community citizens. Perhaps there's a better question: How can all willing contributors, united in purpose, participate in the onerous task of improving the curriculum? This question admits the contributions of those politicians who are inclined to spend less time blaming the schools for their failures and more time campaigning for constructive moral and ethical behaviors and wholesome family living. It admits professional educators with the knowledge and insight to make a difference in what is planned, taught, and learned in schools. It admits leaders in business and industry whose power and access to wealth can support worthy school programs, some of which relate to supplementary education now being provided in the workplace. The question admits further the prospect of carefully guided curriculum planning and evaluation at the community level, with all groups of local participants providing the kinds of input that will be discussed in Chapter 9 of this book.

When one inspects the lists of pupil complaints, one can find in them no suggestion of central, consistent purposing. Several years ago, a list of goals to be reached by the year 2000 was projected by the National Goals Panel. These goals, little known by school administrators and teachers, focus on our national interest in business competition with other nations and on the requisite intellectual and financial health of American corporations. We should have a clearly defined, education-related set of goals leveled somewhere between the above-mentioned goals and the amateurish goals sometimes set by individual school systems. National and state political leaders, working in conjunction with the National Education Standards and Improvement Council established by law in 1994, could, if they would, cooperate in having usable goals accepted by professionals and non-professionals.

The malaise that has come into the schools from the society "out there" has increased the importance of teaching moral values and of changing pupils' attitudes as recognized parts of the curriculum. Objections to this idea are raised by people who are afraid that the morals and ethics taught will come straight from organized religion. The fear of schools' being "contaminated" by religion can be relieved by teaching those values and attitudes that have become universals in civilized societies, regardless of time, place, or theological views. For example, the conservative actor Tom Selleck and the liberal ex-Congresswoman Barbara Jordan have worked with others in the Character Counts Coalition to identify and promote a number of core values: trustworthiness, respect, responsibility, justice and fairness, caring, and civil virtue. When a society has seriously declined, such values become essentials. When schools lose their ability to control pupils sensibly and humanely, to teach them responsibility and diligence, and to convince them of the importance of learning useful subject matter, they need reform that begins with correcting beliefs, attitudes, and standards. The teaching of hard subject matter, which many people think is the only worthwhile function of a school, can occur only if learners have the will and the spirit to work and study. Thus valuing comes before intellectualizing. Trying to interrelate the two suggests one reason that curriculum planning is so complex.

Chapter 1 through 11 in this book are intended to provide information and understanding concerning ways in which decisions about the curriculum can be made and also concerning what processes can be used in stimulating and assuring improvement. The first six chapters tell of essentials of decision making:

Chapter 1: Heed what other people have learned about improving the curriculum, and give thought to the educational philosophies available to curriculum planners.
Chapter 2: Master knowledge and understanding of pupils as learners, and of the ways in which they learn.
Chapter 3: Take into account the full impact of the society and the cultures surrounding each school on what happens to the people, plans, and progress in that particular school.
Chapter 4: Concentrate on what is to be learned, selected from a range of possibilities.

Chapter 5: Consider how the curriculum, or any part of it, is to be designed, so that the design is sensible and operable.

Chapter 6: Think of how all or some of the curriculum is to be assessed so that its worth or lack of it becomes evident.

These hard tasks, if they are to be well performed, need to be accomplished through a process that takes the following into account:

- Details of the improvement process
- Ways of planning that get results
- Enlisting the right people to help
- Passing the word about the worth of what is planned
- Leading people intelligently

These matters are discussed in the five concluding chapters of the book.

This book provides some bottom-line messages:

1. American schools have never been as good as they might have been.
2. Today, considering the handicaps under which they work, our schools are not as deficient as the media and politicians have often declared them to be.
3. Nonetheless, pupils' literacy remains at low levels, their general knowledge continues to be weak, and their mastery of the subject curriculum is only partial.
4. Although schools have not declined precipitously, they are struggling against an unprecedented collection of difficulties.
5. The most potent difficulties originate in American society at large, with its new populations, its disdain of hard work, its confused moral and ethical standards, its toleration of violence and crudity, and its lowered expectations.
6. As educators, we need to do better, perhaps by organizing and operating schools differently.
7. In this competitive world, we face both obvious and hidden barriers that are taller and wider than the barriers we have previously encountered.

Perhaps Carl Henry, in his correspondence with the author, has defined best the condition of many of our youngsters and adults: "intellectually uncapped, morally unzipped, and volitionally uncurbed." Although schools alone cannot remedy this condition, they can be expected to do their part. Those of us with responsible assignments have an unusual opportunity to serve people better than we have served them in the past.

Indeed, if ever we needed curriculum improvement in its fullest sense, it's now.

ENDNOTES

1. Commission on Excellence in Education, *A Nation at Risk* (Washington, DC: Superintendent of Documents, U.S. Government Printing Office, 1983).

2. See the November 29, 1993 issue of *Fortune,* 130 et seq.

DECISION MAKING IN
CURRICULUM IMPROVEMENT

1

HISTORICAL AND PHILOSOPHICAL FOUNDATIONS OF CURRICULUM DECISION MAKING

As long as there have been schools, there has been an obvious need to improve them. Thousands of people have expended time, energy, and money in efforts to make and carry out decisions about how to effect genuine improvement. In the mode of Charles Dickens, these people have often felt that they were living simultaneously in the best of times and the worst of times. Despite the discouraging difficulties they have sometimes encountered, they have, by fits and starts, improved the quality of schooling in this and other countries. What has been done in the past can be done even more insightfully and consistently in the future.

This book, which deals with the decision making and process needed to improve the curriculum of the school, thus begins in a spirit of optimism. Curriculum planners in elementary and secondary schools have learned much by hard experience, especially from the 1920s to the present, about what decisions and actions produce results. In the process, they have often found curriculum planning to be stimulating and enjoyable, the most enlightening of professional activities.

Early in the 1990s, experienced curriculum planners, looking back over a half-century of service in elementary and secondary schools, offered several suggestions to guide men and women new to the field. These suggestions should provide a sense of what it means to plan the curriculum intelligently.[1] As you read this book and experience the planning enterprise yourself, you will develop additional insights.

1. Remember that improvement that counts occurs in *people.* Improvements in institutions, structures, and materials are almost without worth unless they help people improve.

2. Starting small in your planning usually works better than starting in a grandiose manner.
3. The timing of your planning makes a great deal of difference. Strive for timing that receives the commendation "just right" rather than the condemnation "too early" or "too late."
4. Expect that as you plan you will be surrounded by people—especially bright people from outside your specialty—who will try to persuade you that a quick fix or an irrelevant scheme will do what needs to be done. Speak to them courteously, but regard them with a jaundiced eye.
5. If you can make an old, entrenched program or set of practices work by revising it, revise it and use it again.
6. It's possible, however, that only an entirely new program or set of practices will do. If so, don't be afraid to be a pioneer.
7. Remember that several minds, carefully marshalled to a task, can usually produce better results than the mind of one individual.
8. Don't worry about who will receive credit for what is done. Put your emphasis on *what* is done rather than on who does it.
9. Be aware that money helps, but that sometimes you can do much with limited financial resources.
10. Because the wisest planning is usually grounded in curriculum history, become acquainted with that history. It should prevent you from making some of the foolish mistakes that have burdened the past.

You already know that the curriculum represents only a part of the total organism we call the school. Both the curriculum and the body or organism it inhabits live and function. Fundamentally, they do so because they involve living, developing, changing people. These people make both the school and its curriculum what they are. From people—pupils, teachers, administrators, educational specialists, counselors, librarians, nurses, secretaries, custodians, parents, and others—the school derives its spirit and uniqueness, and from them the curriculum gets its potential for conditioning learning.

Within the complex that is the school, the curriculum should never be disregarded. During the past two centuries in the United States, the curriculum has been placed front and center in attempts to answer these and other crucial questions about elementary and secondary education in a free society.

- Who *should* be educated? Who *can* be educated?
- What kinds of educational experiences should be offered to given groups of learners?
- How much can our nation afford to spend for education?
- Are the schools as good as they used to be? If not, why not?
- To what extent should education be made uniform within community, region, state, and nation?
- How can the needs of our great variety of individual learners be met?

Some people have said, "The questions are too hard to answer, so let's not spend time discussing them. Once the curriculum is established in a school, let's not try to change it."

Harold Benjamin wrote in 1939 about the folly in this viewpoint. In his *Saber-Tooth Curriculum,* he described an imaginary school established in paleolithic times to teach fish-grabbing, tiger-scaring, and horse-clubbing. These were the means by which people met their basic needs for food, protection, and clothing. When glacial drift changed the conditions under which people lived, the paleolithic curriculum remained as it had been. The result was sterile, unproductive schooling. Experience shows that because time moves on and circumstances differ, standing still leads to disaster. We cannot afford to give up the effort to make curriculum timely, appropriate, and maximally effective in increasing and improving learning.

THE MEANING OF CURRICULUM

What *is* the curriculum of a school? It has been said that the casual answer to this question depends on where one stands within or relative to the education system or hierarchy. The underinformed curriculum worker or administrative official in charge of curriculum development may say, "It's a catalog or compendium of the experiences pupils should have under the direction of the school." Usually this means preplanned, written subject matter content that the school should teach. To the classroom teacher, the curriculum is often a statement of what the school authorities, the state government, or someone or some group outside the classroom requires the teacher to teach. The youngster in school may put it more simply: "It's what I'm to learn to please the teacher so I can move on to face other teachers and the disagreeable life they make for me."

Most literate adults outside the school environment think they know what the curriculum of their favorite school really is. An informal poll (conducted by the author) of beliefs about the meaning of the word *curriculum* reveals how disparate people's beliefs actually are. To different people, the curriculum represents what is taught; how it is taught; materials for teachers; materials for pupils; and youngsters' experiences in school and out. (Few people in the United States think the curriculum is a document distributed and mandated by a government, state or federal.)

Other people believe they can offer more sophisticated definitions. To some, the curriculum is the accumulated tradition of organized knowledge found in school and college subjects. To others, it consists of modes of thinking and inquiring about the phenomena of our world. To still others, it represents something pervasive and enduring: the collected experiences of the race. People who have wanted to routinize education have used catch phrases like the following to delimit the meaning of curriculum: *carefully guided, preselected experiences; concrete plans for learning; ends or outcomes of being educated;* and *systems for achieving educational production.*

A Continuing Argument

Scholars in the curriculum field have sometimes become lost in arguments about the semantics of curriculum definitions. A definition commonly used during the 1930s and 1940s was "the curriculum of a school is all the experiences that pupils have under the guidance of that school." A counter definition, generally considered to be too broad, was "a child's curriculum in a given day of his life is all that he experiences from the moment of waking to the moment of falling asleep."

The former definition, which survives in much of educational literature, has been modified to read "the curriculum of a school is the engagements that pupils have under the auspices of that school." The term *engagements* is thought to be more accurate than *experiences* because observers can see pupils engaging in educational activities, whereas they cannot see them experiencing the activities. Accordingly, Gordon N. Mackenzie has defined the curriculum as "the learner's engagements with various aspects of the environment which have been planned under the direction of the school."[2] More recently, the term *auspices* has been considered to be more accurate than either *guidance* or *direction* because there is a definite limit to the supervision or control that a school can exercise over the activities of the pupils who attend it. The word *auspices* suggests that the school offers general patronage or sponsorship of the experiences or engagements pupils have within it, without attempting to plan every experience.

Must, in fact, every curriculum experience or engagement be a planned experience? Many attempts at defining curriculum have foundered on this question. Pangs of conscience about what the schools should be planning in order to fulfill their distinctive mission have caused the creation of convoluted definitions like this one: The curriculum is "the planned and guided learning experiences and intended learning outcomes, formulated through the systematic reconstruction of knowledge and experience, under the auspices of the school, for the learner's continuous and willful growth in personal-social competence."[3]

The Curriculum, Both Planned and Unplanned

It is certainly true that every school has a planned, formal, acknowledged curriculum and also an unplanned, informal, or hidden one. The planned curriculum embraces content usually categorized within subjects and subject fields. The unplanned curriculum includes such varied experiences or engagements as teasing boys, pinching girls, advancing oneself inconsiderately in the cafeteria line, learning to like history, developing a prejudice against an ethnic group, protecting one's front teeth from being pushed down hard on drinking fountains, finding new ways to beat the system, and resisting pressure to smoke marijuana.[4] For children and youth today, these and similar informal experiences or engagements are sometimes the most memorable ones in their school careers. They are discussed at family dinner tables, and they obviously color parents' and other community citizens' views of the school. Every school administrator in the United States is held responsible for both the formal and the informal experiences or engagements that pupils have in his or her school.

One of the most memorable experiences of the author's years as an elementary school pupil constituted an informal lesson in physics and physiology. On a morning when the temperature hovered just above zero degrees Fahrenheit, one of the pupils put his tongue on the steel railing leading from the ground level to the first floor entrance of the school building. Why the youngster could not remove his tongue from the railing, why water was used in the removal process, and how the tongue had been affected became discussion topics, all previously unplanned, in classrooms throughout the school building.

The Search for a Workable Definition

A workable definition of the curriculum is the following: *The curriculum of a school is the formal and informal content and process by which learners gain knowledge and understanding, develop skills, and alter attitudes, appreciations, and values under the auspices of that school.* This definition includes both formal and informal aspects of schooling, what one learns (content) and how one learns (process), and outcomes in the forms of knowledge, understanding, skills, attitudes, appreciations, and values. The curriculum, whether planned, unplanned, or hidden, comes into existence under the auspices or general sponsorship of the school, which is able to legislate and control it only in part. The definition is necessarily broad.

The position taken in this book is that the curriculum, viewed in this way, is improvable, within limits, in both its formal and its informal aspects. That which is formally planned and presumably observable in the engagements of pupils can be evaluated and improved. Certain actions can also be taken to improve informal aspects of schooling. Whichever informal aspects are deemed constructive can be modified, reinforced, and supported. Pupil engagements that are considered harmful can sometimes be eliminated or reduced in number or potency. But the "hidden, or unstudied," curriculum, as it is now called in the literature, frequently cannot be dealt with directly. Fundamentally, the hidden curriculum is the pupil's own curriculum, which he or she uses to cope with the school's bureaucratic organization and arrangements and with his or her social relationships within the school. The hidden curriculum represents the realm of unofficial opinion and unexpressed feelings, in much the same way that a hidden agenda represents an unspoken and sometimes bothersome discussion theme in a meeting of adults. A common feature of the hidden curriculum today is the fear children feel in schools where violence reigns.

Another is the feeling of isolation gifted children experience in a school culture in which other children are asking, "Why are you so smart? Why are you always doing what the teacher tells us to?" Minorities of all kinds feel the stigma of simply being what they are.

Another, different discussion has developed among theorists in their attempts to distinguish between curriculum and instruction. Some theorists have tried to make one a subsystem of the other. Still others think of curriculum and instruction as having about equal importance in the overall educational scheme. They consider the curriculum to be the body of subject matter content to be taught, and instruction to consist of carefully organized plans for teaching curriculum content. This author concurs in general with the latter view.[5]

One of the characteristics of failed curriculum plans and programs has been, as we have seen, a disregard of history. An ahistorical attitude can lead planners to imagine that they have invented the curriculum wheel. Before one begins to plan a curriculum, one needs to know what other people with-perhaps equally good intentions have done to meet the same kind of challenge in the past—hence the historical detail in the next sections of this chapter.

THE UNDERPINNINGS: CURRICULUM CHANGE IN EARLY AMERICA

In social and educational movements, patterns of progress are often set by early events. During the initial years of curriculum reform in the United States, change occurred slowly, but it frequently proved to be deep and enduring.[6] The basic curriculum was developed by English-speaking peoples who settled along the Atlantic seaboard. When the British established colonies in America between 1607 and 1733, they transplanted three major types of education from Europe: the church-state type, found in New England; the parochial school type, established in Catholic Maryland and Protestant Pennsylvania; and both private and charity education, commonplace in certain southern colonies, notably in Virginia. Religion dominated all three types but in quite different ways. In New England, church and state served a common purpose: to prepare a ministry capable of propagating the true faith and to educate lay persons in reading and interpreting the Bible, the sure foundation of the faith. In the middle colonies, the prevailing branches of Christianity, whether Protestant or Catholic, founded their own schools to educate children in religion and the fundamentals of literacy. In the South, those who, like Washington, had sufficient means sent their children to private schools oriented to the classics and religion, and those who lacked means shared some prospect of placing their children in charity schools to be trained for apprenticeships. Education everywhere in the colonies was designed chiefly for boys, and the primary method of learning was memorization. The curriculum for children of the privileged was heavy in intellectual studies. Practical and artistic subjects, which were said to "educate the senses," were considered suitable for training the servant class and entertaining young ladies who, because of their sex, could not then realistically aspire to leadership roles. Boys of the upper classes obtained their basic education in a dame school (a school of reading and writing) and their secondary education in the Latin grammar school (a New England institution that had its counterpart in the other colonies). Here, Latin, Greek, the catechism, the Bible, and arithmetic were the chief subjects.

Evident Need for Change

During the mid-eighteenth century, political, economic, and social changes were occurring rapidly enough to bring about at least a minor transformation of the curriculum. Commerce and trade were increasing, and students had not been prepared to engage in them. People were moving away from their original settlements, pioneer life on the frontier was beginning, urban growth was flourishing, and religion was becoming a less powerful force in society. The educational system responded by establishing district schools instead of town schools, by combining reading and writing schools into a new unit called "the school of the three Rs," and by establishing English grammar schools and academies to replace the inflexible Latin grammar school. Meanwhile, private tutors were teaching vocational subjects such as navigation, surveying, and bookkeeping. Franklin's Academy developed a new concept of schooling, extending the traditional list of subjects to include modern foreign languages and natural science, the content of which was deemed useful in educating enlightened men of affairs.

The post-Revolutionary period brought several developments that influenced anew the curricula of American schools. The Ordinance of 1785 set aside land for schools in each township in the new West, and as people moved into the territories they brought with them a dominant pattern of schooling, chiefly that of the New England district school, thus providing the basis for eventual establishment of the free public school. The 1820s and the 1830s were a time of political consciousness, when U.S. statesmen became convinced that children should be educated to love their country and to perpetuate its ideals. In order for education to reach enough children to have a favorable effect on national welfare, the masses would have to be educated. Finally, though many statesmen were espousing the principle without comprehending its full meaning, the people of a democracy were seen as having a right to education, that they might prepare themselves to their own personal advantage.

These startling ideas, so foreign to the European heritage of education for the privileged only, eventually caused curriculum reform. Horace Mann, Henry Barnard, and others spearheaded the drive toward establishment of common, tax-supported schools in which the curriculum would theoretically accommodate the abilities and interests of all learners. By 1860, arithmetic, algebra, geometry, ancient history, geography, and English grammar were being accepted by colleges as subjects that partially fulfilled entrance requirements. The curriculum for girls, who were now being admitted much more freely to schooling, was differentiated to include music, painting, and dancing. Academies prepared, in practical subjects, those pupils who would not go to college; eventually, these academies began to give way to public high schools.

A Unique System of Education

By the mid-nineteenth century, at least some Americans had an educational ladder on which they could climb from primary education to the university level. By 1860, New England had public elementary schools that taught, at primary grade level, reading, spelling, writing, and arithmetic; at intermediate grade level, reading, arithmetic, geography, spelling, writing, and grammar; and in the "grammar school," advanced reading, advanced arithmetic, elementary algebra, spelling, word analysis, penmanship, grammar, composition, declamation, geography, United States history, and general history. (The antiquated label *grammar schools* is still used for elementary schools in many U.S. communities.)

The high school program in New England in 1860 included United States history, ancient history, natural philosophy (elements of chemistry and botany), Latin, advanced algebra, geometry, bookkeeping, and surveying. Curriculum development, by which changes in society were reflected in the addition of school subjects, was under way.

Curriculum Movements from 1860 to 1995

As a nation matures and ages, careful study of its history can suggest movements that have dominated its development. Within the period from 1860 to 1995, a half-dozen movements affecting curriculum change and improvement in the elementary and secondary schools of the United States became clearly identifiable. Three of these movements relate to what the curriculum can and should be:

1. The movement to establish, organize, and reorganize schools and school programs
2. The movement to open, augment, and broaden the curriculum
3. The movement to reduce, contract, concentrate, and tighten the curriculum

Three additional movements identify bases of curriculum planning. These bases are discussed in Chapters 2, 3, and 4 of this book.

4. The movement to focus on children and youth as learners, and on the ways they learn

5. The movement to focus on the problems and requirements of society and the culture

6. The movement to focus on subject matter and pupils' success in learning it

Some of the events that have contributed to each of the six movements are specified below.

1. The Movement to Establish, Organize, and Reorganize Schools and School Programs

1860–1890

The struggle to establish free public schools was ongoing. The arrival of immigrants and the doubling of the population created demands for new and broader types of schooling.

Technical and commercial high schools were organized separately from academic high schools.

In 1873, the first public school kindergarten was opened in St. Louis.

In 1874, the famous Kalamazoo decision legalized establishment of high schools at public expense.

In 1880, the first manual training high school was founded in St. Louis.

In 1886, the first high school specifically for teaching cooking and sewing was established in Toledo.

1890–1920

J. F. Herbart's view of apperception, which was formulated in five steps (preparation, presentation, comparison and abstraction, generalization, and application), encouraged correlation of subject matter, especially in elementary schools.

In 1895, the Committee of Ten on Secondary School Studies said that all subjects taught equally well for equal periods of time had equal educational value and suggested that four programs of study be developed in high schools: the Classical, the Scientific, the Modern Language, and the English.

In 1895, the Committee of Fifteen on Elementary Education urged concentration and correlation of subjects taught in elementary schools.

The first junior high schools were created.

In 1918, the Committee on Reorganization of Secondary Education enunciated the famous Seven Cardinal Principles of Secondary Education.

1920–1970   Organizational plans for rearranging uses of pupils'
                         time appeared. There were calls for making schools
                         more humane, for individualizing instruction, and for
                         nongrading to break children's lockstep through the
                         schools, thus removing another impediment to chil-
                         dren's development.
                            Comprehensive high schools were organized to uni-
                         fy and coordinate secondary education.
                            For economic reasons, some communities refused
                         to authorize construction of additional school build-
                         ings. Pupil population in some schools changed as
                         a consequence of the desegregation movement and
                         busing.

1970–1985   Public schools shrank in size as the population in
                         some sections of some communities declined.
                            Very early childhood education was begun in a lim-
                         ited number of school districts.
                            To a degree, acceptance of mainstreaming ended
                         isolation or separation of several categories of disadvan-
                         taged children.
                            A drive to add "new" subject matter to the curricu-
                         lum brought to the schools programs in drug, alcohol,
                         and AIDS education, as well as other externally imposed
                         special programs.
                            The organization of schools and school programs
                         continued to express the U.S. policy of providing the
                         best possible education for nearly all the children of all
                         the people.

1985–1995   Slowly, the enrollment of elementary and secondary
                         schools increased as the children of the "baby boomer
                         generation" continued to enter the schools.
                            Industrial firms and other businesses contributed to
                         education in varied ways. A notable example is Walter
                         Annenberg's pledge of a half-billion dollars to schools
                         and school systems.
                            The idea of organizing Total Quality Schools entered
                         the United States from other countries such as Japan.
                            The ills of education were given a less discouraging
                         look, as in the Sandia Report which was issued under the
                         auspices of Perspectives on Education in America.
                            The term *restructuring* came to include among its
                         meanings the effort to assure smooth transition of
                         youngsters from school to work.

2. The Movement to Open, Augment, and Broaden the Curriculum

1860–1890

The elementary school curriculum broadened and became somewhat less dedicated to rote memorization. The oral instruction and object teaching proposed by J. H. Pestalozzi took root in the United States. Programs in oral language and mental arithmetic augmented the curriculum.

The content of high school subjects was broadened to include the arithmetic of business, the English of business, American literature, general science, and family care.

Educational experiments included those of Francis Parker in breaking down barriers among subjects; of Batavia, New York, in providing remedial instruction; and of Santa Barbara, California, in preparing parallel courses of study.

1890–1920

In 1899, the Committee on College Entrance Requirements approved "restricted election of subjects by high school pupils, early completion of high school programs by gifted pupils, acceptance of a year's work in any subject as counting toward college entrance, and extension of the high school program to six years, including the seventh grade." The report of this committee marked the beginning of the unit system, which dominates the crediting of courses.

As the number of one-room elementary schools decreased, the curriculum offerings of larger schools with better facilities broadened.

1920–1970

The Eight Year Study was an exciting, if little-heeded, investigation into the effects of loosening the secondary school curriculum.

Combinations of subjects—e.g., general science and social studies—increased in popularity among teachers and administrators.

Life-adjustment education was introduced by some secondary schools to improve the social, community, and work-centered relationships of young people.

Teachers' dissatisfaction with having to rely only on textbooks was overcome in part by an increase in commercially developed and locally prepared instructional materials.

The well-publicized Progressive Education movement began to flourish.

1970–1985   Very early childhood education was thought to deserve particular emphasis because of educators' conviction that early education could facilitate children's later learning.

Underprivileged and minority children became a focus of renewed attention.

"Open schooling" enjoyed temporary popularity in some school districts.

1985–1995   Active, experiential learning (à la John Dewey) was given a name: *authentic learning.*

New attention was accorded the acquisition of real-life language skills. Also, practice in writing increased.

Values education and character education, as seen from a number of vantage points, became more common.

Use of computers and other technical devices was promoted as a way of augmenting learning.

Out of despair concerning the unwillingness of youngsters to learn, there developed the idea of permitting pupils to leave school before graduation with a promise that they could return at almost any time in the future.

3. The Movement to Reduce, Contract, Concentrate, and Tighten the Curriculum

1860–1890   Though this was an era of expansion in elementary and secondary education, it was also a time in which the expenditures for education were very limited, buildings and facilities were sparse, and curriculum offerings were relatively few.

1890–1920   So much money was needed for other kinds of expansion that elementary and secondary education was placed low on the list of causes to be supported. High schools frequently included only the ninth and tenth grades. Elementary education beyond the routine was an exception.

1920–1970   Well-advertised plans for improving teaching and learning (e.g., the project method, the Dalton Plan, the Winnetka Plan, ability grouping, and the activity program) were unknown in the many school districts with pared budgets and limited staffing.

Changes in birth rates affected schools' ability to adopt new programs and to increase teaching staffs.

Attacks on schools resulted from revelations that mathematics and the sciences were not being taught as thoroughly to our widely diverse school populations as they were in other nations where teaching was more rigorous.

1970–1985

Competency-based education, test-based instructional management, and close inspection of teachers' work contributed to constriction of imaginative planning. Curriculum improvement was also discouraged by other factors, such as reductions in the number of specialists in schools, attempts to use various systems approaches in solving educational problems, and the pressures applied by ultraconservative thinkers and authors.

The temper of the times brought about a retreat to "the basics," commonly considered to be only the three Rs. The fine arts, music, and other fields lost some of their former support.

The health of the curriculum was sometimes affected adversely by rapid turnover of top school officials, by a tendency to permit the results of minimum skills testing to determine the curriculum, by an all-too-frequent lack of curriculum balance, and by a general drift toward curriculum chaos.

1985–1995

When helping youngsters feel good about themselves seemed less productive of school achievement than expected, a thrust toward "standards" and toward reemphasizing basics ensued.

Tests that measured "essential" subject matter at the expense of alleged frills sometimes became the curriculum to which teachers taught.

The limited nature of the national goals known as America 2000 had some effect in narrowing the curriculum in those schools in which America 2000 was known.

Implementation and extension of America 2000 was undertaken through establishment of three federal commissions/committees in 1994.

Within the preceding discussion and listings, you have probably identified terms and ideas with which you are unfamiliar. Most of them reappear with explanations in the remaining chapters of the book.

The three additional movements that are reported below center on so-called foundations of curriculum planning: learners and learning, social and cultural forces, and subject matter.

4. The Movement to Focus on Children and Youth as Learners, and on the Ways They Learn

1860–1890	Children in general and pupils in particular were thought of as vessels to be filled, as blank chalkboards to be written upon, as collections of persons to be made uniform. Therefore, the function of schools was to offer a standard curriculum to be learned without modification or variation.
1890–1920	In 1896, at the University of Chicago John Dewey founded his Laboratory School, which had special concern for the interests and purposes of learners. In 1911, the Committee on the Economy of Time in Education advocated child centeredness in learning. Partly as a consequence of the work of this committee, art, music, handicrafts, and health education became recognized subjects in elementary and secondary schools. Though simple and limited studies of learning were increasing, they had little influence on educational practice.
1920–1970	Ways of raising pupil interest levels and of providing special education for the gifted claimed the attention of some parents and teachers. Psychologists and social workers were employed as specialists in school systems. Guidance programs, work experience, functional reading, and other innovations brought children's preferences and needs into focus. Numerous different pupil-evaluation instruments were developed.
1970–1985	Interdisciplinary studies of children increased the availability of information about child growth and development. Psychomotor and affective education (especially education in moral values) became somewhat more prominent. Discipline was loosening seriously in homes, with a consequent effect on discipline in schools.

1985–1995   The need for internal bonding (constructive affiliation) of teachers, pupils, and parents working together in individual schools became more evident.

Alternatives to tracking were sought because competition, as opposed to cooperation, had increased among pupils, sometimes to their detriment.

Terms like *developmental appropriateness,* which applies to young children, and *empowerment,* which applies to older ones, began to have meaning in education.

5. The Movement to Focus on the Problems and Requirements of Society and the Culture

1860–1890   Society and the culture emphasized the importance of "keeping school," maintaining discipline in classrooms, and highlighting "the fundamentals" of learning.

Elementary and secondary education was valued within a framework of the limited purposes of the public schools.

1890–1920   Scientific developments began to put a strain on the schools, as scientists and industrialists began to expect better preparation of pupils in fundamental subject matter.

Job analysis and career studies stemmed in part from the impact of training programs begun during World War I.

Vocational and industrial education was under way.

1920–1970   Curriculum specialists were asking that the curriculum be made relevant to the problems and activities of contemporary life.

Little money was spent for curriculum study; instead funds were expended for school building construction, pupil transportation, bonding and insurance costs, and attorneys' fees.

Schools were ripe for the criticism of their programs that followed the launch of the Soviet Union's Sputnik I in 1957. Shortcuts to increased learning were sought as a means of meeting criticism. Heavy assignments of standard curriculum content and use of teaching machines were considered to be effective shortcuts.

To many people, curriculum improvement came to mean changing programs through adding facilities and materials and altering organizational plans.

In response to demands for improved cognitive learning, schools adopted "projects in instruction," devised mainly by subject matter specialists whose previous contact with schools had been sparse.

Business-sponsored teaching aids augmented an increased supply of curriculum materials.

1970–1985   This was an era of especially heavy criticism of schools. Low College Entrance Examination Board scores and poor achievement records of pupils in both elementary and secondary schools caused much finger pointing in the direction of the curriculum and teachers.

Politicians at state and federal levels of government became especially vocal about deficiencies in schooling.

"Teacher-proof" curriculum materials were imposed from outside the schools.

A major goal of those who advocated tightening of school programs was to bring together three elements of schooling: the curriculum, tests to measure its application, and materials and methods for making it effective.

1985–1995   Sub-movements that were stirring included advocacy of curriculum planning at local sites (site-based management) and of increased involvement of parents.

A contrasting sub-movement encouraged national testing, with more than a hint of a presumed need for a national curriculum.

"Culture wars" erupted in discussions of Outcome-Based Education and in determination of whose values were to be taught in the schools.

An important facet of staff development became the education of teachers about differing cultures now represented in the schools.

6. The Movement to Focus on Subject Matter and Pupils' Success in Learning It

1860–1890   The subject matter that was taught followed traditional lines. In addition to the three Rs, algebra, elocution (declamation), history, geography, simple chemistry and botany, geometry, bookkeeping, and surveying were the subjects commonly taught.

Very little was known about evaluation of educational achievement.

1890–1920   Edward L. Thorndike and Charles Judd began studying the curriculum quantitatively and opened up an era of intellectual ability and achievement measurement.

Experimentation with the teaching of "new" subjects was proceeding very slowly.

1920–1970   The 1920s heralded a long era of scientific studies in education, including immediate attention to testing and measurement.

Combinations of subject matter were effected by means of correlation, block-of-time organization, the core program, the life-experience curriculum, and so on.

Attention to subject matter took the form of updates by scholars of subject matter within their specialties.

The quantity of subject matter available for teaching grew so rapidly that teachers complained of their inability to "cover the books."

Multicultural education became a program element, and subject matter emphasized the multicultural.

Limited instruction in moral and ethical values was made a part of the curriculum.

Toward the end of the period, the teaching of the so-called hard subjects became more rigorous.

1970–1985   More than ever before, schools were called upon to cure the ills of society—by teaching about drug use, alcoholism, permissive sexual behavior, and other human shortcomings.

U.S. schools were criticized for failing to equal the schools of other nations in academic toughness and in pupil achievement.

Preparing pupils to help make U.S. industry more competitive with that of other nations became a prime purpose of elementary and secondary education, at least in the minds of industrialists and politicians. A related purpose was to improve teaching of thinking skills and to increase the amount of subject matter that schools covered.

Political leaders tended to advocate uniform, rigorous curriculum content.

Because of outside pressures, the so-called basic skills were emphasized; meanwhile, building deep understanding and teaching pupils to make decisions were too often neglected.

People outside the schools seemed to assume that whenever the curriculum changed, the change could be accomplished within the current organizational and cultural framework of the school.

1980–1995   New attempts were made at integrating curriculum content.

The theory of multiple intelligences shed new light on the ability of people, regardless of age, to learn varied subject matter.

Increasing evidence of "how to lie with statistics" exposed errors in what had been said previously about deficiencies in schooling.

Realization was more widespread that pupils' failure to learn subject matter can be attributed in part to their failure to be accountable, responsible, and diligent.

A DIGEST OF TRENDS IN THE EVOLUTION OF THE CURRICULUM

Running through the panorama of U.S. education from colonial times to the present are several trends in the evolution of the curriculum.

- Ideas have often been developed in private schools and then adopted by public schools.
- Schools and school systems everywhere have frankly copied plans, procedures, and curriculum content from other schools and school systems.
- New institutions, such as the early academy, the junior high school, and the more recent middle school, have been established to satisfy unmet needs. Alternative schools have increased in number and changed in nature as new alternatives have been sought.
- Educational principles, such as that of schooling for everyone, have been adopted in substance and modified in detail whenever they have struck a popular chord. The goal of educating all the children of all the people has been looked at critically from time to time.
- Experimentation has occurred, but it has usually been informal and its results have remained largely untested.
- National committees have determined general objectives, policies, and programs.
- Psychological and social theories and revelations have turned the efforts of curriculum planners in new directions.
- U.S. educators have been susceptible to the use of plans, some of them delusive, for making the difficult processes of teaching and learning easier.
- Important educational ideas that have been based on the soundest evidence have been adopted very slowly by practitioners.

- The schools, as instruments of U.S. society, have been subjected to numerous public pressures, the nature of which tends to change from generation to generation, depending in part on the interests and concerns of individual groups within the society.
- Parents have become involved in schools in increasingly varied ways.
- Curriculum planning, once an activity centered almost exclusively in public schools, has to some degree moved to private schools and agencies promoting home schooling.

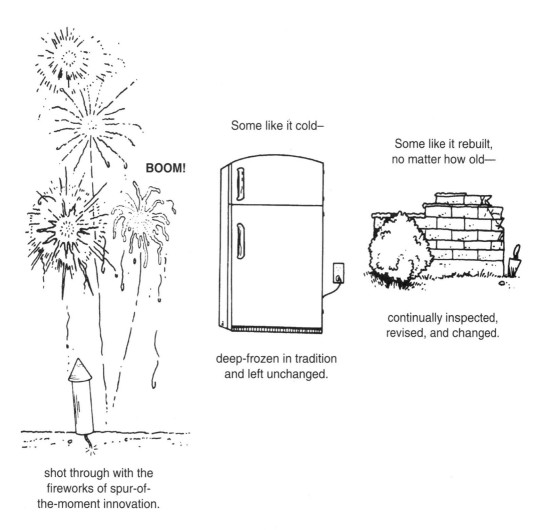

Some like it hot–

BOOM!

Some like it cold–

Some like it rebuilt, no matter how old—

shot through with the fireworks of spur-of-the-moment innovation.

deep-frozen in tradition and left unchanged.

continually inspected, revised, and changed.

FIGURE 1-1 The Curriculum

ACTIVITY 1-1

Identifying Curriculum Concerns in Your Own Environment

List the names of three persons from each of the following four categories who have shown interest in the elementary and secondary schools in your community: teachers, pupils, administrators, and parents. Interview the twelve people about their curriculum concerns. Compare what they say. Tabulate the concerns they express, and then discuss your findings with your class or group.

ACTIVITY 1-2

Recognizing Well-Known People and Movements in the Curriculum Field

Following are the names of some individuals who have influenced the movement toward curriculum improvement in the United States. How many do you recognize? What contribution did each of them make? Which of them apparently thought similarly?

John Dewey	Robert J. Havighurst
W. W. Charters	James B. Conant
Franklin Bobbitt	Benjamin Bloom
Ralph Tyler	George S. Counts
William H. Kilpatrick	Jerome Bruner
Hollis Caswell	Jean Piaget

Some educational leaders produced ideas that have had at least an indirect effect on curriculum reform. What idea does each of the following names suggest to you?

Abraham Flexner	William H. McGuffey
Lewis Terman	B. F. Skinner
Edward L. Thorndike	James S. Coleman

ACTIVITY 1-3

Narrating the Curriculum History of Your Own School System

Every school system or school district has a curriculum history of its own. By searching school system documents and interviewing older administrators, identify several events that have dominated curriculum history in your school district. Determine how these events relate to the timing of developments on the national scene, as indicated in the preceding pages of history. Compare your findings with those of fellow students who have identified events in the curriculum history of their districts.

THE CURRICULUM—LATELY AND PRESENTLY

The nature of the elementary and secondary school curriculum at present is determined in part by the nature of the curriculum as it has been in the past. The events of the 1980s and early 1990s were a prelude to the present. Some of the events proved reminiscent of similar ones in previous decades. The period of the 1980s was, however, a unique era in several respects. Some, but not all, test scores were declining; business people were complaining about the incompetence of their new, young employees; and college professors continued to report the deficiencies they were finding in their students.

You will remember that in 1983 the publication *A Nation at Risk* had warned that the schools were drowning the United States in a tide of mediocrity. Among the prominent national groups concerned with needed improvement of the schools was a task force sponsored by the Twentieth Century Fund. Another group, consisting predominantly of politicians and business leaders, was formed by the Education Commission of the States. On the state and national levels, report of the emergency piled on report. Clearly, curriculum reform was to be imposed from the top down. This impression was reinforced by the fact that teachers and administrators in the schools, as well as scholars in education, psychology, and related fields, had no significant input into the thinking that underlay the reports.

To many a politician, the establishment of higher academic standards meant mainly the addition of courses to secondary school programs. Within a few years, mathematics requirements were increased in forty-two states and science requirements in thirty-four. Attempts were made to identify and encourage master teachers, but their qualifications were ill defined and they were hard to find in an era in which more lucrative employment was available outside teaching.

During the late 1980s, school dropout rates were continuing to increase, presumably as a consequence of the rise in graduation requirements. Simultaneously, the unsubstantiated belief prevailed that 70 percent of all pupils were receiving some benefit from the increased effort and expenditures attributed to the reform movement. The remaining 30 percent included low-achieving pupils, some of whom were unacquainted with the English language.

The decade of the 1980s closed with a governors' summit, hosted by President Bush at Charlottesville, Virginia. Though former Secretary of Education William Bennett called the content of the discussions "pap," the summit did attempt to highlight national education goals that would emphasize increased literacy, more early childhood programs, and greater teacher accountability.

After the summit conference, a resultant half-dozen goals labeled "Goals 2000" were considered by the critics to be desirable but difficult to attain. In late 1994, the Clinton administration, using the catchwords "America 2000," sought to increase federal influence over public schools by promoting the passage of a new Elementary and Secondary Education Act, a $65 billion measure that sets standards, proposes assessment procedures, and deals with such varied topics as gender equity, daycare for unwed mothers, violence prevention, and health maintenance as they affect schools. To assure a degree of federal control, the National Education Standards and Improvement Council was established to constitute a national school board. Obviously, the era of curriculum reform imposed from above is well under way.

The 1990s have seen a rising tide of immigration, chiefly from Latin America and Asia. Meanwhile, people continue to flail about in their efforts to improve schools and schooling. During the decade, pupils have been recategorized, teachers have been certified according to untried criteria, testing has been extended and partially changed, and technological resources have been added. Many persons without professional experience in schools continue to advocate central planning of the curriculum at federal and state levels. As teachers move slowly into planning within their own school districts, the general public remains largely unaware of the importance of school-based planning and of cooperation between teachers and parents. School personnel are forced to pay attention to the problems that society and culture bring to the schools: increases in violent crime, higher divorce rates, single-parent homes, and increased television viewing by pupils.

Several partially developed theories have been posed to guide curriculum reform in the future. All of them have been applied in an uneven manner throughout the nation; some have been applied in combination with others.

The Free-Choice Theory

The free-choice theory holds that pupils learn best when they and their parents choose the settings in which they are educated. The range of choice is increasing. Specialized schools, such as those in mathematics and science, have existed in cities for a long time. More recently, magnet schools have drawn pupils to them because of their rigid standards or their unusual offerings. Private schools of all sorts, including the religious, continue to abound. Home schooling is on a rapid rise in both the United States and Canada. Furthermore, where the law permits, vouchers equivalent to cash benefits may be issued to parents who crave free choice, causing the public schools to continue to weaken in enrollment.

The "Big Buck" Theory

The "big buck" theory, much discussed by business leaders and conservative politicians, maintains that the major reason for improving schools is to make young citizens more competent and productive. In this way, schools will eventually foster the national economic interest. The litany associated with this theory goes as follows: Education is an industry, learning is an asset, and knowledge is a commodity. The basics, "hard" subjects, and skill development for getting along on the job should be essential.[5]

The "More" Theory

The "more" theory says, "Just tighten up; pupils will learn to the maximum, and youngsters who should leave will leave." In practice, this means more teacher-made tests and standardized testing, more frequent and rigorous evaluation of teachers and their work, more stringent requirements for high school graduation, more time spent in school, more teacher-proof curricula, and more regulation in general. Meanwhile, systems of teaching and learning would remain the same.[6]

The Empowerment Theory

The empowerment theory focuses on making competent and confident curriculum planners of teachers, administrators, parents, and other citizens. Decision-making power would be granted to classroom teachers in particular. The theory recognizes variations among pupils leading to the creation of special curricula; it also encourages individualization. It would promote development of additional nontraditional tests and would require new structures and arrangements in schooling.[7]

The Education-in-Balance Theory

The education-in-balance theory emphasizes the theme of balanced curricula for individual learners. Much time and attention are devoted to studying and prescribing experiences that, taken together, effect balance, individual by individual. Education is seen as having intrinsic, as well as instrumental, worth. Teachers help their pupils receive equitable treatment regardless of background, sex, race, mental ability, and other characteristics.[8]

The Transformation Theory

The transformation theory may also be termed the theory of restructuring. It is based on the idea that schools, as they are now structured or organized, lack the ability to provide learners with real education. Each of the two preceding theories contains suggestions of the need for restructuring. Restructuring requires shifting pupils to varied learning sites and allocating time in different ways. Curriculum, then, follows structure. In other words, curriculum is created to make optimal use of space and time in all their varied arrangements.

The theories discussed above mark initial rethinking about curriculum needs in the 1990s and on into the twenty-first century. They highlight the following needs.

1. The need to give selected pupils new opportunities to succeed by moving them to different school environments

2. The need to identify particular strengths in the curricula of individual schools
3. The need to make graduates of our schools genuinely competent and employable
4. The need to strengthen the work ethic, which has become so weak in many schools
5. The need to improve performance and build decision-making power in pupils, teachers, administrators, and other persons associated with schools
6. The need to further individualize teaching and learning
7. The need to minister in new ways to pupils who are products of other cultures and to pupils who have disabilities and deficiencies
8. The need to seek curriculum balance for each pupil who attends school

Keen observers of schools and of the social scene at the end of the twentieth century have suggested additional needs. Put in imperative form, they are as follows:

- Make schools less dismal and uninspiring.
- Empower teachers to make more of the really crucial decisions.
- Improve the use of time during the school day.
- Capitalize on what pupils learn outside the schools—in churches and synagogues, in social contacts, in part-time work, and so on.
- Emphasize social responsibility, decency, courtesy, and ethical behavior.
- Make schools truly humane institutions.
- Promote intellectual endeavor and diligent learning, which are central in the life of the effective school.[9]

When parents are asked what should be done to improve schools for the benefit of their children, they speak of discipline, control, prevention of drug abuse, a secure environment, education in manners and morals, and creation of an atmosphere conducive to learning.[10] Teachers and administrators cannot afford to disregard what parents think about these and other preconditions of effective learning.

The discussion above brings us to three considerations that will probably influence thinking about curriculum and schools in the future. The first consideration is the need to use schools as instruments of social amelioration, redemption, and strengthening. Whether teachers and administrators like it or not, their functions in the future will probably include being reformers and helpers. If social and cultural conditions outside the schools continue to deteriorate as many people believe they have been, school personnel will need to become teachers of what is true, what is right, what is uplifting, and what is helpful to one's fellows. The curriculum will then include additional civilizing content drawn, for example, from literature; from practices found in the other helping professions; and from principles common to religion, ethics, and morals. In a technically oriented civilization in which employers require people with skills far different from those possessed by employees in the past, children will need both basic and more complex skills, as well as increased understanding of matters affecting the progress of business and industry.

The second consideration is the need to redesign the curriculum and restructure schools. Redesigning properly precedes restructuring. Redesigned schools will no longer follow the traditional factory model. They will incorporate curriculum ideas that meet the needs of individual learners. When schools are restructured, they will provide new uses for space and return to some of the approaches thought of in the past: nongrading, team teaching, flexible scheduling, programmed learning, and differentiated staffing. Additional ideas for restructuring will be developed.

The third consideration is the need to emphasize the importance of people within local schools. What happens in classrooms will become the primary focus of attention. New curriculum will be developed and recorded "in the heat of combat"—i.e., in the process of classroom interaction. Careful study will be given to the ways teachers can be involved further in curriculum planning. Teacher-proof curricula, devised in distant places by people who do not know local teaching environments and pupil populations, will be rejected, as will teaching materials and tests that restrict intelligent teaching. More attention will be paid to what is known about thinking, problem solving, higher-order skill development, and learning styles. Classroom publishing and other applications of technology will become commonplace. In short, what is known about learning and its encouragement will be put to use as never before, and teachers will be increasingly respected.[11]

In combination with the general considerations we have examined, several specific future developments will affect the course of curriculum decision making:

- Our knowledge in some fields will probably double every few months.
- Increased computerization will be aided by new, small computers with great reliability, sensitivity, capacity, and program capability.
- Interactive television will permit pupils and teachers to engage in give-and-take across thousands of miles.
- More curriculum planning will be of a projective, if-then variety, patterned after econometric modeling rather than relying heavily on trends of the past.
- The length of the school year will increase because of the facilities available for home schooling and remote study centers, not because of the desires of legislatures or commissions.
- The time allocated to work and vacation will vary according to the wishes of pupils, teachers, and school patrons.
- Distribution and planning networks will help school systems share the curriculum wealth.
- Electronic paging devices will allow curriculum people to communicate with one another.

- Despite certain hazards, drugs will be used to enhance general intelligence and memory.
- New tax bases will be found for supporting education, and funding will be more equitably distributed among federal, state, and local governments.
- Where local school districts are failing, state governments will authorize themselves to take over the schools.
- Lifetime learning will be made literal in some school systems, where diplomas will be granted when learners have shown their readiness to receive them—at age 22, 27, 32, 45, 51, or whenever.

TWO PHILOSOPHICAL VIEWS OF WHAT THE CURRICULUM SHOULD BE

Among the preceding reports of historical events and estimates of things to come, one finds overtones of firmly held beliefs about the nature of learners, the demands of the culture, and the subject matter that is most worth learning. Two major, distinct belief systems are evident in the sweep of historical events and the interpretation of data. They are the positions of the Traditionalists and the Progressivists. The Traditionalists say, "What has been done in the past has been done well; therefore we should hold to it in the future." The Progressivists plead, "Let's look critically at past actions and practices to see what can now be done differently to make learning more satisfying and effective." (Note that the term *Progressivist,* though capitalized here, is not used to imply membership in the historic Progressive Education Association.)

Persons who hold these positions support differing viewpoints and practices in professional education relative to the aims of education in elementary and secondary schools, the issue of authority versus freedom in the schools, and the uses of subject matter in schooling. Of course, the Traditionalist is not uniformly a Traditionalist nor the Progressivist uniformly a Progressivist in responding to given ideas, issues, and problems—just as Republicans and Democrats do not always follow their respective parties' platforms to the letter.

Among the Traditionalists are believers in the "eternal verities" of knowledge and wisdom as enunciated by outstanding men and women of the past. The Traditionalists also include persons who hold that a fixed or standard curriculum meets the needs of children and youth regardless of temporal or geographic considerations.

Among the Progressivists are Reconstructionists who would remake the curriculum and the world according to their own designs. A prominent group of Progressivists is made up of persons who pride themselves on their ability to provide innovation in education.

Although the views of individual Traditionalists and Progressivists vary, the following statements represent the customary positions of Traditionalists and Progressivists concerning the four typical aims of American education, the issue of authority versus freedom, and the uses of subject matter.

The Aims of Education

Aim One: To Develop Learners Intellectually

Traditionalists	*Progressivists*
Certain subjects "train the mind" better than other subjects.	All subjects are potential contributors to intellectual development.
The liberal arts and sciences have intrinsic worth in disciplining the mind and building intellectual power.	Content selected carefully from both the liberal arts and sciences and the practical arts can help in developing effectively functioning human beings.
Pupils in school "learn with their heads." The task of education is to "educate heads."	Pupils learn with their heads, their hearts, and their hands. Education of the "whole child" is the only valid kind of education.
Much desirable education is to be had by absorbing ready-made experience as reported by the written and the spoken word.	Experience that is really worthwhile involves acting, acquiring meaning, and solving real problems.
Education may be conceived of as instruction.	Education may be conceived of as creative self-learning.

Aim Two: To Develop Learners as Functioning Citizens

Traditionalists	*Progressivists*
Intellectual development makes for good citizenship.	Development of good morals and useful skills is the key to preparing functioning citizens.
Knowledge and discipline prepare pupils to exercise freedom.	Direct experiences in democratic living prepare pupils to exercise freedom.

Aim Three: To Develop Learners as Individuals in Our Society

Traditionalists	*Progressivists*
Learners may profitably follow modes of learning that have succeeded in the past within carefully prepared curricula.	Learners should be invited and expected to develop their own learning modes within a flexible curriculum.

Homogeneous grouping, tracking, and special grouping of pupils help learners to develop high levels of competence.	Practices that segregate learners on the basis of what may be false assumptions are undemocratic and un-American.
Individuals should be educated rigorously to accept their roles in society and to cooperate with others in performing common societal roles.	Individuals should be educated to nonconformity, individuality, creativeness, and development of their potential.

Aim Four: To Develop Learners as Actual or Potential Workers

Traditionalists	*Progressivists*
Learners who have acquired necessary knowledge and discipline in liberal studies may then profitably devote time to learning work skills.	Learners should develop abstractions and skills in both liberal and vocational studies. The vocational aspects of education should not be deferred or denigrated.

The Issue of Authority Versus Freedom

Traditionalists	*Progressivists*
Education involves direction, redirection, control, and restraint. Therefore, it should emphasize use of authority.	Real education involves experiencing freedom from imposed authority, with full opportunity to pursue one's interests and to develop one's own potential.
Inasmuch as some knowledge and attitudes are fixed and absolute, pupils may be indoctrinated safely and correctly with this knowledge and these attitudes.	Pupils should be free to pursue knowledge and develop attitudes on the basis of observable data and the tests they apply to their knowledge and attitudes.
Human beings should learn to accept and to manage the environments in which they find themselves.	Human beings should learn to modify the environments in which they find themselves.

The Uses of Subject Matter

Traditionalists	*Progressivists*
Values are fixed, absolute, and objective, inhering in the things being valued.	Values are relative, subjective, and changeable, inhering in the circumstances in which they appear.

What is learned may be worthy because it is inherently good.	What is learned may be worthy because it is good for something.
Subject matter is important in itself.	Subject matter is important as a medium for teaching skills, intellectual processes, attitudes, and appreciations.
Subject matter should be taught mainly for deferred use.	Subject matter should be taught mainly for immediate use.
Because all people are basically the same, they should have basically the same curriculum.	Because individuals differ markedly from one another, they require widely differentiated curricula.

In summary, educators have long been divided into these two major groups, both of which desire for learners improved minds, constructive citizenship behaviors, and other advantages. Traditionalists would achieve desirable ends for learners by filling their minds with information from a wealth of precious sources in the ancient and modern world. Progressivists would encourage learners to take from accumulated human knowledge the data they can use in creating learnings that serve their own purposes. Whereas Traditionalists believe in the superiority of liberal studies, Progressivists consider the liberal and the practical arts to have equal value, particularly when both of them open prospects for easy applicability. Traditionalists would differentiate curricula especially to cultivate an intellectual elite, whereas Progressivists favor widely differentiated curricula to develop the uniqueness of each human being regardless of his or her seeming lack of promise and potential. Traditionalists hold that one must accept the world as it is and then conform to it. Progressivists believe they can remake the world into an environment that approaches ideal conditions.

Conflict among curriculum planners occurs when those who hold positions along a continuum of Traditionalist beliefs encounter those with a range of Progressivist persuasions. Sometimes the conflict becomes so intense that curriculum study grinds to a halt. More often, perhaps, all but the most pronounced differences can be submerged temporarily in deference to the demands of an immediate task. Teachers and administrators who are clearly divided in philosophy, however, can seldom work together in close proximity for long periods of time.

SCHOOLS OF PHILOSOPHICAL THOUGHT AFFECTING THE CURRICULUM

The importance of philosophy in determining curriculum trends and decisions has been expressed by L. Thomas Hopkins:

Philosophy has entered into every important decision that has ever been made about curriculum and teaching in the past and will continue to be the basis of every important decision in the future. ... When a state office of education suggests a pupil-teacher time schedule, this is based upon philosophy, either hidden or consciously formulated. When a course of study is prepared in advance in a school system by a selected group of teachers, this represents philosophy because a course of action was selected from many choices involving different values. When high school teachers assign to pupils more homework for an evening than any one of them could possibly do satisfactorily in six hours, they are acting on philosophy although they are certainly not aware of its effects. When a teacher in an elementary school tells a child to put away his geography and study his arithmetic, she is acting on philosophy for she has made a choice of values. If she had allowed the child to make the choice, she would have been operating under a different set of beliefs. ... When teachers shift subject matter from one grade to another, they act on philosophy. When measurements experts interpret their test results to a group of teachers, they act upon philosophy, for the facts have meaning only within some basic assumptions. There is rarely a moment in a school day when a teacher is not confronted with occasions where philosophy is a vital part of action. An inventory of situations where philosophy was not used in curriculum and teaching would lead to a pile of chaff thrown out of educative experiences.[12]

Hopkins's statement reminds us that we cannot be content with the simplistic black-and-white view of educational philosophy that the conflict between Traditionalists and Progressivists suggests.

Philosophy has the multifaceted effect of helping us to (1) indicate in general what we mean, (2) make what we mean more specific and definite, and (3) develop what we mean into a useful construct. People in curriculum planning groups usually develop more comprehensive, and often clearer, meanings than individual curriculum workers. As they discuss curriculum philosophy, group members tend to become helpfully critical of their original purposes. They deal in the meanings of words, a feature of philosophy making that parents and other lay persons often understand better than educators think they do.[13]

To refine and clarify the range of philosophical viewpoints that have influenced curriculum making, we need to look at general categories into which viewpoints can be classified. These categories include the distinctive beliefs of the Perennialists, the Idealists, the Realists, the Pragmatists, and the Reconstructionists, as well as the less certain beliefs of the Existentialists. The following sections describe educational practice in hypothetical schools operated according to these beliefs.

The School of the Perennialists

The School of the Perennialists, which holds that the cement of education is the common nature of man, wants to cultivate reason and otherwise develop children's intellectual powers. It considers the ends of education to be absolute and universal, for truth itself is absolute and universal. The liberal arts and sciences, the "Great Books," the "eternal verities" drawn from human rather than divine wisdom, and classical sources in general are fountains of truth.

The School of the Perennialists teaches subjects in their customary separate form: history as history, geography as geography, economics as economics, rather than in the combined form called social studies. Similarly, chemistry is taught as chemistry, biology as biology, and physics as physics, rather than in the combination known as general science. The teachers and patrons of this school are sure that some subject matter is too trivial to be included in the curriculum. Only subject matter that is thought to be hard to learn is admissible. Education in the areas of feelings and emotions and of body movement is not to be classed with education to improve memory and thinking. Because the ends of education are necessarily absolute, the curriculum that serves these ends can be fixed. The children who attend the School of the Perennialists must like to study and must strive hard to be able, effective students. Ability to read the classics and other difficult materials is, of course, an absolute essential for these students.

Example

An actual public elementary school that, in general, follows the philosophy of the Perennialists has eliminated all the "extras and frills" it can. These alleged nonessentials include drawing, dancing, and instrumental music. The principal has done everything she can think of to strengthen the teaching of the three Rs by nearly doubling the time spent on this "solid" subject matter, by forming small groups of pupils for intensive study, by extending efforts at tutoring, and by establishing prize contests and an award system for gaining proficiency in oral reading, written composition, penmanship, mental arithmetic, and spelling. She and the faculty are studying the curriculum literature of the past, including research data from the first half of the century, to discover practices that are fundamental to cognitive development and also safe in the view of the school's more conservative patrons.

The School of the Idealists

Teachers in the School of the Idealists believe that reality exists only as it is experienced. Learning is to be pursued to benefit humanity, rather than merely for self-aggrandizement. Because truth is the same today as it was yesterday, teachers are to serve as models of truth and other abiding virtues. They are to administer discipline, knowing that although interest and self-direction are important in the learning process, both must be reinforced with discipline, especially in the earlier stages of learning.

According to the Idealists, learning is, in the last analysis, the realization of goodness and truth. The learned adult and the child protégé try to practice social justice, respecting the opinions of minorities. They are convinced that a curriculum that upholds goodness and truth can be fixed, for these qualities are immutable. Accepted, traditional materials of instruction, with reading as a learning medium, are suitable for implementing a fixed curriculum. In the School of the Idealists, divine control and influence are of central importance; hence this school is oriented toward religious, values-based education.

Example

One private secondary school supported by a Protestant denomination is oriented toward Idealism. Its headmaster takes pride in the high standards of intellectual attainment the school promotes. He knows that many community members correctly say, "If a boy or a girl wants to be well prepared for college, he or she should go to that school." All students are required to attend chapel exercises daily and to participate in Bible study each Monday morning. Discipline is enforced by a system of lengthy detentions, by guard duty (carrying lead-filled muskets during forty-five-minute marches), and ultimately by suspension and expulsion. The football team is one of the most powerful in private secondary school circles, and an active intramural sports program is conducted for the benefit of all the students. The alumni office is proud of the number of graduates who, after further education, have entered the service professions and overseas missionary activity.

The School of the Realists

The School of the Realists is concerned with the world of ideas and things that are fixed within established subject matter and are generally accepted: facts, the mechanics of reading, the certainties of science and mathematics, and the fundamentals in any subject. In this school, theory and principles tend to come first in the learning experience; application or practice follows. The Realists believe that worthwhile knowledge is to be gathered, organized, and systematized in a rational form and then dispensed to the young so that the young may be truly educated, and so that knowledge itself may be preserved. A curriculum that includes only essential knowledge cannot contain fads and frills. In this school, what matters is not whether children are naturally interested in the subject matter to be taught, but only that they somehow acquire interest in, or at any rate a sense of dedication to, the "right" subject matter. Textbooks and other written materials prepared by experts, laboratories, films, testing, and biographical studies are important media for helping children learn what they should learn. The keystone of preparation for further education and for all of life is basic, essential education to be gained by increasingly intensified study of fact-oriented knowledge of subjects.

Example

In a large U.S. city, there is a public secondary school that is popularly known as "the academic high school."

"It's a no-nonsense school," says one of its supporters. "They teach you straight, and they expect you to come out well prepared." In this school, there are few school activities, but there is much after-school tutoring in subject matter that is "most worthy of attention," especially the natural sciences, mathematics, foreign languages, English, history, and geography. No general science or social studies courses can be found in this school. According to the principal, they would, if they existed, be merely bastardized and ineffective versions of the pure subject matter one should be learning.

The dropout rate is high. Students who do not care to study facts and fundamentals without sugar coating soon transfer to other, less demanding high schools in the city. The faculty makes it clear that it is being realistic about school, subject matter, and life.

The School of the Pragmatists

Teachers in the School of the Pragmatists see themselves less as dispensers of facts than as humane moderators of learning, which one really accomplishes for oneself. For these teachers, knowledge is not at all immutable. In a world of rapid change, what the teacher teaches today may not be valid tomorrow. Taking into account the pervasive fact of change, Pragmatists want to relate what they teach to the surroundings and experiences of individual children. They wish to teach children how to think rather than what to think. Because the key test of what is taught is its practical effect on human behavior, subject matter content must encourage development of insight, understanding, and appropriate skills, which are to be acquired whenever possible in creative settings. The new technologies of learning, like the hackneyed textbooks of the past, are useful only insofar as they contribute to relatedness in what is worth learning. The curriculum, then, should be pupil centered, with subject matter geared to stimulating exploration and other practical action by learners. Among really worthy school activities are defining issues, solving problems, and conducting scientific inquiry. Accordingly, experimentation and means-to-an-end instrumental education are especially prized.

Example

In a private elementary school in a suburb, the chief figure is a wealthy teacher called "Mr. Experimentation." He supports the school almost singlehandedly, when it is necessary, from his own inherited resources; accordingly, he has more to say in faculty meetings and the school offices than anyone else. Mr. Experimentation tries to see to it that nothing is taught in his school merely for its own sake as presumably important subject matter. He says, almost without challenge, "If what we teach isn't useful, it isn't worth teaching."

Young as many of them are, the children in this elementary school have numerous experiences in the community—observing, trying their skills, and serving other people. The field trip is an important part of their curriculum. The teachers, having been employed because they have declared themselves Pragmatists, try to judge what subject matter is utilitarian and therefore needed, and to teach it as naturally and openly as they can. Their written tests are designed to measure thinking and application of ideas.

The School of the Reconstructionists

The School of the Reconstructionists holds to an anthropological-sociological philosophy that would put schools in the forefront in remaking society. Teachers in this school will break precedents, if necessary, to rebuild the culture. They regard human heritage as a tool to be used in further inquiry and action as people strive to achieve self-realization. Thus, they try to avoid indoctrinating children; rather, they seek to lead them in rational discussion and in critical analysis of issues. Reconstructionists use multiple teaching materials and consider subject matter to be useful chiefly in serving their central cause. They often involve pupils, parents, and community members in planning to fuse the resources of formal education with social, political, and economic resources to try to better the human condition. Many Reconstructionists are convinced that group life should be a center of school experience inasmuch as groups are instrumental in achieving genuine democracy.

Example

Several years ago, the board of education in a small city permitted the principal and an influential teacher in a public intermediate school to establish a small satellite school three blocks away. By renting a three-room warehouse, the board provided basic facilities for an attempt to "lift the educational level" of a minority population in the immediate neighborhood. The curriculum of the satellite school, created by several teachers who subscribed to Reconstructionism, centered in a number of themes, including self-concept development, relief from powerlessness, ability to work within an established system while seeking to change it, the nature of necessities for getting along, and prospects for improving the social and economic circumstances under which minority people often live. The carefully chosen faculty conducted weekly planning meetings with parents and with community members interested in reform. Resource persons who volunteered to help with the teaching were mainly labor union officials, chairpersons of minority organizations, and social workers. The subject matter chosen for concentration was, in the judgment of the teachers, most useful in alerting pupils to the actual conditions under which they were living and to possibilities for altering these conditions.

The School of the Existentialists

The School of the Existentialists expects children to make their own choices and to reject authority that cannot justify its own existence. Thus, this school tries to free learners to choose for themselves what they are to learn and to believe. In implementing this point of view, teachers in the School of the Existentialists refuse to adhere to course guides, outlines of content, and other documents and instruments of systematic learning. They work hard to help children find their own identities and set their own standards. Necessarily, then, they themselves do their own planning apart from committee or other group arrangements. They seldom talk about curriculum goals because they tend to reject universal or widely applicable standards. Of all available subject matter, the humanities are likely to appeal to them most. These teachers do not moralize, establish numbers of rules, or humiliate or ridicule pupils. The guidance they give youngsters tends to be nondirective. They share with existentialist thinkers in other fields a flexible philosophy which, because of its nebulousness, has been called a "nonphilosophy." In summary, their chief educational concern is to free the individual child "to do his or her own thing."

Example

"I wanted my daughter to find out who she is and what she can do," said a mother who had just enrolled her child in a private middle school that advertised, "We are Existentialists. We teach your children to make their own choices." The school, founded ten years previously, had no fixed curriculum. The teachers prided themselves on listening to learners and on questioning but not telling. They refused to specify what was good or bad, useful or useless, desirable or undesirable. The administration was impatient with requests for information made by governments, local and remote, that seemed to be encroaching on the rights of private school students and faculties to do what they desired. The students made many decisions about what they would study and how they would proceed in their school activities program.

There is probably not a public school anywhere that follows any one of these educational philosophies to the letter. Most schools, public and private, tend to draw eclectically upon more than one or two philosophies to create the kinds of schooling their patrons, administrators, and teaching staffs desire. It is desirable, however, for curriculum planners to know the common, available educational philosophies, to recognize the philosophies that are being blended in the schools they know best, and to help their fellow planners change schools by combining the common philosophies in ways that satisfy them.

Religious schools have been found most likely to conform to beliefs that represent clearly defined philosophical positions. For example, examination of seven schools of the Reform Jewish tradition showed that two factors determined the nature of their curricula: (1) the culture of the individual school as molded by its history, self-perception, self-definition, and the influence of its supporting community; and (2) the nature of Reform Jewish philosophy and institutional standards.[14]

In many a school, little or no thought has been given to settling on a philosophy that the faculty supports. Teachers and administrators come and go without asking the classic question, "What is to be most commonly believed among us?" When this question is left unanswered, teachers and other planners have missed the beginning point in curriculum planning. Without a stated philosophy, aims become nebulous, processes and methods are chosen without valid reason, and results can be anything they turn out to be. Only pressures from outside the school remain as potent forces determining the nature of the curriculum.

On the affirmative side, a glance at curriculum history reveals that events and movements that have created change have had clear and solid philosophical foundations. Cases in point include Dewey's explorations of pupil interest and effort, the Eight Year Study's impact on loosening the secondary school curriculum, and the influence of vocational education programs in promoting training of hands to accompany the education of minds.

ACTIVITY 1-4

Describing the Educational Philosophy of Your Own School

Consult the preceding statements concerning educational philosophy, ranging from the Perennialist to the Existentialist. As revealed in day-to-day practice, the philosophical viewpoint of the school you know best probably represents a combination of philosophies. Write a paragraph or two expressing the particular philosophy of the school you know best.

ACTIVITY 1-5

Defining and Refining Your Own Curriculum Philosophy

A. W. Sturges, writing in the *Bulletin of the National Association of Secondary School Principals,* May 1982, presents an "ideology attitude inventory." The main themes of the inventory, adapted for the present purpose, are (1) human nature and development, (2) process and objectives of education, (3) the ideal curriculum, (4) the structure of schools, (5) the relationship between school and society, and (6) the role and function of the person in educational process.

Consider, with other members of a group, the possible meaning of each of these themes. What agreements develop among the members of your group? What differences appear? What implications do the agreements, the differences, and the processes of your discussion have for the formulation of a curriculum philosophy by the faculty of a school?

EDUCATIONAL PHILOSOPHY IN A CONTEXT OF OTHER CURRICULUM FOUNDATIONS

The preceding discussions of historical events and philosophical viewpoints suggest that learners, the learning process, social/cultural settings, and subject matter are all involved in effecting curriculum improvement. In a sense, curriculum history and educational philosophy form a platform for the real bases of action in planning. Though curriculum textbooks, including this one, characteristically treat history, philosophy, and the other foundations of the curriculum in series, the foundations actually integrate the elements involved in making decisions about the curriculum. Philosophical points of view fairly leap out of accounts of curriculum history, while historical records tell much about the learners who participated in curriculum experiments, how they learned, what social and cultural forces affected them, and what subject matter interested and challenged them. At the same time, the psychological, social/cultural, and subject foundations gain orientation and strength from lessons found in curriculum history and from the directions set by philosophical belief. Clearly, curriculum has to do, first and foremost, with people and their welfare. This fact makes the content of Chapter 2 particularly significant.

SUMMARY

The curriculum of a school may be defined as the formal and informal content and process by which learners gain knowledge and understanding, develop skills, and alter attitudes, appreciations, and values under the auspices of that school.

People's concerns about an elementary or secondary school compel them to try to improve the school's curriculum. Much has happened to the curriculum and to the process of curriculum improvement from colonial times to the present. The private system of education that existed during colonial times and the early days of the republic has been transfigured into a fifty-state system of public education that coexists with local developments in private education. Some of the informal experimentation with the curriculum that has occurred during the past three centuries has resulted in changes in curriculum practices. On several major occasions, national groups and the federal government have initiated change. Increasingly, they and compacts of governors are involving themselves in the curriculum improvement process.

While trends have been appearing and developments have been occurring in curriculum matters, two major philosophical viewpoints of curriculum, one conservative and the other liberal, have emerged: Traditionalism and Progressivism. Distinct, more specific philosophies of education—Perennialism, Idealism, Realism, Pragmatism, Reconstructionism, and Existentialism—are combined in eclectic modes in elementary and secondary schools.

In subsequent chapters, the significance of psychological, social, and subject matter influences on decision making about the curriculum will be discussed. The relevance of these forces can be seen most clearly against the backdrop of historical events that this chapter has presented. The curriculum worker desperately needs knowledge and understanding of the whole curriculum movement, seen in historical and philosophical perspective. So much time has already been lost in making false starts and in pursuing projects of limited worth that we need careful, wise decision making.

ENDNOTES

1. From the author's discussions with experienced curriculum leaders

2. Gordon N. Mackenzie, "Curriculum Change: Participants, Power, and Processes," in Matthew B. Miles, ed., *Innovations in Education* (New York: Teachers College Press, 1964), 402.

3. See Chapter 1 in Daniel Tanner and Laurel N. Tanner, *Curriculum Development: Theory into Practice* (New York: Macmillan, 1975).

4. Compare Ralph Keyes, *Is There Life after High School?* (Boston: Little, Brown, 1976).

5. The magazine *Fortune* has published articles advancing this theory.

6. See an opposing view in Frank N. Dempster, "Exposing Our Students to Less Should Help Them Learn More," *Phi Delta Kappan* 74, no. 6 (February 1993): 433–437.

7. See Mary Ann Horenstein, *Twelve Schools That Succeed* (Bloomington, IN: Phi Delta Kappa, 1993).

8. This theory is described in Mary Hatwood Futrell, "Mission Not Accomplished: Education Reform in Retrospect," *Phi Delta Kappan* 71, no. 1 (September 1989): 9–14; see also C. W. Taylor et al., "Meeting the Needs: Cultivating and Nurturing Student Differences," *Bulletin of the National Association of Secondary School Principals* 76 (February 1992): 78–84.

9. See the results of annual polls, such as those of Gallup and other polling organizations.

10. Gleaned by the author from conversations with parents at parent/teacher meetings.

11. Several projects have helped to center on altering roles and responsibilities—for example, the Coalition of Essential Schools, the National Network for Educational Renewal, and the Mastery in Learning Project.

12. L. Thomas Hopkins, *Interaction: The Democratic Process* (Boston: D.C. Heath, 1941).

13. See Russell L. Hamm and Kenneth T. Henson, "Philosophy: Curriculum Source and Guide," *Contemporary Education* 51 (Spring 1980): 147–150.

14. Michael Zeldin, "The Challenges of Autonomy: Curricular Decisions in Reform Jewish Day Schools," a paper presented at the annual meeting of the American Educational Research Association, Chicago, April 1985. Reported in ERIC # ED 257705.

SELECTED BIBLIOGRAPHY

Association for Supervision and Curriculum Development. *Challenges and Achievements of American Education*. Alexandria, VA: The Association, 1993.

Benjamin, Harold. *The Saber-Tooth Curriculum*. New York: McGraw-Hill Book Co., 1939.

Borman, Kathryn, and Greenman, Nancy P., eds. *Changing American Education: Recapturing the Past or Inventing the Future*. Albany, NY: State University of New York, 1993.

Brubacher, John S. *A History of the Problems of Education*. New York: McGraw-Hill, 1947.

Cremin, Lawrence A. *The American Common School: An Historical Conception*. New York: Bureau of Publications, Teachers College, 1961.

Doll, William. *A Post-Modern Perspective on Curriculum*. New York: Teachers College Press, 1993.

Firth, Gerald, and Kimpson, Richard D. *Curriculum Continuum in Perspective*. Oakland, CA: Peacock, 1992.

Gordon, Peter, and Lawton, Denis. *Curriculum Change in the Nineteenth and Twentieth Centuries*. New York: Holmes and Meier, 1979.

Jencks, Christopher. *Inequality: A Reassessment of the Effects of Family and Schooling in America*. New York: Basic Books, 1972.

McClure, Robert M., ed. *Curriculum, Retrospect and Prospect*. National Society for the Study of Education, Seventieth Yearbook, Part I. Chicago: University of Chicago Press, 1971.

Miller, John P., and Seller, Wayne. *Curriculum: Perspectives and Practice*. White Plains, NY: Longmans, 1985.

Miller, Ron. *What Are Schools For?* 2nd ed. Brandon, VT: Resource Center for Redesigning Education, 1992.

Morrison, George S. *Contemporary Curriculum K–Eight*. Boston: Allyn and Bacon, 1993.

Ornstein, Allan C., and Hunkins, Francis P. *Curriculum: Foundations, Principles, and Issues*. Englewood Cliffs, NJ: Prentice-Hall, 1987.

Phenix, Phillip H., ed. *Philosophies of Education*. New York: Wiley, 1963.

Ravitch, Diane. *Schools We Deserve: Reflections on the Educational Crisis of Our Time*. New York: Basic Books, 1987.

Rich, John M. *Readings in the Philosophy of Education*. 2nd ed. Belmont, CA: Wadsworth, 1972.

Schubert, William H. *Curriculum: Perspective, Paradigm, and Possibility*. New York: Macmillan, 1986.

Seguel, Mary Louise. *The Curriculum Field: Its Formative Years*. New York: Teachers College Press, 1966.

Tyack, David. *One Best System: A History of American Urban Education*. Cambridge, MA: Harvard University Press, 1975.

Venable, Tom C. *Philosophical Foundations of the Curriculum*. Chicago: Rand McNally, 1967.

Wynne, John P. *Theories of Education*. New York: Harper & Row, 1968.

Zais, Robert S. *Curriculum: Principles and Foundations*. New York: Thomas Y. Crowell, 1976.

2

PSYCHOLOGICAL BASES FOR CURRICULUM DECISIONS

How do children grow and develop? What differences are commonly found among learners? How can data about learners be used in curriculum planning? What does the discipline of psychology say about the ways pupils learn? What does psychology say specifically to the curriculum improver?

Psychological factors are at the root of many curriculum decisions, for psychology is one of the mother disciplines in which education finds its rationale. This chapter discusses the psychological bases for curriculum decisions that relate to the five questions above.

LEARNERS–THEIR GROWTH AND DEVELOPMENT

In the United States and abroad, many investigations into the nature of learners have been conducted during the past three-quarters of a century. Much has been discovered about children's sequence of growth and development, about factors that affect growth and development, about the mental equipment that learners bring to their tasks, about the importance of individual personality and personal experiences, and about the effect of the social order on individual learners.

Learners have been studied from several points of view. Arnold Gesell and his followers have used a cross-sectional approach, which involves studying thousands of children at specified ages and then generalizing about children's physical, mental, and behavioral characteristics at these ages. Willard C. Olson has used a longitudinal method by which children are observed and examined at intervals during their development from childhood to adolescence, and their individual patterns of growth and development are plotted. Psychoanalysts have discussed undesirable feelings and experiences which, when present during childhood, cause young people to grow into disordered adults. The sociologist Robert Havighurst outlined developmental tasks from infancy through later life. These four approaches, quite different in nature, often yield different findings about the growth and development of learners. But they do tend toward a view of the learner as a whole being, rather than as a parcel of unrelated skills, understandings, and attitudes. As the findings from these and other approaches generally reinforce one another, the interrelatedness of growth factors becomes increasingly clear. In the physical area, researchers view *growth* as involving increase in the size of individuals and *development* as involving increase in their physical complexity. In the matters of mental and emotional development with which curriculum workers are chiefly concerned, however, researchers regard *growth* and *development* as having generally interchangeable meanings.

Studying groups of pupils comprehensively and comparatively may involve learning about their audiological and ophthalmological status; their auditory, visual, tactile, motor, and visual-motor functioning; their verbal, nonverbal, and emotional patterns; their personality characteristics; and their social, work, and academic skills. Obviously, this list does not exhaust the possibilities for study because human beings are so complex.

A Step Back into History

Gesell, Olson, and Havighurst should be included in any list of psychologists and educators who have manifested a primary interest in children and their welfare. During earlier eras, the assumption was made that youngsters were pliable and therefore amenable to being taught almost anything that adults wanted them to learn. The first major challenge to this concept came from Jean Jacques Rousseau (1712–1778). Rousseau said, in effect, that the nature of the child must be considered more important than the nature of the curriculum. After Rousseau, Friedrich Froebel (1782–1852) proposed a curriculum centering in the nature of the child, having established as his chief goal the child's "self-realization." Froebel held that the curriculum should originate within, not outside, the learner.

Somewhat later, William James (1842–1910) and Edward L. Thorndike (1874–1949) formulated a psychology of education that was used by others to support the child-centered curriculum. Soon studies of child growth and development were under way, and John Dewey was developing a curriculum that emphasized the life activities of children. Outspoken advocates of the child-centered curriculum ran into serious conflict with advocates of the adult-organized curriculum. Opponents of child-centeredness accused Dewey and his supporters of providing "soft pedagogy" for pampered children. The accusation gained strength as a consequence of certain excesses committed by teachers who came to be considered extreme progressives. Dewey himself, writing in *The Child and the Curriculum,* deprecated both the common underestimates of children's maturity and the rising sentimentality about the nature of children. The battle between the Progressives and the Traditionalists had begun. Though the Progressive Education Association is officially dead, the battle continues today. Ours is an era in which curriculum based in what we know about children and youth competes with curriculum prepared in remote places by adults who may have no direct contact with learners.

Characteristics, Needs, and Tasks

In the early 1950s, at a time when data about child growth and development were regarded very seriously by curriculum planners, a curriculum committee in one U.S. school district compiled a list of the characteristics and needs of "representative" youngsters who were attending school within the committee's district. Having recognized that characteristics and needs overlap proximate age levels, the committee observed children in kindergarten and the first grade, in the second and third grades, in the fourth and fifth grades, and so on. In addition, the members explored all the child growth and development literature they could find. Reprinted below, as examples, are the lists of characteristics and needs the committee compiled for two educational levels: kindergarten and grade one, and grades four and five.

Kindergarten and Grade One

Characteristics

1. Children begin to lose baby teeth, causing lisping, etc.
2. Right- or left-handedness is established. No change should be made without expert advice.
3. Bone structure growth is slower than in previous years.
4. Heart growth is rapid. The child should not be overtaxed physically.
5. Eyes are increasing in size. Watch reading and writing habits.
6. Feeling of tension may be evident in thumb sucking, nail biting, and mistakes in toilet habits.
7. Motor skills begin to develop; coordination may be awkward and uneven.
8. Large muscles are much more developed than smaller ones.
9. The child responds to rhythms—skips, beats time, etc.
10. The average child of these ages is full of vitality. He has good facial color, and he stands and sits erect.
11. Children are interested in an activity rather than in its outcome.
12. Self-dependence and a desire to help others are developing.
13. Children prefer activity—climbing, jumping, running—but they tire easily.

Needs

1. Short periods of activity
2. Twelve hours of sleep
3. Vigorous and noisy games so essential to growth

4. Many opportunities to do things for oneself
5. Frequent participation in organized groups—games, dramatics, rhythm
6. Chances for the shy child to join in the routine and be important

Grades Four and Five

Characteristics

1. Small muscles continue to develop, increasing manipulative skills.
2. Coordination is improving, especially hand-eye.
3. This is the period of prepubescence at which time physical growth slows down. Beginning of pubescence may appear in a very few boys and girls.
4. Overtaxing of heart needs watching.
5. Posture needs watching.
6. Eyes need to be considered. Attention now may prevent more serious trouble later.
7. This is a period of untidiness, overabundance of energy, frequent accidents.
8. Children show increased interest span in a wide range of activities.
9. This is the gang age, the age of secret clubs.
10. Children are critical of their families.
11. Relationship to group and approval of peers are important.
12. It is the age of collecting—cards, stamps, etc.

Needs

1. Opportunities to develop independence
2. At least ten hours of sleep
3. Physical equipment (desk, chairs, etc.) carefully adjusted to each individual
4. Uniformity and fairness in rules and punishment
5. Real need of regularity, as opposed to schedule changes
6. Whole body activities
7. Sympathy and understanding of adults
8. Help in finding a place in the group
9. Opportunity to learn to be a good follower as well as a good leader[1]

These lists are noticeably heavy on physical growth factors and correspondingly light on intellectual factors. Subsequent studies of cognitive development have supplemented lists of this kind with data especially important to today's curriculum planners, who are required to keep their eyes constantly on youngsters' intellectual achievement.

Statements of learners' characteristics and needs can be rounded out and made more credible and usable by determining what tasks the learners can perform. Lists of psychological tasks are more than simple statements of jobs or assignments at which youngsters of given age levels are competent. They describe actions, trends, and movements that adults can confidently expect to see in the lives of these youngsters. For example, a list of tasks of middle school or junior high school pupils may be expected to include these items:

1. Self-exploration of one's uniqueness as an individual and one's relationships with other people
2. A continuation of detachment from parents, and of the assertion of autonomy that began at the toddler stage
3. Short-term commitment to work and its diligent performance, followed by a change to aimlessness and moodiness
4. Movement from transient, hit-and-run acquaintances to more stable and rewarding interpersonal relationships
5. Cognitive development that permits abstract thinking, generalizing, and ability to appreciate theorems, figures of speech, and ideologies
6. Examination of one's own and others' values
7. Comprehension of, and sometimes overemphasis on, law and order[2]

In school, early adolescents need opportunities to undertake a variety of activities, to relate to peers and adults in varied ways and settings, to be in charge of the action at times, to be challenged during bursts of effort, to get to know a few persons well, to stretch their minds with abstractions, and to explore values and valuing.

Said one curriculum specialist, "If you want to know what a group of pupils is like, put the group to work on a series of learning tasks. What's inside the pupils will soon show out." Essentially, that is what psychologist Jean Piaget did in a limited but sophisticated way when he presented tasks and questions to children to determine how they developed logical, sequential thought. Piaget found and reported four major levels of development: the sensorimotor level, the preoperational level, the level of concrete operations, and the level of formal operations.

According to Piaget, at the sensorimotor level, from birth to about eighteen months, the child apparently assimilates sensations and interacts with unfamiliar objects. As the child accommodates to his or her physical environment, a system or structure for manipulating objects is developed.

From eighteen months to about seven years of age, the child exercises his or her perception. For example, the child recognizes differences in size and increases in number and uses images and words to symbolize objects and events; however, he or she operates not logically, but rather on the basis of what appears to the child to be reasonable.

Logical thinking operations begin at the concrete operations stage, extending from approximately seven to eleven years of age. The child now recognizes several factors at a time. For example, the child sees that some things can be combined in varied ways to arrive at the same result. He or she manipulates objects more insightfully, noting that whatever is manipulated remains the same in length, or area, or volume, or weight.

The level of formal operations involves using reasoning and applying rules in more abstract situations. Beginning at about age eleven, the child is able to state hypotheses, test them, and formulate conclusions. Meanwhile, he or she can consider possibilities, keep several variables in mind at once, and deal with probabilities. The child is able to answer the question "What would happen now if . . . ?" His or her logical system is steadily developing.

Piaget commented that intellectual development is gradual and continuous, creating a merging or blurring of the four levels. Progress at these levels depends on how mature the child is, how much relevant experience the child has had, and how the child has processed information supplied by people in his or her environment.[3] Piaget considered another factor to be important: equilibration, a search by the child for equilibrium in his or her cognition.

The last three levels of cognitive operation have real meaning for curriculum planners in nursery schools and on through high school. In the middle grades of schooling, for instance, teachers should spend time making the development of logical operations easier at the concrete level, as well as creating readiness for formal operations. Piaget's theory provides hints about arranging subject matter sequence. It suggests that careful development of thought processes produces greater-than-usual individual differences among learners. Inasmuch as already wide-ranging differences are being treated inadequately in schools, this finding suggests an obvious need for careful curriculum planning.

Although some of Piaget's ideas have now been either supplanted or extended, his original monumental work still commands respect.

SITUATION 2-1

Judging What Use to Make of Certain Characteristics and Needs

A committee of teachers of fourth- and fifth-grade children concerned itself with art experiences for children of these grades. Both the learning activities of the children and the facilities the children were to use came within the purview of the committee, which was charged with developing program facilities for a new elementary school. The committee's attention was drawn particularly to the following characteristics and needs of fourth- and fifth-grade children:

Characteristics. Small muscles are developing more and more manipulative power; children are often untidy and energetic, and they have frequent accidents; children are interested in collecting items that they and other people produce.

Needs. Independent creative ability should be developed; children need a wide range of activities in which to expend their energies.

Assuming that the characteristics and needs of children of these age groups as listed above are valid, what are some of the inferences you can make concerning program facilities in art?

The Significance of Learners' Abilities

Sometimes we hear teachers say, "You know, children today are not as bright as children were ten, twenty, or thirty years ago." The appropriate response to this comment is that we have no hard evidence from administering our most respected intelligence tests that children today are less bright in general, according to multiple criteria, than children were years ago. But we do have evidence from a variety of sources, including Scholastic Aptitude and achievement test results, that youngsters do not perform as well nowadays, either on tests or in daily classwork. Something has happened to make the great American experiment of educating nearly all the children of all the people less successful than it had been heretofore. Many of the cultural causes of this decline are discussed in Chapter 3.

There are, however, causes within individual learners. Genetic studies continue to indicate that some children's heredity works against their performing well in schools as they are now organized and conducted. We know that not every youngster's DNA will permit him or her to become a financial genius, a brilliant scientist, or a poet laureate, but parents are naturally dismayed at the thought that their own children seem to be unable to achieve as well as the neighbors' children. Sometimes they find consolation in the idea that such differences result from physical ailments that may have affected their children since birth.[4]

Evidence is increasing that beyond genetic and other physical causes, youngsters' unwillingness to accept responsibility for their achievement is paramount. Thus, the problem of flawed attitudes must become a chief focus. Psychologists often describe the interconnecting roles of heredity and environment as follows: It appears that we inherit many of our traits. However, these traits can be modified by our experiences, especially by experiences we have early in life. Human experience needs to have breadth, and sometimes in crucial matters it needs to follow a pattern that leads to uniform, conforming behavior.

Confirmation of a major cause of difference in pupils' achievement can be found in Howard Gardner's explorations into the meaning of human intelligence. Gardner has concluded that we possess seven kinds of intelligence: linguistic, logical-mathematical, musical, spatial, bodily kinesthetic, interpersonal, and intrapersonal. Testing of most of these kinds of intelligence obviously lags behind their identification by Gardner and others, and also behind present efforts to develop them through education. However, Gardner and his associates have been doing extensive work in these directions in their Project Zero at Harvard University.

Not only are we lax in taking into account variations in intelligence; we also know less than we should about the effect of poor self-concept on achievement. At present, specialists in psychology and curriculum are discussing whether "doses of instruction in self-esteem" are needed to increase children's learning and, simultaneously, whether the self-esteem of pupils is largely a consequence of their ability to meet high academic expectations.

Some of the earlier research findings seem to suggest that individual learners develop and perform according to their self-concepts, that a positive self-concept correlates closely with school achievement, that achievers feel more positive about themselves and their abilities than do underachievers, and that underachievers learn poorly partly because they underestimate their ability to perform well. Educators have, however, been seeing danger in concluding that improved self-esteem has unchallenged effect in improving school achievement.

The Individual Learner

Consideration of learners' abilities inevitably causes us to focus on pupils as individuals. Clearly, exceptions to general findings about children and youth are both numerous and provocative. The challenge to education in a democracy appears much more prominently in the differences among children and youth than in their similarities. In practice, schools unrealistically tend toward treating learners as though they were substantially alike, whereas they actually vary beyond our wildest imaginings. The following are some generally realistic statements about individual differences in pupil growth and development:

1. Many of the obvious differences among learners can be seen in five minutes in any classroom. Other, less obvious differences can be revealed only by careful study.
2. Learners differ in their ability to perform tasks. Thus, according to an arbitrary standard of quality, a child may be good in arithmetic, poor in spelling, and fair in reading. To complicate matters, the same child displays differing abilities in performing different tasks within each of these school subjects.
3. Growth and development apparently occur in spurts, sometimes referred to as the "thrustration" involved in pushing forward; a subsequent period of quiescence and reinforcement follows each push.
4. If individual differences are really taken into account, the school cannot hope to maintain a single or minimum standard for a given group of children, comfortable though this standard might be for teachers. Education should cultivate differences rather than restrict them. If this were done, the range of differences would be even more obvious. Although high schools often tend to teach adolescents as though they were all alike, maturation brings out more differences in learners than were present or obvious when the same learners were young children.
5. Differences in rates of growth, with other factors, cause some children to be "early bloomers" and other children to be "late bloomers." One of the noticeable developmental trends during the second half of the twentieth century has been the tendency of children and youth to mature earlier, presumably because of new mores, changed expectations, and technological gains such as easier communication, more facile transportation, and

wider availability of television. Earlier maturation may make classic lists of characteristics and needs partially obsolete.

6. Given desirable educational conditions, children of whom we have expected little can often give much. Teachers have shown an unfortunate tendency to write off as hopeless those children who have not succeeded well at first.

7. Since factors of growth are interrelated, the causes of learning difficulty at a given time may be found in some factor that we do not presently know— for example, a major, unexpected event in a youngster's personal life.

By noting instances of differences within the pupil populations they serve, competent teachers can identify basic differences among pupils. Consider, for example, cases of four hypothetical nine- and ten-year-old youngsters we shall call David, Doreen, Duncan, and Dixie.

David achieves A's with regularity; spends nearly all his free time reading and studying; has only one or two friends; seems to fear playing with other children; assumes an air of superiority toward others, including adults; and appears on the streets only in the company of a parent.

Doreen is considered to be average in mental ability; finds quiet, subversive ways of getting attention; often cheats on tests and examinations; has many acquaintances but almost no close friends; expends as little effort as possible on schoolwork; and can often be found alone on downtown streets in the evening.

Duncan worries little about school or almost anything else; registers low-average on tests of mental ability; passes to the next grade marginally, mainly because of the social promotion policy of his school; is jovial and humorous; stays out of trouble; and interacts well with his peers, including several ostensible friends.

Dixie sometimes mystifies her teachers; achieves reasonably well in school, despite somewhat limited mental ability; seems to have almost no friends; shows tension by crying often; is chronically absent from school; and fears that she might be punished for her trivial offenses.

Lists and descriptions like these give curriculum workers pause as they begin to consider factors of growth and development that teachers sometimes fail to take into account. Every learner brings with him or her individualized conditioners of learning. These include personality, personal experiences, mental ability, and the effects of the social order. The nature of the learner and of the learner's background has a marked effect on what is learned and on the style of learning. Furthermore, the personality of the learner becomes evident in the learner's emotional organization, which affects sensitivity to social and other phenomena, ties with adults, desire or lack of desire to master the environment, and the extent of preoccupation with personal problems, which may prevent learning. It appears, of course, in the quality of one's relationships with people of all sorts. The learner's insecurities may cause him or her to "show off" abilities by achieving to the maximum, or to undervalue personal powers so markedly that he or she suffers from emotional paralysis. The learner is affected further by physical characteristics such as muscular coordination and visual and auditory acuity.

One's past experience conditions learning in many ways. Interests developed early in life often carry into subsequent years. Sometimes they coincide with the curriculum of the school, but too often they are unknown to teachers, or they seem to have no relevance to anything people do in schools. Socially and in other ways, modern children have more opportunities for wide experience than children had a generation or two ago, and wide experience shows itself in the sophistication, whether real or artificial, that modern children often manifest.[5]

It is important to see how the social order affects the individual learner. First, it affects the learner through his or her socioeconomic status. High status brings advantage and privilege; low status, disadvantage and rejection. Second, the social order affects the individual learner through his or her ethnic or national background. Various ethnic and national groups tend to have different expectations of schooling and of the status in society that a person with their background may hope to reach. Soon the individual learner comes to share these expectations. Third, a learner is affected by the family in which he or she has been reared. The interests learners have acquired, their cultural advantages, and the extensiveness of their travel are but a few variables that relate directly to family life. Other factors that affect learners are their neighborhood, the occupations of the people they know, and the cultural level and aspirations of their associates as they grow up. "Every child learns what he lives, and he is motivated only to learn more about those things which he knows or imagines."[6]

Some Familiar Categories of Difference

Differences among youngsters are so varied and wide ranging that if they were all visible, a school's pupil population would form a kaleidoscopic image. Within this changing image, we can identify several common categories of difference. The descriptions below cover neither all possible categories nor the degrees of difference that appear within categories. Nonetheless, they are familiar to people who know schools and communities today.

At-Risk Pupils

The term *at risk* is an invention of critics of the schools. It appears to define the largest category of difference. When teachers are asked to indicate the percentage of their pupils who are educationally at risk, they usually state a figure that approaches 40 percent.[7] Most teachers apparently believe that "at risk" means poorly motivated. (Teachers do recognize other risk factors, as well, however; see Table 2-1.) Teachers have been taught by supervisors to raise their expectations of learners, to stimulate learners' sense of self-worth, to improve relationships among pupils, to increase opportunities for cooperative learning,

TABLE 2-1   Perceptions of Risk Factors Affecting Pupils' Learning, 1970 and 1990

Factor	Incidence, by percentage, of total pupil population in selected schools	
	1970	1990
Intentionally working below apparent potential	8	19
Having special learning disabilities	6	8
Coming from damaging home and community environments	4	7
Coming from homes that are culturally different from the norm	3	6
Behaving in unusually disruptive ways	2	5
Showing evidence of mental retardation	2	3
Having obvious physical handicaps	2	1
Percentage totals	27	49

Compiled from oral and written comments by thirty men and women with a wide range of experience in elementary and secondary schools (recorded by the author during spring and summer, 1990) and from analysis of thirty-five articles and books concerning pupils at risk

and to respond to differing learning styles. Several elaborate programs for aiding learners at risk have been developed.[8]

Use of the omnibus term *educationally at risk* proves unsatisfying to teachers and others who work daily with children affected by the more definitive influences described in the paragraphs below. We have learned that the condition of being at risk of failing develops early in life. To counteract that condition, school personnel have tried one-to-one tutoring and nongraded primary programs, sometimes preceded by early-early childhood education. Succeeding during the early years of schooling doesn't guarantee a child's success during the later years, but early failure does tend toward later failure. Fortunately, we know much about how to prevent failure during children's early years. For example, schools need to compensate for children's deprivations at home, often by providing books, places to work, and direct help; they need to increase children's wholesome contacts with other people; they must provide the monitoring that parents neglect; and they must decrease social distance between individual teacher and individual pupil.

Pupils with Deficiencies

Terms like *underachiever, learning disabled,* and *retarded* have been used for years in categorizing pupils with deficiencies. Psychologists use subcategories affecting learning—e.g., gross motor development, sensory-motor integration, conceptual skills, language development, and social skills—in defining the difficulties that individual learners experience. Some of the difficulties have a physical base, but most of them originate elsewhere: in mental process and in environmental deficiencies. One of these deficiencies can be found in the school itself, where, as Gerald Bracey has said, we find that underachievers can't handle the bean-jar curriculum, so we give them smaller beans. In other words, an old, stultifying curriculum, when prescribed in limited or diluted form, works less well than a curriculum that allows informal conversation between teacher and pupils, freer movement within classroom and school, and practice in activities that are off the beaten curriculum track but are important to the development of individuals.

The Culturally Different

Pupils described as culturally different characteristically come from homes where English is not spoken, where customs differ from those familiar to long-time residents of the United States, or where other handicapping conditions exist. Prescriptions for helping culturally different youngsters tend to vary with the needs of individuals. Sometimes special education in language is called for; sometimes fragmented portions of the curriculum need to be used; at other times new, miniature program offerings have to be developed; almost always close mentorship and guidance are required.

The Gifted and the Talented

Who's gifted? Who's talented? Parents don't always define giftedness and talent realistically. Unquestionably, gifted and talented individuals are being overlooked and underdeveloped in present-day schools. The characteristics of the gifted pupil include ability to handle abstractions, marked power of concentration, ability to see connections and relationships, a tendency to learn quickly, and possession of extensive information. Talent expresses itself in quality performance in specialties. The gifted and talented need curriculum emphases on symbol systems, interdisciplinary subject matter, individualized learning packets and contracts, and multiple learning resources. In addition, the talented need time and space for emphasizing their individual specialties.[9] Too often, teachers have assumed that gifted and talented pupils can "go it on their own" without encouragement from teachers and considerateness from their peers. The latter are often envious of them and consequently abusive to them. Only the gifted and the talented can understand a remark attributed to Professor Bradford Brown of the University of Wisconsin at Madison: "Doing well in school is cool. Doing great is not."

The Rejected

Many a pupil can feel rejection. Consider the child who has recently arrived from a country where people dress differently than Americans, or the child who exhibits a strange speech pattern, or who seems to prefer isolation from other children. In cases like these, rejection comes from outside the individual, notably from the school environment. At the same time, the individual may be rejecting himself or herself. Accordingly, we say that he or she has a poor self-image. Traditionally, the school curriculum has done little to encourage or otherwise aid rejected pupils. A comprehensive curriculum includes education in social relationships and also in self-enhancement. Learning how to think about others and ourselves need not become caught up in the faddism that sometimes surrounds education in self-esteem. Youngsters are moving toward understanding self-rejection when they can find humor in the words of Goethe that "I do not know myself, and God forbid that I should," or in the words of H. L. Mencken, who described self-respect as "the secure feeling that no one, as yet, is suspicious."[10]

The Disruptive

Where and how does disruptive or violent behavior originate? The following sample comments by classroom teachers suggest some possibilities:

> "Many of the current crop of students have a 'make me if you can' attitude."
> "Youngsters today are busy testing their teachers, having first tested their parents—and having won."
> "Children's respect for adults is no longer automatic."
> "If influence on children were in the form of a pie, you'd see the largest slice going to television, not to parents or teachers."
> "It comes down to this: Too many adults fear children, and too many children don't trust adults."

In 1994, the National School Boards Association advised its members that schools nationwide were taking extra steps to curb violence. The language used in connection with the suggested remedies was purposely harsh: bodily removal of offenders, expulsion from school, criminal charges against parents, "boot camps" for the unruly, and financial liability of parents.

Traditionally, teachers have believed that the best direction for the disruptive pupil to take is toward the door, and his or her best destination is anywhere outside the classroom. Much depends, however, on the degree of disruption. If the population of a school includes a large number of disruptive pupils, a special program, usually expensive in terms of time and money, can be designed. A program of this kind may require a behavioral curriculum laden with skill-development activities and backed up by reinforcers and punishments. It operates best with a small group of pupils, perhaps a half-dozen or so, and also with highly supportive staff members ready to come to one another's assistance. Naturally, many disrupters require extensive individual counseling. In a time of economic stringency, programs of this kind are likely to be rare. There are those who are much concerned with the civil rights of extreme disrupters. They should be at least equally concerned with the rights of other pupils.[11]

The need for increasing attention to the disruptive is presaged by the Heritage Foundation's study of changes in American culture from 1960 to the early 1990s. Violent crime was found to have increased 560 percent; illegitimate births, 400 percent; and teenage suicides, 200 percent.[12]

The Physically Handicapped

Many attempts have been made in the past to help the physically handicapped. Because the teacher in the self-contained classroom sometimes found these pupils difficult to work with, in the early days physically handicapped pupils were consigned to their respective ghettoes of the similarly handicapped. Later, they were mainstreamed in "regular" classrooms. Subsequently, after more careful diagnosis, they were placed in situations that included some of the best features of both mainstreaming and special education.

Curriculum modification for the physically handicapped has had a long history in the United States. The so-called special education curriculum has become commonplace in many school systems. The purchase of materials and equipment for these pupils claims a significant portion of school district budgets.

The Lethargic

Many a pupil shows little enthusiasm for most of what happens in school. Unfortunately, the mental outlook of a lethargic pupil is closer to the American norm than we like to believe. The work ethic ascribed to learners and workers of earlier generations is often rejected by youngsters today. Harold Stevenson and others, having studied pupils and their parents in Japan, Taiwan, China, and the cities of Minneapolis and Chicago during a ten-year period, concluded that Americans have too little confidence in the significance of working hard in school. Asian mothers apparently value, on behalf of their children, hard work and scholastic achievement, but American mothers speak of the importance of their children's popularity and their success in sports and other activities. Where study occurs "around the kitchen table" as a part of family life, children tend to carry the family-approved work ethic to school and become increasingly responsible for their own success or failure.

Victims of Other Hostile Environmental Causes

Today, many learners are being taxed by the pressures and influences of other hostile environmental causes. The first cause that usually comes to mind is poverty. Without doubt, poverty at home diverts learners' attention from school subject matter because of the exigencies of simply living, and it permits no provision of books and other enriching materials. Some of the heroes and heroines of pupil populations are those who have worked around the disadvantages of poverty.

A miscellany of other hostile causes includes the prevalence of AIDS, addiction to alcohol and illegal drugs, and constant threats of harassment. A number of school systems have tried to make the local schools places of refuge. Surely curriculum planners can provide educational experiences that help young people avoid the damaging influences around them. The Heritage

Foundation has noted in its literature challenges to curriculum workers in the estimate that many a youngster has witnessed at least 50,000 acts of murder and more than 10,000 incidents of illicit sex—on television—by the time he or she has completed high school.

Attending Carefully to Individual Differences

As teachers face learners who as individuals belong in one, two, or more of the preceding categories, they are required to think how attention can be given to individuals. To take all significant information about individual learners into account, teachers need a comprehensive scheme for attending to individual differences. One of the best schemes was suggested some years ago by Professor Virgil Herrick. Herrick said that to deal with individual differences effectively, a teacher should make three kinds of decisions:

1. The teacher selects objectives, the topic to be studied, the organizing center for the subject matter content,[13] the instructional plan to be used, and a useful evaluation plan. This is a comprehensive educational decision.
2. The teacher decides how to recognize and respect individual children, how to interrelate teacher and pupil roles, and how to establish the interpersonal dynamics of the classroom. In plain English, this is a set of decisions in interpersonal relations and classroom climate, decisions about how people can get along best in the classroom so that learning can proceed.
3. The teacher determines how the children are to be grouped, how time and space are to be utilized, and how materials and resources of instruction are to be acquired and associated. This is a set of decisions in administrative arrangements and logistics.[14]

Curriculum planners have these three kinds of decisions in mind, usually in a less organized form, each time they develop a major curriculum project in individualization. Some of the subparts of the decisions are obviously more important than others. For example, if objectives are made to express significant generalizations and processes, the individual learner can supply the specifics that seem appropriate to support a given generalization or process. Thus, if genuinely understanding the process of addition in arithmetic is to be highlighted, 148 plus 292 provides only an application of the understanding. Human beings' dependence on other human beings is an important concept; the Grand Alliance—the coalition formed in 1689 by England, Sweden, Spain, the Netherlands, and the Holy Roman Empire—is only one instance of it. Obviously, the learner should be expected to acquire the big idea, not the details of a single instance. Continual fact teaching, still so common in U.S. schools, will not suffice.

Similarly, the way time is used can have a telling effect on the degree to which individualization is attained. Proper use of time should offer maximum opportunity for individuals to perform activities that are different from what members of the class or group commonly do. The idea of time-on-task is discussed later in this chapter.

Teachers can use several strategies in accommodating the educational needs of individual learners:

1. Finding the individual in the group; then giving that individual special attention
2. Varying learning activities and materials
3. Preparing new and different packages of learning materials
4. Varying the time needed to complete prescribed activities
5. Allowing learners to individualize to suit themselves, such as by choosing activities and utilizing time in their own ways
6. Subgrouping learners in numbers of groups formed for different purposes
7. Providing for independent study
8. Preparing varied evaluation instruments and test and inventory items
9. Following the procedures in mastery learning to be discussed in this chapter

Many pupils are capable of planning their own learning experiences within the framework of their regular classroom learning. They need not start this planning at the beginning of a school term but may wait until they have become accustomed to new subject matter. Opportunities for individualized learning may then be presented incidentally to "regular" learning, often in the form of brief episodes. The monotony of working alone will be reduced if some of the learning experiences occur in small groups. Pupils may be encouraged to prepare individual outlines of their proposed activities, specifying the why, what, when, and how of the activities. By attaining self-direction, exceptional pupils—not only the gifted but also those for whom teachers previously held out little hope—can deepen their interests and increase their abilities to an unusual extent.[15]

SITUATION 2-2

Homework for an Eighth-Grade Class

Mr. Simpson's work as assistant principal of a junior high school took him into a number of classrooms. In most of them, he noticed homework assignments given in the following manner: "For tomorrow, read pages 145 to 153 and be ready to talk about what you have read." To Mr. Simpson, this way of assigning homework seemed oversimplified and insensitive. He found a sympathetic spirit in an eighth-grade science teacher, Miss Carey, who felt that assigning homework had become a special problem of which she was painfully aware. On the day she assigned all her pupils ten pages of textbook reading on the age of the earth, she came to Mr. Simpson for help.

"A single assignment for all these dozens of children whom I meet daily doesn't make sense," said Miss Carey. "But earth science is so remote to them! How can I vary my assignments to reach children of differing abilities and interests?"

If you were Mr. Simpson, what facts of human growth and development would you wish to take into account in working with Miss Carey to improve her homework assignments? What assignments other than her routine one would you recommend that Miss Carey make?

ACTIVITY 2-1

Diagnosing the Learning Potential of an Individual Learner

To see the advantages and disadvantages that individual learners possess, one should study individuals carefully. Each learner operates amid a cluster or complex of forces. Some of these forces have been noted above.

Choose an individual learner for study, or encourage a teacher whom you supervise to do so. Through interview, analysis of cumulative records, home visitation, and/or any other means at your disposal, find out all you can about this learner—the pattern of his or her development; his or her personal characteristics, talents, strengths, and weaknesses; and the social forces that impinge upon him or her. Describe your expectations concerning the individual and the extent to which these expectations are being realized. Describe something concrete that the child's school could do to help develop his or her potential.

Recent Changes in Learners

Children and youth are continually changing in biological, intellectual, and other ways. Adults often observe that "children don't remain children as long as they used to." Physically, today's children and youth are taller, heavier, and healthier than children were a few decades ago. Puberty and sex drives appear at an earlier chronological age. Though adolescence begins earlier, by force of cultural mandate it also ends later. Curriculum activities formerly reserved for older adolescents are now in the educational regimen of younger persons. Older adolescents are often discontented with some of the elements of the curriculum that are prescribed for them, so the senior year in high school, for instance, can become a trying time for teachers, parents, and pupils. Adolescents in senior high school and college are often frustrated by their superficial exposure to adult activities, privileges, and problems, especially when their actual adulthood is delayed into the twenties.

One of the major features of the new world in which children and adolescents now find themselves is the prevalence of an excess of information from television, wide-ranging reading materials, and reports of technological achievements. Judging what information to process and knowing how to process it become confusing problems. The curriculum of the future will need to guide youngsters in finding ways to manage both of these problems.

The changed culture in which children grow and develop affects them in other ways. Ours is an age in which most youngsters no longer work with their parents or grandparents, and in which they tend to find parental authority arbitrary. In the words of Grant and Briggs, "us-them feelings" often characterize the relationships between youngsters and their older relatives.[16] Having to deal with an increasingly older adult population is a new experience for young people.

We live in a society in which working mothers and "latchkey children" are commonplace. Leaving children home alone can lead to a lack of moral standards and absence of effective discipline. As one adult who had been left alone excessively during his childhood put it, "No one talked with me about what I should do, so I simply did what the other kids suggested, and I got into trouble." But what if his mother and father had been at home constantly while this man was growing up? Could they have helped him set personal moral standards? Where in our culture could they have found such standards? In most entertainment media, or in most books and magazines? In the behavior of public figures? In the views of relatives and friends?

It can be argued that standards of morality in society and community are moving from uncertainty to deterioration, bringing an increase in child abuse. With their rights increased by legal and social sanction but with moral and ethical standards for exercising those rights largely missing both at home and at school, the younger generation is confused about what is acceptable in people's relationships with one another. Abdication of responsibility by parents can lead to roaming the streets, and free time out of doors can lead to destructiveness, vandalism, and violence. Teachers sometimes wonder how so many of the pupil population can be as good as they are.

Unfavorable comparisons of the achievement of pupils in U.S. schools with the achievement of pupils in the schools of other developed nations have raised the question "What's happened to large numbers of our youngsters?" For too many of our pupils, at least part of the answer lies in a scenario like the following:

> Mother and father are very busy; they both work outside the home. In the evening, hours and tempers are short. As a consequence, time spent with the children is minimal. "Have you done your homework?" is a question seldom asked. "I'll help you with your homework" is heard even less.
>
> Mother, father, and other people in the adult workplaces try to avoid spending long hours at anything that resembles work. Accumulation of more money and instant gratification of desires have become the goals of life. The old-fashioned work ethic seems to be disappearing rapidly.

At school, the children consider the pursuit of easy ways out to be almost a civil right. Many of them seem to resent teachers who try to make them work. Eventually, some of the most conscientious teachers say, "Oh, well, what's the use?"

In school, children have always learned that prejudice comes in multiple forms. For a long time, it's been aimed at races, religions, and genders, and it still is. But now there's a new object of prejudice: the children who try hardest, work hardest, and succeed.

Using Data About Learners Insightfully

We need all the insight we can muster to reckon with the characteristics, needs, and tasks that we can identify in the precious youngsters in our schools. We must realize, first, that characteristics, needs, and tasks overlap among age groups, with the greatest overlap occurring when groups comprise children of two or three consecutive ages (six and seven, eight and nine, etc.) rather than broader categories. Then we must give careful thought to what a particular characteristic, need, or task means for school programs. Some inferences can be drawn immediately—about physical capabilities as they relate to learning experiences, for example. Other inferences are harder to draw, and the school experiences that seem to fit must be tried out before we can confirm their appropriateness. Once a characteristic, need, or task has been validly identified, it must be thought about in relationship to other factors: What relative weight should be given to this particular characteristic, need, or task? Finally, evidence about the growth and development of learners should be checked against the objectives to which teachers and pupils subscribe.

One can point to a number of curriculum guides that are based, at least in part, on the developmental characteristics of children. These publications tend to classify child growth and development into four broad areas: the physical, the social, the emotional, and the mental. Each area may then be subdivided. For example, physical characteristics may be subdivided into growth in height, weight, and body proportions; growth of internal organs; growth of sex characteristics; development of physical abilities; and maintenance of physical health and hygiene.[17]

Curriculum materials can be prepared in such a way that all growth and developmental characteristics of learners show through them. When this is done, the materials are likely to list a wide range of experiences for learners and thus deal with human potential more adequately. In general, curriculum guides in art, home economics, and physical education have been oriented more closely toward the reality of human growth and development than have the guides in other school subjects.

Sometimes a particular view of human growth and development proves especially adaptable to the work of curriculum planners. One of these is Robert Havighurst's concept of *developmental tasks* (tasks such as learning to speak), with their special requirements at given times in the learner's life. Developmental tasks emerge from a combination of factors: maturation, the culture in which the child is reared, and the nature of the individual child. The concept is therefore an interdisciplinary one, originating in individual psychology, human growth and development, and sociology.[18]

Teachers and other curriculum planners who want to use data about learners insightfully should

1. Establish objectives for helping learners find their identities, create their own goals, and make attainment of their goals possible
2. Teach with the needs, abilities, interests, and developmental levels of learners constantly in mind
3. Make the school a personal and social institution as well as an agency for intellectual development
4. Help learners establish roles associated with achieving adulthood, practicing good citizenship, taking responsibility, and making wise decisions
5. Consider what effect proposals calling for major changes in the process of schooling are likely to have on the growth and development of learners

From the broader standpoint of the whole curriculum, study centers where many different role-takers can work together are needed. Curriculum planners should cooperate in determining what is especially worth learning well. Incorporating higher-mental-process material, intensive art experiences, continuing social interaction, and engagement in peak effort helps to increase the worth of learning strategies.

Where Fact Meets Fantasy in Interpreting Data About Learners

Sometimes the developmental data about children and youth appear obvious, clearcut, and factual. At other times, however, they prove so equivocal and uncertain that efforts to act on them lead to disputes. Brief descriptions of two currently controversial issues follow.

1. Do We Know Enough About the Development of Three- and Four-Year-Old Children to Insist That They Be Provided with Formal Schooling?

Compulsory early-early childhood education has been advocated recently in a number of states. The assumption is that if compulsory very early childhood education is good for one population of three- and four-year-old children, it is good for all. A conflict between advocates and opponents of early-early childhood education develops when advocates make the assumption that these children have achieved "mature intelligence," especially as indicated by ability to read, and when they try to legislate across-the-board admission of children to school based on chronological age. Opponents say, "The old-fashioned idea that children who are chronologically old enough to enter school are developmentally ready to do so has proved entirely invalid."

Contradictory findings cause argument and confusion. Tests show that very young children gain immediately from formal schooling but, after several months, have lost most of the gain. Among the advocates of early-early childhood education one finds state governors, mayors of cities and towns, officers of educational foundations, and state education officials. Opponents include child development specialists, educational researchers, and local school personnel. Whereas advocates of early-early childhood education focus on children's intellectual development, opponents look more carefully at physical, social, and psychological development. Advocates show concern about lost opportunity for learning during a learning-productive period of life. Opponents fear the social and emotional effects of taking young children from a nurturing home environment. The discussion is complicated by difficulties in evaluating current programs because of differences in the programs and the uncertainty of evaluation methods that can be used. Realizing that hard evidence about the long-term effectiveness of early-early childhood education is largely lacking, compromisers favor (1) providing this education for children deprived of warm, supportive home environments and (2) offering the same opportunity to other children when it seems desirable.[19] Other persons reject the formalism of instruction in reading, writing, and numbers, opting instead for learning activities better suited to the physical, social, and emotional needs of young children.

2. Do We Know Enough About the Development of Brain Functioning to Urge Speedups and Slowdowns in Our Teaching?

Certain learning content can obviously be mastered more readily at a given chronological age by some pupils than by others. The cause has been attributed in part to increments in the development of the brain, in both brain weight and mental activity. Although states of development in intelligence have been discussed for a long time (by Vygotsky and Piaget, for example), how learners move from one state to the next has only recently come under scrutiny. Epstein and others have said that the advances occur by correlated brain growth and mind spurts, called *phrenoblysis*.[20] As measured by head circumference, brain growth is 5 to 10 percent during each of the age periods from two to four, six to eight, ten to twelve, and fourteen to sixteen. Between the ages of ten and twelve, girls grow at approximately twice the rate of boys. At about the age of fifteen, boys overtake girls in rate of head growth. In most youngsters between the ages of twelve and fourteen, the brain ceases to grow.[21] Epstein and Toepfer have said further that the probable difference between a learner with an I.Q. of 160 and a learner with an I.Q. of 100 is the speed at which new intellectual capacities mature.

Consideration has been given to the differences in function of the right and left hemispheres of the brain. At first, the left hemisphere was thought to be devoted to rationality and the right hemisphere to emotionality and creativity. Although subsequent study has reduced the rigor of this distinction between the two hemispheres, differences continue to appear. For instance, the two hemispheres differ in the contributions they make to perception; the right hemisphere apparently plays a special role in emotion; and for right-handed people, speech seems to be centered in the left hemisphere. The implications of these and similar findings for education have yet to be explored.[22]

Information of this kind interests curriculum planners, but they wonder how it should be applied. Epstein and others have said that schools should increase the potency of cognitive experience during certain age periods and reduce it during other periods—a process called *brain periodization.* The quiescent periods might be used for skill practice and for acquiring certain affective learnings. Although spurts in cognitive development occur when the brain grows, apparently one cannot safely generalize that slowed brain growth prevents the learning of new material. As in the case of early-early childhood education, a major problem arises when application of brain periodization is attempted across the board, without ample allowance for individual differences. In order for brain periodization theory to be successfully applied across the board in a school, the curriculum of that school would need to be changed markedly and the standard teaching materials would need to be revised radically. We are certainly not at a stage at which we can say of a group of pupils, "They can't learn because they're on a brain growth plateau."[23]

A Conflict Between Two Viewpoints

You have already seen, in the first chapter of this book, some of the philosophical distinctions between Traditionalism and Progressivism. Later in this chapter, you will see the differences between two theories of learning: behaviorism and human development. Related to these distinctions are two schools of thought in psychology about how children and youth learn. Both of these schools have influenced the decisions of curriculum makers and therefore the nature of the curriculum.

One school of thought holds that youngsters have measurable abilities that can be expressed in terms of numbers, scores, and percentages. This so-called psychometric school looks for variations in performance that indicate differences in amount or degree of ability among individual learners whose performance is checked from time to time. When individual learners fail to "measure up," something must be done to make them perform better. Frequently, the first thought is to match pupils according to their tested levels of ability: the presumably less bright with the other less bright, the gifted with the gifted, and so on. Careful, separate grouping of the "able," the "less than able," and those somewhere in the middle follows. More than that has to be done with the troublesome poor performers, however. The suggestions flow:

"Let's put more heat on these kids to learn."

"We have to teach the basics with more rigor and vigor because that's where much of the trouble appears, especially trouble that's embarrassing to us teachers, school board members, parents, and employers."

"We should assign more homework to these children and test them more often."

"We've got to take the nonsense out of the curriculum—especially subjects like the industrial arts, home economics, the fine arts, music, and other trifles."

"We must get all the children we can into preschool programs when the children are three or four years old."

"Children should learn to read earlier. Nearly all of them should be reading by the time they leave kindergarten."

Individual psychologists and curriculum workers of the psychometric school have a right to object to some of these statements, because not all of the psychometrically minded accept them. But many persons of influence in state and national politics, as well as many citizens in local communities, accept all the ideas expressed above as gospel truth.

The other school of thought maintains that all learners, except a small minority of handicapped and retarded ones, have abilities that can be developed fairly easily over a period of time. As members of this school study individual learners, they often use the expression "not yet." They are convinced that youngsters may be expected to vary in the age levels at which they develop any particular ability. The curriculum worker's task becomes matching curricula with the levels of children's abilities at the times these abilities appear. Therefore, multiple rather than single curricula are needed. At the least, standard curricula should be utilized in segments, from the extremely easy to the extremely difficult; further, some of the segments should require exercise of general abilities, while others should require exercise of highly specific abilities.

Developmentally minded psychologists and curriculum workers have been heard to say:

"We should let the children grow and develop a while. Most of them aren't ready for what we've been asking them to do."

"Two things we must prize: the idea of active, hands-on learning and education of children in getting along together. Much of what has happened in recent years has deprived children of sufficient activity and socialization."

"Children learn to read, write, and speak best when they see sense in the content in which skills are taught."

"When children develop as learners, we can expect the development itself to occur unevenly, sometimes in spurts. Therefore, comparisons among them cannot always be fairly made."

Specialists in child development realize that their view of learners puts them in opposition to approaches that rely exclusively on whole-group teaching, uniform curricula, and standardized tests. What these specialists have been saying recently has been receiving more credence than the words of their counterparts during the 1970s and the early 1980s.

Certainly curriculum planners can find truth in what both schools of thought have been saying. On one hand, they should deplore the waste of time that has become commonplace in many schools, the less-than-serious attitudes of some teachers and pupils, and the inability of numbers of youngsters to read, speak, and write. Accordingly, they should seek to "toughen" some aspects of the curriculum, to use tests and inventories that identify deficiencies in the school program as well as in learners, and to challenge pupils at every ability level. They should recognize that much time in school is now being spent on subject matter that has been imposed on the schools by outside influences.

On the other hand, curriculum workers should know, as members of a service profession, that learners are more important than the curriculum that is assigned to them. They should respond to the fact that development does occur unevenly within and among pupils. Therefore, they have to admit that sometimes it is appropriate to say, with regard to a given youngster and a given task, "not yet." Finally, they should know that the real curriculum is not a monolithic document to be forced on teachers and pupils by a Grand Vizier who sends spies to observe and test how well the document has been used. This concept has always been grounded in unrealistic thinking about the nature of human beings. To a large degree, when the classroom door is closed, the teacher does what he or she believes to be best to do.

UNDERSTANDINGS OF THE LEARNING PROCESS

Some Generally Accepted Principles of Learning

Much that has been said in the preceding pages has implied the importance of having a point of view about how learning proceeds. Schools of psychological thought are so numerous and so varied in their viewpoints about learning that a real service has been rendered by scholars who have tried to reconcile the differing viewpoints. Two of these scholars were Ernest R. Hilgard and Goodwin Watson. Quotations and paraphrases of some of Hilgard's and Watson's statements are presented below. The statements chosen have special relevance for teachers and other curriculum workers. The ideas are, of course, subject to change as more is learned about psychology and about psychological bases for curriculum decisions. So far, however, they have—with amendments—generally withstood the test of time.

- Tolerance of failure is best taught by providing a backlog of success.
- Individuals need practice in setting goals for themselves: goals that are neither so low and limited as to elicit little effort nor so high and difficult as

to foreordain failure. Realistic goal setting leads to more satisfactory improvement than does unrealistic goal setting.

- The personal history of the individual—for example, his or her record of reaction to authority—may hamper or enhance the ability to learn from a given teacher.
- Active participation by learners is preferable to passive reception of the content to be learned.
- Meaningful materials are learned more readily than nonsense materials, and meaningful tasks more readily than tasks not understood by the learner.
- There is no substitute for repetitive practice in the overlearning of skills or in the memorization of unrelated facts that must be automatized.
- Information about the nature of a good performance, knowledge of one's mistakes, and knowledge of successful results assist the learner.
- Transfer to new tasks will occur more smoothly if, in learning, the learner can discover relationships for himself or herself and has experience in applying principles of relationship within a variety of tasks.
- Spaced or distributed recalls are advantageous in fixing material that is to be retained a long time.[24]
- "Learners progress in any area of learning only as far as they need to in order to achieve their purpose. Often they do only well enough to 'get by'; with increased motivation they improve."[25]
- "The most effective effort is put forth by children when they attempt tasks which fall in the 'range of challenge'—not too easy and not too hard—where success seems quite possible but not certain."[26]
- Learners engage in an activity most willingly if they have helped select and plan the activity.
- When learners are grouped by ability according to any one criterion such as age, I.Q., or reading ability, they vary over a range of several grades according to other criteria.
- Learners think when they encounter obstacles or challenges to action that interest them. In thinking, they design and test plausible ways of overcoming the obstacles or meeting the challenges.
- When pupils learn concepts, they need to have the concepts presented in varied and specific situations. They should then try the concepts in situations different from those in which they were originally learned.
- Pupils learn a great deal from one another. When they have been together a long time, they learn from one another more rapidly than they do from peers who are strange to them.
- The problem of "isolates" appears in every school. Isolates are those children who are generally not chosen by their classmates and who are also likely to be unpopular with teachers.
- No school subject is strikingly superior to any other subject for strengthening one's mental powers.

- Pupils remember new subject matter that conforms with their previous attitudes better than they remember new subject matter that opposes their previous attitudes.
- Learning is aided by formulating and asking questions that stimulate thinking and imagination.

Two Theories—and Half a Theory—of Learning

Much of what Hilgard, Watson, and several other psychologists have said has passed into the commonly accepted lore of learning. Beyond lore, we need current theory that is a product of recent, concentrated thought. Two major theories have influenced curriculum study during the twentieth century. The first of these has been labeled behaviorism; the second, human development.

Behaviorism

Behaviorism speaks of what can be known objectively and therefore of what is accessible to us as observers of the learning process. The language of behaviorism is familiar, in part, to most teachers: conditioning, readiness, stimulus, response, habit formation, connectionism, behavior modification, and programmed learning. Near the beginning of the century, Edward L. Thorndike enunciated his laws of learning: readiness, exercise, and effect. Later, B. F. Skinner and others emphasized the importance of conditioning and behavior modification. The mid-century enthusiasm for programmed learning found its basis in theories of stimulus and consequent response.

Life in schools, as well as practice in curriculum planning, has been dominated during the latter half of the twentieth century by familiar ideas that stemmed from behaviorism. Think, for example, of behavioral objectives, skill training, direct instruction, mastery learning, time-on-task, and the whole sweep of educational technology. Chapter 6 of this book, on evaluation, refers to procedures that owe their rationale to behaviorism. Advocates of this theory speak often of repetition, reinforcement, and shaping. They tend to say to learners, "We want you to have success; you can have it by our structured methods." A curriculum prepared by behaviorists contains learning sequences and opportunities for reinforcement. Usually, the critics of behaviorism find it too mechanistic. As a student of curriculum planning said, "Behaviorism means to me, 'Just prepare the table, and the creatures will eat.'"

Human Development

Development is the process of the human organism's "unfolding" as it interacts with its environment. The human being develops cognitively, socially, emotionally, physically, and spiritually. Piaget, the hero of the human development theorists, described the cognitive development of children according to the successive steps or stages noted earlier in this chapter. Other scholars described three discrete learning steps: assimilation, or taking in curriculum content; accommodation, or finding a place for the content in the program of learning; and equilibration, or balancing the new content with other accretions of subject matter. Jerome Bruner added to the discussion by describing the acquisition of knowledge, its transformation, and its evaluation.

The idea of development opened exploration of levels of thinking. Robert Gagné discussed thinking in the form of a hierarchy (see pp. 80–81). J. P. Guilford spoke of the structure of intellect, which involves operations, products, and contents of learning. Much has been said in education circles during the past few decades about problem solving, reflective thinking, critical thinking, and discovery learning. All of these concepts owe allegiance to the theory of development.

Critics of the human development theory consider it too loose, free, and permissive. Though it has a shorter history in curriculum practice than does management-oriented behaviorism, it has had many adherents among curriculum workers.

The two theories discussed so far are settled and solid. A third, discussed below, may be called half a theory in the sense that it is somewhat nebulous and has uncertain boundaries, outreach, and application.

Phenomenology and Humanism

Coming from philosophy, the terms *phenomenology* and *humanism* have different, though complementary, meanings. The phenomenologist relies for data on observable human experience; the humanist places concern for the human being above all else in the universe. Phenomenology centers on the recent experience of the individual; humanism centers on helping people in a number of ways. Affective education, or education about feelings, attitudes, and self-esteem, finds much of its basis in this half theory. So, too, does clarification of values.

Phenomenologists and humanists commonly speak of wholeness, the holistic approach, the field, continually reorganized perception, self-actualization, nondirectiveness, needs hierarchies, self-fulfillment, and student choice. Some of these terms suggest Gestalt theory and the work of both Karl Maslow and Carl Rogers.

Obviously each of the three theoretical constructs has much to offer curriculum planners as they seek alternatives to the routinized educational viewpoints of earlier centuries.

Three Central Issues in Learning Theory and Practice

As teachers work daily in their classrooms, they are often concerned with three matters: what their pupils can learn, how motivation of learners occurs, and the nature of concept development. These matters have long been in the forefront of learning theory and practice.

What Pupils Can Learn

Most adults think of learning content in schools as consisting of the same content they themselves tried to master in their own school days. These adults include educators and political leaders who ought to know better. Times have changed in the sense that school populations today, notably less homogeneous than they were thirty to sixty years ago, don't always succeed in mastering standard, time-honored curriculum; numerous deficiencies and other difficulties stand in the way. As knowledge abounds, the curriculum undergoes subject matter changes. Thus the American goal of successfully educating all the children of all the people encounters new difficulties. If we are to educate all the children, what curriculum content shall we use? Can everyone learn to read, write, and calculate acceptably? The answer being no (painful though the realization is), can something else be offered to so-called nonlearners? Helène Hodges reports that the young adolescents she taught in New York City could and would learn from what she calls global, tactual-kinesthetic activities in which they were interested: activities that seemed real to them and required that they move about and work with others.[27] Such activities may not constitute the be-all and end-all of experiences for these pupils, but for the time being they keep them in school, satisfying the law mandating compulsory attendance. When one considers alternatives to *some* sort of education, one realizes that society can afford to pay for this kind of schooling, even though it does not suit the American dream in this era of high technology. Meanwhile, the search must continue for ways of improving the teaching of basics and fundamentals, as must the search for other experiences that are constructive and educative. Hence there is a continuing need for curriculum planning.

How Motivation Occurs

When pupils are moved to learn, the motivation actually comes from inside them. They may have been affected by outside influences, but the real movement to accomplish something comes from within. To say it another way, only the individual can motivate himself or herself; other people merely set the stage or provide suitable conditions for motivation. Motivation results from setting and possessing goals. The goals most helpful in inspiring learning are intrinsic in the learning itself rather than extrinsic, immediate rather than deferred, and major rather than minor. Because goals may be set so high as to be frustrating or so low as to be unchallenging, an important aspect of teaching is helping individual learners set goals that are realistic for them.

What can teachers do to help learners motivate themselves? They can show their interest in and appreciation of learners. They can personalize, or tailor, their teaching. They can teach in different ways —that is, sometimes directively, sometimes nondirectively. They can provide study helps and give learners feedback and immediate rewards. Most important of all, they can help learners feel genuinely competent.[28]

The Nature of Concept Development

Concepts are the threads of thought, or universals, that run through the curriculum. Children should indeed learn facts, but facts are most usable and most easily recalled when they help to form a context. In the workaday world, for example, the compounds, or medicines, created by pharmacists constitute the context within which the selected ingredients and allotted amounts are facts. Pharmacists know ingredients and amounts well because they use them in creating medicines.

Suppose we apply this idea to learning in schools. The pupil who is merely taught to memorize a series of historical dates, places, personages, and events without seeing and using them contextually has been cheated. He or she will not remember them long, because they have little relevance to anything bigger and more important. If, on the other hand, the pupil's teacher has related the facts to a king-size thread of thought like teamwork or sacrifice for a cause, the significance of the facts will become clear. Then the pupil merely needs to keep the thread of thought, or concept, in mind in future situations, as other combinations of facts in subsequent learning support, or "feed," it. These facts may well appear in subjects other than history. The well-educated pupil should finish his or her schooling with a store of significant, supportable concepts that are usable in daily living. For most adults, concept development has been casual and fortuitous rather than intentional and planned because we have been merely fact-taught and, hence, partially miseducated. Able teachers become masters at helping learners weave relevant facts into concepts.

SITUATION 2-3

Putting Selected Learning Principles to Work

A central office supervisor and a building principal visited every classroom in the principal's building. As they did so, they spent most of their time observing pupils rather than teachers. They tried to ask themselves, "What are these pupils learning? What difficulties are they encountering? What principles of learning could we help teachers apply to improve the learning in this school?" They identified three chief difficulties:

1. Too many items of content were being learned in isolation and without interrelationship.
2. Most of the reading material used in the school was too far above the comprehension level of the pupils, but most of the classroom discussion, if it could be called that, was simple and repetitive.
3. Pupils were learning under threat of punishment more often than they were learning because the content seemed to them to be worthwhile.

What important principle of learning does each of the difficulties suggest? What concrete activities could teachers perform to apply each of the principles?

Applying Learning Theory in Confronting Pressing Problems of Curriculum and Instruction

Learning theory, like other theory, is worthwhile only when it works. The learning theory available to the school practitioner covers a wide range of current and potential school activities. It soon becomes obvious to anyone studying learning in schools that no one theory can be used to undergird all school activities and experiences. A theory that emphasizes conditioning is helpful in supporting one experience, and a theory emphasizing concept development is useful in supporting another.

Curriculum workers, coming as they usually do from varied academic backgrounds and job assignments, are notoriously weak in specifying learning strategies that teachers can use in implementing curriculum plans. They should know what has happened to the older learning theories: faculty psychology, unfoldment, apperception, and psychoanalysis. They should know the current status of connectionism, behaviorism, and neobehaviorism, as well as of Gestalt-field theory. They should know the range of Piaget's work and Jerome S. Bruner's ideas about discovery. If any of the terminology in this paragraph looks unfamiliar to you as an aspiring curriculum leader, you should go immediately to sources of help in the field of psychology. One cannot derive eclectic learning theories without understanding the theories on which eclecticism is built. There is room in school programs for all kinds of learning activities, from memorization to drill, to inquiry, to creative activity. Curriculum specialists are responsible for helping teachers attain objectives expeditiously. In these days of increasing attention to objectives and performance, applications of learning theory must be made with special understanding and skill.

Perhaps the most significant research in learning conducted during recent decades has been Benjamin S. Bloom's study of human characteristics; Piaget's inquiry into the development of individuals; the work of several investigators concerning physiological approaches to learning and memory; John C. Flanagan's study of the talents of young people in Project Talent; inquiries into the relative significance of nature and nurture; and studies of the effects of environment on the continuing development of individuals. The frontier is only beginning to open, and much remains to be done in the study of the learning process and the conditions that encourage or inhibit learning. Attention is now being given, if only on a fragmentary and limited basis, to several facets of process and environment.

Providing Variety in Learning Experiences

A first instructional problem requiring interrelationship between theory and practice is providing variety in pupils' learning experiences. Robert Gagné has identified eight "learning types" representing eight different kinds of experiences based on differing learning theories. They are signal learning, stimulus-response learning, motor chaining, verbal association, multiple discrimination, concept learning, principle learning, and problem solving.

1. *Signal learning* causes development of reflexive responses to signals by continuing repetition. Examples are children's learning to come to attention when the teacher claps her hands or turns lights off and on.
2. *Stimulus-response learning* is often called *operant conditioning.* An example is learning by practice to pronounce words in a new language.
3. *Motor chaining* consists of connecting stimulus-response learnings. Examples are operating science equipment in a laboratory and putting letters together to form words.
4. *Verbal association* consists of putting words together in association. An example is reciting a poem.
5. *Multiple discrimination* is responding differently to events and objects and distinguishing among them. Examples are making distinctions among makes of automobiles or among geometric figures.
6. *Concept learning* consists of placing objects or events in a class and responding to them as a class. Examples are identifying and responding to a family of objects and identifying and responding to a cellular structure.
7. *Principle learning* means linking concepts to form principles, which may appear as generalizations or formulas. Examples are learning to understand and use statements of principles like "interest equals principal times rate times time" and "objects dropped from one's hand fall to the earth."
8. *Problem solving* is often simply called "thinking" and consists of combining two or more learned principles to create a new principle of higher order. An example is using principles of addition, subtraction, and multiplication to solve arithmetic problems.[29]

All pupils do not respond equally well to the same experience. Learning can be enhanced by varying experiences so that pupils approach the same idea in different ways. Individual differences in learning are thus brought into play.

Giving Direct Instruction

A second instructional problem calling for application of learning theory has real import in our own times. The apparent decline in skill-teaching in elementary and secondary schools has led many a person in the street to say of modern-day teachers and teaching, "If teachers don't teach it, it doesn't get taught." In the thinking of the lay person, *it* refers to basic skills, or essentials for survival. Within the past quarter-century, the basic skills, like almost everything else, have often been taught nondirectively. Although nondirective teaching surely has its place, evidence has been accumulating in favor of teaching "the basics" directively. The importance of concentrated, continuing direct teaching becomes obvious when one watches successful athletic coaches drill their charges in the fundamentals of their respective sports.

After a careful survey of the literature, Brophy reported that direct instruction unquestionably produces pupils' learning of the basic skills. In teaching directly, teachers should focus on academic goals, plan to teach a large amount of content, keep the pupils involved, select and pursue specific objectives, use carefully chosen materials, monitor pupil progress, structure learning activities, provide for immediate feedback, and create a classroom environment that is task oriented but relaxed. Brophy mentions additional obligations of the teacher: to "have a mind" to instruct thoroughly; to use time as a precious commodity; to teach personally rather than through surrogates; to be unafraid to use recitation, drill, and practice; to do whole-group, small-group, and individualized teaching judiciously; where necessary, to encourage overlearning to the point of mastery; and to manage the classroom well. If these responsibilities seem numerous and onerous, they may remind us that many teachers have not been "bearing down hard enough" to ensure success in the learning of fundamentals.[30] Trying hard begins with the will to try. As we shall see in Chapter 3, teachers' will to try has been broken by unfortunate influences in the society and the community.

The same general mandates for learning the basics are usable throughout school systems regardless of the age or maturity of the pupils. Hard work, rigorous drill, and constant trying are necessary at the upper levels of schooling whenever pupils have not learned the basics at lower educational levels.

Peterson agrees that direct instruction should be used in teaching the basic skills. For teaching inquiry skills, the instruction properly may be more indirect.[31] Similarly, Powell points out that pupils learn what they are taught, not what they are not taught, and that the more time teachers spend in direct teaching, the more pupils are likely to learn.[32]

For cases in which following the direct approach is problematic, precision teaching is needed. Precision teaching is a careful application of the techniques used in many tutorial arrangements in public and private schools. It begins with screening pupils, assessing their skills, and initiating remediation. The continuing remedial program is then carried on in both classroom and resource room.[33]

Subsequent research has supplemented these basic ideas about direct teaching with the following guidelines:

- Direct teaching can best be accomplished by having pupils take small steps, checking their understanding and performance, and expecting their full and alert participation. A teacher might use explanations, questions, and suggestions like these:

  "Here are our goals."
  "Let's review what we've done so far."
  "Let's take these steps one at a time."
  "Do you understand the steps?"
  "Now we'll practice the steps in series."
  "I'm going to watch you and correct you."
  "Some of you need special help, which I'll provide."
  "Let's try it again while we evaluate what you do."

"Let's correct, correct, and correct."

"Let's try again and again."

"You seem to be independent and capable now, but I'll keep watching you as long as you're with me."

"When you can, try the steps or the whole activity at home."

"You want to be ready to apply what you've learned and do well when you're evaluated."

- The ablest and most mature pupils do not need attention every minute. For them, excessive attention can lead to boredom.
- Teachers should be sure to repeat practice sessions often, take ample time in presenting material, watch and guide practice sessions, use feedback to keep pupils encouraged, and conduct frequent review of what has been learned.[34]

The coaching of football as it is done in the United States provides a model of direct teaching that incorporates the kinds of activities supported by research on direct teaching. Successful coaches are not afraid to drill their players to achieve correct form and procedures. Once rejected from the vocabulary of professional education, drill has come into its own as an important means of achieving mastery.

This is not to imply that brain and muscle react in the same way to exercise. Properly conceived and utilized, however, exercise and practice do result in mastery, whichever body part or organ is involved.

Teaching Indirectly

Whereas a portion of learning theory supports direct instruction, another portion supports indirect, or more casual, teaching. For a long time it has been known that if learners are to "blossom out," to become creative and self-fulfilling, they must be given time and space within which to operate freely. Open-space education was designed to take pupils from what were alleged to be oppressive school environments into open arenas where they could make free choices as they tried experiencing in ways that were new to them. What has been said in the preceding pages about the need for "tightening up" in the learning of basic skills is not inconsistent with the important goal of retaining in education the freedom to pursue other purposes. Purposes and objectives that require freedom and openness in the learning environment are common to the arts and to almost the whole of the humanities. In free and open environments, pupils learn to work independently and so develop self-reliance; they are not restrained from proceeding at their own rates of learning; they are encouraged to use a variety of learning resources; and their classroom and other learning areas are modified or redesigned so that there is ample space for preparing materials and fostering independent activity. Young children need more space and time for constructive play than they have usually been given. In such settings, pupils' work such as writings and drawings is evaluated individually with reference to the work each of them has done previously. The role of the teacher in this more informal setting is less that of taskmaster and more that of guide, adviser, helper, comforter, and encourager. Pupils should be helped to understand why their teacher proceeds differently in performing a different teaching task.

Encouraging Mastery Learning

Mastery learning is what its name implies: learning to the point of mastery. For a time, it was put to use chiefly within the context of *competency-based education* (sometimes called *performance-based education*), an educational procedure in which the objectives of learning and the evaluation of their attainment, along with the time and circumstances required, are carefully planned.

A major advocate of mastery learning, Benjamin Bloom, expressed the belief that most pupils (perhaps 95 percent) become very similar in learning ability, rate of learning, and motivation for further learning when they encounter favorable learning conditions. The most important conditions are provision of feedback and corrective individualized help. Thus learning characteristics often called good-poor and fast-slow become alterable when conditions are favorable. Bloom was convinced that learning can be made more effective by using mastery learning strategies in which the goal is mastery, no matter how much time and attention are needed to achieve it in the individual case. When pupils achieve mastery, Bloom said, they appear to develop confidence in their capabilities, and their mental health tends to improve.

What, then, are the roles of teachers in promoting mastery learning? Bloom said that teachers need to equalize the feedback and help they give to individual pupils. The procedure should go as follows: (1) group instruction, leading to (2) feedback by means of brief diagnostic tests, leading to (3) individual help usually given by an aide, a peer, or a parent, or through previously prepared materials. Often, just seeing how well mastery learning works for nearly all their pupils increases teachers' faith in learners' potential. In fact, teachers' strong but realistic expectations that their pupils can learn seem to inhere in the mastery learning process itself.[35] Confidence in what learners can do leads teachers to state in sequence desirable learning objectives, to know the reading abilities of their pupils, to model the skills to be learned, to watch their pupils perform, to give learners helpful feedback by reinforcing and correcting what they do, and to evaluate learning with a view toward modifying content and procedures in the future.[36]

Bloom's Learning for Mastery model has been amplified to comprehend broad programs that Bloom would probably never have included. Like *core curriculum,* the term *mastery learning* has become confusing as applications have broadened. However, mastery learning programs, including Bloom's, usually have carefully defined learning objectives, call for frequent evaluation and subsequent feedback, and use for evaluation purposes their own mastery criteria rather than the criteria used in standardized measures of achievement.[37] It appears that applying mastery learning procedures is helpful in achieving a number of learning outcomes.[38] Nevertheless, these procedures need to be experimented with further in elementary and secondary school classrooms.

Mastery learning has been criticized for putting too much emphasis on what adults do *to* learners; for restricting curriculum content to what learners can assuredly do and to what pupil achievements can be measured; and for ignoring much of the need for increased individualization in teaching and learning. The mastery learning idea has led to pupils' spending too much time on uniform content while slow learners struggle to master it and rapid learners wait for the teacher's signal to move forward. Slow learners are embarrassed by their own struggle, and rapid learners become frustrated.

More recent criticism of Bloom's model has centered on its alleged failure to function well in the schools of Chicago. Also, conservative critics in the fields of education and religion have linked it with Outcome-Based Education, which has proved to be a vulnerable target. Thus mastery learning has come, in popular thinking, to be affiliated with attempts to undermine family values and the morality of youth. This, of course, is not the first time that a commendable idea has been twisted to serve an extraneous purpose.

Using Time Wisely

Efficiency in teaching and learning requires that the time pupils spend in school be used wisely. Wise use of time does not imply that youngsters should not have relaxation and change of pace during the school day, but that time dedicated by plan to hard effort should not be frittered away. It has been estimated that up to 39 percent of scheduled instructional time in classrooms is spent on noninstructional matters. These matters include disciplining, restoring attention to the subject matter content under consideration, attending to the personal welfare of individual pupils, attending to interruptions originating in the school office and elsewhere, and providing for transition from activity to activity. Teachers do not realize the amount of time pupils spend merely awaiting instructions. In recent years, a squeeze has developed between the increased quantity of subject matter to be taught and the decreased amount of time pupils have to learn it. At one research center, the time learners have for concentration has been called Academic Learning Time, the three ingredients of which are allocated time, engagement rate, and success rate. As might be expected, pupils who accumulate more Academic Learning Time usually score higher on achievement tests.[39]

Researchers who have studied use of time in elementary schools say that the time spent on teaching and learning in these schools varies from about eighteen to twenty-eight hours a week. At present, most elementary schools have days that are not too long for children to endure and yet are long enough to accommodate all elements of needed instruction. Using time wisely does not, therefore, relate directly to the current attempts to lengthen the school day and school year; rather, it relates to the ways in which time in school is used consistently and constructively for work on worthwhile tasks.

In 1988, Louise McDaniel-Hine and Donald J. Willower reported that, according to their studies, teachers of grades two through four were using only

45.1 percent of school time for instruction. Most of the rest of the time was being used for transitions among activities, supervision of recess periods, clerical-mechanical duties, desk work, moving from the classroom, talking with staff, planning with others, talking with pupils, lavatory duty, and conferences with parents. Secondary school teachers were spending even less time on instruction: 38.6 percent.[40]

In addition to generalized Academic Learning Time, which embodies the total time pupils are engaged in and experiencing success in learning, the literature discusses three other types of time. *Allocated time* is the amount of time actually scheduled for learning. The better-known phrase *time-on-task* refers to engaged time during which pupils are "bearing down" in serious attempts to learn. *Time-off-task* is time when pupils are not involved in learning, whatever the reason. Critics of the schools say, "Time-off-task is not what taxpayers are spending their dollars for." On the other hand, countercritics argue that emphasis on time may deflect attention from the nature of the task, which is the more important curriculum matter.

Things are not always exactly as they seem. When the National Commission on Excellence in Education suggested that the school year might be lengthened to, perhaps, 220 days and the school day to seven hours, it was talking loosely.[41] Research studies on use of time have shown a positive relationship between time used and learning attained, but the variables they have uncovered are so numerous that ignoring them could prove fatal. These variables include the nature of curriculum tasks, the ability of teachers to organize their own efforts and their classrooms to use time productively, the nature of pupil populations, the degree of fatigue, pupils' attendance and attentiveness, whether school was closed because of outside forces and influences, and the general attitudinal stances of professionals and pupils. Obviously, it is not enough to say simply, "Let's beef up what we're doing so that we can equal the Japanese, the Germans, and the English."[42]

Specific advice can be given to teachers for using scheduled time wisely:

1. Analyze how time is presently being used and misused.
2. Establish priorities in the use of scheduled time.
3. As learning proceeds, allot time with discretion.
4. Set deadlines for completing parts of the work.
5. Expect total concentration when the subject matter demands it.
6. Quarantine the classroom against outside demands.
7. Remain conscious of time expenditure.
8. Plan the work, both before and during the activities.
9. Recognize and respond to signs of fatigue.

Helping Pupils Learn to Think

Thinking, an important function of learning, needs to be understood more clearly. Louis Raths categorized the difficulties that learners encounter in thinking as impulsiveness, overdependence, rigidity, the tendency to miss meanings, dogmatism and overassertiveness, underconfidence, inadequate concentration, and unwillingness to think.[43] He and others have made a small start in helping upper elementary school children remove some of their difficulties within these categories. The school has had much to do with helping learners "think straight," but the means of doing so have been largely hit and miss. The thinking done by some learners has been misunderstood. For instance, the person who "thinks at right angles" to his or her group may be considered an eccentric or a deviate, whereas such a person might be described more accurately as a creative thinker.

It is possible to prepare questions that give pupils practice in using the categories of thinking that appear in Bloom's *Taxonomy of Educational Objectives:* memory, comprehension in the forms of translation and interpretation, application, analysis, synthesis, and evaluation.[44] In funded programs, posing questions within each of these categories has proved helpful in teaching youngsters to learn to think. Descriptions of Bloom's categories, along with a sample of teacher questions for each, are given below:

1. *Memory.* Pupils recall or recognize information. Example: Who is the chief character in the story?
2. *Translation.* Pupils change information into a different symbolic form of language. Example: Stated in your own words, what are the ideas in the second paragraph?
3. *Interpretation.* Pupils find relationships among facts, generalizations, definitions, values, and skills. Example: Is the climate of Portland different from or the same as the climate of Seattle?
4. *Application.* Pupils solve a lifelike problem, identifying the issue and using appropriate generalizations and/or skills. Example: According to what we have studied, how would you solve the following problem?
5. *Analysis.* Pupils solve a problem in the light of conscious knowledge of the parts, so that they can describe the step-by-step process by which the problem is solved. Example: It is dangerous to cross the street. The candy store is on the opposite side of the street, so it is dangerous to go to the candy store. What can you do?
6. *Synthesis.* Pupils solve a problem requiring original, creative thinking. Example: Write a poem that describes excitement at receiving an unexpected gift. What's original and creative in what you have written?
7. *Evaluation.* Pupils make a choice of good or bad, right or wrong, according to established, known standards or criteria. Example: Do you think the main character in the story was punished enough?

For a long time, teaching children to think has been regarded as an important function of schools. Before Hilda Taba developed her "thinking strategies" and others began to search for ways of teaching thinking, no systematized methods existed. Any comprehensive curriculum used today in elementary or secondary schools should have within it one or more explanations of relevant ways of teaching thinking. Articles and books by specialists in the subject fields (for example, social studies and science) include many helpful hints concerning ways of teaching learners to think.

Continuing study of the thinking process has suggested that the old-fashioned procedure of asking pupils to think about little parts of a whole problem or situation is less effective than getting them to think holistically.[45] Getting pupils to think with intensity is also mandated by the finding that teachers need to expect their pupils to concentrate to an unaccustomed degree. Principals and supervisors can support concentration in classrooms and at home by insisting that development of the skill of thinking be made a priority in their schools.[46]

One of the problems teachers often encounter when they engage pupils in discussion is pupils' inability to think critically. Lacking background knowledge, learners talk loosely and they talk on and on. In the depths of discussion, they are unable to recognize assumptions, to assess points of view, or to appraise inferences. These abilities can be taught, but the effects of teaching them have not been thoroughly evaluated.

Arthur Costa has reminded us that having pupils do thinking skill exercises apart from the subject matter in which they might be embedded is like having them learn the capitals of the states without making use of that knowledge. The best curriculum materials for teaching thinking combine thinking skill development with pertinent subject matter. To teach subject matter alone and expect that the nature of it will induce real thinking makes little sense. To teach thinking skills without reference to content is about as unproductive. Subject matter content, then, should be selected in part for its ability to stimulate thought processes.[47]

During recent years, many educators have especially valued the teaching of thinking and have campaigned hard for it. Meanwhile, conservative thinkers—mainly outside the education establishment—have pressed the point that additional attention needs to be given first to teaching subject matter content that pupils will presumably use in the act of thinking.

Encouraging Learning That Is Authentic

When they engage in learning that is authentic, youngsters encounter and master situations that are genuinely "practical." By the time the term *authentic learning* became popular, many school people had forgotten to heed what John Dewey and others had said near the beginning of the century: One can learn readily by doing that which is relevant to one's earlier learning and is instrumental, usable, and useful. Currently, a declared purpose of authentic learning is to make some of schooling more like life outside school.

Teachers are tempted to turn what could be concrete activity into abstract exercises. Excessive memorization, constant use of workbooks, slavish following of textbooks, and too-rapid coverage of content mark the stultifying procedures found in many classrooms. When they speak of disconnected learning, bright pupils sometimes say, "The work we do in school has no meaning except to help us pass tests and be promoted." Under these circumstances, learners seldom acquire understanding of how to transfer what they learn in one situation to another similar situation.

Newmann and Wehlage have specified five steps that teachers and curriculum personnel can take to make learning authentic:

1. Encourage high-order thinking.
2. Teach for deep understanding.
3. Connect subject matter with its applications beyond the classroom.
4. Make conversation in the classroom substantive rather than trivial.
5. Solicit positive support, in community and society, for pupil achievement.[48]

Responding to Differing Learning Styles

One's learning style is a combination of one's characteristic behaviors in responding to or interacting with learning environments. Every learner appears to have his or her own learning style, based on a variety of interrelated influences. When learning content really matters to youngsters, they can tell other people how they learn, and they explain willingly.[49]

Cognitive style alone is said to involve three sets of behaviors: the ways in which one gathers information, the ways in which one interprets information, and the ways in which one reasons to reach a conclusion or decision. The first, or information-gathering, set of behaviors includes reading, listening, using all the senses, exercising sensitivity to others' feelings, interpreting staged effects, and understanding body language. The other two sets of behaviors, interpreting information and reasoning, can also be broken into parts. Just as there are modes of learning cognitively, there are modes of learning affectively.

Rita and Kenneth Dunn have identified eighteen elements within four categories representing the ways pupils learn: (1) the environmental—including sound, light, temperature, and casualness as compared with structure; (2) the emotional—involving motivation, persistence, responsibility, and structure; (3) the sociological—involving peers, self, pair, team, adult, and varied input; and (4) the physical—including perceptual strengths, intake, time, and mobility. These four categories provide structure for the eighteen elements or variables associated with teaching styles. The teaching styles also number four: (1) the traditional—representing minimum "grade level" standards; (2) the individualized—in which diagnosing, prescribing for, and guiding each pupil are prized; (3) the open—which permits pupils to select, within limitations, their own curriculum, resources, schedule, and pace of learning; and (4) the alternative—within which pupils presumably have maximum curriculum choice, freedom, and independence.[50] The individual's learning style profile may be matched with available programs to achieve the best possible fit. Specifically, given programs emphasize the achievement of particular skills. The skills developed in a program may be matched with the elements of learning style the pupil needs to function well in that program.

The dimensions of learning style have been extended to include descriptions that can be matched with teaching style descriptions. For example, some learners learn incrementally, or step by step; others learn intuitively, by intuitive leaps. Some are sensory specialists, relying primarily on one sense, whereas others are sensory generalists, using many or all of the senses. Emotionally involved learners want an emotionalized classroom atmosphere; emotionally neutral learners like classroom emotional excitement to be low key. Then there are "explicitly structured" learners who need clear, unambiguous structure to enhance learning, as well as their opposite number, those who want open-ended structure that gives opportunity in the classroom for divergence and exploration. Finally, of course, there are eclectic learners who can draw on several styles, shifting them from time to time.

Teaching styles that, in general, can be made to fit learning styles have been called task oriented, cooperative, child centered, subject centered, learning centered, emotionally exciting, and emotionally subdued. Ideally, schools need to make varied learning environments available simultaneously so that learners with differing style orientations can be accommodated.

To begin responding to differing learning styles, teachers should be given time to interview individual pupils, to note their preferred "learning modalities," and to provide methods, materials, and tests that match the style preferences. Pupils can be asked what methods of instruction they like best, the times of day they study best, how they assess their attention spans, and how much physical activity and structure they need. Interview data can be confirmed by observation. Evidences of cultural diversity should also be considered, as the cultural values of pupils may affect their learning styles.[51] Also, it should be kept in mind that the rigid, traditional ways we manage schools and arrange classrooms can create real barriers to accommodation.

Recognizing but Not Exaggerating Sex Differences

Much of the discussion about sex differences in learning seems to be guided by the lyrics "Anything you can do, I can do better." Public laws have emphasized the importance of having girls and boys do the same things in the formal curriculum and activities programs of schools. In addition to emphasizing the desirability of freeing youngsters of both sexes to have worthwhile experiences in common, the new legislation has aroused interest in the relative capacities of boys and girls to profit equally at any given time from particular experiences. Learning theorists are more interested in the relative capacities of the sexes to learn than in the fairness of new social policies intended to equalize human rights. A possible beginning point in a study of sex equity is analysis of the personal characteristics of girls and boys. Girls seem generally to be better at following directions, are more conscientious, and tend to check their work. In contrast, boys take more risks and appear to be more confident of their abilities.[52]

Learning theorists recognize that the culture affects what girls and boys can do by determining what they are expected to do. During most of the time they spend in elementary school, girls show superiority over boys in verbal tasks. Boys receive more remediation in reading and the language arts, as school personnel and parents expect them to. In elementary school, girls and boys do about equally well in arithmetic. As stereotyping concerning girls' alleged incompetence in mathematics begins, girls tend to steer away from mathematics courses in high school.

Some differences in functioning are real. Young girls exhibit superior hearing; young boys, superior vision. Boys manipulate three-dimensional objects well. Girls who achieve well intellectually are often active, assertive, and outgoing, whereas intellectually inclined boys may be less active, more shy, and more anxious. The unspoken rule in most classrooms is that boys should receive more of almost all elements of interaction—recognition, questions, feedback, and response time—than girls do. In this and other respects, the reform movement has done little to provide equity between the genders.[53] Almost in desperation, some school personnel have concluded that boys and girls should be placed in separate secondary schools.

Given that schooling and the testing done in schools discriminate at different times against both girls and boys, teachers and administrators should do all they can to reduce discrimination. Both standardized and teacher-made tests need redesigning so that they give boys and girls equal opportunities to achieve. The curriculum should balance opportunities for seeing and listening. For hyperactive pupils (frequently boys), additional space should be made available. As boys grow into adolescence, they may be expected to be restless, to write illegibly, to want to disassemble things, and to be loud and clumsy. Girls, on the other hand, need to be accommodated with linguistic approaches to physics and other scientific subject matter. The overall need is for watchfulness in noting differences and for diligence in balancing opportunities.

Cooperative Learning

Throughout the years, there has developed in the United States the popular belief that success and progress are achieved almost exclusively by independent, individual effort. When individuals work independently and alone, they tend to compete with one another. To an entrepreneur who has succeeded in business, competition is the soul of enterprise. Subsequently, the entrepreneur discovers that his or her employees, whom the schools have trained to compete, often have difficulty working together on tasks that require cooperation. Consequently, the entrepreneur finds it necessary to hold two differing views simultaneously—a formidable assignment.

Within a number of school systems, strategies for encouraging cooperative learning have been devised and tried. Existing instructional episodes have sometimes been transposed into cooperative learning episodes. Special attention has been given to specifying what learners do when they work cooperatively; to teaching methods of conflict resolution; and to reinforcing social behaviors that contribute to pupils' getting along congenially and productively. Because critics of cooperative learning say that it will damage pupil achievement, emphasis is given to achievement and the rewards gained from learning are focused on the intrinsics of the learning experience. In general, cooperative learning has a needed humanizing effect in a culture of "dog eat dog."[54]

Highlighting the Rewards of Learning

True learning is not without its rewards. Initial learning, aided by reinforcement, helps the learner improve what he or she will do in the future. Teachers, parents, peers, and other community members reinforce desirable learning by commenting on it favorably, by granting awards, and by signaling in other ways that what the learner has accomplished meets with approval. Rewards of these kinds are called extrinsic, whereas the joy the learner experiences by learning something worthwhile is called intrinsic. Both intrinsic and extrinsic rewards are needed, but neither should be permitted to damage interest, for interest carries the learner along so that he or she continues to do well in the absence of the teacher or other mentor. Interest forms a coating around the priceless pearl of significant achievement, which is to be desired by all learners.

Without promoting an intrinsic-extrinsic reward system, curriculum workers almost guarantee that valuable content will not be learned well. The impact of curriculum materials that accommodate a sensible system of rewards depends on whether teachers follow suggestions like these:

1. Strive to make intrinsic rewards of learning as strong as possible.
2. Judiciously supplement intrinsic rewards with extrinsic ones.
3. Reward only as much of the learner's success as you must.
4. "Get out of the way," so that the best of the rewards do not depend on you or your efforts.[55]

SITUATION 2-4

The Case of Mary Williams

Mary was the youngest child in a family of three children. Her father, a retired engineer, decided to move from the town of Bushville, the site of the plant in which he had worked during recent years, to an apartment in a nearby city. "We can attend the opera and the theater in the city," Mr. Williams said to his wife. "Mary will have a good school that will prepare her for Oberlin just as well as Bushville High School has done."

In the course of time, the Williams family, which now consisted only of the father, the mother, and Mary (the two older children having married and moved away), rented an attractive apartment in Jackson City within three blocks of El Centro High School, which Mary would attend. Fortunately for Mary, the Williams's move to Jackson City occurred when she was about to begin her junior year. If the move had come earlier or later, she might have had more difficulty at El Centro.

At first, Mary found the new school easy. Why should it not be for a girl whose I.Q. was reported to be 130? Mary regarded her peers as being rather dull and uninspired. Perhaps, she thought, this was because she had been in the experimental class at Bushville and these were ordinary students with whom she was now associating.

Then came the first report card. Mary discovered to her shock that it was possible for a student with a nearly straight A average in Bushville to receive a C in English, a B in American History, a D in Latin III, a C in Chemistry, and a C in Algebra II. "Is the work *that* much harder?" her distraught parents asked. "No," Mary replied, "but it's different."

Mary's cryptic remark led Mr. Williams to inquire of the school *how* the work was different, if it really was. After all, wasn't second-year algebra second-year algebra wherever a student took it? Perhaps Mary had changed. To investigate the possibility, Mr. Williams hurried her to a physician, who found no changes in Mary's physical condition that could account for her scholastic decline.

Mr. Williams's visit to El Centro High School elicited varied comments by Mary's teachers, but one remark was common to all: Mary did her homework assignments well, but she could not compete, either in speed or in quality, when she tried the varied activities in which El Centro's teachers asked their students to engage. "We try to emphasize mind stretching," Mrs. Culver, the principal, told Mr. Williams. "Our teachers prepare their key questions in advance to encourage divergent thinking and imagination. We make up 'thinking exercises,' and some of our tests are like nothing you've ever seen. We favor student discussion, provided our youngsters know what they're talking about, but discussion is only one of many classroom procedures we use. The activities in most of our classrooms are really varied."

That night, Mr. Williams turned and tossed while he worried about Mary's situation. The next day he wrote Mrs. Culver: "My daughter came to your school from a good school in which she learned the fundamentals she needs. She memorized her grammar and solved her basic problems in mathematics without difficulty. I have diagnosed her present situation this way: You people are asking Mary the wrong questions, and you expect her to do things she should not be doing. It is your duty to treat my daughter as she was treated previously. If you do not do so, I shall make a complaint at the offices of the city board of education."

What do you conclude about the relative worth of what Mr. Williams wanted done for Mary and what El Centro High School was trying to do for her?

Were the El Centro teachers using valid approaches to learning when they worked with students in general and Mary in particular?

SITUATION 2-5

Identifying Basic Considerations Affecting Learning Style

A curriculum leader surveyed some of the literature of psychology that she thought might relate to a study of the learning styles of children in her school system. Among the generalizations she noted were these:

1. Pupils change their attitudes by identifying with people who are their models.
2. Learning by wholes frequently works better than learning by parts.
3. A learner's success in performing a task depends significantly on the frequency and effectiveness with which his or her learning has been reinforced.

If you had been the curriculum leader, what might you have done to check the validity of these generalizations relative to the learning styles of a sample of fifteen pupils?

The Many Faces of Learning

A review of the preceding pages reveals that learning has many faces, many facets, many features. They include but are not limited to direct instruction, indirect teaching, learning for mastery, wise use of time, learning to think, authentic learning, styles of learning, sex differences, cooperative learning, and the rewards of learning. Taken together, they complicate decision making about what the curriculum should be. Considered individually, each of them forms a sieve through which the curriculum is strained as it passes from idea to statement to practical use. In other words, the faces, facets, and features condition what is finally learned.

Beyond all of this, learning the curriculum depends on what teachers do in the teaching act to really encourage learning. Often, the best judges of what teachers do are the consumers, the pupils themselves. Mosley and Smith reported the answers of 566 pupils in grades seven through twelve of the Little Rock (Arkansas) school district to the question "What do you like about the ways teachers help you learn?" The pupils said they wanted teachers to provide adequate explanations with examples, constructive and relaxed learning situations, individualization of instruction, enough time for learning, and incentives and interest.[56]

A few years ago, the author solicited from upper elementary school and secondary school pupils oral and written comments about their engagement in learning activities in school. The nature of the comments showed that pupils have their own valid, if unsophisticated, views of the classroom learning process. As Rush and his associates said, the final evaluation of any teaching-learning episode is accomplished by pupils, who decide what is worth listening to, trying, and remembering for subsequent use.[57] In any attempt to improve learning in classrooms and schools, the views of learners should be taken into account.

Pupil comments accumulated by the author reflected four views of teaching:

1. Teachers who "madly teach" without giving much thought to their teaching practices sometimes do little to encourage real learning.
2. The best teachers seem to set the stage for learning and then let learning take its course.
3. Teachers can take various concrete actions to assist learning.
4. Probably teachers do best in assisting learning when the school experiences they provide have greatest meaning for learners.

ACTIVITY 2-2

Soliciting Pupils' Comments About Learning

The following question represents the third view of teaching: What can your teachers do in their teaching that would help you most in learning what you are expected to learn?

The following question represents the fourth view: What have you done in your classroom work during the past few days or weeks that has helped you most in understanding or appreciating what you were expected to learn?

Ask the pupils in one or more classes in your school to respond to either or both of these questions. If the response is oral, keep notes concerning what is said or make a tape or cassette recording of what is said. If the response is written, keep the written records. Think about what meaning the pupils' comments have for teachers in their efforts to assist learning. If possible, discuss the pupils' comments with other teachers, and invite them to try the same experiment with their own pupils, with subsequent discussion.

ACTIVITY 2-3

Learning What It Means to Learn

To develop additional insight into the ways pupils learn, teachers may ask pupils to do the following:

Identify a document or a brief selection of material you want to learn. After I approve your selection, study it for a half-hour to an hour, as necessary. Do not try to memorize it. Seek only the meanings you can gain from the material and state these meanings to me.

After the exercise has been completed, the teacher should ask:

- What steps or procedure did you use in learning the material?
- How do you know you have learned the material?

After one month, the teacher may ask the pupils what meanings they can recall and then pose two follow-up questions:

- How do you feel about the learning you have accomplished?
- What does this experience tell you about what you might do to learn more effectively on a similar occasion?

SOME USES OF PSYCHOLOGY IN MAKING DECISIONS COOPERATIVELY ABOUT THE CURRICULUM

So far in this chapter, commentary about learners and learning as it relates to curriculum planning has been focused on teachers and learners in classrooms. This focus has seemed appropriate because, as we have seen, the curriculum is fundamentally made in the classroom by continuing interactive process. This is not, however, the only necessary focus in curriculum planning. What the teacher does in planning for the next day or for the next term is also important. Teachers do not properly teach merely to please themselves by following an instructional program of their own making or choosing. Several curriculum planners are likely to do better, wiser planning than just one. Major decisions about the curriculum and its impact on the lives of people should be made at a third level of planning—cooperative planning by groups of competent people.

The third level of planning is addressed in the following pages in three terms: the psychological basis for finding directions governing learning by children and youth, the psychological basis for selecting and organizing school experiences for pupils, and the current interest in achieving equity while attaining excellence.

Setting Psychologically Based Educational Directions for Children and Youth

For a long time, expectations of pupil achievement have been stated against a background of goals and objectives, which sometimes have been expressed clearly and explicitly but more often have been left obscure. Whereas goals or aims guide the educational thrust of the school, objectives provide specific direction in the selection of experiences to meet pupils' educational needs. Teachers are familiar with the day-to-day objectives of their teaching and particularly with the objectives they have written into their unit plans. They know much less about the goals or aims of the schools in which they work, partly because the schools themselves frequently have no stated goals.

Several key questions reflect the relationship of psychology to the wise selection of objectives:

- Is the objective attainable by the school?
- How long is it likely to take to attain a given objective?
- At approximately what age or ages should pupils be expected to begin attaining given objectives?
- To what extent should objectives be repeated in subsequent years of schooling?
- In what ways do objectives have multiple effects?

As soon as objectives have been accepted, means of evaluating their attainment should be sought. Unfortunately, there are often time lags between formulation of objectives and their evaluation because educators characteristically short-circuit the evaluation process, skipping directly to the experiences through which objectives may be achieved. As soon as the objectives are clear, then, the means of their evaluation should be considered, and these means will in turn suggest learning experiences. Placing the steps in this order tends to prevent teachers from becoming lost in a forest of experiences and activities, the purposes and means of evaluation of which may have been forgotten. In developing course guides and preparing units of instruction, the teacher usually should follow the sequence suggested.

Evaluation procedures should be designed to measure the achievement of every desired behavior expressed by the objectives. Thus, if one of the objectives is development of appreciation, evaluation questions or other evaluation devices should be prepared to show the extent to which appreciation has been developed. Modern teachers often subscribe to several objectives at a time, but the tests they prepare continue to show their success with only one or two objectives, such as garnering of knowledge and attainment of understanding. Changes in attitudes, appreciations, and interests are difficult to evaluate. Pencil-and-paper tests frequently will not fulfill the need; therefore more ingenious instruments must be prepared. Some of these may be both informal and semiprojective—for example, asking a pupil to give oral answers to thought questions, to play out a situation through sociodrama, to create portfolios, or to serve as an interview subject.

Psychology reveals that evaluation can become a powerful force for either good or evil. On the one hand, it stimulates learners to better achievement; on the other, it creates anxieties that inhibit worthwhile learning. What Percival M. Symonds wrote years ago remains largely true: "All of the anxiety inherent in the examination situation comes from the reactions of other individuals—parents and teachers—to examination results. Teachers have the power to make an examination a challenge, or an ordeal to be dreaded and avoided if possible, by the attitude they take toward it and toward the results that individual children achieve."[58] Tests should be used to enhance learning and not merely to effect traumatic checkups. They are used by alert teachers to help pupils learn to take tests; they are sometimes given a second time so that the factor of novelty does not affect the result; and they may sometimes be given for fun rather than for keeps.

By setting objectives and evaluating the extent to which pupils are able to attain them, teachers can determine some of the educational needs of pupils as these needs relate to the psychology of learning. As we shall see in subsequent chapters, other evidences of educational need must also be sought. Determining educational need in a comprehensive way goes well beyond evidence of learning in school to a consideration of the nature and goals of the instructional system, community influences, and other factors.

More comprehensively, educational directions for children and youth are guided by *academic press,* the extent to which all kinds of environmental forces press for pupil achievement. These forces include people's expectations, as well as policies, practices, norms, and rewards.[59]

Selecting and Organizing School Experiences for Pupils

Findings in educational psychology suggest that certain criteria be used in selecting educational experiences that lead to certain objectives:

1. Learning experiences should be designed to allow practice of the behaviors that the objective suggests. The pupil must believe that practice is helping

him or her to learn what the objective specifies. If the opportunity for practice does not seem to the pupil to be relevant to his or her view of the objective, the pupil will tend to reject it.

2. Learning experiences should express what the learner believes he or she is expected to know. The learner's background and present environment suggest that some experiences are worthwhile and that others are fruitless. The perceived worthiness of the experiences has a significant impact on learning.

3. Some learning experiences should be of the self-activating type. Pupils need opportunities to proceed at their own rate through subject matter that suits them. Thus individual learning is justified and necessary. Obviously, keeping pupils in group situations in both elementary and secondary schools too consistently can lessen effectiveness. Invention and creativeness are often aided by the silences during which individual activity occurs.

4. Learning experiences should be fostered, whenever possible, in intimate face-to-face relationships within small groups. Desirable interaction and learning can apparently be achieved more readily in groups of five to eight members than in groups of thirty to forty. Teachers and other curriculum workers should pay more attention to this finding.

5. Learning experiences should be as varied as the objectives they represent. There has been too great a tendency to utilize a few kinds of experiences to achieve several objectives. Ingenuity is needed in devising experiences that achieve given objectives.

6. Learning experiences should be challenging without being frustrating. In recent years, many pupils have found work in their schools unchallenging. When a nation of youngsters fails for any reason to work hard in the process of acquiring an education, that nation is in danger of losing in competition with other nations.

The ways in which learning experiences are put together greatly affect the achievement of objectives. Helpful organization of experiences provides sequence where sequence is needed and continuity where continuity is needed. It also provides balance, so that there is not an overemphasis on one kind of experience at the expense of other kinds. At the same time, it affords enough scope of experiences to guarantee that a broad range will supply all that is needed for total educational development. Finally, organization assists with correlation of subject matter that is closely related—for instance, the history of the westward movement in the United States in clear relationship with the literature of the westward movement. The educational dimensions of sequence, balance, scope, continuity, and correlation demand consideration by master planners of the curriculum. These important elements of planning are discussed in Chapter 4.

At the level of operation of the classroom, where curriculum plans are put into effect, the ideal functional organization of learning experiences is seen by classroom teachers as having certain characteristics:

The good organizing center for learning encompasses ability floors and ceilings of the group.... Some kinds of content, such as mathematics and science, require the development of rigorous concepts. Solving mathematical problems demands high-level insight into concepts of quantity. Learning to read involves acquiring skill in word attack. There are very definite limits to the range of concept or skill development that can be challenged by a single organizing center for learning. When these limits are narrower than the range in group abilities in the particular skill or concept sought, the teacher must plan to make the two more comparable by dividing the class into smaller groups. The development of certain social skills, on the other hand, demands the interaction of individuals varying widely in their interests, abilities and backgrounds. The best organizing center for such learning may be one that plans for inclusion of the entire class....

The good organizing center for learning is comprehensive in that it permits inclusion of several ideas and several catch-hold points for differing student interests. An organizing center of limited complexity is soon exhausted of its appeal and must be replaced by another....But a truly comprehensive center invites exploration at several points and poses a variety of student appeals....

The good organizing center for learning has the capacity for movement—intellectual, social, geographic, or chronological. The class must be able to move somewhere with it. Such a capacity is almost always present in certain favorite units of study....[60]

There are, then, two levels of operation in organizing learning experiences. The first of these involves seeing the curriculum as a whole and letting general curriculum objectives, reflected against a background supplied especially by psychology, determine the sequence, scope, continuity, balance, and correlation that programs of teaching and learning should have. The second involves decision making by teachers about how to organize both their pupils and the blocks of subject matter they study so that the maximum achievement of objectives can be attained. Curriculum leaders are much concerned with the first level, which requires mastery of large segments of the school program. They should be concerned also with the second level, which consists of helping teachers to do better what they have already learned to do in part. On neither level are the tasks simple for their locus is a complex human being—the learner. We must therefore continue to study the learner's reactions to sequences, unit plans, ways of grouping him or her with others, and other strategies of organization.

As learners grow older, they move from the here and now of childhood to what David Elkind has called an extended spatial, temporal, and figurative world of adult thought.[61] Effective teachers gauge the worth of learning content and materials against the effect of these changes on pupils' learning abilities. By selecting and organizing learning experiences, teachers learn to select and organize experiences that are increasingly appropriate.

Finally, the following practical advice to the individual learner suggests approaches teachers and other curriculum workers can use in designing and implementing improved curricula:

- Learn as long as you have to to "get it."
- Learn in whatever environment is best for stimulating your learning.
- Learn from anyone who can teach you.
- Learn especially whatever has prospects of being most useful, presently or eventually.
- Learn with full realization that you are attempting to attain at least one goal.
- Learn by using a variety of facilities and materials.
- Learn, by taking tests, what you need to know and haven't yet learned.
- Learn to the maximum, not just to the minimum that someone else expects.
- Learn by whatever means you can, remembering throughout your school days that you are being given opportunities to learn.

Providing for Equity While Pressing Toward Excellence

Attempts to educate nearly all the children of all the people have been labeled the great American experiment. As the experiment has unfolded, participants have had no real notion of its magnitude or of the factors that could make or break it. Study of the nature and nurture of children has shed the light of realism on the obstacles to be overcome. These obstacles can best be illustrated by considering the case of an individual child called Laura.

To know Laura, at least in a limited way, one must be acquainted with her general mental ability, her achievement record, her stage of maturation, what she thinks of herself, and what impels her to do what she does. Although these are some of the elements in her makeup that an educational psychologist might investigate, they do not tell all one needs to know about Laura. What specifically has she been learning, and how has she utilized time in learning it? What's her home background? What are the cultural influences that have affected her? How does she interact with peer groups inside and outside the school? How does she occupy her leisure time?

The differences between Laura and other pupils make the task of teaching the twenty to fifty children in Laura's classroom extremely difficult. If, at last, the children are to emerge as educated persons from the variety of classrooms they will occupy, great effort must be made to plan for them as individuals rather than merely as members of faceless groups.

The recent influx of minority and culturally different populations has raised the question "Can the schools really help their pupils attain excellence while they are charged with treating all these pupils equitably?" The prevailing fear is that the total learning experience will be diluted by efforts to accommodate a wide range of pupils. Geneva Gay has concluded that equity and excellence need not be incompatible. Excellence is expressed in high standards and expectations; equity, in appropriate curriculum selection and methodologies.[62] Minority and culturally different pupils have backgrounds that must be revealed and talents that must be cultivated through use of ideas and materials tailored to their needs. The object is comparability (equal worth) and not sameness (a uniform curriculum for all). Homework should be special; tests should be appropriately designed; and curriculum plans should have built-in diversity. At the same time, special and different pupils should be expected to work at least as hard as any of the other pupils in the schools. By recognizing and dealing with the real situation, we can yet achieve the American dream.

SUMMARY

This chapter considers questions about the nature of children and youth as learners, about how learning proceeds, and about what we know from psychology that can help curriculum workers. The chapter discusses the characteristics, needs, and tasks of learners as they have appeared to investigators in the past and as they are affected by modern culture. As learning theorists focus on the meaning of learning in the lives of varied individuals, they are preoccupied with what individuals can learn, how they are motivated, and how they develop major ideas and understandings. Learning is a vast theme in the curriculum field because it comprehends such major elements as the effects of teaching directly and indirectly, learning to think, the use of time, individual learning style, and learning cooperatively. Curriculum workers need to gain from modern psychology a sense of how testing should relate to attempts to learn, an ability to judge what constitutes wise selection and organization of learning experiences, and insight into how equity and excellence in schools can go hand in hand.

ENDNOTES

1. From the *Language Arts Guide: Kindergarten and Grades One Through Seven* (Montclair, NJ: The Public Schools of Montclair, 1956). Used with permission.

2. Joan Scheff Lipsitz, "The Age Group," in Mauritz Johnson, ed., *Toward Adolescence: The Middle School Years*. National Society for the Study of Education, Seventy-Ninth Yearbook, Part I (Chicago: University of Chicago Press, 1980), 13–20.

3. For an overview of Piaget's theory, see Jean Piaget, *The Theory of Stages in Cognitive Development* (Monterey, CA: McGraw-Hill, 1969).

4. Deborah Franklin tried to break "the news about heredity" to parents and others in her article "What a Child Is Given," *New York Times Magazine,* September 3, 1989. Note that some recent research suggests that genetic differences do account for much of the variation in pupils' ability to achieve in school. See Jere R. Behrman and Paul Taubman, "Is Schooling 'Mostly in the Genes'? Nature-Nurture Decomposition Using Data on Relatives," *Journal of Political Economy* 87, no. 6 (December 1989): 1425–1443.

5. These facts were known long ago. See Association for Supervision and Curriculum De-

velopment, *Learning and the Teacher,* 1950 Yearbook (Washington, DC: The Association, 1959), 29–32. Note also Calvin W. Taylor's proposal of "multiple talent teaching," a means of giving pupils opportunities to exercise their unused talents, as reported in *Today's Educator,* December 1968, 69.

6. Association for Supervision and Curriculum Development, *Learning and the Teacher,* 33.

7. See "Locus of Control and At-Risk Students," *Phi Delta Kappan* 70, no. 9 (May 1989): 731, 732.

8. Robert E. Slavin, Nancy L. Karweit, and Nancy A. Madden, *Effective Programs for Students At Risk* (Boston: Allyn and Bacon, 1989); see also Robert E. Slavin, Nancy L. Karweit, and Barbara A. Wasik, "Reversing Early School Failure: What Works?" *Educational Leadership* 50, no. 4 (December 1992–January 1993): 10–18.

9. "When Bright Kids Get Bad Grades," *The Harvard Education Letter* 8, no. 6 (November-December 1992): 1–3.

10. Self-rejection and self-esteem were interestingly discussed in the February 17, 1992 issue of *Newsweek* under the title "Hey, I'm Terrific!"

11. For the description of a program in Hartford, Connecticut, see Ray Petty, "Managing Disruptive Students," *Educational Leadership* 41, no. 6 (March 1989): 26–28.

12. William J. Bennett, "An Outrageous Lack of Outrage," *Asbury Park* (NJ) *Press* (January 2, 1994).

13. Organizing centers for subject matter content can be key ideas, people, places, materials, or ways of working.

14. Virgil E. Herrick, "Curriculum Decisions and Provisions for Individual Differences," *Elementary School Journal* 62, no. 6 (March 1962).

15. Barry K. Beyer, "Individualized Learning: Students Can Do Their Own Planning," *Clearing House* 55, no. 2 (October 1981): 61–64.

16. Gerald Grant, with John Briggs, "Today's Children Are Different," *Educational Leadership* 40, no. 6 (March 1983): 4–9.

17. The late James B. Macdonald cautioned against extending the thrust of developmental meanings too far beyond the contexts in which they were formed. See James B. Macdonald, "Myths about Instruction," *Educational Leadership* 22, no. 7 (May 1965): 574.

18. Robert J. Havighurst, *Human Development and Education* (New York: Longmans, Green, 1953).

19. See the discussions of early childhood development programs in *Educational Leadership* 44, no. 3 (November 1986): 4–38.

20. Herman T. Epstein, "Growth Spurts during Brain Development: Implications for Educational Policy and Practice," in Jeanne S. Chall and Allan F. Mirsky, eds., *Education and the Brain.* National Society for the Study of Education, Seventy-Seventh Yearbook, Part II (Chicago: University of Chicago Press, 1978), 343–370.

21. Herman T. Epstein and Conrad H. Toepfer, Jr., "A Neuroscience Basis for Reorganizing Middle Grade Education," *Educational Leadership* 35, no. 8 (May 1978): 656–660.

22. See the four articles under the heading "Educational Implications of Recent Brain Research," *Educational Leadership* 39, no. 1 (October 1981): 6–17.

23. See, for example, Marilyn S. Ballas, "Brain Power," *ETS Developments* 30, no. 4 (Spring 1985): 5–7; Richard McQueen, "Spurts and Plateaus in Brain Growth: A Critique of the Claims of Herman Epstein," *Educational Leadership* 41, no. 5 (February 1984): 67–71; and Kurt W. Fischer and Arlyne Lazerson, *Human Development* (New York: W. H. Freeman, 1984).

24. Ernest R. Hilgard, *Theories of Learning,* 2nd ed. (Englewood Cliffs, NJ: Prentice-Hall, 1956).

25. Goodwin Watson, "What Psychology Can We Feel Sure About?" *Teachers College Record* 61, no. 5 (February 1960).

26. Ibid.

27. Helène Hodges, "I Know They Can Learn Because I've Taught Them," *Educational Leadership* 44, no. 6 (March 1987): 3.

28. For suggestions concerning motivation, see Phi Delta Kappa, *Practical Applications of Research* 5, no. 1 (September 1982): 1–4; see also Deborah J. Stipek, *Motivating Students to Learn: A Lifelong Perspective* (Washington, DC: National

Commission on Excellence in Education, July 1982).

29. Robert M. Gagné, *The Conditions of Learning* (New York: Holt, Rinehart and Winston, 1965), 31–59.

30. Jere E. Brophy, "Teacher Behavior and Student Learning," *Educational Leadership* 37, no. 1 (October 1979): 33–38; see also P. G. Kussrow, "Back to the Real Basics: Preparing Students for Success as Adults," *Bulletin of the National Association of Secondary School Principals* 77 (October 1993): 66–71.

31. Penelope L. Peterson, "Direct Instruction: Effective for What and for Whom?" *Educational Leadership* 37, no. 1 (October 1979): 46–48.

32. Marjorie Powell, "New Evidence for Old Truths," *Educational Leadership* 37, no. 1 (October 1979): 45–51.

33. Ray Beck et al., *Precision Teaching Project: Implementation Handbook* (Great Falls, MT: Great Falls Public Schools, 1977). Reported in ERIC # ED 169 688.

34. For a summary of the research, see Barak V. Rosenshine, "Synthesis of Research on Explicit Teaching," *Educational Leadership* 43, no. 7 (April 1986): 60–69.

35. Gary L. Taylor, "Mastery Learning: A Prescription for Success," *Bulletin of the National Association of Secondary School Principals* 67, no. 464 (September 1983): 84–89.

36. Delva Daines, *Designing Instruction for Mastery Learning* (Provo, UT: Brigham Young University, 1982).

37. See, for example, Thomas R. Guskey, *Implementing Mastery Learning* (Belmont, CA: Wadsworth, 1985); and Z. R. Mevarech, "Cooperative Mastery Learning Strategies," a paper read at the convention of the American Educational Research Association, Chicago, 1985.

38. Herbert J. Walberg, "Improving the Productivity of America's Schools," *Educational Leadership* 41, no. 8 (May 1984): 19–27.

39. Charles Fisher, Richard Marliave, and Nikola N. Filby, "Improving Teaching by Increasing 'Academic Learning Time,'" *Educational Leadership* 37, no. 1 (October 1979): 52–54. (This article was based on work performed at the Far West Laboratory for Educational Research and Development, San Francisco.)

40. Louise McDaniel-Hine and Donald J. Willower, in their lectures and discussions.

41. Other changes in the school year have been suggested. For example, periods of school attendance interspersed with periods of vacation, extending throughout the calendar year, have been proposed for inner cities. This on-and-off arrangement has certain advantages and also some serious disadvantages.

42. See ERIC Clearinghouse on Educational Management, "Academic Learning Time," in *The Best of ERIC on Educational Management,* no. 65, May 1982.

43. Louis Raths, "Sociological Knowledge and Needed Curriculum Research," in James B. Macdonald, ed., *Research Frontiers in the Study of Children's Learning* (Milwaukee: School of Education, University of Wisconsin, 1960), 31–34.

44. See Benjamin S. Bloom et al., *Taxonomy of Educational Objectives* (New York: Longmans, Green, 1956).

45. William A. Sadler, Jr. and Arthur Whimbey, "A Holistic Approach to Improving Thinking Skills," *Phi Delta Kappan* 67, no. 3 (November 1985): 199–203.

46. Monte C. Moses and Jan Thomas, "Teaching Students to Think—What Can Principals Do?" *Bulletin of the National Association of Secondary School Principals* 70, no. 488 (March 1986): 16–20.

47. "On Teaching Thinking: A Conversation with Art Costa," *Educational Leadership* 45, no. 7 (April 1988): 10–13; see also Lauren B. Resnick and Leopold E. Klopfer, *Toward the Thinking Curriculum: Current Cognitive Research,* 1989 Yearbook (Alexandria, VA: Association for Supervision and Curriculum Development, 1989).

48. Fred M. Newmann and Gary G. Wehlage, "Five Standards of Authentic Instruction," *Educational Leadership* 50, no. 7 (April 1993): 8–12.

49. Rita Dunn, "Can Students Identify Their Own Learning Styles?" *Educational Leadership* 40, no. 5 (February 1983): 60–62.

50. Rita Dunn and Kenneth Dunn, "Learning Styles, Teaching Styles," *Bulletin of the Na-*

tional Association of Secondary School Principals 59, no. 393 (October 1975): 37–49.

51. Barbara Cooper Decker, "Cultural Diversity: Another Element to Recognize in Learning Styles," *Bulletin of the National Association of Secondary School Principals* 67, no. 464 (September 1983): 43–48.

52. See the series of articles in *Educational Leadership* 50, no. 7 (April 1993).

53. Myra Sadker, David Sadker, and Sharon Steindam, "Gender Equity and Educational Reform," *Educational Leadership* 46, no. 6 (March 1989): 44–47; see also Jillian Mincer, "Boys Get Called On," *Education Life, The New York Times* (January 9, 1994): 27; and Marcia Linn's address, "Sex Differences in Educational Achievement," at the Conference on Sex Equity, The Plaza Hotel, New York City, October 26, 1991.

54. Paul Chance, "The Rewards of Learning," *Educational Leadership* 74, no. 3 (November 1992): 200–207.

55. Ibid.

56. Mary H. Mosley and Paul J. Smith, "What Works in Learning? Students Provide the Answers," *Phi Delta Kappan* 64, no. 4 (December 1982): 273.

57. Donald E. Rush et al., "Essential Components for Effective Curriculum Development," *Peabody Journal of Education* 53, no. 4 (July 1976): 296–298.

58. Percival M. Symonds, *What Education Has to Learn from Psychology* (New York: Bureau of Publications, Teachers College, 1958), 72.

59. Joseph F. Murphy et al., "Academic Press: Translating High Expectations into School Policies and Classroom Practices," *Educational Leadership* 40, no. 3 (December 1982): 22–26.

60. Association for Supervision and Curriculum Development, *Learning and the Teacher,* 56–58.

61. David Elkind, "Adolescent Thinking and the Curriculum," *New York University Education Quarterly* 12 (Winter 1981): 18–24.

62. Geneva Gay, "Designing Relevant Curricula for Diverse Learners," *Education and Urban Society* 20, no. 4 (August 1988): 327–340.

SELECTED BIBLIOGRAPHY

Armstrong, Thomas. *Multiple Intelligences in the Classroom.* Alexandria, VA: Association for Supervision and Curriculum Development, 1994.

Association for Supervision and Curriculum Development. "Early Childhood Education: Advocates Square Off over Goals." *ASCD Update* 30, no. 2 (March 1988).

———. *Educational Leadership* 45, no. 5 (February 1988): entire issue.

———. *Human Variability and Learning.* Washington, DC: The Association, 1961.

———. *Learning More about Learning.* Washington, DC: The Association, 1959.

Ausubel, David P. *Educational Psychology—A Cognitive View.* New York: Holt, Rinehart and Winston, 1968.

Bloom, Benjamin S. *Human Characteristics and School Learning.* New York: McGraw-Hill, 1976.

Bruner, Jerome S., et al. *Studies in Cognitive Growth.* New York: John Wiley, 1966.

Doll, Ronald C., ed. *Individualizing Instruction.* 1964 Yearbook. Washington, DC: Association for Supervision and Curriculum Development, 1964.

Doll, Ronald C., and Fleming, Robert S., eds. *Children under Pressure.* Columbus, OH: Charles E. Merrill, 1966.

Flanagan, John C. *The Identification, Development, and Utilization of Human Talents: The American High School Student.* Pittsburgh: Cooperative Research Project No. 635, University of Pittsburgh, 1964.

Flavell, J. H. *Cognitive Development.* 2nd ed. Englewood Cliffs, NJ: Prentice-Hall, 1985.

Gagné, Robert M. *The Conditions of Learning.* New York: Holt, Rinehart and Winston, 1965.

Gardner, Howard. *Multiple Intelligences: The Theory in Practice.* New York: Basic Books, 1993.

Gesell, Arnold. *The Child from Five to Ten.* New York: Harper and Brothers, 1946.

Guilford, J. P. "The Structure of the Intellect." *Psychological Bulletin* 53 (July 1956): 267–293.

Havighurst, Robert J. *Human Development and Education.* New York: Longmans, Green, 1953.

Hilgard, Ernest R., ed. *Theories of Learning and Instruction.* National Society for the Study of Education, Sixty-Third Yearbook, Part I. Chicago: University of Chicago Press, 1964.

Hosford, P. L. *An Instructional Theory: A Beginning.* Englewood Cliffs, NJ: Prentice-Hall, 1973.

Jersild, Arthur T. *Child Psychology.* Englewood Cliffs, NJ: Prentice-Hall, 1968.

———. *In Search of Self.* New York: Bureau of Publications, Teachers College, 1952.

Johnson, Mauritz, ed. *Toward Adolescence: The Middle School Years.* National Society for the Study of Education, Seventy-Ninth Yearbook, Part I. Chicago: University of Chicago Press, 1980.

Lefrancois, Guy R. *Of Children: An Introduction to Child Psychology.* Belmont, CA: Wadsworth, 1973.

Mann, John. *Learning to Be: The Education of Human Potential.* Riverside, NJ: Free Press, 1972.

Martin, John H., and Henderson, Charles H. *Free to Learn: Unlocking and Ungrading American Education.* Englewood Cliffs, NJ: Prentice-Hall, 1972.

Noar, Gertrude. *Individualized Instruction: Every Child a Winner.* New York: John Wiley, 1972.

Olson, Willard C. *Child Development.* Boston: D. C. Heath and Co., 1958.

Ornstein, Allan C., and Hunkins, Francis P. *Curriculum: Foundations, Principles, and Issues.* Englewood Cliffs, NJ: Prentice-Hall, 1987.

Piaget, Jean. *The Theory of Stages in Cognitive Development.* Monterey, CA: McGraw-Hill, 1969.

Prescott, Daniel A. *The Child in the Educative Process.* New York: McGraw-Hill, 1957.

Resnick, Lauren B. *Education and Learning to Think.* Washington, DC: National Academy Press, 1987.

Stevenson, Harold, et al. *The Learning Gap.* New York: Summit Books, 1992.

Stipek, D. J. *Motivation to Learn: From Theory to Practice.* Englewood Cliffs, NJ: Prentice-Hall, 1988.

Taba, Hilda. *Curriculum Development: Theory and Practice.* New York: Harcourt, Brace and World, 1962.

Wortham, Sue C. *Early Childhood Curriculum: Developmental Bases for Learning and Teaching.* New York: Macmillan, 1993.

3

SOCIAL AND CULTURAL FORCES
AFFECTING CURRICULUM DECISIONS

Society, the culture, and our American system of values, unclear as these values sometimes are, have a marked effect on efforts to improve the curriculum. Their impact develops at two levels: the remote but significant level of society's influence and the immediate and practical level of a community's contact with its schools.

The first portion of this chapter deals with influences from society and the culture at large. The second section discusses community influences for and against curriculum improvement. The third portion treats examples of curriculum ideas that are of current interest and that demonstrate how American society and culture impinge on the curriculum. The final segment suggests several strategies that curriculum planners can use in dealing with social and cultural influences on schools.

INFLUENCES FROM SOCIETY AND THE CULTURE AT LARGE

We live in a difficult era. Sometimes our only consolation is the thought that other nations and people have lived and are living in difficult times, too. We are faced, for example, with fiscal stress within governments, adverse trade balances, problems of money management in households, deteriorating family structures, the special needs of minority populations, excessively permissive parents, out-of-control youngsters, misuse of drugs and alcohol, and the growing threat of an AIDS epidemic. Some economists believe that after years as a great world banker and an even greater donor, our developed nation is rapidly retrogressing to the status of a developing, poverty-burdened nation. We can gain courage, however, from our country's political stability, the possibilities offered by an eye-opening revolution in communication and technology in general, and the potential that resides in a population with varied and sometimes exceptional talents.

Perhaps more than the general public realizes, our schools are affected by forces from American society and the culture at large. These forces affect the school curriculum in three major ways: by inhibiting change through the power of tradition, by speeding change that stems directly from social and cultural influences, and by creating political pressures. Inasmuch as the school is a reflection of the society that supports it, it receives from the society messages that influence its daily conduct as an institution.

The Boon and the Weight of Tradition

Tradition has sometimes been referred to as a "dead hand"—a potent inhibitor of progress. Actually, it may be viewed either as a helpful preventive of attempts to discard the tried, tested, and true or as a heavy weight that restrains desirable change. Surely the rapid, negative changes that have occurred in our society and culture during recent years should make us willing to retain whatever elements of tradition we have found helpful and useful.

Several forces support tradition and inhibit change. The first of these is legal authority. Laws are frequently enacted more easily than they are repealed. Hence a law that establishes a certain day each year for the planting of certain trees as an exercise in conservation education may have outgrown its usefulness, but the law is likely to remain on the books anyway. A second force, which is of enduring consequence and which exercises desirable restraint, is the generally agreed upon principles of right and wrong. From our Judeo-Christian tradition, we have inherited notions of property rights and individual rights that have often been considered immutable. Thus education in the decent treatment of other people is an objective of the school. A third force, psychological resistance to change, is so potent that it gets full treatment in Chapter 7. Human beings resist change so energetically that, in some areas of their lives, they would rather die than shift their positions. Many teachers cannot prove that their curricula and methods of teaching are actually functioning for improved learning, but they strenuously resist any effort to bring about change.

The curriculum worker must take these and other tradition-assisting forces into account. Almost daily, he or she encounters people who say, "But we've always done it this way!" In a few instances, the response should be, "I agree that we must continue to work in the same manner, because we are dealing here with an unchanging element of our responsibility." Matters of physical safety and the maintenance of intelligently derived morality fall within this category. In many instances, however, a question should be raised about the worth of traditionalized practices. There is nothing sacred, for example, in the methods used in the past to teach arithmetic, though the need to teach arithmetic according to some combination of methods will remain a fixed responsibility.

To illuminate the notion of social and cultural impact within a limited arena, let us consider the effect of tradition on the modern secondary school. By tradition, most secondary schools in the United States do the following:

1. Organize pupil time in several brief periods, generally of equal length
2. Emphasize a limited number of objectives
3. Permit pupils to elect subjects rather freely
4. Conform to established means of evaluation and accreditation
5. Subject themselves to the rigidities of the Carnegie Unit System
6. Add subjects at intervals, but eliminate subjects only with the greatest difficulty

Most of these ideas originated and have been perpetuated as a consequence of what people expect our secondary schools to be and to become.

Curriculum workers who are concerned with secondary schools should look hard at the traditions surrounding the schools. They should ask: Which traditions are imponderables? Which really ought to be preserved? Which could and should be eliminated promptly? Similarly, elementary schools have traditions that ought to be respected, as well as other traditions that need to be challenged.

When changes in the culture are fast moving, as they are today, curriculum workers have to be careful that they don't "throw out the baby with the bath water." The new information era, following our enchantment with television, may readily become a threat to principles and beliefs that have served Americans well through the years. Because youngsters often fail to distinguish between the fictional and the factual, they find it easy to believe and emulate what may prove to be harmful to them. Wanton drug-taking and illicit sex are prime examples.

SITUATION 3-1

Finding Traditions to Challenge

Imagine yourself to be a curriculum coordinator who, with a committee, has sought to identify traditions that need reexamination. The committee has elicited from teachers and lay persons several traditions that they feel should be challenged. Here are six of them:

1. Teachers in the primary grades should be women.
2. Sociology doesn't belong in the secondary school, but history does.
3. Teachers are rightly concerned only with how to teach; lay persons must tell the schools what to teach.
4. The curriculum is appropriately geared to the achievement of the upper classes in society.

5. We must continue to put a premium on verbal comprehension and verbal fluency.
6. Teachers and school board members properly represent mainly the middle classes of our society.

Which of the six traditions operate in the schools you know best?
Which of the traditions that operate in the schools you know genuinely need to be questioned? Why?

Current Social and Cultural Influences

Society influences action for curriculum improvement by bringing to bear on the curriculum those changes that develop in the wider society and culture. As we have seen, the changes can be either negative or positive in their effects. Despite the influence of tradition in holding social forces in check, society is constantly changing. Change is often accompanied by an instability that a society can tolerate unless or until the instability becomes excessive, at which time disorder or revolution occurs.

In many respects, including the following, the United States is moving rapidly.

- Science and technology are continuing to advance, as new discoveries and breakthroughs are made in physics, chemistry, medicine, and other fields.
- Bigness prevails in nearly everything—in government, labor, business, and agriculture; however, small businesses are now receiving increased attention.
- Improved transportation and communications have brought about travel at remarkable speeds and the transmission of messages by satellites. Additional breakthroughs in communications occur regularly.
- Striking changes have been wrought in family patterns of living as traditional family life continues to disintegrate.
- Population continues to grow out of bounds in some areas of the world.
- Social movements that include integration of the races, mobility of the population, and movement of people from lower to higher socioeconomic status are continuing, though the pace of these movements appears to have slowed.
- A value crisis has gripped youth and adults, who have become less clear about what they really believe.

Some of the changes affect schools immediately. For example, when the population of a nation is on the move, new faces suddenly appear in school classrooms. Many Americans are moving each year—from cities to suburbs and, more recently, to small towns and rural areas. The arrival of large numbers of people from Mexico, Cuba, Haiti, South America, Central America, and the Far East has presented new challenges. Schools in larger cities have been forced into curriculum reform by the influx of culturally different children to whom standardized tests are not applicable and to whom American middle-class experiences are foreign.

Other changes have a subtler, more gradual effect. When family life disintegrates, the school finds itself taking on more and more of the responsibilities that the family previously assumed. Although few schools now have to bathe children to eliminate lice, all schools are faced daily with coping with the problems of children whose parents are divorcing, of children who are "on their own" after school, and of children who are feeling the effects of alcoholism, drug abuse, or violence in the home. As a teacher in a city school says, "One thing a teacher learns from years of experience is that a child at risk has one parent, perhaps both, who are also at risk."[1]

In the presence of these and other changes, elementary and secondary schools retain their responsibility for the cognitive development of pupils who represent wide varieties of ethnicity, social status, mental ability, talent, and social outlook. They have become more directly responsible than ever before for affective education, a relatively uncharted domain. So-called simple education of feelings and emotions is never really simple. Today, affective education is made especially complex by societal and academic disagreements about the meaning of moral development and about the determination and clarification of values. Day by day in the schools, there are arguments over matters of morality and values, often with reference to sex, drug, and alcohol education. Where homes have abdicated their responsibility for moral suasion and setting values, many people expect the schools to fill the breach.[2]

Four changes in American society that particularly affect the schools are worthy of brief discussion here. The first change is continuing development and communication of knowledge. Growth in the "knowledge industry" is occurring under the control of big business. Research and development in the invention and use of communications machines are well on the way to dominating the production and distribution of knowledge. As research and development help increase our capacity to learn, education for all persons is likely to take on new meaning. The storage, retrieval, and communication of information will become an even greater industry than it is now. Demand for education will increase beyond its present level.

A second change affects the financial support of the public schools. Prior to the arrival on the political scene of Howard Jarvis and California's Proposition 13, the public was getting tired of paying taxes that had steadily increased in a time of rising living costs. Many a school district was finding its annual budget and its special bond issues unacceptable to the public. Sometimes the movement against higher taxes was statewide, as when legislatures put caps on education budgets. The public was striking out against a visible, reachable opponent. Able to do very little about federal and state taxes, taxpayer groups concentrated their efforts on local property taxes. Among the effects on teachers and pupils were numerous cutbacks in programs and courses and reduction of school activities. A lesson to be learned from this experience is that in periods of extremity, the face and the function of the public school as an institution are subject to surprising changes. In the early 1990s, local property taxes became so high in many U.S. communities that state legislatures are now trying to find new tax bases for the support of public schools.

A third shift is in the realm of human conduct. For some time, discipline and morale in the schools have been deteriorating. As society's standards for guiding and controlling children and youth have become more and more confused, physical attacks on teachers and school property have increased at an alarming rate. For example, the New Jersey State Education Department revealed in 1993 that *reported* instances of violence had risen from 4932 cases during 1989–1990 to 9603 cases during 1991–1992.[3] Violence in the schools has become a frequent topic of discussion in the media, at education conventions, and in living rooms. Teachers are being subjected to indignities that were unheard of two or three decades ago. A high school teacher, writing to one of her more troublesome pupils near the end of a school year, said to him:

> I don't know why you've acted toward me as you have. You seem to be normal, healthy, and good-looking. I think I've tried to respect you as much as I have any of the others. Certainly I've been fair with you. As you know, there have been times in school this year when I have kept you out of trouble, even when what you did was outside our classroom.
>
> You've noticed that I've had to change my home telephone number. I've asked the telephone company to leave it unlisted because of your nuisance calls in the middle of the night. I haven't enjoyed trying to start my car after you were seen putting sugar in the gasoline tank. Also, my neighbor tells me it was you who urinated against my front door.
>
> My telephone calls to your parents have yielded nothing, apparently because they think you can do no wrong. So, unless your subtle attacks stop, I shall have to take stronger action.

On reading a letter of this kind, many a teacher is moved to say, "At least he seems not to have hit her. I wish I could say the same thing about all the youngsters in our school."

Violence has become part of the informal curriculum—in classrooms, in lavatories, in hallways, and elsewhere in schools. In some schools an atmosphere of fear akin to that of the jungle is affecting the lives of pupils, aides, and teachers. A university professor has reported the following experience in a large city high school:

> On a cold February morning I entered the school, to be met near the front door by the principal, a genial but obviously nervous man.
>
> "This is as good a day as any to visit us," he said. "You'll be visiting classrooms in this section of the building. Just go down that hallway,

keeping close to the wall. Some of our male visitors have been at-tacked—by girls as often as by boys—so it pays to put your back to the wall in that event. One of our assistant principals will meet you on your way down the hall. Have a good day, and please come to see me before you leave the building."

Soon an assistant principal arrived to ferry me past an inset in the wall. Through a window, open about an inch, there came the unmistakable odor of burning marijuana. I was quite sure the odor came from the street, which was just below the window. "You probably wonder why we permit marijuana to be smoked anywhere near the building. We made an agreement with ten or twelve of our worst-behaved students: we won't complain if you smoke on the street, and then come back into the building, if you'll promise not to attack teachers or your fellow students. So far the agreement is holding."

Shortly my guide and I reached the first classroom I was to visit. "Please don't leave your coat on that table," said the teacher in charge. "I'll hang it in our closet. Surely you wouldn't want to find it cut or torn into small pieces when you are ready to leave."

That's the way the day started. As for the remainder of the time I was there, I'd like to forget the fights in the cafeteria during the lunch hour, the disturbance in the auditorium during an assembly program, and the other forms of commotion. I saw no guns, but I saw several knives.

Fortunately, few suburban and rural schools have as bad a situation to contend with.

A fourth recent change relates to the mobility of the population of the United States. People are moving from one geographic area to another, sometimes every few weeks. Their children often encounter adjustment problems in school and are enrolled in so many school systems that their total curriculum resembles a crazy quilt. Continued movement of people toward cities is being countered by movement from the inner city to the periphery. Social distance between old and new residents has increased. Assimilation of immigrants into a given culture has become less and less possible. Instead of assimilation, the key problem has been one of communication among cultures, sometimes at the most fundamental level. Children in schools, as well as their parents, now have real difficulty in understanding and accepting the values and ways of life of some of the people around them. Accordingly, education for increased cultural understanding must become one of the most prized goals of the school. Diane Ravitch reminds us that we need to instill in children our shared (common) culture. If we fail to do this by encouraging racial and ethnic separatism instead, our public schools will lose their stake in public support.[4]

Population shifts to the Sunbelt, or extreme southern tier of states, are likely to alter education in the United States in special ways. Education in the north and east will tend to differ from that in the south and west. In the Sunbelt particularly, working mothers may be more numerous, learners may come more often from minority populations, teachers may be in shorter supply, and the pupils coming into the schools may be less well prepared. The public schools must prepare themselves to meet these and other challenges.

These are but four of the several changes in U.S. society that have affected schooling. In the last analysis, the school is a miniature of the society that nurtures it. The school teaches essentially what the society expects it to teach. The values it inculcates differ little from those of the culture that supports it.

Teachers are often hard put, especially in society's fast-moving transition periods, to know what to educate for. Fortunately, there are perennial goals to seek, though emphasis among the goals may change. Education continues its concern for intelligent inquiry, for developing fundamental character traits, and for training children in basic skills. Teachers must stand for principles and ideals in which they strongly believe and, at the same time, cooperate with a general public that is rightly anxious and concerned about what is happening to stability in society. Though diagnosing new developments is difficult, teachers must ask, "What meaning will this societal change have for my teaching next week, next month, and in the years to come?"

During the late 1980s and the early 1990s, the pace of cultural change affecting elementary and secondary schools has quickened. This quickening has often reflected the general permissiveness that pervades the social order. From the standpoint of the structure of the social order, four forces have made a special impact on the ways in which pupils behave and respond within the school environment: (1) the economy as it affects the family has been changing; (2) the racial and ethnic composition of the population has changed without an accompanying accommodation of differences; (3) government policies have seemed increasingly obscure and uncertain; and (4) the meaning of "family" has become more indefinite.[5] The resultant pupil population, say some teachers, is representative of a "raw generation."

In a few schools, youngsters have practiced writing suicide notes or built cardboard models of their coffins, in the name of death education. The English and American literature studied during earlier years has been replaced in part with reading material that can scarcely be described as literature. New textbooks have been published to accommodate the views of all youngsters and their parents, presumably offending none. Teachers in elementary schools have been instructed to watch for evidence of child abuse. As usual, elementary and secondary schools have been expected to "do something, anything" about deficiencies in the society and the culture. Teachers in these schools are, in the words of Thomas Hardy, "people distressed by events they did not cause."

Many school principals wonder what has happened to change the whole climate of schooling adversely during the past two decades. Who or what is at fault? Peter Uhlenberg and David Eggebeen, writing from their vantage points in sociology and family study, have discussed the need to establish policies for strengthening the role of the family, as well as the roles of the church, neighborhood organizations, and volunteer groups, in redirecting American culture from its laissez-faire and often harmful course.[6] If special policies are to be developed, their makers will have to take into account the depth and extensiveness of our sociocultural malaise. When violence, devil worship, sexual promiscuity, prejudice against other peoples, cruelty, and daily disrespect pervade a school, one may safely conclude that they have entered the school from outside it. Similarly, when diligence, honesty, regard for others' rights, graciousness, and decency are the vogue in a school, these traits have shown themselves and have been nurtured mainly at home and in the community.

In brief, blaming teachers and other school employees for the misbehavior of children and youth provides only a partial and sometimes unfair answer to the question "How did the infection start, and what is helping it spread?" Fortunately, fair-minded citizens who know what is happening in schools today realize that, though teachers and other school personnel have themselves been influenced by negative forces, most of them try to resist the worst of these forces when they are manifested within the school.

SITUATION 3-2

Assessing the Effects of Specific Social Changes

The faculties of the elementary and secondary schools in Raysville thought they noted several changes in American society. These changes included increased tolerance of pornography and freedom of sexual expression, reduced interest in the classics in literature and the arts, and preoccupation with self-centered survival in an era of economic uncertainties.

How do you react to the faculties' list of changes? From your vantage point, are all three changes real? What other changes can you suggest?

Select two or three other changes that you consider important. What impact might they have on curriculum in elementary and secondary schools in the United States?

SITUATION 3-3

What to Do About the Plight of Victimized Teachers

The principal of a school in Cranwood brought a guest to the faculty meeting. For reasons he expressed later, the guest wanted to remain anonymous. He had a story to tell the teachers. When he had told it, he wanted the teachers to react to it and to advise him about what he might do.

"What," asked the guest, "would you do about the situation I'm now going to describe? Until this year I've never had trouble with the pupils in my high school classes or around the school, but this fall a new boy arrived and soon began creating disturbances in his classes. One day in one of my mathematics classes I asked this boy to sit down. He refused, we argued, and suddenly he struck me on the chin with his fist. I fell to the floor unconscious. On my way down, according to other youngsters in the classroom, I struck the left side of my head on a chair back. After a week in the hospital with a concussion, I returned to school to find that our principal had suspended my attacker for a month, and that the boy's mother had taken the case to our board of education, protesting that a one-month suspension was too long.

"Because the case had criminal elements, it went to the municipal court, where the boy pled guilty. The judge heard several witnesses, including me, and then dismissed all of us before he passed sentence. The next morning, we at our school learned that the judge had ordered the board of education to readmit the boy immediately and had put him on probation, with a light reprimand. When the boy returned to school (as bold as brass), the morale of the teaching staff went down considerably.

"Now I've come to you as a kind of independent jury to ask what I, and possibly other people, should do immediately and in the future about situations of this kind."

If you had been a member of the faculty hearing the narration of this case, what would you have said?

Society's Political Pressures on the Schools

Every era brings its own kinds of pressures to bear on the schools. During the late 1950s, vocal groups in American society were demanding that our schools help us beat the Russians in the race for space and in technological sophistication. The consequence was pressure within school programs to teach "more of the same" and toughen up for the sake of keeping pupils busy. When the quality of what pupils were learning did not improve as a consequence of this kind of pressure, the funded "projects on instruction" in the sciences, mathematics, and other subjects came into vogue. Schools were urged to install enough projects to give assurance that the curriculum was being improved. Unfortunately for the planners of the projects, the incidence of project adoption was so slight that many projects did not obtain further financial support and disappeared from the scene. Many of those that remained for evaluation did not receive very favorable ratings.

Almost simultaneously, a malaise of softness, a belief that "we'll succeed somehow anyway," afflicted both the United States and a number of other nations of the world. Many parents no longer expected high-level achievement of their children; at the same time they condemned teachers for failing to "make the children learn." Falling scores in standardized tests were only one symptom of a serious disease. Among nations with established educational systems, the United States rated very low in the amount of instructional time it provided pupils *in school*. As to *out-of-school* study, the average pupil in the other nations was spending 216 hours a year more on such study than a pupil in the United States. Although time spent in instruction and study is not the only criterion of learning effort or progress, time spent in learning, within school and outside it, does relate closely to level of learning.

Historians tell us that the United States began slipping into its present cultural malaise during the 1960s. In the view of a number of commentators, we shall find it impossible to eliminate this malaise by passing laws or preparing judicial decisions. Instead, we should spend our time identifying a core of values that can be commonly accepted, and then publicizing worthy applications of these values. Commitment to "political correctness" in its original sense will thus be replaced with another, more productive unity of the culture.

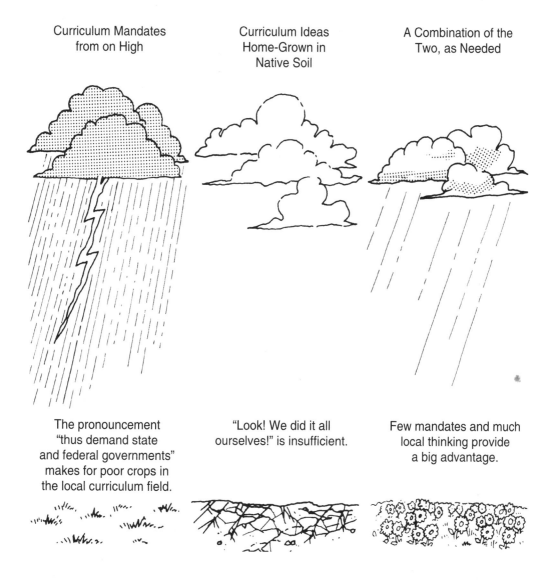

Curriculum Mandates from on High

Curriculum Ideas Home-Grown in Native Soil

A Combination of the Two, as Needed

The pronouncement "thus demand state and federal governments" makes for poor crops in the local curriculum field.

"Look! We did it all ourselves!" is insufficient.

Few mandates and much local thinking provide a big advantage.

FIGURE 3-1   Ways of Making the Curriculum

Politics within communities and school systems sometimes assumes subtle forms. When teachers' lives are filled with numerous duties imposed by the society and the culture, and when school leaders do not emphasize the importance of learning that is truly essential, effort soon diminishes and even the ablest pupils start doing less well than they should. Such has been the situation in many schools, public and private. As attempts have been made to compensate for this decline, schools have been urged to teach the fundamentals better than before, to restore discipline, to emphasize moral and religious values, to prepare youth better for additional education and for making a living, and at the same time to reduce expenditures and to continue discharging duties that are properly within the domains of other institutions and agencies. The task of educating has become more difficult than ever.

Discussion perennially centers on the extent to which control of the schools follows the dollar. During the late nineteenth and the early twentieth century, the funds that the public schools could not obtain from local communities came almost exclusively from state governments. In that era, the effect of financial support in determining control became unclear. The United States Constitution had left to the states the obligation and privilege of operating public school systems. Legal authority itself was nominally sufficient to accord the states the power they needed to implement control. Inevitably, however, the states granted annual appropriations to local school districts. To what extent did these appropriations specifically condition state governments' influence over policy making and management within the schools? This question has brought forth a variety of answers.

Subsequently, a new grantor of funds, the federal government, became a competitor of state governments for the loyalty that necessarily accrues to grantors. Though the federal government had long supplied limited funds to the public schools (for instance, to support vocational education), a flood of money began to issue from Washington. As an entrant in the field of large-scale funding of public education, the federal government, especially as represented by the United States Office of Education, became a threat to school officials who resented the fact that federal grants were customarily made for limited and specific purposes that were determined by a few people at a central place. Reminding objectors to federal control that local school districts were not required to accept federal grants did not silence their complaints. Some local communities feared the growth of a federal colossus whose agents might wheel and deal with friendly state officials in the interest of destroying local control by developing a national curriculum or by strengthening a state curriculum of monolithic design. This threat has seemed more real during recent years.

When the federal government began withdrawing from the funding of public schools through large grants, state departments of education resumed, with increased initiative, their attempts to guide the destinies of individual school systems. For a long time, state education departments had prepared curriculum guides that were meant to be what the name suggests—guides to be followed in a general way by school personnel in local districts. Inasmuch as there was never any real enforcement of the proposed use of the guides, following the guides in local districts was, in fact, optional. One could visit district after district and find untouched guides on office shelves.

During the late 1980s, the decline in the federal government's funding of public schools created serious problems. Between 1980 and 1986, increases in state and local spending for educational purposes only offset what the federal government was failing to spend. By 1986, federal expenditures had dropped to the lowest level in twenty years. The pupil groups most often mentioned as needing additional help include the minorities, the gifted, and the handicapped. Less has been said about the economically disadvantaged, who may well constitute a third of the total pupil population by the turn of the century. In the 1990s, controversy has developed concerning the extent of federal support of public schooling. Using almost the same data, people on opposite sides of the political fence have drawn nearly opposite conclusions.

During the late 1970s and early 1980s, the accountability movement, in some instances backed by legislation, led state departments of education to supervise the work of local school districts more closely. The chief medium of curriculum supervision became minimum competency testing. Having established lists of pupil competencies representing the *least* that the state would require pupils to achieve if they were to be promoted or graduated, state departments of education themselves supplied—or contracted with private testing agencies to supply—measures of the achievement of the competencies, called competency tests. Sometimes the appearance of rigid state control is softened by use of euphemisms like "state guidelines" and "the development of proficiencies." State teachers' associations and school board associations have sometimes condemned proposals of competency-based education unless the benefit from them is sufficient to compensate for the loss of local decision-making power. Teachers feel strongly that their influence in curriculum making has seriously declined.

It may be that state departments of education still make their greatest impact on local schools by allocating funds, scheduling statewide tests, supervising pupil accounting, enforcing state laws and department regulations, and engaging in other tasks formerly regarded as almost purely administrative. Where mandates are tied directly to state grants of funds and where rigorous tests determine whether the schools in a district have "measured up," control by states is assured, but it is sometimes to be questioned. When state governments dominate schools, local control is obviously reduced. The reduction may occur in subtle ways. For instance, the schools are considered to be responsible for achieving socioeconomic effects and especially for making prosperity possible. Although the culture may be imposing obligations in the education of affect, the state government insists that cognitive studies be strengthened. When the curriculum is to be improved by spending more dollars, the state government wants to control the use of the dollars it provides.[7]

State governments in the past have pressured school districts to attain minimum standards and to install new programs like driver education. Now, however, governors and state education officials seem to share an altered vision of what is needed. The methods they use to reach their goals vary, but the goals are the same: quality, equity, efficiency, and choice.[8] The goals themselves are being translated into education presumed to be better geared toward achieving economic growth and success in international economic competition. State leaders see a direct connection between an altered job structure and the school curriculum. That is, they believe that in order to work efficiently at new kinds of job assignments, youngsters must satisfactorily complete a curriculum that really prepares them for these assignments. Presumably, when jobs are done efficiently and well, the United States will grow economically and compete more successfully in world markets.

If one were to ask honest, conscientious school reformers at the state level which of the four goals—quality, equity, efficiency, and choice—they were most interested in seeing achieved, they would probably select efficiency. That goal often counts most in political settings, and research studies show that it is attainable. For example, learning time in schools can be increased, and time can be used more productively. Serious students of the curriculum warn, however, that stepping up efficiency may put such a premium on teaching subjects that teaching pupils to meet their individual needs may be neglected.[9] They doubt whether an efficient school is necessarily a school of high quality.

Of the four goals, quality is usually seen as an end product of all attempts to improve schools. Equity, efficiency, and choice are thought to result from effort expended day after day in the process of schooling. Equity consists of giving all pupils a reasonable break. Evidence has been accumulating that neither excellence in schooling nor the quality of schools is affected negatively by giving pupils full opportunity to learn regardless of racial, cultural, gender, or other status.[10] The notion of choice has been much discussed in the 1990s. Upholding the right of parents and their children to choose the schools the children will attend theoretically could improve the quality of schooling across an entire community, but whether it can do so in fact is not entirely certain.[11] In a really free society, parents can, of course, exercise their own version of choice by withdrawing their children from public schools and having them educated in private schools or by home schooling.

ACTIVITY 3-1

How Much Federal and State Control?

One of the issues in U.S. education is the extent to which local schools should be controlled by federal authority, as opposed to state authority. Some educators have maintained that to balance the many pressures on U.S. schools and to provide a stabilizing force in elementary and secondary education we need a strong United States Office of Education or some other powerful federal agency. Too little has been said about what such an agency would do, under our governmental system of state control of schools, to make its influence fully felt without infringing upon the authority of state departments of education.

Think about ways, if any, in which you would strengthen federal influence or control in curriculum matters. What powers would you give to a federal Office of Education or its equivalent?

In what ways, if any, would you strengthen state influence and control?

What specific help should federal and state governments give in balancing the pressures that are applied to school systems and individual schools by groups in the society at large?

United States Senator Patrick Moynihan has observed that the nearer a state's capital is to Canada, the better are the standardized test scores of the state's eighth graders. Specifically, he has noted an inverse correlation between eighth graders' scores on standardized mathematics tests and the distance of the capitals of their states from the Canadian border. He has noted further that this correlation is stronger than the correlation between high test scores and high per pupil expenditures.[12] As the argument about the effect of high dollar expenditures waxes and wanes, we can come to some basic conclusions. For example, we can conclude that money helps, but that an excess of money doesn't help appreciably. A puzzling task is determining where cutoff points between help and non-help should exist in given situations.

Some Larger Societal and Cultural Developments

A number of larger developments affecting the curriculum have a societal or cultural base. A few years ago, one of the most noticeable of these was declining school enrollments. When enrollment declines, school buildings are often given over to purposes other than the strictly educational and teaching staffs are reduced. The effects on the curriculum can sometimes be beneficial, however, especially where enrollment decline is sufficiently small to prevent the closing of entire school buildings. Possible advantages include smaller class sizes, which benefit certain categories of pupils, more opportunities for multi-level instruction, closer professional contact among teachers and other school personnel, and reduction in the duplication of effort and materials.

Other larger developments related to the society and the culture have been:

1. Admission of unorthodox subject matter content concerning events and preferences on the U.S. sociocultural scene
2. Introduction of facilities and materials that are products of a new industrial technology
3. Identification of special needs of children, through evaluation of their home and community settings

4. Increased accountability of school personnel to the American public for the quantity and quality of their work
5. An increase in educational conservatism and private schooling
6. The thrust toward schools of choice and deschooling
7. Accommodation of the effects of cultural shifts
8. The continuing problem of curriculum bulge

The last four developments, which have special pertinence now, are discussed below.

Conservatism and Private Schooling

Some recent developments include continuations or revivals of earlier phases of evolution in American education. The first of these is the rise of a new conservatism. Following a flurry of activity resulting in the organizing of storefront and other alternative schools that tended toward reconstructionist philosophy, segments of the public began pushing more actively for schools representing other viewpoints. The new "fundamental schools" have been called the new conservative alternative. These schools emphasize discipline and cognitive achievement, sometimes using as "inspirational" means detention and paddling, homework, dress codes, repetition of grades in school, respect for adults, and observance of moral standards. Often schools of this kind are religious schools that are conservative in both moral-ethical precepts and cognitive content.[13] In an era in which a return to old values is becoming more marked, conservative education—which is, of course, not without its excesses—is continuing to make an appearance and an impression.

The movement of the 1980s toward conservatism is reflected strongly in a drive to make private education public policy. The drive is directed not merely toward gaining tax relief for those who pay private school tuition and other costs involved in sending children to private schools. It is directed also toward placing control of education in the hands of parents and teachers who are free to make decisions about their own schools, with minimal interference by local, state, and federal government. Furthermore, it captures the attention and sympathy of parents who look to private schooling as a way to ensure upward mobility and economic advantage for their children. We may expect to see additional private schools established in the future. In them, the roles of staff members will have to be clarified and altered as new expectations of conservative instruction are realized. The bureaucratization that has afflicted and burdened public school systems will need to be avoided.

Movement in the direction of private schooling has been called "privatization." A minority of citizens would like to see public schooling abandoned. The opponents of abandoning or weakening public school systems point to the danger to democratic ideals, especially the unity of people across social class lines and the upward economic movement of the very poor.[14] At heart, the new private school movement has the same fundamental purpose as the Roman Catholic schools of the nineteenth century: upholding a value system that is acceptable to patrons.[15] Private schools independent of religious influences have existed for years in the United States because of the real or presumed intellectual demands they have made on their pupils. Today, patrons' desire for intellectual rigor in schooling remains strong, but the values problems they find in the public schools often loom larger.[16] Naturally, renewed pressure for private schooling raises questions about how it should be financed in times of fiscal emergency. The issue of public financing of private education is about as old as the private school movement itself. Calls have been made recently for compensatory education certificates, a term that is perhaps a euphemism for vouchers, or chits representing funds for the purchase of schooling outside the public sector. Opposition to the idea of public funding for private education has come from such groups as Americans United for Separation of Church and State and other organizations that fear entanglement of religion and government.[17]

Schools of Choice and Deschooling

The 1970s' term *alternative schools* has now been sharpened to *schools of choice*. Interpreted broadly, choice implies not only the opportunity to select a school but also the right to educate one's children at home. In the past, a few critics of both public and private schools called for *deschooling,* or the elimination of both public and private schooling.[18] More recently, critics have pointed to research data indicating that when children attend the schools they and their parents prefer, their attitudes, behavior, and involvement improve. The children's gains in achievement have appeared less striking but nonetheless generally satisfying.[19] Now in the 1990s, disagreement has developed as to whether certain gains in achievement are imagined or real. Furthermore, the administrative difficulties inherent in systemwide choice often discourage school officials.

Schools of choice can exist in either the public or the private domain. In the public domain, they can lead to constructive competition among the schools within a school system. For example, one school may be formal and conservative, another may emphasize activity and learning by experience, and still another may provide ways of individualizing learning. The kinds of schools made available are determined by boards of control and educators at the central office level; the particular school attended by a child is determined by the child and his or her parents.[20]

What might be termed quasi–public/private schooling has been provided in cities like Baltimore, Maryland and Hartford, Connecticut. This form of privatization consists of employing a firm to help run a school system or a part thereof. A partnership is often formed between a firm and a board of education, with the board having the power to dissolve the partnership after proper notice. The results that can be attained by such a firm after continuous use of its services are yet to be determined. The evidence so far is not very encouraging.

As a compromise with the deschooling movement, some schools offer a plan whereby pupils are removed from control of the school for part of each day or week. This might be called education at large or, more cynically, education on the loose. When pupils are released to be educated beyond the confines of school, they are expected to engage in *action learning,* or learning out in the community, where greater activity can be found. One yearbook identified opportunities for action learning under the following headings: learning in the great outdoors, learning in unfamiliar cultures, learning in service agencies, learning in the professional community, learning in construction and urban renewal projects, learning on the road, learning in the political arena, and learning in the world of work.[21] The possibilities for achieving variation in pupil experiences are almost unlimited.

As for total deschooling, parents can make this choice simply by keeping their children at home, to be educated there. Although obtaining legal sanction of this decision has sometimes proved difficult, many states now permit home instruction by parents or other instructors. By the mid-1990s, it was estimated that about a million youngsters in the United States and southern Canada were being educated at home.[22] A few industries now provide ideas, laboratory facilities, and space for educating youngsters in the sciences. In years to come, elementary and secondary education may be based in the home, supplemented by the aid of centers that include laboratories, libraries and media sites, counseling and testing sites, and group meeting facilities. These centers may be provided at public expense.

Isabel Lyman has listed some advantages of home schooling. They include its availability to families of limited income, its flexibility in scheduling, its protection from hazards encountered in public schools, its contribution to building strong family bonds, and its success as gauged by standardized tests.[23] Interestingly, accompanying a decline in enrollments in Roman Catholic schools has been the formation of an organization to assist home schooling: the Catholic Home Educators for Christ the King. As might be expected, home schooling has been criticized because it deprives children of the socializing effects of a life in school and because it prevents them from participating in school activities.

Effects of Cultural Shifts

Another prominent development relates to diversity in ethnic status and national origin. Within recent years, when Spanish-speaking Americans in and near our large cities began their thrust for bilingual and bicultural education, they opened a range of possibilities for both recognizing and dealing with diversity and for achieving true cultural adjustment. Two major curriculum objectives became (1) fostering respect for the national background or ethnicity of each pupil and (2) helping the pupil function effectively within the common culture, within his or her own culture, and within other cultures. If carried to their limits, these objectives would materially assist in the ultimate realization of multicultural education, of which multilingualism is a part. The assumptions underlying the objectives suggest that minority cultures are unique in specific ways, but that all groups share common traits, values, and behaviors, and that individual pupils, whatever their backgrounds, need to know and appreciate the common culture and also cultures other than their own.[24] Furthermore, the prospects for broadened and deepened education in human relations and communication through language are improved by utilizing assumptions that lead to rejection of the melting pot theory, used for years in an attempt to "settle" minority peoples. The United States continues to be a nation of immigrants, partly because of the illegal entrance of new residents.[25] In a recent move toward conservatism, many U.S. cities have shifted from an emphasis on bilingual education to an insistence that English be used as the accepted language.

A significant, continuing, culture-based development can also be seen in the current impact of the labor movement on curriculum planning. Whereas business interests have influenced the curriculum for decades, the influence of labor organizations on the curriculum is relatively new. Labor groups representing teachers are now helping to make curriculum policy. Involvement of teachers in curriculum planning is regarded by teachers' unions as both a right and an obligation of professionals. The unions maintain that legislatures and business groups have often had special interests in mind when they have supported educational programs, whereas teachers' unions have the potential for promoting the general welfare of pupils. Union leaders see the entrance of teacher bargainers into the curriculum field as a safeguard against coercion by other groups in our society. Teachers' unions and associations in a few states have become the most influential labor organizations.

Finally, the attitudes of parents toward children's use of time at home and the inroads of television in preempting children's available time form interrelated influences on the curriculum. Many parents, busy as they are with their own affairs, consign children to sit before a television tube (an assignment they readily accept), thus reducing the time spent helping with homework, discussing around the dinner table the events of the day, and reading to the children. In many American homes, little connection is made between the curriculum of the school and evening activities at home. This fact amazes some immigrant families, particularly those from the Far east.

The Problem of Curriculum Bulge
In an era in which the curriculum, particularly in the public schools, is already overloaded and in which thorough teaching of fundamental subject matter has been made a priority, new demands for addition of subject matter are cropping up everywhere. Schools have become accustomed to feeding and babysitting children, teaching teenagers to drive, coaching youngsters in a variety of sports, and developing pupils' social skills. Today, society and the culture expect that schools will teach AIDS prevention, improve the quality of sex education, warn against unwise use of drugs and alcohol, make youngsters more moral and ethical, counsel against suicide, control violent behavior, and on and on. The consequence is a bulge in the curriculum that makes the responsibilities of teachers and administrators so heavy that the fundamental, origi-

nal work of the schools is done poorly. What *is* the proper function of schools, anyway? Many serious students of elementary and secondary education are advocating a new and careful nationwide review of the aims, goals, and objectives of schooling. To be adequate, the review would have to be more thorough than the one culminating in the list of national education goals issued at the state governors' conference in Virginia in 1989.

INFLUENCES WITHIN THE IMMEDIATE COMMUNITY

The individual community is often considered to be the real locus of decision making about the curriculum. In a sense, this is true. In classrooms, one finds teachers and pupils making fundamental day-to-day curriculum decisions. But, in some states, master planning at local levels of educational programs of large scope and import is becoming less and less common. Some persons maintain that boards of education and administrators in local school districts now have little control over significant matters. Other persons, pointing out that every school district does have its own board of control, continue to insist that local decision making is much in evidence.

What the Community Wants, the Community Can Usually Get—Within Limits

Certainly communities have a great deal to say about some curriculum matters in local schools. But, in the future, some important curriculum decisions such as the determination of broad educational objectives will probably be made on a state, a regional, or even a national basis. As revenue from local property taxes declines and schools' financial support comes increasingly from state and federal governments, control will almost inevitably follow the dollar. In addition, interstate programs such as national testing may take from teachers and other curriculum personnel a considerable amount of control over what is taught.

Some community groups and some educators favor statewide or national uniformity in the curriculum, which, in one form or another, has become a strong prospect. Two major advantages attributed to uniformity are certain financial economies and educational continuity when pupils transfer from district to district and from school to school. John Goodlad and Jeannie Oakes have written that curriculum uniformity can be increased because individual learning differences do not necessarily require radically different curricula.[26] In the American democratic system, however, development of ideas in local communities and local schools needs to be encouraged, for people grow by participating in planning. Some of the consolidations of school districts that have occurred to date have seriously limited participation in planning at the community level. Currently, the United States has a wealth of resources and facilities for planning in and through communities, and the nation must decide if it wishes to lose what de Tocqueville commended years ago—encouragement of groups of people to volunteer for all kinds of community service. In truth, some planning can well be done centrally; other planning requires local participation.

Of course, the school is only one of the community agencies that contribute to education. Child-development specialists say that more education than we realize occurs before the child is four years old, and observers with a comprehensive view of education report the impact of parents, youth-serving organizations, and other community groups on learners. Curriculum workers are involved in continuing controversies as to who has responsibility for particular efforts to educate children and youth. In the areas of sex education, religion, driver training, and the social graces, for instance, there are many differences of opinion about the locus of educational responsibility. With some educators insisting that the schools have already absorbed too much responsibility for child welfare from the community at large, discussions of the total role of the school are likely to increase and become more vigorous.

When the author asked groups of upper elementary and secondary school pupils where they acquired the learnings they consider most significant, many of them said their most important, durable learnings had come from sources outside schools.

The author has also asked youngsters, "What could schools do to educate you in ways that no other agencies could or should?" About two hundred youth provided the following answers (in paraphrase) during tape-recorded interviews:

1. Put what we learn in school into a framework or system that will help us understand it better.
2. Teach us "fundamentals." Nowhere except in school are you likely to gain the tools you need for thinking and serving.
3. Give us opportunities and materials in school to help us inquire, discover, and probe meaning. Getting meaning is perhaps the most important thing schools can help us do.
4. Stop attempting to compete with and destroy what we learn elsewhere. Instead, seek to coordinate what we are taught in school with what we learn outside school.

There is a definite, though evolving, place for the school in the American culture complex, but it is evidently not its current place as arbiter and dispenser of education. Education itself is so universal that it needs to be thought of in broader terms than merely the institutional. Albert Shanker in his weekly column has reminded us that we must not forget the other settings in which learning takes place and where learners can get the kinds of help that schools cannot supply. A complete study of the roles of educational agencies should be undertaken to answer questions like the following: What is the full scope of current educational efforts and activities? What other useful efforts and activities might there be? What agencies should be providing education for children and youth? What responsibilities should belong exclusively to schools? How can schools best discharge their responsibilities?

Communities influence schools in three basic ways: through the communities' own needs, through the limits they set on the curriculum of the school, and through their decisions as to who shall receive schooling. The effect of local needs can be seen in rural communities that insist that pupils study vocational agriculture. It was also exemplified some years ago in a community in which there was a high rate of school tardiness. Curriculum planners in the community at first suspected that there were too few alarm clocks in the homes, but a more thorough and realistic appraisal of the situation revealed that malnutrition was unusually prevalent—children simply did not feel like getting out of bed to go to school. Consequently, instruction in nutrition, as part of a whole community drive for better feeding of adults and children, became a curriculum mandate. The need for vocational agriculture in some communities and the need for better nutrition in others are only samples of the numerous local needs that differ from region to region, from one section of a city to another, and from one small town to another throughout the nation.

The tendency of communities to determine who shall receive schooling is sometimes evident in local unwillingness to establish nursery schools and kindergartens, even when state appropriation of funds encourages their establishment. A less negative example is the planning of vocational and technical high schools and community colleges throughout the nation.

Inevitably, the curriculum is based firmly in home-school-community relationships, and school-community planning is therefore much needed. The great majority of American citizens live in communities of fewer than 10,000 people. Many such communities are quite isolated despite improvements in transportation and communication, and where they are not isolated physically, the people in them are isolated psychologically, often by their own choice. Both the traditions and the planning that touch people are grounded in local communities, so it seems unlikely that the power and influence of the community in educational decision making will be lost. Such power and influence are enhanced by a psychological fact: Learners are best equipped to explore and talk about their own environment, yet they need to have some aspects of it clarified for them. Accordingly, more school assignments should probably be centered in the world of the child and fewer in the world and the universe at large. "How I Diagnose My Own Fears" might be a more worthwhile composition title than "What Astronauts Have Found on the Moon." One of the real obligations of the school is to help learners deal with conditions and situations that confront them, directly or indirectly. To this end, community resources in the form of resource files, directories to community assets and points of interest, and other aids should claim learners' attention.

The legal arbiter of educational decision making in the local community is, of course, the board of education. In most instances, communities get from their board of education members what they deserve. If they are willing to abide the abuses that board members sometimes inflict upon children by their short-sightedness, temporary extravagance, long-term stinginess, or outright corruption, they perpetuate a low level of decision making that has plagued certain U.S. communities for a long time. If, on the other hand, the ablest and most responsible community members are willing to serve on boards of education, the children and the schools are sure beneficiaries.

Board members come from various occupational, religious, and ethnic groups. Naturally, they reflect the predispositions and insights of other community members. Communities contain subcultural groups that hold differing views of the worth of education and its function in the lives of people of different status, aspirations, and potential. Some subcultures value education for its intrinsic worth, its almost mystical or magical impact on the lives of people. Other subcultures value education for its practical worth and are willing to sacrifice to almost any extent to see their children enter prestigious professions and respected businesses. Still other subcultures desire rigor in education and training so that their children, divided in their thinking by their apparent potential or present socioeconomic status, may learn to do their best and be respected for it. Unfortunately, a few subcultures have little faith in the schools as agents for raising their children's position in life. The subcultural group that is perhaps most damaging to the schools is the one that seeks to intimidate administrators and teachers on the ground that parents and other taxpayers own the schools and employ, through a subservient board of education, a coterie of would-be professionals of low socioeconomic status and little influence in the community. Boards of education are expected to listen to the voices of all groups of citizens.

Arthur Steller has suggested several ways of involving the ablest people in a community in policy making about their schools. He favors compiling a local "who's who" of talent, opening and using communication channels, listening to and observing community members, and preparing a "marketing framework" for convincing people of the worth of curriculum ideas. Afterward, detailed ways of proceeding to promote the ideas can be specified.[27] What Steller proposes is good public relations and good politics.

From the preceding discussion, it might appear that making schools what they can be has become the exclusive responsibility of identifiable community leaders. At the grassroots level, however, teachers, parents, and pupils, who are often anonymous, make a real difference. According to a sponsored survey and observations by school administrators, teachers, parents, and pupils are engaged in three concrete actions:

1. They participate in curriculum planning so diligently that it assumes a prime position in their thinking and practice.
2. They put vigor into site-based management by promoting teacher empowerment, campaigning for accountability, and increasing cooperative decision making.
3. They encourage restructuring of schooling.[28]

ACTIVITY 3-2

A Limited Study of One Community

Identify a community you know reasonably well. Ask public school officials in the central administrative offices to permit you to see minutes from meetings of the board of education for the past five years. Note what groups and individuals appeared before the board to present curriculum proposals or to discuss curriculum matters. State the points of view the groups and individuals apparently represented. What do you conclude about formal input by community members concerning curriculum concerns?

ACTIVITY 3-3

A More Comprehensive Study of the Same Community

Conduct a more comprehensive investigation of the same community. By interviewing several leading citizens, including a board of education member and a first-line school administrator, learn what forces are at work in the community to change the curriculum. Inquire about the relative influence of industrial, labor, political, patriotic, professional, welfare, and health groups.

What specific groups seem to wield the greatest influence?

How have these groups become so powerful? Who are the individuals in the community who direct their activities?

What can you generalize from your findings concerning direction, strength, and necessary control of the community's influences on the curriculum?

SITUATION 3-4

When Subcultures and Social Classes Come to School

A group of teachers decided to investigate differences among their pupils attributable to subculture and social class. To do so, they took the following steps:

1. They inspected pupil records and interviewed pupils concerning their home life and general background.
2. They asked the pupils to react in small groups to experiences that the school provided through formal instruction and informal activities.
3. They asked specific questions about the significance of photographs and ideas appearing in textbooks and other teaching materials, as these photographs and ideas reflected subculture and social class.

4. They asked the pupils to respond freely to words and expressions that might evoke particular memories and reactions: Ku Klux Klan, Knights of Columbus, illegal immigrants, Fundamentalist, country clubs, labor unions, etc.

What do you think of these methods of finding out about the subcultures and social classes that pupils represent?

What methods would you use in addition to or instead of the four listed above?

What useful information would you expect to get by employing these four methods and/or your own?

The Impact of Inner-City, Suburban, and Rural Community Environments

The effects of social environment on children and their ability to learn are well illustrated by the impact of life in the inner city and in suburban communities, and of life in what is essentially a new rural environment. Though many of the problems of inner city, suburban, and rural education have existed in the United States for a long time, the full significance of these problems is only beginning to become clear. The arrival of large numbers of migrants and immigrants in U.S. cities, their clustering for social and economic reasons in the centers of these cities, and the consequent move of more privileged subpopulations to the suburbs have highlighted the needs of disadvantaged urbanites. At the same time, a new version of ruralism has replaced the old rural social environment in remote places throughout the United States.

The Inner-City Environment

After the waves of immigrants of the early and later twentieth century had found at least a precarious living place in U.S. cities, migrants and immigrants from numerous states and countries poured into these same cities and frequently found it necessary to accept menial employment and to occupy substandard housing facilities. These newcomers often exhibited the following characteristics: Their backgrounds were rural and impoverished; their levels of formal education were low; they took commendable pride in their own cultural traditions; and they were willing to learn, but on their own terms. These people were not necessarily culturally inferior, but they *were* culturally different. To teach them, the teacher had to accept them and be accepted by them. Several circumstances soon militated against their proper schooling, however:

1. Disappearing taxable property and declining values of real estate in the inner city
2. Segregation of pupils racially and, often more importantly, socioeconomically
3. Frequent displacement and consequent mobility of the poor

4. Impoverished facilities and limited personnel in inner-city schools
5. Cumulative deficits in the school achievement of children
6. Lack of community interest in problems of inner-city schools
7. Impermanence of teaching staffs and lack of preparation of school leadership to help teachers with their more difficult problems

Efforts to overcome these circumstances have been based on the point of view that the more powerful groups in society must help less powerful ones by direct assistance, education, and common involvement in lifting the downtrodden. Culture-free tests, specially prepared and diversified school staffs, an increase in the number of male teachers, textbooks devised to take into account the backgrounds of migrants, varied school experiences, summertime educational programs, work-study projects, and improved preservice and inservice education of teachers have become major devices for achieving assimilation of the culturally different.

The dictionaries define slums as places—usually, but not always, within cities—where poor people cluster, forced to live in undesirable conditions. Classroom teachers who work outside the slums of U.S. cities often believe that teaching in the slums requires the same abilities as teaching anywhere else. Conditions exist in the inner city, however, that make teaching unusually difficult. True, teachers everywhere face some of the same problems encountered in slum schools, but the inner city imposes special stress on schools and teachers because of the social realities of slum life. There is, first of all, density of population with corresponding loss of identity by residents of the inner city. In personal terms, loss of identity means that to an exceptional degree the slum dwellers question who they are and whether or not they are important. Slum dwellers have correctly been described as feeling anonymous, depersonalized, lonely, and hardened in their relationships with people. Big-city bureaucracy, which is replicated in urban school systems, causes teachers and principals to make decisions for the faceless mass of pupils and then attempt to apply these decisions to individual cases. Most teachers in the slums cannot know individual children thoroughly because, as nonresidents of the community, they do not see them in family or community connections.

Furthermore, unusual feelings of powerlessness afflict inhabitants of the inner city. The big city wields big control, which creates this sense of powerlessness in the individual citizen. Forming combinations and seeking cooperation among the citizenry have become especially difficult because large numbers of markedly different people are thrown together in urban life. Both the inner-city community and its schools seem to want to stamp out diversity. Meanwhile, old-fashioned attempts at acculturation, or adding everyone to the "melting-pot," no longer function because of resistance created by diverse cultural groups and because of frequent movement by families within, into, and out of the community.

To many pupils in the slum school, the curriculum seems phony because it relates so poorly to the realities of their lives. Partly for this reason, older youngsters often show contempt for professional personnel in the schools. The individual pupil's impoverished environment contributes to development of a poor self-image and a realistic lack of confidence in his or her own future. He or she lives in a physical world, rather than an intellectual world in which respect and personal success are needed. Communication with teachers is frequently monosyllabic, but the pupil communicates readily with peers. During the school day, the pupil is sensitive to sudden changes in routine, so disorderly and even violent conduct may occur when procedures in his or her classroom are unplanned and unorganized.

As a learner, the pupil in the inner city needs special attention and patience. This requirement is so important that it has been emphasized in the writings and oral comments of experienced teachers who have been deemed successful in slum schools. Though inner-city pupils may learn slowly, they tend to retain what they have learned if it has any meaning for them. Although they are apathetic about most of the content the schools teach, their curiosity can be aroused. Their inarticulateness should not suggest to teachers that their manipulative skills are above normal. Contrary to a popular myth, pupils from the slums are not necessarily adept in the vocational arts.

Too often the curriculum in slum schools follows the patterns of schooling used elsewhere. The "quality school" attains its status in the United States because it teaches the so-called basic skills with maximum success as determined by standardized tests. But the ordinary definition of quality does not apply to schooling in the inner city. The curriculum here needs to be based to a greater extent on the realities of social living in the slum—to help pupils become personally involved in the life situations in which they find themselves, to help them see options for themselves in their environment, to provide opportunities for them to perform and to act out roles in participatory citizenship. The realities of the inner city require young people to negotiate with adults, to relate to and organize people in special circumstances, and to get what they need in ways that are both civilized and effective. The schools should help them learn to do these three things.

Is there hope for the schools of the inner city? The Rand Corporation studied educational innovation in five city school districts in urban centers with a population range of 125,000 to 900,000. Rand found that innovation in these districts waxed and waned, but that the participants in innovation were learning how to do better next time.[29] The future of education in the inner city seems to depend on several factors: ideas and their dissemination, the nature of populations to be served, the political situation, economic circumstances, and social climate.

A few years ago, several urban school systems organized to help one another with curriculum planning and supervisory strategies. The systems achieved measurable gains in a number of areas, including increases in pupils' learning of basic skills and reductions in dropout rates. The success of educational programs in the cities seems to depend on the presence of strong leadership, the willingness of the education hierarchy to increase principals' authority, and the freedom of individual schools to change in any sensible ways they desire.[30]

Suburban Communities

The suburbs have been populated by upper-class and upper-middle-class persons who wanted to avoid the physical dangers, noise, and cultural modes and mores of cities. With them has come, from cities and rural areas, a coterie of lower-class citizens engaged in service occupations. Many people living in U.S. suburbs contribute enthusiastically to the life and growth of their communities, sometimes with the help of the corporations for which they work. Libraries, museums, and parks have been constructed with the generous assistance of local citizens. Because people everywhere are exposed to social evils, harmful beliefs and practices have crept into suburban communities, blemishing what the citizens often imagine to be a near-perfect record. Drugs, alcohol, white-collar crime, and satan worship are four of the several causes of damage and disruption in the lives of youth and adults. The vaunted high ethical, moral, and cultural standards allegedly common to suburban communities have then become a mere state of mind. Many residents of our suburbs cannot believe that the "evils of the big cities" have somehow crept into their presumably temptation-proof communities. Suburban parents often face even more subtle evils. One of these is turbulence in homes that results from having reared strong-willed children whom the parents seem to fear.[31]

Schools in the suburbs are especially vulnerable to community snobbishness, unwarranted competitiveness, and social climbing by children and their parents. In the most snobbish communities, children have been known to arrive at school in stretch limousines and even in helicopters. Also attending these schools are the children of the poor, who live "on the other side of the tracks" in a condition of isolation.[32] The advantages that some of our suburban schools offer are frequently the best that money can buy: superior teachers, equipment, and materials. Many suburbanites would not consider moving elsewhere—at least not until unfamiliar populations begin to encroach upon "their" terrain and influence their lives unduly.

The New Rural Environment

In 1982, the Federal Reserve Bank of Philadelphia reported that, for the first time in 150 years, rural areas of the nation had outstripped in population the cities and their suburbs. Indeed, better transportation and communication and population migration are making the rural areas different from what they once were. Some of the families who lived in rural regions during past decades have moved. They have been replaced by emigrants from cities and suburbs and population groups arriving from outside of the United States. For some, the rural regions have become new lands of opportunity. Multilingual and multicultural influences have made the rural social scene less uniform. The seasonal presence of migrant farm workers has further reduced cultural uniformity. The establishment of new industries and the consequent failure of some of them, together with consolidation and reduction in the size of family farms, have both raised and lowered the hopes of industrial and farm workers. Shopping malls have provided employment but have also burdened highways with heavy traffic. All in all, the rural environment has become nondescript and filled with uncertainties.

Rural America has its indoor and outdoor movie theaters, along with an abundance of television sets. Its greatest cultural void is in the scarcity of libraries, museums, concert halls, and arrangements for formal continuing education. In their general taste and their response to advertising, the modern inhabitants of rural areas resemble people in the suburbs. In cultural sophistication, the resemblance lessens. Lack of exposure to rich and varied cultural advantages proves decidedly limiting.

Within school buildings, small rural schools offer many opportunities that rival the opportunities given pupils in nonrural settings. Rural schools of limited size are, however, disadvantaged by the inaccessibility of varied reading materials, by a lack of interesting places for pupils to visit, by the inability of the staff to assist pupils with special problems, and by limited opportunities for pupils to work and serve within the community. Administrators and teachers have so many and such varied responsibilities that curriculum planning tends to be neglected. The teachers often find that a public too geographically close to them makes unreasonable demands. After all, isn't the school the center of community life? On the affirmative side, however, is the fact that teachers and administrators can interact often. Similarly, pupils can interact readily with teachers, to the end that their curriculum can be individualized.[33]

In large, consolidated rural systems, the size and remoteness of school buildings have created the same general effect one sees in urban communities—poor communication and lack of understanding, which result in a loss of confidence in the schools. Because of this crisis in confidence, budgets are defeated, bond issues are lost, and the local property tax becomes a less and less acceptable base for school support.

Like the inner city, the new rural environment requires that curriculum emphases be altered. The idea of community and of the roles of individuals in it needs to be developed in rural pupils. Field trips to remote places, including centers of culture, are important, as is the study of people's ways of behaving in other cultures. Also to be emphasized is the diligent search for individual talent and for means of developing human potential.

Many rural problems that originate in poverty remind one of the poverty-based problems of residents of the inner city: facelessness, low self-esteem, and limited hope. Improvement of cognitive learning in deprived rural areas will not suffice; carefully planned affective education is a special need.

Small towns have become a feature of the rural scene. Of the nearly 40,000 governments below the state level in the United States, more than 70 percent serve populations of fewer than 3000 persons and about half serve populations of fewer than 1000. These communities generally want to remain small. The people are comfortable with one another and, although privacy and anonymity are scarce, help is quickly available to those who know one another.[34]

Under the illusion that "that's where the votes are," politicians have favored spending money on the cities and have neglected the growing rural areas. The federal money that has helped to support rural education has gone to support primarily the disadvantaged and "special need" populations. Both federal and state programs of aid should be reformed to meet actual rural school needs, new programs should be created, and research activity in rural education should be encouraged.

CULTURE-BASED CURRICULUM IDEAS: TWO EXAMPLES

Curriculum ideas do not spring from the forehead of Zeus. Orlosky and Smith noted that such ideas come from sources both inside and outside school systems. These authors identified the chief external sources as community groups, governments, and foundations.[35] (The 1980s and 1990s have seen the foundations decline in prominence.) Many ideas develop, but, like fingerling fish in lakes and seas, the great majority of them disappear. The ideas that are left vary in magnitude and significance: A few are called seminal, and even fewer take the nation by storm.

The ideas that genuinely succeed appear to have the support both of elements of the culture and of important people in local school districts. A little financial boost from government doesn't hurt, so community groups and government are likely to be, in Orlosky and Smith's terms, chief protagonists. The culture, however, provides the seedbed for planting and nourishing each successful idea.

Ours is an environment in which people often feel alienated and alone; therefore, self-concept development has become a major interest. The federal grants people have shown willingness to fund projects with the term *self-concept development* in them. Communications, one of our greatest cultural lacks, is another reasonably sure bet. The disadvantaged, like the poor, are with us always, so the disadvantaged, handicapped, and discomfited become eligible for attention. Then there are the gifted, who, in the rush to care for the disadvantaged, have often been left to get what they can from routine schooling. In a time of conservatism and the valuing of high-quality human resources, routine schooling for the gifted seems to many people to be inadequate. Special programs are again being demanded.

Some curriculum ideas become especially deeply rooted in the culture. Two of these, used as examples below, are career education and education in an era of high technology.

Example 1: Career Education

Planning and preparing for a career is an important culture-based curriculum idea. Education related to entering and pursuing careers belongs at elementary, middle, and high school levels of instruction.

Educators have shown an interest in career education for a long time. In 1918, the well-known *Cardinal Principles of Secondary Education* contained the following statement under the heading "Vocations":

> Vocational education should equip the individual to secure a livelihood for himself and those dependent upon him, to serve society well through his vocation, to maintain the right relationships toward his fellow workers and society, and, as far as possible, to find in that vocation his own best development.

In 1938, the Educational Policies Commission spoke of "the objectives of economic efficiency," including "occupational efficiency." Later, the Commission advocated development in pupils of salable skills and also appropriate career-related attitudes and understandings. Since 1970, the National Assessment of Educational Progress, providing what is popularly referred to as "national testing," has made career and occupational development one of its subject area interests in preparing tests that are administered throughout the nation.

Career education has never gained the status of a discrete subject, but it has been on the fringes of the formal curriculum since the late 1930s and early 1940s. At that time, the guidance movement was being initiated in a number of school systems after having made its first organized start in cities like Providence, Rhode Island. Guidance responsibilities were divided among the educational, the vocational, and the social. Vocational guidance was dispensed to individuals and small groups, with the later assistance of vocational interest inventories like the Strong and the Kuder. It was intended for all pupils in secondary schools. Entirely apart from vocational guidance, the schools were offering courses in vocational education, some of which were funded substantially by the federal government. Secondary school pupils who had no intention of attending college were the major clientele of vocational education programs.

After a period of quiescence, the emphasis on planning and preparing for careers revived, making an entirely new appearance under the leadership of a United States Commissioner of Education, Sidney P. Marland. Marland used the term *career education* in promoting a nationwide movement combining curriculum, instruction, and counseling. He was interested in seeing pupils prepared for economic independence, personal fulfillment, and appreciation of the dignity of work. He hoped that career education would help remove the distinction between academic and vocational preparation and would consequently affect the education of all pupils.

Interest in career education has become widespread in elementary and secondary schools. Its societal and cultural significance has seemed so obvious that articles, curriculum plans, and course guides relative to it have been created everywhere, filling ERIC files and *Edu-*

cation Index listings. In kindergarten and the first four or five grades, career education usually consists of general orientation; in grades five through eight, exploration of career fields; in grades nine and ten, intense investigation of particular careers; and in grades eleven and twelve, actual preparation experiences. Vocational education itself has grown and improved vastly.

One of the major problems with career education is uncertainty as to what to teach about the careers of the future. Consequently, more attention is being given to ways of making decisions about careers and to general preparation for types of careers through vocational education than to precise career opportunities and preparation for them. Current and near-future opportunities in the local community are not hard to trace, but few graduates of the local schools remain in or return to their native communities. Nevertheless, career exploration in the community is frequently part of career education programs.

ACTIVITY 3-4

A Study of Present and Future Career Opportunities

As a means of aiding curriculum planning in career education, teachers who are specialists in specific school subjects are sometimes asked to investigate present and future opportunities in careers that are clearly related to their subjects.

A similar possibility exists for persons who expect to become specialists in the curriculum field and are already preparing for this role. At the higher levels of preparation, it is possible to specialize in (1) the curriculum of elementary schools, (2) the curriculum of secondary schools, (3) procedures for planning curriculum, and (4) curriculum evaluation. Choose one of these four subspecialties. Review data about present and future opportunities in it, then discuss your data with others who have been conducting similar investigations. Possible information sources are ERIC materials, placement offices in universities, educators already working in the subspecialty, and the literature of futurism.

Example 2: Education in an Era of High Technology

Unlike career education, the kinds of education that relate to high technology as a culture-based phenomenon are, in part, new. High technology is a highly developed, refined methodology by which we provide ourselves, through applied science and engineering, with the material objects of our civilization. No one knows what the long-term impact of high technology on elementary and secondary education will be. However, any force that changes industrial society by altering production methods and shifting the demand for workers must inevitably affect the curriculum.

The reports of commissions and committees referred to in Chapter 1 have emphasized need for the old-style education that has as its goal the education of large numbers of pupils in the sciences, mathematics, and computer operation. If high-technology industry continues to turn to robots, automatic machines, and other self-operating devices, however, the labor force may come to consist of two "classes": a large number of highly skilled, well-educated technical personnel and a far smaller group of workers with minimal skills. The implications for education are obvious. An individual cannot hope to be accepted into the first group of workers without a complete scientific and technical education, whereas he or she can be admitted to the second group with minimal general education, to be trained later on the job. In light of our customary belief in upward mobility, this new prospect is hardly inviting. Under the new circumstances, our broad, democratic, and relatively uniform education could give way to European-style education, where the intellectually elite are segregated in one kind of school or track and the other pupils are trained elsewhere in the cognitive and social basics.

Parents and other citizens who know what is likely to happen in industry (as it has already happened to a large degree in the manufacture of automobiles) are likely to pressure schools in the direction of major curriculum change. In this drive, they may well be supported by business and industry. Poor as the schools are financially, they will be asked to spend even more on salaries of specialist teachers, on expensive technological and scientific equipment, and on sophisticated computers. They will be required to find among their pupils more young women and minority group members who qualify for study of the "new" science, mathematics, and computerization. They will need to search harder for teachers in these fields, in view of the competitive ability of industrial managers to attract young people with higher salaries.[36]

ACTIVITY 3-5

Investigating the Pervasiveness of High Technology

It pays to know what is happening in the industrial firms and business and research organizations to which the local school district sends its graduates for employment. In highly industrialized states, one is likely to find a number of industries and businesses that use or conduct research in high technology. Arrange visits to sites where practice and research are under way. Learn what the prospects are for further development of high technology in selected firms and organizations in your area.

If your school or school district is located in an area in which industry is scarce, try to visit or correspond with industrial and business centers elsewhere to gather your data.

The results of this investigation may prove worth reporting to top school administrators and curriculum personnel and committees in your school or district. If the data are at all striking, they should stimulate new curriculum planning.

STRATEGIES FOR USING SOCIAL AND CULTURAL INFLUENCES

Experience and current observation supply curriculum workers with several strategies to use in dealing with society-wide and community influences. The implication here is not that curriculum workers should seek to resist these influences but that they should use them intelligently as aids to curriculum planning.

First, curriculum workers need to be as open-minded as they can be about influences that affect the schools. Although not all influences are benign, they all deserve hearing and consideration. Too often, educational leaders have been said to take a proprietary attitude toward "their" schools or to be possessive or defensive about existing programs. In the view of some commentators, these leaders have shown too little interest in what the public has had to say, perhaps because they themselves are insecure or insensitive to the feelings of others. A point of view that may well be taken is that schools belong to the people, who employ professional personnel to administer and operate them. These personnel, as professionals, should be autonomous in much that they do, but they must also listen to what other citizens are saying. They must work with today's citizens, but their wisdom comes also from their knowledge of the past and their own estimates of the future.

Second, curriculum workers need to take the lead in using social influences. As they welcome ideas, so also must they help school staffs square the ideas with theory and practice and see that assumptions and premises are tested. They should urge citizens who have ideas to advance them, but they must recognize at the same time that arguments as to whether two and two make four are fruitless, and that persons whose only contact with the schools occurred 25 years ago as pupils are definitely *not* educational authorities. When curriculum workers listen, they should also inform. The need is for dialogue rather than a hearing of witnesses.

Third, curriculum workers should consider fully the feelings of Americans about education and should act according to their best diagnosis of those feelings. Generally speaking, Americans take great pride in their schools. Most of the time they are complacent about them, but in moments of real or imagined crisis they become worried and anxious. It has been said that Americans are satisfied in general with their schools and are dissatisfied in particular. Accordingly, the curriculum person must serve as a troubleshooter of dissatisfactions—but not, of course, on every occasion. All of us have difficulty in knowing when to counterattack and when to remain quiescent, but school personnel seem to have been oversensitive during recent years to every wind of criticism and complaint. Basically, the public's attitudes toward schools are often more favorable than superintendents and other school leaders believe. The public wants to know mainly whether schools are moving forward and in what direction. Curriculum leaders should lead the planning for movement and should cause the plans to be known and talked about.

Fourth, curriculum workers should recognize that they are operating in a special dynamic. The profession that they serve has not been noted for attracting power to itself, probably because teachers behave "like teachers" and are expected to behave thus. In the past, the image of the teacher has been one of a middle-class, unmarried, white, Protestant, conservative female without strong community influence. The curriculum person has real responsibility for encouraging teachers to move outside their own milieu, so that they may learn from other institutions, agencies, and individuals and may contribute to them. One of teachers' occupational hazards is talking too much among themselves. The potential of teachers as both contributors and listeners to the community can scarcely be exaggerated. As teachers are seen in a new and better light, other citizens can help them redesign and reinterpret their role. If they are to deserve favorable reputations, teachers cannot afford to assume extreme, offbeat postures in support of morals and behaviors that are harmful to children and other persons.

Finally, curriculum leaders must realize that they are deep in politics. Theirs is a politics associated with careful planning, which requires balancing of pressures and cooperative policy making. Educators should probably stop talking about administrators' "community relations" when what they really mean is their political acumen and skill. Curriculum leaders are inevitably concerned with pressure groups and with allocations of public funds. These two areas of responsibility alone thrust them into the realm of politics.

Politicians proceed according to tried and tested beliefs about ways in which the human being as a political animal customarily behaves. Without doubt, curriculum planners will need to become increasingly adept in their political behavior. There are sure signs that curriculum improvement activities have been moving, on national and state fronts, into the realm of politics as big projects develop, as governors and other political figures become involved, and as competing interests vie with one another. Within our own era, curriculum leaders have been called upon to deal with the political ramifications of desegregation, negotiations with teachers, the rights of students, and attacks on textbooks and library books.

In the preceding pages, curriculum workers have been urged to be open-minded about social influences, to exert leadership in using these influences, to understand people's feelings about the schools, to appreciate basic weaknesses in their own profession, and to consider themselves practical politicians. If we return to our initial discussion of society and community as they influence the schools, we see possible strategies for curriculum workers in another dimension. Beyond the attitudes and understandings they must have, they need concrete strategies for dealing directly with the influences discussed in the first sections of the chapter.

Tradition is sometimes beneficent, and curriculum personnel must find specific traditions that are good and then see that these traditions are strengthened and used. For instance, certain patriotic observances fall within this category. The curriculum worker's object is to make use of them in educating the young in love of country and then to place them as high as seems desirable on the agenda of experiences that the school provides. Curriculum improvement should never be labeled as action to destroy the desirable learnings of the human race.

Curriculum workers should also take direct responsibility for channeling social and cultural change constructively within the school. For some persons, this action may evade the question of whether educators should serve as social reconstructionists. Whatever their position concerning their role as social engineers, curriculum workers must recognize and use influences that burst or creep up on the school from both society and the immediate community.

As previously mentioned, when social values are unclear to both adults and children, curriculum workers should urge that much time be spent in helping children clarify or alter their values. In a free society, citizens who do not know what they believe are a danger to the society and therefore to themselves. On key issues of morality, patriotism, and ethical standards, learners should be schooled in the alternatives; where only one decision is socially acceptable, they should know what the decision is. Cheating on examinations is dishonest, whatever its causes. Juvenile delinquency is a serious social ill, and alcoholism and drug addiction are serious personal diseases with dire social consequences, whatever may have caused them. There is clearly no sense in avoiding hard reality. In order that values may be clear, the methodology of value formation and reformation should be taught. Respect for cause-and-effect relationships, testing of one's present values against evidence, and the origin and development of a philosophy of life are but three of the matters to be treated in a school where creation and re-creation of value structures are a concern. Much more will be said in Chapters 4 and 5 about the teaching of values.

When content from the society and the culture is forced into the school curriculum and therefore into a teacher's classroom, the teacher has a special problem: that of finding or making relevance. If the new content is not relevant to what is already being taught and learned, it becomes a foreign element; like an organ transplanted into a human body, it may be rejected. Arthur Combs says that teachers' apathy is often a consequence of their having been asked to do the inconsequential and therefore the relatively worthless.[37] Similarly, it has long been known that pupils, when they fail to see the relevance or importance of what is being taught, soon engage in what are politely called off-task behaviors. To make new and strange content from the world outside the school sensible to youngsters, teachers need to ask themselves the following questions:

- Does the new content relate in any way at all to what I would normally be teaching within this subject matter framework?
- How can I organize and present the whole mass of content, including the new element, in such a way that it is most likely to make sense to my pupils?
- Can I organize any of the parts of the content in a logical sequence?
- How, specifically, can I relate the new and strange content to my pupils' life experiences and/or to their probable future experiences?

ACTIVITY 3-6

The Site at Which Political Power Should Be Applied

"The most important election is a school board election," said a candidate for the board in his community.

"If I wanted to affect education permanently and importantly," said a candidate for Congress, "I'd try to influence governors, presidents, and members of Congress."

"Times and places determine which of you is more nearly right," said an impartial citizen.

Analyze these statements to determine which of them you favor. Give full reasons for your answer.

ACTIVITY 3-7

Which Will You Have?

Consider the following continuum. Only you can decide your own position along it.

The school isolated from the community

A position somewhere between the extremes

The school involved with and busily remaking the community

Answer these questions from your own position along the continuum.

1. Should the school remain as separate as possible from the community?
2. Should the school be made to serve as a model of the community as it presently exists?
3. Should the school help to remake the community?
4. What should the school do about the mores and values that large numbers of community members respect? Provide examples of mores and values you have in mind as you discuss this issue.

5. What should the school do about treating the controversial issues that abound in our society? Be specific about particular issues.
6. What should the school do about accepting tasks that other institutions and agencies are not performing or are performing poorly? Give examples of such tasks.
7. What should the school do about the social class values that pupils presently hold? Provide examples of values held by two or three of the following social classes: upper-upper, lower-upper, upper-middle, lower-middle, upper-lower, lower-lower.

People rightly wonder about the destiny of public schools in the United States. Even some of the leaders of teacher unions and associations believe that the future looks grim, assuming that the schools will continue to be regarded in political circles as institutions worthy of only limited support and assuming that the public at large will continue to show little real interest. If our system of public education should be destroyed by forces within our nation or by outright neglect, the effect would probably be deeper division among the various segments of our society. Separate private schools would then educate children of the wealthy and privileged, children of religious parents, children who seemed destined to "hew wood and draw water" because of their lack of intellectual abilities, and so on. Under such a divided arrangement, more children of promise would presumably "drop through the cracks" than at any time since the colonial era. On the other hand, if the public schools are to enjoy new prestige and productiveness, there must be a vast improvement in their general quality, more agreement as to what they are permitted and required to teach, and clarification of their vision of the future. Above all, perhaps, they must gain what they often lack: committed teachers and motivated, energetic pupils. All of these needs are current, major challenges to curriculum planners, as well as challenges to school administrators and political leaders.

Can conditions improve in society and the culture so that schools can be given breathing room? Under the title "Who Says It's Hopeless?" the *Boston Herald* struck an encouraging note. In the early nineteenth century, the rates of crime and degeneracy in American cities were alarming. Then programs to instill moral values were developed, and anti-drinking campaigns became common. Crime rates began dropping by mid-century and continued to fall into the early twentieth century, when community standards of behavior became evident.[38] Schools would indeed be aided by a revival of moral standards that contribute to the development of higher intellectual standards.

SUMMARY

Chapter 3 points out that social and cultural forces have always had a strong effect on decisions made about the curriculum. Certain of these forces, which operate sometimes in support of tradition and sometimes in support of change, form the significant, relatively permanent influences that originate in our nation and our social system. Currently, the U.S. social order seems to demand from our schools achievement of four goals: quality, equity, efficiency, and choice. Since the early 1900s, we have seen an increase in private schooling, marked changes in the composition of U.S. population, a demand for schools of parents' and pupils' choice, a great increase in home schooling, and the pervasiveness of a bulging school curriculum.

Though the society at large influences schools, the immediate cultural impact on them comes from the local community. In the United States, the inner cities, the suburbs, and the rural areas make their respective local contributions and demands.

What to do with the pressures and demands from society and community that can and do affect the schools is a special problem facing classroom teachers and curriculum leaders, who must balance external influences, accepting the valid ideas of the public and of professional personnel.

ENDNOTES

1. Anita D. Bland in the *Asbury Park* (NJ) *Press,* December 5, 1993.

2. Michael L. Berger, "The Public Schools Can't Do It All," *Contemporary Education* 54, no. 1 (Fall 1982): 6–8.

3. Robert J. Braun in The (Newark, NJ) *Star-Ledger,* May 5, 1993.

4. Diane Ravitch, "A Culture in Common," *Educational Leadership* 49, no. 4 (December 1991–January 1992): 8–11.

5. See D. Stanley Eitzon, "Problem Students: The Sociocultural Roots," *Phi Delta Kappan* 73, no. 8 (April 1992): 584–590.

6. Peter Uhlenberg and David Eggebeen, "Hard Times for American Youth: A Look at the Reasons," *Bulletin of the National Association of Secondary School Principals* 72, no. 508 (May 1988): 47–51.

7. Concerning the role of the federal and state governments, see John F. Jennings, "The Sputnik of the Eighties," *Phi Delta Kappan* 69, no. 2 (October 1987): 104–109.

8. Douglas E. Mitchell et al., *Alternative State Policy Mechanisms for Pursuing Quality, Equity, Efficiency, and Choice Goals* (Washington, DC: Office of Educational Research and Improvement, October 1986).

9. Herbert J. Walberg, "Studies Show Curricular Efficiency Can Be Attained," *Bulletin of the National Association of Secondary School Principals* 71, no. 498 (April 1987): 8–12.

10. Jeannie Oakes and Martin Lipton, "Examining Curriculum in 'Best' Schools," *Education Week,* March 7, 1990, 36.

11. See Robert Rothman, "Choice Claims Overstated, A.S.C.D. Panel Concludes," *Education Week,* March 7, 1990, 8.

12. As reported by George Will in his syndicated column, September 15, 1993.

13. Walberg, "Studies Show Curricular Efficiency Can Be Attained."

14. Among others, Albert Shanker has expressed warnings to this effect.

15. James S. Coleman maintains that independent private schools lie somewhere between public schools and religious schools in the balance of power between pupils and their parents.

16. Coleman has suggested in a conference paper that Roman Catholic and other conservative religious schools can hold to a no-nonsense position concerning hard academic work because of the strength and support of their religious communities.

17. John H. DeDakis, "Should Government Help Kids Attend Private Schools?" *Christianity Today,* May 15, 1987, 52, 53.

18. Philip W. Jackson, "Deschooling? No!" *Today's Education* 61, no. 8 (November 1972): 18–22; see also R. W. Burns and G. D. Brooks, eds., "Designing Curriculum in a Changing Society," *Educational Technology* 10 (April 1970): 7–57; and *Educational Technology* 10 (May 1970): 9–64.

19. Mary Anne Raywid, "Synthesis of Research on Schools of Choice," *Educational Leadership* 41, no. 7 (April 1984): 70–78.

20. Mary Anne Raywid, "Public Choice, Yes; Vouchers, No!" *Phi Delta Kappan* 68, no. 16 (June 1987): 762–769.

21. Vernon H. Smith and Robert D. Barr, "Where Should Learning Take Place?" in William Van Til, ed., *Issues in Secondary Education,* National Society for the Study of Education, Seventy-Fifth Yearbook, Part II (Chicago: University of Chicago Press, 1976), 167–175.

22. Isabel Lyman, "Better Off at Home?" *National Review,* September 20, 1993, 61–62.

23. Ibid.

24. James A. Banks has written extensively about this topic.

25. See Richard Pratte, "Social Heterogeneity, Democracy, and Democratic Pluralism," in Kenneth D. Benne and Steven Tozer, eds., *Society as Educator in an Age of Transition,* National Society for the Study of Education, Eighty-Sixth Yearbook, Part II (Chicago: University of Chicago Press, 1987), 148–185.

26. John I. Goodlad and Jeannie Oakes, "We Must Offer Equal Access to Knowledge," *Educational Leadership* 45, no. 5 (February 1988): 16–22.

27. Arthur Steller, "Curriculum Development as Politics," *Educational Leadership* 38, no. 2 (November 1980): 161, 162.

28. See Thomas H. Gaul, Kenneth E. Underwood, and Jim C. Fortune, "Reform at the Grass Roots," *The American School Board Journal* 181, no. 1 (January 1994): 35–38.

29. John Pincus and Richard C. Williams, "Planned Change in Urban School Districts," *Phi Delta Kappan* 60, no. 10 (June 1979): 729–733.

30. Discussion has waxed and waned concerning what can be done to free schools in our larger cities for constructive decision making. Conflict has developed concerning locus of control by a "big board," regional boards, or community boards.

31. Lucinda Franks, "Little Big People," *New York Times Magazine,* October 10, 1993, 28, 31–34.

32. See *The Harvard Education Letter* 10, no. 1 (January–February 1994): entire issue.

33. West Virginia State Department of Education, "Schools in Crisis: Students at Risk," a report by a special task force on rural school districts, published by the department in 1989.

34. Susan Katz, "Places in the Heartland," *Insight* 3, no. 34 (August 24, 1987): 8, 9; see also Stephen L. Jacobson, *Administrative Leadership and Effective Small-Rural Schools: A Cooperative Case Study* (Ithaca, NY: State University of New York, September 1986).

35. Donald Orlosky and B. Othanel Smith, "Educational Change: Its Origins and Characteristics," *Phi Delta Kappan* 53, no. 7 (March 1972): 412–414.

36. Martin Carnoy, "High Technology and Education: An Economist's View," in Kenneth D. Benne and Steven Tozer, eds., *Society as Educator in an Age of Transition,* National Society for the Study of Education, Eighty-Sixth Yearbook, Part II (Chicago: University of Chicago Press, 1987), 100–107.

37. Arthur W. Combs, "New Assumptions for Educational Reform," *Educational Leadership* 45, no. 5 (February 1988): 39.

38. "Who Says It's Hopeless?" *The Boston Herald,* September 4, 1993.

SELECTED BIBLIOGRAPHY

Belanger, Maurice, and Purpel, David. *Curriculum and the Cultural Revolution: A Book of Essays and Readings*. Berkeley, CA: McCutchan, 1972.

Benjamin, Harold. *The Sabertooth Curriculum*. New York: McGraw-Hill, 1939.

Benne, Kenneth D., and Tozer, Steven, eds. *Society as Educator in an Age of Transition*. National Society for the Study of Education, Eighty-Sixth Yearbook, Part II. Chicago: University of Chicago Press, 1987.

Campbell, Duane E. *Education for a Democratic Society: Multicultural Curriculum Ideas for Teachers*. Cambridge, MA: Schenkman, 1980.

Commission on the Reorganization of Secondary Education. *Cardinal Principles of Secondary Education*. Washington, DC: U.S. Government Printing Office, 1918.

Cookson, Peter W., Jr., ed. *The Choice Controversy*. Brandon, VT: Resource Center for Redesigning Education, 1992.

Erickson, Edsel L.; Bryan, Clifford E.; and Walker, Lewis, eds. *Social Change, Conflict and Education*. Columbus, OH: Charles E. Merrill, 1972.

Gordon, C. Wayne, ed. *Uses of the Sociology of Education*. National Society for the Study of Education, Seventy-Third Yearbook, Part II. Chicago: University of Chicago Press, 1974.

Haubrich, Vernon F., ed. *Freedom, Bureaucracy, and Schooling*. 1971 Yearbook. Washington, DC: Association for Supervision and Curriculum Development, 1971.

Havighurst, Robert J., ed. *Metropolitanism: Its Challenge to Education*. National Society for the Study of Education, Sixty-Seventh Yearbook, Part I. Chicago: University of Chicago Press, 1968.

Havighurst, Robert J., and Levine, Daniel U. *Society and Education*, 5th ed. Boston: Allyn and Bacon, 1979.

Jencks, Christopher, ed. *Inequality: A Reassessment of the Effect of Family and Schooling in America*. New York: Basic Books, 1972.

Lieberman, Myron. *Beyond Public Education*. New York: Praeger, 1986.

Margolin, Edythe. *Sociocultural Elements in Early Childhood Education*. New York: Macmillan, 1974.

Miller, Ron. *The Renewal of Meaning in Education: Responses to the Cultural and Ecological Crisis of Our Time*. Brandon, VT: Resource Center for Redesigning Education, 1993.

"Restructuring Schools to Match a Changing Society." *Educational Leadership* 45, no. 5 (February 1988): entire issue.

Sharp, Rachel, and Green, Anthony. *Education and Social Control*. London: Routledge and Kegan Paul, 1975.

Sieber, Sam D., and Wilder, David E., eds. *The School in Society: Studies in the Sociology of Education*. Riverside, NJ: Free Press, 1973.

Tanner, Laurel N., ed. *Critical Issues in Curriculum*. National Society for the Study of Education, Eighty-Seventh Yearbook, Part I. Chicago: University of Chicago Press, 1988.

Van Til, William, ed. *Curriculum: Quest for Relevance*, 2nd ed. Boston: Houghton Mifflin, 1974.

4

SUBJECT MATTER: ITS ROLE IN DECISION MAKING

Schools have always taught subject matter. This statement would indeed be unnecessary if the notion had not been created at one time that U.S. schools are committed to teaching *children* instead of subject matter. The prevalence of this notion was the fault, in part, of the Progressive movement of the 1920s, 1930s, and 1940s. Progressives talked so much about the interests and needs of children that people missed what they said about subject matter. Of course, it has always been impossible to teach human beings without teaching them something.

During the 1950s, people became concerned about whether subject matter was "hard" or "soft" and, when it was considered to be soft, what could be done to make it harder. Some schools sought to toughen the curriculum by teaching a greater quantity of the same content more demandingly. This approach was especially noticeable in secondary education, where teachers assigned forty algebra problems of the same kind instead of the twenty they had formerly assigned and where the parsing of twenty sentences was magnified into the parsing of forty. Little was being learned about selection of subject matter because, even before the scare about the U.S.S.R.'s Sputnik, a major objective was to teach content that had been in the books long enough to be respectable. American teachers knew that almost anything they taught could be made too difficult for pupils to learn or so easy as to prove boring, but most of them apparently did not believe, with the investigators in the Eight Year Study, that what one learned was often less significant than the way one went about learning it.

Of course, teachers had to face certain necessary perennial questions about subject matter. In counseling individual pupils, they had to decide in a given case whether an extra year of science would serve better than a year of home economics. Insightful teachers wanted learners to have balanced programs, by which they meant well-rounded ones. At the classroom level, they were somewhat concerned with improving the quality of teacher-pupil planning, but they showed greater interest in selecting textbooks and other aids to enrich their classroom procedures. Their decision making about content selection was guided by two classic considerations: (1) the nature of the learner and the learning process and (2) the impact of society at large and the local community upon the school. During the 1960s and the 1970s, an additional consideration in decision making was more consciously addressed: the nature and uses of subject matter itself. In the early 1980s, the public awakened to the fact that, though teachers had known for a long time many of the best procedures and methods of teaching all sorts of subject matter, the ease and softness that had pervaded American society generally had encouraged teachers and schools to become easy and soft. The response of the schools was reminiscent of the reaction they had back in the 1950s to charges of curriculum softness: toughening the curriculum by adding more of the same standard content. During the 1990s, the continuing softness has been clearly related to societal and cultural decline, to ever-changing populations, to a lessening of parental interest and cooperation, to a decrease in pupils' enthusiasm and diligence, and to teachers' discouragement.

The present chapter will concern itself with the function of subject matter alone in conditioning the curriculum. In Chapter 5, we shall return to the larger matter of deciding what to teach in terms of a design that transcends the nature of subject matter.

AN OVERVIEW OF SUBJECT MATTER SELECTION AND PLACEMENT

What to teach and when to teach it are of interest to many people today for reasons such as the following:

1. Knowledge has already exploded to the point where it is necessary to select for teaching those items of knowledge that seem most significant and to eliminate much that is inconsequential.
2. The conviction has grown that insufficient subject matter is being taught within allotted learning time.
3. Experiments have shown that subject matter, old and new, can be made to relate to the lives of learners in previously unthought-of ways.
4. When a curriculum consists of a little of this knowledge and a little of that, it cannot be made coherent; therefore something must be done to supplement it, organize it, and integrate it.

The Explosion of Knowledge

Identifying suitable subject matter and placing it in the school curriculum have been complicated by a monumental explosion of knowledge. Anyone who views the educational scene at all perceptively can see that there is much more to be known than can possibly be comprehended. There is more in print than can be read—and much more that no one has time to put into writing or to express in other ways. The increase in knowledge is, however, only part of the problem. Knowledge is useless unless it is made grist for the mill of understanding. As knowledge increases, the time available to combine it into usable concepts decreases, so the learner asks repeatedly, "What meaning can these findings have for my life and the lives of others?" Quandary develops from the effort to find meaning in a world of too many facts and too many events.

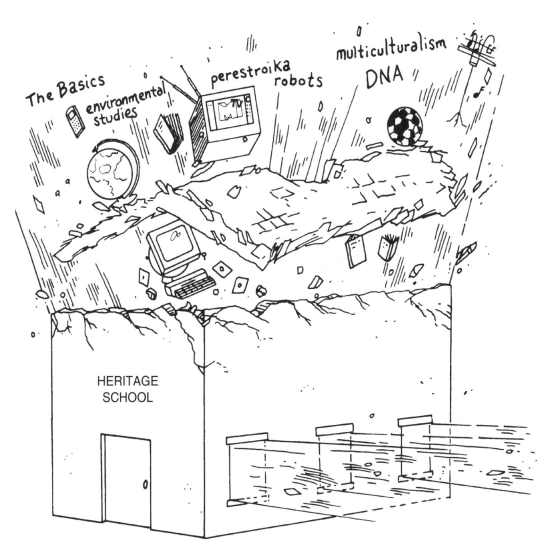

FIGURE 4-1   Knowledge Is Exploding!

Furthermore, the process of increasing knowledge is not merely an additive one. As knowledge abounds, some of that which was known previously is negated and must be discarded. Thus physics textbooks that were completely usable years ago are partially obsolete in a new era of atomic fission, nuclear weapons, space exploration, and space communication. Unfortunately, colleges have not prepared students to distinguish important elements of subject matter from unimportant ones. In fact, few college teachers have thought very much about the organization of the content they teach. Instead, they find it easier to follow the traditional organization of subject matter which they themselves received ready-made from their college teachers. Meanwhile, large blocks and little pieces of newly discovered knowledge overburden old plans of subject matter organization, and teachers become more and more perplexed about how they will cover all the material.

Knowledge is being compounded in a multiplicity of ways: (1) Knowledge that was once a piece of a whole has now become a whole. In mathematics, the theory of sets was once vaguely implied in the solution of certain mathematical problems. After the mid-twentieth century, it became a recognized subject entity. Like other new entities, however, it has not been accorded a clear position in the whole range of subject matter. (2) Blocks of knowledge that were formerly accepted are suddenly destroyed as entities. The unaffiliated pieces may remain, but they no longer form a context or design. This happened to the construct known as Newtonian physics. Part of what was believed by Newton and those who followed him is considered valid today, but Newtonian physics as an entity has been superseded by a newer physics that may conceivably be superseded in the future. (3) The number of theories and hypotheses about phenomena is increasing. Though many theories remain untested, those that are being tested suggest new combinations of the items of knowledge. Examples may be found especially in newer fields like psychology, which abounds in theories and hypotheses about individuals, groups, learning, and other concerns. (4) Specialization has become a phenomenon of modern life. More practitioners are engaging in small segments of practice, and researchers are looking more and more deeply into narrower and narrower expanses of content. A case in point is the field of biology, in which specialization has grown strikingly. In this and other fields, subspecializations have developed within specializations.

Arthur Combs expressed the belief that we cannot make a curriculum that can appropriately be required of everyone at a given level of schooling. The explosion of knowledge itself may prevent such an approach. Combs noted further that the ideas that knowledge is stable and that it comes entirely from the past are mythical. Those best equipped to deal with knowledge are adaptable, problem-solving people. To develop such people, we need to educate pupils to expect continuous change and to explore values.[1]

The question "What knowledge is of most worth?" was posed by Herbert Spencer in 1859. It is a question that must be asked by every generation of teachers. In the late 1990s, the question is as important as ever before. Witness the numbers of persons, professional and lay, who say that the principal function of the school is to teach the fundamentals, or basics, so well that learners can call them to use in every life situation. Witness, too, the persons who believe that schools can teach to all pupils, regardless of background or ability, the general or liberal studies, with the expectation that every pupil will become a reasonably well-educated man or woman. Witness the others who insist that knowledge not directly usable or functional is worthless. The types of subject matter that would be taught to satisfy each of these viewpoints obviously differ widely. Harry Broudy suggested a less simplistic way of considering knowledge than as a product of a kindergarten-through-twelfth-grade education. Broudy said learners should value knowledge in their later lives less for repeating and applying than for forming associations and interpreting phenomena. Thus learners, when mature, use the images and concepts they have become familiar with for thinking and feeling in all kinds of life situations. In this sense, the curriculum contributes the stencils or lenses through which mature learners make their interpretations of what is real in the experiences of life.[2] Hence knowledge becomes the basis of an operation involving analyzing, combining, and interpreting that results in understanding. Usually, merely to know is not enough in encountering the issues of life. To understand is essential in resolving the issues. To behave wisely guarantees the best in choice making.

As the problem of selecting curriculum content from the vast pool of knowledge became real to scholars in the subject fields, they began to interest themselves in the work of the elementary and secondary schools. Previously, they had been content to discover and report knowledge and occasionally to write textbooks and instructional manuals. Many of the textbooks and manuals were written from the viewpoint and in the vocabulary of the mature scholar and could not therefore be appreciated fully by pupils in elementary and secondary schools. The explosion of knowledge, along with other factors, caused scholars to think seriously about what subject matter is truly basic to learning additional content and especially to learning in depth. Some of the wisest scholars in subject fields are able to tell educators what is most important in the subjects, and then leave to the educators the complex task of determining where, when, how, and to whom the content should be taught. In the 1950s, however, scholars were trying to design curricula for children and youth without soliciting much help from practicing educators. After rising in the 1950s and the 1960s, the interest of subject matter scholars in school curriculum gradually began to abate. The scholars found that their curricular plans were sometimes inappropriate or too difficult, that their attempts to influence teachers and administrators were frequently ill conceived, and that medium-size and small schools were notably hard to reach and impress. On the other hand, the scholars' personal prestige helped their cause whenever curriculum reform was expected to originate outside schools rather than within them. In general, cooperation between subject matter scholars and professional educators improved as each group recognized that the other had a special role and competence. Cooperation is still poor in situations where the scholars assume they know just how subject matter can be used in schools, or where educators try to assume the role of subject matter experts.

The Need to Try Harder

Citizens of the United States have long considered themselves strong competitors in almost every human endeavor. Decades ago, several national figures voiced warnings that the graduates of U.S. secondary schools were unable to achieve satisfactorily and competitively, particularly in the sciences and mathematics. At that time, less was known about what had happened to the level of standardized test scores during the prior decade or two, and there were few data comparing the scores of our graduates with those of graduates of foreign schools.

During the 1980s, much was said about falling test scores in the United States. Comparison with data accumulated in New Zealand, Japan, Canada, and a dozen European nations shows that the relative achievement levels of pupils in the United States have seriously declined, particularly in the basic skills and in the sciences and mathematics. Comparative data about achievement in other fields have proved scarcer and less certain. Even the data about achievement in the basic skills and in science and mathematics have been flawed by the differences in the populations tested and observed. In economically developed countries other than the United States, the test subjects have usually been highly selected. One is reminded of attempts to compare apples with oranges.[3]

In 1990, the governing board of the National Assessment of Educational Progress proposed that three standards of performance be established for pupils in U.S. schools. These standards were to be labeled the basic, the proficient, and the advanced. Thus, in the 1990s, a formerly descriptive testing process would become normative. When the three standards, or levels, were specified in detail, they would presumably address the question "How good is good enough in pupil performance?" Critics of the proposal voiced the fear that the plan would open the way to a national curriculum. Further, they noted that the plan followed once again the top-down method of planning and ignored ranges of subtle differences among pupils.[4]

Several questions have arisen concerning the approximately 180 days of schooling per year mandated in the United States: Of how much time does a school day really consist? What happens during the allotted time? How much time do pupils spend learning subject matter outside school? A school day of five or five-and-a-half hours, of which 20 percent is spent on classroom routines and another 7 percent on behavioral and interactional matters, hardly suffices for learning enough subject matter. If, after each school day, pupils spend only an hour or two reinforcing what they have learned and encountering new learning material, their total learning period is shorter than that of pupils in other advanced nations. This fact has been seized upon by lay people whose agenda is the quick, simple fix.

Although much has been said in the media about scores, little has been said about pupil motivation. In the occasional exception, the burden of ideas in an article or column tells of the failure of parents to understand that hard study, encouraged and supported at home, is the stage setter and mainstay of pupil motivation. In the educational caste systems that exist in some European nations, high-achieving pupils are accorded special honor. Their segregation from less able pupils marks them clearly. Although they are often unhappy about what they are required to learn, being told that they are special people on their way to success in the world of work boosts their morale. By contrast, able pupils in the United States have fewer reasons to feel good about their accomplishments. The democratizing influence of being educated with other pupils of widely varying abilities and backgrounds is permitted to supersede demands for high standards. Brilliant youngsters are often denigrated by their peers merely because they are bright and therefore "different," and the honor accorded the intellectually gifted by adults in and around schools usually pales in comparison with the honor accorded skilled athletes.

Entirely aside from the current tendency to emphasize comparisons with pupil achievement and school practices in other developed nations, a central fact is clear: Pupils in the United States have not been working very hard. For example, they spend too little time reading and writing, in school and out. At home, television has become more attractive than books. At school, youngsters spend little time analyzing, discussing, and writing about what they read, and reading instruction itself is not very extensive or in-depth.

Experiments in the Placement of Subject Matter

There has always been a certain amount of experimentation with subject matter placement, but experimentation on a larger scale has been in progress since the 1960s. Obviously, large-scale experimentation cannot be left to individual teachers, who in their lifetimes will achieve only a limited rearrangement of what they teach. What subject matter should be moved up the grade scale? What should be moved down? What can children learn that has heretofore seemed beyond their capabilities?

Various experiments in rearranging old subject matter and taking on new subject matter have been carried out. Many of these suggest that portions of content might be taught earlier in pupil development and that teachers are taking longer than is necessary to help children build certain fundamental understandings. For example, the current grand dispute over early-early childhood education is producing arguments worthy of note.

A second example concerns the work of the curriculum committee of the National Science Teachers Association, which recommended that pupils have experience with all science concepts before they leave elementary school. Part of the content that was formerly taught in junior high school general science courses began to be taught in elementary schools. In senior high schools, science that was formerly taught superficially to junior high school pupils was incorporated within more sophisticated science courses.

Other experimentation has led to the conclusion that some subject matter is being taught too early. One conclusion of experiments in the teaching of arithmetic has been that children gain more understanding of certain number concepts if these concepts are developed later in the primary grades. In the field of physical education, the literature contains reports of attempting to teach physical skills before children's bodies are ready to master them.

During recent decades, creators of learning packages have experimented with moving subject matter up and down age and grade scales. Obviously, moving instructional content vertically is only one way of dealing with subject matter. Other ways are referred to in Chapter 5, in connection with designing and redesigning the curriculum.

Perhaps the most ambitious experiments in placing subject matter have been of a wholesale kind. When junior high schools were created, subject matter was transferred from high school and elementary schools and a minimum of new content was invented to form an educational institution that was expected to meet a serious, special need. Later, schools bearing the names "middle" and "intermediate" were established, usually to replace junior high schools in the gap between elementary schools and senior high schools. The ninth-grade curriculum is often placed in the senior high school, inasmuch as it is the first phase of the college preparatory program and inasmuch as youngsters attain puberty a year earlier than they did some years ago. Founders of middle and intermediate schools hope that they will not become imitations of junior high schools. To keep the middle school or intermediate school curriculum from resembling the usual curriculum of the junior high school, emphasis is placed on homemaking, practice in cogent thinking, the industrial arts, typing, computer use, library and media center orientation, study procedures, and other content not usually found at the same skill and understanding levels in either elementary schools or senior high schools. Block-of-time and individualized scheduling, exploratory experiences, and values studies bring the program in the school closer to the interests and needs of preadolescents and very young adolescents. As long as middle and intermediate schools are established for philosophically clear and altruistic motives rather than merely for administrative convenience, their special curriculum is likely to fit more closely the needs of the pupils who attend them.

Guarding Against the Patchwork Curriculum

Years ago in her classes, Hilda Taba spoke of the "additive curriculum" as being amorphous and disorganized. By this remark, she meant that a curriculum that results from adding piece to piece when the pieces differ from each other is indeed a patchwork curriculum. Amorphous and disorganized, it resembles the quilts people used to make from miscellaneous pieces of the family's discarded clothing. A curriculum of this kind doesn't cohere, or "hold together," and there is usually no semblance of sequence from part to part.

Unfortunately, the curricula most of us experienced as children had these characteristics. Because curriculum making is such an uncertain enterprise, the schools have continued to harbor and value patchwork curricula. Real curriculum coherence often comes from crossing subject lines. The crossover was always difficult, but it is even more troublesome today because the content of individual subjects continues to enlarge greatly. We are tempted at all points to mix the trivial with the significant, frequently just by caprice.

One can readily see why it is necessary to design and plan the curriculum in detail. We need a category system that keeps levels of knowledge separate. When children learn, they adopt our categories (and later propose some of their own), place ideas within the categories, and begin to see relationships among ideas. The remainder of this chapter emphasizes the importance of ideas, concepts, and concept formation within any system of categories we can devise. Whatever is pushed into the schools for pupils to learn, expanding learners' understanding of really important ideas must be given top priority.[5]

ACTIVITY 4-1

Finding Reasons for Changes in Subject Matter Placement

In a time of fast-moving changes in subject matter placement, the reasons for making changes should be considered thoroughly. It is important to know as certainly as possible whether given changes are justified or unjustified.

To learn what changes have occurred, (1) talk with school principals or other persons who see the curriculum as a whole or (2) compare recently published textbooks and other teaching materials with materials published ten years ago. To get behind the facts, ask the teachers why they have made specific changes in subject matter placement. Try to learn whether these changes have resulted chiefly from (1) copying what other teachers have done, (2) falling in with what seem to be national trends, (3) experimenting informally with subject matter to see whether one's pupils learn it readily and well, or (4) following the results of research reported in publications or research done in one's own professional environment. Learn whether the teachers feel satisfied with the new placement of subject matter *as compared with the former placement.*

What do you conclude about the reasons that undergird decisions concerning subject matter placement?

What, in your opinion, should be done to make changes in placement more judicious?

SELECTING SUBJECT MATTER AS LEARNING CONTENT

The potential experience of pupils in modern elementary, middle, and secondary schools covers a respectable portion of what human beings should know and understand, of what they are able to do, and of how they feel about people and things. The subject matter the schools have traditionally taught has been confined to the content of recognized school subjects. In these terms, subject matter is taught merely to be known and understood—as a lay person put it, "School is for getting something into your head." But the best modern schools teach pupils how to do things, and they also help them clarify how they feel and what they value.

Even today, most of what is taught in schools is to be found within bodies of organized knowledge incorporated within school subjects. But much is now being taught apart from the formal structure of school subjects—in handicrafts and in human relationships, for example. Accordingly, the meaning of school subject matter is beginning to approximate the meaning of that which is experienced within the total environment of the school. We may expect to continue teaching subject matter known and understood as *substance*. Subject matter that contributes to skill building or to values development, however, must be taught mainly as *process*. Learnings in both the substance and the process categories form the curriculum of the school. Consider the subject called history. History is now taught primarily as substance, but it is also possible to teach the process of creating history, in the sense of selecting historical data and then recording them understandably. This is done, for example, when pupils select and record the history that comes from interviews, known as oral history. On the other hand, teaching reading is commonly thought of as process, though that which is read is the substance called literature. Both the process and the substance are improvable.

What a school teaches depends partly on the point of view about learning that is accepted by the school's teachers and administrators. One view holds that learning is work to be engaged in sporadically, to be accomplished alone and diligently, to be organized carefully, and then, possibly, to be forgotten. People who accept this view tend to believe that the only worthwhile subject matter consists of the traditional, honored, familiar subjects. An opposing view is that learning is natural, spontaneous, and relatively effortless, and that it requires little in the way of extrinsic rewards and reinforcement. It can encompass the content of traditional school subjects within an informal, social setting. A keyword of the first view is *memorization;* a keyword of the second is *growth*. Many of us were educated in schools that exemplified the first view. But even our traditional schools found informal aspects of learning creeping in. Therefore they came to accept a broad definition of the curriculum.

A Range of Objectives

Liberalizing our views of what subject matter is permits us to utilize a wider range of objectives. Since the mid-1950s, Krathwohl, Bloom, Masia, and others have formed taxonomies of educational objectives of three kinds: the cognitive, or intellectually based; the affective, based in feeling or emotion; and the psychomotor, relating mental activity with physical movement. The taxonomies are meant to embrace all the classifications of subject matter available for teaching in elementary, middle, and secondary schools.

Cognitive Objectives

The *cognitive domain,* which is the domain of intellectuality and thought process, includes

1. Knowing, which has to do with learning and recalling facts, words, and other symbols, classifications, events, trends, principles, ways of working, and theories
2. Comprehending, which involves interpreting content, translating it to another form, and extrapolating elements from one situation to another
3. Applying, or using in new situations what one has already learned
4. Analyzing, which consists of breaking wholes into parts and noting the nature of the parts and their relationships with each other
5. Synthesizing, or putting parts together and showing creativity in combining elements
6. Evaluating, or using criteria to judge the worth of an object

Affective Objectives

The *affective domain,* which is the domain of sensing, feeling, and believing, consists of

1. Receiving, or showing interest in, giving attention to, and indicating awareness of an object
2. Responding, which includes both giving willing response and replying with a feeling of satisfaction
3. Valuing, or accepting a value, preferring it, and becoming committed to it
4. Organizing values by conceptualizing, clarifying, and systematizing them in one's thinking
5. Characterizing values by internalizing them so that eventually they become a philosophy of life[6]

Psychomotor Objectives

The *psychomotor domain,* the most recently described of the three domains, contains five generally accepted levels of human activity. They are

1. Moving physically, including walking, jumping, running, pulling, pushing, and manipulating
2. Showing perceptual ability of visual, auditory, tactile, kinesthetic, and coordinative kinds
3. Showing physical ability related to strength, endurance, agility, dexterity, and time required to react or respond
4. Making skilled, coordinated movements in games, sports, and the arts
5. Communicating nonverbally through facial movements, gestures, posture, and creative expression[7]

Levels of Knowledge

Some of the objectives in the preceding lists deal directly with knowledge as content for teaching. Taba described knowledge for use in schools as being at four levels. The lowest, simplest, and most common level is that of *specific facts and processes*. The date Columbus discovered America is an example. Specific facts and processes constitute data to think with or means for developing basic ideas. Some teachers almost stop their teaching at this level.

Taba's second level is the level of *basic ideas and principles,* which often represent a common core of learning for all pupils. For example, a basic idea in American history is that the American frontier became a safety valve for discontent and also a stimulus to technological development.

The third level is that of *concepts,* such as the concept of human interdependence, the concept of the set in mathematics, or the concept of political democracy. As pointed out in Chapter 2, concepts are the threads of thought, or universals, that run through the curriculum. Several subjects contribute simultaneously to the development of most concepts. A teacher can never legitimately say to a pupil, "I'll give you a concept," because the pupil must develop each concept for himself or herself. The best a teacher can do is to arrange pupils' experiencing in ways that contribute to concept development.

The fourth level is the level of *thought systems,* which direct the flow of thought and inquiry in areas of learning. For example, in theology, John Calvin developed a thought system known as Calvinism. Each thought system includes interrelated concepts, principles, and definitions. With a thought system as a base, mature pupils (especially the abler pupils in secondary schools) ask intelligent questions, relate ideas, and engage in rational and sophisticated inquiry. They become interested in ways of thinking and inquiring within their favorite subjects, as when they develop advanced machines and models for a school science fair.[8]

The Planning of Measurable Outcomes

The two immediately preceding sections of this chapter make quite different contributions to an understanding of subject matter and its uses. The taxonomies prepared by Bloom and others provide a general mapping of large objectives. For daily, weekly, and monthly use, large objectives need to be broken into smaller, directly usable ones.

Taba's descriptions of levels of knowledge organize the cognitive domain into elements that range from simple to complex and that help one to come up with smaller objectives to suit one's intentions and at the same time know where pupils are working within the total domain. (Unfortunately, no one has organized the affective and psychomotor domains in so neat and usable a way.)

Given a level of achievement we hope to see pupils attain as they utilize subject matter, how should the small, usable objectives be stated? Many persons in the curriculum field now say these objectives should be stated behaviorally—that is, according to the behavior to be expected. A leading promoter of behavioral objectives, W. James Popham, has put it this way: "A properly stated behavioral objective must describe without ambiguity the nature of learner behavior or product to be measured."[9]

When this definition is applied literally, it leads to a "tight" method of stating objectives, as seen in *performance-based education* (sometimes called *competency-based education*). Objectives that are performance-based state what the learners will do, under what conditions and at what level of group performance, if the given objective is to be regarded as having been attained. The emphasis is on intended outcomes of instruction, constituting the specific performance of pupils. Performance-based educational procedures often follow a set sequence such as the following: (1) behavioral (performance-type) objectives are stated; (2) learner's behaviors (baseline mastery of the subject matter) are assessed; (3) learners' abilities to perform at an established outcome level are also assessed; (4) alternative paths to achievement of the desired outcome(s) are plotted; (5) post-assessment is used to determine the degree to which the expected performance has been attained (for example, to a degree of 90 percent, established at the time the objective was stated); and (6) learners are passed to the next step or are asked to repeat, depending on the results of the post-assessment.

In performance-based education, the outcomes expected become definite achievement criteria. The usual achievement tests, based on national or regional norms, are not suitable for determining whether a given group of pupils has met its own definite achievement criteria. Consequently, *criterion-referenced tests* have to be designed to meet the need. These tests are expected to fit not only the objectives but also the subject matter content that has been taught. Thus criterion referencing applies to everything in the instructional procedure: content, materials, and evaluation scheme.

Performance-based education can be improved by making the statements of expected performance or competency completely clear, by paying attention to the location at which each competency fits within the curriculum, and by providing resource materials for planners.[10] Its potential seems to lie mainly in the provision it can make for such aspects of effective instruction as individualization, self-pacing, remediation, and experiences in the field.[11]

Performance-based education and criterion-referenced testing are subjected to the same criticisms that have been leveled at behavioral objectives: that they are applications of mechanistic stimulus-response learning theory; that they do not admit the variety of behaviors that occur in classrooms and therefore constitute a closed, unrealistic learning system; that the number of objectives they position behind real performance is staggering; that they make it literally impossible to attend to the needs of individuals; and that, because of the preceding handicaps, they center on a few minor, measurable bits of subject matter.[12] Some of the critics say that performance-based education will inevitably impoverish the curriculum because rich, significant elements of the curriculum will be left untouched while teachers are busy with the little pieces that the tests highlight. Nevertheless, some state officials, boards of education, and lay persons continue to press for performance-based education and its associated strategies because they offer a means of holding teachers accountable for the quality of their work.[13]

Some Themes Governing the Selection of Content

An informal survey by the author of the interests of curriculum planners in subject matter and planning processes has highlighted several favorite themes, including basic education, functional learning, education of affect, and staff development resulting from curriculum planning. The first three themes contribute directly to curriculum content; the last represents strategies, or process elements, that can be used in making curriculum decisions.

Basic Education

As we saw in Chapter 3, pressure to improve the teaching of the basics—skills such as those needed to read, write, and do arithmetic problems, and fundamental knowledge such as that in the sciences, history, or geography—has increased in recent years. Persons in charge of curriculum planning have naturally responded to the pressures by searching for ways of strengthening the teaching of the basics. Actually, methods of teaching reading and arithmetic have been thoroughly explored in the past, though we still hear many discussions of ways of going about teaching reading and arithmetic. Therefore the essential problem, as identified by curriculum coordinators, has been the failure of school personnel to take seriously what is already known and put it into regular practice.

Though deficiencies in basic education have appeared in all geographic locations and in all segments of the U.S. population, the favorable effects of doing something about them can often be seen most readily where the deficiency has been greatest. In Appalachia, for example, improvement in basic education was brought about when two sources of help were utilized: the Appalachian Regional Commission and state-sponsored agencies.[14] In developing countries of the world, the particular need is often for skills in communication, skills that improve the quality of life, and skills that increase production.[15] Thus the meaning of the term *basic skills* varies in accordance with economic status and cultural background. The groups in our society that have cried loudest and longest for improvement in basic education are conservatives in education and religion, employers frustrated with their employees' poor performance in applying basic skills, and parents who recognize their children's deficiencies.

Functional Learning

Identification of subject matter for functional learning has been one response to the public's demand for high school graduates who not only *know* something but also can *do* something. In 1980, the Association for Supervision and Curriculum Development formed a national network of schools to redefine general education in U.S. secondary schools. The network interested itself in the broad range of learnings that are presumably necessary in a high-tech society. The schools of the network expressed a desire to achieve the following results: an increase in total requirements for graduation, more serious study by seniors, augmented mathematics and science requirements, an expectation of competency rather than of mere exposure to subject matter, and careful analysis of the nature of course content.[16] Employers, who are among the chief advocates of functional learning, have expressed themselves similarly. They have become more concerned with broad-based general education than with specialized education, most of which they believe they can provide on the job. Applied science has long been recognized as important functional learning. The applications of science are now considered to include public and social policy matters and ethical issues. In biology, for instance, the emphasis has been changing from instruction in biology strictly for its own sake to instruction in biology with overtones of information management, data analysis, and decision making based on moral and ethical dimensions.[17]

Real and functional learning, which has been talked about for generations, and surely before the time of John Dewey, has been given the name *authentic education,* or its alternative, *authentic learning.* Experienced teachers have found that youngsters' perennial question "Why do we have to study this stuff?" is less likely to be heard when learning content seems real, applicable, and practical.

Education of Affect

Education of affect, or affective education, means more than merely education in personal, religious, political, and social values. Affect, first of all, means feelings and emotions, both of which belong in the learning process. The feelings and emotions pupils bring to the learning of particular subject matter influence the facility with which the subject matter is learned and also the permanence with which it remains in the lives of the pupils. Arthur Combs said that the cruciality of what is learned depends on the subjective experience of the learner. He described four preconditions for relating to and absorbing content. Put in the language of the individual learner, they are

"I think well of myself."
"I feel challenged rather than threatened by what I am to learn."
"What I value accords with what I'm expected to learn."
"I feel I belong in this situation and am being cared for here." [18]

The wisest curriculum leaders know the importance of affect. Therefore they try to meet the challenge of making room for it in planning and in teaching. Whatever they do is likely to take into account a pupil's self-concept, sense of challenge, values, and sense of belonging.

Staff Development by Means of Curriculum Planning

Many people think the end product of curriculum planning is a project, a program, a model, or a printed curriculum guide. We have known for a long time, however, that changes in the behavior of teachers and other persons who come into contact with pupils constitute the real product. With the advent of programs of staff development, curriculum coordinators have turned their attention once more to using curriculum planning intentionally to assist teacher growth.

An example of the change-in-people emphasis on a national scale has been the National Writing Project.[19] The project started at Berkeley, California in 1974 and was subsequently funded by the National Endowment for the Humanities, by an ESEA grant, and by state grants. Although it has provided for input by scholars and use of discovery learning, the project's greatest strength has been its careful and thorough involvement of teachers. In staff development groups, teachers have learned to write through extensive practice and are thus prepared to teach both their colleagues and their pupils to write. The project has taken the almost unprecedented step of treating teachers as professionals, and therefore has differed from earlier instructional projects in which production of written materials (curriculum packages) was more important than the direct development of people.

If teachers are to use curriculum planning as a means of self-development, they must be involved in the planning from its inception; they must have sufficient time, competent help, and adequate facilities, clerical assistance, and materials; and most of all they must be encouraged by their supervisors to stay with the tasks of planning. When teachers work closely with a portion of a subject, identifying facts, experiences, activities, and materials and concerning themselves with scope, sequence, evaluation, and other professional matters, they use varied talents that enrich the planning process and help make the ultimate selection of subject matter especially appropriate.[20] Teachers beginning their service during recent years have sometimes proved to have decidedly limited knowledge and understanding of their subject matter. Staff development in the learning of subject matter is thus essential.

Criteria for Selecting Content

Several criteria have been proposed for selecting appropriate subject matter content from an embarrassing wealth of choices. They include the following:

• *The validity and the significance of the content.* Some items of content available to learners are likely to be of little worth because they are inconsequential or trivial. Such items should be ruled out.

• *The balance that is being maintained between content for survey and content for study in depth.* Pupils need to see the broad sweep or scope of subject matter. After moving for a while on the surface of the content, however, they should have opportunities for digging deep, or "postholing." Points on the subject matter terrain at which the individual pupil postholes may be peculiar to personal needs, or they may be the same points at which his or her classmates go into depth. The problem for the curriculum planner is to achieve a reasonable balance between scope and depth. Curriculum planners who do this best are generally those who know most about the entire range of the subject matter with which they are dealing.

• *The appropriateness of the content to pupil needs and interests.* Casual interest is not hard to identify. Lasting interest and real need are much more difficult to determine. Only the passage of time permits curriculum planners to know pupils' enduring interests. Needs of which the pupil is unconscious appear only to outside observers and must be assessed by those who have the necessary maturity to weigh the gravity of various needs. The value of teachers as diagnosticians of need depends on their previous experience in living as well as on the criteria they use in the identification process.

• *The durability, or lasting quality, of the elements of content that are being emphasized.* Determining how long an item of content will last as a desired and desirable element is difficult. Subject matter has changed so rapidly in fields like physics and chemistry that prediction of its durability has sometimes seemed impossible. In general, however, the closer an item of content is to a main idea or concept, the greater its chance of being durable.

• *The relationship of facts and other minor content to main ideas and concepts.* The comment above concerning the criterion of durability relates to this criterion. The webbing that holds a body of subject matter together is big ideas and concepts. An item of subject matter that is not related to a major idea may conceivably be dispensable.

• *The learnability of the content.* Obviously, no attempt should be made to teach pupils that which they cannot learn. Trying to teach the same basic content to nearly all the children of all the people has been one of the major failings of the American experiment.

• *The possibility of illuminating the content with data from other fields of knowledge.* Some subject matter has potential for relating readily to content from other subjects. In modern studies of ecology, for example, ecological principles found in pure science have implications for the social studies and have their base in psychology, morals, and ethics. Teaching content that is capable of crossing subject lines in this way facilitates reinforcement of learning as the learner is reminded of his or her previous contact with it in other settings.

Persons especially interested in human development and those with a realistic view of the difficulties teachers of reluctant learners face day by day may be expected to list additional criteria: the evident needs of individual learners, their achievement status, and their expectations; the context within which the subject matter is presented; and the relevance that the learners find in the content.

As time passes, curriculum planners continue to be reminded of what John Dewey said in 1916: that knowledge is "the working capital, the indispensable resources, of further inquiry; of finding out, or learning, more things."[21] Later, Dewey wrote that educators are to consider the current experience of learners and then seek to extend that experience. What the learner knows becomes the means of opening the way to new knowledge. Educators thus serve as agents to help learners achieve connectedness in their development.[22]

In selecting and placing subject matter, building experience on experience appropriately, as Dewey advocated, is a difficult task in itself, but curriculum leaders are called upon to do much more. One of their additional assignments is to see that the schools accept and discharge responsibilities that are theirs, and to screen out all the unjustified responsibilities the society and the community try to impose on the schools. Another additional assignment is to encourage articulation of learning from level to level of schooling. Another is to urge strictness in the learning process when the subject matter requires strictness, and to urge relaxation and openness when the subject matter calls for exploration, inquiry, and discovery. Still another is to be the immediate source of equipment and materials that facilitate the learning of the subject matter to be taught. These assignments are so staggering in their proportions that new administrators, supervisors, and coordinators do not usually realize their magnitude and significance. Certainly, most members of the public do not.

ACTIVITY 4-2

Planning Improved Selection of Subject Matter

Read the following questions, and ask yourself whether you know the answer to each question. If you do not, inquire within your school district or another district you know reasonably well concerning the issues with which you are unfamiliar. When you report to your class or group, discuss with the members how far the school district you have studied needs to go to develop adequate bases for selecting subject matter competently, in light of your answers to the questions.

1. In this school district, have curriculum planners reviewed the district's educational program to see that the schools are accepting as their responsibilities tasks that really belong to them? How have such tasks been defined?
2. In this district, have administrators and other personnel tried hard to screen out tasks that obviously do not belong to the schools? What example of such a task can you give?
3. In the district, have teachers, department chairpersons, and other planners tried to make sure that, in curriculum fields where obsolescence is common, the subject matter taught is really up to date? What example of this kind of action can you give?
4. Have system-wide planning groups attempted to achieve articulation among parts of the curriculum so that pupils' movement from developmental level to developmental level in learning is continuous and smooth? What evidence of these attempts can you give?

5. Have curriculum planners in the district made certain that the curriculum contains at every developmental level subject matter that, by its nature, must be taught rigorously and also subject matter that is rightly taught in a relaxed and open way? What evidence do you have that teachers are paying attention to the distinction between these two kinds of subject matter?
6. Have administrators in the district made equipment and materials available for the teaching of required and recommended subject matter? How do you know?

Learning Experiences for Achieving Objectives

No matter how wisely subject matter has been selected to aid in the achievement of objectives, teachers need to prescribe and administer specific subject matter to pupils. They do this by creating and using learning experiences, alone or with the help of their pupils. Teachers find several criterion questions useful in creating appropriate learning experiences:

1. Can the experiences profit the pupils we teach?
2. Do the experiences help to meet the evident needs of our pupils?
3. Are our pupils likely to be interested in the experiences?
4. Do the experiences encourage pupils to inquire further?
5. Do the experiences seem real?
6. How do the experiences accord with the life patterns of our pupils?
7. How contemporary are some of the major experiences?
8. How fundamental to mastery of total learning content are they?
9. Do the experiences provide for attainment of a range of objectives?
10. Do the experiences provide opportunities for both broad study and deep study?

Practical hints for preparing and stating learning experiences were listed by a group of teachers as follows:

1. If you are going to describe learning experiences at all, spell them out in sufficient detail to make them understandable.
2. Know the purpose or function of each experience within your curriculum plan.
3. If possible, have each experience serve more than one of your objectives. For instance, a single experience can easily serve a cognitive objective and also an affective one.
4. Try to organize each experience within a hierarchy of experiences. For example, move from the concrete and experientially close to the abstract and experientially remote, or from the easy to the difficult.
5. Make increments in experiencing "bite size." Instead of providing substantially bigger bites for bright pupils, try preparing alternative experiences for them.

6. Try rotating *types* of experiences, like the following:

a. Experiences for intake
b. Experiences for expression
c. Experiences for assimilation of big ideas and concepts, through planned practice
d. Experiences for accommodation or restructuring of big ideas and concepts, through making them functional in real situations
e. Experiences to sensitize or to otherwise develop feeling
f. Experiences to stimulate intellectual growth, including gaming, puzzles, and simulation
g. Experiences to interrelate mind and physical movement, as in sophisticated practice in sports

7. Use within the experiences varied ways of learning, including reading, writing, observing, analyzing, dramatizing, making art objects, working individually, working in groups, and making maps and charts. Keep a master list of possibilities like these.

SITUATION 4-1

Resolving Problems in Subject Matter Selection and Assignment Making

The principal of an elementary school received the following letter of complaint from the mother of a fifth-grade boy who was enrolled in the school:

Dear Mrs. Rumson:

My son Gilbert, who is in Miss Axtell's fifth-grade section, brought home a strange assignment last Friday. The assignment was given to the entire fifth grade at your school, the fifth-grade teachers having got together to make it up.

I was upset when I saw the assignment, which called for making a booklet about poets. You may already know about it yourself. Anyway, the teachers had listed twenty-four names, eight names to the column. The first column was headed 1700s, the second column 1800s, and the third column 1900s. I guess each column was supposed to contain the name of at least one poet, maybe more.

Gilbert and the others were to choose one poet from each period of time, write a biographical report about each one in script, copy at least three poems written by each poet, and make a bibliography.

I checked the lists of poets in a dictionary and an encyclopedia and found no poet in the list for the 1700s and two poets in the 1800s list that belong in the 1900s.

The poems written by many of the poets are long and hard. The kids can't understand them, and they don't want to copy all that stuff.

Didn't anybody guide the teachers in selecting the poets before the assignment went out all over town? It looks as though the teachers don't know the poets or what they wrote either.

I talked with Miss Axtell about this. She said the teachers worked very hard researching the assignment and they were going ahead with it even if it had a mistake or two. I told her nobody researched it. I have an anthology at home where I found lists of poets almost the same as the ones the teachers gave out. Some of the teachers' poets wrote only one poem.

Gilbert will complete his assignment because his mother will help him. But this does *not* solve the problem.

Other than moving or sending Gilbert to a private school, what can I do about such ignorance? What are you going to do?

Grace Oreo

1. What abuses of subject matter and pupil experiences are described in this letter?
2. What hidden abuses can you detect?
3. What *should* the principal do to help the teachers with their subject matter problems?

Ventures in the Selection of Subject Matter— Here and Abroad

In the United States, subject matter selection finds its basis in two sources: (1) classic subjects and subject fields and (2) available informal content. The classic subjects and subject fields have included the English language arts, foreign languages, reading, mathematics, the sciences, social studies, art, music, physical education and health study, vocational and technical education, home economics, and business education. Developments in these subjects proceed slowly to rapidly depending on specific trends that affect their popularity and use. Curriculum planners need to follow the work of organizations such as the National Council of Teachers of English and the International Reading Association to recognize the latest developments in specific subject fields. The presence of these developments can be discovered by utilizing *Education Index* and research journals.

Outside the bounds of subjects and subject fields, informal content works its way into the curriculum, especially as society makes its demands. The variety of informal topics is amazing. The topics range from strategies for dealing with teen pregnancy to techniques for warding off attackers on the streets, to ways of knowing whether a youngster is too intoxicated to drive, to methods of performing skillfully and humanely in hospital service. Departures from ordinary experiences are, metaphorically, only subject matter islands in a sea of curriculum change.

Curriculum planners can learn from international education journals and other resources what changes are being made in curricula in foreign countries. Planners may want to know whether national, standard curricula are common in Europe and the Far East. They may find, for example, that the national curriculum in Great Britain is undergoing revision. Further, they may learn that, whereas local autonomy is increasing in a number of nations, centralized planning, its opposite, operates in France, Spain, and Sweden. Variety in curriculum planning is demonstrated by Russia's flirting with religious instruction, Turkey's use of our U.S. taxonomy of educational objectives, Poland's education in marriage and family life, Malaysia's reform of its science program, South Africa's introduction of anti-apartheid instruction, Australia's adoption of a daily program in physical education, and Scotland's preparation of thematic units for English teaching. In the United States, our propagandists of negative bent continue to laud the effectiveness of teaching and learning in countries other than our own. In doing so, they ignore two important facts: (1) Achievement levels of dissimilar pupils in the respective nations naturally differ, and (2) pupils and teachers in Japan and Germany, our chief competitor nations, have become critical of their own education systems.

A CLOSER LOOK AT SUBJECT MATTER

In the recent past, subject matter as learning content has been examined more critically than ever before. There has been much talk about the role of the various disciplines in learning, a *discipline* being defined as a way of making knowledge and as the domain occupied by particularized knowledge. Thus the phenomena of chemistry have been discovered by a given set of methods known to the chemist from training in laboratory science, and the content the chemist has discovered is distinctively different from the content that has been discovered by the historian or the philosopher or even by other scientists like the physicist and the biologist. Each discipline, according to the definition, has its own integrity—an integrity that is worth respecting because it has been built by the regulated efforts of so many intelligent and creative persons. A few authors, as they write about the disciplines, seem to be thinking of applications of organized knowledge, as in the field of medicine. Actually, a discipline has a history, has its own domain, follows its own rules, and should be based in testable theory.

Some of the thinking about subject matter as learning content has followed these lines: Subject matter includes what people know and believe, together with reflections of people's ideals and loyalties; and subject matter may validly be selected for use in teaching and learning when it is significant to an organized field of knowledge, when it has proved appropriate down through the years, when it is useful, when it can be made interesting to learners, and when it contributes to the growth and development of our society.[23] Of these criteria, the first is highlighted within the context of the present chapter. The criterion of significance to an organized field of knowledge implies that the items of knowledge within that field must be interrelated so that the structure formed by the items can be seen and understood. According to this thesis, there are big and significant principles or concepts on which lesser principles, concepts, and facts depend. A first, major task of the scholar and of the learner alike is to identify clearly these big principles or concepts.[24] For example, in the view of a leading economist, there are four principles on which all of economics depends. Know these and you have the hooks on which the minor principles and the facts of economics hang. The details of economics as a discipline may change—time may retire some of them and new details may replace old ones—but the fundamental structure of economics will remain, and it is the fundamental structure that counts. Although the fundamentals often develop from observation of details in the first place, the steadfastness of the fundamentals is a basic consideration in studying the structure of a discipline. Detail is hard to remember unless it is related to the fundamentals. Transfer of training, so long argued in U.S. education, seems to proceed best when learners understand the fundamentals of what they are learning and transferring.

These ideas bring one to the thought that different elements in the structure of a discipline can be taught at different developmental levels. Thus attention must be given to more than the facts of mere readiness as a function of the human organism. Readiness for *what* becomes a central question. Piaget has maintained, in Bruner's expression, that "any subject can be taught effectively in some intellectually honest form to any child at any stage of development." This would mean, for instance, that some portions of algebra and geometry can validly be taught to children in the primary grades. These portions must necessarily be concrete. More importantly, they must accord with the child's perception of the world's phenomena. Piaget points out that children advance through three stages of development in learning subject matter and that young children tend to be at the first stage. At this stage, learners perceive phenomena in terms of their own experiences, and they try to establish relationships between their own experiences and the actions that are being taken. At the second stage, children engage in concrete operations with present phenomena, being competent enough to attempt trial-and-error experiments in their heads. At the third stage, they go beyond working with present phenomena to work with hypothetical ones.[25] Each successive stage calls for more abstract thinking. A prime difficulty in selecting subject matter is to find content that is abstract enough to challenge without being so abstract as to frustrate. When this is done, even crudely, it is possible to build a spiral curriculum in which the same subject, but not the identical subject matter, is taught on several occasions during one's school experience. For example, selected portions of American history may be taught profitably in the fifth grade and then again in the eighth and eleventh grades of a pupil's schooling.

Differing Views of Subject Matter

People have differing views of what subject matter is acceptable and usable for teaching. Scholars or experts in subject fields think that the schools should teach subject matter that is "ideal" in the sense that it makes contact with principles and abstractions and facilitates idea development. These experts believe that emphasizing principles provides learners with knowledge that is centrally significant. By understanding principles and abstractions, learners become capable of drawing inferences that have meaning for them. Having made a principle or a concept their own, they can infer the need for additional principles or concepts and then proceed to develop and state them. In this way, learners stay close to the heart of subject matter and are en route to becoming subject matter experts in their own right.

Representing a second view, the authors of textbooks and curriculum guides draw on "ideal" subject matter, but they keep their eyes also on the culture and the local community to find trends, developments, and cautions therein. Furthermore, they take into account what they think the users of their materials need to know. What they incorporate into books and guides thus becomes a compound of big ideas, cultural input, local demands, and learners' presumed needs. Textbooks and curriculum guides that take this approach usually gain great respect from school administrators, many of whom have been taught that an approved curriculum can be laid out in detail for teachers to follow. These administrators say to themselves (with fingers crossed), "Woe be unto the teacher who doesn't follow the prescribed curriculum."

A third view of subject matter is just a bit more realistic. It embodies what supervisors and other observers think they see being taught in classrooms projected against what these observers believe should be taught. A written record or a videotape can provide suggestions about the structure and the details of the subject matter presented in a teaching episode. What observers think they are seeing is not always, however, what teachers think they are teaching.

Thus a fourth view of subject matter—and not always a sophisticated one—is the view held by classroom teachers who, while they may be willing to listen to the advice of scholars and supervisors, use in the privacy of their classrooms subject matter that conforms to the needs of their pupils. In interviews, teachers can tell us what they think they have been teaching, but their impressions are not always the same as those of their pupils.

Finally, then, there is the subject matter that pupils are actually learning. Youngsters take from their classrooms understandings and attitudes that sometimes surprise and disturb adults. Their learned subject matter frequently consists of principles, warped versions of reality, offbeat revelations, memorable incidents, the reactions of others, disorganized facts, and casual comments by teachers and fellow pupils. All of this constitutes a wide range of learnings, most of which would not gain the respect of subject matter specialists. Is it any wonder that, except in highly restrictive environments, "respectable" subject matter competes constantly with the joyous, and sometimes disheartening, subject matter of childhood and youth?

Two Kinds of Knowledge

Curriculum planners work with two kinds of knowledge. The first of these is called *substantive* knowledge. Knowledge of this kind concerns the essential substance, or content, to be taught. The substance comes chiefly in three forms: central concepts, organizing principles, and factual data. Central concepts and organizing principles are, of course, most important; factual data, or details, hang on the framework represented by concepts and principles and are dispensable and replaceable. As mentioned earlier in this chapter, Hilda Taba defined a fourth, even more sophisticated element of substantive knowledge: thought systems, which formalize knowledge and induce further inquiry.

A second kind of knowledge, of how to inquire or how to make new or different knowledge within a subject matter field, has gained educators' attention. Called *syntactic* knowledge, it helps teachers become inquirers within their own specialties. As one teacher remarked, "It helps us avoid misrepresenting part of what we teach."[26]

If we ask a subject matter expert what syntactic knowledge is, he or she may say that it is knowledge of how to make new knowledge. If we ask a teacher who has used the so-called discovery process with pupils, he or she may say it is a way of discovering and rearranging preexistent knowledge to make new interpretations. That is, pupils in schools can discover for themselves established, accepted knowledge by inquiring about phenomena and inferring meanings. John Dewey noted that when learners are ready to inquire as a prelude to discovering, they take the following steps, though not necessarily in an established order: They sense a difficulty; they locate and define it; they suggest a possible solution; they develop by reason the details of their suggestion; and they observe and experiment until they accept or reject the suggestion.[27]

If pupils studying history are to discover elements of historical events that matter, they need to ask questions like these:

> What kinds of events in the period we are studying seem most important?
> Where can we find accurate reports of the kinds of events we have selected as being most important?
> How do the best available reports of these events differ?
> When historians disagree in their interpretations of the recorded events, why and how do these disagreements seem to have developed?
> What original or different interpretation of the events can we ourselves think of?
> What can we do further to judge which interpretation is right or most nearly right?
> As a consequence of what we now know, how would we write an accurate history of the period we have been studying?

In France, copies of historical documents have been made available to the schools so that pupils can construct portions of the history of France *de novo*. An important objective of the discovery process is to *feel* like the historian, the scientist, or the mathematician. The act of discovery can obviously be engaged in only at intervals. Time is too short. But the discovery method is badly needed in a society that seeks excellence in its youngsters—a society in which pupils are presently able to enter college chiefly because they are effective rote memorizers rather than effective critical thinkers. In every discipline, pupils need to understand the workings of that discipline—how it is made and put together and how it is refined and polished. Unfortunately, in recent years the discovery process has fallen into disuse.

Philip H. Phenix thought of the disciplines as being peculiarly suited for teaching and learning. He maintained that all curriculum content should come from the disciplines rather than from the needs, concerns, and problems of learners. To make knowledge useful for teaching and learning, he said, we must accomplish three goals: (1) provide analytic simplification through which we can make understandable the classes and generalizations that are formed of particulars; (2) provide synthetic coordination by which we make evident the patterns and relationships that exist in subject matter; and (3) ensure the presence of dynamism, the "lure of discovery," or the force that leads us on to new knowledge. In the disciplines, said Phenix, we can find the answers to our needs, concerns, and problems. Therefore the source of all that teachers and learners require is the disciplines themselves.[28]

Having seen what analysis of subject matter might contribute to decision making about curriculum, the educator comes full circle to the old problems of motivation, interest, and effort with which Dewey and others have wrestled. Both Phenix and Bruner expressed the hope that learners will find motivation in the fascination of working over subject matter that is intrinsically fascinating. But the problem of getting an "optimum level of aroused attention" from pupils must continue to challenge all who call themselves teachers.[29]

Miel raised several cautions about proposals for analysis of the disciplines. In brief, these cautions may be stated as follows:

1. There is disagreement as to the definition to be assigned to the term *discipline.*
2. Scholars within a given field will probably not be able to agree on what constitutes the structure of that field.
3. Structure can easily be regarded either as abstract and static knowledge or as the dynamics of inquiry by which knowledge has been developed. Of the two, the dynamics of inquiry is the more valuable for learning.
4. The structure of a discipline changes as the discipline evolves. Pupils cannot be "handed" structure; they should be helped to understand structure gradually.
5. Distinction should be made between the understanding of structure that is needed by the specialist in a discipline and the understanding needed by the nonspecialist—the pupil in a general education program.
6. Overemphasis may be given to disciplines in which structure is most obvious (for example, in mathematics and the sciences) at the expense of other disciplines.

7. If they are not careful, those who try to teach structure will be tempted to teach adult-ordered, logical structure without regard to the pupil's perceptions and needs.
8. The problem of integrating the learnings derived from individual disciplines remains.[30]

Mauritz Johnson pointed out that discovery is by no means new as an educational idea. He quoted William C. Bagley's statement made in 1905 in *The Educative Process:*

> The pupil is not to be told but led to see....Whatever the pupil gains, whatever thought connections he works out, must be gained with the consciousness that he, the pupil, is the active agent—that he is, in a sense at least, the discoverer.[31]

Bagley owed a debt for the idea to Frank and Charles McMurry (1897), who in turn were indebted to David P. Page (1847) or else to Herbert Spencer (1860). Of course, many years earlier, Plato had referred to discovery through the asking of questions. Once again, an idea that seemed novel to many educators when it was advanced proved to be nearly as old as educational history.

Some Additional Understandings About Knowledge

Behind the search for structure and the revival of the discovery process are understandings about knowledge and its use in curriculum making that every curriculum planner should possess. The first of these understandings returns us to the problem of identifying and utilizing objectives. Most of the objectives to which curriculum committees in school systems customarily subscribe fall under the headings of acquiring knowledge, developing ability to think, effecting attitude change, and developing skills in a variety of learning areas. Of these four kinds of objectives, only the first is implemented directly through selection of content. The others are implemented mainly through stating learning activities and experiences for pupils and then stating teaching strategies for helping pupils engage in these activities or have these experiences. Also, coming to *know* something requires a different kind of learning process than does learning to think, achieving attitude change, or increasing and refining skills.

A second understanding about knowledge and its use in curriculum planning is that by avoiding fact and topic teaching we can deal with the problem of having too much knowledge to teach. Teaching should be planned around and within the largest, most significant elements of knowledge. These elements are concepts or big ideas. Within and beneath these larger elements are useful topics and pertinent facts in a variety of subjects and subject fields. If, for example, we decide to teach justice as a concept, we must select from the great body of available topics and facts those that will probably have the most telling effect in helping pupils to make the concept their own. Some of the topics and facts may be on the frontier of knowledge and, therefore, nowhere to be found in books. No matter. It is the pertinence and potency of the topic or fact that count.

A third understanding is that subject matter content is often conveyed by means other than words. This is true today, for example, in multicultural education. Teachers' nonverbal behavior may tell more than their spoken words about their liking for or aversion to given cultural groups. Also, assumptions implicit in written content may easily be at variance with what the words of the content seem to say.[32]

The interest of curriculum planners in the structure of knowledge has, at least for the present, declined. The discovery method, on the other hand, has continued to attract moderate interest in a few school systems. Occasionally, deeper investigation of subject matter gives promise of leading to useful application in the schools. For example, traditional views of subject matter for developing cognition have been considered by Joe M. Steele, Herbert J. Walberg, and Ernest R. House in light of pupils' perceptions of their own experiences with the subject matter. These researchers worked with 121 secondary school classes in four subjects, recording pupils' perceptions of the subject matter they were learning cognitively. They found that the content of the four subjects had three significant functions: convergence-divergence, syntax-substance, and objectivity-subjectivity. Mathematics was considered by the pupils to be convergent, the language arts divergent. Both the language arts and mathematics were labeled syntactical, whereas science and the social studies were thought to be substantive. Science appeared to the pupils to be objective, social studies subjective. Inasmuch as pupils seemed to be learning the four subjects in these terms, Steele, Walberg, and House asked whether mathematics is in fact convergent and, if it is not, whether it must be taught convergently. They wondered whether there are syntactical aspects of science and the social studies that should be given greater emphasis and whether subjective aspects of science and objective aspects of social studies and the humanities can be taught.[33]

ACTIVITY 4-3

Discovering What's Inside a Discipline

To help other persons become acquainted with the nature of subject matter, curriculum leaders should see for themselves what is fundamental in as many disciplines as possible. Select a discipline such as mathematics, biological science, or modern language. Learn from one or more specialists in this discipline what is considered most important to be comprehended. (You may find that the specialists disagree.) Then study the textbooks used in teaching the discipline.

When you have completed your investigation, answer these questions:

1. Can I now clearly see the fundamentals of this discipline?
2. How well are the fundamentals understood by experts in the discipline, including textbook authors?
3. What should be done to clarify for curriculum workers the meaning of the discipline for instruction in elementary and/or secondary schools?

ACTIVITY 4-4

Working with the Discovery Process

The text illustrated the use of the discovery process in history classes; the process can be duplicated in other school subjects. For example, in general science, pupils can develop a test for starch and apply it to a variety of commercial products. In physics, they can approach experiments in mechanics and optics intuitively. Each experiment should be open ended—that is, the result should not be predetermined.

With teachers of a subject you know well, design several experiences that require pupils to discover the content of that subject. Work with the teachers as they use, refine, and evaluate the results of these experiences. Note for your own subsequent reference the ways teachers proceed in freeing pupils for discovery, as well as the materials needed. Observe what happens to individual pupils as they discover hidden abilities of their own in mastering subject matter.

ORGANIZING AND REORGANIZING SUBJECT MATTER FOR TEACHING AND LEARNING

How educators organize subject matter for teaching and learning depends very much on their view of the uses of subject matter in curriculum planning. Some accept the "don't skip a thing, everything's important" point of view. Others think the training or discipline one gets from studying the subject matter counts most. Still others say that only "hard" subject matter is worth learning, or that the process of learning subject matter is more important than the substantive outcomes of learning it, or that subject matter is worth learning only if it proves useful in a very practical way.

In these terms, subject matter is organized around its key ideas; around materials of instruction, as in learning activity packages; around ways of working, or the processes by which one usually makes and dispenses knowledge in a subject or subject field; around significant places that are symbolic of what is being taught; or around people, as when biography is used in teaching. Someone who is especially interested in learners may organize subject matter around the centers of learners' interests; around their developmental tasks, as Havighurst has done; around social, scientific, and other problems that concern people; or around evolution in human events, treated chronologically or otherwise. In brief, the options open to us are numerous.

For use in actual teaching, subject matter may be divided into units, into themes or topics, into analyses of life problems, into cases, episodes, or anecdotes, or into incidents of real and direct experience.

The preceding discussion concerns subject matter as it is organized and then taught by classroom teachers. For curriculum planners, there is necessarily a broader prospect of what is to be taught and learned. A master planner of curriculum content must hold a definite philosophical viewpoint about what is really worth teaching and learning. Should the content consist of that which individual subjects have to offer, of that which combinations of subjects to form subject fields can provide, or of something else? A half-dozen possibilities are considered below. Some of them call for the integration of diverse elements of subject matter in the interest of serving a cause.

Organizing by Subjects

The first and most-used possibility is organizing strictly by subjects. This way has seemed obvious and easy to curriculum planners, who have majored in given subjects and who have had their own school programs organized in this manner. Learning subjects emphasizes the use of chronology, prerequisites, whole-to-part mastery, and deductive learning. It is considered respectable partly because it is laden with verbal activities and utilization of logic. It permits both required and elective subjects to have places in the school program. It attempts to care for individual differences through extra and differentiated assignments. In the subject-centered organization, the teaching time granted to a subject depends on the alleged relative worth of that subject. Organizing by subjects tends to compartmentalize learning, to emphasize memorization, and to make the subject, rather than learners' activities and interests, central.

Organizing by Correlation

In an effort to relate proximate bodies of subject matter, curriculum planners have attempted simple correlation of content. Leaving subjects intact and side by side, they have correlated elements of history, geography, and literature, as in studies of the westward movement in U.S. history. They have made similar correlations between mathematics on the one hand and one or more of the natural sciences on the other. Sometimes correlation occurs fact to fact, sometimes principle to principle, and sometimes viewpoint to viewpoint. Obviously, correlation cannot occur without at least elementary planning. It is the first organizational step beyond the use of subjects in their "pure" form.

Organizing in Broad Fields

Becoming a bit bolder, the planners have developed the broad fields, or fusion, approach. This organizational plan permits surveys of subject matter within a category like the social studies or general science. Some of the subject matter in the surveys can be developed inductively by learners, who may be said to be preparing themselves in the survey process for later specialization in depth. Sometimes fusion occurs around general principles, as in courses in the problems of American democracy. The principles themselves may appear in hierarchies so that they are called themes on one occasion and topics on another. The broad fields idea actually dissolves subject boundaries by finding sensible arrangements among parts of subjects. Furthermore, it offers greater flexibility in choice of content than does subject-centered organization.

Organizing Core Programs

The plan of organization known as the core was moderately popular during the 1940s and 1950s. Programs were developed to allow pupils to have a core of experience with one teacher during a period of time that was longer than had been customary. This unified core of experience could be centered in subject matter on the one hand or in pupil needs and interests on the other. Four kinds of core programs came into prominence: (1) the unified studies core, closely analogous to simple correlation; (2) the culture epoch core, an attempt to study a lengthy period in human history by introducing all content that could help with understanding the period; (3) the contemporary problems core, in which subject lines were crossed to permit the study of problems in popular elections, crime prevention, modern art, and so on; and (4) the adolescent needs core, which dealt with the presumed common problems, interests, and needs of American youth, including planning one's career, establishing appropriate boy-girl relationships, and determining one's beliefs. As the last type suggests, core programs were directed primarily toward educating the adolescent population. To do this, teachers had to assume unaccustomed viewpoints concerning subject matter, pupils, and learning. One of the serious problems in core teaching and administration lay in the scarcity of teachers specifically prepared to teach in core programs. Specialized preparation of teachers is so important that without it core programs are almost certainly doomed to failure.

During the years in which the core was moderately popular, such a plethora of almost unclassifiable core programs developed that the meaning of the term *core* became obscured. Nevertheless, two advantages of organizing core programs appeared: (1) James B. Conant and others began to advocate a somewhat similar block-of-time idea for loosening and improving the secondary school schedule, and (2) the needs, concerns, and interests of young people sometimes replaced rigidly traditional subject matter as the prominent feature of curriculum designs. In the 1990s, one still occasionally hears of thriving core programs. Thus the core idea is by no means dead, especially in an era in which the demand for commonality of school experiences is so often heard. For example, some educators insist that two-thirds of secondary school curriculum content should be taught to all pupils. If this were done, the kind of core needed might resemble the contemporary civilization/humanities core that was assigned to all students, including the author, at Columbia College of Columbia University in the 1930s and beyond.

An application of a version of the core has appeared at San Diego's Crawford High School, where the pupil population has been about equally divided among Asians, Hispanics, African-Americans, and whites. Beginning with the class of 1994, pupils at Crawford have taken a subject-centered core that has mandated study of biology, algebra, and geometry. Thus an effort has been made in San Diego to "toughen the high school program."[34]

Organizing Around Persistent Life Situations

A fifth plan had its base in persistent life situations.[35] Initially, Florence B. Stratemeyer and other creators of the plan tried to define the characteristics of individuals and society, leading to a listing of "persistent life situations which learners face." Next, they listed these situations in detail. For example, one of the persistent life situations is need for growth in ability to deal with economic, social, and political structures and forces. Under the subhead "Earning a living," there are additional subheads: "Deciding what work to do" and "Assuring that needed work will be done." Under "Deciding what work to do" are four categories of activity listed according to developmental levels: early childhood—"assuming responsibility for simple tasks at home or at school"; later childhood—"deciding on work responsibilities with or without remuneration"; youth—"studying vocational possibilities and making vocational choice"; adulthood—"selecting and/or carrying forward chosen vocation."[36] Sample activities appear under each subhead, and there are nearly two dozen pages of subheads and activities related to persistent life situations involving growth in ability to deal with economic, social, and political structures and forces. The persistent life situations idea was a valiant effort to move attention from subject matter to the life needs of people.

Organizing Around the Pupil's Experience

Life needs are represented further in the experience-centered curriculum, in which the pupil's own experience becomes the starting point for planning. For example, in a geographically remote community, pupils may experience helping other people start a community store. As they work with others in this enterprise, they learn something of reading, writing, arithmetic, designing, group planning, human relationships, and many other "subjects." They learn the subject matter incidentally, while having an exciting experience in which the learning materials are multiple and teachers' roles are decidedly nontraditional. In modern schooling, few opportunities occur for experience-centered programs to flourish. Alternative schools and schools-within-schools, when organized and operated informally, present one opportunity. An additional, limited opportunity is work-experience programs in which subject matter is taught for the instrumental purpose of aiding pupils in work sponsored jointly by the school and a local business or industry. The magazine *Fortune* reported extensively in its issue of November 29, 1993 on what American corporations were doing to supplement the curricula of schools, especially in science, mathematics, technology, and health education.

The most extreme form of curriculum organization in regular use—organizing curriculum around pupils' experiences—has support from experimental philosophy, interactional sociology, and Gestalt psychology. It promises to be used increasingly in the future. Suggestions about its probable future use appear prominently in the action learning projects that school systems are undertaking.

Changing the Placement of Subject Matter and Adding New Subject Matter

Because schools are continuing institutions, the subject matter they teach needs periodic reorganization or change in placement. Perhaps the easiest way to change the placement of subject matter is to move it up or down grade scales and other educational levels. Items of subject content and major blocks of experience have been moved from one part of the school program to another. New subject matter has often been added. On rare occasions, subjects and subject matter have been eliminated. The following are some well-known actions that have been taken to change subject matter placement and to add subjects:

1. Subject matter formerly taught in colleges is being taught in secondary schools.
2. Multicultural education has been added to the curriculum.
3. The kindergarten has now assumed certain of the earlier functions of the first grade.
4. Driver education has long since entered high school programs.
5. Career education has become common in the curriculum of both elementary and secondary schools.
6. Education on sexual behavior, the abuse of drugs and alcohol, and the prevention of AIDS has been added.

Curriculum reorganization proceeds on the assumption that rearranging and altering pupils' experiences can improve the quality of learning. Placing subject matter content in different sequences, substituting new experiences for old (or old for new), and combining subjects to achieve greater psychological unity can sometimes facilitate learning. Much more evidence is needed, however, concerning the results of many changes in curriculum organization. So far, the results have appeared discouraging.

The organization of the curriculum has both vertical and horizontal dimensions. Vertically, children progress from level to level on the ladder of learning experiences. Thus they move from third- to fourth- to fifth-grade arithmetic in vertical sequence and with some assurance that a thread of continuity runs through their three years of arithmetic experience. Viewed horizontally, the curriculum has breadth or scope. That is, ideally it provides sufficiently varied experiences to comprehend the child's life needs at present and, to a degree, in the future. Because all of one's life needs cannot be prepared for in a single year of schooling, specific needs must be attended to year by year according to the child's current intellectual, physical, and social development. The horizontal dimension assumes an integration of educational experiences. Integration, which must actually be achieved by the child, consists of relating experiences to one another in such a way as to create wholeness out of the collection of little pieces that constitute the usual experiences in schools. Though children must achieve integration for themselves, curriculum workers believe they can aid them by placing similar and related areas of subject matter together, as in social studies or the language arts.

In many school systems, adding subjects and courses has resulted in a strange combination of offerings, which has been called a "crazy quilt." Teachers themselves often find it reasonably easy to organize each new course *logically,* but there may not be much reference to either the needs of learners or the structure of subject matter. Later, they let the relevance of the course content to real-life situations diminish further as the course becomes crystallized and institutionalized. Course deletion, which is often much needed, has seldom occurred when courses that have been added have outlived their usefulness. Usually, educators remove even minor items from the curriculum with great trepidation. On the other hand, the additive method of curriculum development has lost much of its acceptance because of the difficulty the curriculum planner has in selecting appropriate content from the large body of available subject matter.

The modern elementary school has discarded ten- and fifteen-minute periods for the teaching of twelve to fifteen separate subjects each school day. Instead, the school tends toward the scheduling of longer periods in the language arts, social studies, the general arts (music, drawing, handicraft), arithmetic and science, and health and physical education. Similarly, the program of studies of a smaller number of up-to-date secondary schools contains broad-field offerings like general mathematics, the dramatic arts, family living, general language, and problems of democracy. The movement toward the broad-field approach often seems incidental or accidental. As a consequence, some offerings have proved to be as far removed from reality for pupils as the original, fragmented subjects. Nevertheless, when they are carefully designed, offerings in the broad fields of knowledge can be much more vital than logically organized subject matter by virtue of their interesting, meaningful organization of material.

Experimentation that respects, but is not limited by, the differences and distinctions between subjects or disciplines has led to the creation of more varied and often more intelligent ways of reorganizing subject matter for sensible use. These ways tend to follow themes that are chosen because they are specially valued. Throughout the history of curriculum development in the United States, a number of themes have been tried as organizing centers for the curriculum, among them the following: the activities in which pupils may be expected to engage as adults, experiences in being a good citizen and in serving humankind, the interests and evident needs of children and youth, ways of solving problems, orientation to careers, education for work, situations in daily living that persist throughout life, and education for aesthetic appreciation. Few themes are sufficiently comprehensive to form a core of respectable learnings of both length and breadth, but they do make the traditional subjects the servants rather than the masters of the curriculum. Some themes, especially those based primarily in the humanities, become important steps on the way to formulating school programs that educate pupils both broadly and deeply. The struggle to reorganize the placement of subject matter will last beyond the creation of apparently satisfactory, widely accepted organizing centers, because subject matter that makes a marked difference in the quality of human life will continue to be discovered and will need to be put in strategic places within any schema adopted.

The compendium of ways of organizing subject matter, as reported in the preceding pages, should supply curriculum planners with options to consider in making their plans.

SPECIAL PROBLEMS IN ORGANIZING AND PRESENTING SUBJECT MATTER

Though common and pervasive problems in organizing and presenting subject matter are many, some special ones demand attention. They are the deeper problems of curriculum planning and include the sequence of the curriculum, its continuity, its scope, and its balance. In general, *sequence* is the time order in which educational experiences are presented, *continuity* describes the continuousness with which the same kind of experiences are offered over a period of time, *scope* is the latitude or breadth of the curriculum, and *balance* defines the fit of the curriculum in providing varied but appropriate amounts of experience for learners at given times in their development.

Sequence

Sequence deals with the question "What learning content is to follow what other among prescribed, established learning experiences?" The problem of finding appropriate sequence is encountered in subject matter in which certain ideas and developments necessarily build upon others. This is the case, for instance, in mathematics and foreign languages. It has seemed in the past to be much less the case in social studies, a field in which an active search for sequence has been occurring. The generally accepted view of sequence is that it should depend directly on the nature and structure of particular subjects and subject fields. If, instead of thinking immediately of subject matter, the curriculum planner were to think of developmental tasks for learners—tasks to assist their *becoming*—sequence would be determined by the competence of learners in performing tasks at various stages of their development. In this way of proceeding, sequence is associated with learners rather than with subject matter. The notion of developmental stages might be reinterpreted as referring to stages of mental growth or the changing status of interests of growing, developing children.

Traditional Attempts to Establish Sequence

Certain traditional ways of allegedly establishing sequence have been used in U.S. elementary and secondary schools. They include the following:

- Movement from the simple to the complex
- Study based on prerequisite learning
- Movement from part to whole
- Movement from whole to part
- Chronological ordering of events
- Movement from the present into the past
- Concentric movement in ever-widening circles of understanding or involvement
- Movement from concrete experiences to concepts

One or more of these ways may seem ideal to a teacher or to a specialist in a subject, but an entirely different way may appeal to an individual pupil or group of pupils. Actually, different sequence modes suit different pupils. For example, some children need to use manipulative materials in arithmetic for extended periods of time before they work with numerals; other children proceed almost directly to working with numerals. Spelling presents a particular problem. There are simply no ordered ways of learning to spell that can be used with all pupils or even a majority of pupils.

Sequence in the curriculum cannot be achieved merely by casual reordering of topics. Why, for example, should study of Native Americans precede study of the Greeks—or vice versa? Endless argument has occurred in curriculum committees because some of the members have had unfounded preferences for particular topical arrangements. There are so many available topics and possible orders of those topics that only a more careful, comprehensive basis for making choices will do.

Sequence Governed by Concept Development

The most comprehensive basis for making choices about the ordering of learning content is the concept. Once a concept has been recognized by curriculum planners as constituting a worthy educational focus, the planners may freely search for content that "feeds" the concept. This content may then be ordered in a way that makes sense in terms of chronology, movement from simplicity to complexity, or some other way of proceeding. Suppose we use the concept of change as a focus. Any topical or other content that helps pupils develop the concept of change is eligible for use; that is, we may provide pupils with alternative content relative to changes in people, weather, color, living conditions, economic circumstances, musical effects, preferences for clothing, and so on, and then help them make sequences to suit their abilities and their preferences. Concept development can be made to occur most readily if content is ordered so as to make the optimal contribution to it. Satisfactory sequence is often intuitive rather than logical in its origin.

Continuity

Continuity inevitably relates to sequence. An established order of events in learning raises questions about how long certain events should be allowed to continue. Thus continuity can be vertical, determining the continuousness with which certain experiences will be scheduled during consecutive periods of time. In a sense, it can also be horizontal, determining the continuousness of a particular kind of experience on a given school day, An example of vertical continuity is the teaching of a modern foreign language for four consecutive years. An example of horizontal continuity is teaching about the geography and history of the Oregon Trail during a two-and-a-half-hour block of time on Tuesday, January 14. Continuity involves large questions of articulation among levels of the school system, as among elementary schools, junior high schools, and senior high schools. Articulation of school experiences among levels of schooling is so difficult that no school system has devised an ideal set of procedures for achieving it.

Like sequence, continuity is seen differently by individual children and adolescents.[37] It is patently impossible, considering what we know about individual differences, to plot a uniform plan of continuity for all children. Although the experiences of all may be continuous in time, the differences among these experiences need to be wide. In a given school system, planning for continuity may be three-way: for continuity in subjects and subject fields, for continuity between and among levels of schooling, and for continuity in experience for individual pupils. The first of these ways may be shared by planners in national curriculum projects and authors of educational materials. The second and third are clearly the onerous responsibility of individual school systems.

Possible Routes to Continuity

Alice Miel has suggested that children need to experience continuity in three respects: in developing strategic concepts, in developing ways of processing information, and in developing ways of feeling about and relating to people.[38] Development of strategic concepts was discussed briefly above. Processing information results in the development of thought processes related to three levels of tasks (an effect Hilda Taba sought to promote when she developed her cognitive strategies). The levels are grouping and labeling, interpreting and making inferences, and predicting consequences. Developing ways of feeling about and relating to people involves maintaining good feelings toward one-self and other people and learning skills for improving one's interaction with other people. Schools should attempt, then, to make concept development, information processing, and learning in the area of interpersonal relationships continuous thrusts throughout children's school years.

Scope

The scope of the curriculum can be seen in the weekly program of an elementary school. The breadth of elementary school programs is usually great. Several school subjects and one or more informal learning experiences are sandwiched into the week's work so that the total program accommodates experiences in the language arts, arithmetic, social studies, science, health, physical education, art, music, assembly program rehearsal, and homeroom activities and insertions of community-supported and society-demanded experiences. The scope is so broad that many elementary school teachers, uncertain as to how to accomplish all that is expected of them, develop a kind of curriculum schizophrenia. The problem of scope does not end with listing subjects and activities, however. Each subject and activity may grow entirely out of bounds. For example, the language arts as a subject field was once heavy in reading and writing alone. Then speaking as a specific art and skill assumed increased prominence. Now listening, and to some extent the history and structure of language, has been added to the language arts area. Spelling and penmanship once took much time without being related very consciously to written composition. Now, in the face of multiple tasks to be performed within the language arts, they may be suffering from underemphasis. The problem of too broad a scope indicates again that the world of education is not afflicted with a scarcity of knowledge; rather, perspective is needed if a profusion of knowledge is to be fitted into limited periods of time at varied stages in the development of learners.

The scope of the curriculum can perhaps be kept within bounds most readily by cultivating allegiance to a limited number of carefully selected objectives. Among the prized general objectives in U.S. elementary and secondary schools are the achievement of skill in communication, skill for continuing learning, understanding of people and their world, physical and mental health, desirable citizenship behaviors, and aesthetic, moral, and ethical values. If the scope of the curriculum is to stay within bounds, the specific objectives within these general categories must be kept from becoming too numerous and diffuse.

Balance

A balanced curriculum for a given learner at a given time would completely fit the learner in terms of his or her particular educational needs at that time. It would contain just enough of each kind of subject matter to serve the individual's purposes and to speed his or her development. General balance in the curriculum can be partly achieved, in the sense that certain kinds of experiences can be planned for large groups of learners according to what we know about them and about the subject matter they might learn. Within the whole group, the individual learner receives an input of experiences that are of two sorts: those presumably suitable for and common to large numbers of learners and those that are tailor-made to his or her own needs and interests. However, true balance among experiences is very difficult to attain. For one thing, what constitutes somewhat acceptable balance today is imbalance tomorrow. Also, tailor-made experiences are difficult to plan in schools that have traditionally planned only for masses of pupils. Perhaps the best that can be done in working toward balance is to be clearer about what is valued for the growth of individual learners and then to apply these values in selecting curriculum content, grouping pupils for instruction, providing for articulation, and furthering guidance programs.[39]

A school can do much to provide a generally balanced program by seeing that all major areas of human competence are included in its curriculum. These major areas, which are comparable to those mentioned above in connection with continuity, may include skills in communication, opportunities for problem solving, understanding people and their world, knowledge of the activities of citizens, ability to care for one's mental and physical health, interest and skill in aesthetics, and recognition of specialized interests. Within each area, the individual should be permitted to perform to the maximum of his or her capacity. In order to do so, each pupil will necessarily need to spend enough time in each curriculum area to satisfy his or her own learning requirements. A school program that is truly balanced for individuals can be created only with a system of flexible scheduling and within a curriculum that contains varied experiences among which the pupil is reasonably free to select. Working toward balance may involve taking actions like the following: attending to educational goals in proportion to their importance, knowing individual pupils better than we now know them, providing improved facilities and materials for teaching and learning, preventing pressures and special interests from destroying balance, and organizing pupil time around activities of appropriate kinds.

Conditions for Seeking Balance

If a school or school system were to seek curriculum balance for individual pupils energetically, it would need to assemble a staff of professionals and paraprofessionals of varying competencies to work in a large, well-equipped learning center. The staff would work with persons inside and outside the school or school system to determine appropriate goals of schooling and out-of-school education. According to the goals that were formulated, ideas, time arrangements, facilities, and materials would be made available, the nature and needs of individual pupils would be assessed, studies made by futurists would be consulted to provide a forward look to individualized programs, the status and progress of each pupil would be carefully charted, and, after continuing reevaluation, summary data would be assembled at intervals for each pupil. This is obviously an expensive way of proceeding—according to a "hospital model" rather than a "factory model" of schooling. As Walker and Doll said, however, it seems to be the only route by which curriculum balance for the individual learner can be approached.[40] Some practitioners of Individually Guided Education (IGE) sought to effect individualization in this way, but the limited budgets within which they operated would not permit them to proceed to the ultimate step of developing genuinely balanced programs for individual learners. Educating children at home, if supported by instructional insight and suitable equipment and materials, could allow individual children to experience nearly balanced programs. As restructuring of schools proceeds during the 1990s, the quality of pupils' school experiences will be conditioned by the degree to which balance among the experiences can be achieved.

Problems of sequence, continuity, scope, and balance obviously remain largely unsolved. During the years to come, these four problems must be given more attention by curriculum planners if the much desired goal of carefully individualizing instruction is to be attained.

ACTIVITY 4-5

Becoming Acquainted with Curriculum Literature Relating to Special Problems in Organizing and Presenting Subject Matter

Curriculum literature abounds on the role of subject matter in curriculum planning. For example, general works on the curriculum by Hilda Taba, Virgil Herrick, and Smith, Stanley, and Shores contain information of a comprehensive sort. Some of the yearbooks of the Association for Supervision and Curriculum Development and the National Society for the Study of Education deal with more specific problems in utilizing subject matter, such as problems of continuity and balance.

Become acquainted with these and other sources. Take notes from the sources you consider most helpful.

SITUATION 4-2

Responding to the State's Criticisms of the Yalta Pass Curriculum

For three years, the public schools at Yalta Pass had been under fire from the state department of education for providing too few learning opportunities for their pupils, considering the total amount of money being spent on the schools. Specifically, the complaint had detailed the following deficiencies:

1. Insufficient attention to the teaching of the three Rs in the elementary schools
2. Too few elective courses in Yalta Pass's small high school
3. The obsolescence of some of the subject matter currently being taught at the secondary school level
4. "Excessively compartmentalized organization of subject matter in both the elementary and the secondary schools" (each subject taught in distinct separation from every other subject)
5. The presence of too much unchallenging subject matter in the required curriculum of both the elementary and the secondary schools

Realizing that a formal evaluation by the state department of education was to occur within two years, the superintendent of the Yalta Pass schools formed the Special Committee on Subject Matter, consisting of eighteen teachers and administrators. The committee was asked to suggest ways of meeting the state's criticisms—"ways that are likely to succeed and that can be put into effect immediately."

Yalta Pass had never been noted for its activity in curriculum planning. Lacking experience, therefore, the committee quickly developed one proposal to meet each of the state's criticisms, as follows:

1. Provide "coaching classes" to drill pupils in the three Rs. These classes, assigned to especially competent teachers, would meet partly on school time and partly after school.
2. Add elective courses to the high school curriculum in accordance with the findings in a survey of parents' opinions of the need for particular electives.
3. Form study groups of teachers who know most about given subjects to update the content of these subjects as they are taught in the schools.
4. Try team teaching across subject lines as a way of making the subjects interrelate.
5. Ask the administrators to urge teachers to add more difficult subject matter to what they are teaching now.

What actions can you suggest to meet the five criticisms more adequately?

THE STATUS OF SUBJECT MATTER SELECTION AND PRESENTATION

Newer developments in selecting and presenting subject matter may be discussed under three main headings: subject matter selection at local and state levels, new versions and selections of subject matter, and special resources for presenting subject matter.

Subject Matter Selection at State and Local Levels

Subject matter selection by local school districts and by state departments of education is not an innovation. As Chapter 1 indicates, the first active curriculum planning was accomplished in city school districts. Later, state departments of education began to develop course guides that were distributed among their respective school districts.

Beginning in 1957, subject matter specialists initiated the planning of national instructional projects. Most of the projects that thrived owed their support to foundations and the federal government. A majority of them were intended to affect secondary education. Not unexpectedly, persons who planned them gave little thought to the processes that influence teachers to try new ideas, and they were out of touch with the realities in local school situations. This latter fact helps to explain the early demise of nearly all the projects.

Some of the projects, which received their start in either elementary or secondary education, later became kindergarten-through-twelfth-grade projects or projects covering a major portion of this span. At first, the projects were chiefly in the natural sciences and mathematics. Subsequently, the modern foreign languages, social studies, and the English language arts were emphasized. The National Education Association formed its Project on Instruction to sort out subject matter in selected fields and to encourage wise use of it in the schools. Some of the project sponsors and titles are still familiar: University of Illinois Elementary Science Project, Syracuse-Webster Elementary Mathematics Project, Physical Science Study Committee, Biological Sciences Curriculum Study, School Mathematics Study Group, Commission on English of the College Entrance Examination Board, and High School Geography Project.

The sciences and mathematics received more attention than other subjects or disciplines during the heyday of the projects. In 1980, when nine groups of teachers, administrators, parents, school board members, and "neutrals" were asked to comment on the curriculum reforms wrought by the National Science Foundation, they agreed that teachers had listened to the NSF proposal and then had done what they wanted to do. Teachers in the nine groups said that they were usually unaware of what was happening in other teachers' classrooms; rather, they were concerned with their own "survival" and with attaining goals that had been established in their school systems.[41]

Robert James expressed the view that if projects and programs are to succeed, their promoters must consider the stages of teachers' concern, ranging from general awareness to specific awareness to varied thoughts about issues like the teachers' own involvement and the quality of the teachers' work with pupils and colleagues during project life. James also emphasized the significance of levels of use of project ideas by teachers. Use seems to range from negligible to mechanical and routine to integration with the work of colleagues. Ignoring stages of teacher concern and levels of teacher use can result in disaster for any project or program.[42]

During the 1970s, school systems and entire states varied widely in the rates at which they adopted subject-centered innovations. Many school systems abandoned their earlier commitments to projects. Through their associations and unions, classroom teachers were expressing resentment at having been pushed aside in the process of deciding what subject matter should be taught. Administrators complained that the energies of school personnel were being drawn from tasks of permanent significance so that instructional projects of uncertain worth could be staffed. The stampede for dollars that caused people to write proposals continued for a time, but other interests (such as better schooling for handicapped pupils) replaced interest in teaching "right" subject matter in "right" ways.

Studied, comprehensive efforts at updating subject matter declined during the 1980s, an unfortunate circumstance in an era in which new knowledge abounded and in which the schools could have profited from capitalizing on mistakes made in connection with earlier programs and projects. The obligation to select subject matter returned largely to local school districts and state departments of education, with occasional help from professional associations. Individual school districts, working largely alone, began plotting learning content in subject matter areas where they felt most pressure. Sometimes they were able to do this with financial help from federal or state governments. Too often, limited budgets prevented them from getting help from people who knew the subject fields or the planning processes under consideration, or from releasing teachers to plan together on school time.

State departments of education experienced the same waves of pressure that affected the personnel of local school districts. Pressures such as those to teach the three Rs better and to "do something" about the use of drugs by pupils and about the increase in pregnancies among young girls consumed the attention of state officials. The results were a flood of pronouncements and a few hurriedly prepared documents. Careful, deliberate planning of subject matter offerings, incorporated within updated state guides, was neglected so that state officials could meet emergencies in the areas of attitude, morality, and social relationships—elements of the curriculum for which schools are only partly responsible.

At the end of the 1980s, large-scale subject matter planning focused not on the so-called solid subjects, but on related matters. For example, educators in the sciences, social studies, and environmental studies sought to cooperate in developing a science/technology/society theme. With limited financial support and without assurance of implementation, they designed several programs with environmental education components.[43] Program proposals were often surface-survey in nature, without deep examination of what could be done to teach specific subject matter successfully.[44] One of the valid reasons for issuing surface-survey materials is to provide background data for the setting of policy. Policies on planning procedures in social studies were considered in Michigan.[45] In New York, policies to guide administrators in keeping language arts innovations alive were stated in a space of eleven pages.[46] In Illinois, second language and international studies were upheld as essential to the interests of the state.[47]

The welter of apparent confusion concerning whose responsibility is whose remains no less present during the 1990s. The term *national curriculum* has been replaced by the less distasteful-sounding *standards*. The "big standards" that might be set for pupils, educational level by educational level nationwide, would presumably be established at a single federal center. They would be tied closely to a program of national testing and would encompass learnings that all pupils at a given age-grade level would be expected to acquire.

"Little standards" would become the responsibility of state and local functionaries and would take into account needs peculiar to particular locations and situations. For example, the nature of local industry and employment might dictate thorough teaching and learning of content in technology. State education departments and local school systems have been busy for a long time creating standards that have been left largely voluntary.[48]

New Versions and Selections of Subject Matter

The curriculum field needs scholarly study of what knowledge is of most worth amid the great quantities of available subject matter. At present, some consideration is being given to subject matter long regarded as classic, but more attention is being given to content that provides a response to sociopolitical pressures. Examples of efforts in the former category can be seen in recent planning in mathematics, the sciences, and the language arts. Examples of the latter type of attention include the addition to the curriculum of education in AIDS prevention and education to combat drug abuse. A great need exists to restructure teaching and learning in the standard subject fields. Meanwhile, societal pressure compels attention to the particular topics that evils in the culture have forced into the schools—subject matter relating to unwanted pregnancies, AIDS, drug and alcohol addiction, and ignorance of our religious heritage.

Evidence has been accumulating that the curriculum is more out of balance than ever before. Elementary and secondary schools are struggling to provide learning experiences in what's new as well as in what's traditional in subjects like science, social studies, and language. Time devoted to music and art has been decreasing, while exposure to newly imposed areas of learning has been increasing. The special interests of the 1980s continue to make an impact: global education, programs in economics education and in management of personal finance, death education (now given the less forbidding title of grief education), development of thinking skills, improvements in educating the gifted, and training in using computers.[49]

The newer special interests include technology education; ecological studies; study of our religious heritage; values education; energy resources education; the "new" sex education, slanted toward preventing AIDS and unwanted pregnancies; and alcohol and drug abuse education. Brief descriptions of several of these follow.

Technology Education
Technology education often provides a background in technological nomenclature and ideas; in drafting, electronics, robotics, electricity, basic engineer-

ing, and architecture; and in advanced computing, energy use, and telecommunication. Programs at present are in a primitive and changing state,[50] but new insight concerning what should be taught is coming from industrial firms like Apple Computer, Inc. and the American Telephone and Telegraph Corporation.[51] The popular version of educational assistance being provided by business and industry is that it consists mainly of education for literacy, a kind of help the elementary and secondary schools should be expected to provide. This view persists while business and industry are spending time and money helping workers gain technological and human relations skills.

Ecological Studies

Current preoccupation with the condition of the earth, its flora and fauna, its water, and its surrounding atmosphere has resulted from an appreciation of the great waste of our natural resources. In the United States, where nature's bounty once seemed unlimited, destruction and pollution have been the rule long enough to cause scientists and government officials to foresee ecological disaster. As is usually the case, schools have been expected to impress upon youngsters the significance of the problem. Elementary school children are being taught the simple steps that people can take to care for our environment; secondary school pupils are learning the applied science and sociology necessary for saving our resources. Notably, organized programs and courses are fewer than incidental incursions into knowledge about ecology. Only a small portion of instructional time in science, social studies, and literature is now devoted to ways of preserving the environment,[52] but ecological studies seem destined to increase.

Values Education

Generally related to concern about the study of our religious heritage is a demand for reconsideration of the teaching of moral and ethical values in schools. Dissatisfaction with constructs prepared by Louis Raths, Clive Beck, and Lawrence Kohlberg has sparked a movement to standardize and stabilize the values taught.[53] The fear of facing lawsuits as a consequence of teaching values tinged with religious perspectives is not a valid reason for ignoring values education. It is possible to teach positive, definite values in public schools without being seriously attacked by community members or civil rights organizations. A design proposal for such an effort appears in Chapter 5.

The "New" Sex Education

The so-called new sex education is intended to meet two emergencies that have developed in school and society: the increase in teenage pregnancy and the AIDS epidemic. One of the hazards of this effort to "put out fires" is departure from systematic study of sexuality. Attention needs to be given to preparing organized, sequential programs that teach understandings and values of an enduring kind.[54]

Of the two emergencies, the AIDS epidemic looms larger. When the AIDS scare in a locality becomes sufficiently terrifying, free and unbridled sexual activity diminishes—slightly. Teenagers' lack of knowledge about how disease develops and how pregnancy occurs has shocked many teachers and other adults. The best immediate remedy has been thought to be increased and improved sex education in the schools—that is, education emphasizing the study of human physiology and the details of sexual practice. Accordingly, elementary and secondary schools in some communities have taken pains to prepare instructional materials that represent the new sex education. In a few communities, cooperation between public health agencies and schools has been attempted. Often, curriculum materials in sex education have been roundly criticized.

Because AIDS infection usually brings death, excitement about AIDS education as a curriculum element has become unusually intense. It is startling to realize that only in 1981 was the presence of AIDS infection first reported in the United States. Since that time, branches of the federal government, state agencies, the Red Cross, insurance associations, the National School Boards Association, and numerous other groups have sought to alert the public. Magazine and other polls have found that the public expects the schools to "do something" to educate youngsters about a danger that may become the cause of millions of deaths before the end of the century.[55]

The Association for Supervision and Curriculum Development has suggested that AIDS education begin when children reach the age of eight. The Association has described proposed curriculum content in kindergarten through grade three, in grades four and five, and in grades six through twelve. Beginning with generalized discussions of body appreciation and wellness, curriculum materials for use during early childhood should, according to the ASCD, avoid scaring children but alert them nonetheless to AIDS as a hazard that affects mainly adults. At the other end of the grade scale (six through twelve), the ASCD would place emphasis on knowledge of the disease, healthy behaviors that prevent it, and the relevance of other sexually transmitted diseases, all in an atmosphere of honesty and forthrightness.[56]

In the language of television and radio commentators, all curriculum workers should "stay tuned" for further developments in matters of sex education and AIDS prevention. A flood of ideas will be coming from a variety of sources. Tragically, valid scientific findings about the prevalence of AIDS are sometimes covered up, even by U.S. government agencies. The British, on the other hand, have been much more forthright in their discussions of the AIDS epidemic. Interestingly, both here and abroad only religious organizations have been active in making statements and publishing materials about abstinence from sexual activity as a means of overcoming social problems related to sex.

Alcohol and Drug Abuse Education

Alcohol abuse education is often classified with drug abuse education under the general heading "Preventing substance abuse." Usually the two are kept separate in school programs, which range in level from kindergarten through the twelfth grade. This program expansion has been made necessary because of the ease with which young children acquire habits that jeopardize their futures. Research has shown that whereas gaining knowledge of what alcohol and drugs do to the human body is easy, modifying attitudes toward them is much more difficult. Because the real test of the educational effectiveness of a program is refusal of the individual exposed to the program to abuse his or her own body, conclusive data are hard to collect. Meanwhile, programs of varied kinds continue to appear in school systems across the country.[57] A few communities have pushed their schools hard to feature substance abuse education in their curriculum planning.

Futurists expect the late 1990s to bring more active learning, higher levels of cognitive skill development, education in the service occupations, development of skills for coping with human diversity, education across subject lines, education for improved communication, new versions of early-early childhood education, and increased attention to global education.[58]

Special Resources for Presenting Subject Matter

One of the really serious problems in presenting subject matter has been lack of, or inconvenient placement of, materials and facilities of instruction. Prominent resources for solving problems encountered in presenting subject matter are the media center, the resource room, and minicomputers.

The Media Center

The media center is sometimes called the instructional materials center (IMC) or the learning center. It is intended to maximize opportunities for learning, serving as a kind of control center for the facilities and services that can be found in the school building. Active, helpful media centers are conveniently located within school buildings and are adequately staffed. They become work centers for teachers and pupils and thus implement teaching strategies. They are storage sites for all sorts of instructional materials, housing audiovisual equipment, the latest in teaching and copying machines, computers, books, monographs, pamphlets, magazines, and everything else that stimulates and satisfies learning. Media centers in the newer school buildings are large enough to accommodate meetings, work space, individual study, and whatever other activities and arrangements are necessary.

The Resource Room

The resource room is separate from classrooms and the media center, but it is related to both. The interior of the resource room is arranged to be functional and to include materials of interest, especially to nonacademic pupils. The room houses basic audiovisual materials, the wherewithal for gaming and simulation, and materials for art and handicrafts. Often, resource rooms contain learning centers in mathematics, reading and the language arts, social studies, science, and life skills. Experiences that cannot be had in the usual classroom for lack of time, space, and facilities are available here. Frequently, the establishment of resource rooms depends on the funding of programs for the mentally retarded and other pupils in special need of attention. A decline in adoption and use of textbooks is making the materials in resource rooms, along with computerized materials, increasingly attractive to teachers and pupils.

Minicomputers

Great expectations have developed for computers of small size, known as minicomputers, which have come into use in elementary and secondary schools. As purchase of computers and software proceeds apace, use of these relatively new additions is occurring in three main ways. First, in the well-known CAI, or computer-assisted instruction, the computer serves as a tutor, employing software prepared by specialists and alleged specialists in the subject fields. When the computer presents subject matter, the pupil responds. The computer then evaluates the response, reports to the pupil how well he or she has done, makes the next presentation, and finally records how well the pupil has succeeded overall. Most school people are familiar with this use of the computer.

Second, the computer is a tool for calculating, word processing, retrieving information, and maintaining records. When properly programmed, the computer can simulate real-life problems for resolution by pupils. Examples are pressing problems in ecology and potential strategies in sports.

Third, the pupils program or "teach" the computer. Whereas in the first two uses the pupils respond rather than taking initiative, here pupils dominate the computer. Even young elementary school pupils can make simple programs. Critics of the computer as a tool have condemned this third use as involving pupils in learning more than they need to know and do.

Elementary and intermediate schools have been using computers for basic skills instruction, remediation, and enrichment of learning. Secondary schools have tended to use them chiefly in computer science courses. When pupils have learned to use computers in these courses, they are able to extend their application to other subjects and circumstances.

The Ultimate Reality? The High-Tech Multimedia Classroom

Whereas the classroom is an ancient tradition, radical modification of its interior is necessary to make it look new and forward-looking. In the next century, one may eventually find novel classroom "stations" that implement different purposes—for example, a teacher's station containing a main computer and interactive keypads, a learner's station with personal computers, and a station for small-group instruction.

Let us imagine what might happen in a classroom equipped and ordered for a new era. Suppose, in a study of biology or general science, the life of the dolphin becomes the topic. Teacher and pupils make contact with a biologist by way of a high-speed data line. At the biologist's suggestion, they use a video segment from a laser disc to learn about the dolphin's anatomy. Then they poll a series of resource people long distance to inquire about the dolphin's capabilities, responses to human beings, and apparent level of intelligence. Individually, the pupils compare what they have just learned with information supplied in articles and portions of textbooks. Some of the pupils meet with the teacher at the small-group station to discuss their findings; others gather additional data by means of the interactive computer system linked to a satellite dish. The pupils have another helpful resource in the hook-up of the main computer with a video disc player and a CD-ROM drive; they look forward to a future connection with a cable television station that will provide direct program transmission into the school and the community.

The technological millenium hasn't arrived, but there are many signs that it is on its way.

SUMMARY

From the time of Herbert Spencer to today, confusion has existed about what knowledge is worth teaching. Chapter 4 begins with a report of the current situation. Knowledge is exploding; youngsters in our nation are not learning as much as they should; the old problem of where to place worthwhile subject matter remains bothersome; and the tendency to create a diffuse, unrelated pattern of subject matter is a greater danger than ever before.

When we select subject matter for teaching, we should specify our objectives, establish criteria for making selections, detail learning experiences for our pupils, keep up to date with developments in subject fields, and learn from the successes of educators in other nations who are charged with selecting subject matter. These preliminary steps provide the foundation for organizing the subject matter we have chosen. In doing so, we face familiar curriculum problems like those of assuring proper scope, achieving sequence in learning tasks, and maintaining balance among elements of the curriculum. Our difficulties are compounded by the addition of a number of unprecedented topics and themes that cry for attention because of the exigencies of our times. Can anyone doubt that the selection, organization, and placement of subject matter to be taught lie at the heart of curriculum making?

ENDNOTES

1. Arthur W. Combs, *Myths in Education* (Boston: Allyn and Bacon, 1979), 77–83.

2. Harry S. Broudy, "What Knowledge Is of Most Worth?" *Educational Leadership* 39, no. 8 (May 1982): 574–578.

3. For discussions of this situation, see articles written by Gerald Bracey.

4. Robert Rothman, "NAEP to Create Three Standards of Performance," *Education Week* 9, no. 35 (May 23, 1990): 1, 8. For background, see Harry S. Broudy, "Becoming Educated in Contemporary Society," in Kenneth D. Benne and Steven Tozer, eds., *Society as Educator in an Age of Transition,* National Society for the

Study of Education, Eighty-Sixth Yearbook, Part II (Chicago: University of Chicago Press, 1987), 247–268; see also Herbert J. Walberg, "What Works in a Nation Still at Risk?" *Educational Leadership* 44, no. 1 (September 1986): 7–10.

5. Marion Brady, *What's Worth Teaching?* (Albany, NY: State University of New York Press, 1989), 9, 10; see also Allan S. Vann, "The Curriculum Cup Runneth Over," *Educational Leadership* 46, no. 1 (September 1988): 60.

6. Cognitive objectives are presented in Benjamin S. Bloom, ed., *Taxonomy of Educational Objectives: Cognitive Domain* (New York: David McKay, 1956). Affective objectives appear in David R. Krathwohl, Benjamin S. Bloom, and Bert Masia, *Taxonomy of Educational Objectives: Affective Domain* (New York: David McKay, 1964).

7. See, for example, Anita J. Harrow, *Taxonomy of the Psychomotor Domain: A Guide for Developing Behavioral Objectives* (New York: David McKay, 1972).

8. Hilda Taba, *Curriculum Development: Theory and Practice* (New York: Harcourt, Brace and World, 1962), 174–181, 211–215.

9. W. James Popham et al., *Instructional Objectives* (Chicago: Rand McNally, 1969), 34, 37.

10. William Habermehl, "Competency-Based Education—Will It Rob Peter to Pay Paul?" *Bulletin of the National Association of Secondary School Principals* 64, no. 439 (November 1980): 54–57.

11. Gerald D. Bailey and Robert K. James, "Competency-Based Education: Its Elements and Potential," *School Science and Mathematics* 81 (November 1981): 563–571.

12. For a critical article, see Arthur Wise, "Why Minimum Competency Testing Will Not Improve Education," *Educational Leadership* 36, no. 8 (May 1979): 546–549.

13. Note that *competency-based education* was the term first applied to the accountability movement in teacher education.

14. Mercy Hardic Coogan, "A Double Dose of Basic Skills...for Appalachian Alabama," *Appalachia* 14, no. 2 (November–December 1980): 24–32.

15. Abdun Noor, *Education and Basic Human Needs,* Staff Working Paper No. 450 (Washington, DC: The World Bank, 1981).

16. Association for Supervision and Curriculum Development, "Network Schools Define What Students Need to Know," *Curriculum Update* (October 1983): 1–8.

17. National Association of Secondary School Principals, "Public Policy, Social Implications, Ethical Issues...New Emphases in Biology," *Curriculum Report* 10, no. 3 (February 1981): 1, 2.

18. Arthur Combs, "Affective Education or None at All," *Educational Leadership* 39, no. 7 (April 1982): 495–497.

19. Jane Zeni Flinn, "Curriculum Change Through Staff Development," *Educational Leadership* 40, no. 1 (October 1982): 51, 52.

20. Ronald C. Doll, *Supervision for Staff Development: Ideas and Application* (Boston: Allyn and Bacon, 1983), 172–175.

21. John Dewey, *Democracy and Education* (New York: Macmillan, 1916), 186.

22. John Dewey, *Experience and Education* (New York: Macmillan, 1938), 90.

23. B. Othanel Smith, William O. Stanley, and J. Harlan Shores, *Fundamentals of Curriculum Development* (New York: Harcourt, Brace and World, 1957), Chapter 6.

24. This idea and many additional ones in this section have been developed by Jerome Bruner. See also David Ausubel's theory of concept development involving subsumptive ideas, as he treats it in *The Psychology of Meaningful Verbal Learning* (New York: Grune Stratton, 1963) and in other writings.

25. See Jean Piaget, *The Origins of Intelligence in Children* (New York: International Universities Press, 1953). Dewey had said earlier that children develop hypothetical thinking as they mature.

26. For a discussion of substantive and syntactic knowledge, see Paula L. Grossman, Suzanne M. Wilson, and Lee S. Shulman, "Teachers of Substance: Subject Matter Knowledge for Teaching," in Maynard C. Reynolds, ed., *Knowledge Base for the Beginning Teacher* (New York: Pergamon Press, published for the American Association of Colleges for Teacher Education, 1989).

27. John Dewey, *How We Think* (Boston: D.C. Heath, 1910), 72.

28. Philip H. Phenix, "The Use of the Disciplines as Curriculum Content," *Educational Forum* 26, no. 3 (March 1961): 273–280.

29. Jerome S. Bruner, *The Process of Education* (Cambridge, MA: Harvard University Press, 1961), 72.

30. Alice Miel, "Knowledge and the Curriculum," in Association for Supervision and Curriculum Development, *New Insights and the Curriculum,* 1963 Yearbook (Washington, DC: The Association, 1963), 79–87.

31. Mauritz Johnson, "Who Discovered Discovery?" *Phi Delta Kappan* 48, no. 3 (November 1966): 120–123.

32. Compare Mary M. Williams, "Actions Speak Louder Than Words: What Students Think," *Educational Leadership* 51, no. 3 (November 1993): 22, 23.

33. Joe M. Steele, Herbert J. Walberg, and Ernest R. House, "Subject Areas and Cognitive Press," *Journal of Educational Psychology* 66, no. 3 (June 1974): 363–366.

34. *ASCD Update* 34, no. 2 (February 1992): 1, 4, 8.

35. Florence B. Stratemeyer et al., *Developing a Curriculum for Modern Living,* 2nd ed. (New York: Bureau of Publications, Teachers College, 1957).

36. Ibid., 296, 297.

37. See Association for Supervision and Curriculum Development, *A Look at Continuity in the School Program,* 1958 Yearbook (Washington, DC: The Association, 1958).

38. Alice Miel, "Sequence in Learning—Fact or Fiction," *Elementary Instructional Service,* Stock Number 282–08810 (Washington, DC: National Education Association, n.d.).

39. Association for Supervision and Curriculum Development, *Balance in the Curriculum,* 1961 Yearbook (Washington, DC: The Association, 1961).

40. Cheryl D. Walker and Ronald C. Doll, "Curriculum Balance for the Individual Learner: A Continuing Need," *Educational Leadership* 32, no. 3 (December 1974): 208–211.

41. "National Groups Tell Why Curriculum Didn't Work," *The Teacher Educator* (Ball State University) 16, no. 3 (Winter 1980–1981): 34, 35.

42. Robert J. James, "Understanding Why Curriculum Innovations Succeed or Fail," *School Science and Mathematics* 81 (October 1981): 487–495.

43. John F. Disinger and Terry L. Wilson, "Locating the 'E' in S/T/S," *ERIC/SMEAC Information Bulletin,* no. 3, 1986, published in Columbus, Ohio, by the ERIC Clearinghouse for Science, Mathematics, and Environmental Education.

44. Ohio State Department of Education, *Integrating the Language Arts,* Minimum Standards Leadership Series (Columbus, OH: The Department, 1985).

45. Anga A. Youssef and Jemil Metti, "Proposal for Revising Social Studies Curriculum, Grades K–12," an unpublished discussion of a study conducted in Michigan.

46. Joseph Sanacore and Sidney J. Rauch, "Sustaining Language Arts Innovations: Implications for Administrators," an unpublished discussion of a study conducted in New York State.

47. Illinois State Board of Education, *Second Language and International Studies: Policy Study and Recommendations* (Springfield, IL: The State Board, 1986).

48. Walter C. Parker, "The Standards Are Coming," *Educational Leadership* 51, no. 5 (January 1994): 84, 85.

49. This evidence comes from surveys conducted by education organizations and from commentary by panels and discussion groups at education conventions.

50. See, for example, Christopher Dade, "The Evolution of Information Technology: Implications for Curriculum," *Educational Leadership* 47, no. 1 (September 1989): 23–26.

51. Nancy Ramsey, "What Companies Are Doing," *Fortune* 128, no. 15 (November 29, 1993): 142–162.

52. Ecological studies have constituted one of the curriculum novelties that have claimed attention during recent years.

53. Larry P. Nucci, ed., *Moral Development and Character Education* (Berkeley, CA: McCutchan Publishing Corporation, 1989).

54. See, for example, Peggy Brick, "AIDS Forces the Issue: Crisis Prevention or Education in Sexuality," *Curriculum Update* 29, no. 7 (October 1987): 1–12.

55. See Sally Reed, *Children with AIDS: How Schools Are Handling the Crisis* (Bloomington, IN: Phi Delta Kappa, January 1988).

56. Association for Supervision and Curriculum Development, *ASCD Curriculum Update* (Alexandria, VA: The Association, October 1987).

57. David J. Hanson, "The Effectiveness of Alcohol and Drug Education," *Journal of Alcohol and Drug Education* 27, no. 2 (Winter 1982): 1–13; see also Claudia Grauf-Grounds, *Desk Reference Manual on Student Drug and Alcohol Use: A Comprehensive Planning Guide* (Trenton: New Jersey State Department of Education, 1985); and American Council for Drug Education, *Building Drug-Free Schools: An Educator's Guide to Policy, Curriculum, and Community Consensus* (Rockville, MD: The Council, 1986).

58. Steve Benjamin, "An Ideascope for Education: What Futurists Recommend," *Educational Leadership* 46, no. 7 (March 1989): 8–12.

SELECTED BIBLIOGRAPHY

Brady, Marion. *What's Worth Teaching?* Albany, NY: State University of New York Press, 1989.

Brandt, Ronald S., ed. *Content of the Curriculum.* 1988 Yearbook. Alexandria, VA: Association for Supervision and Curriculum Development, 1988.

Drake, Susan M. *Planning Integrated Curriculum: The Call to Adventure.* Alexandria, VA: Association for Supervision and Curriculum Development, 1993.

Goodson, Ivor. *School Subjects and Curriculum Change,* 3rd ed. Philadelphia: Taylor and Francis, 1993.

Grossman, Pamela L. *A Tale of Two Teachers: The Role of Subject Matter Orientation to Teaching.* Palo Alto, CA: School of Education, Stanford University, 1987.

Halverson, Paul M., ed. *Balance in the Curriculum.* 1961 Yearbook. Washington, DC: Association for Supervision and Curriculum Development, 1961.

Kealey, Robert J. *Curriculum in the Catholic School.* Washington, DC: National Catholic Educational Association, 1986.

Maurer, Richard E. *Interdisciplinary Curriculum: Reconstructing Secondary Schools.* Boston: Allyn and Bacon, 1994.

McClure, Robert M., ed. *The Curriculum: Retrospect and Prospect.* National Society for the Study of Education, 70th Yearbook, Part I. Chicago: University of Chicago Press, 1971.

Ornstein, Allen C., and Hunkins, Francis P. *Curriculum Foundations, Principles, and Issues,* 2nd ed. Boston: Allyn and Bacon, 1993.

Overly, Norman, ed. *The Unstudied Curriculum: Its Impact on Children.* Washington, DC: National Education Association, 1970.

Phenix, Philip H. *Realms of Meaning.* New York: McGraw-Hill, 1964.

Piaget, Jean. *The Origins of Intelligence in Children.* New York: International Universities Press, 1953.

Progressive Education Association. *The Story of the Eight Year Study.* New York: Harper, 1942.

Ravitch, Diane. *The Schools We Deserve: Reflections on the Educational Crises of Our Times.* New York: Basic Books, 1985.

School of Education, University of Wisconsin. *The Nature of Knowledge.* Milwaukee: Edward A. Uhrig Foundation, 1962.

Smith, B. Othanel; Stanley, William O.; and Shores, J. Harlan. *Fundamentals of Curriculum Development,* rev. ed. New York: Harcourt, Brace and World, 1957.

Swenson, Esther J., ed. *A Look at Continuity in the School Program.* 1958 Yearbook. Washington, DC: Association for Supervision and Curriculum Development, 1958.

Taba, Hilda. *Curriculum Development: Theory and Practice.* New York: Harcourt, Brace and World, 1962.

Whitfield, Richard. *Disciplines of the Curriculum.* London: McGraw-Hill, 1971.

Wilhelms, Fred. *What Should the Schools Teach?* Phi Delta Kappa Fastback No. 13. Bloomington, IN: Phi Delta Kappa Educational Foundation, 1972.

5

MAKING DECISIONS ABOUT THE DESIGN OF THE CURRICULUM

We come now to the difficult decision making that eventuates in the actual design of the curriculum and its subparts. In the preceding chapters, consideration has been given to distinct, separate foundations on which decisions about the curriculum can be based. The present chapter is meant to interrelate foundational data and to suggest curriculum designs that can ensue. Furthermore, the chapter is intended to clarify the designing process; one of its underlying beliefs is that both product and process are important in curriculum planning and neither can be separated from the other.

The curriculum planners in an elementary school might interrelate the foundations discussed in the preceding chapters in the following way:

> In our school, with an eye to the general background of the curriculum movement and the traditions of our own school, we are developing a common point of view or philosophy about what is to be emphasized in *our* education of *our* children. We know our children as members of groups and, insofar as we find it possible, as individuals. Because we know also something of the ways they learn, we are trying to adjust school life to them and their learning modes. In doing this, we are influenced by what the society, the culture, and the community seem to want of us. As we learn to work within (and sometimes in spite of) these influences, we know that we are usually encouraged and aided by them. We try to select subject matter and provide experiences for our children according to valid principles so that they learn what's worth learning, in the most effective ways.[1]

With this kind of thinking as background, the school's committee on curriculum planning would be ready to design proposals for improving the total school program.

THE NATURE OF DESIGN AND DESIGNING

The history of U.S. education is filled with examples of designs that fulfill the criteria of a particular definition of the term *curriculum design*. One definition says that a curriculum design is a way of organizing that permits curriculum ideas to function. Diverse ways of organizing subject matter content are exemplified by the project method, Summerhill, the open access curriculum, persistent life situations, the process approach, and the activity school. Glancing at these terms, one discerns immediately how different they are. Using any one of them as a content organizer, designers can create big designs or little ones.

Another definition says that a curriculum design is a carefully conceived curriculum plan that takes its shape from (1) what its creators believe about people and their education and (2) how its creators would like to see their beliefs expressed. A curriculum design takes into account a number of interrelated and interdependent elements: what its creators want done, what subject matter they wish to use to fulfill the design's purposes, what instructional strategies they favor using, and how they will determine the success or feasibility of the design. As designers become more sophisticated, they include other elements: diagnosis of need, organization as well as selection of subject matter, and organization as well as selection of learning experiences.

A third definition refers to design as the organizational pattern or structure of a curriculum. Viewed this way, curriculum design involves two levels of choice: (1) what the designers value as outcomes or consequences of the design and (2) what the designers want to do to plan and implement the design. In practice, designers begin thinking about a potential design by considering what subject matter is to be taught, the nature of the learners to be taught, and what the community and the society at large seem to be requiring. As designing proceeds, one of these data sources usually gains preeminence over the other two.

If a curriculum design is to prove genuinely commendable in an era in which excellence is prized, it must generate affirmative answers to a half-dozen questions: (1) Will this design treat an educational malaise, rather than merely the symptoms of the malaise? (2) Does it go straight toward meeting particular needs of learners? (3) Is it directed toward achieving broad and acceptable goals rather than narrow and selfish ones? (4) Will it involve all the people who should be involved in planning? (5) Will it lend participants courage and hope and so raise their expectations? (6) Will it contribute to democratic as opposed to elitist schooling?

Intellectually, the test of a curriculum design is whether its elements "hang together." First of all, the four nearly universal elements—the objectives of the design, the subject matter to be taught, the learning activities to be engaged in by pupils, and the evaluation methods necessary to indicate what kinds and degrees of learning have occurred—need to be consistent with one another. These elements are generally accepted and supported by both theorists and practitioners.[2] To determine whether the four elements are internally consistent, we ask, "Do the evaluation means fit the objectives, and do the subject matter and the activities meet the requirements set by the objectives?"[3] Beneath the four design components, there should lie a foundation of careful thinking on the part of the designers about their basic beliefs concerning people, their worth, their development, and what the proposed design should do for them. If and when the design components are properly interrelated, they are said to be aligned. It is likely that alignment can be achieved more readily in elementary schools than in secondary schools.[4] The difference may stem largely from the personal knowledge that elementary school teachers can have of their pupils during their long and continuing contacts with them in self-contained classrooms. At any rate, the meaning that one design component has for each of the others needs constant consideration. For example, if an objective proves unrealistic in light of available subject matter or learning experiences, it may have to be altered or eliminated. If the effect of a learning experience that "feeds" an objective cannot be properly evaluated, it may need to be replaced with another learning experience. Vigilance is the rule.

The thinking that underlies planning of designs takes into account the availability of four models: the academic, the experiential, the technical, and the pragmatic. The meaning of each of the models can be deduced from the meaning of the word applied to it. Practitioners often use parts of two or more of the models in order to suit their purposes.[5]

Curriculum workers are sometimes confused about the distinction between curriculum design and instructional design. Curriculum design is, in a sense, the parent of instructional design. It involves a higher level of generalizing based on principles and problem solving, and it encompasses fundamental beliefs, major aims, and projected outcomes. Instructional design, on the other hand, treats beliefs and aims as givens and does the best it can to establish technically sound teaching procedures based on those beliefs and aims. These procedures are established by answering questions like the following: What resources and materials should we use? How much time will we need? How much space and what environmental conditions must we have? How shall we group our pupils? What teaching methods shall we try? How can we validly test what has been done?

Inasmuch as the designing of instruction is assuming the earmarks of a fairly careful, accurate set of procedures, why spend time on curriculum designing, which has a less favorable record in these respects? When curriculum planners fail to design, they soon begin to improvise, and improvisation often leads to chaos. Also, when they fail to design, capricious and selfish interests may easily come to govern what is done. The planners' salvation lies in their knowledge of their purposes and in their incorporating into the decision making, against a backdrop of acceptable philosophy, the three major elements discussed in Chapters 2, 3, and 4: learners and learning, the society and the culture, and available subject matter.

As planners begin their design making, they must consider what kind of product they wish to develop. In their study of eighteen nations, Klein and Goodlad found five kinds of curriculum models:

1. *The ideal:* a curriculum the schools *might* implement, if conditions were just right
2. *The formal:* a curriculum expressing intended learnings
3. *The instructional:* a curriculum mirroring what teachers think they are do-ing
4. *The operational:* a curriculum indicating what is really being done in the schools
5. *The experiential:* a curriculum demonstrating what pupils actually experi-ence or think they experience[6]

Only the first two kinds qualify as sufficiently forward looking for potential use as curriculum designs. The remainder fall into the general category of cur-riculum notation and analysis, a procedure used in an increasing number of schools in Great Britain.[7]

SOURCES OF IDEAS THAT UNDERGIRD CURRICULUM DESIGNS

Fundamental to designing the curriculum are curriculum planners' views of the nature, nurture, and destiny of human beings. In the center of the nature-nurture-destiny trilogy is nurture, or education, which expresses what can be done with and for people. What can be done with them and for them is affect-ed by their nature, and what can be done with them and for them in turn af-fects their destiny. Persons who want to improve the quality of education for themselves and other people must face an initial question: What are the sources of the ideas that will determine the kind of education to be provided? The an-swers to this question will imply much about the curriculum improvers' view of the nature of human beings. The answers will also suggest what the curric-ulum planners think about some of the phenomena in their world. Most of all, however, the answers will suggest points of view that curriculum planners can comfortably take toward the substance and process of education.

It is a truism that as we think, so we are. One's personal philosophy molds and determines one's thinking about the issues in planning for anything of significance. In formulating a philosophy, the individual must consider what he or she will accept as truth. In deciding what is true, one has access to sources or bases of truth.

Accordingly, in making decisions within the realm of curriculum plan-ning, school faculties try to agree on an educational philosophy or point of view. This philosophy needs to be thought through and discussed so as to re-veal the basic beliefs about people and things the philosophy represents.

There are several classifications of basic beliefs that underlie curriculum philosophy. In a somewhat oversimplified and rigidly stated form, these and their origins are detailed below without emphasizing any one at the expense of the others.[8] Each has its merits, and each is usable to a major extent in given situations. In general, however, the faculties of most schools would need to draw eclectically upon the classifications described below. Too little time during recent days has been spent sorting out our common beliefs.

Science as a Source

According to persons who rely on science as a source of belief, the scientific method is the most reliable method for establishing truth. Students should be taught to solve problems in terms of scientific procedures, and curriculum improvement itself should be accomplished scientifically; that is, valid and reliable data should be assembled in support of any curriculum change that is made. Thus heavy reliance is placed on rational procedures, especially as found in problem solving. Judgment and valuing are of limited usefulness in strict application of scientific methodology because the results so gained are neither measurable nor certain.

As a source of ideas for the curriculum and its improvement, science enjoys much prestige in an era and a society in which science is assigned so much credence and respect. For years, scientific methods have been used in determining the characteristics of learners, the nature of their growth and development, the extent of their learning, the worth of teaching materials, and to a degree the effectiveness of instructional methods. It would be possible to take the position that no curriculum change should be initiated until the validity and reliability of the change have been confirmed by research and evaluation. One of the deficiencies of this position is that much of the judging and valuing that curriculum workers prize would be eliminated by the scientific method. Also, some people do not accept the premise that educational data derived by scientific means constitute the whole truth.

Society as a Source

Society may be regarded as the ultimate source from which ideas about the curriculum are to be derived. According to this view, the school owes its being to the society that has fostered it, and the school should acquire ideas from the social situation it observes. There are various interpretations of what society is and ought to be, however.

Some persons say that society's views can be determined by gathering a consensus of what people think. This consensus is usually gathered in a local community and therefore does not show the thinking of people who are geographically remote from the local scene but still highly important in a highly mobile society. Nevertheless, it would be possible to base a curriculum strictly on a series of opinion polls.

Another variation consists of thinking of government as the agent of society. According to this view, the curriculum should be changed only by legislative enactments and the decrees of the administrative and judicial branches of government. Many persons would say immediately that a society is more than its government and that curriculum making by governmental authority limits the whole process unnecessarily.

Still another variation assumes that society in its present state is to be studied not only by curriculum makers but also by pupils in schools. The object is to perpetuate the present society by involving the pupil in studying it. A curriculum stemming from this view would be devoted to extensive study of the society both in school and out, with details of the society itself forming the subject matter.

A final variation is known as the reconstructionist view. It holds that the school's role is to remake society. The curriculum would emphasize ideas for changing the social order, and curriculum improvement would be bent toward inventing ideas for that purpose. All of these variations make society the central source of ideas about the curriculum.

Eternal Verities from the Human Past as a Source

Eternal truth, in the view of Robert Hutchins and others, can be found in the works of great persons of the past. This view has been expressed in studies of the "great books" in adult education and in college curricula, but it has not completely found its way, as a significant emphasis, into our elementary and secondary schools. As held today by humanists, the notion that lasting truth inheres in the writings of the past depends on human reason for an ordering of truths in primary, secondary, and consequent importance.

In 1987, Allan Bloom shook the college and university establishment with his book *The Closing of the American Mind,* which is in part an attack on what John J. Byrne calls trendy and depthless courses. E. D. Hirsch, Jr. has moved the discussion to elementary and secondary schools with his *Cultural Literacy: What Every American Needs to Know.* Hirsch's plan for increasing children's background knowledge involves using a list of 5000 names, other identifications, and proverbs in a kind of "trivial pursuit" evaluation process.[9]

A curriculum derived from this source would depend, of course, on the literature of the past. Any changes in the curriculum would call for a reordering of ideas in the hierarchy of truths. Since these truths are considered eternal, they need not be found in new experiences; therefore reordering them would not involve reflective or creative thinking about present and current phenomena but intuitive and deductive thinking for discovery of first principles, the status of which is allegedly fixed and invariable in any age. The alleged invariability of the first principles does not prevent arguments about them: principles that are put in first position by one authority may well be put in second position by another. Furthermore, the application of fixed principles suggests that the conditions to which they are applied are unchanging, whereas change is a known rule of life. Difficulties of these kinds have prevented eternal verities from the past from becoming accepted as guides for elementary and secondary school curricula.[10]

Divine Will as a Source

The Divine Will position maintains that God has revealed His will to human beings through the Bible and especially through the inspiration of the Holy Spirit of God in the lives of Christian believers. It received support in colonial New England, but its influence was subsequently weakened by the emergence of antithetical viewpoints and the divergent interests of an increasingly less uniform population. A curriculum developed according to these ideas—even if the ideas were modified to accommodate religions other than Christianity— would rely heavily on religious, moral, and ethical teachings found in Holy Writ and church doctrine. Persons who use Divine Will as a curriculum source hold that it encompasses study of secular content so that learners may be prepared to fulfill God's will in their future lives. For public school systems in the United States, this curriculum source is largely unavailable because of legal sanctions against its use. For parochial and certain other private schools, it is a most important curriculum source. The use of Divine Will as a source is likely to increase if numbers of private schools with a religious emphasis are established as a consequence of the growing secularization of the public schools.

Use of God's will as an ideational source of the curriculum is not limited to private Christian schools. It appears in private schools sponsored by Jewish congregations and also in schools maintained by religious groups separated from the Judeo-Christian tradition. The influence of religion in American life has caused this ideational source to affect the teaching about morals, ethics, and human values in public schools, even when God's existence and authority are left unmentioned.

How Particular Philosophies Relate to Sources of Ideas

The philosophies of education discussed in Chapter 1 owe their nature, in part, to the classifications and sources of ideas just mentioned. Sometimes the relationship is clear and direct. For example, society as a source "feeds" reconstructionism. In other instances, the relationship is partial. For instance, some Perennialists use Divine Will as a definite and usually unvarying source, and some Realists make science an important source. The fact that one soon fails in an attempt to find exact relationships indicates that other thinking, much of it recent, influences philosophies of education. Thus humanism, which was not mentioned in Chapter 1 as one of the classic philosophies, represents part of the "other thinking." Humanism and one or two other philosophical viewpoints of recent application will be discussed later in this chapter.

It should be clear from the preceding discussion that none of the four sources of beliefs—science, society, the eternal verities, or Divine Will—can be used exclusively to guide the making of a philosophy for a public or a private school. Perhaps the most obvious instance of direct influence is science as a source guiding the preparation of a philosophy for a high school of science in one of our larger cities, but, even in such a specialized high school, eclectic viewpoints enter. Therefore one must say that differing eclectic choices guide philosophy making in differently oriented elementary and secondary schools.

The curriculum design one advocates at a given time and place obviously depends greatly on what one wants to do for learners at that time and place. Knowing what one wants to do, however, is only a first step. The complexity of designing can be glimpsed by considering the curriculum planning operations in two school systems.

Example 1: Decision Making in the Guise of Scientific Respectability

School System Number One was part of a suburban community inhabited by many business executives, engineers, and scientists who were employees of local industry. More than half the members of the board of education were executives and professionals. The board members, and other citizens with whom they frequently associated, were much interested in science and its applications.

The school system staff had never taken time to state its philosophy of education. The only standard belief of teachers and administrators was that they had better do what the board and more influential people of the community wanted them to do. One of the more interested and enthusiastic members of the Parent-Teacher Council learned from a friend that listening skills were being taught as a part of the language arts program in the elementary schools of the friend's district. Soon the superintendent of School System Number One was inspired to form a committee on listening skill development to determine how these relatively unknown skills should be taught to elementary and secondary school pupils.

The committee believed that, because so little had been done anywhere to develop listening skills, the members should learn everything possible about listening as an art and skill, and that studies about listening should be accomplished by searching the literature. Eventually, teachers in the district should be encouraged to conduct some experiments of their own regarding listening. In effect, then, the committee said that the methods of science have something to offer in studying problems of this kind.

Having decided the bases on which it would operate, the committee proceeded to analyze the problem along the following lines:

Question: What sort of discipline is listening?
Answer: It is so new to us we don't know. Let's explore it.
Question: Can anyone possibly object to our studying listening?
   Are there, for instance, priorities of curriculum study that should delay this study?

Answer: Both questions may be answered negatively. Let's go ahead.

Question: Doesn't the nature of the learner make a difference in learning listening? What if he's a dull pupil? What if she comes from a deprived social class?

Answer: These things worry us. We'd better investigate them.

Question: Are there some listening experiences that ought to come earlier in life and some that ought to come later?

Answer: This is a matter of readiness that we may be better equipped to deal with if we know more about listening as a discipline. We'll probably find too that we'll need to know more about the learning processes involved.

After two years of investigation and discussion, the committee produced its "Curriculum Guide to Listening" and proudly gave a copy to the Parent-Teacher Council member who had suggested the study. She was no longer interested, partly because she was currently pressuring the superintendent to do something about educating adolescents against drug abuse.

Example 2: Decision Making to Serve Two Philosophical Viewpoints Simultaneously

School System Number Two was in a rural area where the residents were mainly farmers and tradespeople. These people valued what the American social system could give their children—opportunities to get ahead in the world of work and to rise on the social scale. For these utilitarian purposes, they valued the eternal verities from the human past as long as time spent with the verities did not interfere with their children's achievement in practical learning.

The teachers and some of the administrators in School System Number Two came and went rapidly. Most of them were young and inexperienced because the board of education discharged teachers and principals on slight provocation before they could become tenured. This, of course, was a convenient way of keeping school personnel from rising too high on the salary scale in a community where the taxpayers were happiest when the school district budget was smallest.

No one within System Number Two had time to think very much about educational philosophy, but the administrators knew that parents were clamoring for a mix of what students of philosophy would have called perennialism and pragmatism. In their eagerness to do something about curriculum reform, the administrators agreed to employ a consultant who would foster attention-getting curriculum projects to serve the ends the community seemed to desire.

After she had stimulated and indoctrinated committees and study groups of volunteer teachers, the consultant helped form a study group on helping children write creatively. The committee doubted that old, time-honored procedures for teaching English composition would produce the desired results. Accordingly, the members began a search for new ideas in books, articles, and the experiences of other teachers with whom they corresponded. Eventually, they developed the hypothesis that, if learners were freed of mechanical restrictions such as neatness of penmanship, correctness of punctuation, and grammatical accuracy, they might create more worthwhile stories, poems, and essays. To test the hypothesis, the committee had to establish criteria of quality in creative writing. This led to a question: What does creativity in literature really consist of? Their experiment subsequently involved a "brakes off" approach, a freeing of learners to write as they wished. The committee worried about community opinion only to the extent of wondering what parents would say when poorly punctuated, poorly constructed papers came home. The experiment did result in considerably increased creativity according to the committee's criteria. However, the mechanical quality of pupils' writing declined to the point where an "editing and reinforcing period" was used to restore lost mechanical skills.

At the conclusion of the experiment, School System Number Two reported through the press that the experiment was indeed a success and that many youngsters in the schools were well on their way to becoming creative writers.

What Happens in the Usual Designing Operation

The designing operation in each of the two school systems was subject to influences that transcended thoughtful philosophical consideration. In each instance, philosophy was "on the back burner." Curriculum designers touched base with a system of beliefs when they perceived that system to be approved by people in the community who "mattered." Curriculum workers who feel pressed to produce results tend to look for quick, expedient, and (they hope) efficient methods of planning.

At the classroom level, if teachers are quarantined by the school administration or their union or association from outright interference by the community or the state, they make many of their curriculum decisions according to the nature of their pupils and the ways they learn. When teachers move from their own classrooms to curriculum committee membership, however, they are faced with additional influences. In curriculum committees, they hear about social demands on the schools, the planning activities in neighboring school districts, topics at recent national conventions, and new subject matter developments. If guidelines for designing are not made available through wise curriculum leadership, teachers and other members of curriculum committees are at sea. One person's opinion then seems about as valuable as another person's opinion, and progress becomes highly uncertain. Obviously, progress can be reasonably assured only by using models that feature matters to be thought about in preparing curriculum designs. Behind the designs should lie quantities of knowledge about new developments in subject fields, about current modes of designing, and about the respective strengths of alternative designs. As we have seen, more than one or two design models will almost inevitably be followed within any one school.

Before they appear at a curriculum planning table, teachers who value what their pupils think may consult with them about what works best in learning bodies of subject matter. At a laboratory school, for example, pupils concentrated on content and materials that they considered worthy, formulated questions to guide their study, and helped design useful learning activities.[11]

ACTIVITY 5-1

Thinking About Sources of Educational Philosophy

If the curriculum maker takes an eclectic view of the uses of sources, the nature of practical school problems will condition the emphasis placed on given sources. Think about the problems listed below. Which of the four sources—science, society, eternal verities, Divine Will—would you utilize in solving each of the problems? Discuss your conclusions with others to discover differing viewpoints and to clarify your own thinking.

1. The senior class of a high school is planning a two-day trip to a seaside resort. Sponsors of the trip are trying to help the class make up a code of social conduct to be followed by class members.
2. The eighth-grade art class has been invited to submit plans for a new fountain to be erected in the town's public square. Two art teachers are working with five pupils who are superior in art to determine an aesthetically desirable design for the fountain.
3. During late October, three civics classes are trying to learn about people's motives for voting in the November election. The social studies department is considering what activities and procedures should be recommended to pupils for their use.

SITUATION 5-1

Using Curriculum Foundations in Planning Improvement

Professor Morris Shamos of New York University proposed that mathematics be presented within the framework of science (*New York Times,* February 14, 1962). In Professor Shamos's view, mathematics should be incorporated within science, with examples of mathematics being "taken from the sciences rather than from the farm or the grocery store; from mechanics, for instance, or from the gas laws or geometric optics."

If you were to explore this idea further, what would you need to know about each of the following?

- The nature of mathematics
- The nature of science, with particular reference to physics
- Social demands and influences on the teaching and learning of mathematics and science
- Relevant principles of learning
- The needs and problems of adolescents who are required to learn advanced mathematics and physics

Which of the curriculum foundations would, in your opinion, deserve greatest play in establishing a desirable relationship between mathematics and science? Why?

SITUATION 5-2

Making Further Use of Curriculum Foundations and Viewpoints

A committee of first-, second-, and third-grade teachers wished to build a social studies program to satisfy the needs of primary-grade children in their community. Key comments by the teachers about points to consider are listed below:

- "It may be that children's thinking doesn't necessarily proceed from the here and now to the there and then. Does a young child necessarily think more about home and community than he does about definite places in the state, the nation, or the whole world? Does his horizon really broaden according to a set pattern?"
- "We need to learn more about children's interests and the needs they presently feel. Shouldn't we, therefore, find ways of studying children that have special relevance to social studies experiences? What could we possibly invent for this purpose?"
- "We're free as far as demands upon us are concerned. The community doesn't care what we teach young children in the social studies. (People in the community are much more concerned about reading.) Furthermore, teachers in the fourth and fifth grades don't try to tell us what to do in the social studies."
- "We may have to develop some of our own materials to suit the program we devise."

What curriculum foundations do you consider most significant in solving this kind of problem? Do you take at face value the teachers' comments as they relate to foundations?

What innovations are needed for pioneering in use of the foundations? For instance, if we do not yet know enough about the learning of social studies concepts by young children, what should be done to explore this matter?

Also, what could be done to learn more about how interests and needs of these children could be met by an improved social studies program?

A CLASSIC MODEL FOR CREATING CURRICULUM DESIGNS

The complexity of the designing operation caused Ralph W. Tyler to posit a series of necessary steps, which he incorporated in a syllabus at the University of Chicago decades ago. This syllabus can still be found in a classic paperbound volume.[12] The Tyler rationale has been described as a linear model for curriculum planning consisting of four elements: objectives, activities, organization of the activities, and evaluation. Tyler proposed that objectives be selected on both philosophical and psychological grounds. The objectives in turn became bases for selecting activities, often called pupil experiences. The activities were to be organized sequentially and to be interrelated. Evaluation was to be used to determine whether the objectives were in fact being attained.

The Model's Reception by Curriculum Planners

The systematic, sensible nature of this plan has made it *the* plan for designing curriculum in many planning centers. Some practitioners consider it to be as American as baseball, hot dogs, and apple pie. School districts that do not use it consciously often use it unconsciously.

When the Association for Supervision and Curriculum Development polled six of its prominent members concerning the worth of the Tylerian model "for current curriculum development," four of them favored it. They said it is useful to practicing, responsible school people who need a reliable mode of thinking about the curriculum. They maintained also that its critics have failed to invent a more suitable rationale for planning.

Criticisms of the Tylerian model have centered on conceptions of how objectives should be stated. The argument is that Tyler provided no real basis for selecting objectives, that he established a confining system of means-ends reasoning with objectives always the point of beginning, that he offered a system of mechanized planning in which learning can be divided too conveniently into subparts, and that he neglected the long view—human beings' delayed or latent response to education.

Two of the respondents in the ASCD poll criticized the model for failing to address questions of value, specifically questions of a moral, political, ethical, or aesthetic nature. In this sense, they found the model too rational and thus insufficiently real.[13] There are critics who simply do not like behavioral objectives because they limit the work of creative teachers. Other critics prefer to style objectives in particular ways to meet standard criteria. For them, Tyler's objectives are too simplistic and crude.[14]

Changes in the Model

Over the years, Tyler's design model has been supplemented and tightened in practice. The following is a mandate, representing a revision of the model, that a curriculum steering committee might send to curriculum planners in a school system:

1. State the need for your proposed design. Base your statement on a preliminary investigation of need. Think of need as being educational, social, and/or personally developmental.
2. Indicate the objectives the design is to serve. State a few prime or major objectives of the design, making them succinct and clear. Be sure that each objective has at least two major parts: an indication of what is to be done and an indication of how you will know when it has been done.
3. Say what subject matter content will be used within the design; then say how the content will be organized for teaching and learning.
4. Provide examples of learning experiences that pupils will have—sometimes thought of as pupil activities—using the subject matter content indicated in 3, above. Show just how these experiences will be organized to profit pupil learning.
5. Propose an evaluation schema that fits the objectives and the learning experiences in particular.

STRATEGIES OFTEN USED IN CREATING CURRICULUM DESIGNS

Curriculum designs come in varying sizes and shapes. Most attempts at designing are made on a limited "retail" basis, within limited areas of subject matter. The titles of the following proposals suggest the limited scope of many designs.

- A Unit on Nutrition for High School Pupils
- Relating Social Studies and Science in Kindergarten
- A Plan for Peer Group Teaching
- Experiences in Sensitivity Training for High School Pupils
- New Experiences in Bilingual Education
- A Look at the Local Community: A Three-Week Minicourse for Incoming Seventh Graders
- A Plan for Parent Workshops on Drug Education
- Creating a Sixth-Grade Social Studies Learning Center
- Helping Preadolescents Adjust to New School Experiences
- An Inquiry into Meanings of Success (Twelfth Grade)
- A Plan for Developing Better Eating Habits
- Experiences in Earth Science to Develop a Scientific Attitude
- Painting School Murals to Inspire Improved School Citizenship

Limited though their scope may be, consider how much time during a school year might be needed to fulfill the terms of each of these proposals as you perceive them from the titles.

Sometimes designing is done more comprehensively and thoroughly. The following titles of actual designs suggest the magnitude of comprehensive designing:

- The Happy Kindergarten: What We Learn
- A Four-Year Design for a Business Education Work/Study Program
- The Secondary School Program Design for the _____ Unified School District
- A Constructive K–12 Sex Education Program
- A Language Development Program for Language-Impaired Pupils (K–12)
- The Study of Mankind: A Program in Junior High School Science
- People and Culture: A Humane Approach to the Social Studies
- An Elective Program in Urban Ecology

These titles designate programs requiring much time and effort to prepare and put into effect.

Designs for both large programs and smaller projects are needed. Program development is very time consuming, but when well executed it can provide for sequence and continuity in instruction. Projects, on the other hand, are often placed in little niches in the curriculum mosaic, and creating numbers of them may result in more fragmentation within the curriculum structure.

Both programs and projects must be designed and planned with care if curriculum improvement is to occur. Curriculum leaders and major planning committees are responsible for maintaining a balance between program development and project development.

Halting, spotty, and uncertain as curriculum designing in the United States appears to be, it is at least more democratic than it is in most other nations. In this country, top and middle management administrators are not the only ones involved in planning. The 1990s have brought an enhancement of the roles and contributions of teachers and parents in curriculum designing and planning.[15] The schools that use the resultant designs often provide the originators with feedback about the designs' success or failure.

Democracy does not, of course, necessarily make for proficiency. Because of the difficulty of the task, people who participate in creating curriculum designs should show particular competence. If they desire to reduce differences between what is taught and what is learned, they should know possible ways of ensuring this result. If, on the other hand, they want to pose alternatives, they should know how to present them and how to be sure they are viable. The most effective designs are well-described ones. Some of them include additional descriptions of follow-up procedures in supervision.[16]

The Importance of Preplanning

Preplanning for the act of designing comes in two forms: the general and the specific. Before designers become specific in their work they need to think about how their proposals can make contact with pupils' general needs.[17] General designing in the 1990s relates to facts like these:

1. Job opportunities are changing from industrial–blue collar to service and technology oriented.
2. Functions in the workplace are becoming concept related and dependent on integration of the subjects studied in school.
3. Knowledge of how to live well stems from practicing behaviors that improve health, from relating ethically and morally to other people, and from building in oneself inner discipline and the ability to work independently and also cooperatively.

The specific planning that precedes creation of an actual curriculum design may be represented by a series of questions:

1. What do you think you might want to design? What are the possibilities or alternatives?
2. What level(s) of schooling are you thinking of?
3. What is the nature of the pupil population you have in mind?
4. If you're ready to narrow the possibilities, what do you think ought to be done under terms of the design you favor?
5. What subject matter, both classic and different from the usual, do you think you should include?
6. How might you organize the subject matter to make possible the best teaching?
7. What three or four activities or experiences occur to you as being typical of what you think pupils ought to do?

The cardinal rule for whoever preplans is THINK, THINK, THINK. Thinking takes time. It is better to take a long time in the preplanning stage than to choose a design option that proves to be uninteresting or unproductive. One of the major shortcomings in the process of designing curricula in the past has been a tendency to limit the involvement of people who are to participate in the implementation of the program or project that is eventually chosen. Again, involving people takes time.

Steps to Be Taken in Designing

Once preplanning has been accomplished, the action has only begun. The yearning for a program or project may be intense, but so far no evidence has been accumulated showing that it is needed. Prior to elaborate goal setting, therefore, need should be assessed. This is not the detailed needs assessment that is discussed in Chapter 8. It is the limited determination of the need to design a particular project or a major program.

Determining Need

Need determination should probably begin with an attempt by the designers to specify the outcomes desired. Often it is easy to think loosely and talk glibly about something that apparently needs to be done without stating, preferably in writing, the proposed outcomes. When the outcomes have been stated so that they make sense to people outside the planning group, these people—teachers, administrators, pupils, parents, and other citizens, as appropriate—should be asked what they think of the project or program in comparison with other possibilities and in light of the aims or goals of the school or school system. Next, the planners should collect evidence about the status of the pupils to be affected, lest it be found later that the pupils are already achieving most of the objectives that the proposal is designed to help them attain. The planners should then review the local scene to gauge the community's response to a new project or program. Conversations and discussion with community groups may accomplish this purpose more readily than written surveys, which sometimes arouse suspicions about the motivations of the surveyors.[18]

When need seems to have been established, the planners should see to it that administrative arrangements are made for the formal steps in designing, beginning with establishing aims, alternatively called goals.

Stating or Reviewing Aims or Goals[19]

A new project or program should fit with previously established aims or goals of the school or school system. It is necessary, therefore, that the aims be reviewed or, if aims have never been stated (as in the case of newly founded schools or of school systems that have never done serious curriculum planning), clearly prescribed.

Lists of aims or goals are sometimes prepared by boards of education, administrators, and professional staff people, who may involve pupils and selected citizens from the community. Or they may be formulated by first polling community members concerning their expectations for their schools and then stating the aims on the basis of consensus of community opinion. A third alternative, the one perhaps most common today, is for representatives of the school system and the community to rank aims previously prepared by educational organizations such as Phi Delta Kappa.

Most model lists of aims seem to be reworded versions of the Phi Delta Kappa list, which was produced by the staff of the Program Development Center of Northern California at California State University in Chico, under a grant from the United States Office of Education. The Phi Delta Kappa list calls for development by schools of skills, understandings, and attitudes in family living; management of time, money, and property; general education; character and self-respect; reading, writing, speaking, and listening; changes occurring in the world; examining and using information; a desire for learning; pride in one's work; health and safety; respecting and getting along with other people; democratic ideas and ideals; using leisure time; becoming good citizens; making job selections; and appreciating culture and beauty.[20] The Phi Delta Kappa model suggests three phases in program development. In Phase I, planners rank the aims or goals and determine the current level of achievement. In Phase II, they prepare performance objectives for the school district. In Phase III, they allocate resources to achieve their aims.

Earlier, the Midwest Administration Center had prepared a set of omnibus aims under four headings: intellectual dimensions, social dimensions, personal dimensions, and productive dimensions.[21] Similarly, Tyler had summarized the aims of U.S. schooling as the development of self-realization in individual learners, the making of literate citizens, provision of opportunities for social mobility in the population, preparation for the world of work, preparation for making wise choices in nonmaterial services (education, health, recreation, and so on), and instruction in learning how to learn.[22] Even earlier, the Commission on the Reorganization of Secondary Education (1918) and the Educational Policies Commission (1944) had developed standard lists of aims.

In a speech to the New Jersey Council of Education on March 10, 1989, former U.S. Commissioner of Education Francis Keppel noted that well-publicized aims or goals often show remarkable similarity. In our era, he said, we need a limited number of national goals, perhaps in the range of six to ten. The act of stating these goals would not predestine the establishment of a national curriculum. Yet when President Bush asked the governors of the states and others to formulate a set of aims or goals that he might include in his State of the Union address at the beginning of 1990, he was apparently asking for more than he realized. *Education Week* and other publications have reported since that time how difficult it was to reach an accord on goals.[23]

The very general (national) goals stated at the "education summit" organized by President Bush bore collectively the name *Goals 2000*. These goals were to be reached by the year 2000; a cynic called them "the stealth bomber of reform." To implement them, Congress during the Clinton administration enacted the *America 2000* concept. As a number of legislators noted, the goals as stated are unrealizable products of the wishful thinking of politicians or, as George Will said, "puffs of legislative cotton candy." Implementation of America 2000 has been supported nonetheless by major teachers' organizations. In brief form, the goals actually specify six major wishes:

1. By the year 2000, all children in America will start school ready to learn.
2. By the year 2000, the high school graduation rate will increase to at least 90 percent.
3. By the year 2000, all children will be competent in core subjects.
4. By the year 2000, U.S. students will be first in the world in mathematics and science.
5. By the year 2000, every adult American will be literate.
6. By the year 2000, every school in America will be free of drugs and violence.

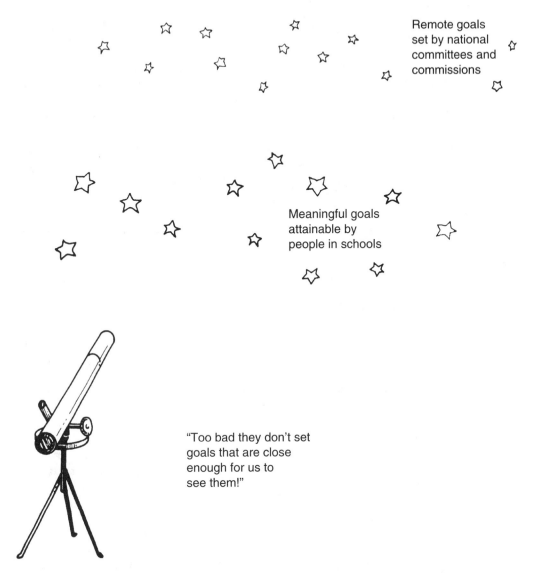

FIGURE 5-1   Goals? What Goals?

Naturally, omnibus lists of national, state, and school system goals provide only general guidance to curriculum planners in expressing aims or goals for their individual schools. Every school, as a separate institution, should have its own aims, stated more specifically and clearly than the aims proposed above. Some of the individual school's aims should be identical to the aims of the system to which the school belongs; others should be adaptations of system-wide aims; still others should be distinctively the property of the individual school. Aims that will be respected and supported are formulated by representatives of all the persons and groups who are to live with the aims. Thus representative teachers, pupils, administrators, parents, and other citizens of the school community should be involved in establishing aims for a school. As usual, however, the competence of individual representatives is more important than their representativeness.

A resurgence of interest in the preparation of aims or goals has raised questions about the functions of schooling that will be debated for a long time. One of the issues concerns the place of schooling in the total range of educational experience offered to children and youth. Alternatives to formal schooling have grown up in many communities. The nature of some of the alternatives suggests that the school may in the future limit itself to activities that it is preeminently successful in performing and that must be performed in schools. Additional educational input may be provided by other media and agencies: television, paperbacks, radio, clubs, labor unions, businesses, religious education programs, community programs, and youth centers.

A second issue concerns central and peripheral missions of the school. The American school was originally created to educate pupils in the directions of intellectuality and values development. Subsequently, the school was seen to be an agency of social interaction and uplift and, later, a means of integrating different racial and cultural groups. During recent years, many of the actions taken in the field of education by high officials in state and federal government have been directed toward the aim of social uplift and the integration of peoples. The prevalence of these actions has caused some critics of the schools to suggest that the central mission of the school, as perceived by many state and federal officials, is to provide schooling less for education's sake than for improving the social status of disadvantaged subpopulations. Similarly, teachers' organizations have viewed the thrust toward accountability as being inspired by social reformers rather than by persons with fundamental interest in the quality of schooling *qua* schooling.

A third issue is clearly values centered. It relates to perpetuation of closed-ended aims versus the adoption of open-ended ones. The American school has traditionally served closed-ended aims by keeping pupil experiences within bounds—teaching established modes of writing, speaking, and behaving in general and assuming the rightness and the propriety of given books, songs, and conclusions in particular. Recently, the voices of a few individuals and small groups of people with different values orientations have been heard. These individuals and groups, which do not usually include parents, want school to admit experiences that enlarge the functions of the school and that sometimes fall far outside traditional functions of schooling. Experiences of the latter sort might include, for example, providing social services for the indigent and teaching pupils how to subvert the U.S. political system.

A fourth issue concerns the limits to be placed on various aspects of formal education. For instance, development of the ability to read effectively has been considered the birthright of every U.S. citizen. Experience in the teaching of reading has revealed, however, that some children never learn to read as effectively as we would like them to, regardless of the time, energies, and methodologies that are employed. Failure to recognize this fact has resulted in widespread criticism by the public and self-flagellation by teachers. Social conscience and faith in the limitlessness of human potential have kept the issue from being thoroughly considered and discussed. Without denying the wonder and the exceptionality of human potential, realists admit that although the potential of every individual is wide ranging, covering varieties of human endeavors, the range of an individual's potential may not include effective performance in every one of the three Rs.

Still other issues and questions are age-old: Beyond basic education, should the schools provide mainly instrumental education or mainly esoteric education? Will the American public support its schools well enough to permit them to fulfill their aims, whatever those aims may be? Are nearly all the children of all the people to receive formal education?

Stating Program or Project Objectives

Within a framework of institutional aims or goals, it is necessary to state objectives that the program or project being designed is to meet. At first, most such objectives were vaguely stated. But notations such as "achieving correct use of language in speaking and writing" proved so general as to be confusing. A change to the pupil objective "to demonstrate in specific ways one's ability to speak and write effectively" seemed useful only to a degree. The big problem was lack of specificity. Whether a program or project objective is to be stated from the vantage point of teachers or of pupils, it should obviously be clear, definite, and limited in size. Shifting to behavioral objectives was perhaps inevitable, inasmuch as people designing programs and projects need to show clearly what pupils are to *do*.

For a program or project, then, the planners may state a general objective like "improving arithmetic learning in our upper elementary school," but to show what pupils are to accomplish specifically, they must state a series of specific objectives beneath the general one. Suppose the planners wanted to touch base with the three identifiable kinds of objectives—cognitive, affective, and psychomotor. Below are samples of an objective within each category:

1. *Cognitive.* To help pupils acquire an understanding of the process of division as revealed by their attainment of a 90-percent proficiency level in teacher-made tests

2. *Affective.* To increase pupils' interest in division of numbers, as indicated by their choice, during four of every five opportunities, of "division options" during independent study periods and by their favorable comments, with the same degree of frequency, about division during interviews and group discussions

3. *Psychomotor.* To improve pupils' perception of number size as a means of making more accurate judgments in the process of dividing, as revealed by their attainment of a 95-percent proficiency level in number estimation exercises taken from standardized and teacher-made tests

An incidence of 90 percent, four of every five, or 95 percent is chosen on the basis of the planners' best judgment and has no other basis.

Objectives like these bear the label "behavioral" or "performance." Though they are not unmixed blessings, behavioral objectives have been instrumental in increasing learning and in relating the intent of pupils and teachers to the aims of the school. Worthwhile behavioral objectives express behaviors that are observable, and they also state the outcomes to be anticipated from behaving in given ways. Reservations about stating objectives behaviorally include the fact that not all subject matter learning can be expressed in behavioral terms, that behavioral objectives sometimes set a ceiling on learning, that such objectives can perhaps be stated accurately only after instruction has occurred because they emerge only in the processes of teaching and learning, and that objectives in general are not always products of rationality.

Some of the critics of behavioral objectives point to the fact that curriculum planners who are skillful in verbalizing objectives are not always capable of formulating objectives that are worthy and attainable.[24] Values questions arise in selecting the objectives to be used. Other critics suggest that formally stated objectives should be eliminated in favor of a mutual refining of ends and means until a curriculum plan is developed that relates the best ends to the best pupil experiences available for attaining these ends.[25]

Despite the criticisms, behavioral objectives remain front and center on the curriculum planning scene. Planners are constantly searching for patterns, order, stability, efficient management, a logical approach, structure, system, and predictability.[26] Many of them believe they are achieving these effects when they prepare behavioral objectives to guide whole curriculum projects. Creators of behavioral objectives at this level should first look to the outcomes they wish to attain, make certain that the behaviors mentioned in the stated objectives are clearly observable, reduce the number of their objectives as they refine a gross list to an essential one, and distribute their objectives appropriately among the cognitive, affective, and psychomotor domains.

Whatever the method used in stating program and project objectives, the statement should be clear and precise.

Identifying Evaluation Means

"If we were to try to achieve the objectives we have just stated, how would we know when, in fact, they had been achieved?" This question should be asked at this juncture by persons designing a project or a program. The answer lies in finding or making evaluation means that will suit the requirement. Among the potential evaluation means are the following: teachers' observations, recording of pupils' behaviors, interview schedules, rating scales, checklists, questionnaires and opinionnaires, teacher-made tests, standardized (norm-referenced) tests, criterion-referenced tests, and semi-projective instruments. Some instruments can be purchased; others must be made within the school system. Achievement standards must be made rigorous enough to make certain that achievement of the objectives has occurred. If the objectives themselves do not express achievement levels (for example, 90 percent, reflecting satisfactory performance in nine of every ten attempts), acceptable levels must be described elsewhere.

The evaluation means are put to use as the curriculum design goes into operation and continue to be used throughout its life span. (Details of program and project evaluation are presented in the next chapter.)

Choosing a Type of Design

Modeling and preplanning lead naturally to specification of design types. A number of design types are being used in improving the whole curriculum or part of it. They represent planners' choices of worthwhile knowledge and functional ways of organizing it.

1. *The subject design,* which is the most common design type, follows the traditional idea of making school subjects the basis for designing. It is orderly as a consequence of its neat divisions and subdivisions of subject matter. Because of the strong presence of the Carnegie unit system, it is difficult to dislodge from high school programs. Variations of the subject design have already been discussed in Chapter 4.

2. *The societal activities and problems design* is based in perceived realities of institutional and group life. It is intended to reinforce cultural traditions and also to meet some of the community's and society's unmet needs. Designs highlighting persistent life situations and reconstruction of the society are included here. The content generally consists of a discussion and examination of social problems or of human activities or needs. Curriculum workers especially interested in social reform are often attracted to this design type.

3. *The specific competencies design* has been represented in recent years by performance-based or competency-based education. Having formerly emphasized descriptions of occupations and training in occupational skills, this design has been tightened in an attempt to show direct relationships among objectives, activities, and performance, especially relative to so-called essential skills. The objectives are usually stated behaviorally. Industrialists and other persons particularly concerned with how graduates of the schools perform on the job often give lay support to the specific competencies design.

4. *The individual needs and interests design* is based in the felt and unfelt needs and the particular interests of individual pupils and small groups of pupils. It utilizes findings about human growth and development and prizes individualization of instruction. Furthermore, it recognizes what the society and

the community are doing to learners. The experiences of learners are often made a beginning point. Additional experiences are varied as they touch the needs and interests of particular learners. Curriculum planners discover these interests and needs in part by consulting and testing the learners themselves. Alternative schools often adopt this design type; child development specialists have long supported it.

5. *The process skills design* emphasizes how to learn and how to solve immediate and lifelong problems. Development of life skills thus becomes an important component of the process skills design on the theory that if learners know how to confront and deal with current problems, they can continue and improve the confrontation in the future. The process skills cross subject matter lines because they are generalized—for example, observing, classifying, hypothesizing, and making decisions. They extend beyond the cognitive domain to the affective, as in valuing. Enthusiasts of lifelong learning have helped prepare process skills designs.

Ornstein and Hunkins maintain that all curriculum designs are variations of three design types: the subject-centered, the learning-centered, and the problem-centered.[27]

Choice of design type is governed in part by the planners' philosophical positions. It also is governed by objectives of the program or project being planned. The planners should not be surprised, therefore, if a particular project falls within a design type that is philosophically quite different from viewpoints commonly held by teachers and administrators in the planners' school.

Selecting Learning Content

"What learning content shall we select?" Aims and objectives point the way to the content that pupils are to learn. Some of the content may be formal subject matter. Part of it, especially in the affective domain, is likely to be informal and may not even be classified as content. What is the content, for example, that is to be used in teaching self-realization or civic responsibility? Much of it is necessarily drawn from the world of affairs, from the life experiences of human beings. Some of it, of course, can be found in subjects and subject fields, such as psychology and the social studies.

Selection of content taken from the subjects and subject fields has been discussed in Chapter 4. The more informal content may be said to fall within categories or domains like the following:

1. Personal development, which includes human communication, values determination and clarification, the inventorying of interests, and self-analysis
2. Acquisition of life skills, which includes listening, discussing, analyzing issues, solving practical problems, and retrieving information (These are skills not usually taught in schools in a sophisticated manner.)

3. Improvement of human relationships, involving use of languages, practice in social interaction, participation in community affairs, and human relations troubleshooting
4. Extended development, which encompasses specializations learned by work experience, individual study, and community service

In selection of learning content, the options are open. There is much less danger in trying varied content than in restricting learners to content that, though tried and true, may in fact be less educative than any one of several alternatives.

Determining and Organizing Learning Experiences

"What shall our pupils do under the aegis of the design we propose?" The answer to this question depends on the answers given previously to other questions: What outcomes do we want, and what, therefore, are our objectives? What means of evaluation have we chosen to fit the objectives? What is the design type within which we are operating? What learning content shall we select? Many teachers and administrators want to determine learning experiences for their pupils before they have answered the preceding basic questions. When they do so, they are likely to select and create dead-end, irrelevant, and inappropriate experiences.

Choice of experiences deserves careful thought, as reflected in the criteria suggested by Hopkins:

> While all interaction of the individual with the environment is experience, the school cannot promote experiences of low educative quality. Pupils, teachers, and others can find too many of these in every walk of life. The school must be concerned with experiences of high educative quality since it should aid each individual to raise the level of his experiencing in all aspects of living. To do this, educators must have some criteria for testing incipient experiences to see whether they warrant study through the school....
>
> 1. The experience must begin with and continue to grow out of the real felt needs of pupils.
> 2. The experience must be managed by all of the learners concerned—pupils, teachers, parents, and others—through a process of democratic interaction.
> 3. The experience must be unified through evolving purposes of pupils.
> 4. The experience must aid each individual to increase his power to make intelligent choices.
> 5. The experience must aid each individual to mature his experiences by making progressive improvements in the logic of such experiences.

6. The experience must increase the number and variety of interests which each individual consciously shares with others.
7. The experience must help each individual build new and refine old meanings.
8. The experience must offer opportunity for each individual to use an ever-increasing variety of resources for learning.
9. The experience must aid each individual to use a variety of learning activities compatible with the variety of resources.
10. The experience must aid each individual creatively to reconstruct and expand his best experience in the developing situation.
11. The experience must have some dominating properties which characterize it as a whole and which usually give it a name.
12. The experience must close with a satisfactory emotional tone for each participant.[28]

Experiences for pupils, whatever their source or nature, need to be organized in ways that fit the curriculum designs to which they contribute.[29] Organizing centers, around which subject matter can be learned and experiences can be clustered, should be created. Common organizing centers include life activities (ways of making a living, utilizing leisure time, and the like), pupils' needs, and pupils' interests.

Virgil E. Herrick developed a different categorization of organizing centers that was based on five qualities:

1. Significance, which means usefulness in teaching, interest to pupils, and general worth
2. Accessibility of a physical nature, an intellectual nature, or both
3. Breadth and scope in meeting the needs of a diverse pupil population, in moving several curricular elements along together, and in serving as a stimulant in dealing with significant life problems
4. Capacity for organizing and relating so that teacher and pupils can "tie things together" in related wholes
5. Capacity for development—permitting children to "catch hold" of content and "run with it"

Herrick decided that five organizing centers had the qualities noted above: ideas; materials; displays, collections, exhibits, and the like; places; and people.[30] He developed his thesis in this way:

The deceptive and yet enchanting thing about the whole concept of organizing centers is that, instead of qualities such as those outlined above being inherent in a given center, the center is itself described, defined, and created by the qualities. In effect, the qualities are in the mind and eye of the viewer. The milkman kicks a pebble at the doorstep, and to him it is only a pebble. The geologist residing there picks it up and enchants his children for several nights with stories of how it came to be. The girl in the match factory watches the clock and thinks of the weekend ahead, while box after box passes under her scrutiny on the production line. The woodsman picks up a single match and brings forth endless tales of woodland giants, raging fires, and reforestation. To the geologist and the woodsman, a stone and a match are organizing centers for learning and teaching. An organizing center is whatever a teacher and a class can get their hands on and their minds around to enrich the quality of classroom living. Visualizing in the center the qualities that make it worthwhile determines the usefulness of that organizing center.[31]

Note that ideas, materials, exhibits, places, and persons are only beginning points for development of experiences. The experiences themselves need to be extended so that they have meaning. Sometimes they can be adapted to be used differently within given organizing centers. Publishers of packaged learning materials have tried interesting variations and combinations of this kind. (Chapter 4 offers a detailed discussion of learning experiences for achieving objectives.)

Evaluating Programs and Projects

Still another step in the designing operation is determining the worth of the design. As might be expected, this action may require considerable time. The worth of the design is revealed by comprehensive evaluation of the resultant program or project. The evaluation occurs both during and at the terminus of a project or program. Evaluation is so significant a step in curriculum design that it is treated at length in Chapter 6.

Evaluation should reveal that the design has flaws. The question is "To what extent does the design accomplish what it was intended to accomplish?" A subsequent question is "What went right, what went wrong, and why?" One must gauge a design's worth with reference to its reason for being and its functioning with reference to the ease with which it has been initiated, implemented, and maintained.

Evaluation may result in establishment of an alternative way of proceeding in the future, or in modification of the current design.

ACTIVITY 5-2

Moving from Philosophical Sources to Objectives

Consider society as the major source of educational objectives. What particular point of view do you take toward the role of society as a source of objectives? That is, should schooling be conditioned by a consensus of citizens' views, by government on behalf of society, by the present social scene, or by a society that has not yet come into being?

State several behavioral objectives that you believe would stem from whatever point of view you take. For instance, if you believe that a society that has not yet come into being should condition schooling, you will value experiments by pupils that will lead them to think about establishment of a new society. Hence several objectives written from the pupils' standpoint might begin with the words "To design experiments..." or "To experiment with...." Suppose, on the other hand, you believe that government should condition schooling on behalf of society. You might propose objectives beginning "To understand legislation...," "To acquire an attitude of acceptance toward regulations about...," and so on. As you state objectives, think of the processes by which pupils are to learn, and also of the content they are to learn.

SITUATION 5-3

Selecting Evaluation Means for a Middle School Project

"Manners have really deteriorated in this school! Courtesy is a rare thing. People don't hold doors for each other. If someone drops books on the floor, no one helps pick them up. While we're thinking up projects, let's think one up on good manners."

The speaker was a member of the faculty of Cloister Middle School. The occasion: a meeting of the school's Curriculum Planning Committee.

Another member of the committee responded: "I'm for that. We need a project of that kind. It would be about as good for the teachers as for the kids."

In due time, the Good Manners Project was designed. Several objectives, mainly repetitious of one another, were stated and accepted. All of them said, in effect, "Let's treat each other in more courteous, decent ways."

Before the committee began planning project activities, the members gave much thought to a troublesome problem—how to gauge improvement in manners when and if the improvement did occur. After having spent time at home considering the problem, the members were able to suggest a number of evaluation means, five of which were determined to be most promising:

1. "Do before-and-after observation (by a team of teachers and pupils) of the status of our manners, with instruction or activities coming between."
2. "Give a manners test before and after instruction. See how we do."
3. "Write descriptions of several school scenes showing good and poor manners. Ask the people to comment on them before we teach and after we teach."
4. "Get the PTA to prepare and publish a manners code. Expect everyone to study it. Give a test on it."
5. "Invite three adult citizens to come in and observe our manners. Show films on etiquette in the auditorium. Have the citizens come back to observe again. Compare."

What do you think of these five ideas? How would you change any of them to make them usable? If you had been a member of the committee, what else would you have suggested?

ACTIVITY 5-3

Suggesting Concrete Actions in Selecting and Ordering Learning Experiences

From the following kinds of objectives, select one and prepare a list of actions you would take in selecting and ordering learning experiences to achieve it:

- Objectives for developing interests
- Objectives for altering attitudes and values
- Objectives for improving skills
- Objectives for developing appreciations
- Objectives for improving quality of thinking

You may wish to carry out this activity with other teachers in a group setting.

SOME NEEDS AND TRENDS REFLECTED IN CURRICULUM DESIGNING

If a curriculum designer were to ask a sampling of people on the street what conditions in the United States call most urgently for curriculum reform, the answers might focus on the three Rs or else on teaching about one or more of the maladies that have originated in the social system—for example, substance abuse, AIDS, or unwanted pregnancies. If the three Rs and other curriculum components have not been learned very well during recent years, the problem may lie in part in the attitudes and values of the persons most concerned with children's learning, especially pupils, parents, teachers, and school administrators. As we have seen, attitudes and values affecting schooling are often acquired from society and the culture.

Certain needs for new curriculum designing have become evident in the era in which we live. Stated in question form, they are as follows:

1. What values should be taught in schools as universals?
2. How can youngsters be taught to care for other people?
3. What special attention should be given to educating children of migrant workers and illegal aliens?
4. What should be done to provide special education to youngsters whose impairments schools have often overlooked?
5. What more should be done to identify and teach children who have exceptional gifts and talents?
6. What should schools do to educate youngsters to care for the environment?
7. What should be done about educating children in multiculturalism?
8. What else should schools do to prepare youngsters for the world of work?

The issues that these and other needs raise will be discussed in future years. The purpose of the following text is to illuminate the eight needs posed above and to offer initial help and words of caution to curriculum designers.

Teaching Values of Universal Import

Citizens of the United States often do not know what to believe about the issues of life because they lack a basis for determining viable beliefs and because they have had too little experience both in clarifying any values they may currently have and in selecting and adopting new ones. To help resolve this values dilemma, which is sometimes a values vacuum, some elementary and secondary schools include, within their curricula instruction in values development, instruction that may not be available to pupils elsewhere in their lives.

Teachers in public schools often wonder what values they can teach without getting into trouble with the law or with community prohibitions. To identify values that can be taught safely to all pupils, curriculum designers can go to two sources: general/universal values and values stemming from the wisdom of the ages. General/universal values are those ordinarily accepted in civilized societies and in citizenship education and human relations practice. C. S. Lewis called them "fair play" and "harmony among people" values. They include cleanliness, orderliness, truthfulness, diligence, honesty, and respectfulness. They can be thought of as everyday values that make schools, homes, and communities run smoothly. On a more exalted level, the general/universal category embraces harmony among people, excellence in achievement, moral responsibility, and democratic consent—values that are hard to teach and harder to evaluate when practiced. Although different socioeconomic and cultural groups have different conceptions of these values, the basic values are sensible and generally accepted and therefore safe to teach.

The basis of wisdom-of-the-ages values is just what the name suggests. Sometimes they are simply the classic "cardinal virtues" of prudence, temperance, justice, and fortitude. When they are screened through the generational experiences of the Egyptians, Babylonians, Greeks, Hindus, Chinese, Jews, and Australians, these values embody the doing of good; beneficence in special circumstances; one's duty to one's elders, ancestors, and children; good faith and veracity; and all-round large-heartedness.

Lists of values like these satisfy the demands of teachers who believe that it is desirable to teach universal values universally. To those who hold that anyone's values, whether beneficent or not, are as respectable as anyone else's, standard lists are anathema. For teachers working in private religious schools, general/universal and wisdom-of-the-ages values do not suffice. These teachers need another category of values to encompass those coming directly from the Ten Commandments and the Sermon on the Mount. These values, which might be termed "thus saith the Lord" values, include compassion, kindness, humility, gentleness, and patience.[32]

Even public school teachers can choose to teach a wider range of values than they commonly do, without evoking lawsuits or protests. To this end, they can be helped by persons affiliated with state departments of education. These persons need to give special attention to the process by which selected values are brought into the schools for careful teaching.[33]

Values education has two distinctions at present: (1) It is attractive to school personnel who feel pressed to help pupils deal with dilemmas related to character, morals, and social conventions, and (2) it is supported by a large quantity of research data, gathered over several decades.

Research and experience have taught us that our values come mainly from two sources: morals and conventions. Morals tend to be based in religion; conventions, in the culture. Children are able to distinguish between values that are morality-related and values that are convention-related. Even young children can be taught values of universal concern, such as fairness and justice. Such values can be taught independently of religious instruction and therefore are legitimate subject matter for public schools. These values can be seen and applied in classrooms where firmness, fairness, and flexibility prevail.

Experiences in values development need to be provided on a continuing basis rather than in an occasional unit or project; otherwise, the effect is lost. The experiences should be made more sophisticated as the maturity of pupils increases. Guided discussion and other peer-to-peer interaction seem more productive than lecturing or telling by teachers.

Learning to Care

A group of teachers in a private school accepted at face value the words of one of their members: "People don't care for one another anymore." After much discussion, the teachers summarized what they thought was wrong: (1) A too-common theme in modern society is "What's in it for me?" and (2) holding to one's homemade moral code may not lead to practicing caring because there are all kinds of homemade codes.

The teachers decided to show youngsters what it means to care. To do this, they tried to improve their own relationships with individual pupils, to assign reading materials containing episodes in caring, to form groups of pupils for cooperative learning, to create opportunities for community service, and to involve parents in assisting with their children's homework.

Clearly, caring has to be learned. Every pupil needs to learn that caring for others does not negate caring for oneself; in fact, caring for oneself can make a person more ready to care for others. In group settings, youngsters gain commitment; therefore they should be organized into groups that foster pro-social values. Gradually, pupils learn that, in caring, little things (as well as big ones) count: sending greeting cards to the ill, celebrating others' birthdays, holding the swinging doors so that others may pass through safely, picking up the debris left carelessly by others, and so on. An aura of desirable attitudes appears slowly, but it appears. What teachers and parents inculcate can be reinforced by peer interaction. Of course, improvement of pro-social behavior takes time.

Educating the Children of Migrant Workers and of Illegal Aliens

Some parts of our nation are especially subject to the ingress and egress of migrant populations. Immigrant processing centers, resettlement sites, and agricultural areas with variable demand for labor are a few of the places that attract and hold migrants for limited periods. The children of migrating families have brief contacts with school after school and thus receive instruction that has little continuity.

Most school systems with shifting pupil populations simply do the best they can. Tangipahoa Parish Schools in Amite, Louisiana went further and developed a plan for working with migrant children. It began with measurement of pupils' individual skill deficiencies and proceeded to instruction in the skills individuals needed. Lists of skill activities and materials were color coded according to educational level and were correlated with computer software, the National Migrant Skills List, and appropriate tests. The school system prepared a guide containing a compendium of resource materials and suggestions for teachers.[34] The Tangipahoa plan suggests the kind of attention that curriculum workers should give to pupils with special problems.

Educating the children of illegal aliens poses yet another kind of problem. Dealing with the children of illegal aliens in appreciable numbers is a new experience for most educators. With their families in flight and their parents' employment uncertain, these children usually come from poor environments where they receive little help or encouragement in their quest for an education. Sensing the instability in their lives, they show an unusual degree of psychological trauma, which is not lessened by a limited ability to speak English or by the effects of culture shock.[35] Like the children of migrant workers, they need planned programs of instruction that are of short duration, designed in the form of brief units. Plug-in and plug-out units of the kind needed have been tried in sites such as the Red Hook section of Brooklyn, New York, where children of seafaring and other migrant populations have been admitted to the public schools for brief periods before they have moved on.

A prolific population within the legal and illegal categories is continuing to arrive during the 1990s, subject to some changes in immigration regulations.

Educating Children with Impairments

Special education of the mentally and physically handicapped has occupied the attention of curriculum planners for a long time. The educables, the trainables, the blind, the partially sighted, the deaf and hard-of-hearing, the orthopedically handicapped, and many other groups have been identified and specially taught. As medical science makes the characteristics of other kinds of handicapped children and youth more clearly identifiable and makes the needs of these youngsters clearer, the schools are being called upon to do something special for each of the newly identified groups. Where specialized educational offerings are needed, they should be provided. Youngsters with nervous disorders are a case in point. The victims of impairment and illness may need the kind of specialized attention that cannot be provided in regular classrooms. For them, the mainstreaming that has become common in schools is rarely appropriate.

Other kinds of impairments loom today. Large numbers of pupils in our schools remain at risk not only of dropping out of school early but also of leaving school eventually without, for example, the ability to find information, to interrelate ideas, and to make generalizations. Minor gains in imparting such skills were reported in 1990. The gain in so-called basic learning, according to data from the National Assessment of Educational Progress, was greatest among blacks and Hispanics.[36] Where learning deficits exist, lack of sufficient education and/or intentional or unintentional miseducation have been blamed. The efforts at reform that have been commended by politicians and the media having largely failed, curriculum planners must return to what has actually worked with educationally impaired pupils who have improved. Five stratagems, sometimes taken together, have succeeded where gimmickry has failed. They are (1) harder work, (2) flexible scheduling, (3) opportunities for personalized learning, (4) focus on sociocultural factors (especially family life), and (5) increased emphasis on affective education. Need it be said that despite the insistence of many that special funding is unnecessary, money from some source is needed to put these stratagems to use? If teachers were physicians, they would probably have rebelled long ago against the inflexibility and impracticality of a system that keeps them from ministering properly to the needs of individuals and small groups. The tendency today is to provide for impaired persons in such obvious ways as reserving parking spaces for them, while some of the needs of impaired pupils are left unmet.

Finding and Teaching Additional Children with Gifts and Talents

The gifted and talented will be with us always, though not in the numbers that fond parents like to imagine. The problem of dealing with the gifted and talented is twofold: (1) identifying within the mass of pupils the truly gifted and talented and (2) finding significant subject matter for them to learn by appropriate methods. Portions of curriculum designs can be devoted to content that is beyond what these pupils quickly learn in company with their classmates. In mathematics, for example, operations research, logic, statistics, and computer applications can provide challenging and useful subject matter for gifted children.

Planning and designing on behalf of these pupils should be comprehensive. This requirement is complicated by the necessity to both accelerate and enrich programs; to offer individualized instruction; and to provide stimulating environments, resources, and materials, especially outside of school buildings. Because the gifted and talented are our potential leaders of the future, they should be kept alert to developments in technology, in leadership theory and its practice, and in world events.[37] The frozen and reduced school budgets of the 1990s do not bode well for development of better advanced and enriched programs. Even if and when the gifted and talented have been correctly identified and properly treated, they may not achieve at expected levels. The ennui of the age has afflicted some of these youngsters, too.

Educating Pupils About Hazards to the Environment

Hazards to the environment are increasing so rapidly that pupils need to understand the nature of those hazards and to develop a sense of what can and should be done to reduce them. Pollution, overpopulation, depletion of food supplies, loss of natural resources, partial elimination of the ozone layer, and the greenhouse effect are bringing dire consequences. These and other hazards are now being discussed at different times in earth science, biology, and geography. There is need for coordinated programs and projects that emphasize the current emergency and that consider solutions to problems of the environment. Youngsters have difficulty in making sense of what they read in textbooks and journals unless they have opportunities to see the effects of environmental hazards firsthand. Giving them these opportunities requires field trips and, if possible, actual service in the field.

Care of the environment is one of those thrusts in modern living in which there is no accounting for zeal. Pupils should become acquainted with the fact that some amateur ecologists would stop the wheels of progress in their strong desire to protect wildlife and natural resources. The presence of knowledgeable ecologists and fearless politicians is limiting the making of irrational decisions about the relative welfare of human beings and preservation of nature's bounty.

Educating Children in Multiculturalism

The United States is rapidly becoming a nation of such diverse cultures that people's mores and expectations are changing with head-spinning rapidity. A plan for multicultural education begun in Portland, Oregon emphasized at its outset a study of six major geocultural groups. Its thesis, which is now accepted in many school systems, was that all pupils need to know and understand the cultures represented by fellow pupils in their schools.[38]

Constructive multicultural education brings recognition of the unfortunate tendency of some programs to deprecate traditions of the western world. Lesser-known traditions—e.g., those of Latin America, Africa, and Asia and those of Native Americans—should be studied *with* traditions of the western world. Well-planned multicultural education will not divide our nation. Information and examples can be used in a number of school subjects. Textbooks and supplementary readings are helpful in transforming pupils' attitudes toward groups other than their own. In schools, teachers' efforts to encourage cooperative learning and to arrange social contacts are proving productive.[39]

Educating Youngsters for Work

After years of supporting vocational and technical education in American schools, curriculum planners find that schooling and work in business and industry remain fundamentally unrelated. Work-experience programs and after-school jobs have helped to narrow the gap somewhat, but real concentration in schools on projecting the experiences of pupils about to enter the world of work has been largely lacking. Americans do not enjoy the seamless integration of school with workplace that some of our competitor nations have sought to establish and maintain.

The facts speak for themselves. Employers in the United States find that they can place most high school graduates only in unskilled jobs. The average male graduate holds seven jobs during the first ten years after his graduation and is unemployed 20 to 25 percent of the time during those first ten years. As to the nature of jobs, some of the jobs that once required individual performance are being replaced by those calling for group effort and interaction. A curriculum design taking these and other facts into account might have the following characteristics:

- A requirement of solid academic skills developed in cooperative settings
- Advisement of non–college preparatory pupils away from weak "general" programs
- Provision of practical school-day training in industries and businesses linked with formal classroom learning
- Assignment of mentors and masters to work sites, their chief function being to work on the job with young people
- Provision of youth apprenticeships involving job training at work sites; school-based learning in core subjects like mathematics, English, geography, and science; and assessment of academic, technical, and employment qualifications[40]

Three Trends That Stir Controversy

Growing up alongside the needs for curriculum designing that have been discussed in the preceding paragraphs have been trends of a controversial nature. Three of these are described below: application of the philosophy of humanism, the idea of standardization and a national curriculum, and Outcome-Based Education. Sometimes curriculum workers are cajoled into fighting fires that need not have been set. Failing to investigate presumably bright ideas, their history, and the motives of their supporters has cost curriculum designers valuable time and professional energy. Each of the three trends has useful features. The greatest danger lies in going all the way with any one of them.

The Place of Humanism in Schools

The term *humanism* is used in the literature of educational philosophy to designate two sets of beliefs: (1) the beliefs of persons who have formed what *Webster's* calls a "cult bearing allegiance to Humanist Manifesto I and Humanist Manifesto II" and (2) the beliefs of educators of goodwill who would do their best to exalt and develop human potential.

The official Humanists (the first group mentioned above) are convinced that human beings determine their own destinies without intervention by a divine being. Thus they reject the miraculous, the mystical, and the supernatural. Humanist Manifesto I rejects creationism, worship, prayer, and "religious emotions and attitudes" as impediments to self-realization and personal fulfillment.[41] Humanist Manifesto II, which appeared in 1973, cast aside salvationism, faith in a prayer-hearing God, revelation of truth, divinity as a source of moral values, and puritanical views of human sexuality.[42] Persons who trust these documents follow a logical progression in believing that there is no God; that human beings therefore were not created but evolved; and that there are no moral absolutes. Unfortunately, some may conclude that it is consequently all right to be amoral.

In many public and private schools and in much of current educational literature, humanism has become a generic term that is often confused with humaneness. Teachers who want the best for their pupils and are willing to help their pupils achieve, freely call themselves humanists. Surely, humanistic philosophy as applied in schools has set the direction of several breakthroughs in elementary and secondary education, such as those emphasizing self-concept development and attention to the productive abilities of human beings. This is a result of what Arthur Combs called the commitment of applied humanism to "freedom, value, worth, dignity, and integrity of persons."[43]

Many conservatives maintain that, largely as a consequence of court decisions against the teaching of religion in public schools and the actual indifference of some parents to what happens to their children's values, humanism has become the prevailing "religion" in many schools, replacing all others. Their views have come to the fore in the debate concerning creationism versus evolution. When curriculum projects and materials seem to uphold what conservatives call secular humanism, objections are often loud, parents hunt for new schools for their children, and public schools lose some of their support. Although people who call themselves humanists deny that their beliefs constitute a religion, conservatives continue to maintain that humanism has filled the gap created by the forced withdrawal of Judeo-Christian teaching, and that its presence in schools constitutes a violation of church-state separation. Humanistic philosophy is obviously one of the themes that curriculum coordinators need to be informed about as they meet with planning groups in the schools. They need to distinguish between two themes that are often discussed interchangeably at the same meeting by the same group of planners: (1) humaneness in the treatment of people in schools, and (2) subscription to the philosophy or religion of humanism. Unfortunately, many serious textbooks and articles in the curriculum field confuse the two themes. In meetings for curriculum planning, it pays to ask the question "Just what are we talking about?"

Standardization and a National Curriculum

Professionals within several subject fields—e.g., art, mathematics, and physical education—have been working to create national curriculum standards in their specialties. For a long time, a degree of standardization (by which we mean the teaching of the same subject matter in all schools) has prevailed as a consequence of teaching to commercial tests, using uniform textbooks, and distributing mandated curriculum guides. At present, further standardization depends on two circumstances: the willingness of teachers to adopt what professional societies specify and the aggressiveness of federal and state authorities in issuing and enforcing standardization mandates. When enough standardization has occurred, educational literature will begin to tell us that we have a national curriculum.

The opponents of further national standardization fear that government edicts can bring about in America what was once alleged to have happened in France, where the minister of education was reported to have said that he could tell what was being taught in any classroom at any given educational level on any Thursday morning at eleven o'clock. Opponents base their resistance on the fact of known variability in human development; on uncertainty as to what might happen when children fail to meet the standards; on probable discouragement of spontaneity among pupils and teachers; and on the inadequacy of measuring pupils' real accomplishments on the basis of standardized performance.[44]

Thus the argument about standards as a point of entry for a national curriculum goes on and on. Most professionals in education agree that items of knowledge and skill exist that should, even must, become the property of all learners. These items may be few, but they are nonetheless important. They should be supplemented with other items that differ from one another but that, taken together, form contexts and contribute to concept development.

Outcome-Based Education

Experienced teachers have always looked for specific outcomes of their teaching. During the past few years, a takeoff from this benign feature of good teaching has been sweeping the country. This adaptation is called Outcome-Based Education. In some people's thinking, it is affiliated with another enterprise, mastery learning, which has always been counted worthy in its original state.

Advocates of Outcome-Based Education say that more than traditional subject content is needed in our information age—that curriculum content must include learning of skills and behaviors that successful adults use, and that these authentic experiences must not be considered attitudinal or values related. They maintain that emphasis should be put on youngsters' motivation, courage, and will to demonstrate knowledge and competence.

Critics express the fear that the somewhat vague statements of OBE's advocates will lead to behavior modification of a pernicious kind. Their objections are twofold: OBE will encourage the teaching of non-traditional values, and it will replace respectable subject matter with vague, non-objective learning materials. They see pupils as pawns in a great social experiment, what someone has called a "dumbed-down scheme" to delude parents and to lower academic standards.

Several states have shown interest in Outcome-Based Education. In other states, especially Pennsylvania, parental resistance to it has developed.[45] The flurry over OBE demonstrates that a basically valid idea can easily be perverted and subsequently surrounded with an aura of suspicion.[46]

EXAMPLES OF CURRICULUM DESIGNING

Although the five major design types discussed on pages 225 and 226 are not the only ones available, they provide bases for much curriculum designing. The first two examples that follow are based on the subject design; their slant is toward extensive involvement of teachers in the planning process. The third example is centered on the individual needs and interests design. The fourth example represents the societal activities and problems design; the fifth example, the specific competencies design; and the sixth example, the process skills design.

Example 1: Organizing to Improve Subject Teaching

The following procedure was used in developing curricula in three school districts where involvement of teachers was especially valued.

Four teams were organized, made up of teachers who were interested in the subject matter area to be reconsidered. Where possible, teachers were given released time for planning. The first of the four teams determined why the subject matter was important for teaching and what concepts and skills needed to be emphasized. The second team decided on grade level content in concept development and skill development. The second team also examined textbooks and multimedia programs that might be of use. The third team prepared methods of evaluation. The methods included minor testing, observing, interviewing, analysis of pupils' writing, and criterion measures within a comprehensive framework of cognitive and affective evaluation. The first draft of a report was then prepared for distribution.

The next step was pilot testing and revision. To these ends, the fourth team tried units and subunits in classrooms, having developed criteria for judging their worth. The fourth team was also responsible for making changes in the design and distributing the revised version. The fourth team then planned for implementation of the design.

The design was implemented by reeducating the school staffs on group and individual bases. A feature of this procedure was close personalization of inservice teaching relative to the design.

The last step called for the participation of teachers and pupils in demonstrating at public meetings their work products under terms of the design, which was now in reportable form.[47]

Example 2: Increasing and Improving the Learning of Basic Skills

Under the leadership of a new principal, the teachers in an intermediate school took seriously the failure of many of their pupils to achieve satisfactorily in reading, writing, and arithmetic reasoning and computation. They considered a majority of the pupils to be "at risk"—at risk of failing to receive high school diplomas and, subsequently, at risk of failure on the job. They agreed with Secretary of Education Cavazos's remark in 1990 that the educational reform movement of the 1980s had not worked, and that a restructuring of schools and a revolution in teaching and learning were needed.[48]

The teachers asked themselves: "How can we restructure the school?" and "How can we change teaching and learning?" After much discussion, they concluded that they themselves had to work harder and, more importantly, work smarter. To this end, they planned to reorganize the learning system of the school in several ways:

1. They would free themselves to work more closely with children who were clearly at risk. To accomplish this, they would petition for use of reserve funds in employing aides. They would also work within the parent-teacher organization to enlist parents as volunteer helpers and then assign them according to their interests and competencies.
2. Beginning with a part of the pupil population (perhaps a single grade level), they would create flexible scheduling plans that would permit teachers to work with smaller groups of pupils and, whenever possible, with individual pupils.
3. They would try to build pupil morale by inculcating a "you can do it" spirit and by removing the threat of too-frequent testing and grading.
4. They would try to reach pupils "where they were" with respect to their sociocultural backgrounds and their feelings and values. To accomplish this, they would do a lot of listening and prescribe

      reading materials and learning exercises to which the pupils could relate.

5. By getting to know individual pupils better, they would seek to bring out and put to use the multitude of talents to be found in the school population.

6. They themselves would volunteer to work during lengthened school days with children in special need of their help.

7. The cornerstone of their plan was the belief that all pupils could, under the right conditions, do better than they were then doing. To show faculty approval of the children's progress, they would honor them in a variety of ways, making sure to recognize a range of the differently talented.

The principal realized that the decisions needed to implement a plan of this kind had to be made cooperatively by the teachers and himself, with the understanding and support of parents. He and the teachers expressed willingness to let the plan stand or fall on the basis of standardized test results, though they knew that standardized tests were inadequate to measure all that the plan would provide in educational opportunity. If the plan succeeded, he and the teachers would recommend it to the teachers and administrators of other schools.

Example 3: Creating a Humane Environment Where Communication Is Improved

Curriculum planners in Cumberland County, a rural county of New Jersey, proposed that a project be developed to make the elementary schools of the county more humane by improving the ability of children to communicate with one another and with adults. The thesis underlying this approach to humanization was that children are likely to consider their teachers and the other adults and children in their environment humane if these persons listen to them and otherwise appear to honor and respect them. This humane attitude on the part of others presumably causes the children to feel better about themselves and their potential. An ability that is especially helpful in improving one's feelings about oneself is competence in communicating effectively with other people. The planners of the project thus hypothesized that the individual child's self-concept, together with selected, related skills of communication, could be improved by implementing a program of instruction that simultaneously emphasized enhancement of the child's self-concept and improvement of his or her communication skills. The planners thought of the proposed project as being in three parts: a curriculum planning segment directly affecting pupils, a planning segment in the inservice education of teachers and administrators, and an evaluation scheme encompassing the two preceding segments.

Five assumptions about people's needs were made:

1. Many disadvantaged minority children and other disadvantaged children in the schools of the county have poor self-concepts.
2. The low self-esteem of these children tends to generate below-normal achievement in communication skills.
3. The below-normal achievement of these children tends to affect unfavorably their teachers' expectations concerning the children's ability to learn—especially to learn communication skills.
4. Some administrators tend to think in much the same ways as the teachers about disadvantaged children's ability to learn.
5. Some teachers and administrators are partially unaware of important considerations relative to learning and cultural differences.

Evidence about the validity of each assumption was sought and in most cases clearly discovered.

The overall, most significant objective of the project was pupil centered: to improve the self-concepts of disadvantaged minority children and other disadvantaged children by enhancing their ability to communicate with other people. The specific objectives of teachers, which were intended always to relate to this major objective, were formulated at the time each teaching unit or exercise was planned.

The Human Development Program, a commercially operated program in which personal awareness, mastery of tasks, and social interaction were the central themes, was utilized exclusively in attempting to improve the self-concepts of the children.

Because communication skill development was not provided for directly in the Human Development Program, it was necessary to prepare a series of pupil experiences relating self-concept development to concrete development of communication skills. Accordingly, Ronald C. Doll and Cheryl D. Walker developed a series of communication exercises with four themes: getting ready for better speaking, writing, and listening; communicating to develop in individual children awareness of themselves and their environment; communicating to develop in individual children self-confidence and a sense of mastery; and communicating to improve social interaction.

The inservice experiences for adults were involved directly with the ideas and materials for self-concept and communication skill development described above. A programmed series of conferences and workshops for both teachers and administrators was conducted throughout an entire calendar year.

The plan for project evaluation was divided into two parts: the formative and the summative. The entire evaluation system, formative and summative, was intended to answer three questions:

1. To what extent have the objectives of the project been met?

2. How is the curriculum content of the project, at pupil level and adult level, better (or worse) for pupils, teachers, and administrators than the ordinary or routine content?
3. What side effects has the project had, and how are these side effects better (or worse) than the corresponding previous conditions in the schools?[49]

Example 4: Designing a Plan in Moral Education for Use in the Seventh Grade

An enterprising seventh-grade teacher in a traditional junior high school designed a plan for teaching morals and ethics to the twenty-three pupils in her self-contained classroom. She diagnosed the needs of her pupils as follows:

- Coming mainly from middle-class homes, these youngsters were unclear about the few "sure" beliefs they had. Therefore their current values needed clarifying.
- Most of the youngsters did not value truthfulness or honesty, and they showed little respect for their elders.
- The youngsters had widely differing ideas of what constitutes wholesome personal living.

A miscellany of other values also needed development or clarification, but the teacher decided that she had enough to do in fostering truthfulness, honesty, respect, and wholesome personal living.

The teacher decided that the objectives of her group should be multiple: to clarify the meanings of the four selected values; to establish standards for recognizing when these four values had been learned; to develop sensitivity to the effects on human behavior of cherishing the values; and to permit the pupils to make constructive changes in their behavior with respect to the four values.

The subject matter to be used included the following:

- Historical and cultural data about the meanings of truthfulness, honesty, respect, and wholesome personal living as seen by people in a variety of civilizations—ancient, medieval, and modern
- What religious and other documents have to say about these four values
- Data gathered by pupil observation within the school and elsewhere of youth and adult practices in situations calling for the values
- Data gathered by interviewing people about their moral and ethical points of view

Experiences (activities) for pupils varied widely:

- Listening to lectures and sermons
- Reading about historical and current views of the four values
- Talking about the values in small groups, during brainstorming, and during strength bombardment
- Writing about the four values in "I believe" and "sources I can trust" statements
- Watching films, slides, and filmstrips that provide values data
- Analyzing cases, presenting role-playing episodes, participating in psychodramas and sociodramas, and using simulated materials in general
- Engaging in action learning in community agencies, stores, hospitals, churches, and synagogues
- Finding and commenting on models of human behavior exemplifying the four values

The teacher knew that what pupils say they do provides an inadequate basis for determining what they have learned. Instead, she chose to make the observed behavior of her pupils in varied situations the real test. Accordingly, she set up situations in which her pupils could demonstrate truthfulness, honesty, respect, and wholesome personal living. To this end, she manufactured situations in which it paid pupils to lie, to abscond with money or other valuables, to show disrespect for adults and peers, and to eschew cleanliness, seemly behavior with the opposite sex, and so on. The observed behavior of the pupils was reported by scheduled observers both in writing and in group discussions. A generalizations-and-insights session with groups of pupils concluded the immediate evaluation activities. After three months, pupils' behavior was evaluated again in "conflict situations" similar to those used earlier.

Example 5: Helping Pupils Demonstrate Specific, Useful Competencies

Planners in a high school that was growing very rapidly were charged with designing and developing a program of vocational and technical education. Prior to the start of the designing operation, the school, which then enrolled 850 pupils in grades nine through twelve, offered two courses in woodshop, a course in cooking, and a course in sewing. The planners wanted to provide proper vocational and technical education for a pupil population projected to number 2000 by the year 1990. They decided to create a curriculum design based on the best available evidence.

To determine what competencies pupils should develop, the planners conducted in-school and community/societal searches. In connection with the former, they arranged for periods of testing to determine pupils' skills and abilities in activities common to vocational and technical education, and they inventoried and interviewed pupils concerning their interests. The planners also assessed the availability of competent instructors and of needed facilities. Then they proposed a program budget.

Next, the planners read about the probable future need for labor of varied sorts in the United States. Locally, they surveyed the future needs for employees, by type and number, in the industries that were being established in the nearby industrial park. They inquired into the actual and proposed vocational-technical programs in local high schools and the county's two-year college. They consulted statistics concerning population trends, and they asked about the degree of support that government officials favored giving to budding industries.

The resulting design was based on the data gathered concerning these and other matters. The planners determined that the objectives of the design had to comprehend preparation for high-technology and small-industry employment for those young people who were likely to attempt to work in or near the community. The subject matter to be taught ranged from basic mechanical skills to the technology of modern small-industry machines and equipment. Room was left for future revision of this content. The skills of reading, speaking, and writing received special attention because of previously revealed deficiencies in these areas.

In addition to classroom instruction, the program provided for laboratory practice and visits to industries. A senior-year internship program was in the process of being prepared. Evaluation of program results began with routine testing and observation of skills and concluded with post-graduation follow-up of the on-the-job achievement of former program participants.

Example 6: Cultivating a Skill Beyond the Basic Ones

A teacher in a middle school was struck with how frequently she heard her pupils say, "I'm bored." Many of her pupils had the advantages that abound in affluent society, such as easy access to transportation; expensive, trendy clothing; and mass entertainment. After talking extensively with the youngsters, the teacher decided that they were bored because they were preoccupied with the froth of civilization rather than its substance.

Under the rubrics "process skills" and "life skills," the teacher found a skill that especially needed cultivating: the ability to use time wisely and productively. She talked with her pupils about what causes boredom. Together, they stated their objective: to have worthwhile experiences that give feelings of satisfaction and real pleasure. The activities they used to give substance to this kind of experience included considering the circumstances of people in the community who needed help; examining the nature of creativity in the arts, especially music, writing, and the fine arts; participating in games that challenge the mind and in those that challenge the body; engaging in hobbies previously left untried; exercising skills involved in building, decorating, and refurbishing; identifying the uses of mathematics in life pursuits; making constructive applications of science to human life; and undertaking volunteer and paid work in local businesses and institutions. Learning required more time than the normal school day allowed and therefore extended to after-school, home, and community activities.

The pupils and their teacher evaluated the success of this design by registering evidences of boredom and evidences of satisfaction and pleasure that appeared after the project went into operation. The former decreased in number and intensity, while the latter increased.

THE PURPOSES AND THE NATURE OF OLD AND NEW CURRICULUM DESIGNS

New designs like the ones just described are made with the obvious intention of improving education for children and youth. Elements of the curriculum wear out and need to be replaced. New knowledge usurps old knowledge and must be incorporated into the curriculum if education is to remain realistic and functional. New ways of teaching subject matter sometimes prove more satisfactory than the old ways and should therefore be highlighted. The thrill provided by the new may constitute at least a temporary reason for emphasizing it at the expense of the old. For these and other reasons, the curriculum is changed in pieces and parts.

Curriculum planners must decide what innovations they want and why they want them. The options are numerous. Much more can be done with the teaching of subject matter than has been done heretofore. The interests and concerns of pupils always make a promising source of new curriculum proposals. Parents, too, can make significant contributions of curriculum ideas.

Instrumental materials can easily become a focus as well as a medium for planning. Moral and spiritual teachings form a basis for projects in values education. The biographies of the great suggest lessons in affective education. Experimentation can be made the means of promoting innovation. Emphasis can be placed on learning process rather than on the products of learning. Attention can be given through new curriculum materials to preserving or reforming social systems. In brief, the possibilities are limited only by the scope of life itself.

Some Choices of Design Themes

Curriculum planners today are putting emphasis on what they consider most important in human life and behavior. Some planners continue to put extreme faith in the disciplines; other planners, in preparing learners to be vocationally competent; others, in preparing learners to engage in constructive activities of direct benefit to our society; and still others, in helping learners develop enlightened self-interest. When practitioners in the schools are given encouragement, time, and resources to propose curriculum projects, they can create truly functional designs. Such designs now emphasize, for example, practical ways of teaching basic skills, educating for work, views of the global interaction of peoples, experiences in community service, teaching for equity, and improving thinking skills.

Perhaps everyone who casts about for a major curriculum plan is hoping to create a grand curriculum design that will become a model. The search for a grand design has been undertaken on several major occasions in the history of the curriculum movement. One of these was preparation of the Thirty Schools experiment; another was the proposal of a plan for the General College of the University of Minnesota. The Thirty Schools experiment, commonly called the Eight Year Study, was based on an attempt to answer four questions: What is to be done within the school? What subject matter is to be used in doing it? What plans of school organization and what classroom procedures are to be followed? How are the results to be appraised? The General College Project gave attention to elements necessary in making a well-balanced curriculum: philosophy of life and education of those responsible for education programs, the needs of society and resources of the school, the needs and interests of pupils, and purpose or outcome.

These two attempts resulted in partial rather than comprehensive designs. To be comprehensive, curriculum design must show a pattern of relationships among numbers of elements of curriculum. A comprehensive design defines these elements and shows their interrelationships, states the means used for selecting and organizing learning experiences, and indicates the roles of teachers and other personnel in curriculum planning. It should show the emphasis given to subject matter for its own worth or importance versus the emphasis given to the needs of pupils, since these needs also are worthy and important. Certainly, it should reveal the organizing centers around which elements of subject matter are to be taught. Also, a comprehensive design should clarify the roles of teachers, pupils, and aides in continuing the curriculum planning that inevitably goes on in classrooms. Teachers naturally want to know, "How free am I? How far can I go in making changes?" About pupils, curriculum designers should ask, "Are they more than sounding boards for determining how the curriculum is functioning? What other responsibilities should pupils have in curriculum development?"

If federal and state mandates increase, tending toward national and state-wide curricula, many decisions about ways of implementing large designs will still need to be made at local levels.

A Strict and Classic Mode of Designing

The systems approach is a strict and classic mode of designing the curriculum. It has been known for some time to be a carefully guided and tightly operated mode. The primary connotation of the term *system* is interrelatedness, inasmuch as the parts of the total procedure are closely related to one another. Systems of education contain interrelated components like people, buildings, books, and equipment and are designed to create carefully planned changes in people's behavior.[50]

The systems approach is helpful in making decisions among alternatives. In general, this process consists initially of gathering criterion information about each alternative, applying "decision rules" or regulations (about, for example, regard for teacher rights) that must condition the final decision, choosing one alternative, reviewing this choice of alternative, and finally confirming or rejecting the choice. Following the application of this rigorous initial thinking process, three procedures are commonly available for use.

One procedure is called the Management Information System. It is designed to provide data about current performance, to suggest modification and adjustment of objectives, and to propose additions to and deletions from the present program.

A second procedure, originally known as the Planning-Programming-Budgeting System (PPBS) and more recently renamed the Planning, Programming, Budgeting, and Evaluation System (PPBES), projects programs into the future, answering the question "What would be the effect of _____?" The programmer provides information about subject matter, educational level, the target group of pupils, the object of the effort, specific activities planned, support services, and the like. PPBES focuses on planning according to aims and objectives, considering relative costs and anticipated benefits of alternative procedures, and basing future decisions on concrete findings. Inherent in the procedure are improvements in program through elimination, expansion, revision, and addition. PPBES is heavily cost oriented and therefore offends the sensibilities of curriculum planners who like to ignore costs whenever possible in the interest of other considerations. However, in an era of budget watching, this system and others like it will inevitably be used.

A third procedure is the relatively simpler Input-Output Analysis. The questions answered by this system are "What do we give?" and "What do we get?" These questions can be answered for several programs or projects that have been tried in a given school system. The answers tend to sharpen the judgment of decision makers, who must still make value judgments about elements of cost in relation to effectiveness, benefit, or utility.

After having used one or more of the three procedures, curriculum planners may use the critical path method in determining what routes to take in implementing decisions. The Program Evaluation and Review Technique (PERT) is a commonly used critical path charting method.[51] PERT is used for ordering events in planning to meet target dates. Developed in the late 1950s by the Navy and the Lockheed Aircraft Corporation and applied to the development of the Polaris Weapon System, PERT follows a six-step procedure:

1. Significant events in the accomplishment of a desired result are selected, defined, and stated specifically.
2. The necessary sequence and the interrelationships of events are determined. The events are noted on a flow chart called a network and are connected sequentially by arrows. No event is considered to be complete until its preceding events have occurred.
3. Each action is given three time values, the values being "optimistic," "most likely," and "pessimistic."
4. The three estimates of time value indicated above are used in this formula to determine the anticipated time for completing an action: $t = (a + 4m + b) \div 6$, where a is optimistic, m is most likely, and b is pessimistic.
5. A computer is used to determine the "critical path" by computing expected times along every possible path on the flow chart. Only by reducing the time of the critical path can the project be completed ahead of the scheduled time. However, taking some actions at parallel times or highlighting highly critical actions may reduce the time needed to complete the project.
6. Computer printouts provide information concerning need for corrective action while the PERTing process occurs.

A variation of PERTing extends systems-oriented planning in other directions. For example, it is now possible for the central office of a local school district to learn from the state department of education or a nearby university whether the scores in arithmetic earned on a standardized achievement test by pupils in the fourth grade of a given school would be improved more by adding another fourth-grade teacher or by securing the services of an arithmetic consultant.

The systems approach provides information that is not available through ordinary inferential methods. Like other "managed" ways of proceeding, however, it does not create original ideas. Instead, it offers cues that lead to idea modification.

Some Challenges to Designers

An important mandate to designers in our day is "Think, think, think." It's easy to get caught up in the mechanics of designing without thinking thoroughly about the reasons particular new designs should be created. It is easy to jump aboard bandwagons driven by people who are inexperienced in the curriculum field. This is especially true when the bandwagons are made enticing with blandishments of ready cash.

Some challenges that designers face are proving to be especially potent and pertinent. These challenges are presented below in the form of questions:

1. *How can we make the schools more humane?*

To make education humane is to take coldness, aloofness, joylessness, and negativism out of schooling. Humane practices and procedures encourage interaction among people. The real key to making schools humane is obviously willingness of teachers and administrators to change their attitudes and consequently their practices. The curriculum in a humane school highlights experiences in displaying interest in other people, in having success, in evaluating cooperatively, in inquiring and discovering, and in living closely with others. Teachers give positive attention and praise to pupils within a school atmosphere of friendliness, openness, informality, and uninhibited communication.

2. *What can we do to educate the diverse populations coming into the schools?*

Pupils of varied cultural backgrounds need varied learning procedures and materials. For example, no single set of reading materials and methods can be used equally well with all pupils. Materials and methods should reflect the social contexts and ways of working that are peculiar to different cultures. In learning situations, the people of some cultures are assertive, quick, and ready to move. The people of other cultures are deliberative, slow, and hesitant, but thorough. Ethnically different pupils need curriculum content and teaching illustrations relevant to their own experiences.

3. *How can we achieve excellence and equity at the same time?*

A curriculum design that emphasizes equity with excellence expresses priorities to be recognized and learning outcomes to be sought. Then it details content, materials, and activities that offer experiences of quality and worth leading to respected outcomes. One of the cardinal rules of curriculum designing is that different experiences can be chosen to lead to the same desired results. Thus the curriculum need not be watered down or made inferior in any way, but parts of it should be different.

4. *How can we restructure schools to learners' advantage?*

What sort of restructuring do we need? A longer school year? A rigorous core program? A standard curriculum? More difficult graduation requirements? Additional standardized testing? An argument can be made for each of these prospects. Considering the differences within our school population, the more pressing needs would seem to be for flexible grouping formats; more functional buildings and facilities; community involvement, with direct participation by parents; an increase in individual and machine-assisted learning; enhanced affective and psychomotor education; and, of course, constant attention to basic and life skills.

What Else Is There?

Curriculum literature contains many discussions of ideas underlying various kinds of designs. Some of the designs emphasize process as opposed to product in learning; others have a values orientation; others are directed toward reforming our social system; and still others depend on altering school organization.

In the field, interesting designs—many of them unknown to curriculum specialists—are being worked out by teachers and administrators. One of these is a plan for instrumental learning prepared by one of the author's former students. Given four partially finished buildings (double-car garages on school grounds), he pondered what could be done to provide a worthwhile educational experience for a group of upper elementary school children. Suppose the four buildings were to be used as a science center, a workshop center, a home center, and a crafts center. What kinds of experiences might the children have in finishing, decorating, and furnishing the four buildings? After the buildings were completed, what might they learn about science, the industrial arts, home economics, and arts and crafts? What might the children learn about gardening, masonry, well drilling, or even rocketry? The plan answered these questions within a framework that expressed the need for the project, the objectives of the proposed design, the nature of the subject matter to be learned, the kinds of experiences open to pupils, ways of evaluating the project as it progressed and after it was completed, and media for influencing other decision makers to help bring the plan to fruition.

The fun and the challenge of creating original curriculum designs are available to teachers, parents, pupils, and administrators who are willing to think and imagine beyond ordinary limits.

The Bottom Line for the Year 2000 and Beyond

A dependable topic of living room conversation in the 1990s is "the failure of our elementary and secondary schools." During such a conversation, many a participant will offer a single, simple, exact answer concerning what can be done to treat our educational malaise. Do we need more money? better teachers? more modern buildings and facilities? brighter pupils? longer school days or years?

If a group of curriculum planners were asked to narrow the options and then to identify one constructive action that should be taken, what might that action be? As often happens in human affairs, problems in the schools originate with people, especially with pupils, teachers, and parents. Crucial to recovery from our end-of-century educational malaise is the will to do, a virtue that doesn't exist alone. Rather, it is clustered with diligence, responsibility, persistence, ambition, caring, and the other virtues that we often verbalize as we seek to describe functioning, productive human beings. Inasmuch as children and youth in the United States have not been blanketed suddenly with suffocating stupidity, we must conclude that despite their language deficiencies, poverty, and other handicaps, their failure to achieve often lies with lack of will to do and lack of desire to succeed.

These facts tell curriculum designers that their efforts are almost certain to be frustrated unless they emphasize the values and attitudes that one needs in order to learn subject matter, whether it be easy or difficult. These values and attitudes must be taught not only in classrooms, but also in homes and communities. Though brilliant curriculum designs will not automatically improve people's values and attitudes without continuing help from national, state, and community leaders who advocate and promote hard work and achievement, such designs are sure to prove deficient if they attend only to subject matter without putting concurrent emphasis on why learners should and must learn it.

The status of American education in the year 2000 and beyond may be lower than it is today unless we learn the beneficent hardness that is tough love.

ACTIVITY 5-4

Identifying Curriculum Designs

In a school you know or one described in the curriculum literature, find a design that is characterized by one of the following:

1. Emphasis on preselected subject matter content
2. Attention to the interests and concerns of pupils
3. Reliance on sets of instructional materials
4. Emphasis on moral and spiritual teachings
5. Dependence on biographies of the great
6. Attention to experimentation in teaching and learning
7. Emphasis on process rather than on product
8. Attention to reforming or revolutionizing the social system
9. Emphasis on letting pupils mainly do as they wish
10. Dependence on changed organizational patterns

Discuss the design.

SUMMARY

Decision making about how a curriculum should be designed is a complex matter. Usually, it is helpful to follow a set series of steps in the designing process, although the steps are not invariable. Ideas for designs come from four major sources, not all of which can be drawn upon in individual schools. The sources are what science and a science-oriented culture suggest, what society seems to mandate or require, what eternal or permanent values from the human past say to us, and what Divine Will dictates. Several current needs and demands now affect curriculum designing. Among them are, for example, an insistence that the schools teach values, morals, and ethics; that children with a variety of impairments be taught better than they have been heretofore; and that children who are gifted and talented be offered better programs of instruction. Several terms now in common parlance among curriculum workers suggest possible future emphases in designing: the systems approach, the humane school, educating a more diverse population, achieving equity with excellence in schooling, and restructuring schools so that they really improve. Curriculum workers need to regard with care certain controversial trends: application of humanistic philosophy, standardization of content and a national curriculum, and Outcome-Based Education.

ENDNOTES

1. Submitted, with a wish for anonymity, by a member of a school's committee on curriculum planning.

2. Geneva Gay, "Conceptual Models of the Curriculum Planning Process," in Arthur W. Foshay, ed., *Considered Action for Curriculum Improvement*, 1980 Yearbook (Alexandria, VA: Association for Supervision and Curriculum Development, 1980).

3. For an explication of curriculum foundations, see Robert S. Zais, *Curriculum Principles and Foundations* (New York: Thomas Y. Crowell, 1976).

4. Steven A. Melnick and Robert K. Gable, "High School Curriculum Alignment: Much Work to Be Done," *Clearing House* 62, no. 6 (February 1989): 245–249.

5. Gay, "Conceptual Models of the Curriculum Planning Process," 121–143.

6. M. Frances Klein and John I. Goodlad, "A Study of Curriculum Decision Making in Eighteen Selected Countries," National Academy of Education, Stanford, California, September 1978. Reported in ERIC # ED 206 093.

7. Tom Simkins, "Some Management Implications of the Development of Curriculum Information Systems," *Journal of Curriculum Studies* 15, no. 1 (January–March 1983): 47–59.

8. See B. Othanel Smith, William O. Stanley, and J. Harlan Shores, *Fundamentals of Curriculum Development* (New York: Harcourt, Brace and World, 1957), 529–544.

9. John D. Byrne, "E. D. Hirsch, Jr., Is Alive and Well and Living in Brooklyn," *Clearing House* 62, no. 7 (March 1989): 289–292.

10. For further discussion of this and other curriculum sources, see National Society for the Study of Education, *Modern Philosophies and Education*, Fifty-Fourth Yearbook (Chicago: University of Chicago Press, 1955); see also John S. Brubacher, *Modern Philosophies of Education*, rev. ed. (New York: McGraw-Hill, 1950).

11. J. Ron Nelson et al., "Can Children Design Curriculum?" *Educational Leadership* 51, no. 5 (February 1994): 71–74.

12. Ralph W. Tyler, *Basic Principles of Curriculum and Instruction* (Chicago: University of Chicago Press, 1949).

13. Association for Supervision and Curriculum Development, "Is the Tyler Rationale a Suitable Basis for Current Curriculum Development?" *ASCD Update*, December 1980, 4, 5.

14. See James S. Fogarty, "The Tyler Rationale: Support and Criticism," *Educational Technology* 16, no. 3 (March 1976): 31.

15. See current issues of publications devoted to cooperative learning and parent participation.

16. Douglas D. Christensen, "Curriculum Development: A Function of Design and Leadership," *The Executive Review* 1, no. 3 (December 1980): 2–8.

17. Tony Wagner, "Improving High Schools: The Case for New Goals and Strategies," *Phi Delta Kappan* 74, no. 9 (May 1993): 695–701.

18. See John D. McNeil and Louis Laosa, "Needs Assessment and Cultural Pluralism in Schools," *Educational Technology* 15, no. 12 (December 1975): 26.

19. In this discussion, the terms *aim* and *goal* are used synonymously.

20. For a thorough analysis of goals, see the series of articles in *Phi Delta Kappan* 72, no. 2 (December 1990): 265–314.

21. Lawrence M. Downey, *The Task of Public Education* (Chicago: Midwest Administration Center, University of Chicago, 1960), 22–26.

22. Ralph W. Tyler, "Purposes for Our Schools," *Bulletin of the National Association of Secondary School Principals* 52, no. 332 (1968): 1–12.

23. "Accord on Goals Hard to Attain, Executives Find," *Education Week* 9, no. 19 (January 31, 1990): 1.

24. Helen F. Durio, "Behavioral Objectives: Where Have They Taken Us?" *Clearing House* 49, no. 5 (January 1976): 202.

25. Robert I. Wise, "The Use of Objectives in Curriculum Planning: A Critique of Planning by Objectives," address delivered at the annual meeting of the American Educational Research Association, Washington, DC, April 1975.

26. William Strong, "The Ant and the Grasshopper: A Didactic (and Somewhat Moral) Fable," *Media and Materials* 11, no. 7 (March 1975): 26.

27. Allan C. Ornstein and Francis P. Hunkins, *Curriculum: Foundations, Principles, and Issues* (Englewood Cliffs, NJ: Prentice-Hall, 1988).

28. L. Thomas Hopkins, *Interaction: The Democratic Process* (Boston: D. C. Heath, 1941), 218. Used with permission of the author. Compare Gail M. Inlow, *The Emergent in Curriculum,* 2nd ed. (New York: John Wiley, 1973).

29. This is an aspect of the internal consistency of the design as discussed by Francis P. Hunkins in his *Curriculum Development: Program Planning and Improvement* (Columbus, OH: Charles E. Merrill, 1980).

30. Virgil E. Herrick et al., *The Elementary School* (Englewood Cliffs, NJ: Prentice-Hall, 1956), 110–111.

31. Reprinted by permission of Prentice-Hall, Inc., Englewood Cliffs, NJ, from Herrick et al., *The Elementary School* (©1956), 110–112.

32. The three values categories—general, traditional, and religious—come from the writing and speeches of the author of this book.

33. New Jersey is representative of states that could have given more careful consideration to process.

34. Billie J. Pietri, *Tangipahoa Parish Migrant Education 1982–1983 Program: Guidelines for Implementation* (Amite, LA: Tangipahoa Parish School Board, 1982).

35. See Maxine Greene and Mary Anne Raywid, "Changing Perspectives on Schools and Schooling," in Kenneth D. Benne and Steven Tozer, eds., *Society as Educator in an Age of Transition,* National Society for the Study of Education, Eighty-Sixth Yearbook, Part II (Chicago: University of Chicago Press, 1987), 226–246.

36. *The Newark* (NJ) *Star-Ledger,* January 10, 1990, 15.

37. A. Harry Passow, "Issues and Trends in Curriculum for the Gifted," a paper presented at the annual conference of the National Association for Gifted Children, Las Vegas, November 2–7, 1986.

38. See *Educational Leadership* 49, no. 4 (December 1991–January 1992): 4–81.

39. See James A Banks, *Multiethnic Education: Theory and Practice,* 3rd ed. (Boston: Allyn and Bacon, 1994).

40. See the entire issue of *The Harvard Education Letter* 9, no. 2 (March–April 1993).

41. *The New Humanist* 6, no. 3 (May–June 1933).

42. *The Humanist* 33, no. 5 (September–October 1973).

43. Arthur W. Combs et al., *Humanistic Education: Objectives and Assessment* (Washington, DC: Association for Supervision and Curriculum Development, 1978), 9.

44. "Opinions Clash on Curriculum Standards," *ASCD Update* 36, no. 1 (January 1994): 6, 7.

45. See articles in the March 1994 issue of *Educational Leadership.*

46. See miscellaneous literature published by conservative groups, religious and secular.

47. David S. Martin, "Reinventing the Curriculum Wheel," *Educational Leadership* 39, no. 2 (November 1981): 130, 131.

48. *The Newark* (NJ) *Star-Ledger,* January 10, 1990, 15.

49. Reports of the project, with full explanation of its design, appear in the fifth edition of this book (1982) and in ERIC # ED 127 229.

Chief co-planners of the project were John N. Falzetta, Jean K. Nocon, William D. Fenton, Patricia Horton, Leon Trusty, and Ronald C. Doll.

50. See, for example, J. Alan Thomas, *The Productive School: A Systems Analysis Approach to Educational Administration* (New York: John Wiley, 1971).

51. Carleton A. Shore, "PERT Philosophy and the Curriculum Supervisor," *Education* 102, no. 1 (Fall 1981): 77–81.

SELECTED BIBLIOGRAPHY

Association for Supervision and Curriculum Development. *What Are the Sources of the Curriculum?* Washington, DC: The Association, 1962.

Beauchamp, George A. *Curriculum Theory,* 3rd ed. Wilmette, IL: Kagg Press, 1975.

———. "Curriculum Design." In Fenwick W. English, ed., *Fundamental Curriculum Decisions.* 1983 Yearbook. Alexandria, VA.: Association for Supervision and Curriculum Development, 1983.

Benne, Kenneth D., and Tozer, Steven, eds. *Society as Educator in an Age of Transition.* National Society for the Study of Education, Eighty-Sixth Yearbook, Part II. Chicago: University of Chicago Press, 1987.

Casciano-Savignano, C. Jennie. *A Systems Approach to Curriculum and Instructional Improvement.* Columbus, OH: Merrill, 1978.

Cawelti, Gordon, ed. *Challenges and Achievements in American Education.* 1993 Yearbook. Alexandria, VA: Association for Supervision and Curriculum Development, 1993.

Choate, Joyce S., et al. *Curriculum-Based Assessment and Programming,* 2nd ed. Boston: Allyn and Bacon, 1992.

Eisner, Elliot W. *The Educational Imagination: On the Design and Evaluation of School Programs.* New York: Macmillan, 1979.

Foshay, Arthur W., ed. *Considered Action for Curriculum Improvement.* 1980 Yearbook. Washington, DC: Association for Supervision and Curriculum Development, 1980.

Golby, Michael; Greenwald, Jane; and West, Ruth, eds. *Curriculum Design.* New York: John Wiley, 1975.

Goodlad, John I., ed. *The Ecology of School Renewal.* National Society for the Study of Education, Eighty-Sixth Yearbook, Part I. Chicago: University of Chicago Press, 1987.

Grundy, Shirley J. *Curriculum: Product or Praxis.* Philadelphia: Taylor and Francis, 1987.

Maurer, Richard E. *Interdisciplinary Curriculum: Restructuring Secondary Schools.* Boston: Allyn and Bacon, 1994.

Miller, John P. *The Holistic Curriculum.* Toronto: Ontario Institute for Studies in Education, 1988.

Ornstein, Allan C., and Hunkins, Francis P. *Curriculum: Foundations, Principles, and Issues,* 2nd ed. Boston: Allyn and Bacon, 1993.

Posner, George J., and Rudnitsky, Alan. *Course Design: A Guide to Curriculum Development for Teachers,* 4th ed. New York: Longman, 1994.

Schubert, William H. *Curriculum: Perspective, Paradigm, and Possibility.* New York: Macmillan, 1986.

Slavin, Robert E.; Karweit, Nancy L.; and Madden, Nancy A. *Effective Programs for Students at Risk.* Boston: Allyn and Bacon, 1989.

Snyder, Benson R. *The Hidden Curriculum.* New York: Knopf, 1971.

Swenson, Esther J., ed. *A Look at Continuity in the School Program.* 1958 Yearbook. Washington, DC: Association for Supervision and Curriculum Development, 1958.

Thomas, J. Alan. *The Productive School: A Systems Analysis Approach to Educational Administration.* New York: Wiley, 1971.

Tyler, Ralph W. *Basic Principles of Curriculum and Instruction.* Chicago: University of Chicago Press, 1949.

Warwick, David. *Curriculum Structure and Design.* Mystic, CT: Lawrence Verry, 1975.

Wilson, L. Craig. *The Open Access Curriculum.* Boston: Allyn and Bacon, 1971.

Zais, Robert S. *Curriculum: Principles and Foundations.* New York: Thomas Y. Crowell, 1976.

6

EVALUATION OF CURRICULUM PROGRAMS AND PROJECTS

Chapter 5 emphasized the importance of designing programs and projects intelligently and functionally. Casual mention was made of the significance of evaluating thoroughly any program or project that is introduced. The current chapter is devoted entirely to evaluation.

Professional literature about evaluation as a general theme exists in profusion, but relatively little has been written about evaluating programs and projects intended to improve the curriculum.[1] As a consequence, ways of evaluating programs and projects have not always been as sophisticated as they might have been, and many major actions to improve the curriculum have been evaluated poorly when evaluated at all. Extraneous considerations like the prestige of the author of a proposal have sometimes been permitted to replace evidence of the proposal's real effectiveness.

Evaluation may be defined as a broad and continuous effort to inquire into the effects of utilizing educational content and process to meet clearly defined goals. According to this definition, evaluation goes beyond simple measurement and also beyond simple application of the evaluator's values and beliefs.

In writing about evaluation for curriculum improvement, Albert Oliver identified three thrusts: (1) within the curriculum, as in evaluation by teachers in classrooms; (2) about the curriculum, as in evaluation of the curriculum's success in reaching its goals; and (3) about the process used in improving the curriculum.[2]

Within recent years, stirrings of curriculum improvement activity have been evident in both developing and developed countries. In developing countries, this movement has generated efforts to determine whether the major curriculum changes made in previous years have constituted real improvements. In developed countries, dissatisfaction with current curricula has required status evaluation of long-standing school programs and projects, as well as early evaluation of newly installed curricula, to determine whether they are producing expected gains in pupil learning and teacher satisfaction. In the United States, funding agencies, school personnel, and school patrons have asked for precision in evaluating the effectiveness of new programs.[3]

In everyday language, the common reasons for wanting to evaluate curriculum improvement programs and projects may be stated as follows:

- "I'd just like to know whether this plan has been worth anything!" (Evaluation to satisfy one's curiosity)
- "I may be asked whether the time, talent, and money expended on this project have yielded results." (Evaluation to fulfill an accountability requirement)
- "I wonder how our plan compares with theirs." (Comparison of programs)
- "We need to know how nearly ideal this plan is." (Evaluation to distinguish among the best)
- "We want to know what moves to make next." (Decision evaluation)[4]

EVALUATION AS IT IS GENERALLY KNOWN IN SCHOOLS

Teachers, administrators, and other school personnel commonly think of evaluation in three terms: the evaluation of pupil progress by teachers in classrooms; the evaluation of schools and school systems by outside agencies, usually for purposes of checking up but also as part of national, state, or regional projects; and the evaluation by the National Assessment of Educational Progress and state departments of education, often called national testing and state testing.

Evaluation in the Classroom

The classroom may, in fact, become the site of important data gathering that leads to curriculum improvement and that assists with the evaluation of programs and projects already under way. Within the classroom, curriculum leaders can help teachers administer evaluation instruments and then help them interpret the results. The instruments that are most often used fall within the following categories:

Achievement tests	Journals
Anecdotal records	Observation schedules
Appreciation tests	Personality inventories
Aptitude tests	Portfolios
Attitude inventories	Projective techniques
Checklists	Rating Scales
Diaries	Semiprojective techniques
Interview schedules	

Sociometric devices	Vocational interest inventories
Tests of mental ability	Writing samples[5]
(intelligence tests)	

Teachers who are unfamiliar with standardized instruments in any of these categories are in obvious need of help from curriculum or guidance personnel.

Every day, teachers informally evaluate on the basis of their own tests or their own subjective judgment. In its informal sense, evaluation is simply a part of living. Inasmuch as we are all being evaluated with great frequency, everyone needs to become familiar with evaluation instruments that are fair and accurate. Teachers must improve their own evaluation skills and also help their pupils respond effectively to evaluation instruments. The teacher's self-evaluation of his or her own work offers one of the most promising ways of improving schools. Teachers need help in studying the differences between their intent and the outcomes they are achieving. Their objectives may need changing or amending; their methods may be faulty. To know that such circumstances exist, teachers need to observe skillfully and to record data carefully. Because the evaluation process, including self-evaluation, is probably an unfamiliar one, supervisors and administrators should be prepared to help teachers at any point in the process.

The reasoning of professional evaluators is not always understood by people in the schools. There, program evaluation and standardized testing are often considered to be synonymous. King and Thompson made a study of program evaluation as seen by school administrators (chiefly principals and superintendents), 1600 of whom were asked to participate. Of the 686 who responded to the evaluation instruments, 61 percent said that program evaluations are useful. More superintendents than principals were represented in this 61 percent; principals, especially in large school districts, were more skeptical than favorable. Most of the respondents said that information from the evaluations was being used, though 28 percent of them thought the evaluations had not succeeded in getting to what they really needed to know. It was clear that practitioners within the schools had too little contact with the program evaluators.[6] Obviously, a need exists for further study of evaluation process.

Evaluation of Whole Schools and School Systems

Entire schools and school systems may be involved in evaluation in the form of surveys, opinion polls, follow-up studies of graduates and pupils who leave school early, standard evaluation instruments, and large cooperative projects. Teachers are aware that omnibus studies are being made, but they frequently have little part in them except to answer a few questions and demonstrate their teaching skills for a few minutes. The studies are usually conducted by agencies outside the local school district; the evaluators are usually strangers. Some of the better evaluation studies within this category have been cooperative, involving both external experts and local administrators and teachers.

Surveys

Comprehensive studies of schools and school systems resulting in recommendations for their improvement are called *surveys*. Teams of university staff members and the personnel of survey firms have customarily conducted surveys from the outside looking in. After a series of visits, conferences, and interviews, the surveyors usually prepare written reports to communicate their findings and recommendations. Within recent years, external surveys have been partially replaced by self-surveys and cooperative surveys.

In self-surveys, staff members of school systems organize to study their own curriculum and facilities. Often, they use as criteria the objectives of teaching and learning that they have previously developed or that they have borrowed from educational literature or other school systems.

Cooperative surveys represent a compromise between external surveys and self-surveys. They call for the joint efforts of school system personnel and specially employed external surveyors. Cooperative surveys are said to avoid some of the disadvantages of both external surveys and self-surveys. External surveyors sometimes know so little about the institution being surveyed that their reports contain inaccuracies. On the other hand, self-surveys show incompleteness and improper balance because local personnel frequently lack the necessary experience and vision for the survey task. Cooperative surveys tend to bring together the understandings and skills required.

Opinion Polls

Another procedure for studying curricula of schools and school systems is relatively quick and informal. It consists of asking people within and outside the schools what they think of various aspects of schooling. Opinion polls have been used comprehensively by several polling firms. For instance, the Gallup organization regularly asks people throughout the nation what they think of their schools. In individual school districts, the purpose of opinion polls is often to discover agreement regarding strengths and weaknesses of school curricula. Polls have certain public relations values, and they may set the stage for curriculum improvement. Teachers and administrators often use opinion polls to identify points along the educational front at which gains can be made with maximum public support, as well as points at which nonsupport is probable.

Follow-Up Studies

Both graduates and pupils who leave school early are the subject of follow-up studies of educational, occupational, and personal accomplishments. These studies help to answer questions like the following:

1. What kinds of experiences do graduates and those who leave school early believe the schools should offer their pupils?
2. To what extent have the schools in question offered these experiences?
3. How well has subject matter content been taught within the range of these experiences?

4. How successful have graduates and those who leave school early been in applying to life situations what the schools have taught them?
5. What modifications in the school program should be made for similar groups and individuals in the future?

High school guidance personnel sometimes make statistical follow-up studies of college students and business employees who are graduates of their schools. These studies are often so superficial that one wishes more studies could be made in depth. Deeper studies could include assembling individual alumni and small groups of alumni for interviews, conferences, and meetings to reveal genuine feelings and to develop creative ideas about appropriate schooling for children and youth of varied backgrounds.

Standard Evaluation Instruments

Evaluation of several areas of the curriculum may be accomplished by using standard evaluation instruments. Perhaps the most widely used is a document called *Evaluative Criteria,* which was prepared by the Cooperative Study of Secondary School Standards assisted by the American Council on Education, the National Association of Secondary School Principals, the National Education Association, and the United States Office of Education. It is applied by a half-dozen regional accrediting associations, such as the Western Association of Colleges and Secondary Schools and the comparable New England Association. The evaluators who use it review each school's curriculum organization or design, its pupil activities, its plant, its administration, its guidance and library services, and its faculty personnel. Standard questions arranged within categories are asked about every school in which the *Criteria* is made the evaluation document. A roughly comparable instrument has been developed for use in evaluating elementary schools.

State departments of education often develop their own evaluation instruments. Regional associations like the Southern Association make cooperative evaluations of schools; the instruments they use become nationally known and are borrowed throughout the country. Study groups in New England, the southwest, and elsewhere have tried to prepare comprehensive instruments. Standard evaluation instruments meant to be generally applicable are obviously not tailored to the evaluation needs of any one particular school. Therefore when they are used, they should be supplemented with questions and other evaluation items that conform with the situation in the school being evaluated.

Large Cooperative Evaluation Projects

School systems sometimes have opportunities to participate in evaluation and research projects that are of national, regional, or statewide scope. In the past, the federal government, universities, foundations, educational associations, and private business concerns were among the agencies sponsoring large-scale projects. Government funds, foundation grants, and private capital were once used for what was nominally evaluation and research activity. Developing spelling lists, experimenting with educational television, developing learning machines, and trying out materials to be published in connection with projects in science, mathematics, and other subjects highlighted the lists of activities simultaneously under way in school systems.

Within the past sixty-five years, a few large projects have been developed to improve elementary and secondary school curriculum. Two of them were noted in Chapter 5: In the 1930s, a total of thirty schools engaged in the Eight Year Study,[7] and the Stanford Social Education Investigation was carried out by Stanford University with a grant from the General Education Board.[8] The Eight Year Study examined the relationship between high school and college; the purpose of the Stanford project was to encourage experimentation in social studies teaching and to stimulate cooperation in curriculum study between school systems and the university. Other projects on a smaller scale followed, as both the federal government and the educational foundations did more than they are doing today to promote curriculum improvement. Currently, expenditures for this purpose are few; limited projects receive support from state departments of education.

National Assessment and Statewide Testing

The National Assessment of Educational Progress (NAEP), begun in 1964 as an agency for nationwide testing of pupils' skills, understandings, and attitudes, has some effect on what is taught in individual schools. Governed by the Education Commission of the States, a nonprofit organization of legislators, governors, and educators financed by the United States Office of Education and the Ford and Carnegie Foundations, the NAEP has tested samplings of pupils aged nine, twelve, and seventeen, as well as young adults twenty-six to thirty-five years of age, in ten academic areas within five-year cycles. The questions asked in the ten areas—science, mathematics, reading, writing, social studies, citizenship, literature, art, music, and career and occupational development— have partly determined, in those schools where the tests are being administered, what teachers consider worth teaching.

The thoroughness with which National Assessment operates is indicated by the series of steps taken by the evaluators in developing the assessment program. The first step was the determination of educational objectives for each academic area. Every usable objective had to be considered (1) important by scholars in the academic area or subject field, (2) acceptable by school personnel for use in schools, and (3) desirable by groups of lay persons. The second step was the laborious preparation of evaluation items. The third step was the random selection of schools, pupils, and out-of-school personnel for participation in the testing. The test items, ranging from easy to difficult, are theoretically not to be used for comparison of persons, schools, school districts, or states. No norms or individual scores are reported, and the data are analyzed in census form by region of the nation, size and kind of community, parents' education, race, and sex. The NAEP releases to school systems and state departments of education some of the test items used in recent tests. Therefore it is possible for teachers to teach subject matter in anticipation of the nature of future tests. This is often referred to as "teaching to the test" or as using standardized tests, past and probable future, as a main source of curriculum content. Some curriculum personnel regard this fact to be a warning that a national curriculum looms as a threat to determination of curriculum in the individual school.[9] Their fear has been strengthened by the call by America 2000 for a new series of achievement tests.

The famous Scholastic Aptitude Test has undergone revision to put more emphasis on critical thinking and on critical issues. Bearing the new name Scholastic *Assessment* Test, the revised version has fewer but longer reading passages and fewer multiple-choice items in mathematics. The appeal is to higher mental processes, and a hope is that our newer population of pupils will be aided in developing critical-thinking abilities.[10]

The efficiency with which this national program of testing and evaluation has operated has encouraged a number of the states to install programs of statewide testing. Sometimes the purpose is comparison of schools, with the hope of reducing the number of ineffective ones. Sometimes it is improvement of teaching, so that the high school diploma will have more meaning than it has had in recent years. Whatever the purpose, teachers and administrators soon feel the influence of statewide testing, and the power of state departments of education inevitably increases. Near the mid-1990s, the Educational Testing Service reported on the nature of statewide testing. The ETS had found that all states were testing pupils in mathematics and language, and that most were also using tests of science, writing, and social studies. Thirty-eight states required writing samples, and thirty-four used norm-referenced tests and criterion-referenced tests. Seventy percent of the tests were of the multiple-choice type, 12 percent were in the form of writing samples, and 18 percent were termed multiple-subject performance in nature. Eighty percent of the tests were of the achievement type; the remainder focused on vocational interests, school readiness, and a miscellany.[11]

SOME PRINCIPLES AND PRACTICES OF EVALUATION

It should be obvious from the preceding discussion that for most teachers and administrators, evaluation has remained a peripheral function in which they have had no real part. The exception, of course, has been evaluation of pupil progress in classrooms. Although teachers and administrators have participated in planning new programs and projects, too often the planners have given little thought to their evaluation. As a consequence, the curriculum has come to resemble a boat accumulating barnacles. The accretion of unevaluated material has added weight, but nothing has been done to provide streamlining. Evaluation gauges worth, thereby permitting some programs and projects to be retained and others to be eliminated.

Before an evaluation committee or other group becomes involved with the technicalities of evaluation, it should consider the context within which the work is to be done. Some key questions should be asked: Is our faculty capable of helping with this particular evaluation? If not, where can we obtain the best help? Is our administration amenable to having a serious evaluation conducted? Will our financial and material resources support a thorough evaluation? Are there interpersonal or other barriers within our school district or community that might thwart our evaluation plans? To an amazing extent, the problems of people affect practice and performance in evaluation.

When evaluation of programs and projects is conducted in schools, it ranges from the highly informal to the highly formal. At a basic level of informality, it consists of judging, estimating, or giving opinions about the extent to which certain changes in school programs have occurred. At the more formal level, it involves carefully collecting and treating data about progress toward prescribed goals. In all circumstances, it has as an important characteristic the collection of evidence of some sort. This evidence may merely indicate that movement has occurred from the beginning to the end of an allotted period of time, or it may indicate the presence of carefully directed, goal-oriented movement. The difference between the two is usually a difference between aimless movement and purposeful action.

Thus the nature of evidence varies with respect to an informality-formality continuum. For instance, an evaluator may judge informally that people's attitudes have changed in a given direction by observing one or two behavioral cues, or he or she may undertake a formal evaluation of attitude change by conducting interviews and observations and by administering attitude inventories, with all instruments having been chosen or developed to suit given purposes. Formality thus implies scholarly care.

Many a planning or evaluation committee, eager to begin evaluating, has moved too fast in its desire to evaluate *something*. False starts can be avoided by arriving at correct answers to questions like the following:

1. What project or program is most in need of evaluation?
2. What degree of support and help are we likely to have in performing our evaluation tasks?
3. How fast need we move in the evaluation process?
4. What are the common pitfalls that we want to avoid?
5. What methods and instruments should we use in our evaluation effort? Are they readily available to us?

Once these basic questions have been answered, other questions of strategy arise:

1. To whom will our findings go?
2. What do we hope will happen as a consequence of putting into operation the project or program we are evaluating?
3. Are there people we can rely on as data sources? If so, who are they?

4. Of what use to us might a "reference drawer" be? (This drawer might contain statements from planners, scholars, boards, study groups, commissions, survey administrators, and regulatory agencies.)
5. What descriptions, charts, and statistics do we need to prepare?

When the time comes to begin, it is important to keep in mind the following characteristics of evaluation.

The Presence of Values and Valuing

One of the characteristics of evaluation is the acknowledged presence of values and valuing. The act of valuing—a conscious recognition and expression of the values that an evaluator holds—is a necessary initial step in the evaluation process. For instance, the Council for Basic Education has valued, in the past, intellectual experience in the three Rs for elementary school children at the expense of certain social and emotional experiences. Accordingly, the Council has encouraged the kind of inquiry that discovers evidence of intellectual rigor. Whenever an evaluation project is initiated by any group, it expresses beliefs the group holds about what is worth evaluating. At the conclusion of the evaluation episode, the investigators make value judgments about the effects of the episode. These value judgments help determine what will be evaluated on subsequent occasions. Sometimes a consortium of people outside the schools give their group an indecipherable name and thus succeed in hiding their identities and their values.

Orientation to Goals

A related characteristic of evaluation is usually orientation to goals. Most evaluators believe that without setting goals one cannot tell much about the nature and direction of a program's progress or achievement. A thorough program of education subscribes to many goals: information getting, understanding, skill development, feeling and perceiving, critical thinking, and attitude change. When goals have been adopted, ways of evaluating their achievement should be considered immediately. Such testing serves a dual purpose: (1) to gauge the clarity of the goals and the feasibility of their attainment and (2) to sort out the evaluation means most likely to register their attainment. Achievement of goals is accomplished by designing experiences that fit, or accord with, the goals; then the effects of experiences can be evaluated with reference to the goals. Consistency of both evaluation devices and learning experiences with an established list of goals is a necessity of good educational planning that is too often ignored.

Incorporation of Norms

To evaluate, one may (and usually should) establish norms, or standards, for judging the quantity and/or quality of an educational accomplishment.

Norms come in different forms to answer different questions: (1) Is the desired behavior present? (2) Is the behavior what it could be, considering factors such as ability, environmental circumstances, and resources? (3) Is the behavior socially desirable? (4) Does the past record suggest that the behavior is suitable for future use? (5) Does the behavior result in the attainment of significant and worthy ends? (6) How much behavioral change is to be anticipated?

Norms are commonly derived from what similar people or similar programs have accomplished in the past. Some norms are not based on comparisons, however; they simply permit judgment of the quantity and quality of accomplishment in a particular educational endeavor. Such norms are suited to particular, even unique, situations. When the same nonstandard norms are used repeatedly, the endeavor is sometimes said to have been "measured against itself." Nonstandard, or criterion-referenced, norms specify levels of task performance and expert judgment that are considered acceptable in specific cases. They are useful, for example, in computer education. Also, they are helpful indicators of status and change in curriculum projects in which the use of standard, customary norms seems inappropriate.

Comprehensiveness

Another characteristic of effective evaluation is comprehensiveness. Evaluation must, as we have seen, be as broad as the goals to which it relates. Making it broad is not easy, a fact indicated by the difficulties one encounters in evaluating changes in attitudes and appreciations. To be comprehensive, evaluation must make use of numerous and varied media, some of which may have to be invented.

Continuity

Still another characteristic of thoroughgoing evaluation is continuity. In most education textbooks, the chapter on evaluation appears at the end of the book. The consequent implication might be that evaluation comes last in an educational enterprise. Actually, it should be frequent and recurrent—continual, if not continuous. It is needed at almost every stage of every enterprise, and it should be accomplished with imagination, skill, and appropriateness.

Diagnostic Worth, Validity, and Reliability

Appropriateness of evaluation suggests a need for two additional, related characteristics—diagnostic worth and validity. Instruments of evaluation must be capable of diagnosing specific aspects of educational situations. In this sense, they should achieve "diagnostic fit." The instruments should also be valid; they should have the ability to describe what they purport to describe. Needless to say, many instruments in use today lack validity and also reliability, which—as applied to the curriculum—consists of the ability to measure the effects of an educational experience accurately on repeated occasions.

Integration of Findings

Finally, evaluation should serve to integrate findings about educational phenomena. The ultimate object of evaluating is *not* to leave data in a diverse and unintegrated state but to combine significant findings so that their real meaning is evident. Organization and interpretation of data thus become important tasks in evaluation, creating that desirable characteristic called integration.

Progress Toward Goals

Inasmuch as most evaluation is concerned with progress toward goals, it is important to know whether, when, how, and in what directions progress is occurring. To this end, criteria of progress like the following need to be established:

1. Are we really moving toward our goals? (*Theme:* perceptibility of movement)
2. How much movement is present? (*Theme:* time and space)
3. How fast is movement occurring? (*Theme:* rate)
4. What, precisely, can be said about direction(s) of movement? (*Theme:* directed and aberrant motion)
5. How does the general movement we have discovered relate to other movements toward change or improvement? (*Theme:* relevance within the whole complex of improvement)

These criteria have implications for the nature and the evaluation of curriculum improvement programs and projects. They imply that such programs and projects should "get somewhere" and should move as far within their allotted life spans as possible. In the United States, we expect movement to be rapid. Movement may not always occur in a straight line, though, because variations in movement may create significant side effects that supply new outlets for study and growth. Fundamental movement, with its variations, almost inevitably relates to other movements, and effects of the whole complex of movements should be seen in perspective.

A Crucial Question: How Fitting Are Our Evaluation Instruments?

When one gets down to where the curriculum is—in the classroom and in its school and community environs—one's thinking must leave behind the mere technology of preparing useful evaluation instruments. The fact is that most instruments we know and use do not gauge elements of teaching and learning that we respect as constituting genuine improvements. If tests and other devices are to relate closely to the curriculum, they must (1) include more of the knowledge and performance that we are to expect from pupils; (2) give pupils more opportunity to create ideas and to solve practical problems; (3) evaluate pupils' higher-order thinking processes; and (4) reflect books read, ideas discussed, essays written, discoveries made, problems solved, art objects created, and music composed—all by the test subjects themselves.

DIMENSIONS AND PHASES OF PROGRAM AND PROJECT EVALUATION

John Bowers describes the sweep of planning for program evaluation as beginning with concerns and questions with which the evaluation might deal and proceeding to a summary of information about the program to be evaluated. Further planning includes three steps: making elements of the program clear, determining priorities for further planning of the evaluation, and arranging for the collection and use of evidence. Each of these planning steps encompasses outcomes anticipated for learners, the nature of curriculum content, the way the content is sequenced, the instructional approach used, and the extent and nature of program support.[12] When an evaluation plan has been finally reviewed, it should be ready to be put into operation.

Some practitioners begin with decision making about whether or not to evaluate. Having decided to proceed, they learn all they can about the nature of the program or project and the setting in which it has developed, about the identities of the persons who will help to make final decisions, and about questions to be answered by the evaluation. Matters of cost, impact on existing school programs, potential effect on pupils, and extent of parental support also are often considered before actual planning of the evaluation process is undertaken.

Somewhere in the planning process, a major question must be answered: How much of a given program or project should be evaluated? This is a question of quantity or scope. It is relevant because many programs and projects are large—too large to be evaluated as thoroughly as one might like.

A parallel question is one of quality of the evaluation: What goals are being highlighted in the evaluation because attainment of these goals is believed to ensure the worth of the program or project?

The Dimension of Quantity

Programs are larger than projects because projects are meant to fit into the general theme of things, each project being part of a program (see Endnote 1). An important decision about programs is whether one should elect to evaluate the whole program comprehensively yet superficially, or to concentrate on carefully selected aspects of the program for thorough evaluation. Most projects, on the other hand, can be evaluated as a whole, but the series of steps in the evaluation is carefully limited and defined.

Evaluating a Whole Program

The amount or portion of a program to evaluate is a matter for careful consideration. It is possible to evaluate programs generally. Such evaluation is often of a survey sort and is necessarily superficial. Nevertheless, the survey helps participants in curriculum improvement see "the whole forest" in which they work. When the goals of a program have been determined, criteria under general headings such as those proposed by the Association for Supervision and Curriculum Development should be prepared with direct reference to the goals. Under several general headings—Educational Objectives, Role Perception, Organizational Structure, Group Action and Morale, Experimentation, Communication, Resources, and Evaluation—the association has listed specific criteria of effective leadership for program improvement. Criteria noted under the heading Group Action and Morale are typical of the specific criteria that appear under the general headings:

Group Action and Morale

1. Administrative officials encourage cooperative planning and deliberation by school staff and other groups.
2. Groups evidence movement toward mutually held goals, productivity in achieving these goals, and maintenance of group solidarity.
3. Individuals and subgroups evidence high morale as they work together.
4. Human relations skills are in evidence in all aspects of the school's functioning.
5. The staff acts rationally in resolving issues and in seeking solutions to problems.
6. Qualities that enhance interaction of persons in the group may be described in terms such as initiative, originality, communication, empathy, cooperation, understanding, cohesiveness, morale, productivity.
7. Decisions regarding program changes are cooperatively made on the basis of the most objective data obtainable.
8. The total staff is encouraged toward realizing its potential.
9. Teachers encountering teaching or other difficulties feel free to seek assistance.[13]

Criteria may be made more general than these. For example, only five general criteria were stated and justified by reference to educational literature in evaluating effects of the International Paper Company Foundation's assistance to secondary education in six school districts:

Criterion I: In the total context of the teaching-learning situation, there should be provided, through varied subject matter, materials, and methods, opportunities for individual pupils to acquire habits, skills, information, and attitudes which will aid them to become contributing citizens in a democracy.

Criterion II: The organizational, administrative, and supervisory pattern, through cooperative planning, implementation, and evaluative procedures, promotes the continuous improvement of the school program and the competence of the professional staff.

Criterion III: The members of the professional staff display a unity of purpose, a sense of worth, and an appreciation of their efforts, and those of others, in the improvement of the school program.

Criterion IV: Student personnel services should result in a continuous process of pupils, parents, teachers, counselors, and other specialists working together to assist each pupil in achieving greater self-understanding, self-direction, and self-realization in a democratic society.

Criterion V: The school, through community study, interpretation of the school program, use of community resources, and working closely with lay citizens, strives to become an integral part of community life.[14]

When criteria are too numerous, their use in evaluation becomes an unduly protracted affair. Professor Howard Gardner and his aides, working in Harvard University's Project Zero, appear to have emphasized pertinence as a criterion. They have found that standardized testing, which is so useful in evaluation of achievement in the usual subject matter, should be replaced with other evaluation means when one is assessing imaginative writing, musical competence, and artistic skill.[15] For these and other achievement areas, interesting activities need to be devised to engage pupils' interest and effort over periods of time. Here is the proper locus for portfolios, personal records of performance, commentary by observers, and statements of where the activities may lead next. Of course, the first thought of beleaguered teachers may well be "Who has time to make fancy evaluation instruments?" As school leaders become more conscious of the need for "evaluation fit," they will perhaps seek help in instrument making and will in turn give help to teachers in classrooms and in committees.

Evaluating Component Elements of a Program

Despite the temptations and dangers, evaluators often seek to evaluate component elements of a program in depth. Here, their purpose is not merely to avoid the potential sloppiness or incompleteness of whole-program evaluation or to avoid expending time and energy. They seek to "cut away clean" a section of the program so that they may evaluate it with care, then possibly isolate another section for evaluation. Each section or part has, presumably, a peculiar identity or separateness about it. Sometimes evaluators make their evaluation of component elements first and then go on to evaluate the program as a whole. Evaluating a portion of the program may provide a slanted view of the whole, but careful concentration on it can yield more valid returns than whole-program evaluation usually does.

Evaluation of parts of programs has to do with the usefulness of subject matter in achieving desired results, usefulness of materials, effectiveness of school organization and groupings of pupils, and the worth of the process by which given programs are conducted. Another way of subdividing the total evaluation task is to evaluate just learners, or educational environments, or learning, or instruction. Evaluating learners consists of studying pupil achievement and performance. Evaluating educational environments deals with characteristics of the curriculum and of school and community influences on learning in the school. Evaluation of learning is a study of changes in pupil behavior as a consequence of instruction. Evaluation of instruction includes study of pupil characteristics within a set of environmental circumstances as they affect learning. Instead of dealing directly with questions of learning and instruction, some evaluators have tried gauging programs in terms of their effects on teacher performance or their effects on teachers' attitudes toward their work.

One example of the evaluation of a part of a total program is the evaluation of a component element in a new reading program: the series of reading materials used in the program. Questions to be answered include the following: How useful is the series in helping to achieve the program goals? With what segments of the pupil population is the series most effective? How does the series compare with the miscellaneous reading materials used in the program when the contributions of all the materials to the attainment of program goals are assessed?

A program element often needing evaluation is the effectiveness of the delivery system. The question here is not "How effective has the program proved to be?" but "How effectively has the program been put into place?" To answer the latter question, evaluators should begin by selecting indicators of effective delivery. Two of the most common and satisfactory kinds of indicators are observation of applicable teacher behaviors and observation of applicable pupil behaviors. For example, what does the teacher do to offer alternative instructional approaches, to connect new learning with former learning, to stimulate pupils to action, to supply a variety of correctives, to give pupils opportunities to show their increasing abilities? Meanwhile, what do the pupils do to demonstrate enthusiasm and involvement, to ask for help when it's needed, to show ability to solve their own classroom problems, to indicate mastery of project learnings?[16] Balanced use of indicators like these can result in a complex of findings that helps to explain the effectiveness or ineffectiveness of a program.

Evaluating a Curriculum Project

A curriculum project, as defined here, is a part of a whole curriculum program, but it is a special part. For example, the curriculum program in District K had been in operation for years. In 1976, the program included the activity of four task forces and two study groups. Suddenly, in 1977, funds were made available by the state department of education for a work dear to the hearts of members of the program's steering committee. The steering committee voted unanimously to have its project designers plan a special project, which was funded handsomely by the state. The special project was considered to be a part of District K's ongoing curriculum improvement program, but it was a special part with its own goals, ground rules, personnel, equipment, materials, and funding. Because of requirements made by the funding agency, it had to be evaluated separately from the program as a whole.

The process often used in evaluating a curriculum project can best be expressed in a series of steps. Assuming that needs assessment—which helps to justify the project—has already occurred, the first major step is to define the goals of the project. This step usually has two components—making a workable statement of the goals of the project and identifying quantitative measures to be used in evaluating performance relative to the goals. Great care is needed in stating the project goals. The Educational Testing Service has found that the goals as first stated by program and project planners often bear only a slight resemblance to what the program or project in fact does.[17]

The second step in the process is to collect the data necessary for determining the project's effectiveness. The data may include findings about pupil characteristics; about the nature of the project and the processes used in it (its duration and the varied treatments it provides groups of pupils, for example); about the cost of resources committed to the project; and about pupil performance as revealed, for instance, by standardized test scores and dropout rates.

The third and final step is to determine the cost-effectiveness of the project. Here, levels of progress toward achieving the project's goals are noted against amounts of resources used in reaching these levels. If pouring in additional resources produces no better results, the maximum extent of desirable resource input has been reached.

Recently, two developments have affected the relative emphases on these three steps. Charges that the schools have failed have led to increased concentration on pupil learning, or the lack thereof, and the shortage of funds for special projects has led to more intense dollar-watching. Factors like these can readily affect in turn the nature of projects chosen for attention.

The Dimension of Quality

Some Pertinent Steps

Clearly, improving the quality of evaluation is a major need. Reliable evaluation data will help the curriculum worker determine whether to continue a program or abandon it. In the hope of ensuring quality in evaluation procedures, evaluators have sometimes used a sequence of steps:

1. The goals of the program are specified, along with the desired outcomes and alternative ways in which these outcomes might be achieved.
2. A sample of pupils is selected for the evaluation study. These pupils should be representative of all the pupils who will be exposed to the program.
3. Pupils in the sample are "measured" to determine their status with respect to relevant characteristics. For example, their levels of achievement are sought, and their learning skills gauged. Since pupil characteristics go *into* the evaluation design, they are called *input variables.*
4. The program is tried with the sample of pupils. Since alternative ways of proceeding are built into the program for the sake of evaluating it, portions of the sample of pupils will receive separate "treatments."
5. The effects of the alternative treatments are now gauged. This monitoring goes on while the program is under way and is often referred to as *formative evaluation.* Evaluation also occurs at the conclusion of the treatment process. This is *summative evaluation.* Evaluation of both kinds is accomplished through tests, inventories, interviews, planned observations, and other means.
6. The results, or *outputs,* are reviewed, and conclusions are drawn.
7. The conclusions dictate what shall be done with all or part of the program. The program may be continued in its present form, modified according to what has been discovered in the evaluation process, or abandoned. If it is continued without change, or modified, it may well be subjected to future evaluation.

Prior to the start of a program or project, judgmental data supplied by experts can be helpful in determining the probable worth of the proposal. Experts are asked to express in writing their views of the proposal, their views are assembled and a consensus formed, and modifications are made in the proposal to conform to the consensus. The modified proposal is then returned to the experts for final commentary.[18]

Formative evaluation has proved to be an important resource in refining evaluation procedures. The quality of such procedures is improved more by formative evaluation than by summative evaluation not only because formative evaluation is involved in the development of the project but also because summative evaluation does not directly deal with the subtle events and circumstances that appear en route to the conclusion of the change process.

Formative evaluation occurs prominently at three stages: the stage of needs assessment, the stage of program planning, and the stage of program implementation, which is called *process evaluation.*[19] Summative evaluation is almost always thought of as occurring after the actual implementation. Accordingly, it must be comprehensive and thorough. Interestingly, however, summative evaluation can also take place during the formative period, as sections or phases of the program or project come to their natural conclusions.

Difficulties in Managing Variables

Within the process of evaluation, there are three classes of variables: input variables—what pupils bring with them; output variables—what pupils have when they come away from instruction; and treatment variables—teaching methods, emphases in subject matter, class size, characteristics of fellow pupils, and characteristics of teachers. When output variables relate directly to the objectives of the instruction, they are called *criterion measures*. The three classes of variables interact. Thus pupil characteristics (input) affect school climate (treatment); differing methods of teaching (treatment) affect pupil achievement (output); and pupils with given characteristics (input) succeed in a given project (output). The complications are startling.[20]

Specialists in educational evaluation can usually find variables in need of control. For instance, a commentator on a social studies project in St. Louis identified eight variables and related difficulties that the project managers did not take into account: differences among districts in which the project was tried, differences among participating teachers, the effects of administrative liaison, goal ambiguity, conflicts in teacher roles, inadequacy of conceptual skills, complexities in administering the project, and defects in conceptual design.[21]

In other projects, the results could conceivably be affected by involvement of given personnel as opposed to involvement of other potential participants, the evaluation process chosen from among alternative processes, and the particular means used to infuse the evaluation outcomes into decision making. Obviously, managers of projects must seek to control all the variables and other procedural factors they can.

A Variety of Other Treatment Difficulties

Beyond trouble with interacting variables, other difficulties appear in what would seem to be a neat evaluation sequence. First, it is hard to assign pupils randomly to the various treatments. If the lists of pupils assigned to the different treatments are not closely comparable, clashes occurring between learning environment and pupil characteristics affect outcomes. Second, it is hard to specify treatment conditions that effectively take into consideration the impact of the environment. Third, troubles with tests will appear if tests that do not measure given outcomes are applied just because they are available. Fourth, when data are collected in grouped form but analyzed on an across-the-board basis, the analysis hides important conditions and exceptions. Fifth, there is often the *Hawthorne effect,* resulting from the elation induced by novelty, which covers the real significance of the effort. Sixth, long-range effects of that which has been evaluated necessarily remain obscure. Finally, the nagging thought remains that funds expended for the program might have been better spent in another way.[22]

Improving the Process of Evaluation

Hulda Grobman has suggested that program evaluators take a series of process steps to achieve better evaluation. These steps include:

1. Using tests that are valid and reliable and making one's own tests when necessary
2. Reviewing materials of the program so as to be thoroughly familiar with them
3. Making visits to the sites of programs, some visits being unstructured and others being for feedback of precise data
4. Asking teachers what they think of programs in which they are involved
5. Using questionnaires wisely to gather data
6. Utilizing small-scale tryouts of evaluation ideas[23]

As C. M. Lindvall and Richard C. Cox point out, evaluation can become a process tool of worth in ongoing efforts to improve the curriculum, and it can emphasize the importance of evaluating instruction with reference to individual pupils in an attempt to distinguish between individuals who succeed and individuals who do not.[24]

Any plan of evaluation should, first of all, be workable. To be workable, it should be technically adequate. Its worth should be considered in terms of four categories: the philosophical, the psychological, the social, and the subject related. Thus a viable plan makes contact with the foundations of the curriculum discussed in the initial chapters of this book. In addition, any viable plan must be politically feasible.

Evaluators are necessarily interested in outcomes. Decker F. Walker and J. Schaffarzick analyzed curriculum projects dating from 1959 to 1972, emphasizing relative outcomes in the form of pupils' subject matter achievement under old and new curriculum plans. They found that each curriculum tended to be superior in its own terms and that students' patterns of test performance were different under differing plans, reflecting mastery of subject matter that had been included and highlighted.[25] Their findings are reminiscent of the strict test-test-test philosophy that has afflicted curriculum evaluation.

The evaluation process can often be improved by recognizing that tests designed to measure the attainment of goals may overlook positive outcomes of a curriculum treatment that were not foreseen in the goals specified at the outset of the project. For this reason, some of the prominent curriculum thinkers since 1950 have turned to goal-free evaluation. The effect has been to instill freedom and imagination into the curriculum planning process.

The evaluation process can be improved also by collecting data other than those that are specific to pupil achievement on tests—data on pupils' motor skills and attitudes, on effects of the project on teachers and schools, and on the appropriateness of given instructional objectives. Some highly informal data may prove to be extremely worthwhile.

Still other data about outcomes may be derived from sideline experimentation done by teachers as they depart from the strict terms of the project, from reexamining the design of the project in light of the participants' experience with it, and from reconsidering what is educationally valuable or even acceptable in projects of the kind. Evaluation of curriculum programs and projects must not be confused with evaluation of instruction, however. Evaluation of programs and projects opens the process to include outcomes well beyond those associated merely with pupil achievement as gauged by tests, inventories, and other routine measures.

Accumulated evidence concerning what makes for really effective programs suggests that staff expectations and morale need to be high and that teachers need to have considerable responsibility for decision making about matters affecting teacher and pupil learning and also about inservice education of staff. Further, the school needs to be an orderly place presided over by a capable leader and guided by a clear set of goals.[26] Since they were originally formulated, these conclusions have been reinforced again and again.

SOME SAMPLE EVALUATION MODELS

An evaluation model is a widely applicable format in which the major elements in a program or project evaluation are expressed in such a way as to make their functions and interrelationships clear. Samples of evaluation models often referred to in the literature follow.

The Eight Year Study

Probably the oldest of the oft-mentioned evaluation models is the Eight Year Study, which has been referred to in previous chapters. The purpose of the study was to determine whether secondary school curriculum could be freed from domination by colleges. The study attracted attention—though not as much attention as it should have—because it was ambitious and extensive and because the curricula of high schools were being criticized for being so monolithic. Within the thirty high schools included in the study, questionnaires, tests, inventories, scales, logs, and checklists were administered. These and other instruments were designed and used as part of a seven-step format suggested chiefly by Ralph Tyler, who directed the research:

1. Establishment of goals or objectives
2. Classification of the objectives
3. Definition of the objectives in behavioral terms
4. Identification of situations in which achievement of the objectives could be shown
5. Selection or creation of measurement procedures
6. Collection of data about pupil performance
7. Comparison of findings with the stated objectives

The seventh step in this format could lead to revision of the objectives, thus making the evaluation process a live, cyclical one.

The Provus Evaluation Model

A second noteworthy model was known initially as the Pittsburgh Evaluation Model. It was devised by Malcolm Provus to evaluate projects funded under the Elementary-Secondary Education Act. Using a taxonomy of program content developed by Robert E. Stake, Provus identified five stages of evaluation.

Stage I has as its task obtaining a definition of the program based on the program content taxonomy. The steps within it are represented by certain questions: Is the program defined? If not, is a corrective action adequately defined? Is the corrective action installed? If not, is a corrective action defined for securing installation? Is the corrective action so defined now installed? The theme of Stage I is, then, *definition of the program.*

The theme of Stage II is *installation of the program.* Concerning implementation of this theme, the same questions that formed the steps in Stage I may be asked. Stage III has as its theme *process.* Here, the key question is "Are the enabling objectives being met?" The theme of Stage IV is *product* or *outcomes,* with the key question being "Are the terminal products achieved?" Finally, Stage V consists of *cost-benefit analysis.*

Practitioners have further clarified Provus's five steps or stages as relating respectively to (1) the quality of the curriculum design; (2) the faithfulness or care with which the designed program is installed; (3) the processes used in installing and implementing the program; (4) the products or results of the program; and (5) the cost of the program considered against the benefits derived.

The Provus plan has been called a discrepancy model because it compares performance with standards to determine whether a discrepancy exists between the two. This model, as complicated and systems oriented as it looks at first, has the advantage of appealing to practicing school administrators who wish to gather "hard" evidence.[27]

Stake's Congruence-Contingency Model

Robert Stake has said that evaluation is not complete unless three categories of data are made available. The first of these is titled *antecedents,* or bases from which one starts. Included in this category are data on pupil and teacher characteristics, the curriculum to be evaluated, facilities and materials, the organization of the school, and the community context. The second category is labeled *transactions.* Transactions have to do with time allotment, sequence of steps, social climate, and communication flow. The third category, *outcomes,* encompasses pupil learnings in the form of understandings, skills, and attitudes, as well as the effects of the program or project on teachers and the school.

The term *congruence* in the name of the model refers to the degree of agreement between what was desired and what has actually come to pass. *Contingency* applies to the relationship between one variable and another—for example, between time allotment and the learning of skills.[28]

The CIPP Model

A very significant model is Daniel L. Stufflebeam's CIPP, an acronym for Context, Input, Process, and Product. From the original CIPP, there developed CDPP, which represents Context, Design, Process, and Product. CIPP and CDPP have been twin bases for several other program evaluation plans. In the case of CDPP, the term *context* refers to investigation of pupil needs and related problems, as well as other possible context factors. *Design* suggests program development in which money, personnel qualifications, facilities, scheduling, and the like are instrumental. *Process* is actually in-process quality control monitoring of the program. *Product* means measurement of the effectiveness of the program at its conclusion.[29]

The EPIC Model

Another well-known model is EPIC, or Evaluative Programs for Innovative Curriculums. The model is pictured as a cube, one panel of which is *behavior,* which is subdivided into the cognitive, the affective, and the psychomotor. A second panel is *instruction,* which has within it organization, content, method, facilities, and cost. A third panel is *institution,* which has the following parts: student, teacher, administrator, educational specialist, family, and community. The users of EPIC confront five categories of variables: Category I—prediction sources, calling for examination of types of instruction; Category II—descriptive variables, including instructional techniques and institutional constraints; Category III—objectives; Category IV—behavior, instruction, and institution, as specified in the cube; and Category V—criteria of effectiveness, requiring analysis of all data collected.[30]

Eisner's Educational Connoisseurship and Educational Criticism Model

Elliot Eisner goes beyond the usual, routine variables in his data gathering. His educational connoisseurship and criticism model calls for deeper, more wide-ranging observation, the results of which can be expressed in a written statement. This statement does more, however, than merely describe: It provides interpretation and appraisal. The interpretation gives reasons or causes for what has happened, and the appraisal consists of a judgment of the educational value of happenings in the program or project. Eisner believes that written statements can be adapted for different categories of readers without reducing the accuracy of what is said. Though Eisner's model displeases some traditionalists in evaluation because it does not follow customary methodological procedures, it does breathe freshness into an activity that can be considered stale and boring.[31]

Eisner, coming from a background in the arts, refers to connoisseurship as the art of appreciating events that have educational significance.[32] He would use criticism to make appreciation public. To be worthwhile, he says, criticism should have "referential adequacy," which is proper grounding in experience. It should also possess "structural corroboration," or evidence that the parts of the criticism fit together. Eisner's evaluators would analyze pupils' work very carefully, describe in detail what happens in classrooms, and try to capture the spirit pervading classroom and school. Always, the emphasis would be on the quality rather than on the measurable quantity of learning and interaction.

What the Models Reveal About the Evaluation Process

Obviously, evaluation of programs and projects is a decidedly complicated operation. Evaluation specialists usually say that well-prepared evaluators are needed to perform difficult evaluation tasks. But this point of view should not discourage young curriculum workers from learning all they can about the evaluation process or from trying evaluation procedures that look sensible and promising.

It would be convenient if evaluators in school systems could use one or more standard models and rest assured that these would fit their situations. Unfortunately, each available model was originally devised to meet the demands of a particular situation. Therefore models prove useful mainly in offering suggestions as to how evaluators might solve their own problems of design and implementation.

All of the above-mentioned models except Eisner's are constructed similarly in that they follow presumably logical steps that are to be taken in sequence. Some of them borrow steps from the procedure called *systems analysis,* which follows an eight-step pattern. The steps are stating need, defining objectives, indicating major constraints, developing a number of alternative systems, selecting the best alternative or alternatives, putting a chosen alternative into operation, evaluating the resultant system, and receiving feedback to create modifications.

Eisner's model, on the other hand, is suggestive of the work of the phenomenologists, who place confidence in describing phenomena in various areas of experience. Phenomenological inquiry as applied to curriculum evaluation generally calls for seeing events in a program or project through the eyes of the participants rather than through those of outside observers. Thus pupils, teachers, and administrators who are involved in the action become the judges. To gather data from these people, it is necessary to use interviews, autobiographies, questionnaires, and similar instruments. In a final report, the data are organized and summarized as their nature seems to require; then they are interpreted.

Recently, standardized tests have lost some of the favor they once enjoyed as evaluation instruments. A group known by the nickname Fair Test (the National Center for Fair and Open Testing) has advocated reduction in the number of standardized tests that measure "knowledge, laundry-list style." In response to their own similar thinking, the evaluators serving the National Assessment of Educational Progress have shifted some of their emphasis from traditional objective test items to performance-based features like open-ended questions and writing samples.[33] Similarly, the Scholastic Assessment Test, which has replaced the Scholastic Aptitude Test, includes, in the language of the popular press, fewer "guess items" and additional "figure it out yourself" questions.[34]

Apparently, a distinction needs to be made between what Michael Scriven has called "payoff evaluation" and fundamental "intrinsic evaluation."[35] Payoff evaluation answers the question "How well does this program or project achieve its goals?" To provide an answer, evaluators may need hard data derived from careful testing. Intrinsic evaluation, however, answers the question "How good for learners is this program or project?" Determining the essential worth of a curriculum design, together with its long-term effects, involves more than testing and inventorying. Awareness of ongoing events, observation, appreciation, interpretation, and criticism become key terms and objects in the evaluation process. The consequent evaluation results, though less exactly gauged than results of a more rigorous system, produce data of a different kind.

The United States has been lagging behind a number of other developed nations in "loosening" its evaluation schemata. Since the early 1970s, nations such as Australia have been replacing some of their comprehensive, externally developed examinations with teacher-moderated tests administered school by school. In this way, Australian schools are tending away from assessment that culminates in comparison of marks and grades and are tending toward measuring achievement to chart the progress of individual pupils. The Australians, the English, and others have found it possible to use criterion-referenced tests in association with school-based curricula. Their procedures usually consist of (1) defining objectives clearly, (2) making or adapting evaluation measures that suit the objectives, (3) stating acceptable standards of achievement, and (4) saying how well learners must achieve to meet the standards. Under this plan, the final object is to develop evaluation schemes that describe what pupils can do, thereby making pupils more obviously central in the teaching-learning process.[36]

None of the evaluation models above, with the exception of Eisner's, involves this kind of informal evaluation. School personnel who have used such evaluation point to the importance of enlisting bright teachers who are able and willing to help create new evaluation devices that fit the curricula they are involved in planning. If teachers are to become the ultimate professionals, they will probably need to become involved in the invention, the development, and the classroom application of the so-called newer evaluation media.

Evaluation models can prove useful in making clear distinctions among the intended curriculum, the implemented curriculum, and the attained curriculum—that is, distinctions among "what we thought we wanted to do," "what we tried to do," and "what our pupils actually learned." In a number of developed nations, recognition of the differences in individual pupils' learning achievement has pointed the way to systems of school organization like the one that has been tried in the Netherlands. In effect, the Dutch system has embraced nine distinct curricula, each with its accompanying evaluation means:

1. Pre-university education
2. Higher general education
3. Intermediate general education
4. Elementary technical education
5. Elementary nautical education
6. Elementary domestic science education
7. Elementary agricultural education
8. Elementary tradesman's education
9. Elementary commercial education

Apparently, even the nine curricula have proved insufficient. A combination of pre-university education and higher general education has been made; so too have other combinations.[37]

According to a commonly accepted philosophy of education in the United States, such an arrangement is discriminatory and therefore highly undemocratic. One must, however, give the Dutch credit for trying to face a problem that pervades elementary and secondary education everywhere: the problem of dealing with individual differences that result in varied degrees of achievement.

TOWARD THE AGONY AND THE ECSTASY

To comprehend the joys and the hardships of putting evaluation models into action, we need to see in full the application of a particular model. The model chosen for this purpose is the Analysis Package, which was developed for use in New York City public schools.

The Analysis Package emphasizes cost-benefit, or cost-effectiveness, analysis. The steadily increasing popularity of the computer has made analysis of cost effectiveness more and more feasible. The Analysis Package, which is also known as ANAPAC, is a computer program "designed to perform a basic statistical and cost-effectiveness analysis of data from educational programs and to display the findings of the analysis in a narrative format for the use of nonstatisticians."[38] The evaluation process is divided into three steps: defining program goals, collecting pertinent data, and analyzing cost-effectiveness.

In the ANAPAC system, goals are stated with care. A distinction is made between program elements that are policy issues and those that are matters to be evaluated. The ANAPAC evaluators do not determine objectives; rather, they are interested in how well a program achieves its objectives. They prefer objectives that are stated in terms of tangible results—higher reading ability, lower dropout rates, or improved attendance. They believe that "qualitative objectives are legitimate goals of an educational program, but to be useful they should be defined as precisely as possible."[39] A "qualitative" objective might be improving the self-image of minority groups.

A second aspect of defining program goals is identification of measures. This might include standardized achievement test results and more informal data like degree of attendance and participation in classes or use of library and other school facilities. The evaluators recognize that the data gathered will have varying degrees of "tightness," ranging from the results of administering valid tests to the judgments of educators. They believe that whatever measures they decide to use will be "acceptable indices of a program's goals only if the appropriate policy makers accept them as such. To insure acceptance, the evaluator should discuss the measures he plans to use with the policy makers."[40]

The next phase of ANAPAC evaluation is collecting pertinent data, which fall into four categories:

1. *Pupil characteristics,* including ethnic and socioeconomic background, age, sex, behavioral patterns, maturity, aptitude levels, and achievement levels
2. *Program factors,* among them the extent and nature of treatment, length and variation of treatment, and data about the program staff
3. *Cost factors,* including the cost of all resources committed to the program— salaries and fringe benefits for staff, training expenses, equipment, materials, use of space, rentals, leases, consultant fees, custodial costs, and administrative costs
4. *Performance measures,* such as test scores, grade averages, rates of attendance, promotion data, and dropout rates, and also genuinely subjective data

Recognizing the difficulty of controlling variables, the evaluators seek to identify single factors serving as "proxies" for related variables. "For example, average program treatment time (e.g., two hours per week) might be an acceptable proxy for all the factors which constitute the overall program treatment."[41]

As a final major step, ANAPAC comes to the analysis of cost-effectiveness. Here, an effort is made to trace the relationship between gains in performance achieved by pupils in a program and the resources that have been put into that program. Cost-effectiveness can be attained by minimizing resources to achieve a stated result or by maximizing the result gained with given resources. Estimated levels of progress toward achieving the program's objectives can be calculated for different levels of input resources. Points of diminishing returns might be found—the points at which addition of resources becomes fruitless.

Example: The Use of ANAPAC

As an example, consider cost-effectiveness evaluation of a mathematics laboratory program. The objective of the program is to improve pupil computational skills as indicated by gains on standardized

Table 6-1

Group	Per-pupil cost	Achievement gain	Gain over control	Cost-effectiveness ratio
Control	—	4 months	—	—
Two-hour	$200	8 months	4 months	$50
Four-hour	$400	9 months	5 months	$80

achievement tests. During a five-month period, two plans are used for administering the program to two experimental groups of pupils. One experimental group uses the laboratory two hours a week; the other experimental group uses it four hours a week. A third group of pupils— considered the control group—receives no instruction in the laboratory. Assume the average cost per pupil for each hour of laboratory instruction to be $100 and the average gains in achievement for the control, two-hour, and four-hour groups to be four months, eight months, and nine months, respectively (see Table 6-1). At a cost of $200 per pupil, the two-hour group showed a gain of four months over the control group (which obviously had no cost for this specific instruction). The four-hour group produced a gain of one month over the two-hour group, at an additional cost of $200 per pupil. Persons making policy might well decide that the four-hour group had not gained enough in relative terms to warrant the extra expenditure of $200 per pupil. Two hours in the laboratory seems to bring worthwhile results. Therefore, as funds permit, more and more pupils might be offered a two-hour laboratory experience.

ANAPAC states a cost-effectiveness ratio that is calculated by dividing the gain of each experimental group beyond the gain of the control group into the experimental group's per-pupil cost. The cost-effectiveness figure (called a ratio) for the two-hour group is $50 for each month of achievement gain (a four-month gain divided into $200). For the four-hour group, the ratio is $80 for each month of gain (a five-month gain divided into $400). The ratio is used for comparing the effectiveness of different treatment methods within the same program. It may also be used for comparing the effectiveness of quite different programs which, nevertheless, have the same objectives and use the same performance measures.

Issues Concerning Process
Throughout the preceding discussion, the emphasis has been on methodology grounded in experimental research. Some significant problems in attempts to evaluate projects and programs come from evaluators' unwillingness to relate cause and effect by means other than those used in experimental research. M. C. Wittrock asks whether we have "the methodological knowledge to esti-

mate the cause and effect relations in naturalistic situations, such as instruction in schools." He reports a study by Fellows of the Center for Advanced Study in the Behavioral Sciences, Stanford, California, in which the literature of sociology, econometrics, statistics, political science, and psychology yielded cues about the uses of non-experimental methods in making causal inferences.[42]

An approach known as path analysis—the computing of path coefficients for each chain or network of variables thought to be influencing one another in a causal way—has been tried. The search must continue for ways of collecting the hard data needed to make instructional decisions intelligently and confidently without consuming excessive amounts of time in trying to establish causal relationships.

A different issue raised by the ANAPAC method is whether project and program evaluators should do more than describe changes that occur in pupils' learning and school situations. Specifically, should they also judge whether or not the changes are acceptable? Numbers of evaluators believe that the judging of worth and acceptability need not be left to the policy makers referred to by ANAPAC.[43] This is an issue in educational decision making that social forces will continue to influence.

Evaluators are becoming more and more interested in varied evidences of pupil performance for later consideration and assessment. Joseph Waters and Howard Gardner, working in the APPLE Project at Harvard University, have found portfolios useful to this end. They note, using a science exhibit as a case in point, that pupils' contributions can be documented by saving and analyzing photographs, reading journal entries, and studying audio and video tapes of people's interactions about features of the exhibit. Evaluation procedures will be refined as they are used repeatedly.[44]

SITUATION 6-1

Evaluating an Entire Curriculum Program

To comply with terms of the Colorado Accountability Act, the Mapleton Public Schools took several steps in evaluating the curriculum program. These steps included

1. Performing a needs assessment survey, in part by applying a needs assessment questionnaire
2. Using tests and inventories to find a "satisfaction index" and priority rank scores for each curriculum area in elementary and secondary education
3. Collecting demographic information[45]

What else might be included in a system-wide program evaluation for the purpose of demonstrating the school system's accountability?

SITUATION 6-2

Fitting an Evaluation Scheme to a Curriculum Plan

School faculties inevitably include people of differing points of view about learners, learning, worthwhile curricula, and evaluation schemes that work.

The ten-member Program Evaluation Committee at Beakerville High School is meeting today. You have been invited to attend the meeting as a nonparticipating guest. During the meeting, you hear some dramatic and memorable remarks:

Member A: Why evaluate? Some of the kids we are trying to teach shouldn't be in school in the first place. After all, you can't make silk purses from sows' ears.

Member B: Whatever we ask the youngsters in tests and examinations, they should be capable of answering. I'm in favor of admitting students to courses whether they seem to be ready for them or not.

Member C: What kind of school will this become if we keep on making simple projects of the kind we're expected to evaluate?

Member D: As a committee, we have to be tough. That means the evaluation items we approve have to be hard, hard, hard!

If you were the chairperson of this committee, what could you possibly do to get agreement about anything important?

Could you bypass some of the obvious differences in philosophy to arrive at the crucial matter of making an evaluation scheme to fit the project? Explain.

IMPLEMENTING MODELS AND PLANS

In a field as complex as curriculum evaluation, it is not surprising that procedures have had to be developed for implementing models and plans. The implementation prepares the way for further thinking about how programs and projects are to be designed, altered, and extended. It may begin with reporting and describing events that have already occurred and/or are about to occur.

Preparing Written Materials

Routinely, the report of an evaluation might follow an outline like the one below:

I. A summary statement of the nature of the program or project
II. The purpose(s) of the evaluation

III. Basic information concerning the program or project
   A. Origin
   B. Goals
   C. Description
   D. The population of pupils involved
   E. Faculty members and other persons involved
IV. Description of the evaluation study
   A. Evaluation design
   B. Measures of outcome(s)
      1. Evaluation instruments used
      2. Procedures used in collecting data
   C. Other evaluation measures used, with purpose(s) stated
V. Results of the evaluation study
   A. Formal evaluation results (outcomes and all else)
   B. Informal evaluation results
VI. Commentary and conclusions regarding the evaluation results
VII. Cost-benefit analysis
   A. Costs of the program or project in dollars and other terms
   B. Benefits of the program or project in educational terms and dollar terms
VIII. Recommendations concerning the destiny of the program or project
   A. In the immediate future
   B. In the long run

King and Thompson have pointed out that very often evaluation reports are not read. Nevertheless, school administrators seem to believe that reports have real communication value.[46] Certainly, those who write evaluation reports need to be cautioned that people who read them differ widely as to the information they want and need and also as to their ability to understand statistical and other complicated forms of presentation. Reporters can do nothing about the criteria people use in judging the programs and projects described, but they can present information clearly and concisely.[47]

Reports take many forms: descriptive writing, graphics, recommendation or suggestion lists, case studies, test score summarizations, questions and answers, multimedia presentations, and, of course, oral presentations. Sometimes reports combine several methods, as in the case of a report prepared concerning Minnesota's Technology Demonstration Program.[48]

The ERIC Clearinghouse on Educational Management has prepared a compendium of manuals and handbooks on conducting program evaluation. The compendium refers to official publications from Oklahoma, California, Wisconsin, Australia, the Los Angeles Unified School District, and elsewhere.[49] For example, the Oklahoma State Department of Education has prepared a handbook to guide the review, evaluation, and revision of mathematics programs at school and school district levels.[50]

Varying Ways of Gathering Data

Another way of extending models and plans is to open the evaluation process to different ways of gathering data. Marlow Ediger has prepared a brief report titled "How Should Student Achievement Be Determined?" In it, he suggests three methods of appraisal: (1) measurement, (2) problem solving, and (3) decision making. Measurement requires objectivity, presumably attainable by means of achievement tests. Problem solving places learners in active roles in which their efforts and work can be observed. Decision making emphasizes learners' involvement in choosing among alternatives and finding ways of completing tasks, with both product and process subject to observation and analysis.[51]

To assess the quality of school improvement strategies, a Pennsylvania school district tried collecting data by means of a so-called microanalytic case study approach. Attention was given to gathering case data about school staffs' understanding of project goals, assessment of school climate, and discussions and action proposals made by curriculum committees.[52]

The Greater Albany (Oregon) Public School District's music teachers developed their own tests to determine how successfully pupils in the third, fifth, eighth, and eleventh grades were achieving and performing in elements of the music program. The tests for grades three and five centered on musical notation, listening skills, and design, whereas the tests for grades eight and eleven dealt with interpreting notation, listening skills, and the relationship of music to people's historical development.[53]

The task force for evaluating the success of Chapter 1 activities in the School District of Philadelphia chose "indicators" as a basis for making policy decisions to guide future action. The indicators defined by the task force included a pupil stability indicator, an age-grade appropriateness indicator, a pupil exit-return rate indicator, a percentage of success indicator, and a standardized curriculum support indicator for analyzing scores from curriculum-referenced items on city-wide tests.[54]

Customizing Evaluation Instruments

A further method of extending evaluation models and plans consists of customizing standardized tests and other instruments that have been produced commercially. A prime example of customization has appeared in the New York City Public Schools, where a curriculum-related mathematics test was created in 1986 and revised in 1987. The source of test items was the Metropolitan Achievement Test.[55] The items were altered as needed to suit the evaluators' purpose.

Tests and other instruments need not be revised to be customized. That is, they can be related to a given curriculum by deleting items that are inappropriate to the instructional levels of pupil groups. Because many pupils seem to learn better when they are taught at instructional levels where they already know 93 to 97 percent of reading material and 70 to 85 percent of skill-development material, items can be selected that conform to their knowledge and skill levels.[56]

Clifford Perkins refers to the short, timed evaluations used in curriculum-based assessment as "skill probes." The plan he recommends falls within the strategy called Curriculum-Based Assessment, which can be used with individuals and small groups. Because the evaluations are accomplished in so brief a time, they can be repeated, for example, two or three times a week.[57]

MAKING OR SELECTING AN EVALUATION DESIGN

In contrast to an evaluation model, which presents an overall strategy, an evaluation design is a specific plan for attaining a set of objectives by following a series of implementation steps. Making a suitable design is not easy. Inasmuch as schools are not ideal laboratories because of the complexity of physical conditions and human interactions within them, there is no ideal design. The validity of the data collected under the terms of almost any design is subject to question. Of the numbers of designs available,[58] the first three discussed below have had the widest and most enthusiastic use.

The True Experimental Design

The first is a so-called true experimental design. The pupils involved in the experiment and the pupils in a control group are randomized (randomly divided), and the teachers are selected for their similarities according to established criteria. Randomization is meant to decrease error, but it is notably difficult to achieve. After randomization, the experimental pupils are given the special curriculum treatment prescribed in the terms of the project, while the control group receives no special treatment, continuing with the customary subject matter content and educational practices. Then, evaluation of specific learning outcomes and other outcomes is conducted for both experimental and control groups by using the same evaluation strategies and instruments for both groups. Whenever the true experimental method can be utilized, it should be selected because of its relative freedom from error and because of the confidence that evaluators usually place in it.

The Nonequivalent Before-and-After Design

The second evaluation design uses a control group that is not equivalent to the experimental group or groups—that is, no randomization is undertaken. An attempt is made to compensate for this lack by collecting both pre-test and post-test data,[59] by using multiple curriculum treatments with experimental groups in contrast to the treatment received by the control group, and by making across-the-board comparisons of outcomes for groups of pupils rather than for individual pupils. Thus more than one experimental group is formed; pre-tests are given to all the experimental groups and to the control group; differing curriculum treatments are given to the experimental groups and, of course, to the control group; and all groups, experimental and control, receive the post-test. This design is often selected when parents might object to dramatic and obvious experimentation with their children and when the evaluators foresee difficulty in assigning teachers, some of whom might affect outcomes negatively.

The Time-Series Design

The third design is a time-series one. Again, no randomization is attempted. Also, no control group is established. If a time-series project is expected to cover two years of schooling—the years 1996–1997 and 1997–1998, for instance—the pupils involved in the project are tested, inventoried, and observed during the autumn of 1996 as the project gets under way, are exposed to a special curriculum treatment throughout the two-year period, and are tested, inventoried, and observed in the spring of 1997 and again during both the autumn of 1997 and the spring of 1998. This design has the advantage of providing some basic data quickly, of permitting comparisons to be made within the population, and of allowing the evaluators to plot progress over a reasonable period of time (which may, of course, exceed two years).[60]

Naturalistic Designs

In Great Britain, curriculum workers have been practicing *illuminative evaluation,* a form of explanatory and critical evaluation that does not rely on statistics. As we have seen in the United States, the *educational criticism* movement counters the stock methods and external examination that characterize curriculum evaluation by emphasizing careful perceiving and thoughtful decision making by persons directly on the curriculum scene. Both illuminative evaluation and educational criticism admit types of data that are not accepted in more traditional evaluation.

In the process of educational criticism, data are gathered by means of four major strategies. The first strategy is observation by skilled observers to answer the question, "What is happening here?" The second is description, which should be an accurate portrayal of the situation that has been observed. The third strategy is interpretation, which is accomplished by discovering meaning relative to theoretical, historical, socioeconomic, or other standards. The fourth strategy is judgment of the worth and importance of what has been done, in answer to questions like "Was it worth doing?" and "How well was it done?"

This kind of activity is sometimes referred to as *naturalistic evaluation.* Departing from the technical, it capitalizes on human abilities, honed to proficiency. In answering questions about what is true and what is valuable, naturalistic evaluation encourages the participation of people in making intelligent judgments. The more the participants practice evaluation strategies with understanding and care, the greater the quality or validity of the results. The deficiencies so often found in the quantitative (or counting) methods of evaluation discussed previously in this chapter will drive many curriculum workers to try naturalistic (or quality) evaluation.[61]

Although naturalistic evaluation has strengths, it also has weaknesses. The greatest strength is often said to be the presence of informed and skilled viewers, who can act as translators and interpreters and can thus help other viewers make wise judgments. The weaknesses are thought to be as follows:

1. The curriculum is a motion picture rather than a still picture—an ongoing work of art rather than a completed one.
2. Because critics, as individuals, differ, there is no assurance that what one critic sees will be even similar to what another critic sees.
3. Standards of criticism in themselves necessarily vary.
4. What can be seen may easily be less than what can be tested.[62]

ACTIVITY 6-1

Describing an Evaluation Design

Identify a curriculum project in your own or another school. Be sure the project you identify has a recognizable evaluation design. Describe the design in detail, noting the sequence of steps that have been taken or are yet to be taken in the evaluation process. Based on what you have read to this point in the chapter, what do you think of the evaluation design? What could be done to improve it?

ACTIVITY 6-2

Selecting an Evaluation Design

Suppose you were required to select one of the first three evaluation designs described on pages 288 and 289 for use in evaluating a curriculum project either under way or under consideration in a school you know well. Which design would you select? Why? What deficiencies do you find in the three designs that make you wish for an improved design? What might be done in the designing process to satisfy your objections?

A COMPENDIUM OF PRACTICAL IDEAS

Programs, practices, and materials for use in elementary and secondary schools are changing. The practices, devices, and arrangements that new ideas and materials supplant have dominated the educational scene for years and even generations, with little evaluation to gauge their worth. Now there is danger that the innovations and reforms will themselves remain unevaluated. If this occurs, educators will be faced with another accretion of uncertain ways of behaving in a field that is so important to so many people. Despite limitations in evaluation designs, lack of skill in measurement, and educators' tendency to overgeneralize on the basis of limited data, we do know enough about ways of evaluating to insist that evaluation occur. In the process of trying to evaluate all sorts of projects and programs, educators will become more sophisticated in the evaluation process.

Consider the varied methods now being used to achieve individualization. The most desired of the effects of curriculum change, individualization is obviously a complex matter. Part of the problem is that there are potentially so many routes to individualization. Educators do not know very clearly which practices to uphold and which to abandon. Thoroughgoing evaluation, attempted from various vantage points, needs to be conducted, for we can no longer afford to be satisfied with demonstrations. We need evidence.

The object is not to resist innovation or to uphold tradition merely for the joy of doing so; rather, it is to validate programs and practices, whether old or new. Although this action cannot be taken on nearly enough occasions, funds *should* be set aside and personnel *should* be made available for the purpose. Otherwise, curriculum improvement programs must proceed largely by caprice. From evaluation data, curriculum workers derive not only assurance concerning what they have done and are doing but also goals that guide their future actions.

The state of the evaluation art can perhaps best be seen by noting several findings which will, of course, need further checking. One finding is that what teachers do with classroom time is the most important element in determining the quality of a school. Specifically, teachers who lecture excessively or are consistently directive in other ways achieve poorer results than teachers who emphasize small-group work, individual work, discussion, laboratory work, pupil reporting, and demonstration. Another finding is that reduced class size can encourage learning, depending on what is done within the newly formed classes. It has been possible to establish critical breakpoints that mark maximum functional sizes.

Direct evidence now supports the belief that substitute teachers, most of whom perform in a "babysitting" role, have little instructional effect. This is partly because they emphasize ineffective classroom activities: test taking, watching movies chiefly for entertainment, engaging in question-and-answer recitations, and lecturing. Some evidence has appeared that having more than one adult in a classroom is less effective than the enthusiasts of team teaching used to believe it was. Further investigation is needed to discover the times of day at which pupils should have certain learning experiences and what effect the sex of the teacher has on learning.[63] These and similar questions are so interesting that failing to explore them deprives curriculum workers of half the fun of being in an exciting, fast-moving profession.

Mary Heller reported the results of inquiries into experience with the evaluation of presumed changes in programs and projects. Although the findings are not startling, they do appear to be reliable:

- Evaluation comprehends more than mere testing.
- Matters like changes in organization and changes in materials are easily caught up in the evaluation of curriculum change, as though they were all synonymous.
- Standardized testing as an evaluation means falls short because of its lack of relevance to classroom situations and the absence of useful statistical conversion tables.
- Criterion-referenced testing has therefore replaced in part older-fashioned standardized testing.
- The timing of evaluation is important. If evaluation occurs too often, it interferes with the learning process. If it occurs too seldom, the progress of change is not properly gauged.[64]

Recognizing that evaluation of programs and projects is a significant professional activity, the joint Committee on Standards for Educational Evaluation, representing twelve organizations, stated four groups of standards to be used as guides for evaluating procedures and results. The first group consists of utility standards, the second of feasibility standards, the third of propriety standards, and the fourth of accuracy standards. The four standards were meant to answer, respectively, four questions:

Utility: Does the evaluation satisfy the need for practical information?
Feasibility: Is the evaluation realistic and wise?
Propriety: Is the evaluation being conducted legally and ethically?
Accuracy: Does the evaluation uncover and communicate technically suitable information?[65]

Hard experience teaches central truths, like the following, about evaluation:

1. Tests and other evaluation devices do not always reach the depths that they are intended to plumb. The curriculum worker who places undue confidence in standardized devices makes a serious mistake.
2. Test makers are rarely divinely inspired. Classroom teachers, after having been taught the technique of test making, can sometimes do as well as ex-

perts in creating test and inventory items that tap what teachers need to communicate and what their pupils need to know.

3. Worshipping a course guide and teaching to the tests that fit the guide may please an administrator or supervisor who does not know the process of curriculum improvement, but these actions can provide no assurance that youngsters will learn more or achieve better in school.

4. Prominent lay people, including persons who ought to know better, sometimes pressure teachers to test for what the teachers insightfully avoid teaching in the first place. Teaching will never become a truly respected profession until teachers are so well prepared that they can confidently resist demands and suggestions that are patently nonsensical.

5. Evaluation remains a wide-open field. Human imagination will do much to extend and refine it during the years to come.

OVERRIDING PRINCIPLES OF DECISION MAKING AND PROCESS

It is time now to look backward and forward within the pages of this book. The present chapter has highlighted the importance of making wise decisions about ways of evaluating curriculum programs and projects. It constitutes one of six chapters that have been devoted to decision making. Implied within the six chapters are principles that can influence the manner in which decisions about the curriculum should be made. The principles, stated below with accompanying explanations, form a backdrop for the remaining five chapters of the book, which address the process of curriculum change and improvement.

Principle 1: Curriculum decisions should be made for valid educational reasons, not for specious or noneducational ones.

Much of our tendency to "jump aboard bandwagons" results from our failure to ask the question "Why?" Some innovations in education originate in pressures that make no contribution to achieving quality in education. Often, they proceed from vague feelings about "what society wants or needs" or from localized, specific feelings about what community pressure groups will do if the schools fail to heed their demands. Curriculum workers must think carefully about the consequences of the decisions they anticipate making. Are they within the context of purposes of the school? Are they likely to benefit the education of children? Do they spring from worthy and defensible motives?

Principle 2: Curriculum decisions of a permanent nature should be made on the basis of the best available evidence.

Most of the curriculum decisions made in the past have rested on little or no evidence. As the number of decisions we need to make increases, we shall surely need evidence to support some of these decisions. To do research concerning every proposed change in the curriculum is obviously impossible. But curriculum planners can develop a rationale for inquiry that takes into account how changes work experimentally in their own school systems, how they work in other school systems, what hard data are available concerning the quality of their function, and what other people think of the changes. Obviously, tentative decisions based on limited evidence must remain within the decision-making process.

Principle 3: Curriculum decisions should be made in a context of broadly conceived aims of education.

The American public will not approve of or submit to limited education of its children. Those who have asked parents about their aspirations for their children's education know that they demand much more than the three Rs. Most Americans seem to believe that citizenship education, character training, functional skill development, and improvement of social relationships come within the responsibility of elementary and secondary schools. Both education for improved thinking and education for improved feeling fall to the lot of the schools, because education is ill conceived and limited if it does not serve objectives ranging from increasing children's understanding to developing their appreciations, and onward to helping them clarify and reorient their values.

Principle 4: Curriculum decisions should be made within a context of previously made decisions and of needs for additional decision making so that balance and other important curriculum considerations may be safeguarded.

Previous decisions cannot and should not be entirely discarded. There are, of course, standing in the wings, demands for decision making that may be more pressing than those the schools are now attempting to meet. The wide range of previous decisions and of needs for decision making adds to the problem of overload, which appears in the form of having too much to teach in too little time. Curriculum workers might analyze a number of pupil cases in each of their schools to determine just what educational experiences individual pupils are having.

Principle 5: Curriculum decisions should be made by achieving a resolution of forces originating in the nature and development of learners, the nature of learning processes, demands of the society at large, requirements of the local community, and the nature and structure of subject matter to be learned.

Bases for making curriculum decisions may be summed up in these three phrases: learners and learning, social forces, and subject matter. Education that overemphasizes one of the three and largely ignores the other two is not fair to pupils. Imbalance, whatever its source, can swamp the curriculum.

Principle 6: Curriculum decisions should be reached cooperatively by persons who are legitimately involved in the effects of the decisions, with full participation being accorded those persons who are most concerned with the effects.

An imminent danger lies in having the curriculum imposed on classroom and school by interests outside the school. No one knows the children in a given school as well as the teachers and the principal of that school. The best those of us outside a particular school can do to improve the curriculum of that school is to provide general guidelines, data, and suggestions. Curriculum planning of a large-scale or general sort should be done cooperatively, involving as many of the users of the curriculum as possible. Although wide, continuous participation of the users is usually impossible, participation through suggestion making and trials of ideas can readily occur. Such trials should intimately involve an underconsulted group in the body educational: our pupils. Even when pupils are too young to tell us orally how satisfactory or unsatisfactory our ideas are, our own powers of observation can often tell us what we seek to know from pupils.

Principle 7: Curriculum decisions should take into account new facts of human life such as the proliferation of knowledge and a need for a new sense of unity within our diversity.

Americans are living in a new era. Knowledge is increasing so rapidly that teachers cannot hope to "cover the book," for the book is already too large. More and more careful selection of content is needed.

Certain understandings, skills, appreciations, attitudes, and values may need to become universals in the United States. This fact does not make a national or state curriculum necessary, because behaviors people exhibit in common can be developed through a multiplicity of curriculum experiences. But a set of sensible, attainable national goals is needed to guide education. The need for such goals becomes evident when we ask adolescents or adults to name goals or purposes around which Americans are united. The result is often silence.

Principle 8: Curriculum decisions should take into account the many differences among learners, especially with reference to learners' potential for development, their intellectual powers, their styles of thinking, their ability to withstand peer pressures, and their need for education in values and appreciations.

In the schools' anxiety to deal with groups and to make neat administrative arrangements, they have not dealt adequately with individuals. Plans for reorganizing the school and altering uses of pupil time may well stand or fall according to their success in attending to the needs of individuals. The curriculum must be made broad enough to permit development of human potential that is now going to waste. The progress being made in analyzing styles of thinking should be applied to treatment of individual learners. The schools will need to investigate further the mental and physical hazards in applying undue pressures, and they must help many confused children clarify and shift their values.

Principle 9: Curriculum decisions should be made with a realistic view of certain organizational or engineering matters that can affect the quality of the decisions themselves: correlation versus separation of subjects, the distinction between curriculum content and pupils' experiences, and the uses of time, for instance.

Some subject matter can be correlated naturally, some cannot. Content set out to be learned obviously differs from pupils' real learning experiences. What the teacher *does* is so important in pupil experiencing that teachers should receive ample help in choosing the details of content and in setting the stage for pupils to learn in varied ways. Either lengthened or shortened periods of time may be needed to effect economy in learning effort. In sum, much depends on how teachers proceed in putting curriculum decisions into operation.

Principle 10: Curriculum decisions should be made with some forethought about ways in which they may be communicated and shared.

A curriculum decision may be of excellent quality, but unless it is appropriately communicated and shared, it may soon enter the limbo of lost ideas. In many instances, more attention should be given to a plan for communicating decisions than to their original development.

Principle 11: Curriculum decisions should be made only with reference to subject matter and pupil experiences that cannot be offered as satisfactorily outside the school.

The school has sometimes exaggerated its educative function. The home, community agencies, labor unions, and industry already provide more education than some people realize. The impact of extraschool agencies on total educational programs is likely to increase. The schools need to reexamine their functions, determine which are legitimate for elementary and secondary schools, and retain those that can best benefit children and youth.

These criteria condition much that will be said in the next chapter about curriculum change.

ACTIVITY 6-3

Using Process Evaluation

Process evaluation is inquiry concerning how a program or project is proceeding while it is en route to its termination. It is meant to discover or predict, during the implementation of the project, both defects and strengths in its design and/or in ways of implementing the design. Further, it is intended to show whether changes in pupil performance under a given curriculum treatment can in fact be attributed to that treatment.[66]

Do the preceding statements mean to you that a project may be altered en route in order to strengthen it? If so, to what extent may it be altered without destroying its basic terms and intent? If possible, use an actual curriculum project as an example to demonstrate your views. If this is not possible, think of a project in which two or three changes might be made during its lifetime.

SUMMARY

This chapter emphasizes the importance of evaluating the content, process, and effects of curriculum change. Evaluation, as it is known in schools, assumes a variety of forms, from simple daily evaluation of pupil learning to evaluation of large curriculum programs and projects. Evaluation usually follows standard principles and practices that make it acceptable and respected. The data it yields may be quantitative or qualitative in nature, or both. As a convenience, people often seek standard evaluation models to follow, but they usually do their best evaluating when they create schemata to fit their own situations. In creating their own designs, evaluators may find it helpful to model after one or more of the standard designs: an experimental design, a before-and-after design, a design relying on time series, or a so-called naturalistic design. Implementing models and plans involves reporting, gathering data, and customizing evaluation instruments, along with utilizing practical ideas that result from evaluators' experience.

Chapter 6, the last of the chapters on decision making, concludes with an overview of principles that should guide decision making about the curriculum.

ENDNOTES

1. With specific reference to curriculum improvement activity, a *program* is a carefully planned, comprehensive, and continuing operation for improving as many elements of the curriculum as possible. A *project* is an operation involving a portion of the total curriculum or of a particular program, also carefully planned but relatively limited in purpose and scope.

2. Albert I. Oliver, *Curriculum Improvement: A Guide to Problems, Principles, and Process,* 2nd ed. (New York: Harper and Row, 1977), 300.

3. Frederick A. Rodgers, "Curriculum Research and Evaluation," in Fenwick W. English, ed., *Fundamental Curriculum Decisions,* 1983 Yearbook (Alexandria, VA: Association for Supervision and Curriculum Development, 1983), 142–153.

4. Compare Harriet Talmadge, "Evaluating the Curriculum: What, Why, and How," *Bulletin of the National Association of Secondary School Principals* 69, no. 481 (May 1985): 1–8.

5. See periodical publications of the Educational Testing Service, Princeton, NJ.

6. Jean A. King and Bruce Thompson, "How Principals, Superintendents View Program Evaluation," *Bulletin of the National Association of Secondary School Principals* 67, no. 459 (January 1983): 48–52.

7. Wilford M. Aiken, *The Story of the Eight Year Study* (New York: Harper & Row, 1942).

8. I. James Quillen and Lavone A. Hanna, *Education for Social Competence* (Chicago: Scott, Foresman, 1948).

9. Further information is available from National Assessment of Educational Progress, Educational Testing Service, Rosedale Road, Princeton, NJ 08541–0001.

10. *Asbury Park* (NJ) *Press,* February 27, 1994, C7.

11. See *Testing in America's Schools,* available from Editor, ETS Developments, Mail Stop 16 D, Educational Testing Service, Rosedale Road, Princeton, NJ 08541-0001.

12. John J. Bowers, *Planning a Program Evaluation: An Educator's Handbook* (Philadelphia: Research for Better Schools, 1978).

13. Association for Supervision and Curriculum Development, *Leadership for Improving Instruction,* 1960 Yearbook (Washington, DC: The Association, 1960), 166–167.

14. From information supplied by the late Dr. David B. Austin, a consultant to the foundation relative to this study.

15. Howard Gardner, *Multiple Intelligences: The Theory in Practice* (New York: Basic Books, 1993).

16. Stephen F. Hamilton and Albert Mamary, "Assessing the Effectiveness of Program Delivery," *Bulletin of the National Association of Secondary School Principals* 67, no. 465 (October 1983): 39–44.

17. Samuel Ball, *Evaluating Educational Programs* (Princeton, NJ: Educational Testing Service, 1979), 6.

18. See Arieh Lewy, "Utilizing Experts' Judgment in the Process of Curriculum Evaluation" (Los Angeles: Center for the Study of Evaluation, UCLA, 1973).

19. Walter Dick, "Formative Evaluation: Prospects for the Future," *Educational Technology* 27, no. 10 (October 1987): 55–57.

20. See A. W. Astin and R. J. Panos, "The Evaluation of Educational Programs," in Robert L. Thorndike, ed., *Educational Measurement,* 2nd ed. (Washington, DC: American Council on Education, 1971).

21. James A. Phillips, Jr., "A Context for Considering Curriculum Research," a paper presented at the annual meeting of the American Educational Research Association, Washington, DC, April 1975. Reported in ERIC # ED 106 206.

22. Textbooks in measurement and evaluation are filled with both the joys and the hardships of evaluation. Books on evaluation procedures, such as those by Grobman; Tyler, Gagné, and Scriven; and Wick and Beggs listed at the end of this chapter, extend the ideas presented here.

23. Hulda Grobman, *Evaluation Activities of Curriculum Projects: A Starting Point,* American Educational Research Association, Monograph Series in Curriculum Evaluation (Chicago: Rand McNally, 1968), 48–82.

24. C. M. Lindvall and Richard C. Cox, *Evaluation as a Tool in Curriculum Development: The IPI Program,* American Educational Research Association, Monograph Series in Curriculum Evaluation (Chicago: Rand McNally, 1970).

25. Decker F. Walker and J. Schaffarzick, *Comparing Different Curricula: A Review of Research and Some Speculation on Its Implications* (Palo Alto, CA: Stanford University, 1972).

26. See Stewart C. Purkey and Marshall S. Smith, "Too Soon to Cheer? Synthesis of Research on Effective Schools," *Educational Leadership* 40, no. 3 (December 1982): 64–69.

27. For details, see Malcolm Provus, "Evaluation of Ongoing Programs in the Public School System," in *Educational Evaluation: New Roles, New Means,* National Society for the Study of Education, Sixty-Eighth Yearbook, Part II (Chicago: University of Chicago Press, 1969), 242–283.

28. Robert E. Stake, "Language, Rationality, and Assessment," in Walcott H. Beatty, ed., *Improving Educational Assessment and an Inventory of Measures of Affective Behavior* (Washington, DC: Association for Supervision and Curriculum Development, 1969), 14–40.

29. See, for instance, Daniel L. Stufflebeam, "The Relevance of the CIPP Evaluation Model for Educational Accountability," *Journal of Research and Development in Education* 5 (Fall 1971): 19–25; see also R. S. Randall, "An Opera-

tional Application of the CIPP Model for Evaluation," *Educational Technology* 9 (March 1969): 40–44.

30. R. L. Hammond, "Evaluation at the Local Level," Project EPIC, Tucson, Arizona, n.d.

31. Elliot W. Eisner, "Using Professional Judgment," in Ronald Brant, ed., *Applied Strategies for Curriculum Evaluation* (Alexandria, VA: Association for Supervision and Curriculum Development, 1970), 41–47.

32. See Eisner's argument in his book *The Educational Imagination: On the Design and Evaluation of School Programs,* 2nd ed. (New York: Macmillan, 1985).

33. A proposal to increase the role and responsibility of the National Assessment of Educational Progress was criticized, for example, by Matthew G. Martinez in "Proposal for NAEP Is 'Recipe for Disaster,'" which appeared in *Education Week,* March 14, 1990.

34. As reported by the public media in March 1994.

35. See Michael Scriven, "The Methodology of Evaluation," in J. R. Gress and D. E. Purpel, eds., *Curriculum: An Introduction to the Field* (Berkeley, CA: McCutchan, 1978), 337–408.

36. Jim Butler and Leo Bartlett, "School-Based Criterion Referenced Assessment and Curriculum Design: Some Comments on the Queensland Scene," *Studies in Educational Evaluation* 15, no. 1 (1989): 91–107.

37. T. J. H. M. Eggen, W. J. Pelgrum, and T. Plomp, "The Implemented and Attained Mathematics Curriculum: Some Results of the Second International Mathematics Study in the Netherlands," *Studies in Educational Evaluation* 13, no. 1 (1987): 119–135.

38. Richard Vigilante, *Evaluating Educational Programs: ANAPAC User's Guide* (New York: Board of Education, City of New York, 1972), 4.

39. Ibid., 6.

40. Ibid., 7. This reservation stems, perhaps, from the attack in big cities on standardized achievement tests as being unfair to minority groups, and from disputes about the locus of the right and the power to make policy.

41. Ibid., 8, 9.

42. M. C. Wittrock, "The Evaluation of Instruction: Cause and Effect Relations in Naturalistic Data," *UCLA Evaluation Comment* 1, no. 4 (Los Angeles: Center for the Study of Evaluation, UCLA, 1969), 9–14.

43. See the earlier statements of M. Scriven, "The Methodology of Evaluation," in R. W. Tyler, R. M. Gagné, and M. Scriven, eds., *Perspectives of Curriculum Evaluation,* American Educational Research Association, Monograph Series in Curriculum Evaluation (Chicago: Rand McNally, 1967); and of G. Atkinson, "Evaluation of Educational Programs: An Exploration," in W. H. Strevell, ed., *Rationale of Education Evaluation* (Pearland, TX: Interdisciplinary Committee on Education Evaluation, Gulf Schools Supplementary Education Center, 1967), 2; see also Mary Alice White and Jan Duker, "Models of Schooling and Models of Evaluation," *Teachers College Record* 74 (February 1973): 293–307.

44. From a description of APPLE (Assessing Projects and Portfolios for Learning) supplied by Professor Gardner in 1994.

45. Mapleton Public Schools, *Educational X-Ray of Mapleton Public Schools* (Denver, CO: Mapleton Public Schools, 1972). Reported in ERIC # ED 081 709.

46. King and Thompson, "How Principals, Superintendents View Program Evaluation," 49, 50.

47. Rodgers, "Curriculum Research and Evaluation," 147.

48. Minnesota State Department of Education, *Technology Demonstration Program: Final 1984–85 Evaluation Report* (St. Paul: The Department, 1985).

49. ERIC Clearinghouse on Educational Management, *Program Evaluation: The Best of ERIC on Educational Management,* no. 68 (Eugene, OR: The Clearinghouse, 1983). Reported in ERIC # ED 226 404.

50. Eugene Hobbs et al., *Curriculum Renewal Handbook: Mathematics, 1981–82* (Oklahoma City: Oklahoma State Department of Education, 1982).

51. Reported in ERIC # ED 301 582.

52. Wesley C. Pugh, "Moving into the Next Phase of 'School Effectiveness' with Heavy Baggage: An Evaluation of a Districtwide School Improvement Project," a paper presented at the annual meeting of the American Educational Research Association, San Francisco, March 1989. Reported in ERIC # ED 307 294.

53. Bert Stoneberg, Jr., "Music Curriculum Evaluation Report" (Albany, OR: Greater Albany Public School District, 1989). Reported in ERIC # ED 304 391.

54. Stephen H. Davidoff et al., "Indicator Based Evaluation for Chapter 1," a paper presented at the annual meeting of the American Educational Research Association, San Francisco, March 1989. Reported in ERIC # ED 308 226.

55. Constance Goldsby, "Norm Referenced Test Customization: Curricular Considerations," a paper circulated in 1988 by the New York City Public Schools. Reported in ERIC # ED 300 430.

56. James A. Tucker, "Guiding Instruction Effectively by Using Curriculum-Based Assessment," a paper presented at the annual convention of the Council for Exceptional Children, San Francisco, April 1989. Reported in ERIC # ED 304 871.

57. Clifford B. Perkins, "Curriculum-Based Assessment: A New Approach," *Principal* 89, no. 2 (November 1989): 44, 45.

58. See Donald T. Campbell and Julian C. Stanley, *Experimental and Quasi-Experimental Designs for Research* (Chicago: Rand McNally, 1963).

59. *Pre-test* and *post-test* are used here as symbols of whatever instrumentation—including tests and a variety of other instruments—is used in determining pupil status before and after curriculum treatments have been applied.

60. For a helpful discussion of the three designs described, see Maurice J. Eash, Harriet Talmadge, and Herbert J. Walberg, "Evaluation Designs for Practitioners," TM Report 35, ERIC Clearinghouse on Tests, Measurement, and Evaluation (Princeton, NJ: Educational Testing Service, December 1974).

61. See, for instance, Elliot W. Eisner, *The Educational Imagination: On the Design and Evaluation of School Programs* (New York: Macmillan, 1979); see also George Willis, "Democratization of Curriculum Evaluation," *Educational Leadership* 38, no. 8 (May 1981): 630–632.

62. See Elizabeth Vallance, "The Critic's Perspective: Some Strengths and Limitations of Aesthetic Criticism in Education," a paper presented at the annual meeting of the American Educational Research Association, Los Angeles, April 1981. Reported in ERIC # ED 163 166.

63. See Martin N. Olsen, "Ways to Achieve Quality in School Classrooms: Some Definitive Answers," *Phi Delta Kappan* 52, no. 1 (September 1971): 63–65.

64. Mary F. Heller, "The Process of Curriculum Development: An Overview of Research," February 1981. Reported in ERIC ED # 221 938.

65. Joint Committee on Standards for Educational Evaluation, *Standards for Evaluations of Educational Programs, Projects, and Materials* (New York: McGraw-Hill, 1981).

66. Daniel J. Macy, "The Role of Process Evaluation in Program Development and Implementation," *Educational Technology* 15, no. 4 (April 1975): 42–47.

SELECTED BIBLIOGRAPHY

Anderson, D. C. *Evaluating Curriculum Proposals: A Critical Guide.* New York: Halsted Press, 1981.

Bellack, Arno A., and Kliebard, Herbert E., eds. *Curriculum and Evaluation.* Berkeley, CA: McCutchan, 1977.

Bowers, John J. *Planning a Program Evaluation: An Educator's Handbook.* Philadelphia: Research for Better Schools, 1978.

Davis, Ed. *Teachers as Curriculum Evaluators.* Winchester, MA: Allen and Unwin, 1981.

Eisner, Elliot W. *The Educational Imagination: On the Design and Evaluation of School Programs,* 2nd ed. New York: Macmillan, 1985.

Grobman, Hulda. *Evaluation of Activities of Curriculum Projects.* Chicago: Rand McNally, 1969.

Hill, John C. *Curriculum Evaluation for School Improvement.* Springfield, IL: Charles C Thomas, 1986.

Kindvall, C. M., and Cox, Richard C. *Evaluation as a Tool in Curriculum Development: The IPI Program.* Chicago: Rand McNally, 1970.

Lemlech, Johanna K. *Curriculum and Assessment Reform.* New York: Taylor and Francis, 1989.

Ornstein, Allen C., and Hunkins, Francis P. *Curriculum: Foundations, Principles, and Issues,* 2nd ed. Boston: Allyn and Bacon, 1993.

Payne, David A. *Curriculum Evaluation: Commentaries on Purpose, Process, Product.* Boston: D.C. Heath, 1973.

Phi Delta Kappan 46, no. 7 (March 1988): 486–513. (Articles on educational indicators.)

Rippey, Robert M., et al. *Studies in Transactional Evaluation.* Berkeley, CA: McCutchan, 1973.

Salvia, John, and Hughes, Charles. *Curriculum-Based Assessment: Testing What Is Taught.* New York: Macmillan, 1990.

Taylor, Peter A., and Cowley, Doris M. *Readings in Curriculum Evaluation.* Dubuque, IA: William C. Brown, 1972.

Theory into Practice 25, no. 1 (Winter 1986): entire issue.

Tuckman, Bruce W. *Evaluating Instructional Programs.* Boston: Allyn and Bacon, 1979.

Tyler, Ralph W., ed. *Educational Evaluation: New Roles, New Means.* National Society for the Study of Education, Sixty-Eighth Yearbook, Part II. Chicago: University of Chicago Press, 1969.

Tyler, R. W.; Gagné, R. M.; and Scriven, M., eds. *Perspectives of Curriculum Evaluation.* American Educational Research Association, Monograph Series in Curriculum Evaluation. Chicago: Rand McNally, 1967.

Wick, John W., and Beggs, Donald L., eds. *Evaluation for Decision-Making in the Schools.* Boston: Houghton Mifflin, 1970.

Wilhelms, Fred T., ed. *Evaluation as Feedback and Guide.* 1967 Yearbook. Washington, DC: Association for Supervision and Curriculum Development, 1967.

PROCESS IN CURRICULUM IMPROVEMENT

7

THE GENERAL PROCESS OF CURRICULUM CHANGE AND IMPROVEMENT

HOW DECISION MAKING RELATES TO PROCESS

In the first six chapters, this book has dealt with decision making in curriculum improvement. The question now arises, "How does decision making relate to the process by which the curriculum is improved?"

We have seen that such decision making is in itself a process, which involves borrowing from various disciplines—history, psychology, the social sciences, and subject matter to be taught in schools—and then using insights derived from these disciplines in ways that are peculiar to professional education itself.

Curriculum improvement as an evolving discipline of real power and promise depends so heavily on process for its own subject matter that attention is directed in the second part of this book to certain elements of process. In the following chapters, consideration is given to how change and improvement occur, the planning process, who makes the curriculum, how communication aids improvement, and the leadership methods and strategies that can be used; these matters represent the general concerns of curriculum planners. Inasmuch as curriculum improvement is greatly facilitated by a thorough understanding of process, this understanding is a necessary concomitant of and supplement to the curriculum worker's knowledge of the bases and methodology of decision making.

SOME INITIAL OBSERVATIONS ABOUT CHANGE AND IMPROVEMENT

It is obvious that curriculum improvement does not occur automatically. In most situations, it requires the expenditure of much time and effort within an environment rich in helpful and stimulating influences. Curriculum improvement results primarily from improving individual persons and organizations of people. Such improvement follows a course that can be charted in a general way. This chapter deals with the basic process; subsequent chapters describe certain ramifications of and corollaries to the process.

In discussions of process, curriculum workers are often viewed as change agents on the one hand and clients on the other, whereas in discussions of decision making, these persons may be called curriculum planners. When an entire school needs to be reformed, the reform is sometimes called "school renewal."

Meanings of Change and Improvement

To repeat what was said and implied previously: The dictionary defines *improvement* as enhanced value or excellence. In a broader sense, it is all of the following: betterment, amelioration, and enrichment. *Change,* on the other hand, involves a shift in position that may go in either a favorable or an unfavorable direction. One's orientation may change, for example, from total innocence of narcotics to drug addiction, but few persons would call this change an improvement. Improvements are labeled as such according to sets of values, and improvement can best be ensured by evaluating the true effects of change.

In education, many changes, though often small and slight, have occurred during recent years. Certain persons, using their own systems of values, consider given changes to be improvements, whereas others may regard the same changes as backward steps. Thus a lay committee of engineers and scientists who seriously proposed to a board of education that physical education, home economics, and all the arts be eliminated from the curriculum of their local high school made the recommendation because the committee valued a strengthening of the basic subjects at the expense of "the frills." This change was regarded by other lay persons and by organizations of educators as a decidedly backward step. Usually, precise evaluation procedures are needed to determine whether a given change is an improvement. For instance, if a plan for reorganizing elementary schools has been put into operation, planned evaluation is needed to discover whether the ultimate result has been mere reorganization of the school or actual improvement in children's learning experiences. The two are obviously not the same, although they are repeatedly being confused as U.S. education rushes into change.

In educational literature, the process of curriculum change or improvement has sometimes been referred to as *educational engineering,* a term that suggests the existence of a technology of improvement. It has also been termed *planned social change,*[1] and *change in the dynamics of human relationships.*[2] Much of what is known about the process is of a practical or commonsense nature. Most knowledge of planned social change and the related significance of human relations comes from fields other than education. Inasmuch as improvement is really change directed toward excellence, betterment, amelioration, and/or enrichment, it should be recognized as especially worthwhile change but as change nevertheless. Whatever social scientists and educators have learned about the process of change in individuals and groups may be generally applied to the process of improving persons and institutions. With reference to improvement of the curriculum, educators must, of course, make further applications of the findings of social psychology, sociology, and the other social sciences to their own field.

Identifying Common Mistakes

What are some of the mistakes that have prevented constructive curriculum change?

Suppose, taking a cue from science fiction, that the Great Leader who wields his power on another planet has recognized that improvement on earth can be wrought, in part, by improving the quality of children's schooling. Improvement of earthlings and their functioning, he thinks, must be prevented at all costs. Thus, to have a long-term advantage over us, the Great Leader needs to discourage genuine curriculum improvement. After deliberating, he and his cohorts make the following concrete proposals for preventing improvement:

- Keep school personnel ignorant of how effective their schools currently are.
- Organize as many commissions and committees as possible to represent their own and other special interests.
- Expect each commission to prepare a report backed by few valid data and many loose assumptions.
- Find governors, mayors, and other political leaders who are willing to preside over large-scale curriculum planning, mainly according to their own views.
- Explain that improvement can come in across-the-board sweeps without recognition of the differences among very different schools.
- Keep teachers, school administrators, and parents from helping in any important way with curriculum planning.
- Inform parents and other community members that they should expect immediate curriculum change because quick change is always possible.
- Teach the brightest, most influential people in the lay public that schools exist to be manipulated.
- Plan curriculum as far from the site of its implementation as possible.
- Don't be concerned about whether school personnel are ready for a given change; put the change into effect anyway.
- Concentrate on having curriculum plans made; don't give thought to why, how, and when they are to be implemented.

- Influence curriculum planners to put "progress" before quality.
- Advertise the slogan "Do something! Do *anything!*"[3]

We must face the tragic fact that these proposals have come not from a distant planet but from some of our own leaders, who fail to recognize that real improvement requires the participation of knowledgeable professionals and lay persons who work where implementation is to occur and who are willing to resist the temptations that specious schemes pose.[4]

Many recent reform efforts have consisted merely of tooling and fooling around and about the curriculum. Other efforts have scarcely touched the curriculum. Tragically, people who have little or nothing to do with the operation of schools have, in the words of Theodore Sizer, succeeded in "putting the screws on the existing system" without proposing a viable alternative.[5]

To identify common mistakes, one need only examine what self-appointed "curriculum experts" have done in recent years. They have condemned U.S. elementary and secondary education as a whole. They have oversimplified and perverted data about pupil performance. Further, they have adopted and relied on a set of national goals for education that fails to meet the requirement of sensible goal-setting. And they have exaggerated the role of schools in the decline of our competitiveness in world markets. These and other miscues were identified in the controversial Sandia Report, which originated in the federal Energy Department. The report was withheld from publicity by federal education authorities for reasons that remain unclear.[6]

The Lore of Change Process

Practice in curriculum planning has influenced development of a planning lore. This lore suggests that the learner's curriculum improves largely in consonance with improvement in his or her teacher's insights, skills, and attitudes. According to this viewpoint, emphasis needs to be placed on the growth of individual teachers, whether they are assigned to classrooms or rove about as teachers of teachers, bearing the title of curriculum coordinator, supervisor, principal, or consultant. *If the curriculum is to improve, teachers must be committed to the significance of self-improvement.* Obviously, some teachers are interested in improving themselves, whereas others are not. There is, of course, no teacher who cannot do his or her work better, and the basic question then becomes "How can the teacher who is more or less concerned about personal improvement be helped to improve?"

We can *pretend* to help teachers improve by

1. Causing them to feel forced into improving. The teacher says, "I'd better try to improve or 'they' won't like it."
2. Indoctrinating them to follow a prescribed, accepted set of procedures. The teacher says, "In our workshop, we were told how to do it. I'm just following instructions."

3. Expecting them to do as a model person does. The teacher exclaims, "I've never seen anyone teach earth science the way Mr. Agronomy does!"
4. Putting them in groups where they feel group influence. The teacher explains, "We talked about it a long time in our group. I'm convinced it's the thing to do."
5. Rewarding them so that they will be good, cooperative boys and girls. The teacher confesses, "Now that I've been given so many advantages, I wouldn't want to go against our principal's ideas."
6. Trusting the tide and letting them flow with it. The teacher remarks, "When something new comes from our state department of education, I try it and expect it to turn out well."[7]

Obviously, these expedients fail to take into account the factors that give meaning and depth to the improvement process, such as felt need, consequent motivation, appropriate school environment, and encouragement provided by school leaders, peers, and other people who count.

Social scientists have stated that change probably occurs in three stages. The first stage is that of *initiation,* in which ideas for change are launched and decisions are made regarding the nature, direction, and extent of change. The second stage is said to be one of *legitimation,* in which the sentiment on behalf of change is communicated. The third stage involves *congruence* of the separate systems of values held by the person or persons seeking to create change and by the person or persons who are the targets or subjects of the proposed change.[8] The process of change may be assisted by permissiveness and support in accordance with a helpful human relations approach. It may also be aided temporarily by manipulating extrinsic rewards such as affection, favor, promotion, and additional income. Disaster has sometimes been used as an excuse to make changes seem reasonable and necessary. In the presence or imminence of disaster, action seems necessary even when the particular action to be taken violates principles and values that are long established and widely accepted. In organizations, including school systems, change occurs as a result of (1) planning by equals, (2) indoctrination by superior officers, and (3) outright coercion by the same officers.[9]

The process of change may be viewed from any one of three different perspectives. The first of these is the *technical.* According to this perspective, an innovation can be designed carefully and put into action in a rational manner and with all necessary technical assistance. Trouble may develop only if the proposal is of low quality, sufficient time and data are not made available to the planners, or the proposal is not adequately discussed and properly amended.

The second perspective, commonly called the *political,* leads to identification of the special interests of participants in the planning. This perspective has to do with the nature of people's incentives and their relative power within a political setting. When the technical perspective fails to account for failures that develop, attention is drawn to the interaction of participants in a political milieu.

The third perspective, the *cultural,* locates each proposed change within a complex of beliefs, norms, and values. Each change, no matter how small, has potential for disturbing or altering the culture. According to this perspective, cultural setting means much more than we have imagined heretofore.[10]

Sometimes agents of curriculum change move from perspective to perspective as their work proceeds: from consideration of the technical quality of an innovation to consideration of the performance of the innovation in reality, to consideration of the cultural context in which it will succeed or fail. Consider a committee of teachers and principals that makes a carefully conceived and liberally supported proposal for lowering the dropout rate in the secondary schools of its moderate-sized district. The committee believes that, technically, it has done its best. As a next step, the committee finds a dozen influential teachers who have a sincere interest in seeing the dropout rate lowered. These teachers accept responsibility for communicating to school faculties, especially in the secondary schools, the importance of providing new and different curriculum experiences for pupils most likely to leave school. They find that their work is supported by some influential members of the school faculties and hindered by others. Customary faculty politics is operating, but fortunately the "right" teachers were on the job in the first place. As planning proceeds, the committee finds that the nature of the experiences selected must vary according to the requirements, expectations, and beliefs of pupils and other members of the community who are clients of particular schools in the district. The culture of the individual school makes a difference.

Critics of attempts at school reform have said that many reforms ignore the power of people and emphasize instead the usefulness of things, have their basis in worn-out or partially incorrect assumptions, and capitalize on ready-made plans that admit little thinking by people in the field. Real change, in contrast, is more likely to occur when key persons, including teachers, make decisions about what is to be planned, begin their planning within local settings, struggle to eliminate barriers to reform, and stimulate people's will to change even at the risk of making mistakes.[11]

Decade after decade, curriculum specialists have tried to make change occur widely and effectively by employing certain strategies. Beginning with Hollis Caswell's and Doak Campbell's efforts to stimulate statewide curriculum study and continuing with experimentation and study sponsored by universities and associations, the central focus throughout the years has been on the cooperation and collaboration of school people and outside personnel with various responsibilities and specializations. The recent tendency to mandate curriculum reform from the top down and to prepare teacher-proof ideas and materials is now creating revulsion among educators.[12]

How Change Occurs in the Individual

Changing or improving the individual often becomes a very special problem. Consider the case of a teacher named Lucretia and her critic:

I remember Lucretia. She and I taught in the same high school, though hers was a different generation from mine. I can recall Lucretia's long dresses, straight hair, and wan face that had seemingly never known cosmetics.

"Lucretia's the kind of teacher who defeats school bond issues singlehandedly," said a mutual friend. He may have been right. Both her appearance and her attitudes toward youngsters and subject matter were unappealing.

Lucretia expected much of her pupils but less of herself. Her understanding of her subject was limited, and she obviously cared little about the adolescents she taught.

I've often thought about Lucretia since those days in Stockville High School. Where should curriculum improvement have begun in *her* classroom? With her—probably! But how and under what circumstances?

Just incidentally (and maybe it shouldn't be so incidental), I wonder what Lucretia thought of me. How might her brash young neighbor in the classroom across the hall have improved himself so that *his* pupils' experiences could have improved in turn?

The preceding vignette raises some serious questions about process. Among them are these: Granted that Lucretia represents "a type," are there some common ways that can be used in helping people everywhere improve themselves? What different approaches are necessary and desirable for use with widely differing individuals? Are we vain enough to believe that improvement is only for persons other than ourselves? Can curriculum leaders become so preoccupied with the intrinsic worth of a proposed innovation that they forget that real improvement occurs in *people,* including *themselves?*

Sometimes curriculum leaders encounter teachers who seem to improve as a consequence of a particular incident or circumstance. A classic case is that of a teacher named Alice:

Alice, considered by her supervisor to be a run-of-the-mill teacher, had in her sixth-grade class an underachieving boy named Roy. This boy, who had recently lost his mother in an automobile accident, was clearly at risk of failing. During the autumn months of the school term, Alice had written Roy off as an obvious failure.

The day before the beginning of the Christmas vacation, Roy and his fellow pupils came to school with presents for their teacher. A child of poverty, Roy brought Alice a used red scarf and a ring with one of its five rhinestones missing.

"I thought you'd like these," Roy told Alice. "My mother wore both of them before she died. Every day, for months, she wore the scarf. Sorry I don't have something else to give you."

When the children had left for the day, Alice sat down at her desk and cried. She thought to herself, "Whatever else Roy is, he's good-hearted. Maybe I can do something special to help him."

When the children returned after Christmas, Alice began to give Roy extra attention. She noticed that he began to blossom when he was praised and helped. When the spring months arrived, he was in the top half of his class. And Alice had worn the red scarf every day since Christmastime.

For Alice, the years passed quickly. One day, a half-dozen years later, she received a note from Roy that read simply, "Dear Mrs. Fortesque, I'm now the salutatorian of the senior class of Eastham High School. Thought you'd want to know." Alice was pleased and a bit surprised.

Four years later, Alice received a second note from Roy: "Dear Mrs. Fortesque, I wanted you to know that I was graduated *cum laude* from the State University last week. I've been admitted to law school. Thanks for your help." Alice wrote a congratulatory note in reply.

Within less than three years, Alice heard from Roy again.

> Dear Mrs. Fortesque:
> On May 28, I'm being graduated with honors from our law school here at the State University. Inasmuch as neither my mother nor my father is living, I've saved a commencement seat reservation for you. Will you please come to represent my mother? (You needn't wear the red scarf!) You'll be my guest for the weekend."

Alice cried a second time. She knew she had received an offer she couldn't refuse.

Obviously, curriculum leaders cannot afford to rely on such fortuitous circumstances to cause changes in teachers. Instead, they need to set educational stages and scenes that create and encourage genuine, traceable improvement in teachers and consequently in youngsters. This improvement must be so significant as to have a broad impact and be reasonably permanent.

Causing Change in the Individual

Change in the individual seems to come about in the following way. Some of the stimuli in the individual's environment contribute to readiness for change by creating a felt need for something different, a dissatisfaction with what now exists. The need is met, at least in part, by a planned or fortuitous experience. Largely as a result of the experience (or series of experiences), one sees oneself and one's environment in a new light. Consequently, one develops new values and subsequently new goals, which may be closed-ended (fixed) or open-ended. Sometimes the new goals arouse additional needs, and one finds oneself in another orbit of planned change. Encouragement, help, and stimulation are needed during the entire process of change. The nearer a person's newly developed values are to the values he or she has held dear, the more permanent the change is likely to be. Some persons change rapidly, others slowly. Differences in rate of change are therefore to be expected.

This brief description, oversimplified as it probably is, contains several ideas that need examination and extension into practice in the schools. When the ideas have passed through the sieve of the educator's experience, they become a set of tentative principles like the following:

- *People improve with greatest enthusiasm when they detect a desire on the part of the stimulator of improvement to improve himself or herself.* The argument "You need improving and I am here to improve you" has very little effect. "We have a common problem; to solve it, we should all improve our competencies" has a pleasanter, more convincing ring.

- *The direction of improvement should be determined cooperatively.* People's goals differ; however, if they are to work together effectively, they must determine cooperatively the direction their efforts are to take.

- *To achieve improvement, people must identify and examine each other's centrally held values.* This action is difficult and time consuming. It requires the best in communication—the careful listening that Carl Rogers talks about and the careful observing that Daniel Prescott recommends to teachers. It demands lengthy talking together and prolonged watching of one another's behavior, so that the persons involved may truly say, "We know each other."

- *People improve through experiencing.* The kind of teacher one is may be determined largely by the kinds of experiences one has had. School systems should seek to provide their teachers with the best of inservice education.

- *Stimulators of improvement should divide their time between contacts with individuals and contacts with groups.* Research and practice show that both individual conferences and group work are effective in helping teachers improve the quality of their work. The balance between these two general procedures cannot be predetermined; it can be judged only in consideration of prevailing situations.

- *People's resistance to the efforts of others to help them improve constitutes a major individual difference.* Not only are some people more generally resistant than others, but individuals vary in their resistances to specific new proposals.

- *Whenever possible, improvement should be induced in situations that involve problem solving.* People improve most when a stimulator of improvement helps them solve their own problems. Some problems pose a threat and therefore cannot be dealt with immediately and directly. For instance, teachers who have trouble with classroom control are often unable to discuss their control problems dispassionately. Curriculum workers should do their best to put such professional problems into appropriate forms for discussion and solution.

- *Stimulators of improvement should try to create and maintain a climate of freedom for those with whom they work.* This statement rests on the thesis that people improve when they feel free to improve. Where there is a feeling of restraint expressed in declarations like "My boss won't let me," that feeling should be eliminated by carefully chosen words and behavior that point clearly to greater freedom in the whole situation.

• *Stimulators of improvement should help keep channels of communication open.* Psychological static easily gets between the sender and the receiver of a message. Much of this static can be cleared away by face-to-face communication. Curriculum workers should try to ensure that they hear what others say by listening carefully, trying to understand their messages, and then repeating or rephrasing people's comments.

• *Stimulators of improvement should use their power and influence with great care.* Educational leaders have largesse to distribute in the form of position, salary, approval, knowledge, prestige, disciplinary control, and even affection. Their status often begets in teachers an acquiescence that is easily mistaken for a genuine desire to improve. When the threat or the paternalism is gone, acquiescence disappears too.

• *Stimulators of improvement should operate on a limited number of fronts at a given time.* Curriculum workers are learning that sweeping, comprehensive improvements rarely take place. Rather, progress is made on a broken front, a little at a time, in manageable form.[13]

Actions to Be Taken

The preceding principles should be considered carefully by those who would improve the curriculum. They suggest the following specific actions that the curriculum leader should take:

1. Work *with* people, not *over* them.
2. Show that you too desire to improve.
3. Help the people with whom you work know you and know each other.
4. Help teachers enjoy a variety of inservice experiences.
5. Work with both individuals and groups, balancing your time between individual conferences and group work.
6. Recognize that some people improve more slowly than others, both in a general sense and in specific activities.
7. Try to use problem solving as a means of improvement.
8. Help teachers feel free to improve.
9. Keep channels of communication open.
10. Use your status, whether it is real or imagined, with great care: You can easily be a threat and an impediment.
11. Be sensible and modest in your expectations, doing well that which you undertake.[14]

No matter what is done to help individuals change, the expenditure of time and the occasional presence of turmoil appear to be constants in the process.[15]

The general process of religious conversion, whatever the religion, provides a model of change in individuals. This process begins with an individual's sensing a pressing need for change. The individual recognizes the presence of an opportunity to change constructively. Finally, the individual accepts this opportunity, and conversion to new beliefs and behaviors occurs.

The Importance of Care in Working with Teachers

Among the specific factors that assist change and improvement in the individual, motivation is evidently one to be reckoned with. At the beginning of the change-improvement process, the person is thought to receive motivation from "dissatisfaction or pain associated with the present situation"—dissatisfaction that results from "a perceived discrepancy between what is and what might be," external pressures to accomplish change, and an undefined "internal requiredness" that presses the individual to change.[16] After the initial stages of the process have passed, the person who is changing or improving may be motivated by a feeling of need to complete the task and to complete it with appropriate speed. He or she may be motivated further by the existence of desirable relationships between himself or herself and the stimulator of change or improvements.[17] Since these ideas are in no way final, curriculum leaders should check them against their own continuing experiences in dealing with teachers.

Motivation is thought to be inhibited at times by certain "resistance forces." These forces include opposition to any kind of change, opposition to a particular change, desire to cling to ideas or actions with which one is well satisfied, and poor relationships between the person to be changed and the stimulator of change. Sometimes change, no matter how constructive, costs "the client" more than he or she had originally expected it would, and he or she becomes discouraged with it. Sometimes, too, the client is diverted to other projects, and change is inhibited by the diversion.[18]

Arthur Combs discusses a myth that is prominent in professional education; he calls it "the myth they won't let me." Administrators' alleged prohibition of constructive activity on behalf of schools is, in fact, often a crutch on which teachers lean to avoid participating in curriculum planning. Combs points out that professionals employed in schools usually have more freedom than they care to believe. Frequently, the prohibition does not exist,[19] but the fact that teachers and others think it exists raises questions about the ways school leaders respond to curriculum ideas and to the people who communicate them.

William Reid is not the first to assert the importance of being fair in dealing with teachers. And assuming that the curriculum is something to be brought into schools from the outside, ready-made by "experts," does not do justice to members of teaching staffs. To be right in relationships with teachers, curriculum planners need to see teachers as rational people who are able to make choices and to improve the quality of their work. Curriculum leaders should prize and practice ethical behavior, avoiding bias against any group of people. They should view education as purposeful, though not necessarily as "preplanned purposeful." That is, they should generally eschew prewrapped curriculum packages that allow teachers little or no opportunity to participate in curriculum planning or development. At the same time, planners should consider schools to be only part of a broader educational system that has a number of contributing elements in each community.[20]

Lessons gleaned from business, professional, and social organizations suggest that teachers should be treated with respect, that new ideas originating at the grassroots level should be given full consideration, and that teachers' readiness to do curriculum work should be handled gracefully. Another lesson upholds the idea of starting small, lest teachers feel lost in a vast sea of novelty. Still another lesson stresses the importance of open and informal communication, along with careful listening. In summary, in schools where teachers are respected as mature people with worthwhile ideas, where projects are small enough to be satisfying, and where communication is open, care in dealing with teachers is likely to become an operating feature.[21]

Other Means of Encouraging Change and Improvement in Individuals

Although much change and improvement occur through individualized, person-to-person contacts, group work also is known to have a marked effect in changing people. This is true especially when the stimulator of change and the persons to be changed interact consistently in the same group. To be effective as a change medium, the group must, of course, be attractive to its members. The members accept new ideas and values most readily if the new ideas and values relate closely to those that group members already hold. The stimulator of change must diligently seek to cause the pressures for change or improvement to arise from within the group itself. The more the group talks about the need to change, the more pressure for change is built within it and thus within its individual members.[22]

When they are at their best, groups engage in a high quality of problem solving. Change is believed to be created most readily by keeping problem solving openly experimental, cooperative, task oriented, and educational and/ or therapeutic.[23] People who work together may be said to go through three steps in altering their views. They express compliance, usually in an effort to keep or enhance their own reputations; next, they identify with one or more other persons in their group or organization to achieve "a satisfying self-definition"; finally, they internalize the ideas and values in their environment, making these ideas and values part of themselves.[24]

The individual being referred to in the preceding paragraphs is preeminently the classroom teacher. Inasmuch as change in schools occurs primarily in classrooms, and inasmuch as the classroom teacher is still in charge of the classroom, those who desire change in schools must "get to" classroom teachers, whose role automatically builds around them certain resistances. In the first place, the teacher's role is characteristically ego rewarding, for in the classroom the teacher is the cynosure of all eyes, the main font of knowledge, the chief performer. When a board of education or an administrator installs in the teacher's classroom kits of learning materials which are advertised as being "teacher proof" and which substitute for part of the teacher's role, the teacher's resistance to the new materials is likely to be automatic.

If all the constructive work that has already been done with individual teachers in a school or school system is not to be undone, the innovations with which administrators and boards of control often become enamored must be presented to teachers with great care. The problem of moving the teacher out of a central role must be dealt with frankly and openly. Naturally, one of the first questions the teacher asks is "What's in this for the children—and for me?" The change agent must show what the proposed innovation can do to improve learning and how the teacher's time can be used more profitably in a somewhat altered assignment. Later, the teacher may ask embarrassing questions about the intentions of the innovators who devised the scheme, about which pupils are likely to gain most, about the precise gain usually attributable to the innovation when compared with doing nothing or doing something entirely different, and about the added cost of the innovation. The change agent can never be too well prepared to answer questions like these.[25]

The difficulties inherent in inducing change in individuals suggest that the personal characteristics of the change agent should be "special." Morin found that these special characteristics should include enjoyment of high professional esteem, ability to stimulate or to provide inspiration, openness to change in one's own ways, prudence and social awareness, ability to work well with others, and ability to lead and so to influence.[26] As is often true, attaining all the qualities in this list sounds impossible for human beings.

At its best, implementation of curriculum ideas consists of putting the ideas into operation in the most expeditious, skillful, and efficient ways possible. What actually happens when ideas affecting individual teachers are implemented in schools depends on the particulars of the situation. In Ohio, the state's department of education developed an implementation model for diffusing the ideas that were part of the new Environment Curriculum Adaptation Project. Later, the department assessed the factors causing success or failure in the implementation of the project. Three elements proved to be most important in causing teachers to accept ideas intended to teach pupils the importance of protecting the environment: the curriculum guides that had been produced, the interest generated by and in teachers, and the implementation of workshops as an inservice device. The obstacles were largely managerial: lack of time in the teachers' work week, the higher priority placed on other curriculum content, and conflicts in crowded school schedules.[27]

In Canadian schools, the Ontario Institute for Studies in Education traced the implementation of a packaged program designed to develop pupil skills in using concepts. Implementation was blocked in part by focusing too much on the project of instruction, or on the program's structure; by using illogical ways of diffusing the program; and by utilizing oversimplified strategies of change.[28]

In the developmental process, teachers move from orientation toward self, which can turn into a kind of professional selfishness, to task orientation, which occurs as they begin to use the new plan, and then to impact orientation, or realization of the effect of the plan on pupils. When they begin implementing a plan, teachers first become oriented, then behave mechanically, then engage in routine use of the plan, and at last succeed in refining or adjusting the plan.[29]

Wise school leaders have known for a long time that participation by teachers is vital to the success of any curriculum project that teachers are expected to implement. Unfortunately, planners from the outside seldom recognize the importance of teacher participation. As Joseph McDonald points out, the 1983 report *A Nation at Risk* implied that teachers are necessarily "dumb instruments of school policy."[30] Three years later, however, the Carnegie Task Force Report referred to teachers as chief agents of implementation. Clearly, sensible, knowledgeable people accept and use the truth that teaching and learning are interactive. If bright ideas are to be implemented, they must be implemented by people who are closest to learners. If they are to be put to real use, they must be developed and put into practice with the cooperation of classroom teachers.

Support, other than financial and material, depends on trusting relationships between teachers and administrators. The professionals need to commend the new plan and to encourage one another as they undertake it. Teachers do not respond well to overloads of innovations, to lack of time to do what is expected of them, to opposition from their peers, or to ignorance of what is happening of a similar nature elsewhere.[31] Perhaps the biggest block of all is a pervasive climate of mistrust in the school or school system. Underlying outright failure to cooperate, one often finds items of a hidden agenda, such as an administrator's dislike of teachers (or vice versa), fear of potential tragedies, or the personal quirks of staff members. Matters like these must be faced and dealt with first. Surely, encouraging change and improvement in individuals lies at the heart of school renewal.

Obviously, change in the individual is a process, not an event. The process can be aided by lengthening worthwhile staff development activities, by relieving teachers of their traditional isolation in the workplace, by meeting the differing needs of teachers to learn and develop, and by permitting teachers to be "disloyal" to a monolithic project without feeling guilt.[32]

Changes in individual teachers occur slowly. Sometimes, too, they occur subtly. When they prove permanent, they result in a strong sense of conviction and may be accompanied by a sense of pride.[33]

According to John Dewey's philosophy, ideas put to use in American schools should be both intellectual and democratic. Teachers, like other people, develop ideas from facts. Today, it is easy to receive and accept facts from machines—and then stop there. Richard Gibboney rightly criticizes "the amazing passivity of mind and imagination" that has characterized attempts at reforming schools in this technology-bent era. The machine, as opposed to the functioning individual intellect, Gibboney reminds us, cannot respond to changes that are occurring continually in our social system. Technological mindset thus becomes "the killing field of reform." Meanwhile, individual teachers continue to change their behavior in the old-fashioned way: by making thinking the progenitor and predecessor of their actions.[34]

How Change Occurs in Organizations

If change occurred only in one-to-one relationships and in small-group settings, it would be difficult enough to understand and accomplish. But it also takes place in large organizations containing many subparts. A particular subpart—for example, a subject department in a high school—may be ready for improvement while the remaining subparts lag. In organizations, hierarchies and channels are present; through them, plans for change or improvement must pass if they are to be acceptable to the organization as a whole. Hubert S. Coffee and William P. Golden, Jr. describe the general situation:

> Institutions usually develop a formal social structure as a method of performing their work. The structure is characterized by a hierarchy of offices which have distinctive responsibilities and privileges. These are exemplified in a status system which is based on differential prestige and a prescribed set of roles and procedures....
>
> The process of change can be productive within an institution only if conditions permit reassessment of goals and the means of their achievement....
>
> The most significant barrier to institutional change is the resistance which persons express when such change seems threatening to roles in which they have developed considerable security....[35]

Tested Processes of Institutional Change

Hierarchies, goals, procedures, and roles are all involved in the process of institutional change.[36] The existence of rigid hierarchies and standardized views of procedures and roles may inhibit change. Cooperative examination of goals does, on the other hand, encourage permanence of change provided that the altered goals are put into functional use by the hierarchy. At any rate, of the three methods of institutional change mentioned previously—planning by equals, indoctrination by superiors, and coercion by superiors—planning by equals seems to have the greatest long-term and desirable effect.

David H. Jenkins has proposed a methodology of encouraging teacher-pupil planning—and for creating other educational changes—that follows four classic steps in social engineering: (1) analyzing the situation, (2) determining required changes, (3) making these changes, and (4) stabilizing the new situation to ensure its maintenance.[37] Jenkins recognizes the existence of a "force field" (as suggested originally by the late Kurt Lewin) in which there are "driving forces" that push in the direction of change and "restraining forces" that oppose change. The present or current level of an educational situation is "that level where the sum of all the downward forces and the sum of all the upward forces are equal." An example of a driving force is the conviction that if teachers involve their pupils in planning, the teachers themselves will receive greater satisfaction from the act of teaching. An example of a restraining force is teachers' lack of skill in helping pupils plan.

In Jenkins's words, "changes will occur only as the forces are modified so that the level where the forces are equal is changed." To modify the forces, one may (1) reduce or remove restraining forces, (2) strengthen the driving forces or add to their number, or (3) change the direction of certain forces. For instance, one may remove lack of skill in teacher-pupil planning through training, strengthen or add to competence in planning, and change the direction in which the objective "good citizenship" is achieved *from* telling pupils how to be good citizens *to* planning citizenship activities with them. In analyzing the force field, the curriculum leader may seek answers to the following questions: What forces are there in the field? Can the directions of some of the forces be reversed or altered in another way? Which restraining forces can probably be reduced with least effort? Which driving forces can probably be increased?

To become permanent, says Jenkins, change must be stabilized—the stability of the new condition must be ensured. This can be accomplished by making sure that the restraining forces have been made impotent and that the driving forces continue in action.

In making a comparison of diffusion and adoption of innovative techniques in agriculture on the one hand and education on the other, Robert G. Owens explains the relatively slow rate of change in education in the following ways. First, education has an insufficient scientific base. As a consequence, school personnel are uncertain which ideas and procedures are most valid. Second, education lacks change agents comparable to county agents in agriculture. Certainly, school administrators do not create or encourage change as readily. Third, schools lack incentives to adopt new ways of proceeding. One of the important missing incentives is direct evidence that given practices work. Fourth, the U.S. public school, in particular, is a "domesticated organization" rather than a "wild" one. That is, it is protected and secure, unexposed to the risks that business organizations often encounter. As a result, it develops less vigor than it should.[38] There is evidence that less vigorous organizations exhibit less desire to change.

On the affirmative side, E. G. Guba believes that it is possible and necessary to have a strategy for diffusion of innovations. As to technique, the strategy can utilize telling, showing, helping, involving, training, and/or intervening. Guba points out that a regional educational laboratory may be expected to tell, show, or involve people. A state department of education can intervene. An individual teacher can tell and show. People in all of these agencies need to be careful about using techniques that do not come naturally to them or are seen as being outside their prescribed roles.[39]

Very often, several categories of persons are involved in a given curriculum change. Some of them are likely to support the change; others, to resist it; and still others, to be lukewarm about it. Suppose the categories included teachers, pupils, parents, other taxpayers, local employers, college personnel, and representatives of two or three government agencies. An initial step in determining locus and degree of support can be to ask questions like the following: Which of these groups seem likely to support the change? Which seem likely to oppose it? In the former instance, why the support? In the latter instance, why the opposition? How can persons in supporting populations become most helpful in inducing opponents to support the change?

For a number of years, the prophets of structural change in institutions held that if schools were organized differently, school populations were shifted in given ways, and time schedules were constructed differently, learning would improve and everyone would be happier. In the early 1970s, however, Seymour Sarason's emphasis on the culture of the school as the more significant key to organizational change began shifting the thinking of professionals.[40] The school culture most conducive to constructive change has been found to have certain characteristics: high-quality administrative leadership in crucial situations; teachers who are willing to work together, to stay with important projects, and to pay careful attention to cooperative problem solving; and the availability of help and resources.[41] Lively discussion among professionals, open communication with other schools within the same system, and identification of knowledge that is truly new mark the educational institutions with real prospects of improving.

Recently, "restructuring" has become a magical word, causing confusion with the multiple meanings that are being applied to it. The main intention of many persons today is to restructure elementary and secondary schools. Without restructuring, we cannot have real institutional change. The semantic problems are compounded by rejecting restructuring as a mere rearrangement of old stuff and by approving in its place something called renewal, which is akin to rebirth. Meanwhile, people strain to find or invent the best strategies for rearranging the school as an institution.[42] As a consequence of the straining, we have any number of goals and versions of school restructuring:

1. *To change school buildings.* Here we move from one-room schools to eight-room schools, to megaschools, to "open" schools, to schools with all-purpose facilities.
2. *To alter time arrangements.* We move from strict time allocations to blocks of time, to "free schooling," to time allocations to serve different persons and purposes.
3. *To create new roles, relationships, and routines.* We have specialist teachers, groupings to satisfy varied needs, shifting schedules, and more.

4. *To encourage goal-setting, goal attainment, and outcome-based education.* This is, in part, a return to some of the fundamentals of education.
5. *To permit parents and pupils to select magnet schools and other schools of choice.* This strategem suggests different thoughts to different people: "Let's scare the poor schools into becoming good ones," or "Let's establish a system of elite schools," or "What if some of the impoverished children in the poor schools have no way (for reasons of transportation or other) to escape from them?"
6. *To follow the technological route from audiovisuals to teaching machines to microcomputers and beyond.* For decades, people who like machines have tried to substitute them for human beings.
7. *To achieve democratization.* Why not have school leadership exercised increasingly by committees of teachers?[43]

When the dust raised by conflict about these and other ideas has settled, viable institutional change in a given setting will suit the culture that pervades that setting. A school's culture focuses on (1) agreements shared by local people about what is and (2) expectations shared by the same people about what ought to be. The professionals inside a given school may be expected to differ concerning what can be done. (So, too, will parents and other community members.) Nonetheless, the comprehensive goal of the people in and around the school should be general or basic agreement as to what practices originating in the past ought to be challenged and what practices in the prospect ahead hold greatest promise. Once again, people count in the process.[44] Restructuring that takes into account the importance of people is discussed in Chapter 8.

Lieberman and Miller have suggested five "building blocks" that should underlie new structures. First, the designers should think about what can be done to promote quality and equality for all pupils. Second, they should rethink the current structure of the school. Third, they should seek to make pupils' learning environment richer while preparing a supportive work environment for adults. Fourth, the designers should assist in the building of partnerships and networks among teachers and adults outside the school. Finally, they should make special efforts to involve parents and other community members in the restructuring.[45]

Charles E. Moore focuses on whether a restructured school has really been changed. He wants to know, first, whether people's beliefs and behaviors have been altered. Then, he uses words like *pride, sharing, valuing, participation,* and *wise expenditure* to indicate actual, constructive change.[46]

The Psychology of Institutional Change

The persons who are subjects of change may be viewed in any one of seven ways: as rational beings who can be convinced, as untrained persons who can be taught, as psychological beings who can be persuaded, as economic beings who can be paid or deprived, as political beings who can be influenced, as members of a bureaucratic system who can be compelled, and as members of a profession who have professional obligations. The way a change agent chooses to view the persons for whom he or she has responsibility depends significantly on the state or condition in which the agent wants to leave them after dealing with them.[47]

In organizations, there are usually conditions that become psychological barriers to progress. One of these is the requirement that people work together when they are unaccustomed to doing so. Another is that roles become obsolete and thus preparation for existing roles becomes outdated. Another is that decision making takes time, and the passage of time builds tension in people who are waiting for the decisions. Still another is that real control is often diffused, so responsibility remains unclear, and subsequent feedback is uncertain or ambiguous.

Persons who would create change in an organization of the size and complexity of the average school system need to keep in mind several phenomena relating to the peculiarities of people in groups. The first of these is what happens when supporters of an innovation are labeled as "good guys" and the opponents or neutrals as "bad guys." If a change agent applies the labels too prominently, the insecure opponent or neutral is likely to conclude, "If my old way of doing things is no good, then the implication is that I am no good." Polarization of supporters and detractors is a natural consequence of such labeling, and the detractors may begin to hope that the innovation will fail and to work to defeat it. Labeling is often a subtle, even unconscious, action. The change agent should declare a given innovation to be *one* of the bright new prospects on the educational horizon, giving about equal time to each of the other prospects in which people in the school system have become interested.

A related phenomenon occurs when one member of a group becomes the "fair-haired" one, or an object of favoritism. Special contributors to the success of an innovation may easily be regarded by less enthusiastic and less diligent contributors as "fair haired," chosen, or specially favored. Such persons are then envied, deprecated, or hated by the rank and file. Though the fair haired are thus damaged, damage to the managerial system is even greater; the distrust of the rank and file then becomes management's chief handicap in dealing with many of the people in the school or school system.

The so-called bandwagon effect is a third phenomenon. Teachers tend to be suspicious of the motives of administrators who continually board new educational bandwagons for short-term rides. The alleged innovations that the bandwagons represent are sometimes not innovations at all. (The same bandwagon actually came through town years ago; it looks like something new only because people have forgotten its design and the color of its trappings.) Wise school leaders control their enthusiasm for innovations until they know and understand them. This restraint helps to screen out unworthy prospects among the range of innovations.

A fourth phenomenon peculiar to adverse economic situations is the faculty's sense of insecurity. When budgets are being reduced, teachers are being dismissed, and new positions are not being approved, incumbent teachers tend to look at new projects with suspicion, especially if the projects are expensive or if they substitute in some way for service by teachers. In this circumstance, the facts of the matter are less important than the perceptions of faculty members. To campaign successfully for adoption of an innovation, the school leader must keep the facts that support the adoption at his or her fingertips, but the real battle will be won only when the leader has worked honestly and forthrightly to correct the perceptions of the staff (if correction is needed).

Affirmative and negative feelings of people within organizations come in waves. One may encounter initial enthusiasm, followed by disillusionment. In emergencies, there may be panic, a search for the "guilty," and inadvertent punishment of the "innocent." Sometimes praise and honor go to nonparticipants rather than to deserving hard workers. Such is the nature of curriculum planning as it affects and is affected by people.

Finally, a school system is what its name suggests—an organizational system with many people serving different functions. Proposals for change that cause the least disruption within the system usually have the greatest chance of being accepted and therefore of succeeding. Life in organizations is normally filled with enough disturbance to make manufactured disruptions of questionable value unless they are seen as contributing in the long run to constructive results.

Attempts at Effecting Change in Organizations

An approach to effecting change in organizations is organization development (OD), which is based on some of the more humane points of view about motivation that have been expounded in social science literature. Organization development attempts to change schools and other institutions from their mechanical orientation to a living, social one, thereby encouraging the reeducation of people, emphasizing learning-by-doing in confronting organizational problems, and ultimately improving the functioning of the organization. Though organizational change usually concentrates heavily on tasks, technology, and structure, OD has as its main concern the organization's human social system. It emphasizes goals and potentials, data collection and feedback, open communication, effort by a number of groups within the organization, involvement of all parts of the organization, and dedication of people, money, and time to improvement.[48] An abbreviated form of organization development known as organizational consultation uses the same strategies as OD, but it consumes less time because it is less comprehensive.[49]

A second attempt at organizational change, lately emerging, is *systemic reform,* or change in an entire educational system. The partisans of systemic reform say that changing a part of an educational system inevitably causes changes in the other parts of the system. Thus it involves a range of school system issues. Suppose planners begin with need for curriculum change. Soon they realize that effective curriculum planning requires staff development, which costs money. The mention of money leads to consideration of budget policy. When planning has gone this far, the realization dawns that the school system should consider community ramifications. These ramifications may include alliance with private schools and with enterprises in home schooling. Subsequently, they could bring about wide use of a voucher system.[50]

John O'Neil has said that a viable system has a unifying vision and accompanying goals that express what ought to be. It provides ways of developing knowledge, skills, and problem-solving capacities of all pupils. It may value state-proposed outcomes and standards along with locally determined ways of achieving desired results.[51]

Most persons who have studied the change process intensively seem to agree that if people in organizations are to change from old modes to new, they must first be made aware of the possibility of changing. Next, they must be made interested in a proposed change. Third, they must have time to consider the worth of the change. Fourth, they must try it for themselves on a small or limited scale. Finally, if the change withstands the test they apply, they may accept the change for use in the future.

The Prospects for Planned Institutional Change

How will change in schools fare in a difficult era—the immediate future? People who have worked in schools throughout the past four or five decades tend to agree that the current era in elementary and secondary schooling is the most difficult one they have known. The public's faith in schools has eroded to a significant degree. Increased imposition of minimum standards of pupil achievement has altered local curriculum requirements. This imposition is evidence of greater centralization of power in state governments, which has destroyed part of the power and influence of educators and other persons in local communities. These facts would seem to indicate that the schools can become puppets moved to and fro by outside forces, and that their destiny as mainly self-controlled institutions is dangerously uncertain.

Other factors, however, are making planned institutional change at the local level more effective and promising than ever before. In the first place, curriculum leaders are better prepared for their work. They are harder to delude. They know how to work around unwise (and sometimes downright idiotic) mandates. Whether or not they have had careful instruction in the change process, they sense the necessity of working in ways that encourage desirable change. They know more about innovations and practices that have passed both formal and experiential tests of worth. At the same time, their suspicion of quack schemes promises less going-through-the-motions just for the sake of being active. They are learning gradually what better balance in programs and activities can mean in achieving high-quality schooling. Accordingly, the schools themselves are becoming better planned and more nearly self-renewing institutions. As pressures change and eras pass, the substantial element in institutional change will continue to be an element that has been respected too little: constantly improving the quality of personnel who operate instructional programs. One of the barriers to employing well-prepared curriculum leaders is the proposal that the leaders be people who have been successful in distantly relevant roles; too often, such people are totally inexperienced in schools.

The importance of increasing the competence of local school system personnel argues for improved programs of staff development. School system staffs need two kinds of development in particular: (1) reeducation, leading to a redirection and a refinement of competencies, and (2) resocialization, or realignment of roles and role relationships. In any institution, the latter tends to be more difficult to achieve than the former. People do not mind being "updated," but they dislike having their roles and functions changed and having their role relationships altered or destroyed. Nevertheless, both kinds of development are necessary, regardless of the cost in time and money.[52]

Both reeducation and resocialization can be enhanced by freeing teachers to interact during longer periods of time than staff development programs usually permit. The ultimate need is for collegiality and collaboration leading to shared decision making. To achieve these effects, everything possible needs to be done to recognize that teachers have long been independent artisans, kept isolated by the customary organization of schools. Teachers simply do not trust one another fully until they have been together long enough and congenially enough to overcome the "veiling of conversation" common to teachers' rest rooms. Surely, we need to eliminate the expression "When I leave my classroom, I always erase my chalkboard—for a reason other than tidiness."[53]

SITUATION 7-1

Resistance to Change: Trouble in a Faculty

It was October, a month after the start of Jim Downes's third year as principal of Martinsville High School. Previously, he had been in charge of a similar high school in Townsend Terrace.

He came home at the end of the day much discouraged. Sitting in his favorite armchair in the living room, he looked disconsolate.

"What's the trouble, Jim?" asked Eunice, his wife. "Why don't you come to dinner?"

"I'm disheartened and disgusted," said Jim. "We had a faculty meeting again today. Our curriculum consultant from the college was there, and we thought everything would go well. I say 'we.' Sam and I were the only two people who seemed to have any such hopes. If it weren't for Sam and his leadership of the science department, I believe I'd quit. Well, nine-tenths of the faculty members just sat there. When the consultant and I asked what problems the faculty would like to deal with during the coming year, we drew a blank."

"You mean no one said anything?" Eunice inquired.

"Well, practically so. There was a long, dead silence, and then Old Ben Oppenheimer spoke for the group, as usual. 'This is a smooth-running faculty,' Ben said. 'It's been smooth for years, Mr. Downes. It was smo-o-o-th before you came. We just don't see any need to manufacture problems.'

"That was the end of Ben's speech and practically the end of the meeting. I'm glad the superintendent wasn't there. If he had been, he'd have seen how little I've been able to jar that faculty in two years...."

What might have caused the Martinsville faculty to resist change as it seems to have done?

What dynamics or forces are frequently at work in situations of this kind?

What do you suppose Jim Downes might do to reduce apathy and stimulate change?

SITUATION 7-2

Misdirected Change: The Tendency to Move in Too Many Directions at Once

Curriculum change was popping in Plainsburg. The curriculum steering committee for the school system had invited individual teachers and groups of teachers to suggest and develop curriculum projects of any sort they wished. No machinery for selecting or screening projects had been established. The consequence was a flood of projects big and little, well conceived and ill conceived. The steering committee began to express concern as to how many of the projects represented the real needs of the school system and whether there was danger in permitting school personnel "to ride off in too many directions at once."

What is your position regarding control of the number and nature of projects leading to curriculum change?

Which of the ideas about change that appear in the initial part of this chapter relate to the problem of moving in too many directions at once and should therefore be communicated to participants in curriculum improvement?

ACTIVITY 7-1

Statements About Change Process That Are Open to Discussion

Investigate and discuss the validity and the associated implications of the following statements:

1. Parents and other groups of lay persons in most communities do not exert direct influence on the adoption of new instructional programs, but their influence is decisive on the rare occasions when it is exerted.
   Implication: In organizing new programs, it is not necessary to arouse the active enthusiasm of parents, but it is necessary to avoid their active opposition.
2. The board of education in many a community is not a strong agent in determining the path of educational innovation, but its influence is decisive when it is exerted.

Implication: New programs must be developed in ways that will not arouse the opposition of boards of education.

3. New instructional programs are usually introduced by school administrators. Contrary to general opinion, teachers play a relatively insignificant role in educational innovation.

Implication: It pays to convince administrators of the worth of proposed new programs and to gain their support in putting the programs into effect.

4. Classroom teachers can make only three kinds of instructional change in the absence of administrative initiative: (1) change in classroom practice, (2) relocation of existing curriculum content, and (3) introduction of single special courses at the secondary school level.

Implication: Inservice programs for teachers should be limited to these three matters.

5. The most persuasive experience a school person can have is to observe a successful new program in action. Speeches, literature, research reports, and conversations with participants are interesting but relatively unconvincing.

Implication: Recommended new programs must be demonstrated to persons who are expected to become involved in them.

6. The most successful innovations are those that are accompanied by the most elaborate help to teachers as they begin to use the innovations.

Implication: Instructional innovation should be accompanied by substantial continuing assistance to teachers.

PRACTICAL APPLICATIONS OF CHANGE PROCESS IN IMPROVING THE CURRICULUM

Some notable attempts have been made to apply change process in improving the curriculum. For example, the five classic steps in the change process—awareness, interest, evaluation, trial, and adoption—were incorporated, with minor alteration, in the planning accomplished by the Northwest Regional Educational Laboratory. This plan, called Research Utilizing Problem Solving Process (RUPS), specifies the following five steps:

1. *Identifying a need for change:* developing awareness, sensing problems, judging who is causing and who is affected by problems, classifying problems, and specifying goals for proposed change

2. *Diagnosing the situation in which change is to take place:* identifying favorable and unfavorable forces and assessing the strength of each force

3. *Considering alternative courses of action*

4. *Testing the feasibility of a plan for change:* running a trial phase during which further attempts are made to understand the situation; the people who are conducting the testing are trained for it; and evaluation of outcomes and process is effected

5. *Adoption, diffusion, and adaptation of successful change effort:* institutionalizing successful actions, sharing successes and failures with persons else-

where, and returning to the first step to see whether there are now new needs for change[54]

The CLER model, developed by H. S. Bhola, was concerned with configurations, linkages, environments, and resources. Configurations and linkages position data to achieve change; environments and resources encompass elements external to the change process itself. All are thought to be necessary for determining the domain and the time within which change is to occur, for establishing a range of action choices, and for helping with program implementation and evaluation.[55]

Another change model is PARA, an acronym for profile, action, response, and analysis. The first step, involving the *profile,* relates to the participating teacher's aspirations in the direction of better task performance. The second step calls for creating an *action* plan expressing exactly what the teacher will do within an allotted period of time. The third, or *response,* step consists of gathering information from pupils and other persons in the school about ways in which the plan has affected pupil behavior. In the final step, action substeps are *analyzed* to determine their relative worth.[56]

In more recent days, Theodore Sizer has led the Coalition of Essential Schools in using change methodologies. Sizer began his planning with a commitment to helping pupils learn to think and to become involved in actions they consider important. He believes that teachers need to know their pupils well, and that testing should be replaced in part by exhibits and demonstrations. Sizer refuses to create a model because "time and context are everything." Absence of a mandate has resulted in varied experimentation in numbers of school. Foundations and corporations have been providing support for the coalition.[57]

Earlier, the public schools of Montgomery County, Maryland had prepared a five-year plan for developing and installing revised systems of instruction in four subject fields. Within the latter part of the five-year period, announcement was made of a program for reeducation of personnel, incorporating a series of steps in inservice education. These steps included orienting the staff to the philosophy and nature of the proposals; instructing teachers and others about placement tests, curriculum guides, reports, and assessments; providing activities to help teachers use features of the instructional plans; demonstrating exemplary classroom practices; and teaching principals and aides what they needed to know to implement the proposals.[58]

Finally, Project Zero at Harvard University has developed ATLAS communities, which are communities for *A*uthentic *T*eaching, *L*earning, and *A*ssessment for all *S*tudents. ATLAS schools emphasize unorthodox inquiries like the following: What is justice? What does it mean to be alive? Can teachers become coaches rather than lecturers or judges? Can all adults in a school community have a voice in decision making? How can authentic learning environments be created? How can standards of accomplishment be set? In

ATLAS schools, an attempt is made to enhance coherence in pupils' educational experiences and to individualize pupil learning.[59]

Levels of Specific Curriculum Improvements

Changes that are judged to be improvements are produced at several levels of operation. Improvements can be accomplished by substitution, alteration, variation, restructuring, or value-orientation change. If, for example, a group of teachers and administrators were proposing to improve a reading program, they might simply substitute a new series of readers for the current series because the newly adopted books had features that made them superior. On the other hand, they might alter the curriculum by declaring that reading would henceforth be allotted thirty additional minutes of instructional time each day on the ground that increased instructional time would yield improved results. Or they might try variation by importing a reading program that had succeeded reasonably well elsewhere into their own school, where conditions were such that it might have even better success. They might decide to restructure, a more hazardous means of improvement, by organizing teams of reading teachers made up of reading specialists, classroom teachers, and aides to provide maximum instructional impact. Or, finally and most precariously, they might attempt value-orientation change, asking classroom teachers to turn matters of routine reading instruction over to computer-assisted instruction and teacher aides while the teachers themselves became responsible for diagnosis, prescription, search for materials, and other more difficult aspects of reading instruction. Changing teachers' roles in this way requires a shift in their values, a shift that most adults make only with difficulty, though they may give temporary signs of having made it. Although the five levels may appear, for purposes of analysis, to be separate and distinctive, more than one of them may be used at any one time to promote a curriculum project.

An Overview and Analysis of Changes and Improvements

Donald Orlosky and B. Othanel Smith studied major changes and improvements in curriculum and ascribed to them times of origin, sources, and ratings of success (see Table 7-1). The times of origin are specified as pre-1950 and post-1950. The sources are internal to school systems (I) and external to school systems (E). External sources include community groups, government, and foundations. The ratings of success range from 1 to 4. The rating 1 applies to a change that has not been implemented in the schools and would be hard to find in a school system anywhere. The rating 2 means a change that has not been accepted widely but has had some influence on educational practice. The rating 3 refers to a change that has been installed in schools and is quite evident there. The rating 4 indicates a change that has successfully permeated schools and school systems.[60]

TABLE 7-1

Major change or improvement	Time of origin	Source	Rating of success
Activity curriculum	Pre-1950	I	2
British Infant School	Post-1950	I	3
Community school	Pre-1950	I	2
Compensatory education	Post-1950	E	3
Conservation education	Pre-1950	E	3
Core curriculum	Pre-1950	I	1
Creative education	Post-1950	I	1
Driver education	Pre-1950	E	4
Elective system	Pre-1950	I	4
Environmental education	Post-1950	E	3
Extraclass activities	Pre-1950	I	4
Home economics	Pre-1950	E	3
International education	Pre-1950	I	3
Physical education	Pre-1950	E	4
Safety education	Pre-1950	I	4
Sex education	Post-1950	E	2
Special education	Post-1950	I	4
Thirty School Experiment (Eight Year Study)	Pre-1950	I	1
Unit method	Pre-1950	I	2
Updating curriculum content	Pre-1950	I	3
Vocational and technical education	Pre-1950	E	4

It would be interesting to conjecture what social and other forces have made for ratings of 3 and 4 in the cases of programs like driver education, safety education, and vocational-technical education. The high ratings of these programs contrast with the ratings of the core curriculum, sex education, and the famous Thirty School Experiment, the Eight Year Study. Contrary to an assumption shared by many professionals and lay persons, at least as many durable innovations originate inside schools as originate outside them. Evidently, when both the pressures internal to schools and the pressures external to them operate simultaneously in favor of an innovation, its success is assured. The history of curriculum innovation shows, however, that changes in the curriculum can be discarded more readily than changes in school organization.

Although the Orlosky-Smith data are now antiquated, they provide a look at classic movements to create change and the fate of these movements over three-quarters of a century. These authors came to the conclusion that planned change should be based on a combination or interaction of planned experiences, current points of view, and analysis of aspects of the educational field. They found that curriculum change is easier to achieve than change in methods of teaching, that adding subjects and updating content have more permanent effects than reorganizing or restructuring the curriculum. Changing an entire curriculum pattern is hazardous even if teachers support the change at the outset. Changes are made impermanent by lack of external social support and by resistance within school systems. When a diffusion plan is lacking, change is aborted. A change that causes teachers or administrators to lose power or to shift their roles drastically will probably be resisted by the very people who can make it effective. In summary, the source of a change has less to do with its success or failure than the support the change acquires and the strain it places on teachers and administrators. For example, the core curriculum and education for creativity have demanded too much of teachers, in consideration of the limited external and even internal support these innovations have received, and they have therefore had limited success. However, international education, supported moderately by school personnel and lay persons, has required little extra effort from teachers and administrators and has been accepted reasonably well.[61]

In supplementing the Orlosky-Smith version of what happens in the change process, Parish and Arends support the argument made by anthropologists that many innovations are put to use only when adaptations are made to the culture within which the innovations are expected to thrive. Curriculum planners need to understand the culture of each school in which they work. Within a school, teachers have their own subculture, and administrators have theirs. Therefore, if curriculum change is to begin and continue, strategies for achieving cultural change are more significant than strategies for achieving technological change, though the latter have long been emphasized.[62]

Heckman and others agree that research, development, and diffusion (the familiar RD&D) are less effective in stimulating change than is responsiveness on the part of schools to the needs of their occupants. These needs are determined in large part by looking at the sense the occupants of schools make of their settings and situations. Pupils and teachers go along, though often unenthusiastically, with what other people want them to do. Thus the curriculum often provides learners with answers to questions they do not have and probably never will. How much better it is to raise and answer questions that have real meaning for *these* people *here!*[63]

The culture of which school people are a part is a combination of established ways of doing things and the meanings people affix to these ways. Changing what school personnel do demands that they accept not only new ways of doing things but also new sets of meanings that belong with the new ways.[64]

Agencies and Media for Achieving Change

Change-promoting agencies and media come in varied forms and guises. Four of the major ones are the support of official leaders, staff development and in-service education, systems of collaboration, and educational materials.

Support of Official Leaders

Many reports of changes in curriculum do not indicate how crucial the support of official leaders of schools and school systems is to the success of innovations. Considerable curriculum literature is available, however, to show that the support of leaders is indeed necessary. A cross-cultural comparison of the effectiveness of school leaders in five nations indicates that support by leaders and a leadership demeanor (as opposed to a limited management outlook) are essential in building teachers' enthusiasm for curriculum change.[65] The specific help that principals and other administrators are especially able to give includes putting teachers in contact with curriculum resources, helping them clarify the directions in which they wish to go with instructional projects, assisting with adaptation and development of materials, and marshaling the support of other school personnel and community members.[66]

Obviously, not all principals are star performers in helping to improve schools. Consider the distinctions among three categories of leader: initiators, managers, and responders. Initiators (activists) appear to surpass managers and responders in several dimensions of performance. Initiators apply to their work an understanding of the culture of the school, the nature of the pupil population, and the lore of curriculum planning, all backed by both theoretical and practical knowledge. Managers do only what the name suggests; they may be former business people without any background in education. (Tragically, some government officials would have only manager-types chosen as principals.) Responders merely pick up on the ideas of others, following along dutifully without thinking very hard about what is being done.[67]

Leadership also resides in persons other than principals, curriculum coordinators, and supervisors. Any school faculty is likely to include one or more individuals without official portfolio but with a remarkable ability to marshal personnel, get plans moving toward fruition, and elicit support from higher-ups. Inexperienced administrators sometimes fear unofficial, emergent leaders who prove more effective than they themselves are.

Staff Development and Inservice Education

The chief function of staff development and inservice education as agencies of curriculum change and improvement is to cause teachers to want to initiate worthwhile changes in their classroom practices. Several means are believed to assist in achieving this end, including released time, summer institutes, inservice programs before and after school terms, and visits to other teachers' classrooms.

In the past, one way in which educators have attempted to update teachers' knowledge of subject matter is by conducting institutes such as those supported with federal funds under provisions of the National Defense Education Act. Apparently, many of the professors who taught in NDEA institutes knew little "about the limits, possibilities, and politics of teaching in the schools— about what can be changed, and how change happens in a school or a school system." A study reported further that the professors were "not much concerned to learn."[68] They lectured much and listened little to elementary and secondary school teachers who had been specially chosen because of their competency. The teachers complained that they were given too little opportunity to talk back, to consider key issues, to observe ranges of teaching strategies and techniques, and to relate their newly acquired information to their own teaching. Not only did these findings lead to changes in the institutes, but the experiences of these able teachers as students in summer institutes provided insight into the importance of process in the inservice education of teachers elsewhere. Teachers need opportunities to help determine inservice agendas and procedures to be used in inservice sessions.

Giving teachers such opportunities allows new and unaccustomed content to be introduced during inservice sessions. For example, segments of a session may be devoted to "what we know about the curriculum in our district," "how we can all participate in curriculum change," or "coming to a common view of what real change is."[69] Teachers should come to realize that change can produce learning and that having educational problems is natural. Finally, inservice education can be extended beyond the customary institutes, conferences, workshops, graduate courses, and staff meetings so that it offers occupational experiences, field trips, exchanges of teachers among departments and schools, community surveys, professional writing, consulting, and speaking.[70]

Generally, inservice education has the earmarks of an externally imposed regimen. The idea of staff development has been formulated to "loosen" inservice education so that responsibility for teacher change and growth is placed on the shoulders of the teachers themselves. Staff development usually proves most helpful when it focuses on crucial elements of teaching, such as the teacher's sense of purpose, the teacher's perception of pupils, the teacher's knowledge of subject matter, and the teacher's mastery of technique. Always, the emphasis is on the teacher and his or her development, which occurs by participation, peer assistance, individual study, and the making of alternative choices. "We did it ourselves in an informal setting" is the theme of many staff development activities, in contrast to the "here's what you are to do" attitude that pervades many inservice projects.[71]

Systems of Collaboration

Years ago, Stephen M. Corey emphasized in his consulting assignments how important it is for teachers and principals to work together. By collaborating, he said, school people ease the process of curriculum change. Corey advocated action research procedures (described in Chapter 11 of this text) as a medium of collaboration as well as of evidence-getting.

Ideas in education have a way of flourishing, then dying away, and eventually, if they are worth anything, returning as though they were brand new. Nowadays, the collaborative school, in which climate and structure favor teamwork, appears to many people to be a new invention.[72] Actually, a few such schools existed during the early decades of the century.

The culture of a collaborative school features cooperative planning by the staff, the work of a building-level curriculum steering committee, close cooperation with parents and other community members, and cooperative learning in classrooms. Collaborative schools within a district can form a network for supplying curriculum help.[73] The old, threatening lines of authority become blurred as personnel of several ranks and specialties work together on common problems. Furthermore, as Fullan and Miles state, change is effected most readily in cross-role groups: groups consisting of teachers, department heads, service personnel, administrators, and sometimes parents and pupils.[74] To paraphrase the words of a song, getting to know people, getting to know all about them becomes a basis for changing oneself, others, school practices, and the curriculum in general.[75]

Educational Materials

Materials have become a special avenue to change and improvement. For instance, packaged learning programs have come into vogue. In their simplest forms, packages are boxed assortments of materials; more complex packages are complicated learning systems. Packaging of worthwhile learning materials holds promise of helping teachers achieve flexibility in meeting the needs of individual pupils. When the instructional objectives contained in a package tell pupils the quality of performance they should achieve, they have a standard that is seldom communicated to them by other means. Some of the activities in packaged programs are model building, large-group instruction, small-group instruction, role playing, simulation, gaming, field trips, independent study, and laboratory experimentation. Packages are, of course, only one of the kinds of materials found in multimedia centers, which also house books, slides, pictures, filmstrips, transparencies, models, telecasting equipment, instructional machines, and, occasionally, computers. These centers serve also as production areas or educational laboratories. Most centers are in individual schools, to be used directly by pupils and teachers. A few serve as system-wide facilities for use in inservice education, materials production and servicing, and curriculum planning. They can contribute to school quality because having a wealth of materials available is an important criterion of quality.

ACTIVITY 7-2

Teachers' Views of Curriculum Change

Teachers are obviously very important in initiating and perpetuating curriculum change. Interview a randomly selected sample of classroom teachers in an elementary or a secondary school to determine what the teachers think concerning curriculum change. A possible initial question: "If you had your way, what major change would you make in the curriculum of this school?" Formulate other questions that have to do with sources of change, reasons for acceptance of given changes, and the change process as it affects people in the school. Share your findings with other persons in your class or discussion group.

FOUR ACTIONS THAT FACILITATE CURRICULUM IMPROVEMENT

Four actions by curriculum workers seem to be especially effective in facilitating curriculum improvement. Stated in imperative form, they are

1. Change the climate and the working conditions in your institution to encourage curriculum improvement.
2. Achieve and maintain appropriate tempo in curriculum improvement.
3. Arrange for a variety of activities that lead to improvement.
4. Build evaluation procedures into each curriculum improvement project.

Each action will be discussed in some depth.

Establish Suitable Climate and Working Conditions

Climate and working conditions, like employee morale, result from many little actions and influences. The little actions and influences within an organization may, however, be categorized under five larger headings: the general attitudes of participating personnel, the quantity and quality of personnel (especially the competencies they bring to their tasks), the presence of peer tutors and helpers, the physical resources and materials at the disposal of staff members, and the absence of undue and detrimental pressure and influence.

Attitudes of Participants

Certain attitudes of participating personnel seem to be especially helpful in planning curriculum improvement. One of these is acceptance of people's right to feel and express legitimate dissatisfaction with the curriculum. Perhaps all who strive to progress in their work feel some dissatisfaction with what they are presently doing. Legitimate feelings of dissatisfaction lead not to arbitrary complaining but to affirmative steps that eventually result in satisfaction. Curriculum workers should seek to learn the exact causes of dissatisfaction felt by their peers and subordinates and should encourage co-workers who feel dissatisfaction to channel it constructively into new activity.

A second attitude encourages acceptance of the contributions of many kinds of people to improving the curriculum. Obviously, not all contributions of ideas and all gestures of helpfulness are of equal worth. Nevertheless, all who are qualified to belong to a faculty group may be expected to have unique contributions to make, if only because all are individuals. They should also be able to make certain contributions in concert with other members of the group. Curriculum workers should provide ample opportunity for people to express themselves and to offer their own talents in performing commonly approved tasks.

A third attitude expresses willingness to permit other persons to work on problems they themselves identify as worthy of attention. Real live problems are those that are real and live to those who face them and desire to solve them. Thus the principal who is concerned with his or her own problems is often certain that the teachers wish to help solve them. The teachers have their own problems, however, and may soon become impatient or even hostile if they are forced to help solve the principal's imposed or imported problems. Curriculum workers should help teachers clarify and solve the problems that the teachers themselves perceive as being well worth solving. The same teachers are then likely to greet with favor occasional opportunities to help solve problems for which they feel no direct personal concern. (Curriculum matters do not always constitute problems in the adverse sense. Sometimes, as when they are given a chance to spend funds suddenly provided for educational materials, curriculum personnel experience pleasant challenges rather than puzzling problems. Inasmuch as so many curriculum matters require solutions to weighty problems, however, the term *problem* appears frequently in this text, as in other curriculum literature.)

A fourth attitude consists of open-mindedness about new educational decisions and practices. Perhaps every specialist in curriculum improvement agrees that the improvement process is aided materially by an attitude of open-mindedness about the new and different, as well as about the tried and tested. So little in education is known assuredly that school personnel are acting presumptuously when they cling to ideas merely because they are supported by tradition. To some persons, open-mindedness means having an experimental attitude, a willingness to use the "method of intelligence"—commonly called the problem-solving method—in dealing with educational problems. To others, it implies merely an attitude of "wait and see" while other staff members try new practices. Whatever the degree of an individual's personal involvement in a project, open-mindedness is necessary to the project's success and to prospects for future experimentation.

A fifth attitude is one of willingness to work with others to achieve common ends through commonly agreed-upon means. This attitude affects all members of every working group—leaders and followers. However significant the contribution of the talented person working alone may be, well-coordinated groups usually prove wiser in plotting the means and ends of projects. Curriculum workers should become well acquainted with procedures that facilitate group work and should become competent in leading groups of differing sizes and kinds.[76] In addition, they should seek to reconcile the means they use with the ends they desire. One evidence of autocracy is a tendency to use unfair means to achieve desirable ends. Even the best curriculum workers can become careless about the means they use.

Studies of attitude change in teachers reveal that humanely conducted staff evaluations can serve as a starting point.[77] Also, arranging helpful contacts with other persons—fellow teachers, counselors, consultants, and community members serving in relevant occupations—can offer new perspectives.

Quantity and Quality of Personnel

A stimulating, friendly climate and helpful working conditions are aided by the presence of able personnel in sufficient numbers to accomplish worthwhile tasks. Few school systems have too many full-time coordinators, consultants, and specialists in fields like school social work, psychology, reading, and speech therapy. Surveys of the staffing of schools and school systems usually reveal that more work is being accomplished by limited numbers of persons than even the most conservative of personnel analysts expect. Nevertheless, these persons are often discharging responsibilities that should not be theirs or are discharging their responsibilities in ineffective ways.

In spite of the fact that present-day schools are frequently understaffed in the fields of supervision and curriculum services, the quality of assistance that classroom teachers are receiving could be improved in at least three respects:

- *The very best available persons should be utilized to discharge each major responsibility* (even though employing a new person may be costly). Too often, teachers or principals with full or partial work loads are being made part-time specialists in reading, art, music, physical education, speech, psychology, and other fields in which they may have received only limited preparation.
- *The role of the school in the total community should be examined at intervals.* This examination will determine whether all the functions the school has adopted truly belong to an educational institution. Many teachers, administrators, and lay persons suspect that certain social work services for children and the community at large have been preempted by the school from other institutions and agencies. Though the school may in many instances supply these services speedily and efficaciously, the wisdom of making the school responsible for them in the first place is questionable. Of course, children whose only source of necessary services is the school may legitimately expect the school to continue providing the services.
- *Special teachers should be assigned in different, more helpful ways.* Varied and sometimes questionable uses are being made of special teachers in subjects such as physical education. Reading specialists often devote their full time to helping individual pupils instead of spending a portion of their time helping classroom teachers become competent identifiers and eradicators of common reading difficulties. Specialists should ask themselves a key question: "How can we provide the greatest long-term help to classroom teachers?"

Two additional sources of personnel to improve teaching and learning are (1) the staffs of universities, state departments of education, county education offices, and school systems other than one's own and (2) well-informed lay persons who give advice strictly within their own specialties. These two sources provide part-time consultants who may be called upon for a few hours or days of assistance at almost any time. The factors that affect the success of consultants have been described in the literature. Alert boards of education and school administrators are making increasing use of consultant services. Many school systems maintain resource files of community citizens who volunteer their help in instructional fields ranging from the physical sciences and the arts to citizenship education. Classroom teachers are usually the best judges of which lay persons are most effective in reaching pupils with the content they have to teach.

Of course, no substitute has been found for competent classroom teachers who work patiently and insightfully with children day after day. The quality of the schools depends chiefly on the quality of the classroom teachers who teach in them. Consequently, employing superior teachers and then helping them grow personally and professionally is the best way to ensure that American children receive excellent schooling.

The morale of able teachers can be improved by reducing the load of clerical and custodial duties that now burden many of them. Obviously, professional employment carries with it responsibility for certain routine operations, but studies of the duties of classroom teachers often reveal numerous and sometimes unnecessary clerical and custodial loads. An enlightened school administration seeks to free competent persons for activity at their highest level of performance. Recent attempts to use wisely the services of teacher aides have brought revelations of their potential for helping classroom teachers with the semiprofessional and menial aspects of teaching. As "career ladders" of school personnel are built to distribute responsibility for paraprofessional, clerical, and other non-teaching tasks, the role of the classroom teacher as it is now conceived can change markedly. Consequently, school officials will need to be more certain than they are at present that teachers are using their time to maximum advantage.

Individual teachers tend to feel their own roles are valued if other teachers within the building are competent. In times of emergency licensing of marginally qualified teachers, the problem of maintaining teachers' self-respect as well as mutual respect among staff members becomes especially difficult and significant. The effect of quality of personnel on faculty morale is readily apparent.

Peer Tutors and Helpers

It is possible to increase the personnel resources of a school geometrically by preparing a cadre of pupil tutors and helpers who teach their peers and, not incidentally, learn by teaching. Frank Riessman estimated in 1989 that 20,000 peer tutor/helper programs existed in the United States. The number has increased since that time, with the greatest increase occurring in our larger cities. Peer tutor/helper programs tap the strength of youngsters, many of whom might otherwise become bored and obstructive. Young people can often surpass teachers in communicating with other youngsters. For this reason, some schools involve all the pupils they can in teaching and helping. On the fringe of the peer help movement are innovative programs in which selected youngsters arbitrate peer disputes, provide drug education, and conduct AIDS awareness sessions. Most of the older pupils succeed in teaching or helping the younger ones.[78] Certainly, the adoption of peer teaching can lead to restructuring of teacher responsibilities and of the uses of building space and time.

Peer teaching and helping should not end with pupils, however. The idea of collaboration includes interaction among adults for teaching and learning within schools and school systems. The days of the reclusive teacher should be long gone. We cannot admire teachers who erase their chalkboards quickly lest other teachers or supervisors borrow and disseminate their ideas. If knowledge is the wealth of school systems, it should be shared at least within the systems.

Availability of Physical Resources and Materials
Studies of working conditions in schools have revealed that teachers feel satisfaction in having varieties of usable instructional materials at hand and in understanding how to use them. When materials and equipment accord with the requirements of the instructional program, and when the persons who use materials and equipment have a major part in choosing them, the usefulness of these resources can be ensured.

One of the great difficulties with learning materials continues to be their failure to serve differing ability levels, socioeconomic groups, and special interests among the pupil population. Many teachers doubt that superior materials exist in quantity for children of any developmental level or status. The school that seeks to improve the curriculum for its pupils searches continuously for materials and equipment that will best take into account the range of individual differences the school encounters. The principal of a school of this sort tries to make physical resources quickly available to teachers by arranging for purchase of materials as they are needed and by moving them to points of use as speedily as possible. One of the major complaints of classroom teachers is that administrators and custodial staffs fail to move materials from storerooms according to a reasonable schedule, or even to communicate to teachers the fact that materials have arrived. An additional hazard of school administration is the tendency of principals to become overzealous about amplifying systems and electronic machinery generally and thus to spend precious funds in purchasing equipment that teachers would gladly trade for materials of more direct use to them.

Absence of Undue Pressure and Influence
Studies of teacher morale show clearly that the effectiveness of a school can be ruined by the conniving and perfidy of irresponsible politicians. Promises that are made and not kept are one of the major sources of trouble. Another is graft (which has now been eradicated from most school districts, but which is known to be present in a few and is strongly suspected in others). Tenure laws

have generally been successful in preserving teachers' employment, but teachers are sometimes under pressure to behave in politically acceptable ways if they desire salary increments, promotions, and privileges. Some political scientists maintain that control of the public schools should be placed more and more in the hands of municipal and state government officials and accordingly be removed from the authority of local boards of education. It is possible that this change would create more political interference with schools and teachers than now exists. The unfortunate effects of undue influence and pressure should be reduced and avoided at almost any cost.

Wilbur A. Yauch gave helpful advice about morale and its improvement:

1. Be willing to make haste slowly.
2. Take the easiest problems first.
3. Treat people as human beings.
4. Make their experiences in school pleasant.
5. Operate on the assumption that teachers can be trusted.
6. Try a little of the "Golden Rule."
7. Encourage and accept criticism.
8. Don't act like a stuffed shirt.[79]

Research and experience show that if curriculum changes are really to go into effect, varied actions must be taken to support teachers, personnel must be designated to do the supporting, and ample time must be allowed for the effectuating process to be completed.[80]

SITUATION 7-3

A Special Problem of Attitudes

Consider the words of a curriculum coordinator who has a complaint to make:

> Mr. Acornley, our superintendent, came to our K–12 social studies meeting and wanted the whole job we'd been working on for a long time to be done over. The teachers were all hopped up about some experiments they'd been designing. One of them was describing her plan when Mr. Acornley arrived. After about five minutes of sitting and looking wise, he turned to me and said, "Now I hope you're not misleading these teachers. I think they're getting themselves involved in things that don't concern them. I'm not much in favor of some of the ideas that teachers like to try out on other people's children. Now I'll tell you what we need—and the board reminded me of it just last week—a good social studies course of study. Preparing one in meetings like this would be more profitable, I'll bet a cookie, than listening to each other talk, especially when the conversation is over the heads of some of the folks anyway. I'll tell you what to do: Prepare a course of study and have it ready within two months. Then you'll be making a real contribution." When

he'd said all this, Mr. Acornley got up and ambled to the door. Well, you'd have thought a wet blanket had descended on that committee! All we could say was "It's time to go home."

The effect of this sort of commentary by an important leader is obviously serious and highly detrimental.

What could the curriculum coordinator and the superintendent have done to prevent this outbreak?

Is it possible that the superintendent feels somewhat threatened by the curriculum co-ordinator's relationship with the teachers or by the importance of the coordinator's role in instruction? How common are such feelings, in your estimation? If they are at all common, what should be the responsibility of curriculum coordinators in preventing them?

What might have been done in this situation to reestablish cooperation and enthusiasm among the teachers?

SITUATION 7-4

Some Common Problems in Getting and Using Instructional Materials

Mrs. Martinson, the new principal of Clemson High School, looked straight at her assistant. "Henry," she said, "in your fifteen years around here, have you visited all the classrooms in the building?"

"No," replied Henry, as he fumbled with a pad of late-admission slips, "Mr. Davies had me working on administrivia—you know, administrative details—all the time. I hope things will be different under the new regime."

Dodging her assistant's hint, Mrs. Martinson explained: "Within the past eight days, I've been in all the classrooms looking for places to help improve working conditions for the teachers. I'm sure we have at least one handle to take hold of. It's the way our teachers are getting and using instructional materials. Here's a list of problems as I see them."

Henry looked at Mrs. Martinson's notebook. Half a dozen problems appeared prominently at the top of the list:

1. Most teachers seem to be using only a single textbook. In some classes, there are too few copies of the single textbook to go around.
2. Teachers complain that they must order audiovisual materials a half year in advance of their use. When films and filmstrips arrive, the pupils sometimes say they have seen them two or three times in previous years.
3. A visit to the school library during almost any period of the day reveals that one could shoot a shotgun through the library without hitting any pupils.
4. Workbooks seem to be used to provide busywork or to keep pupils quiet.
5. Teachers say that many of the books their pupils are using are too difficult.
6. There seems to be a feud between the high school's audiovisual specialist and most of the department heads. The department heads charge that the audiovisual specialist is trying to "build her own little empire."

In view of the importance of adequate and well-used materials in achieving desirable climate and working conditions in a school, indicate both immediate and long-term actions Mrs. Martinson and her staff might take in dealing with each of these problems.

Achieve and Maintain Appropriate Tempo

A second major action that facilitates curriculum improvement is achieving and maintaining appropriate tempo. Curriculum workers are soon compelled to learn that the timing of curriculum improvement activities is vital. Their fundamental problem is one of maintaining balance between gradualism and rapidity. Many school systems work so gradually at improvement that they scarcely make any effort to improve at all. Eventually, groups of citizens in their communities or in the nation at large surpass the professional staffs of these school systems in thinking and planning and thus are able to create changes in the schools. Too much gradualism, or outright lack of curriculum leadership and action, has contributed to an externally planned revolution in the teaching of mathematics, physical science, and certain other subjects in U.S. schools. Teachers of these subjects have been making changes in curriculum content that they would probably have been very slow in making if they had not been "pushed." Other externally planned revolutions are obviously in the making.

The opposite of extreme gradualism is, of course, excessive and ill-founded speed. Many a noble experiment has come to grief because its supporters have moved ahead of the rank and file of classroom teachers. Many another project has been lost because popular thinking in the community in which it was initiated was not prepared for its appearance on the educational scene. Careful watching of the forces that promote or impede improvement provides the only real guide to appropriate speed. Good timing results from responding cautiously to questions like these: Are we ready for this change? How fast can we comfortably move? How does the speed at which we are effecting this change relate to the speeds at which we are making other changes? If we are not ready for a significant, timely change, how can we develop readiness for it? Are there any ideas and actions that could be helpful in sparking change?

Tempo of change or improvement relates directly to the thoughtfulness with which improvement is sought. For instance, a group of teachers may write a course guide during six weeks of occasional meetings with little effect on the practices of other teachers who are later introduced to the guide. Instead, an inservice project requiring three years may be directed to the same ends, and the improvement resulting from it may be profound and longlasting. The distinction between the two activities is not only in time expended but in careful, early consideration of the kinds of activities that might make a genuinely lasting difference. One of the major functions of leadership is to emphasize the importance of certain projects in relationship to other projects.

Those that are really important to teachers' growth usually deserve the most time for completion and the most preplanning of the procedures by which they will be effected. Furthermore, the time of their initiation must depend chiefly on how soon they have to be accomplished and on the number and nature of other tasks that must be performed.

One of the striking features of curriculum activity in school systems during the late 1980s and the early 1990s has been the presence of excessive hurry in planning situation after planning situation. Particularly in light of the complexity of many curriculum projects, curriculum planners would do well to heed Sizer's comment that good schools do not suddenly appear like prepackaged dinners that have spent fifteen seconds in a microwave. Rather, they simmer until their ingredients have blended.[81]

Specific Problems of Tempo

Practitioners of curriculum planning often encounter problems that affect the tempo of their work. One of these is taking on too much because they fail to recognize the varying sizes of the different tasks. Curriculum planners need to estimate the amount of time particular tasks deserve. If the tasks are large, one, two, or three of them may be all that a school can undertake within a year. Usually, some tasks look small and others loom large. For instance, considering word analysis in the reading program of upper elementary school children is a smaller task than determining sequence in the whole language arts program. The former task might be performed rapidly in conjunction with several other activities, but full consideration of sequence in an important subject field might legitimately claim a faculty's undivided attention for at least a year. Of course, both big and small tasks are being undertaken in most school systems at the same time. It is important to keep the total number and total size of tasks small enough that curriculum study can be thorough rather than superficial.

A second problem of tempo relates to the manageability of projects. Some projects are so large or complicated that they simply cannot be dealt with by the personnel of a single school system. Significant experimentation with the uses of computers, for instance, usually requires large-scale financing and the cooperation of several school systems. Unwise selection of projects that are too large or too involved not only leads to frustration among personnel, but also wastes their valuable time.

A related difficulty is, of course, selecting projects that make no real difference in instructional improvement. Many tasks being performed today are unevaluated, so little is known about their relative or intrinsic worth. One may make expensive rearrangements of personnel and materials, demonstrate the materials, and advertise them widely, and still not know whether the changes make a difference to learning. Time spent on unevaluated demonstrations may easily be time stolen from other, more demonstrably useful projects.

Finally, tempo is affected by injudicious rescheduling of tasks that have been performed on one or more occasions previously. One of the common complaints of teachers is "Someone has decided that we ought to study the English (or some other) program again. I thought we gave it a good overhauling just three years ago." Teachers become frustrated when curriculum leaders seem to "ride" their own hobbies, calling for restudy of given educational problems at too-frequent intervals. Careful pacing of tasks is a special need in those school systems in which curriculum study has been under way for many years.

The rule, then, about tempo, timing, or pacing may be summarized as follows: *not too fast, not too slow, not too carelessly planned, not too big, not too insignificant, not too recently considered.* This is obviously a rule easier to state than to live by, but it is extremely relevant to the process of improvement.

SITUATION 7-5

The Emergencies in Pennsatonic

Pennsatonic is a big town geographically though it's not a very populous one. The principals of its sixteen schools seldom see each other except at monthly meetings in Superintendent Moody's office. Maybe it's the twenty-mile distance from one side of town to the other that makes the problems of the schools so different. Anyway, at last Tuesday's meeting two completely different kinds of problems developed. As a result of them, good old Pennsatonic may not settle down for a long time.

Ned Graves, who's in charge of Adams School, reported that he'd recently been descended upon by a group of parents who wanted to "see the curriculum of Adams School." The group was dissatisfied with the fact that ancient history is being taught in the fifth grade and that long division is postponed until near the end of the sixth grade. There were other complaints about the curriculum too. Ned found some copies of courses of study in the social studies and arithmetic and handed them to the complainants. Now he's sorry he did. The parents soon noticed that the courses of study are nearly eighteen years old. Some of the complainants want the teachers to spend their spare time during the next two weeks describing in writing what they teach in these two subjects. Later, they will want the teachers to describe what they teach in other subjects too.

From the north side of town, Rita Corson had a different tale of woe. The teachers in her junior high school are up in arms because half of them are expected to do team teaching in a block-of-time program. Rita says there is likely to be a strike unless she helps eliminate the block-of-time program and makes an entirely new schedule. A few of the teachers broke up a faculty meeting last week with the complaint that Rita and two of her "favorite teachers" had planned and installed the block-of-time program during the summer without the knowledge and participation of the other teachers.

State the differences (and similarities, if any) between the two problems presented above.

What could have been done to prevent each of these problems?

What should the superintendent and the principals do both immediately and in the long run to solve each of the two problems? How could they relate their long-term actions to newly developed system-wide policies in curriculum improvement?

Select Among a Variety of Activities

A third major action that assists the process of curriculum improvement is to select among a variety of activities directed toward improvement. The provision of varied activities has been referred to as a shotgun approach. When a shotgun is fired, no one knows exactly what will be hit by the pellets. Similarly, curriculum improvers who use varied activities are sometimes unsure who will be attracted to and who will be most affected by each of several activities. The best that we can do is to narrow many possibilities to a few according to ascribed purposes and the exercise of good judgment. If, for instance, the goal is to increase the familiarity of a given group of teachers with research procedures, a staff development project might be organized for them, an experience in using research procedures in their classrooms might be devised, or an apprenticeship to the research director of the school system might be arranged. Reason dictates that any one of these activities would prove more beneficial than merely inviting the teachers to read about research methods. But which of the three preferred activities should be engaged in by a given group of teachers? If all three cannot be utilized simply because there is not enough time to organize them or because all three are unnecessary when one would be sufficient, which one will have greatest effect on the teachers? Though a curriculum leader may judge that the least sophisticated of the activities may serve best, other considerations affect such a decision, and so the answer to this question isn't self-evident.

As has been said, curriculum improvement may be equated in many respects with supervision, inservice education, or staff development. Accordingly, the activities used in these three connecting avenues to school quality are fundamentally the same. They exist in some profusion under these headings: group activities, contact with individuals, and use of literary and mechanical media. Following are some of the available activities under their appropriate headings:

Group Activities

committees	clinics
study groups	institutes
workshops	courses
conferences	seminars
work conferences	

Contact with Individuals

interviewing and counseling individuals	demonstration by individual teachers or supervisors
observation of individual teachers in classrooms and elsewhere	inservice advisement of individual teachers
assistance to the teacher in his or her classroom	directed reading

Literary and Mechanical Media

written bulletins	bulletin boards
research reports	tape recordings of meetings and
policy statements	decisions
course guides	educational television
computer printouts	

The reader will probably think of other activities belonging under these headings. Since the days when course-of-study construction was almost the exclusive activity in curriculum improvement, the problem has not been a lack of activities but uncertainty as to which ones should be used in given situations.

Curriculum workers appear to spend most of their time in activities of a group-work nature. They spend the second most amount of time interacting with individuals. In the future, they will probably give more attention to the third category—literary and mechanical media—as the application of technology increases the possible uses of mechanical media. Many curriculum leaders hold that, of all the separate activities, workshops and conferences with individuals achieve most satisfactory results.

Free and open involvement in activities should not be short-cut. Naturally, expenditure of time by school personnel costs money, so administrators should insist that adequate funds be allocated in school district budgets for curriculum study. Unfortunately, the public often expects schools to produce near-miracles at bargain rates. No one should be surprised, however, when the investment of few dollars yields meager returns.[82]

SITUATION 7-6

Homework for the General Curriculum Committee

Someone turned on the lights in the curriculum office. It was 5:45 on a Tuesday afternoon, and the general curriculum committee was torn between leaving for dinner and other appointments and staying to plan ways of carrying out four distinct activities within the next two months.

"Since we've rejected the idea of having a subcommittee make the plans," said Dr. Stogdill, chairwoman of the general committee, "let's think about possibilities during the next two days and meet here again for an hour on Thursday afternoon."

"I'm not sure I remember all four activities," drawled Herschel Odom. "Ruth, will you put all of them on the blackboard?"

The chalk scraped and clicked as Ruth Hadley listed

1. Sensitizing high school mathematics teachers to new content and sequences in mathematics
2. Getting teachers' suggestions about names of local citizens to add to the resource file

3. Hearing from the child study division of the state department of education concerning the topic "Newer Findings about the Development of Elementary School Children"
4. Presenting to all the teachers in the school system a "buddy plan" for the orientation of new teachers next fall

Assume that you are a member of the general committee. List one or more activities you think you might emphasize in dealing with each of the four goals. Keep in mind the possibility of combining activities that belong to these three categories: group activities, contact with individuals, and preparation and use of literary and mechanical media. Discuss with a group of fellow students the feasibility of your plans.

Build Evaluation Procedures into Each Project

A fourth major action to help the process of curriculum improvement is building into each project, from its very inception, procedures for evaluating the effects of the project. This action is taken so infrequently that the quality of both old and new educational practices usually goes unassessed. After a while, the accumulation of unevaluated practices becomes so large that no one can defend with assurance the ways in which schools are operated.

If the chief end of curriculum improvement is improvement of pupils' engagements in learning under auspices of the school, the significance of every important step toward this end is evident. The evaluation may, because of the pressures of time and work, be done quite informally, but it should be done nevertheless. The presence of evaluation data lends assurance to practitioners, and it supplies evidence to the people who pay school costs and want to know whether money is being well spent.

Evaluation is meant to gauge the extent to which objectives of a project or activity have been achieved. A desirable relationship between evaluation and objectives appears in Figure 7-1. The diagram suggests that as soon as the objectives of a project are stated, ways of evaluating the achievement of the objectives should be considered. Activities should then be chosen for their pertinence to the objectives and also with reference to possible means of evaluation. The thinking process should follow this sequence: from objectives to evaluation to activities that are useful in achieving the objectives and have effects that can properly be evaluated. Too often, curriculum workers think of activities first and then either ignore or defer consideration of objectives and evaluation.

Suppose a committee of second- and third-grade teachers wants to develop a social studies program for primary-grade children that is based less on the imaginings of adults concerning what is good for young children generally and more on the expressed interests of the children themselves in a particular school system. The committee's major objective then is to develop a program centering upon the expressed interests of given groups of children. As soon as the committee has set this objective, it should raise the question "How can

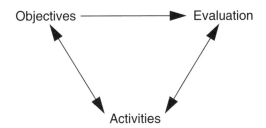

FIGURE 7-1 The Relationship Among Major Parts of a Curriculum Project

teachers know when this objective has been achieved?" The answer might be formulated thus:

> Teachers can know when their objective has been achieved by examining the products of their work in determining children's interests within the field called social studies. One of the products will be the teachers' guide, written at the conclusion of the study. A more important product will be the choices of social studies content that teachers are observed making in their classrooms. Therefore, although we shall inspect carefully the completed teachers' guide, we shall also conduct before-and-after observations of choice making by teachers in their classrooms. Both our objectives and our methodology of evaluation imply that teacher activities like the following will be suitable: conducting interviews with children, administering a three-wishes test, asking children to draw pictures to express their wishes, recording ways in which children complete unfinished stories, and engaging children in group discussions. In this way, objectives, evaluation procedures, and activities used in curriculum study become closely bound together and evaluation tends to become a continuous process.

The same general principles of evaluation that were stated in Chapter 6 apply here also. Note that evaluation can be extended to assessment of the planning process used and to assessment of proposals for future action in light of past experience.[83]

ACTIVITY 7-3

The Prevalence of Built-in Evaluation

Review several curriculum improvement projects to see whether methodology of evaluation was discussed immediately after the nature and purposes of each project were described. If you have had no direct contact with curriculum improvement projects, search for a few reports in educational literature, which can be identified by using *Education Index* or the specific directions provided by your instructor.

In how many instances have plans for evaluation been built into the projects from the start? In how many instances have plans for evaluation been mentioned at all?

What do you conclude about the esteem in which evaluation is held by those who believe they are improving the curriculum? What is your own present view of the significance of evaluation?

SITUATION 7-7

Reducing Illiteracy—A Growing Concern of the Schools

In a school district you know, an increasing number of pupils have been entering the high schools unable to read effectively and unable to interpret symbols in subject matter. High school teachers with long experience in the district are up in arms about the "lowered quality" of pupils now entering the secondary schools. The central office staff realizes that something must be done. After the staff has determined that the pupil population is in fact considerably less able to achieve in the three Rs than were pupil populations of five to ten years ago and yet is only slightly less able mentally than were these former populations, what basic steps should the staff and other persons take to help improve the system of teaching and learning in order to reduce illiteracy? In light of what you have read in this chapter, discuss what might be done with both the people and the equipment and materials in the learning environment.

SUMMARY

Chapter 7 is the first of five chapters concerning process in curriculum improvement. There can be no improvement in the curriculum without a change in the people who design the curriculum and make it function. Changes, constructive and destructive, occur continually in the lives of both individuals and organizations. Psychological and sociological factors, in particular, operate in creating change in both individuals and the institutions of which they are a part. Within past decades, practical applications of the change process have been evident in all sorts of attempts at improving the curriculum. Among the agencies and media that encourage constructive change are direct and indirect support by school leaders, education and reeducation of school staffs, systems of collaboration, and helpful educational materials. Four well-recognized actions by change agents move the curriculum toward improvement: seeking a more helpful climate and working conditions, striving to achieve an appropriate change tempo, sponsoring varied activities that contribute to improvement, and specifying effective evaluation procedures.

ENDNOTES

1. Alice Miel, *Changing the Curriculum* (New York: Appleton-Century-Crofts, 1946).

2. Kenneth D. Benne and Bozidar Muntyan, *Human Relations in Curriculum Change* (New York: Dryden Press, 1951).

3. Ignorance of what has been taught for decades about change process results in do-it-yourself change as it is described here.

4. For an insightful discussion of flaws in reform movements, see Ralph W. Tyler, "Education Reforms," *Phi Delta Kappan* 69, no. 4 (December 1987): 277–280

5. Theodore R. Sizer, "Common Sense," *Educational Leadership* 42, no. 6 (March 1985): 21.

6. Daniel Tanner, "A Nation 'Truly' at Risk," *Phi Delta Kappan* 75, no. 4 (December 1993): 288–297

7. Ronald C. Doll, *Supervision for Staff Development: Ideas and Application* (Boston: Allyn and Bacon, 1983), 114.

8. Charles P. Loomis, "Tentative Types of Directed Social Change Involving Systematic Linkage," *Rural Sociology* 24, no. 4 (December 1959): 383–390.

9. Warren G. Bennis, "A Typology of Change Processes," in Warren G. Bennis, Kenneth D. Benne, and Robert Chin, *The Planning of Change* (New York: Holt, Rinehart and Winston, 1961), 154–156.

10. H. Dickson Corbett and Gretchen B. Rossman, "Three Paths to Implementing Change: A Research Note," *Curriculum Inquiry* 19, no. 2 (Summer 1989): 163–190.

11. Arthur W. Combs, "Changing Our Assumptions about Educational Reform," *The Education Digest* 54, no. 2 (October 1988): 3–6.

12. See "Signs of a Changing Curriculum," *Change* 24 (January–February 1992): 49–52.

13. Compare J. C. Hampsey, "Anguishing over Curricular Change," *Academe* 78 (July–August 1992): 49 et seq.

14. The principles stated here appeared originally in Ronald C. Doll, "Our Orbits of Change," *Educational Leadership* 17, no. 2 (November 1959): 102–105.

15. Carol Red and Ellen Shainline, "Teachers Reflect on Change," *Educational Leadership* 44, no. 5 (February 1987): 38–40.

16. Ronald Lippitt, Jeanne Watson, and Bruce Westley, *The Dynamics of Planned Change* (New York: Harcourt, Brace and World, 1958), 73, 74.

17. Ibid., 75, 76.

18. Ibid., 83, 88; see also Amitai Etzioni, "Human Beings Are Not Very Easy to Change After All," *Saturday Review,* June 3, 1972, 45–47.

19. Arthur W. Combs, *Myths in Education* (Boston: Allyn and Bacon, 1979), 209–213.

20. See William A. Reid, "Schools, Teachers, and Curriculum Change: The Moral Dimension of Theory-Building," *Educational Theory* 29, no. 4 (Fall 1979): 325–336.

21. Vincent Rogers, Cynthia Talbot, and Ellen Cosgrove, "Excellence: Some Lessons from America's Best Run Companies," *Educational Leadership* 41, no. 5 (February 1984): 39–41; see also Thomas J. Peters and Robert H. Waterman, Jr., *In Search of Excellence* (New York: Harper and Row, 1982).

22. Dorwin Cartwright, "Achieving Change in People," in Bennis, Benne, and Chin, *Planning of Change,* 698–706.

23. Kenneth D. Benne, "Deliberate Change as the Facilitation of Growth," in Bennis, Benne, and Chin, *Planning of Change,* 230–234.

24. Herbert C. Kelman, "Processes of Opinion Change," in Bennis, Benne, and Chin, *Planning of Change,* 509–517.

25. See Noojin Walker, "What a Great Idea! Too Bad It Didn't Work," *Educational Technology* 16, no. 2 (February 1976): 46, 47.

26. André Morin, "An Innovator's Odyssey: How to Become a Thoughtful Change Agent," *Educational Technology* 15, no. 11 (November 1975): 43–45.

27. Dennis M. Wint and William R. Kennedy, "Strategies Affecting Successful Implementation of an Environmental Curriculum into Ohio Schools." Reported in ERIC # ED 144 779.

28. See Ellen M. Regan and Kenneth A. Leithwood, "Effecting Curriculum Change: Ex-

periences with the Conceptual Skills Project." Reported in ERIC # ED 136 440.

29. Susan F. Loucks and Ann Lieberman, "Curriculum Implementation," in Fenwick W. English, ed., *Fundamental Curriculum Decisions,* 1983 Yearbook (Alexandria, VA: Association for Supervision and Curriculum Development, 1983), 130.

30. Joseph P. McDonald, "The Emergence of the Teacher's Voice: Implications for the New Reform," *Teachers College Record* 89, no. 4 (Summer 1988): 471–486.

31. Loucks and Lieberman, "Curriculum Implementation," 132–133.

32. See Sheila W. Valencia and Joellen P. Killian, "Implementing Research-Based Reading and Writing Programs; Overcoming Obstacles to Teacher Change: Three Case Studies," Technical Report No. 462, Center for the Study of Reading, University of Illinois at Urbana, February 1989. Reported in ERIC # ED 305 595.

33. Judy Kwiat, "Perspectives on Fostering Change in Teachers of Language Minority Students," a paper presented to the annual meeting of the American Educational Research Association, San Francisco, March 1989. Reported in ERIC # ED 306 767.

34. Richard A. Gibboney, "The Killing Field of Reform," *Phi Delta Kappan* 72, no. 9 (May 1991): 682–688.

35. Hubert S. Coffee and William P. Golden, Jr., in *In-Service Education,* Fifty-Sixth Yearbook, Part I (Chicago: National Society for the Study of Education, 1957), 101.

36. See Ray Sorenson and Hedley Dimock, *Redesigning Education in Values: A Case Study of Institutional Change* (New York: Association Press, 1955).

37. David H. Jenkins, "Social Engineering in Educational Change: An Outline of Method," *Progressive Education* 26, no. 7 (May 1949): 193–197.

38. Robert G. Owens, *Organizational Behavior in Schools* (New York: Prentice-Hall, 1970), 145–148.

39. E. G. Guba, "Diffusion of Innovations," *Educational Leadership* 25, no. 4 (January 1968): 292–295.

40. Seymour B. Sarason, *The Culture of the School and the Problem of Change* (Boston: Allyn and Bacon, 1971). Note that the May 1990 issue of *Educational Leadership,* volume 47, number 8, is devoted largely to the theme "Creating a Culture for Change." Interestingly, the articles advance knowledge of culture and change very little beyond what was being reported in the 1950s, 1960s, and 1970s by scholars like Sarason, Stephen M. Corey, and staff members of the Horace Mann-Lincoln Institute of School Experimentation, Teachers College, Columbia University.

41. Paul Heckman, "Understanding School Culture," in John I. Goodlad, ed., *The Ecology of School Renewal,* National Society for the Study of Education, Eighty-Sixth Yearbook, Part II (Chicago: University of Chicago Press, 1987), 68–71.

42. See Bruce R. Joyce, "The Doors to School Improvement," *Educational Leadership* 48, no. 8 (May 1991): 59–62; see also Jane L. David, "What It Takes to Restructure Education," 11–15.

43. See Larry Cuban, "The District Superintendent and the Restructuring of Schools," in Thomas J. Sergiovanni and John H. Moore, eds., *Schooling for Tomorrow: Directing Reforms to Issues That Count* (Boston: Allyn and Bacon, 1989), 251–270.

44. H. Dickson Corbett, William A. Firestone, and Gretchen B. Rossman, "Resistance to Planned Change and the Sacred in School Cultures," *Educational Administration Quarterly* 23, no. 4 (November 1987): 36–59.

45. Ann Lieberman and Lynne Miller, "Restructuring Schools: What Matters and What Works," *Phi Delta Kappan* 71, no. 10 (June 1990): 759–764.

46. Charles E. Moore, "12 Secrets of Restructured Schools," *Education Digest* 59, no. 4 (December 1993): 23–26.

47. Guba, "Diffusion of Innovations."

48. See, for example, Wendell L. French and Cecil H. Bell, Jr., *Organization Development* (Englewood Cliffs, NJ: Prentice-Hall, 1973); see also Warren G. Bennis, *Organizational Development: Its Nature, Origins, and Prospects* (Reading, MA: Addison-Wesley, 1969).

49. Charles P. Ruch et al., "Training for Planning: Organizational Consultation to Design and Install Constituency-Based Planning," *Planning and Changing* 13, no. 4 (Winter 1982): 234–244.

50. Michael Holzman, "What Is Systemic Change?" *Educational Leadership* 51, no. 1 (September 1993): 18.

51. John O'Neil, "Turning the System on Its Head," *Educational Leadership* 51, no. 1 (September 1993): 8–13.

52. Jerry L. Patterson and Theodore J. Czajkowski, "Implementation: Neglected Phase in Curriculum Change," *Educational Leadership* 37, no. 3 (December 1979): 204–206.

53. "Will Teachers Open Their Doors to Change?" *The Harvard Letter* 8, no. 4 (July–August 1992): 3–5.

54. Reported by Charles C. Jung, Northwest Regional Educational Laboratory, 400 Lindsay Building, 710 S. W. Second Avenue, Portland, OR 97204.

55. Ivor K. Davies, "The CLER Model in Instructional Development," *Viewpoints in Teaching and Learning* 58, no. 4 (Fall 1982): 62–69.

56. Ted R. Urich, Marlene Mitchell, and Judith P. LaVorgna, "PARA: A Mutually Reinforcing Model for Self-Directed Change," *Bulletin of the National Association of Secondary School Principals* 67, no. 464 (September 1983): 104–107.

57. Mark F. Goldberg, "A Portrait of Ted Sizer," *Educational Leadership* 51, no. 1 (September 1993): 53–56.

58. Marilyn E. Nelson, "In-Service Training for Curriculum Change," Montgomery County Public Schools, Maryland (1978). Reported in ERIC # ED 195 535.

59. From publications of Project Zero, Harvard University.

60. Adapted from Donald Orlosky and B. Othanel Smith, "Educational Change; Its Origins and Characteristics," *Phi Delta Kappan* 53, no. 7 (March 1972): 412–413. Used with permission.

61. Ibid.

62. Ralph Parish and Richard Arends, "Why Innovative Programs Are Discontinued," *Educational Leadership* 40, no. 4 (January 1983): 62–65.

63. Combs, "Changing Our Assumptions about Educational Reform."

64. Paul E. Heckman, Jeannie Oakes, and Kenneth A. Sirotnik, "Expanding the Concepts of School Renewal and Change," *Educational Leadership* 40, no. 7 (April 1983): 26–30.

65. Linda Weller Ferris, "What Teachers Tell Us about Administrators and Administration as Sources of Professional Enthusiasm and Discouragement: A Cross-Cultural Comparison of Five Countries," a paper presented at the annual meeting of the American Educational Research Association, San Francisco, March 1989. Reported in ERIC # ED 308 601.

66. Earl B. Russell, "Upgrading Curricula through Change-Oriented Teachers," *Theory into Practice* 14, no. 1 (February 1975): 27–31.

67. See Gene Hall, William L. Rutherford, Shirley M. Hord, and Leslie L. Huling, "Effects of Three Principal Styles on School Improvement," *Educational Leadership* 41, no. 5 (February 1984): 22–29.

68. Donald J. Gray, *The Lessons of Summer Institutes*, a monograph published by the Consortium of Professional Associations for Study of Special Teacher Improvement Programs, April 1970, 16.

69. Toni Griego Jones, "School District Personnel Speak Out on Change," a paper presented at the annual meeting of the American Educational Research Association, San Francisco, March 1989. Reported in ERIC # ED 307 705.

70. Russell, "Upgrading Curricula through Change-Oriented Teachers," 28.

71. Thomas R. Guskey, "Staff Development and Teacher Change," *Educational Leadership* 42, no. 7 (April 1985): 57–60.

72. See the articles in *Educational Leadership,* volume 45, number 3, November 1987.

73. Collaborative schools can assist each other across district lines, as within a region or a state. See Richard L. Egelston, "The New York State Model for Sharing Successful Programs: A Decade of Implementation and Evaluation," a paper presented at an annual meeting of the New England Educational Research Organization, Portsmouth, New Hampshire. Reported in ERIC # ED 308 588.

74. Michael G. Fullan and Matthew B. Miles, "Getting Reform Right: What Works and What Doesn't," *Phi Delta Kappan* 73, no. 10 (June 1992): 745–752.

75. J. H. Young, "Collaborative Curriculum Development: Is It Happening at the School Level?" *Journal of Curriculum and Supervision* 8 (Spring 1993): 239–254.

76. See references on group work, two of the most helpful of which have been Matthew B. Miles, *Learning to Work in Groups* (New York: Bureau of Publications, Teachers College, 1959) and Halbert E. Gulley, *Discussion, Conference, and Group Process* (New York: Holt, Rinehart and Winston, 1960).

77. William A. Rieck, "Staff Evaluation: Strategies for Continuous Instructional Improvement," a paper presented at the annual meeting of the National Association of Secondary School Principals, New Orleans, February 1989. Reported in ERIC # ED 306 648.

78. Frank Riessman, "A School Change Paradigm," *Social Policy* 19 (Summer 1988): 2–4.

79. Wilbur A. Yauch, *Improving Human Relations in School Administration* (New York: Harper and Row, 1949), 257–263. To learn from negative examples, see G. A. Griffin, "Dehumanizing the School through Curriculum Planning, or Who Needs Hemlock?" *National Elementary Principal* 49, no. 9 (May 1970): 24–27.

80. Shirley M. Hord and Leslie Huling-Austin, "Effective Curriculum Implementation," *The Elementary School Journal* 87, no. 1 (September 1986); 97–115.

81. Theodore R. Sizer, "Common Sense," *Educational Leadership* 42, no. 6 (March 1985): 21, 22. (An exceptional article.)

82. Eugene Eubanks and Ralph Parish, "An Inside View of Change in Schools," *Phi Delta Kappan* 68, no. 8 (April 1987): 610–615.

83. James E. Michaletz, "An Effective Approach to Curriculum Change: Planning, Implementation, and Evaluation," a paper presented at the annual meeting of the National Catholic Educational Association, St. Louis, April 9, 1985.

SELECTED BIBLIOGRAPHY

Bennis, Warren G.; Benne, Kenneth D.; and Chin, Robert. *The Planning of Change.* New York: Holt, Rinehart and Winston, 1961.

Corey, Stephen M. *Helping Other People Change.* Columbus, OH: Ohio State University Press, 1963.

Fine, Michelle, ed. *Chartering Urban School Reform.* New York: Teachers College Press, 1994.

Fullan, Michael. *The Meaning of Educational Change.* New York: Teachers College Press, 1982.

Goodlad, John I., ed. *The Ecology of School Renewal.* National Society for the Study of Education, Eighty-Sixth Yearbook. Chicago: University of Chicago Press, 1987.

Goodson, Ivor. *School Subjects and Curriculum Change,* 3rd ed. Philadelphia: Taylor and Francis, 1993.

Gordon, David. *The Myths of School Self Renewal.* New York: Teachers College Press, 1984.

Guild, Pat Burke, and Garger, Stephen. *Marching to Different Drummers.* Alexandria, VA: Association for Supervision and Curriculum Development, 1985.

Havelock, R. G. *The Change Agent's Guide to Innovations in Education.* Englewood Cliffs, NJ: Educational Technology Publications, 1973.

Joyce, Bruce, ed. *Changing School Culture through Staff Development.* 1990 Yearbook. Alexandria, VA: Association for Supervision and Curriculum Development, 1990.

Joyce, Bruce; Wolf, James; and Calhoun, Emily. *The Self-Renewing School.* Alexandria, VA: Association for Supervision and Curriculum Development, 1993.

Lippitt, Ronald; Watson, Jeanne; and Westley, Bruce. *The Dynamics of Planned Change.* New York: Harcourt, Brace and World, 1958.

Miel, Alice. *Changing the Curriculum.* New York: Appleton-Century-Crofts, 1946.

Ornstein, Allan C., and Hunkins, Francis P. *Curriculum: Foundations, Principles, and Issues.* Englewood Cliffs, NJ: Prentice-Hall, 1987.

Owens, Robert G., and Steinhoff, Carl R. *Administering Change in Schools*. Englewood Cliffs, NJ: Prentice-Hall, 1976.

Peters, Thomas J., and Waterman, Robert H., Jr. *In Search of Excellence*. New York: Harper and Row, 1982.

Reid, William A., and Walker, Decker F., eds. *Case Studies in Curriculum Change*. Boston: Routledge and Kegan Paul, 1975.

Rossi, Robert J. *Schools and Students at Risk*. New York: Teachers College Press, 1994.

Sarason, Seymour B. *The Culture of the School and the Problem of Change*. Boston: Allyn and Bacon, 1971.

Sergiovanni, Thomas J., and Moore, John H., eds. *Schooling for Tomorrow: Directing Reforms to Issues That Count*. Boston: Allyn and Bacon, 1989

Skeel, Dorothy J., and Hagen, Owen A. *The Process of Curriculum Change*. Pacific Palisades, CA: Goodyear, 1971.

8

THE PLANNING PROCESS

"Let me show you our curriculum," said the principal to the visitor in his school. Proudly, the principal removed from his desk a mimeographed document that told teachers what to teach, subject by subject.

The visitor scanned the document and replied, "Now let me see your *real* curriculum."

"What do you mean?" the principal asked.

"I mean that I must spend at least a few hours in your school. I need to visit several classrooms at random. I want to stand aside in hallways as the children move through them and wander through the cafeteria while children are eating and while they're talking freely. If an assembly program is scheduled for today I want to attend it. And I'd like to visit the library and then follow the children out to the playing field while they're under a teacher's supervision and while they're on their own. By doing these things, I'll get at least a limited view of your *real* curriculum."

This dialogue between a principal and a visitor suggests a number of ideas about school curriculum. The first, and most obvious, idea is that the curriculum cannot actually be reduced to a lifeless sheaf of papers. A second idea is that the curriculum belongs in two categories: that of objective reality and that of mode and style. Thus, although the curriculum should be viewed as a product, it should also be viewed as process. That is, the curriculum is in part a way of working with what has been set out to be done. Inevitably, the two categories become interrelated.

A third idea is that a given curriculum has a life span, determined largely by its usefulness and timeliness. Within its lifetime, a curriculum may be revised at intervals and in both major and minor ways so that its usefulness and timeliness may be increased. A fourth idea is that the real curriculum, no matter how formally and carefully planned it is alleged to be, has aspects of the unplanned. Every practicing teacher knows that what "creeps in" as a consequence of pupil-teacher and pupil-pupil interaction in the classroom goes beyond the bounds of the most carefully expressed mandates and suggestions. In addition, some of the real curriculum remains unplanned.

A fifth, and most important, idea is that the curriculum, being of the human spirit, is active and changing. It is affected by wishes, thoughts, and restraints. As we have seen in Chapter 7, to change the curriculum is literally to help people change themselves. The real curriculum of the school has already been defined in the prologue as "the formal and informal content and process by which learners gain knowledge and understanding, develop skills, and alter attitudes, appreciations, and values under the auspices of that school." This definition is meant to include both formal and informal aspects of schooling, what one learns (content) and how one learns (process), and products or outcomes in the forms of knowledge, understanding, skills, attitudes, appreciations, and values.

Thus the curriculum involves what happens in classrooms, auditoriums, gymnasiums, cafeterias, and hallways and—in connection with school activities—school-sponsored community service, field trips, and organized work experience programs. It is as big, broad, and all inclusive as the lives of people in a major, thriving American institution.

The action called improvement of the curriculum may be defined as follows: *Curriculum improvement refers not only to improving the structure and the documents of the curriculum but also to stimulating learning on the part of all persons who are concerned with the curriculum.* These persons include, of course, pupils in schools, teachers, classroom aides, supervisors and administrators, and assisting parents and other community members. They have opportunities in a program of curriculum improvement to gain both cognitively and affectively. Obviously, curriculum improvement deals directly with the improvement of people.

HOW THE PROCESS OF CURRICULUM PLANNING HAS EVOLVED

Though improvement of the curriculum has been occurring slowly for generations, conscious efforts to plan for it have been expended only during the past three-quarters of a century. Some of the planning procedures used during the 1920s are being treated today as though they had just been invented. Other procedures have the gloss of novelty because they were made possible by late twentieth-century technology. Still other procedures—some now considered useful, others useless—were in vogue twenty to sixty years ago. Thus there can be no clear distinction between the antiquated and the new.

The process of curriculum improvement was made manifest only when it was first reported in the literature. Prior to 1920, practically nothing concerning this topic was written in professional journals. A curriculum was considered by many persons to be the courses of study and other written materials that a given school system or individual school produced. Customarily, the superintendent of schools assembled several persons who were believed to be competent "to write the curriculum." In the larger school systems during the 1920s, committees of representative teachers met with one or more assistant superintendents and directors of subjects to prepare courses of study, which were then submitted to the system's board of superintendents for approval and subsequently to the board of education for authority to print them as school documents.[1] Participating teachers were selected on the basis of teaching ability, interest in curriculum work, college preparation, and ability to write.[2]

The actual authority for curriculum planning centered strongly in superintendents and their immediate staffs, with teachers, parents, and pupils taking minor parts. Courses of study contained, from the teacher's viewpoint, precise "ground to be covered," and supervisors urged teachers to cover this ground in quantity and sequence. Most administrators in the cities reported that their programs of improvement were continuous, though they centered upon only a few recurrent problems in "revising subject matter."[3] One, two, or three subject matter areas were revised at a given time, and revision was "completed" within a few months, to be resumed by rearranging the same subject matter a few years later.

Generally, teachers were not asked what instructional problems needed attention. Decisions of this sort were made by top administrators, who tended to think of curriculum improvement as being a rewriting of courses of study and the addition or elimination of subjects and course offerings. Curriculum decisions were made on the basis of individual opinion and consensus of groups, inasmuch as experimentation, research, and evaluation were relatively unknown.[4]

Subsequent Developments in Curriculum Planning

An enlarged definition of curriculum improvement, application of newer findings in psychology and sociology to the process of improvement, and increased experience in attempting to improve school programs have opened the whole educational enterprise to these trends:

- Changes are being planned both in the environments within which people operate and in the individuals who occupy these environments. Changing an environment requires setting or resetting the stage for learning; helping individuals to change themselves requires deep understanding of the dynamics of human behavior. Both also demand a thorough knowledge of the best practice in education.
- In more and more school systems, curriculum planning is being considered a necessity and a continuing activity. Improvement in schooling will be merely incidental unless we plan for it. Moreover, if teachers are not active in planning their own teaching-learning programs, ill-informed persons soon appear on the scene to "help" them.

• Today, there is more and more variation in the kinds of activities that curriculum planning encompasses. These activities range from the planning of experimental projects to selection of teaching materials, to development of teaching units, to formation of study groups, to plotting of guidelines for action, and so on.

• Many activities now occur at the same time—a far cry from the one, two, or three concurrent activities in the 1920s. The number of activities, which include large projects and small, is determined chiefly by the energies and talents of school staffs.

• Improvement is now commonly considered to occur on a broken front. This means that "modifications in practice have small beginnings with a few teachers taking the lead in the difficult process of testing new ideas. As new practices are demonstrated to be feasible, more teachers take over their use. Thus change in the actual curriculum is represented by a jagged line of emerging practice in response to new ideas and needs.[5]

• Curriculum planners are demonstrating renewed concern about overall goals of education and about specific objectives. Many curriculum ideas, new and old, should be assessed in light of their contribution to achievement of accepted goals and objectives.

• Teachers are becoming involved in curriculum study in various ways. Some teachers contribute helpfully to group discussion; others organize programs successfully; others write and edit materials well; and still others succeed in experimentation, tryout, and evaluation. All teachers make decisions about the curriculum within their classrooms. But the present expectation of curriculum leaders is usually that teachers will also work in group planning and that they will involve themselves at differing levels and to differing degrees in the improvement tasks the school undertakes.

• Whereas pupils were once involved very little in curriculum planning, they are now consulted at least informally in classrooms and school activities and are asked about certain minor matters of curriculum design. The learners, though they are neither experts nor professionals, sometimes provide significant clues about actions to be taken.

• Involvement of lay persons has passed through stages that began with minimal involvement and that continued with random, unplanned uses of the talents of community members. Lay persons who have been utilized beyond their depth have sometimes revolted or have created disturbances by constituting themselves rivals to boards of education and professional staffs. Consequently, curriculum leaders have come to realize that the purposes of education and certain broad, general policy matters are suitable subjects for public discussion and that lay persons can sometimes be helpful in other direct ways, but that clear distinctions must be made between matters of lay concern and matters of professional concern.[6]

• Curriculum planning is not thought of as a series of distinct and fixed steps. No single pattern, beginning, for instance, with stating objectives, will suffice in solving all curriculum problems. The dynamics of given school situations and the resources provided by interdisciplinary study and practical experience in curriculum planning determine the ways in which problems should be attacked.

• Curriculum materials, which formed a major starting point of activity in the 1920s, are still widely produced and used. The course of study has given way to the less prescriptive course guide, however. Aids for teachers include manuals accompanying textbooks, resource units, and audiovisual lists. The focus during recent educational history has been increasingly on helping competent professional persons rather than on further limiting teachers' opportunities to make decisions. During the late 1960s, many teachers interpreted the insistence of school administrators on curriculum innovation and the availability of materials produced by national curriculum projects as constituting a limitation of their power to make certain fundamental curriculum decisions. Their power was scarcely enhanced by the development of systems, programming, and packaging during the 1970s.

• The heritage of experience described in this chapter suggests that many of the important developments in the curriculum field occurred before the past two or three decades. For this reason, many of the references appearing in the footnotes of the chapters to follow bear dates from the 1930s to the early 1960s.

THE BASES OF CURRICULUM PLANNING

What happens when a group tries to plan the curriculum? Obviously, one has to begin with something. Many planners begin merely with the curriculum as it is, resolving to patch it here and there. Occasionally, planners attempt to build something brand new, as when people first considered educating children in the use of computers. Traditionally, planners have gone into action without thinking much about fundamentals of the planning operation. These fundamentals may be called the usable bases of curriculum planning.

Before we look at the bases, however, let us see what school people commonly do as they begin to plan. At the start, many curriculum planners take the following series of steps:

• They become aware of a way in which particular needs of pupils can be met.
• They learn more about this way.
• They wonder how adopting this way would affect them.
• They think about what would happen in their relationships with other people if they adopted this way.
• They consider the amount of time that might be needed.
• They speculate about what would be necessary to adjust or refocus the proposed way to overcome objections to it.

Planning at this stage is merely an initial thrusting about without real direction. When planners turn to thinking about direction, they tend to adopt the "measured curriculum approach." This approach involves reducing learning tasks to a number of components, specifying behavioral objectives, choosing learning experiences to accord with the objectives, monitoring pupils' use of time and task achievement, and utilizing tests to assess progress in a relative sense.

Thoughtful planners do not make measured planning their only approach. They use other methods to explore such non-traditional aspects of learning as thinking critically and solving problems.[7] One is equipped to plan most comprehensively if one knows the bases of planning, both institutional and personal.

Bases That Are Institutional in Nature

Some of the bases of curriculum planning are indigenous to schools as particular and peculiar institutions. They include the domains of planning, the characteristics of the school situation as it is, the impact of current trends and issues, and the arrival of strategic planning.

The Domains of Planning
Most people begin to plan without knowing what it involves. A first logical consideration may well be the direction or directions in which the planners want to go. What are the aims or goals to be attained? What objectives should be achieved en route to the attainment of these aims or goals? What areas and reaches of knowledge should be tapped?

When planners have given answers to these questions, they should be prepared to suggest a design comparable with the curriculum designs discussed in Chapter 5. The design then requires implementation, during which process (modes of treating the design in classrooms) comes to the fore. Ways of teaching, instructional resources and media, and organization of classroom and school for learning need to be considered in planning for implementation. At intervals during and beyond implementation, planners must evaluate what has been happening in two terms: improvement (if any) in pupil learning and the worth of the curriculum plan in attaining desired aims.

Realizing that no curriculum is made in heaven, good planners make use of the feedback obtained as plans go into effect to change the answers to their original questions of intent, to alter their designs, to improve their implementation, and to modify their evaluation systems. Thus the curriculum moves, changes, lives.

The Characteristics of the Situation as It Is
Curriculum planners have to work within the situations in which they find themselves. Often they know too little about their own situations and circumstances. Surely, they should know about the local scene. Planners should inquire about the qualifications of personnel, the morale of district employees,

the special talents of staff members, material resources available for curriculum work, the degree of support given by top administrators, the pressures applied by the community, and other such matters.

The British have developed a scheme for situation notation and analysis known as the curriculum information system. This system performs two actions: (1) gathering and noting information about curriculum status and (2) analyzing the information collected during the first action to generate a summary showing the nature of curriculum patterns. Specifically, gathering and noting information, called *notation,* results in knowledge of what is taught, by whom it is taught, to whom it is taught, and how it is taught. Imagine the head start that knowing these things can provide! Common sources of such information used in the United States during past decades have been curriculum documents of several kinds and the recollections of a number of people in the schools, but especially of classroom teachers. The raw data constitute such a mass that one must filter them to adduce specifics about curriculum organization, sequence, and "distribution" among the pupil population. Aptly, the British call this process *filtration.*

The second action, analyzing the information, involves what the British refer to as *transformation,* or the manipulation and changing of what is taught so that it suggests design or pattern. Transformation may occur, for instance, in the focus of the curriculum or in the deployment of resources. Analyzing information with a view to taking next steps obviously represents the beginning of planning.[8]

Examination of one's work situation may be conducted in two major ways: (1) by viewing the entire school or school system scene as it affects the prospect of curriculum planning and (2) by learning as much as possible about the current curriculum.

The Impact of Current Trends and Issues

Observers see a number of trends in American society and its schools that should serve as cues to curriculum planners. The deterioration of moral and ethical values has led to a decline in discipline in homes and schools and an increase in drug use, alcoholism, and sexual promiscuity. Demands have been made of the schools that they "tighten up" in many respects, but especially in the teaching of the basics. Pupils' in-school experiences have been called irrelevant to their subsequent life experiences. The purposes and formats of schooling are said to be creaking. Advocacy groups that should be helping the schools are disunited.

These and other trends sharpen issues in the fields of elementary and secondary education. Some of these issues are perennial ones; others have arisen recently:

- What can be done to improve the quality of new teachers and administrators who enter service in the schools?
- What can be done to help present school personnel improve?

- How can preparation in the so-called life competencies be included in the curriculum?
- How can the responsibility for forming policy about the curriculum be distributed more equitably?
- What can be done to improve the morale of school people and to heighten their desire for excellence?
- How can the real weaknesses in the curriculum be discovered and overcome?
- What can be done to coordinate the educational efforts of schools with the educational efforts of outside agencies and organizations?
- How can relationships between state education personnel and school district personnel be improved?
- How can the new demands and expectations of the federal government be reconciled with the intentions of local school personnel?
- How can lay persons be involved more appropriately in curriculum planning?

Beneath and in addition to general issues like these are issues that relate directly to specific planning tasks. For example, if a curriculum committee wishes to add to the school program a curriculum offering that is novel, some of the issues in the list above may apply: those related to responsibility for policy making, identification of pertinent life competencies, and ways of preparing staffs to implement curriculum plans. Other issues are likely to be associated with particular subject matter content and implementation of new projects.

Some of these questions fall under the shadow of a larger issue: Do people in the United States want good schools or merely effective ones? Although effective schools are sometimes good according to certain definitions of goodness, a distinction must be made between the two terms. A rise in Scholastic Assessment Test scores, for instance, may indicate that a school has become effective. If its dropout rate increases dramatically at the same time, however, can one label it a good school? Perhaps the truest measure of the goodness of a school—that is, its goodness for pupils—is the answer to the question "Would I want to send my children to this school?" Feeling to some extent dictates how one answers this question, but information and reason are also involved. Reason, based on investigation and study, tells whether the school is bent toward the total development of youngsters or is preoccupied with a narrow academic focus, "standards," and test scores.[9] Today, the narrow viewpoint evokes the enthusiasm of many would-be reformers, whereas the actual needs of pupils dictate that a broader viewpoint be cherished.

In the 1990s, the federal government is taking an enlarged role in curriculum planning. The goals of America 2000 have been approved with a stipend for assisting the states in setting minimum knowledge levels to be attained by their pupils. America 2000 establishes, in effect, a national school board to determine, at least indirectly, what is to be taught in local schools. The specific actions yet to be taken will require watching by curriculum personnel in school districts.

The Arrival of Strategic Planning

The terms *master planning* and *long-range planning* have been popular in curriculum matters for many years. The planning that these terms imply anticipates events that are reasonably certain and that should come to pass within a few years. The newer *strategic planning,* on the other hand, has become an instrument for dealing with uncertainty. The questions that strategic planners ask are "What might happen?" and "What scenario is most probable?" Strategic planners deal with threats and opportunities as well as with shortcomings and strengths. In our era, strategic planning is coming to be considered a necessity.[10]

Bases That Affect People Directly and Personally

The need for change in a school as an institution has to be translated into statements of needs of the people who study and work in the school. Along with personal needs, one encounters within the local setting curriculum problems, which are actually the problems of pupils, teachers, administrators, parents, and local employers. In order to solve their problems, people must exhibit competencies. In the process of problem solving, people are subjected to pressures originating inside and outside themselves. Taken together, needs, problems, competencies, and pressures influence people in direct and highly personal ways.

The Needs of the School Population

Many curriculum planners believe that identification of needs of all sorts has in the past been casual, even careless. In practice, people's needs sometimes represent a gap between established goals and actual conditions in a school. At other times, needs have not been previously recognized and are therefore unrelated to any established goals, in which case they must be examined carefully in order to determine their nature and validity and, eventually, to find some ways in which they might be met. The identification method called *needs assessment* permits determination of needs either in broad, general terms, with reference to several goals, or in specific terms, with reference to pinpointed goals. If curriculum planning in a school or school system has been either nonexistent or minimal, the broad, general approach is usually followed. If the school or school system is experienced and sophisticated in planning, it may be ready for specificity. In effect, needs assessment is an evaluation of "where we are" so that planners know how to expend time and energy in planning for future activity to meet genuine needs.[11]

The goals of the school, then, are a common takeoff point in needs assessment, although needs determination in rough form may precede the setting of either aims or goals. Preliminary discussion and investigation usually suggest which goals are to be attended to most closely. Possible ways of determining the current degree of attainment of these goals may be proposed next. Partial data on goal attainment may already be at hand in the form, for example, of pupil records, survey reports, and curriculum documents.

The following outline suggests the kinds of data that often prove useful in needs assessment:

I. Data about pupils
    A. Data about the pupil population as a whole
        1. The general pupil population
        2. Specific subgroups
        3. Enrollment statistics
        4. Indications of pupil progress
        5. The incidence of and reasons for leaving school
    B. Data about the growth and development of pupils
        1. Physical growth and development
        2. Achievement in specific school subject matter
        3. Values status with respect to responsible behavior, hard work, and so on
        4. Emotional and social development
        5. Psychological needs
        6. Intellectual and creative development
        7. Personal traits
    C. Data about pupils' homes, families, and community conditions
        1. Conditions of home and family life in general
        2. Extent and quality of attention given children by parents
        3. Nature of the school's adult constituency
        4. Specifics concerning the nature of the community
    D. Data about pupil opportunities
        1. For part-time current work within the community
        2. For eventual career
        3. In terms of economic projection and forecasts
II. Data about social and cultural matters to be dealt with by the school
    A. The need to transmit and to alter the culture
    B. The need to orient and to adjust the young
    C. The need to preserve and to alter the social order
    D. The need to prepare pupils specifically for adulthood
    E. The need to relate the individual pupil to the social and cultural milieux
    F. The need to explore with pupils
        1. Values
        2. Expectations
        3. The political power structure
        4. Community issues
        5. Trends of the times

III. Data about learning—how pupils learn
   A. What learning is
   B. What it means to be motivated to learn
   C. The nature of learning styles
   D. Problems with self-concept
   E. The nature of readiness
   F. How transfer of learning occurs
IV. Data about subject matter—what pupils should learn
   A. What subject matter, old and new, is of most worth
   B. Criteria for selecting subject matter content
   C. Organization of subject matter content
   D. Criteria for selecting and making instructional materials
   E. Criteria for determining relevance of content to pupils' life experiences

A complete range of diagnostic devices is required for identifying and clarifying needs: tests and inventories of all sorts, interviews, open-ended questions and written protocols, unfinished stories and incidents, records of discussions, records of reading, sociometrics, socioeconomic analysis, reports of critical incidents, analysis of drawings, interpretations of pictures, and, of course, observation and recording of performance. The needs easiest to identify are naturally the felt, immediate ones. Needs originating in social and cultural settings are likely to be unfelt and obscure to individual pupils. Sometimes identification awaits the judgment of wise adults.

In most school systems, a large portion of the data about needs that are helpful in edifying teachers, administrators, and other persons who make curriculum policy must be collected anew. These data should be useful to planners in determining whether the school or school system is attaining its goals. If it is not, the planners have two choices: (1) to review the goals to judge whether all of them are still valid or (2) to plan what should be done about pursuing realistic goals more effectively.

When needs assessment has proceeded to this point, the rating or ranking of unmet needs is yet to occur. This rating or ranking has usually been accomplished by largely unplanned group discussion.

The rating of needs can be accomplished by using any of the following methods:

1. *Sorting cards.* A statement of need is put on each of a number of cards that are given to individuals or small groups to rank in order of importance. This convenient and common method is superficial because participants in the sorting need think very little about the meaning of the work they are doing.

2. *Rating sheets.* Rating sheets function like sorting cards, but they are less cumbersome to manipulate. The rating is accomplished on a single sheet or two, as in the implementation of Phi Delta Kappa's model.

3. *The critical incident technique.* This technique requires educators, pupils, or parents to recall incidents that suggest the need for improvement (or for commendation) of the educational system. The technique works best when the incidents reported are not limited to just one or two aspects of educational activity.

4. *The Delphi Technique.* To improve planning and to introduce forecasting into selecting unmet needs, the Delphi Technique requires a group leader to prepare a list of statements indicating the intentions of his or her planning group. The statements are in the form of goals, value comments, or program suggestions which are sent to curriculum specialists with the request that the specialists indicate the years in which they believe the statements will be accepted and put into use. Sometimes the statements are refined and sent to additional consultants. Summaries of these predictions may then be sent to all consultants, with the request that the consultants comment on them and attempt to justify any views of their own that are markedly different from the modal responses. This procedure may be followed on several occasions until further convergence in the views of the consultants has occurred.[12] The technique provides a trend-oriented view, and is in fact an application of strategic planning, as are TARGET and FTA, described below.

5. *TARGET.* An acronym for "To Assess Relevant Goals in Education Together," TARGET combines the Delphi Technique with gaming. People meeting in groups write their needs statements anonymously. The statements are divided into five categories and are analyzed according to the categories. Time and cost are lessened by keeping the activity within the groups, but judgment by experts is not available.

6. *Fault Tree Analysis (FTA).* This method identifies ways in which failure in a program or project is most likely to occur. The method has been used to analyze the design of new programs prior to their implementation. Fault Tree Analysis starts with the proposal of an undesired event (UE) that people wish to see avoided in the curriculum. Given this undesired event, the analysis leads to construction of a "logic tree," the branches of which are series of events. Small groups of participants are trained to suggest these events, which may number several hundred. Experts are assigned to consider the relative frequency and importance of the events. The shapes of the events on the tree show the relationships among the events. These interrelationships reveal the sequence of events that is likely to cause the UE. B. R. Witkin, a proponent of Fault Tree Analysis, reports that by using this technique the Seattle School District found a need for changing its mathematics program for vocational education pupils. He expresses doubt that the relationship between mathematics instruction and vocational program requirements would have been found by any other method of needs assessment.[13]

In the initial discussion portion of assessment, planners should ask one another questions about the unmet needs of pupils and teachers in the system. Needs assessment as it is being practiced calls for collection of data from many constituents, determination of priorities by as many groups and individuals as possible, and evaluation of the gaps between what is and what might be.

Experience has shown that curriculum planners are inclined to favor practical considerations in planning at the expense of "fancier" methodology. Some of the practical questions they raise are the following: Do the teachers really want the changes we propose? How can the changes be incorporated within the curriculum—for example, by adding instructional units, by creating minicourses, by improving school activities, or by supplying new instructional materials? Does our proposal get at the problem we want to solve, or does it deal only with the symptoms? Would this proposal throw the curriculum out of balance? Would we be devoting an inordinate amount of attention to only a limited pupil population?

David J. Mullen has described a game called "Bonanza" that provides a baseline through which people's involvement in needs assessment can begin. The game requires each player to spend $100 twenty times. Possible goals or aims of the school are shown in comic strip form. The players spend their money on the goals they perceive to be most important. The advantages claimed for this game are simplicity, ease of administration, involvement, and inexpensiveness. One group of players chose the following curriculum emphases: the three Rs, the arts, health, physical development and safety, development of the self, relationship with others, the world of work, the physical world, making choices, and the social world.[14]

Interestingly, the durability of curriculum reforms is clearly related to the satisfaction of specific needs. When needs are met by changing institutional structure, by bringing in new and helpful personnel, and by offering data indicating that improvement is occurring, a given reform is likely to last.

Local Curriculum Problems

In curriculum planning, as in the military, the term often used for a challenge to action is *problem*. The term is meant to carry no negative connotation. It implies instead an opportunity to use one's capacities and resources in an honest effort to improve teaching and learning for children and youth. When the needs of pupils and teachers have been discovered, these needs may lead planners to specify the problems involved in meeting those needs. Like the needs, some of the problems may be identified in the teaching and learning of subject matter; others in specific pupil attitudes, behaviors, and welfare requirements.

Needs having been noted, the next challenge lies in solving problems created or raised by the needs. Perceptions concerning what constitutes a proper focus for curriculum problem solving vary from group to group. Young children view curriculum problems differently from the way adolescents view them, and teachers often see them differently from the manner in which supervisors see them. Problems that seem pressing in one school appear insignificant in another. Many ways can always be found to improve the program of a school if one looks about with care, perceptiveness, and sensitivity. Typical problems include providing for individual differences, providing experiences for minority children, developing programs of citizenship education, and obtaining citizens' responses to what the schools are doing.

Classroom teachers may see that problems like these are big and general and thus not concrete enough to concern the teacher "where he or she lives." Another reaction may be "None of these problems concerns us just now, but we can name a currently 'hot' and significant problem." School personnel should recognize that having problems is natural and legitimate, that not having them would suggest dullness and insensitivity. The size of a problem, whether large or small, should not make its proponent ashamed of it. If it proves to be either too large or too small to manage, it can be modified. There is another aspect to the expression of problems:

> Teachers and administrators frequently voice their problems in a form that is more respectable than real. For example, the teacher may say that the principal's office bothers him with frequent interruptions of his classroom routine and that, because of these interruptions, his pupils lose interest. When this respectable statement of his problem has been "pushed back" far enough, one may find that the teacher is really troubled by his own failure to vary his teaching procedures. Obviously, he needs help in clarifying and stating his true problem (which is in part his relationship with the principal) and especially in accepting it as being respectable and worthwhile.[15]

Teachers are often encouraged when they find that other teachers have the same or similar problems.

Numerous curriculum problems cut across the specialized fields of supervision, inservice education/staff development, and curriculum improvement. A common question is "When should a problem be identified as a problem of curriculum improvement rather than of supervision or inservice education/staff development?" An unrealistic trichotomy has come to exist among these three elements. If the major objective of these three fields is to improve teachers in service so that the experiences of their pupils in turn may be improved, the substantive distinctions among them become less sharp. Their interrelationships are diagrammed in Figure 8-1; clearly, there are large overlaps among the fields. Since the distinctions among these elements or strategies affect process much more than they affect substance, activities in supervision, inservice education/staff development, and curriculum improvement should be regarded simply as complementary means of implementing a solution or amelioration of a curriculum problem. The focus of attention should be placed on the problem itself.

A significant basis for getting started in curriculum planning is to *give attention to matters that concern teachers in their daily work*. These matters often have to do with methods of "reaching" individual pupils, selection of content for teaching particular groups of children, classroom organization of children and facilities for better learning, and ways of ensuring that children are motivated to learn. The master planning of facilities and organizational arrangements with which administrators are frequently preoccupied can make a genuine and lasting contribution to children's experiences under school auspices. Teachers are not likely to show deep interest in such problems and proposals, however, when they face their own distinctive problems at their respective teaching stations. Curriculum leaders should generally plan to begin with these distinctive problems.

Voices in support of the preceding statements are being raised today, as they were at mid-century. Ron Brandt proposed in an editorial that both curriculum theorists and practitioners hold to the idea of locally based problem solving.[16] Similarly, the Schools Council and other professional groups in England have advocated making the local school the chief center of curriculum planning, and making development of the curriculum and self-development of the teacher functionally interrelated.[17] We do not yet know what encouraging or dampening effect federal legislation in education will have on local curriculum planning in the United States. If legislation has a dampening effect, the result may be permanent injury.

Problems with which to begin planning emerge from many settings. Some of them are products of given classroom situations and groupings of pupils; others are peculiar to individual schools; others stem from the developmental levels at which children are living and learning and can thus be categorized as grade-level problems; others extend from kindergarten through the top grade; others come from community pressure groups; and still others emerge from the mandates of state governments and from the exigencies of the national scene.

There are two major steps in starting problem solution—identifying a problem and then defining it. The discussion to this point has centered on some basic considerations in problem identification. Attention will now be given to the second step—problem definition. Actually, the first step merges

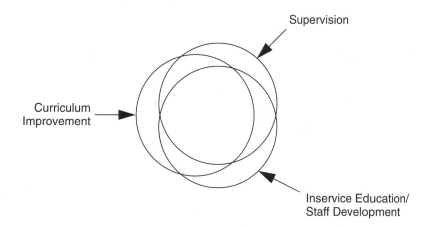

FIGURE 8-1   The Interrelationship Among Three Strategies for Improving Curriculum

into the second. A problem, whatever its source, is likely to be stated rather crudely when it is first identified. It expresses the concern of an individual or a group about a school situation that is believed to need attention. The problem need not relate to a situation that is serious or especially troublesome. Rather, it may relate to a situation that has great prospects for improvement because it has already proved profitable in stimulating learning. Once again, it must be said that the existence of problems need have no negative implications.

As one looks critically at problems as they are originally proposed, one sees that frequently they are too big in overall size or have too many dimensions to be manageable. For instance, problems of child study are frequently proposed in such comprehensive form and with so many sources of data used in gathering initial evidence that one does not know where to take hold of them or how to handle them. On the other hand, problems may be too narrow or limited, particularly when they are expressed by classroom teachers, who tend to be so close to daily problems that they become myopic. Moreover, problems suggested by persons far removed from classrooms may have, for teachers, a totally unrealistic ring, so teachers resist dealing with them. The object of the initial stage in problem definition is to limit the scope of oversized problems, to extend and bolster narrow ones, to make certain that the problems are real and practical, and in general to ensure the manageability and usefulness of the problems to be solved. Sometimes a problem can be described in nearly the same way as its corresponding curriculum need, but usually it must be described more exactly.

Discussion of the meanings of problems can become so boring and impractical that some of the planners complain that a given problem is "being beaten to death." Or a problem may fall prey to persons with axes to grind or with tendencies to view the problem in traditional rather than fresh ways. Some of the difficulties in problem definition can be resolved by pursuing a plan that proceeds as follows:

1. The already identified problem is defined until it is judged to be a single problem rather than multiple ones, manageable in size, and worth solving.
2. The problem is thought about further with a view to formulating hypotheses concerning what could be done to solve it.
3. When several promising hypotheses have been formulated, they are tested intellectually through discussion, and those that do not seem fruitful or relevant are eliminated.
4. A new problem focus now forms around the hypotheses that remain. These are tested by accumulating evidence confirming or denying their worth in solving the problem. Much of the evidence stems from the elements in decision making: children and their developing and learning, social forces that affect the schools, and the nature and structure of subject matter.

5. Now that the problem has been reasonably well defined, tasks in testing hypotheses are assigned to staff members on the basis of their competence and interest.
6. Inquiry of this kind often leads to at least a minor redefinition of the problem, as staff members find hidden factors and influences they had not previously considered. The danger here is in "going off on strange rabbit trails," which may lead too far afield and pervert the original intent of the inquiry.
7. Problems often prove to be interrelated, so that recognition of one of them speedily leads to recognition of another. This fact makes curriculum improvement a fascinating activity.

These procedures need not, of course, be followed seriatim in all situations. The indispensable ingredient in the processes of problem identification and definition is careful, critical thinking about the meanings of problems and about ways of solving them.

ACTIVITY 8-1

Finding Curriculum Needs and Related Problems in the Field of Moral Education

The decline of the American family and several other causes have impressed upon Americans the need for moral education in their schools. Assume that moral education has been clearly identified as a need in the school or school system you know best. Convert this generalized need into statements of four or five curriculum problems that should be attacked in your institution. The following questions may guide your thinking.

1. How can we determine what is moral and what is not, and therefore what moral education should be?
2. How can we take stages of human development into account in planning a program of moral education?

Discuss the suggestions that are made by members of a group in answering these questions.

SITUATION 8-1

Sorting the Problems

The Curriculum Steering Committee of the sixty-eight-teacher Cormorant Unified School District was conducting its second meeting since the time of the committee's formation three months previously. At its first meeting, the committee had decided to poll all teachers in the district to determine what pressing curriculum problems and concerns the teachers could suggest. Forty-nine teachers had responded to a simple questionnaire asking for one or more open-ended statements of problems and concerns that should receive prompt attention.

When the returned questionnaires had been read and the responses interpreted and categorized by a subcommittee of the Curriculum Steering Committee, the following problems and concerns were listed in rank order:

Item	*Frequency of Response (N = 49)*
Excessive clerical work required of teachers	30
Scarcity of locally developed curriculum guides	23
The prevalence of gum chewing in classrooms	18
Frequent interruption of classroom work because of announcements, drives, campaigns, and essay contests	17
Too much interference from community members not connected with the schools	17
Children's weakness in language skills	16
Lack of knowledge of what teachers in grades above and below are doing	15
Failure to concentrate sufficiently on the three Rs	14
Children's poor study habits	12
Uncertainty about what the principals want done	9
Poverty (lack of richness) in the arts—music and the fine arts particularly	7
Poor discipline in some classrooms	6
A top-heavy emphasis on football	3
The presence of certain incompetent teachers	2
A weak science program	2
Poor arithmetical skills	2
Lack of supplies	1
Too many chiefs and too few "Indians"	1
Ineffective leadership by the administrators	1
Limited funds for audiovisual aids	1

If you were a member of the Curriculum Steering Committee, how would you contribute to a further categorization of these problems and concerns? For instance, which of them seem to relate closely to teachers' own feelings about their jobs? What other categories can you find?

Which of the problems and concerns seem to you to be respectable coverups for *real* problems and concerns? Why? How could you be reasonably sure that you are right?

Select one of the problems or concerns that interests you particularly. What would you do to help teachers begin solving or ameliorating it?

If you have an opportunity to do so, conduct a similar survey in a school with which you are familiar; then consider actions you can take in exploring teachers' initially expressed problems to determine the full and accurate meanings of these problems.

The Competencies of Participants

Much will be said in the next chapter about the roles of several categories of curriculum planners. The present discussion deals instead with the kinds of competencies needed in the planning process, without identification of the persons in whom they may be found. The competencies of participants form an important basis for planning. Naturally, some school systems have been able to employ more competent persons than have other school systems. The reasons are often salary schedules, geographic locations, and cultural advantages.

At any rate, several competencies contribute notably to the formation of the best possible plans. Effective planners are capable of planning alone, with the help of pupils, and in groups of fellow professionals and lay persons. The total staff should include people with the following different competencies:

1. *Ability to create ideas.* This competency may well head the list.
2. *Ability to reconcile conflicting viewpoints.* This ability causes planning to begin in a favorable emotional climate and causes it to continue despite expected ups and downs in relationships.
3. *Ability to contribute to the overall quality of group work.* Working successfully in groups requires understanding of and skill in many aspects of group work.
4. *Ability to direct and coordinate.* Organizing people and things, as well as pulling people and things together, constitutes a talent definitely needed by administrators and coordinators, and also by teachers and others who have part-time responsibility for direction and coordination.
5. *Ability to analyze situations and interpret actions.* Often, this competency falls under the category of troubleshooting.
6. *Ability to recognize and choose alternatives.* This competency rests on a firm base of knowledge and understanding about children, youth, learning, community influences, national trends, available philosophies, historical precedents, and developments in the subject matter fields.
7. *Ability to plan and conduct experimentation and research.* Special preparation is obviously required for exercise of this competency.
8. *Ability to ask the "right" questions.* This competency rests on a sense of where a project has been, what its prospects are for the future, and what is possible.
9. *Ability to present ideas in writing*
10. *Ability to present ideas orally*
11. *Ability to use machines, including computers, to facilitate planning*
12. *Miscellaneous abilities,* including the ability to serve as recorder or secretary, to entertain visiting personnel, or to anticipate people's needs[18]

Another way of considering planners' competencies is to test their abilities, understandings, and attitudes in simulated situations. Below are three competencies, defined in terms of concrete tasks.

Competency 1

Can recognize from the following list eight problems of the school or school system that belong clearly within the province of curriculum planners:

Making case studies of pupils from minority groups
Contracting with trucking firms to haul equipment from school to school
Planning a work-experience program for high school pupils
Surveying pupils' attitudes toward smoking marijuana
Conferring with alumni about their experiences in the school
Providing space and other physical arrangements for a new computer
Developing a course guide in learning how to speak more effectively in
     public
Supervising the installation of air conditioning units in school buildings
Organizing a learning center in an old school building
Planning an interpersonal communication system to bring faculty mem-
     bers closer in their thinking
Plotting bus routes for the new school year
Employing a new assistant business manager for the school system
Organizing an arrangement for teacher self-supervision using videotapes
Assigning teacher aides to lavatory duty
Sponsoring a campaign for improving courtesy in the school
Organizing a research team to work on a title project using federal funds

Competency 2

(1) Can identify three of the eight problems chosen above that will probably require for solution close relationships between the current curriculum planners and other persons, such as administrators, supervisors, child study personnel, business administrators, etc. (2) In each of the three cases, can name the categories of personnel to be consulted.

Competency 3

Can suggest three ways of getting planning started that are at least as useful as the method described below:

A question was posed in writing to the faculty: "If you were to have school time for curriculum planning next year, what curriculum problems would you identify as needing most immediate attention? Name three if possible." The miscellaneous responses of the faculty were placed, with a minimum of editing, in a questionnaire that was distributed to the faculty for final response. The curriculum problems that were mentioned with highest frequency in the questionnaire returns were accepted as the problems for study.

ACTIVITY 8-2

Helping Participants Improve the Use of Their Competencies

It's never too early to think of ways in which people who are endowed with talents or abilities can be helped to use them better. Look again at the list of twelve abilities on page 375. Consider possibilities for increasing, improving, or strengthening these abilities. Possibilities include (1) giving people opportunities to exercise their abilities; (2) giving suggestions for improving use of abilities; (3) monitoring use by assigning people to observe what others do; (4) providing specific learning experiences within courses, visits, conventions, institutes, and workshops; (5) recording what people do so that they may analyze their own actions; and (6) employing consultants to consider how well people's abilities are being exercised. What else occurs to you?

Pressures Outside and Inside the Self

Seeds of curriculum planning are planted consciously in numerous places. Still other seeds drop fortuitously on fertile soil. Persons and agencies that apply pressure to have curriculum improvement activities started are doing conscious planting. Many of these persons and agencies can be found within school systems. They include alert superintendents, curriculum coordinators, and principals who want to see schools move forward in using the best available knowledge of children, learning, teaching methods, subject matter, and the demands of a changing society. In addition, each school is likely to have its unofficial or emergent leaders who stimulate other personnel to improve their practices. Nearly every teacher can name one or more problems that he or she would like to see acted upon, though they may be other people's problems.

Pupils themselves, the live consumers of education, demand attention, which often leads to curriculum improvement. Many a promising improvement program has resulted from administering standardized or teacher-made tests, even though the data derived from the original testing may have been of doubtful worth. Careful interviews with an individual pupil can be useful in determining the nature of that pupil's self as a basis for learning what makes him or her "tick."

Teachers and other personnel carry ideas from meetings, conventions, intervisitations, college and university courses, and other inservice and staff development ventures. Professional literature is now so profuse as to challenge teachers to remain current in their reading, even in their own teaching field. These are but a few of the influences that promote improvement from within the schools.

Ours, however, is an era in which demands for change also come from persons and organizations outside school systems, such as the following:

- State officials
- Bureaus of the federal government
- Private educational testing organizations
- Private foundations
- Authors of popular books and articles
- Regional associations of colleges and secondary schools
- Colleges and universities
- Individual subject matter specialists and groups of specialists
- Patriotic organizations
- Trade associations and industries
- Labor unions

The truth of a statement made years ago by curriculum specialists is now being realized: The school that avoids improving its own curriculum will soon have its curriculum "improved" for it. Many school systems have been so negligent in planning for curriculum improvement that they have become fair game for competing interests outside the schools. Without question, many individuals and groups external to the schools are now performing beneficent and valuable services for education, but they should never be allowed to become complete substitutes for school personnel who are working with pupils day by day.

In addition to external pressures, there are pressures within the minds of potential and actual participants in curriculum planning. People conjure up all sorts of notions about how strong tradition is; about their shortages of time, energy, and resources; about what is worth doing; about difficulties in the tasks ahead; and about complications in gaining support and working with other people.

Internal pressures sometimes go even deeper. Some school people are afraid of experimenting with other people's children and with public money. Others are afraid of wasting time and energy by making wrong starts. Others feel insecure about what they might be asked to do. Still others are simply predisposed to "let sleeping dogs lie." Teachers and other adult curriculum planners are sometimes beset by handicaps originating in their own backgrounds. Having been reared in a society in which values and attitudes are awry, some of them are ill-equipped to plan for pupils with similar values and attitudes.

SITUATION 8-2

Whose Concerns Should Have Priority?

Orangeville Elementary School was a brand new school in a desert that had recently been made to bloom by irrigation and was accordingly attracting a number of young families. Many of the parents of Orangeville's children worked in industrial plants in a city thirty miles away. A few were skilled laborers, but the majority were scientists, engineers, or highly specialized technicians.

When the school opened a year ago, Beth Ransom, the principal, organized the Curriculum Improvement Council to identify curriculum problems and to begin dealing with several of these problems immediately. During its ten months of operation, the council had met with all teachers who were not council members and had identified two pressing concerns that seemed worth exploring in depth. One was the need to choose enriching materials for a school that had little more than basic textbooks. The other was the need to develop programs in art and music, inasmuch as these subjects were being largely neglected in favor of the three Rs, science, and the social studies. The council was certain that the teaching staff was committed to pursuit of these two concerns.

Then lightning struck. A committee of parents, intent on maximizing their children's opportunities for college admission, called on Beth and insisted that the previously publicized concerns of the teachers be overridden in favor of the following alleged needs:

1. Homogeneous grouping at all grade levels from first through sixth
2. Investigation of why some children do not learn to read as rapidly as others
3. Establishment of special coaching classes in the three Rs
4. The teaching of "ninth-grade general science" in the fifth and sixth grades
5. Increase in homework assignments
6. Greater competition among children in the primary grades

Later that week, the commander of a patriotic organization discussed with Beth the importance of eliminating the social studies from the curriculum, of returning to separate teaching of history and geography, and of requiring every sixth grader to memorize the Declaration of Independence.

Indicate the degree to which each of these concerns deserves respect, given its origin and intrinsic nature.

In this situation, what should Beth Ransom do? the Curriculum Improvement Council? the faculty as a whole?

The Orangeville Elementary School was new and had had little opportunity to get under way. How do you account for the presence of insistent external forces at this stage of the school's career?

What principles might be applied to balance and reconcile the internal and external forces in a situation of this kind?

SEEKING TO DEAL WITH A RANGE OF PROBLEMS

As we have noted, problems facing schools come from a variety of sources and are themselves varied in nature. Pupils become addicted to drugs and alcohol. Schools are called upon to accommodate and help poor and disadvantaged children. Need exists for the care and early education of an increasing number of children. Working parents have too little time to help and supervise their children, some of whom are appropriately designated "latchkey children." Society seems to have lost its touch, if it had ever gained one, in dealing with racism. And this little catalog of problems constitutes only a beginning.

One can posit the existence of an 8000-pupil school system in which all of these problems appear simultaneously. The system is hard put to determine how its resources are to be used and where resources can come from in the first place. Near the turn of the century, as we face increased involvement in curriculum planning by federal and state governments, organization for planning will become especially necessary. As Alice Miel said years ago, organization becomes useful when it facilitates group endeavor and when it is truly functional, permitting free-flowing interpersonal relationships and widespread participation. It must serve the institution's fundamental purpose and goals, provide for continuity of problem solving, and achieve coordination among groups of planners.[19] Some of the discussion that follows is directed toward achieving organization that truly works.

SITUATION 8-3

An Agenda for Hating School

Miss Baker, a teacher in Tamrack Middle School, was upset. "Are the children becoming savages, or do I imagine it? Twenty or thirty years ago, the children in this school didn't seem to be so impolite, even brutal, to one another," she said to Mrs. Rourk, the teacher in the next classroom.

"You aren't imagining anything," Mrs. Rourk replied. "You must remember that children today don't always have home influences or community standards like the influences and standards of years ago. I've been troubled about the same thing. Why don't we try observing our children to see what we might do to help them with their manners?"

After their conversation, the two teachers began making note of the behaviors of their children, incident by incident, as the children interacted with one another during a two-week period. What they saw formed a catalog of behaviors, too many of which consisted of offenses against plain human decency.

"Let's each choose one incident we find especially troubling and make the two incidents a start toward doing something about this problem," Miss Baker suggested.

Mrs. Rourk agreed. "We should say why the incidents we choose are so troubling to us," she added.

Miss Baker was disturbed because her two brightest pupils were being picked on by most of the other twenty members of her homeroom class. She recorded their comments to the individual "victims."

"Why are you so smart? What are you trying to do—show us up?"

"You're always answering the teachers questions. Why don't you give us a chance?"

"You won't show us your answers to the questions when we're taking tests. You're the very one who should be helping the rest of us."

"You always have your homework ready. Let up! You're just making things tough for us."

"No, we don't want to be with you. You're different. You're weird!"

"If you don't take it easy like the rest of us, you'll go home some day with a big lump on your head."

Miss Baker commented that, after her observations, she was upset for two reasons: "I don't like hearing people say nasty, uncivilized things to one another, and I hadn't realized the extent to which this class is engaging in a voluntary slowdown. I guess people who don't like to work resent people who try hard. Aren't good work habits in fashion anymore?"

Mrs. Rourk had admitted a new pupil to her homeroom class two months before the observation period began. The newcomer, named Lucy, came to school daily in clothes that were threadbare. Mrs. Rourk soon referred her to the school nurse because Lucy showed signs of malnutrition. Mrs. Rourk learned that Lucy, who came from a broken home, lived with her partially blind grandmother, whose annual income was below the poverty line.

On three separate occasions, Mrs. Rourk saw Lucy standing in a corner of the playground taking verbal abuse from a half-dozen girls and boys who seemed to resent her presence. Lucy stood looking down at her dirty sneakers while she clutched the fingers of her left hand alternately with the fingers of her right. Mrs. Rourk recorded the remarks of the other children.

"Why do you always look so crummy?"
"Do you come up out of a sewer every morning?"
"Where do you get those clothes? Why don't you dress like the rest of us?"
"Why don't you ask someone in the cafeteria for food that's left over?"
"Do you know you stink?"

Mrs. Rourk had a special reason to be upset. "I came from a home almost like Lucy's," she told Miss Baker. "I can't stand seeing poor children mistreated like this."

Miss Baker and Mrs. Rourk were sure they had seen the tip of a big iceberg of uncivilized behavior. How could they use their observations in planning immediate and long-term curriculum change to counter problems like these?

PLOTTING, STARTING, AND CONTINUING THE PLANNING PROCESS

As we have seen, human needs come in bundles. Some needs are intellectual, some are skill related, some are emotional, some are physical, some are moral or spiritual. Planners investigate these needs as they manifest themselves within the planners' own environments; investigations reveal people's thoughts and feelings, unique circumstances, and data of many kinds. To discover and sort data, planners use means like the problem census, inservice and staff development media, cooperative study and surveys, experimentation, formal evaluation, and development of philosophies and sets of objectives.

The Problem Census

A time-honored way of initiating curriculum improvement programs is to ask teachers and other personnel to state their problems orally or in writing. At best, this procedure is carried out face to face in an informal, unstructured situation. This procedure was used in Corpus Christi, Texas[20] and in the Illinois Curriculum Improvement Program.[21] A more formal way of inventorying concerns and problems is to ask in writing for open-ended statements or to present a written list of possible concerns to be ranked in order of importance. These methods of census taking remain the most common ways of locating curriculum problems and concerns. The following census form was distributed to elementary school teachers in Cumberland County, New Jersey by the county's "helping teachers" and a team of consultants:

As a consequence of meeting with the administrators of public elementary schools and also with a representative group of teachers in the county, we have listed below a variety of possibilities for study by teachers and administrators, and perhaps also by members of boards of education and other citizens.

Will you please select from the list the four topics which you believe are most worthy of study by people who really want to benefit the schools of the county? Then please place the number 1 next to that topic which you think is absolutely tops as an important study topic. Finally, place a 2 next to your second choice; a 3 next to your third choice; and a 4 next to the topic you rank fourth.

Please note that the placement of a topic in the list does not suggest the degree to which it is favored by the helping teachers or the consultants.

When the returns are in, we shall report them to you, with an indication of the top preferences of all of you. You as an individual will then be asked whether you care to join a study group, which you may choose freely from the several groups studying the most-preferred topics. A teacher who decides to join a study group will be working partly on his or her own time to learn all he or she can about new ideas and materials related to the topic.

Possible Topics for Study

_____ Learning Centers and Learning Stations
"There ought to be places in the classroom and the school where learning is easier."
_____ Developing Listening Skills
"Why don't these kids hear anything?"
_____ Ungraded School Units (Nongrading)
"Kids don't grow in grades; they grow by years and in spurts."
_____ Inquiry Training
"What's this 'inquiry approach' all about?"
_____ Behavioral Objectives and Criterion Referencing
"Do the children and I know where we're going, and when we've gotten there?"

_____ Evaluation as Feedback and Guide
"How can we learn from test results, and how can we report to parents?"
_____ Gaming and Simulation in the Classroom
"How can I make it like the real thing?"
_____ Strategies for Individualizing Instruction
"How can I sort out the individuals in my group, and then do something for them?"
_____ Classroom Discipline and the Curriculum
"Does how children spend their time in school have anything really to do with their getting into trouble?"
_____ The Roles of Teacher Aides
"Lavatory patrol, hall duty, checking papers—what?"
_____ Diagnosing and Correcting Reading Difficulties
"I'm not sure how to find out, and then I don't know what to do after I've found out."
_____ Working with Underachievers
"If he isn't doing as well as he can, why isn't he?"
_____ New Developments in the Teaching of the Social Studies
"What's that about the Third World?"
_____ New Developments in the Teaching of Science
"Having competed with the Russians, there must be something else."
_____ New Developments in the Teaching of Arithmetic
"They say they can tell what kind of teacher you are by watching you teach arithmetic."
_____ Making the School a More Humane Place
"The school is an institution where people should be valued!"
_____ "Opening" the School
"How can they have new experiences without tearing the roof off the building?"

Brainstorming

To shift from the negative emphasis, which a problem census sometimes seems to involve, faculties may use their own adaptations of the brainstorming technique, originally created for idea development in the field of advertising. Brainstorming consists of free, rapid-fire suggestion of ideas by group members, no matter how impossible the achievement of some of the ideas appears to be. One member's suggestion is followed immediately by another member's suggestion, without critical or other comment being made by any member of the group. However, a member may elaborate, or "piggyback," on his or her predecessor's suggestion. A recorder, human or mechanical, keeps a list of the ideas, sixty or seventy of which may be proposed within a very few

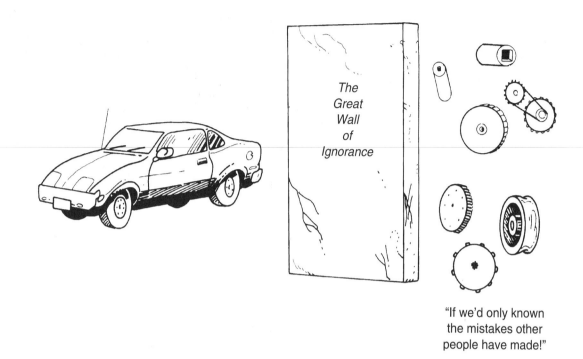

FIGURE 8-2   The Trouble with Trying to Reinvent the Curriculum Wheel

minutes. At some time after the brainstorming episode, a subgroup or special committee outside the group analyzes the ideas in depth for possible follow-up. Commonly, one or more ideas prove worthy of being put into effect. Interestingly, the accepted ideas may include those that initially seemed totally unreasonable and impossible to effectuate. Dramatic developments in program planning have been known to occur as a result of using the brainstorming technique.

Inservice and Staff Development Media

Institutes, workshops, and conferences have sometimes provided opportunities for identifying curriculum needs. At an institute, a challenging talk by a curriculum specialist may be followed by productive group discussions. One of the time-honored institute series in the nation was sponsored in the counties of Pennsylvania on prescribed "institute days." Capitalizing on another medium, some school systems have utilized workshops as a means of identifying problems and concerns that transcend the themes of the workshops themselves. National, state, regional, and local conferences have become sites for in-depth discussion of difficulties encountered in local school districts.

One of the barriers to profiting from these media is intentionally "forgetting" to put newly communicated, worthy ideas to use.

Cooperative Study and Surveys

Sometimes curriculum improvement starts when a faculty engages in formal or informal study of professional books and other materials. Learning centers in school buildings may be stocked with professional materials for use in formal study by faculties. Media specialists now have the arrangements and facilities necessary for selecting useful materials for nearly any faculty effort.

Self-surveys of schools—surveys conducted by staff members themselves—and cooperative surveys involving school systems and college staffs—such as that conducted several years ago in Great Neck, New York in cooperation with Teachers College, Columbia University—yield important topics for further study. All-purpose surveys have declined in recent years in favor of surveys to determine the progress being made in limited areas of the curriculum, such as in uses of selected resources and materials, in personalization of teaching, in teaching of particular skills, and in putting "trendy" ideas into practice.

Experimentation

Experiments conducted by teachers individually or in small groups have led to exploitation of bigger fields for study. By beginning a program with isolated instances of experimentation, a school system can maintain the valuable "broken-front" approach, which may be described as "a little improvement here and a little there." For years, the Horace Mann-Lincoln Institute of School Experimentation, Teachers College, Columbia University sponsored experimentation based on the interests and desires of personnel in local school systems. So, in general, did the Illinois Curriculum Program. Later developments in the subject fields encouraged teachers to try patterns of teaching created by national committees of subject matter specialists. Thus experimentation varies in nature from the free and unstructured to the prescribed and limited. Often, it prepares the way for experimental research, a rigorous form of inquiry.

Though teachers obviously cannot conduct experimentation in their efforts to solve every problem they face, every curriculum problem or issue can serve as an invitation to experimentation. To be induced and encouraged to experiment, teachers need dynamic, skilled leadership. When most of the members of a faculty experiment cooperatively under the guidance of skilled leaders, the faculty is likely to demonstrate growth in its insights and skills. Interrelating diverse experiments often requires special leadership skill.

Formal and Informal Evaluation

The results of administering tests and inventories, particularly tests of pupil achievement, have touched off numerous efforts at curriculum change. Item analysis of test data can be especially helpful in indicating weaknesses that need correcting. When teachers readminister in October the final examinations they gave the preceding June, they often discover how shockingly ineffective their teaching has been. In general, teacher-made tests and other locally developed tests and inventories do more to convince teachers of learners' needs than do so-called national tests based on alleged national norms and prepared by remote commercial agencies. Experience shows also that teachers tend to respect their own tests more than the tests prepared in other school systems. Within recent years, National Assessment and statewide testing have had as their primary purpose revelation of deficiencies in pupil achievement that the schools can presumably remedy.

Apart from testing, ways of evaluating pupils' learning include interviewing pupils, conducting case studies of individuals and small groups, preparing anecdotal records, diaries, and logs concerning pupils' behavior, taking still pictures and motion pictures, and using rating scales. Evaluation of pupils' journal entries has assumed a major place among informal methods.

Development of Philosophies, Goals, and Sets of Objectives

For a time, statement of philosophies, goals, and lists of objectives fell into disrepute because the procedure is time consuming and is sometimes said to keep teachers from dealing with real, live problems. Subsequently, a reaction occurred when many school systems appeared to be operating in a rudderless way, devoid of acknowledged purpose. Accordingly, there developed a moderate upswing in the attention given to stating goals and objectives. Many school systems continued to borrow statements of objectives from standard lists rather than attempting to devise their own. One of the most respected standard lists was developed by Will French and a large committee of educators in the Survey Study of Behavioral Outcomes of General Education. This so-called behavioral goals study concentrated on objectives for high schools under four headings: attaining maximum intellectual growth and development, becoming culturally oriented and integrated, maintaining and improving physical and mental health, and becoming economically competent.

Sophistication in ways of stating goals and objectives improved during the 1980s as people in schools gained more experience in expressing them. Behavioral objectives were written to express outcomes anticipated or desired as a direct result of instruction. Although behavioral objectives have been both defended and attacked, they are favorably regarded in current efforts to make teachers and other school personnel accountable for the outcomes of their work. Outcomes of teachers' work are to be taken seriously, for they indicate successes and failures in implementing a curriculum. Outcome-Based Education, which began flourishing during the early 1990s, has become a special "brand" of education to achieve outcomes that bear the earmarks of defensible learning. The critics of Outcome-Based Education allege that it encourages weakened cognitive academic learning while it supports social/affective outcomes that replace traditional values and attitudes. The critics say further that many state and federal officials support Outcome-Based Education because they have found it to be "politically correct."[22]

Some Other Ways of Starting to Plan

Curriculum personnel have tried other ways of getting planning started. Several promising ones follow:

1. Help teachers identify one general area of emphasis for the year.
2. Set aside a day a week. Call it "Teacher Day," and use it for conferences with teachers about their problems.
3. Utilize a school and community pupil-personnel survey.
4. Keep publications like the *Encyclopedia of Educational Research* handy for teachers' use as they puzzle about problems.
5. Display recent books and other materials and aids where teachers can see them.
6. Encourage teachers to develop small experimental projects in their classrooms.[23]

Even the smallest school may be too complex an institution to rely very long on just one procedure for initiating curriculum planning. Teachers with searching minds think of varied ways of pursuing the common objective of improvement. Following are narratives of the beginning stages of three improvement programs:

> *Program 1:* The curriculum coordinator conferred with the superintendent and other administrators regarding the budget, aims, and underlying principles of the new program and concerning the present condition of the curriculum. A council of administrators prepared a general plan for the program, and "study committees," consisting chiefly of teachers, identified problems for study. A "pilot committee" then looked for materials that would be helpful in solving the problems. In addition, a review of the present curriculum was undertaken.[24]
>
> *Program 2:* The faculty of a high school formed a Curriculum Improvement Committee charged with referring specific problems to special committees. In its first year, the committee made several proposals for curriculum revision, reviewed existing course outlines, led several research-type projects, revised school brochures, helped plan an inservice program, tried to keep abreast of national developments, and served in a continuing curriculum advisory capacity.[25]
>
> *Program 3:* In its early stages, this program featured a concentrated effort to locate needs and resources of the school system. Its leaders accomplished their purpose by conducting a census of teachers' problems, con-

sulting administrators, utilizing testing programs, sponsoring classroom visitations, conferring with individual teachers, using parent contacts, and analyzing personnel records.[26]

Other ways in which planning has been initiated are as follows:

1. A school system established a committee on inservice education to plan college extension courses, workshops, and local courses to suit the interests of its teachers.
2. Another system allotted funds to permit teachers to attend selected national conventions of professional associations. It required reports in the form of "ideas worth pursuing."
3. A school dedicated half its faculty meetings to brainstorming solutions to major instructional problems.
4. Another school established an instructional materials allocation of twenty-five cents a pupil to be spent cooperatively by teachers for improvement projects. (Imagine! Twenty-five cents.)
5. Still another school scheduled its outstanding teachers to conduct inservice courses and key faculty meetings.
6. A school system planned quarterly clinic sessions concerning the educational needs of atypical pupils.
7. The schools of a rural region conducted a twice-yearly show-and-tell program for reporting and demonstrating experimental, innovative projects.
8. The "myth and error conference" at a county high school revealed untruths about public education that were being reported in popular magazines and newspapers and then stimulated a search for needed changes and corrections in programs and procedures in the schools.
9. A city school made Saturday a day of informal schooling during which learners' interests were explored. Jewelry making, the molding of ceramics, and other activities eventually came into the formal curriculum and the pupil activities program as a result of a few Saturdays of exploration.
10. A group of school systems applied measures of quality developed by a regional school study council and a state department of education.
11. A school system provided "alertness experiences" for teachers by sending them on interstate trips to visit selected schools and teachers.
12. Another school system established, in cooperation with a college, a curriculum study center in which teachers could investigate possible solutions to instructional problems.
13. An alliance of schools planned cultural workshops for teachers on the theory that teachers' personal development is at least as important as their professional development.
14. A school district paid selected teachers for summer work in planning experiences for pupils, and these were tried out during the following scholastic year.[27]

The variety of approaches employed in these programs shows how unwise it is to pattern one program after another. Varying situations call for creating new ideas and using differing combinations of procedures.

Initial identification of curriculum concerns has often proved to be a crude and invalid process. Criteria can be preestablished for analyzing concerns with some care in order to accept or reject them for treatment. Among possible criteria are these:

1. Will dealing with the identified curriculum concern prove worthwhile? Is it really worth the necessary expenditure of time and resources? How meaningful could the process and the results be to the participants?
2. Can the concern be properly dealt with at this time? Is the timing appropriate?
3. Is dealing with the concern within the competence of the participants? Specifically, is it any of their business, and *can* they deal with it?
4. Is the plan for dealing with the concern of such size and scope as to be manageable?
5. If help is needed, is competent help available?[28]

Staffs of schools and school systems have real difficulties in setting priorities among the concerns to be dealt with. The values held by participants in curriculum study are, of course, important in determining priorities. These values should be permitted to surface during lengthy periods of probing, questioning, and conferring. Great danger to morale and productivity lies in assuming that values emerge quickly and that problems finally identified are being considered in their appropriate order of importance. In their haste to get projects and programs under way, curriculum planners must not fail to take time for initial deliberation.

SITUATION 8-4

Procedures to Fit the Situation

Glovers Central School District has been in operation seventy-two years. Recently, a superintendent of twenty-eight years' tenure retired. During his regime, only occasional and sporadic activity to improve the curriculum occurred. Several other factors are affecting the school district at this turning point:

1. Few of the 329 teachers have taken any inservice courses within the past five years.
2. The community has recently experienced a wave of fiscal conservatism that has resulted in the defeat of two bond issues to pay for new school buildings.
3. A local resident has created disturbances at board of education meetings about the presence of "radical" textbooks in the schools.
4. The teaching staff likes to think of itself as a collection of individualists.

5. John Dewey's name is generally despised in the schools and, where it is known, in the community at large.
6. Teachers' concerns are directed largely toward improvement of reading and English composition.
7. An evaluation committee from the regional association of colleges and secondary schools has recently called Glovers High School "twenty-five years behind the times in program and in teachers' understanding of what constitutes a modern program."

Assume that you have been appointed curriculum coordinator in charge of the school system's curriculum program and that the teachers' concerns about reading and English composition are bona fide. Assume that the new superintendent is a forward-looking person who has given you a free hand. What would you do to probe these concerns in depth?

Which of the procedures enumerated in this section of the chapter do you think might prove helpful in opening a wedge to improvement?

Whom would you need to work with in making decisions about the procedures to be used? How, exactly, would you hope to proceed?

PLANNING MODES

Since the 1920s, when formal planning of the curriculum was begun in some of the larger cities in the United States, a number of factors to be considered in planning have emerged. Among them are the nature of pupil populations, the importance of teachers as change agents, participation by parents, establishment of program goals and objectives, quality of evaluation procedures, and the presence of what Mary Heller called "sequence interlock" to ensure that planning steps are carried out in rational order. Heller pointed out that planners have developed systems of renewal strategies that provide for continuous input by different categories of people, careful planning of staff development projects, and full recognition of people's expressed needs and concerns.[29]

Some school systems have tried to do their planning in yearly cycles during which goal setting, actual curriculum planning, and application of accountability measures occur.[30] A few systems are preparing scenarios as planning tools. Used frequently in the social sciences, the scenario is a visionary projection of what future conditions may be;[31] thus it becomes an instrument of strategic planning. Whatever the procedures used, curriculum planning is regarded, in both developed and developing nations, as being of paramount importance to progress.[32]

Despite the availability of newer planning procedures, most school systems follow customary planning modes. Representations of customary modes appear below.

School System A Has

1. Described a proposal briefly, specifying its purpose or intent
2. Considered the actual need for this proposal

3. Made a list of aims or goals for the proposal
4. Had the aims ranked by numbers of participants
5. Had the aims restated so that each of them expressed a desired learning outcome and proved capable of subdivision into functional objectives
6. Reexamined the aims to see whether they covered the intent of the program
7. Added and deleted several aims
8. Stated usable objectives that belonged under the aims to which they seemed to relate
9. Thought how the staff would know when each of the objectives had been attained
10. Described experiences or activities for pupils
11. Determined evaluation means for checking pupil achievement and also for gauging the worth of the proposal
12. Communicated the proposal in the form of a curriculum guide

This school system has obviously spent a great deal of time setting and clarifying aims and objectives.

School System B Has

1. Developed guidelines for planning
2. Organized a system-wide curriculum review committee
3. Established goals and objectives, general in nature
4. Required the review committee to prepare forms for submitting curriculum proposals
5. Found representative personnel to staff curriculum committees
6. Asked these committees to submit concrete proposals to the review committee for its approval
7. Valued uniformity in programs and proposals followed in schools throughout the system

School system B has apparently relied heavily on a centralized approach to planning.

School System C Has

1. Designated a curriculum coordinator to supervise all planning
2. Decided to revise each part of the program every four or five years
3. Prepared time lines for the accomplishment of planning tasks
4. Appointed a central curriculum council
5. Searched for ideas and supporting materials
6. Decided via the central curriculum council just what to plan, from kindergarten through twelfth grade
7. Adopted an evaluation system
8. Gathered teaching/learning materials and evaluated them

9. Determined inservice needs of the staff
10. Filed, at intervals, summaries of what has been done
11. Evaluated the planning operation annually

This system seems to have assumed some large tasks in a cavalier manner, perhaps without knowing their magnitude.

School System D Has

1. Identified general curriculum aims or goals
2. Stated goals specifically for subjects
3. Made scope and sequence charts
4. Identified the competencies of staff members for planning
5. Stated instructional objectives, subject by subject
6. Prepared and distributed curriculum guides in a number of subjects
7. Considered means of evaluating parts of the curriculum
8. Planned for subsequent curriculum revision

Placing a heavy emphasis on subjects, school system D has seemingly only scratched the surface, after the manner of curriculum planners in the 1920s and 1930s.

School System E Has

1. Formulated a logical design for planning
2. Stated within each facet of the design a series of tasks
3. Begun planning by analyzing what might be done
4. Proceeded to design several new proposals
5. Elaborated on the proposals so that each of them could be used by teachers
6. Observed teachers while they put the proposals into effect
7. Provided evaluation means (chiefly questionnaires) for assessing the worth of each proposal
8. Sought feedback often during implementation of each proposal
9. Searched for ways in which each proposal might be revised

This school system has worked carefully in utilizing the design it has created.

The planning modes used by school systems differ widely. Occasionally, a particular way of working is associated with the mode utilized. The Ontario Institute for Studies in Education, for instance, proposed the use of innovation profiles, which are detailed descriptions of what teachers actually do to implement classroom practices and make innovations work.[33] The goal of implementing the use of profiles suggests certain planning actions.

Adoption of major blocks of content can also help to determine planning modes. For example, certain steps would have to be taken if the following proposal for a "world core curriculum" were to be accepted in nation after nation, including the United States:

Theme: Our Planetary Home (understanding the universe, the biosphere, and the ecosystem)

Theme: The Human Family (world population, human migration, geography, health, and living standards)

Theme: Our Place in Time (past, present, and future events)

Theme: The Miracle of Human Life (clear thinking, communication, and physical, mental, moral, and spiritual health).[34]

Choice of modes can be influenced more subtly by the rationale that underlies an attempt at curriculum improvement. The most common rationale, which Geneva Gay has called the *academic,* relies basically on four classic foundations of the curriculum—philosophy, learners and learning, society and culture, and subject matter. Curriculum planners sometimes add interpretation, which includes ways of knowing, thinking skills, decision making, problem solving, valuing, and concept development.

Departing from traditional subject matter, a second rationale—the *experiential*—features learner-centeredness and activities that especially develop the individual and frequently are chosen by individual learners. This rationale has led to the planning of Montessori schooling, open education systems, minicourses, schools without walls, and extensions of the humanities and the arts.

A third rationale—the *technical*—is marked by terms like *systems, production,* and *management.* A natural concomitant of similar perspectives in business and industry, the technical rationale is analytical, systems oriented, and behaviorally centered. From it have arisen computer-assisted instruction, performance contracting, and competency-based education. Our technological revolution may encourage further use of this rationale.

A fourth and final rationale has been called by Gay the *pragmatic* because it is heavily endued with practical political and social/cultural influences. This rationale has its basis in pressure brought by school boards, local administrators, associations, donors of grants, the courts, scholars, business firms, federal bureaucrats, and civic organizations. The interaction of these groups with one another and with school systems results in many kinds of curriculum plans which differ from community to community.[35]

It should come as no surprise that these widely differing rationales give rise to very different planning modes.[36]

A COMPENDIUM OF STEPS USED IN PLANNING

What has been said so far in this chapter suggests several steps that may be used in planning. A given situation may not require all these steps or may not require them in the order in which they are listed below. Nevertheless, all of them are eligible for inclusion in the planning process. They are surveying the scene, assessing needs, identifying and defining problems, recalling accepted aims and goals, making and evaluating proposals, preparing designs, organizing the work force, supervising the planning process, utilizing the products of planning, applying evaluation means, and anticipating the future.

Surveying the Scene

Surveying the scene involves knowing what makes a particular school system the same as other systems and what makes it markedly different from the rest. Included in the curriculum scene are tradition, expectations, people, funds (or the scarcity thereof), school system organization, and several other features. What has been said previously about the domains of planning is relevant.

Assessing Needs

Needs can be thought of in two ways. The first is singular: *need* for any change. The second, or plural, form expresses the *needs* of pupils and teachers. Pupils have their recognizable educational needs; teachers have needs related to performing their work effectively and improving their own functioning.

Identifying and Defining Problems

As a result of assessing needs, planners can identify problems of teaching and learning. Additional problems not initially identified in the needs assessment may be discovered as the planning process proceeds. Any curriculum problem that is deemed worth solving and that can be managed should be defined to clarify its meaning and implications.

Recalling Accepted Aims and Goals

Aims and goals that, when formulated, had the support of a broad constituency in the school system should be reviewed and used as guides whenever curriculum planning is done within that system. Two questions should arise as each new curriculum proposal is made: "How does this proposal accord, in general, with one or more aims or goals our school system has accepted?" and "From which goal or goals can we generate objectives that are specific to our proposal?" Goals specified at the federal level are likely to augment goals that have already been adopted locally.

Making and Evaluating Proposals

The crucial curriculum problems that have been identified can form the basis for making proposals. Some of the most promising proposals can eventuate in carefully developed designs. Proposals can be evaluated informally by considering whether they conform to accepted goals and then by asking relevant questions about them. These questions should be answered by the most competent school system personnel and, if possible, by outside consultants.

Preparing Designs

Designing that eventuates from the most promising proposals usually follows steps such as those that appear in Chapter 5: stating program or project objectives, choosing evaluation means, selecting a type of design, identifying learning content, determining and organizing learning experiences, and evaluating the program or project summatively.

Organizing the Work Force

Organizing the work force requires finding the best available personnel to perform designated tasks, and then judging how to organize these personnel so that their talents are used well. Constant scouting or inquiry among present staff members is needed for personnel search. Occasionally, new personnel can be brought in to provide certain necessary abilities. The identified personnel are then organized into study groups and committees to do the most difficult part of the planning and to perform the easy tasks too.

Supervising the Planning Process

Planning cannot proceed smoothly without direction. Central steering committees often make policy and arrange for resources. Daily direction usually comes, however, from leaders such as curriculum coordinators and school principals. The special functions of leaders are discussed in Chapter 11.

Utilizing the Products of Planning

Whatever has been planned needs to be implemented. Implementation, or the act of putting plans to intelligent use, is usually done by classroom teachers. Because that which is new or different is likely to be puzzling, teachers need help and encouragement from supervisors who know what to expect in the implementation process.

Applying Evaluation Means

Applying evaluation means could be called applying the test of reality. Many projects and programs look good on paper, but the crucial question is "Do they work?" This question often yields offhand judgments, only some of which are valid. The validity of a judgment can be checked by formal evaluation of the project or program, as described in Chapter 6. It is impossible to tell what a plan has accomplished in action without applying appropriate evaluation means.

Anticipating the Future

The future begins with feedback of information regarding the apparent success of a plan. This information includes data from formal evaluation as well as little items of news about the experiences that teachers and pupils have had with the plan. When conditions change rapidly, as when the details of subject matter change, the plan should be revised. Looking to the future can be systematized by projecting revision schedules in subject matter fields and other curriculum areas.

SITUATION 8-5

What Was Done in the Planning Process?

Consider the steps in planning that have just been described. Think of a program or a project that has been planned during the past five years in your school system or in a system you know. Learn which of the steps were actually used in the planning. In what order were they used? Which of them were omitted for good reason? How successfully were some of the steps used? Were actions taken that cannot be classified under any of the steps?

What is your final conclusion about the quality of the planning that was done?

Organization for Putting Plans into Effect

The planning steps just described can be put into place only if an organization is developed for allocating and assigning people and material resources. Experience in curriculum planning offers several guidelines that are helpful in organizing people and materials:

1. Start small by involving only a few persons at first.
2. Choose these people carefully. They should be interested, able persons who are eager to see the schools improved.
3. Hold planning sessions when they are needed, having due regard for the time schedules of the planners.
4. Give credit to the planners, rewarding them sensibly and openly.
5. Provide the planners with necessary time, resources, and materials.
6. Fix responsibility for the subparts of the planning operation.
7. Establish time limits for completing portions of the work, but do not rush the participants.
8. Help the planners see what is important by personally emphasizing the important as opposed to the trivial.
9. Have some criteria for determining what is to be done. For example, the first proposals should help solve commonly recognized problems and should be of the right size and complexity to be pursued successfully.
10. Encourage participants to get the job done well—without stress—remembering that what happens during the first attempt will color or condition subsequent attempts.

One of the theses of this book has been that curriculum improvement occurs chiefly where the teacher is—in the individual school.[37] This would imply that most organizational arrangements should be centered at the building level. To a large extent this is true, but the need for developing programs vertically for the sake of sequence and continuity, the importance of articulation among educational levels, and the necessity for teachers to associate with teachers in other schools at the same grade or educational level mandate that the organization for curriculum improvement be larger than an individual school, and that strategies for putting plans into effect comprehend the whole school system or a vertical or horizontal portion of it. Thus it is unwise to center organization either in individual schools or in central offices. What has come to be known as a centrally coordinated approach is needed in facing both those problems originating in the individual school and those problems that are of concern to the total system or to a level within the system.[38] The centrally coordinated approach encourages activity in either the central office or the local building, depending on the kind of problem being attacked. For example, the central office may be concerned with teacher morale throughout the system, while the local school wishes to develop a social studies program for children of a given socioeconomic background. Small school systems containing only one or two schools tend to operate according to a local building or decentralized approach, and some traditionally oriented systems retain strong central control. But the centrally coordinated approach is the most common today.

In individual schools, teachers organize in grade-level groups, departments (secondary school), teams, school councils, planning committees, and working (ad hoc) committees. Sometimes large schools are broken down into schools within schools. In the individual school, the leadership of the principal is obviously very important. Committees in individual schools develop resource units, adapt outlines and course guides to the school's needs, consider school-wide problems like the quality of assembly programs and the power to be given to pupil government organizations, and perform a multitude of other local functions.

In whole school systems, curriculum planning is initiated by means of system-wide faculty organizations, central steering committees (as well as vertical ad hoc committees), lay advisory committees, and central office supervisors, to mention only a few of the groups in the organization. Central organization often provides guidelines for planning, general curriculum leadership, machinery for getting under way, duplicated or printed curriculum materials, and means of evaluating the programs.

The Central Steering Committee

Centrally coordinated organization really requires the formation of a central steering committee for a given school district. Often called the central curriculum committee, it performs tasks such as the following:

Surveying curriculum needs
Getting action started
Facilitating communication
Approving the accomplishments of ad hoc committees
Locating help—personnel, facilities, time, and materials
Coordinating curriculum activities
Arranging for and guiding evaluation
Maintaining relationships with individuals and groups outside the committee and also outside the school system

Records of the life and times of central steering committees can make interesting reports.

Advice concerning the dos and don'ts in forming central steering committees follows:

1. Committee members should know why they are being appointed. Some of the members should help in the preliminary exploration of reasons for forming the committee. The list of reasons should be specific enough to set direction, but general enough to allow latitude.[39]
2. Committee members should be chosen for definite terms, possibly on a rotating basis. Interest in curriculum planning should be a major factor in selecting committee members. The matter of representation should depend on one's view of curriculum improvement and of the committee's function.[40] Representation can be arranged, for instance, by region, by position, or by educational level.
3. Whether the committee is appointed, elected, or chosen from volunteers, it should have the approval and support of personnel throughout the system. Without such approval and support, curriculum activity lags. Administrators should probably not be in the majority in any committee membership.
4. Lay persons usually serve best on an adjunct advisory committee. Generally speaking, they do not perform as comfortably and competently as members of the steering committee itself.
5. The size of a steering committee should be guarded with care. Six persons are likely to be too few for idea development, whereas sixty persons can become an unmanageable group, useful for reaction only.
6. Steering committee members perform so important a function that they should be granted released time for at least some of the meetings.
7. If agenda-planning subcommittees seem necessary, the members must be kept sensitive to what the whole committee is discussing.
8. A steering committee functions best when its members pay attention to the current agenda and help to plan subsequent agendas.
9. The *spread* of participation in steering committee meetings is as important to morale as the *quality* of participation.[41]

The Ad Hoc Committees

Committees to perform special functions, called ad hoc committees, should be organized to serve clearly defined purposes, such as preparation of a pupil-reporting schema for intermediate schools of the district. Obviously, these committees should arise from definite, pressing concerns and should not be organized just for publicity. Membership should be based on competence and interest, and it should terminate at a prearranged time. Committee members should see their task broadly, in the context of a program that has other facets. Also, they should know the scope and the probable duration of their service.

Ad hoc committees come in varied sizes and organizational forms. Some are short-term task forces; others become long-term enterprises. For example, a school system may have two major kinds of ad hoc committees: "A" committees, which are at grade level for elementary schools and subject-specific for secondary schools, and "B" committees, which work on selected problems or themes. An interesting study by Elizabeth Lowe revealed that no apparent differences exist among the process problems affecting vertical, horizontal, and building committees and that, in programs based on volunteering for committee membership, there are several levels of involvement, with persons who carry out interim assignments being most involved. Lowe found also that ad hoc committees of four to ten members meeting about five hours a day and centering their attention on tasks prove most satisfactory. As might be expected, ad hoc committees tend to deal with problems of substance or content, ignoring problems of group process.[42]

Keeping Them Honest: The Call for Curriculum Mapping

Many top administrators in school systems feel the pressure to monitor what actually happens in classrooms. When a plan in the form of a curriculum guide specifies content to be taught and the amount of time to be allotted for its teaching, the pious hope expressed by administrators is that the guide will be followed. Guides may not be followed, however, and therefore a system of quality control called *curriculum mapping* has been devised. This system is intended to assure agreement among the contents of the curriculum guide, the actual subject matter taught within allotted time spans, and the results of testing. Teachers are asked to give anonymous evidence about their teaching practices. Maps (charts) are made from these data, which presumably indicate subject matter emphasized and time spent teaching each component. This process generates the information needed to adjust the time variable to suit the needs of pupils and teachers. Thus curriculum mapping appears to be a humane and sensible vehicle for making adjustments, although it sometimes seems to teachers to assume the visage of Big Brother.

Compilers of the data solicited from teachers frequently find that the terms of the curriculum guide have not been met, but occasionally they find that the terms have been exceeded. In the former case, teachers' compliance is doubted and "new directives" are issued. In the latter case, a higher level of performance may be made a new standard.[43] The value of curriculum mapping, then, rests on the assumptions that (1) what appears in guides represents learning content of quality and worth and (2) teachers can be required to follow it. These may or may not be valid assumptions.

SITUATION 8-6

The Shortcomings of the Curriculum Steering Committee

To listen to the teachers in the Mannheim School District, one would think that everything was wrong with the newly organized Central Curriculum Committee. In teachers' rooms and out-of-the-way places, the staff is complaining:

"Whoever said we needed a big committee to tell us to do what we're already doing?"

"It's the group of administrators who thought of the idea. I notice that no teacher was in the group that made the decision to have a Central Curriculum Committee."

"I think each school can take care of its own business. We don't need a big central committee, even though there are twelve schools in the system."

"There is some need for a central committee. I say that because I believe every fifth grade all over town should be doing the same thing at about the same time. Someone or some group has to police the teachers."

"The big trouble with a group like the Central Curriculum Committee is that it becomes a debating society—all talk and no action."

"Why doesn't the superintendent spend more time preparing the principals to do their jobs? Then they could take the lead in developing curriculum instead of having the leadership centered in a group like this."

"In the eight months it's existed, the committee hasn't done a thing to help the eight groups that were already started in an informal way before the committee was organized. I know. I'm a member of the committee on reporting to parents."

"I guess someone on the inside is bucking for promotion."

Which complaints seem to you to represent the real shortcomings of the committee? Why?

How do you account for the presence of each of the comments that you rejected?

What democratic principles of organization for curriculum improvement can you adduce?

THE COMPUTER AS A PLANNING INSTRUMENT

People in schools today know very well that we have entered the computer age. Development of the microchip has made computers available at such reasonable cost that they are now commonplace in elementary and secondary schools.

To many people in schools, the computer is obviously more than a fad in need of refinement. They consider it useful enough to favor expending the public's money on the inservice education of staff members in computer operation and programming, as well as on purchase of additional computers. The number of national and regional organizations promoting computerization is astounding. For school personnel who want to do more with computers than they are now doing, help is on the way.

In a chapter on curriculum planning, discussion of computer uses needs to emphasize the planning operation itself. Just how helpful are computers in curriculum planning?

In beginning to answer this question, one may note the school management uses to which microcomputers have already been put. They include storing and retrieving information according to given requirements; printing this information in varied displays like lists, charts, and graphs; preparing forms to suit particular purposes; correcting records of people's performance by deleting invalid and outdated information and inserting new data; and sorting and putting in order the records currently in files. These uses are obviously on the mundane side, but they are time savers.

Larger computers in the central offices of some school districts have been performing four separate functions. The most common one is financial management, in which electronic spreadsheets show budget projections and fund accounting. A second function, and one of greater interest to curriculum planners, is information management. Information kept in databases is retrieved for use in making inventories, scheduling classes and programs, assembling grade reports, indicating attendance records, and maintaining personnel records. An interesting third function called telecommunication, or networking, permits users to contact other computers by using a telephone. (Four previous editions of this book were made possible in part by contact between a computer in New Jersey and a master computer in California.) A fourth function is word processing for producing form letters, updating mailing lists, editing manuals, and preparing guides. A less used function is simulation of situations or conditions by means of graphics.

Using Computers in Initial Curriculum Planning

Whereas computer-assisted instruction (CAI) is utilized chiefly in tutoring pupils, computer-managed instruction (CMI) is used in curriculum planning and other management operations. At the grassroots or local school level, microcomputers can help to retrieve and assign goals and objectives, to recall test and observational data, to link objectives with performance, and to display achievement data for program evaluation. Obviously, what one puts into a computer determines what one gets out, and the information may be treated and then exhibited in different forms. In both individual schools and entire school systems, computers help primarily with planning tasks like surveying the scene, assessing the needs of pupils and teachers, and identifying and defining curriculum problems. In addition, they can effect certain statistical treatments.

The planning done by individual teachers can be improved by permitting the teachers to use computers for recording answers to test items; analyzing pupil achievement status, item by item; and determining pupil averages.

The examples so far have dealt largely with "local data." Ideas, trends, and developments of national scope also have relevance for curriculum planning. A competent librarian can help planners become familiar with the Educational Resources Information Center (ERIC), the National Information Center for Educational Media, and the Exceptional Child Education Resources. The publications *Resources in Education* and *Thesaurus of ERIC Descriptors* are used daily in libraries. Many an agency throughout the country can make contact with database sources such as ERIC centers. Within the agency, a search analyst conducts an on-line search to aid the client in learning what data are available about given topics. The client may then limit, broaden, or refine the data until he or she can specify just what is needed. The desired articles, speeches, and other data are then printed at the distant center and sent to the client.

Can More Be Done?

Experience with computers as management tools has resulted in our ability to specify major functions of computers in curriculum planning. The computer can help us form, develop, and focus the curriculum; fit the curriculum to designated learners' needs and abilities; and give computer projects a place in curriculum planning.

In its memory bank, the computer can store information about pupils—their interests, abilities, and achievements. It can also store data about subject matter in the form of descriptions, narratives, charts, and graphs, as well as lists of objectives, learning materials, and suggested pupil activities. This information can help planners build what is commonly known as the written curriculum. As an example, the middle school in Skowhegan, Maine has provided assistance for pupils in preparing computer projects in mathematics, science, the language arts, social studies, and other subjects. Five interdisciplinary teams of teachers have supervised the use of computers as tools in writing stories, illustrating science content, graphing data, creating interactive reports, and other ventures. A twenty-seven-station computer laboratory and in-classroom computers have constituted the major facilities and hardware available for idea development.[44]

Fitting the curriculum to learners is a function that has been performed in the past by classroom teachers, without technological help. The result has been the curriculum as taught. Now, computers can help planners identify the curriculum as it is actually learned by individual pupils. What pupils succeed in learning can be permitted to remain in the official curriculum. Furthermore, the computer can report teachers' and pupils' perceptions of the curriculum's worth, as well as teachers' experience with it. It can also, if desired, make available a record of the achievement of learners, objective by objective.[45]

Curriculum planners are still not satisfied with the extent of the help they receive from the computer. Some planners would like the computer to think for them, dropping pearls of wisdom. They place their hope in literature that reports the development of "artificial intelligence." The psychologist Eugene Galanter reminds us that the hope of creating artificial intelligence existed more than a quarter-century ago. The computer was the means by which this hope was to be realized. The fact now is that computers can work for planners, but they cannot substitute for them.[46] As Howard Peelle put it, we have a partnership in which both computers and human planners do their respective work well.[47] There is no question as to which partner does the more difficult work.

The literature of technology continues to abound with data from experiments in making computers more "intelligent." We would be foolish to deny that progress is being made in refining uses of the computer. Some theorists have guessed that the era of artificial intelligence will arrive during the 1990s—at a cost of $40 billion. They believe that by the end of the present century the ability of machines to recognize almost every word in the dictionary will represent only a beginning, that "expert systems" will provide expert knowledge, and that use of computers in planning will have advanced. They do not say, however, that the computer will ever be able to substitute for the professional worker in any field, including curriculum development. Instead, the professional and the machine will constitute an unbeatable combination.[48]

Meanwhile, planners have continued to try to use computers in sophisticated ways. For example, in 1982 the schools in Gilbert, Arizona wanted to develop a program in which "curriculum unification" (uniformity) would be achieved. The equipment at hand in the Gilbert schools consisted of a used IBM System/34 computer and a new optical scanner for reading answer sheets. The planners stated and monitored objectives from grade one to grade twelve in reading, English communication, science, mathematics, and the social studies. A record of pupils' performance in achieving the objectives was then plotted, stored, and printed. The objectives themselves were distinguished as being "milestone" and "minimum" objectives. The former represented essential learnings; the latter, minimal learnings to permit graduation. Information became available about pupil performance status and the efforts made by teachers in working toward curriculum unification. In addition, gifted pupils took criterion-referenced tests to determine their progress, and data about other pupils in the special education program became clearer and more accurate. For planners who want to keep the curriculum continuous, uniform, or "intact," this procedure holds possibilities.[49] However, the Gilbert experience suggests dangers in relying too heavily on the computer as an instrument of large-scale planning. Excessive reliance on a machine can decrease deliberation by planners, cause the planning process to become unduly centralized, and inhibit teachers from exercising their own initiative and creativity.

Well-developed expert systems can, of course, make major contributions in the areas of planning and supporting decisions already made. In planning, an expert system has potential for inferring steps to be taken in sequence, for gauging the amount of time and money needed to take the steps, and for specifying strategies to be used in attaining goals.[50] Expert systems seem intelligent because they can give reasons for answers to questions. The Institute for the Study of Exceptional Children and Youth at the University of Maryland has developed an expert system called CAPER (Computer-Assisted Planning for Educational Resources). A similar expert system has been put to use at the Developmental Center for Handicapped Persons, Utah State University. Of course, computerized planning can succeed only if valid data are provided.[51] Providing the same data to human experts would presumably yield the same or very similar results.

It is believed that computers will soon be capable of supporting curriculum decisions already made. In the fields of medicine and pharmacy, computers are now being used for support purposes. In giving second opinions, expert systems can apparently perform as well as the best of human experts.[52] Although using computers to support decisions is proving easier than using them in original planning, there remains the big problem of deciding whose expert knowledge is to be introduced into the system—for example, the teacher's, the administrator's, or the researcher's.

Although, in general, the intrinsic worth of human judgment surely exceeds that of computer-generated "judgment," the help that computers can give makes them potentially valuable in both planning and evaluation. Computers have already proved helpful in assessing skill learning, diagnosing exceptionality, evaluating and selecting materials, and suggesting means to instructional effectiveness.[53] In order to work with computers, planners must become acquainted with (1) database management programs for keeping, filing, and retrieving records; (2) programs for treating large amounts of numerical data appearing on spreadsheets; and (3) word processing programs for preparing and editing written materials.

SITUATION 8-7

Beginning to Use the Computer in Planning

In your own school system, there are probably curriculum proposals that offer opportunities for using microcomputers or larger computer units in planning. Through discussion, identify one or more of these opportunities and evaluate them with reference to the following criteria:

1. The curriculum proposal is large and important enough to make computerization worthwhile.
2. At the same time, the proposal is small enough to make computerization manageable.
3. The proposal has in it elements that can be tested or managed in part by computerization.
4. Computerization would apparently be economical of the planners' time and energy.
5. Commercial software is obtainable for at least a minimal portion of the programming.
6. One or more persons are available to program the computer(s) further.
7. The proposal chosen seems to provide satisfactory content for a first effort at computerizing curriculum planning.

TOWARD THE ULTIMATE IN PLANNING: RESTRUCTURING THE SCHOOL

One of the speakers at the 1990 convention of the Association for Supervision and Curriculum Development said, "Our attempts at school reform will get almost nowhere without a restructuring of the school itself. The factory model of the school, with its assembly line tactics, must go."

The speaker is not alone in this thinking. Educators are becoming convinced that foundations and state departments of education are wasting effort and money in two major ways: by promoting reform proposals that touch only the periphery of massive problems and by attempting to shore up what is essentially a fallen structure. Professionals in the schools agree that the population of youngsters being educated in the public schools is more diverse now than ever before in the history of the nation. Somehow, something other than traditional means must be used to reach them. At the same time, our "best and brightest" are not learning as much as they are able to learn. Somehow, they must be challenged. To fill our classrooms (numbering about 2,400,000), we need well-qualified professionals. Somehow, we must find more of them. Teachers today do essentially the same things most of the time. Somehow, their tasks must be varied to take advantage of their talents and to meet the differing needs of the pupils they serve. Inevitably, then, the curriculum of each school must change to reflect needed changes made in the structure of that school.

Discussion waxes hot as to what restructuring means. No universally accepted definition of it now exists. Evidently, it does require a redefinition of the roles of people in schools, the rules by which they should operate, and the relationships they should maintain with one another. What, exactly, could this redefinition mean? To some planners, it means site-based management, or decision making at the local school level. To others, it suggests teacher empowerment, or increased decision making by classroom teachers. To still others, it implies improved tests and changed evaluation procedures. Persons who balk at undertaking curriculum improvement sometimes call for (1) free choice of schools by parents of children who need, or seem to need, a change of schools; (2) shifts and tradeoffs in the power exercised by federal, state, and local agencies in regulating schools; or (3) employment as teachers and administrators of bright but underprepared citizens drawn from occupations unrelated to elementary and secondary education.

Wise planners are becoming convinced, however, that restructuring must embody definite steps that actually alter the old system of education and that center reform where teachers and learners are. Suppose these steps were put in place tomorrow. Then restructured schools might be characterized by descriptions that resemble the following ones:

- Classrooms are no longer used exclusively for whole-group teaching. Teachers, paraprofessionals, and aides work with individuals and small groups of pupils. Remarkably, teachers talk less. Head teachers have responsibility for moving pupils here and there within the school environment according to the needs of individuals. Close diagnosis and prompt remedy are the rule.
- The curriculum is no longer simply a monolithic document. What is written is in segments and adaptable sections; content elements can be called up from computerized storage for use with particular individuals and groups. At the same time, technology assists in meeting goals and in maintaining curriculum continuity. The record of previous deliberations and actions is present in the computer.
- The school itself is no longer a massive institution. When excessive size inhibits or threatens its operation, it is divided sensibly into schools within a school.
- Teachers are no longer regarded as second-class citizens. New incentives include those that teachers have always wanted and needed: truly professional status, the respect of the public, released time for developing the curriculum, awards and rewards for real rather than imagined accomplishment, and a standard of living that reflects the importance of their work.
- Time is no longer wasted so freely. Onerous clerical chores, interruptions of the school day, failure to supervise pupils' work and recreation, and time lost in shifting from activity to activity have yielded to a tighter system for assigning responsibility among school personnel.
- The phenomenon of the impoverished curriculum is no longer commonplace. Basic skills are taught thoroughly, but they are supplemented with higher-order skills in the realms of thinking, creative activity, work and preparation for work, and social relationships.
- Education is no longer thought of as the exclusive responsibility of teachers and schools. Youngsters receive some of their education in the community, in work and service assignments, and at home, all of which offer what no school can provide.
- Parents are no longer occasional school visitors, concerned strictly with the welfare of their own children. Continual communication between

school and home has increased home-school cooperation and offers parents new ways of participating in school affairs.

- Pupils' peers are no longer youngsters strictly within their immediate age range. Multi-age grouping places individual pupils in contact with younger and older peers. Thus having older pupils provide tutoring and help is more feasible, and children's understanding and appreciation of one another are broadened.
- In the elementary schools, children are no longer passed like hot cakes to different teachers, school year after school year. Instead, each child remains with the same teacher for several years in succession unless there is a valid reason for making a change.
- Commercially produced textbooks are no longer the main instructional materials. Teachers are increasingly in the "publishing business," producing text materials within individual schools and school systems to suit their varied purposes. New technology permits publication of materials to supplement texts and allows reference sources and other information to be recalled from computer storage.
- Teachers no longer view accountability as a threat or punishment. The goals to which they subscribe and that they desire to attain provide motivation, and tests that they respect give them feedback about goal attainment. Teachers are eager to serve the cause of education, and they do so by helping to make decisions rather than merely implementing decisions made by others.

Some of these descriptions may sound idealistic. Nonetheless, they embody the kind of consideration the most thoughtful planners have been giving to the problem of devising a new system of education.[54]

A carefully crafted summary article by Jane Davies about the meaning of restructuring highlights its chief features: a supportive learning environment, a compelling invitation to change, provision of authority that makes flexibility possible, access to needed knowledge, and availability of time to do the work.[55]

EXPECTATIONS, AND AN EYE TO THE FUTURE

Curriculum planning is most likely to succeed if certain expectations are kept in mind:

1. Persons in local schools and school systems should accept responsibility for planning. This responsibility should be distributed among numbers of people.
2. Feelings of personal security and worth, as well as satisfactory interpersonal relations, are essential.
3. Adequate time, facilities, and resources should be provided.

4. Curriculum workers should attempt to solve problems that seem real and important.
5. Effective communication about plans, policies, procedures, and achievements should be established and maintained among persons who have a stake in the projects.
6. Curriculum development should be considered a continuous, normal activity and not a stop-and-start activity.[56]
7. All persons affected by a given project should be involved in it in some way.
8. Nothing of real importance should be undertaken without developing an understanding of its purpose.
9. Continuous evaluation of improvements should be built into the design of each project.
10. Balance must be achieved in both the types of activities to be performed and their positions in the ongoing experience of learners.
11. Consistency must be maintained between the means and the ascribed ends of each project.

Persons who undertake curriculum improvement should not expect that great changes will necessarily occur within a period of a few months. Initially, growth may come only in the form of people's sensitization to themselves, to one another, and to the nature of the curriculum and its changes. Values, attitudes, and skills change to some extent almost immediately, but progress of lasting significance takes time.

How teachers feel about curriculum planning can make a great deal of difference. One of the biggest challenges in education consists of helping teachers remain alert and "alive" so that they do considerably more than just keep school. Curriculum leaders often oversimplify the reasons teachers either participate in curriculum planning or stay out of it. Leaders do themselves a favor by listening to teachers when they tell why they accept or reject a project, given the other activities that are available to them.

Leaders of planning actually have three options: They can rely on the authority of persons, the significance of knowledge, or the stringencies of a system.[57] Reliance on the first of these has been overused by zealous principals and superintendents who have wanted to see quick progress. Reliance on the second, based in research and well-communicated practical experience, has been used to a limited extent. Reliance on the third, which is relatively new, usually focuses on a particular way of proceeding. The keynotes of the first and third are power; the keynote of the second is information.

If planning is to have a suitable knowledge base, competent people must be assembled to provide input. For example, personnel from the City University of New York examined the health occupations education programs in New York State by holding meetings of members of the health professions and persons representing high schools, colleges, technical institutes, and regional agencies.[58] County school systems in New York State enlisted the help of competent people in testing a "futures-envisioning process," called ED QUEST, to identify educational trends, to assess their significance, and to adopt strategies for coping with them.[59]

An interesting way of projecting the curriculum into the future is to raise questions concerning how the curriculum is to be viewed. Answers to the questions may suggest metaphors that can determine the focus of planning. Anglin and Dugan projected five metaphors: (1) the curriculum as medicine for educational ills; (2) the curriculum as a greenhouse that encourages growth; (3) the curriculum as a route for traveling to a destination; (4) the curriculum as a means of production; and (5) the curriculum as a resource for developing and using human abilities.[60]

SITUATION 8-8

How the Teachers Felt

William A. Fullagar conducted an investigation of teachers' feelings about a newly started curriculum improvement program. Among the statements he collected from teachers were these:

> "Look at the beginning of the program. It didn't come from any suggestion of ours. It was thought up by the board of education or someone else at the top. They get the ideas but expect us to do the work."
>
> "After the program was decided upon, no one gave us any clear picture of what it was all about."
>
> "We would have gotten more out of our program if we could have met in groups made up of those who teach the same grade."
>
> "Speaking of the administration, they contributed their share of problems for us. Some of our principals were quite open in their hostility to the program and criticized the ideas we brought back from our meetings."
>
> "In a sense, we were our own worst enemy. We were suspicious of the motives of those who were working with us—the consultants and the administrators."

On the basis of your own experience with teachers, select one or two of these comments that sound like remarks made by teachers you know. How are feelings like these acquired?

What other feelings might teachers be expected to express at the start of an improvement program? Which of these feelings are legitimate and to be expected?

SUMMARY

Chapter 8 provides a comprehensive look at curriculum planning. Beginning with a brief history of planning endeavors and ways of working, the chapter describes domains, situations, and trends affecting educational institutions and then focuses on people—their needs, their local circumstances, their competencies, and the pressures they feel. Ways of organizing to deal with a range of problems are then detailed. The chapter continues with descriptions of strategies used in planning and gives illustrations of planning modes. A compendium of concrete and oft-used planning steps follows. Two themes that are so modern they could not have been discussed in the early editions of this book are detailed in the chapter: the uses of computers in planning and our necessary preoccupation with restructuring schools. Chapter 8 concludes with a statement about prospects for planning.

ENDNOTES

1. National Society for the Study of Education, *The Foundations and Techniques of Curriculum Construction* (Bloomington, IL: Public School Publishing Company, 1926).

2. C. C. Trillingham, *The Organization and Administration of Curriculum Programs* (Los Angeles: University of Southern California Press, 1934).

3. Edwin S. Lide, *Procedures in Curriculum Making,* Bulletin No. 17, National Survey of Secondary Education (Washington, DC: U.S. Government Printing Office, 1933).

4. W. W. Charters, *Curriculum Construction* (New York: Macmillan, 1923).

5. Hollis L. Caswell, *Curriculum Improvement in Public School Systems* (New York: Bureau of Publications, Teachers College, 1950). For an informative discussion of the work of Caswell and others during the early years of formal curriculum planning, see Mary Louise Seguel, *The Curriculum Field: Its Formative Years* (New York: Teachers College Press, 1966).

6. H. W. Hill, "Curriculum Legislation and Instructional Decision Making," *Elementary School Journal* 73 (May 1973): 407–411.

7. See the entire Winter 1986 issue of *Theory into Practice,* volume 25, number 1.

8. See, for example, Tim Simkins, "Some Management Implications of the Development of Curriculum Information Systems," *Journal of Curriculum Studies* 15, no. 1 (1983): 47–59.

9. Carl D. Glickman, "Good or Effective Schools: What Do We Want?" *Phi Delta Kappan* 68, no. 8 (April 1987): 622–624.

10. See the major articles in *Educational Leadership* 48, no. 7 (April 1991).

11. Note that the *need* for a specific program is different from the *needs* of learners for curriculum experiences. In the former instance, the question is "Is this program needed?" In the latter, the question is "What are the needs of our pupils for elements of educational experience within broad ranges of potential experience?"

12. See Kae Hentges and Michael C. Hasokawa, "Delphi: Group Participation in Needs Assessment and Curriculum Development," *Journal of School Health* 51, no. 8 (October 1980): 28–32.

13. B. R. Witkin, *An Analysis of Needs Assessment Techniques for Educational Planning at State, Intermediate, and District Levels* (Hayward, CA: Office of the Alameda County Superintendent of Schools, 1975).

14. David J. Mullen, "Involving Parents, Students, and Staff in Determining a Needs Assessment of Educational Priorities," a paper delivered at the annual convention of the National Association of Elementary School Principals, April 1974. Reported in ERIC # ED 093 036.

15. Association for Supervision and Curriculum Development, *Research for Curriculum Improvement,* 1957 Yearbook (Washington, DC: The Association, 1957), 260, 261. Used with permission.

16. Ron Brandt, "When Curriculum Should Be Locally Developed," *Educational Leadership* 44, no. 4 (December 1986–January 1987): 3.

17. See working papers of the Schools Council published by Evans/Methuen, London, various dates.

18. Ronald C. Doll, *Supervision for Staff Development: Ideas and Application* (Boston: Allyn and Bacon, 1983), 172–182.

19. Alice Miel, *Changing the Curriculum* (New York: Appleton-Century-Crofts, 1946): 64.

20. Corpus Christi, Texas Public Schools, "Curriculum Bulletin," mimeographed, October 2, 1951, 1.

21. Harold C. Hand, *What People Think of Their Schools* (New York: Harcourt, Brace and World, 1948), 195–217.

22. Randy Zitterkopf, "A Fundamentalist's Defense of OBE," *Educational Leadership* 51, no. 6 (March 1994): 76–78.

23. Jeff West, "Improving Curriculum Procedures," *Bulletin of the National Association of Secondary School Principals* 43, no. 244 (February 1959): 77–82.

24. Itrice E. Eubanks, "Initiating a Program of Curriculum Improvement," *School and Community* 46, no. 9 (May 1960): 21.

25. Eugene Kitching, "Curriculum Improvement in Action," *Educational Administration and Supervision* 43, no. 3 (March 1957): 165.

26. Jack Rand and Robert Burress, "Case Study of a Curriculum Improvement Program," *School Executive* 73 (April 1954): 50–53.

27. Additional planning arrangements emphasize local cooperation. The titles of some of them are suggestive of what happens. Note, for example: Tamar Ariav, "Collaborative School-Based Curriculum Development: A Case Study," a paper presented at the annual meeting of the American Educational Research Association, Chicago, April 1985; and Susan Toft et al., "An Effective School's Program and Its Results: Initial District, School, Teacher, and Student Outcomes in a Participating District," *Journal of Research and Development in Education* 19, no. 3 (Spring 1986): 35–50.

28. See Heidi Hayes Jacobs, "Planning for Curriculum Integration," *Educational Leadership* 49, no. 2 (October 1991): 27, 28.

29. Mary F. Heller, "The Process of Curriculum Development: An Overview of Research," February 1981. Reported in ERIC # ED 221 938.

30. Victor J. Ross, "To Achieve the Kind of School Operation You Need, Use This Step-by-Step Goal-Setting Plan," *American School Board Journal* 167, no. 9 (September 1980): 30, 31.

31. Christopher Dede and Dwight Allen, "Education in the 21st Century: Scenarios as a Tool for Strategic Planning," *Phi Delta Kappan* 62, no. 5 (January 1981): 362–366.

32. Boris K. Kluchnikov, "Reflections on the Concept and Practice of Educational Planning," *Quarterly Review of Education* 10, no. 1 (1980): 27–39.

33. Kenneth A. Leithwood and Deborah J. Montgomery, *Improving Curriculum Practice Using Innovation Profiles* (Toronto: Ontario Institute for Studies in Education, 1987).

34. This plan, proposed by Robert Muller, Assistant Secretary-General of the United Nations, was reported by Gordon Cawelti in *Educational Leadership* (December 1986–January 1987): 5.

35. Geneva Gay, "Conceptual Models of the Curriculum-Planning Process," in Arthur W. Foshay, ed., *Considered Action for Curriculum Improvement*, 1980 Yearbook (Alexandria, VA: Association for Supervision and Curriculum Development, 1980), 120–143.

36. See the reference to cases in Peter Knight, "The Practice of School-Based Curriculum Development," *Journal of Curriculum Studies* 17, no. 1 (January–March 1985).

37. This thesis is strongly supported by the accumulated evidence that reforms will endure if teachers support them willingly and actively. See Michael Kirst and Gail Meister, "What Reforms Last?" *Curriculum Inquiry* 15 (1985): 176–181.

38. Ronald C. Doll, A. Harry Passow, and Stephen M. Corey, *Organizing for Curriculum Improvement* (New York: Teachers College Press, 1953), 1–10.

39. Paul M. Halverson, *Group Work in Cooperative Curriculum Development*, doctoral dissertation, Teachers College, Columbia University, New York, 1952.

40. Association for Supervision and Curriculum Development, *Action for Curriculum Improvement*, 1951 Yearbook (Washington, DC: The Association, 1951).

41. Halverson, *Group Work in Cooperative Curriculum Development.*

42. Elizabeth Lowe, *An Analysis of the Activities of Three Curriculum Committees,* doctoral dissertation, Teachers College, Columbia University, New York, 1952.

43. Fenwick W. English, *Quality Control in Curriculum Development* (Arlington, VA: American Association of School Administrators, 1978); see also Donald F. Weinstein, *Administrator's Guide to Curriculum Mapping* (Englewood Cliffs, NJ: Prentice-Hall, 1988).

44. Mike Muir, "Putting Computer Projects at the Heart of the Curriculum," *Educational Leadership* 51, no. 7 (April 1994): 30–32.

45. See Donald P. Ely, "Trends in Educational Technology: 1989," ERIC Clearinghouse on Information Resources, Syracuse, N. Y., September 1989; see also Northwest Regional Educational Laboratory, *Planning for Computers in Education: A Resource Handbook, Revised* (Portland, OR: The Laboratories, 1988).

46. From an address presented by Galanter at Columbia University in 1984.

47. Howard A. Peelle, "Computer Metaphors: Approaches to Computer Literacy," *World Future Society Bulletin* 16, no. 5 (November-December 1982): 9–11; see also Anna M. Burford and Harold O. Wilson, "Artificial Intelligence in Business: Technocrat Jargon or Quantum Leap?" a paper presented at the annual meeting of the American Vocational Association, St. Louis, December 1988, and J. D. Fletcher, "Artificial Intelligence in Education and Training: The Promise and the Reality." The Burford and Wilson paper was reported in ERIC # ED 309 756; the Fletcher paper was reported in ERIC # ED 309 756.

48. Both the *Wall Street Journal* and the Association for Supervision and Curriculum Development reported in 1989 that computers were being purchased by school districts for more than simple classroom use. The ASCD's survey of 511 districts revealed that 43 percent of the districts were using computers for curriculum development and/or management. See *ASCD Update* 31, no. 8 (November 1989): 6.

49. Bradley K. Narrett and Michael J. Hannafin, "Computers in Educational Management: Merging Accountability with Technology," *Educational Technology* 22, no. 3 (March 1982): 9–12.

50. Jacqueline A. Haynes, Virginia H. Pilato, and David B. Malouf, "Expert Systems for Educational Decision-Making," *Educational Technology* 28, no. 5 (May 1987): 37–42.

51. Ibid.

52. J. D. Parry, "The Development and Validation of an Expert System for Reviewing a Special Education Practice," a paper presented at the convention of the Association for Behavior Analysis, Milwaukee, Wisconsin, March 1986.

53. Compare Stephen W. Ragan and Thomas D. McFarland, "Applications of Expert Systems in Education: A Technology for Decision-Makers," *Educational Technology* 28, no. 5 (May 1987): 33–36.

54. Some of the most helpful information about restructuring can be found in the following sources: *Phi Delta Kappan* 71, no. 5 (January 1990); *Educational Leadership* 47, no. 7 (April 1990); *Educational Leadership* 45, no. 5 (February 1988).

55. Jane L. Davies, "What It Takes to Restructure Education," *Educational Leadership* 48, no. 8 (May 1991): 11–15.

56. These six expectations have been taken from Doll, Passow, and Corey, *Organizing for Curriculum Improvement,* 16–27, 29, 30.

57. James L. Martin, "Building Curricula When You Don't Have the Answer," a paper presented at the annual meeting of the American Educational Research Association, New York City, March 1982. Reported in ERIC # ED 216 978.

58. The City University of New York, *Examination of the Health Occupations Education Curriculum from a Futurist Perspective: II* (Albany: New York State Education Department, 1981).

59. Thomas B. Mecca and Charles F. Adams, "ED QUEST: An Environmental Scanning Process for Educational Agencies," *World Future Society Bulletin* 16, no. 3 (May–June 1982): 7–12.

60. Leo W. Anglin and Therese Dugan, "Teachers' Perception of Existing and Ideal School Curriculum: An Analysis of Metaphors," a paper presented at the annual meeting of the American Educational Research Association, New York City, March 1982. Reported in ERIC # ED 217 037.

SELECTED BIBLIOGRAPHY

Caswell, Hollis L., et al. *Curriculum Improvement in Public School Systems*. New York: Bureau of Publications, Teachers College, 1950.

Dick, Walter, and Reiser, Robert A. *Planning Effective Instruction*. Englewood Cliffs, NJ: Prentice-Hall, 1989.

Doll, Ronald C.; Passow, A. Harry; and Corey, Stephen M. *Organizing for Curriculum Improvement*. New York: Teachers College Press, 1953.

Eisele, James E., et al. *Computer Assisted Planning of Curriculum and Instruction*. Englewood Cliffs, NJ: Educational Technology Publications, 1971.

English, Fenwick W. *Curriculum Management for Schools, Colleges, Business*. Springfield, IL: Charles C Thomas, 1987.

French, Will, et al. *Behavioral Goals of General Education in High School*. New York: Russell Sage Foundation, 1957.

Hunter, Madeline. *How to Change to a Nongraded School*. Alexandria, VA: Association for Supervision and Curriculum Development, 1992.

Macdonald, James B.; Anderson, Dan W.; and May, Frank B. *Strategies of Curriculum Development*. Columbus, OH: Charles E. Merrill, 1965.

Natriello, Gary, and McDill, Edward L. *Schooling Disadvantaged Children: Racing against Catastrophe*. Colchester, VT: Teachers College Press, 1990.

Penrose, Roger. *The Emperor's New Mind: Concerning Computers, Minds, and the Laws of Physics*. New York: Oxford University Press, 1990.

Pogrow, Stanley. *Education in the Computer Age*. Beverly Hills, CA: Sage Publications, 1983.

Pratt, David. *Curriculum Planning: A Handbook for Professionals*. San Diego: Harcourt Brace, 1993.

Tanner, Laurel N., ed. *Critical Issues in Curriculum*. National Society for the Study of Education. Eighty-Seventh Yearbook, Part I. Chicago: University of Chicago Press, 1988.

Waterman, D. A. *A Guide to Expert Systems*. Reading, MA: Addison-Wesley, 1986.

Wood, George H. *Schools That Work: America's Most Innovative Public Education Programs*. Brandon, VT: Resource Center for Redesigning Education, 1992.

9

PARTICIPANTS AND THEIR ROLES IN CURRICULUM IMPROVEMENT

As a curriculum improvement program begins, the question soon arises, "Who shall participate in curriculum planning?" Today, problems of defining roles of participants in curriculum improvement loom as large as ever. The key issues concerning participants' roles include the following: What responsibilities should various personnel take in planning and improving the curriculum? What special backgrounds, skills, and abilities do they need? How may the talents of participants be used in coordinated ways? Can the effectiveness of participants be damaged or destroyed by modern-day politics?

These and related issues are sharpened by widespread criticisms that are being leveled against the schools. Persons who have worked for years in professional education are sometimes being replaced in curriculum planning by nonprofessionals whose programs for changing schools and school curricula receive wide publicity. Indeed, media coverage makes some of the most complex problems of teaching and learning look easy enough for professional educators to have solved years ago. As broadly based participation in curriculum planning increases and intensifies, however, intelligent participants develop more respect for the complexity of problems with which they must deal.

Curriculum planners from varied segments of the population tend to see the curriculum strictly as a product. As long ago as 1927, curriculum planners in Long Beach, California rightly saw that "the chief value of curriculum revision does not lie in the product made, but in the process of the making."[1] To the school people in Long Beach, the process contributed especially a "rekindling of the intellectual life" of the participants. This rekindling is, of course, most important to those who are closest to the curriculum day by day: teachers, pupils, principals, supervisors, counselors, and others in individual schools. Of these, teachers and principals are clearly most closely involved in curriculum decision making.[2]

So many sources contribute ideas and impetus to curriculum planning that lists of contributors are always long. The contributors include individuals, small groups of people, institutions, agencies, and the documents they have produced. Influences from the sources are often attitudinal rather than substantive. Consider a list composed by two curriculum workers:

National studies
Administrators' attitudes
Board members' concerns
Ideas of theoreticians
Teachers' proprietary rights
National/state testing
Other districts' curricula
Old or traditional curricula
Needs assessments
Pressures from universities
Grants
State curriculum frameworks
Graduate education requirements
Published materials
Proficiency inventories
Parents' concerns
Teachers' concerns[3]

Another list of contributors specifies minority groups, boards of education, superintendents, other administrators, children and adolescents, teachers, community citizens, colleges and universities, the United States government, state legislatures and governors, state education departments, organizations of state and city officials, foundations concerned with education, and the courts. The fact that the two lists differ as they do indicates diversity in ways of thinking about participants' roles.

Pat Cox identified three categories of "assisters" in the planning process: the principal, the change agent from outside the school district, and the central office staff. These assisters focus in part on the content of curriculum change and in part on the context of it. The latter has to do with approval, resources, facilities, and personnel.[4]

Misjudgments about roles in curriculum improvement are easy to make. In times of real or imagined emergency, people assume roles that, on reconsideration, seem entirely inappropriate for them. Also, in times of emergency more people accept roles than in times of calm and the role-takers come from more varied backgrounds. As more people become interested in the curriculum, the likelihood of maintaining productive dialogue among them diminishes. In general, participants in curriculum improvement activities fall into two large classifications: those who operate within local school districts and those who operate outside the districts. It is possible to identify other classifications such as those of professional and nonprofessional personnel, but the crucial issues of the times tend to center about the respective roles of community personnel, both professional and lay, who are willing and able to exercise local control, and persons and organizations beyond the confines of local communities.

Currently, we are faced with an unaccustomed situation. Since the late 1950s, people with little knowledge of elementary and secondary education have been proposing panacea after panacea for our education ills. One after another, their remedies have failed. Consequently, in the 1990s we have come up against a hard, central question: What can we possibly do now to upgrade the school achievement of the children and youth in our charge?

It is clear to informed people, both professional and lay, that changes we can see and respect must occur where children and youth are. This fact weakens the prospects for a number of schemes: creating magnet schools and leaving a majority of children outside the range of the magnets; evolving off-beat ideas for certifying teachers and administrators; accepting into the teaching function "warm bodies" who lack pertinent cognitive preparation; and pursuing pie-in-the-sky, no-cost enterprises of any kind. Reaching and teaching individual pupils, organizing pupils in varied groupings, finding resources and help beyond the walls of school buildings, and utilizing the new technology of an information age are just a few of the more realistic prospects for achieving reform.

As previous discussion in this book has indicated, the seeds of curriculum improvement are sown within populations of pupils, teachers, and teachers' helpers. Unless these populations demonstrate responsibleness, caring, and trustworthiness, their abilities are ill used or used only to a minor extent. Curriculum planning, then, needs to center more and more on cultivation of personal virtues and responses that make for success in learning and teaching.

ROLES OF INDIVIDUALS AND ORGANIZATIONS WITHIN LOCAL SCHOOL DISTRICTS

Persons responsible for curriculum improvement activities within local school districts should be held sensibly and appropriately accountable for the quality of their work in improving the curriculum. The individuals and organizations within local districts who have special roles in improving the curriculum are teachers and their assistants, pupils, administrators and supervisors, local boards of education, parents and parent associations, and other members of the community.

Teachers and Their Assistants

There is little need to reemphasize the fact that classroom teachers and their assistants largely determine the details of the curriculum that is in use. Regardless of curriculum plans made elsewhere, when the classroom door is closed, the predispositions, insights, and skills of teachers and their immediate designees (called paraprofessionals or parateachers) determine in large measure the quality of learners' school experiences. Inasmuch as the teacher, prepared and credentialed, is ultimately responsible for what happens in classrooms, in the following discussion the term *teacher* will comprehend in meaning assistants to the teacher as well as the teacher himself or herself.

Teachers perform three tasks that make them effective improvers of the curriculum: (1) They work and plan with pupils, (2) they engage in individual study, and (3) they share experiences concerning the curriculum with other teachers. By learning from children, from books, and from one another, they grow in insight and skill so that they may provide better experiences for their pupils. Among these three tasks, teachers often prefer group activity with other teachers. Teachers in elementary schools like grade-level meetings; teachers in secondary schools, department meetings. Perhaps the loneliness and isolation of the teacher's life cause this predilection for group work with peers. To influence curriculum planning on a broad front and in favorable ways, teachers need to pool their thinking—for only by knowing, accepting, and promoting the goals of their schools can they be lastingly helpful in curriculum planning. Group thinking, of course, does not always result in wise decisions, but it does raise morale, maintain interest, and create a willingness to change. The quality of group problem solving, including that of the evidence collected during the problem-solving process, determines the quality of the decision making and hence the extent of improvement.

What happens in the group should transfer in part to the classroom and to individual teachers' planning. By the same token, what happens in the classroom and teachers' planning should enrich the life of the group. In performing the three tasks, teachers should keep a central goal in mind: to improve the quality of decision making as they come to educational crossroads on frequent occasions during each day. Much more needs to be learned about ways in which teachers' ability to make decisions can be improved and enriched by both preservice and inservice education.

Certainly, however, the curriculum the teacher tends to honor is the so-called enacted curriculum, which is the curriculum the teacher puts into operation "in the heat of daily combat." The written or recorded curriculum, so much respected in the past by many administrators, supervisors, and lay persons, provides at best a skeleton. To this skeleton the competent teacher adds substance in the process of interacting with learners. Meanwhile, of course, in order to avoid upsetting the supervisor, the teacher may have to write into lesson plans what Eva Weisz has called the "situated events" that constitute the formal, respected lesson. But what the teacher and the pupils do when the supervisor is not looking becomes a matter that is strictly *entre nous*.[5] This behavior may be called subversion, but it will surely continue. When teachers are well prepared, could it not be considered professionalism comparable to the professionalism exercised by practicing physicians?

We have been passing through a period in which teachers have been permitted to make fewer independent decisions. The author's discussions with elementary school teachers have inspired the following composite picture of a classroom teacher in a district in which mandates from above have become common:

> Things have changed somewhat during the twenty-one years I've been teaching. I used to make my own lesson plans and expect them to be reviewed by our principal about twice a month. Now, neither the principal nor I can control the planning for the youngsters I teach. We've both been told by the superintendent's office, which has been told by the state or somebody, that I'm to spend most of my time teaching the "basics." I've found I'd better do that because the standardized tests that we must give seem to emphasize basic learnings. Meanwhile, they leave out any reference to other important learning content. But I don't want a bad rating so I do what our principal calls "teaching to the tests."
>
> I've always emphasized reading because I think learning to read is the most important thing a child can do in school. Lately, our reading program has changed a lot. I spend less time on reading for meaning and for personal development and more time on reading for skill development. About the same thing has happened to arithmetic. I sense that the fun and practical use in solving life's problems are to be put aside until our children have developed enough skill, skill, skill. I believe we teachers need help in getting the two together and in getting the children to go well beyond the simple minimum in mathematics.
>
> As for writing, we don't do much of it in my classroom. That may be my fault, but I realize that there are always more blanks to fill. Now I hear we're to teach thinking. We need it. Right now, the children aren't getting much practice in drawing conclusions, making inferences, sorting out what's worth valuing, or coming up with imaginative ideas. "Right" answers and mechanical responses—are they what we should be looking for?
>
> Who said anything about a rich curriculum!

Ways Teachers Participate

Clark and Astuto have cited three elements of teachers' life in schools that can contribute to their functions as curriculum planners: What motivates the behavior of the individual teacher? How ably is this teacher performing in making plans and implementing them? What level and type of direct contribution does the teacher make in helping to attain the acknowledged outcomes of schooling in this place?[6]

How teachers become involved in curriculum projects and how they participate from that point onward makes an interesting study. A two-year case analysis of the participation of eight teachers seemed to show that there are five steps in the process of participation: orientation of the teacher to his or her role, orientation to "choice points" and alternatives, orientation to practical application of what has so far been theoretical, actual use by the teacher of the theoretical-practical ideas of the project, and modification by the teacher of his or her choices and actions in light of interaction in the classroom and outcomes for pupils.[7]

Leslee J. Bishop described the customary involvement and participation of teachers as occurring in the following sequence. The teachers hear about the ideas, the policy, the design, the materials, and the process to be used in putting a project into effect. They have probably attended meetings about the project and have been made to feel the pressures for change and for their own participation. Their personal commitment to the project depends on the degree to which they accept project ideas, the compatibility of the project with their own ways of working, and their estimate of the project's efficiency in their own classrooms. If they agree with the project and believe they can do what it requires, they comply with its terms and endorse it. Teachers' overt responses range from token moves to enthusiastic participation. As Bishop said, if conditions are just right and the teachers participate, the project is now in operation and the change has come into effect—almost.[8]

David Crandall and others, in their organization called Network, studied the implementation of 61 innovative practices in the schools and classrooms of 146 school districts. They found that teachers were the chief implementers of the new practices, and that they were implementing the practices successfully. The identifiable factors in the implementation proved to be commitment by teachers, the extent to which teachers found practices exemplary, training of teachers in utilizing the practices, and leadership by administrators. Interestingly, commitment occurred largely *after* implementation, whereas the conventional wisdom holds that teachers become committed first and then willingly implement. This finding suggests that, in cases where curriculum planners know practices will work, they can follow a "try it, you'll like it" philosophy with teachers. Once teachers have tried the practices and liked them, they will become committed to them.[9]

Jere Brophy said that teachers do not perform successfully in setting objectives, preparing really useful curriculum materials, and evaluating instructional outcomes. One reason is that they lack time. When they meet in planning groups, they tend to adopt, adapt, and select as they encounter ideas and materials. They seek help for the "intended curriculum" by consulting publishers' manuals and locally made curriculum guides. Improving these materials, said Brophy, would be a constructive measure.[10] Note that as mandates by the federal government increase, teachers may be expected to accept and utilize ideas that have been created elsewhere.

Teachers' commitment to a curriculum they help plan can be increased in several ways. Kerry Kennedy has told how skill training in process can increase teachers' understanding and acceptance of curriculum decisions they assist in making.[11] Rolland Callaway found that, in planning instructional units, teachers should be urged to give more attention to pupil interests and motivation. Currently, he suggests, teachers show too much concern for "covering the book" and beating the major tests imposed from outside the classroom.[12] A book by Connelly and Clendenin treats teachers' down-to-earth experiences in planning and provides details that are not available elsewhere.[13] Revival of action research, a procedure described in Chapter 11 of this text, can put classroom teachers back into the center of interesting planning operations. Similarly, reflective teaching can stimulate educational inquiry in classrooms. (Reflective teaching is a strategy for learning unfamiliar instructional behaviors while using one's own teaching style.[14])

Suppose we put into teachers' own words some of the statements about teacher roles that have come into the literature directly from classrooms:

Teacher 1 says: "I identify and evaluate a variety of curriculum materials under a given theme or topic. Then I select what seems appropriate to what I want to do in the classroom."[15] This statement suggests a paucity of imposed plans.

Teacher 2 declares: "I identify and evaluate a variety of curriculum materials, too, but I see myself as a free person, an authority figure in my own right, a manager, a decision maker, an individualist. Also, I'm a producer, not a mere consumer. *I* interpret what seems at first glance to wear a 'mantle of nobility and righteousness.'"[16] Here is a teacher with extreme initiative, one who is probably difficult for the principal to direct.

Teacher 3 announces: "In planning, I don't like the 'objectives first' way of proceeding. I can enrich planning by calling to mind my preparation in teaching, my interests, the materials I know, and what the administration will let me do. Stating objectives can follow in due time."[17] This teacher would please the growing body of educators who favor free as opposed to structured planning.

Teacher 4 remarks: "I'm influenced by my own beliefs, but I recognize that I have to yield to pressures coming from outside myself. I don't really know how I balance personal belief and pressure."[18] Ambivalence is characteristic of uncertain persons in an unstable profession.

Teacher 5 states: "I know what I value. When an idea comes along that is close to my values, I can accept it immediately. I'm then seen as a cooperative person. But I have trouble with ideas that are far removed from what I value—enough trouble that I balk and drag my feet. Then I'm considered subversive."[19] Perhaps this is a reminder to planners and administrators that they should know teachers' values and at least *begin* by working in accordance with these values.

Finally, Teacher 6 expresses herself thus: "When something new comes along, I usually try it. One thing bothers me, though. I don't want to give up old curriculum content for new. It doesn't seem right to meet new requirements and, at the same time, discard the good in traditional ones."[20] "Preservers of the faith" are found outside the bounds of religion.

The six teachers obviously differ in their perceptions of their role. All of them would probably agree, however, that they are important gatekeepers relative to what is taught in their classrooms. The shyest of them would say that he or she has at least an advisory function in curriculum decision making. Studies show that the actual roles of teachers depend on the teachers' positions, their teaching (grade) levels, the social organization of their schools, the areas of decision making in which they are to voice judgments, the professionalism of their fellow teachers, and the size and wealth of their school districts.[21] Though much planning is done in groups, teachers like to act informally and privately because they are often uncertain how much influence they have in the arena of curriculum policy making.[22] Two influences on teachers' behavior seem to predominate: their own philosophical beliefs and their own versions of their roles.[23] As *Focus in Change* says, feeling like a real professional comes from inside the individual.[24] We must never forget that most teachers, working alone, choose most of what they teach, and they determine to an even greater degree how they will teach it.[25]

The basic reason for emphasizing the teacher's role can be seen in a recent turn of events. Not long ago, people with no involvement in classrooms or schools were advocating tightened control of teachers. They sought standardization of procedures and results, but they were unable to compel standardization of either. Instead, they succeeded, to a degree, in deskilling and demoralizing even the best of teachers. Actually, alert people in and around classrooms know that standardization as it is commonly conceived does not necessarily produce high standards. More recently, parents and other persons in communities have realized again that teachers determine to a major extent what happens in the education of children. They are ready to see well-prepared, diligent teachers given authority to make a positive difference. While they rightly worry that some teachers are incompetent and others are unenthusiastic and even neglectful of duty, they are willing to empower capable teachers and then expect them to act like real professionals.[26] They should show concern in other respects: Just what sort of person is this teacher? How does this teacher rate across a morals/ethics continuum involving, for example, being fair, honest, responsible, trustworthy, and hardworking? A teacher who fails the test of careful observation may well be a direct product of a "cut the corners" family life and community environment.

Though irrational ways of reforming teaching and learning are still being advocated, the chances of freeing good teachers from undue pressure and influence are improving. Of course, to merit confidence, teachers need better preservice and inservice preparation. Well-prepared teachers will see to it that differences in pupils are recognized and that unrealistic goals are changed into realistic ones. In these ways, they will do much to counter demands that "quick fixes" be pursued in the push toward reform. The source of their strength and power will be knowledge of youngsters, of how they learn, and of what they are to learn, along with a moral sense that surpasses similar sense in the people around them.[27] Teachers must also be willing to spend time and energy beyond the call of duty. The importance of this expenditure can be seen in a study of dedication and commitment among Vermont teachers over a 100-year period.[28]

Pupils

Changes have occurred in the role of pupils, especially at secondary school level, in planning the curriculum. The revolutionary movement in colleges in the 1960s had almost immediate effect on many high schools and indeed on some elementary schools. Student rights came to include the right to participate with adults in planning the uses to which pupils' time in schools was to be put. Though this right had existed in some better-known schools for many years and had been advocated to a limited extent by authors in the curriculum field, it now meant permission to speak freely and at length in curriculum meetings, often on a footing equal to that of experienced adults. To some teachers and principals, pupils' newly acquired status represented a refreshing view of human potential and a deserved position in the educational hierarchy; to others, it seemed an especially time-consuming and plaguing form of contemporary insanity. Without question, pupil participation was sometimes carried to ridiculous limits. The student rights movement, as it developed during the 1970s, was generally supported by the courts, which by their decisions gave courage to persons who wished to extend participation by children and adolescents.

Studies of pupil involvement usually show that pupils consider themselves capable of helping with planning and that, in the abstract, teachers and administrators agree. In fact, however, actual involvement by pupils is minimal. It usually begins with the professionals' consulting with individual youngsters or with groups of youngsters.[29]

Children and youth may be said to be the consumers in the educational process. As such, they deserve to be consulted informally at intervals as teachers plan with them. Also, they may be consulted formally and at length at various times in curriculum planning. Consultation with pupils may take several forms, including oral questioning beginning "How do you feel about...?" At times, pupils may be requested to fill out questionnaires, engage in group discussions of curriculum proposals, or subject themselves to intensive interviews. The older the pupil, the more sophisticated his or her participation may become.

But pupils can do more than give quick reactions. They can participate for periods of time in certain curriculum studies. In a junior high school in which the teachers felt especially secure, selected pupils who had suggested that they and other pupils were sometimes disorderly because the teachers "talked too much" in their classroom lectures were asked by a curriculum committee to help the teachers find ways of reducing their lengthy oral contributions in classrooms. The consequent study resulted in teachers' discovering teaching methods they had not previously considered or tried.

Robert Loar suggested that secondary school pupils can participate by helping parents conduct surveys, by conducting their own surveys, by serving on curriculum committees when selected agenda items are discussed—especially matters like discipline and dress codes—and by being paid to help with committee work during the summer. Among the special duties of pupils may be contributing during brainstorming sessions, writing their own ideas, and criticizing existing programs.[30] In addition, pupils can "model" the behaviors required in new projects, take tests containing unaccustomed items, and use innovative materials. As pupils work in these ways, they exhibit skills and other learnings that they have not exhibited previously.

Schooling that ignores what learners think and feel does more than create deep-seated resentment—it inhibits the learning that is possible when the teacher knows the thoughts and values of the learners. One of the interesting ways in which educators can learn what schools are doing to and for youngsters is "shadowing" individual pupils as they move through one or more school days. Shadowing consists of observing individual pupils' behavior in classrooms, corridors, lunchrooms, and elsewhere within schools. One of the conclusions often drawn by panels of observers after they have shadowed secondary school pupils is that the pupils talk little in classrooms and much more elsewhere in the school environment, whereas their teachers talk almost incessantly in classrooms. Down-to-earth findings of this kind can be helpful in starting curriculum improvement that is of real practical use to the participants.

Frank Riessman has described a peer strategy in which pupils are prepared by teachers and counselors to help and tutor other pupils. Treating pupils as "prosumers" of learning—that is, consumers who also produce—puts them into the center of the teaching act. By leading small groups of their peers, for example, pupils become implementers and interpreters of the curriculum. Their changed function causes them to participate inadvertently in restructuring the school and in conserving time and resources for learning.[31]

A final word of caution is needed. Asking children and youth to go beyond their depth in helping with curriculum planning and other curriculum-related activities is of advantage to no one. The maturity and experience of participants should be taken into account in assigning tasks. Two additional ideas are worthy of note. Involving pupils does not mean allowing them to dictate the entire curriculum. At the same time, a curriculum that is not created in part by learners may be weak.[32]

Administrators and Supervisors

Administrators and supervisors of school programs have very special roles to fulfill. Though they administer the curriculum remotely while teachers administer it directly and immediately, the impetus they provide has an important effect in making programs succeed. Evidence has been accumulating that the power of money in stimulating curriculum improvement has definite limits. When additional money, expended for a variety of purposes, no longer makes any real difference, forward movement can result chiefly through bringing new and effective leadership personnel to the task. Truly effective administrators and supervisors know teaching-learning processes, have an understanding of learners and of the intellectual disciplines, and possess knowledge and skill as educational leaders. (These facts overwhelm the argument of state officials and industrialists who say that anyone competent in management and experienced in business or industry is qualified to become a school administrator or supervisor.) Competent administrators invite the persons with whom they work to participate freely in making decisions, both big and little. During recent years, one of the valid criticisms of administrators and supervisors has been that they tend to "take the play away" from teachers and other important participants. Administrators and supervisors perform best when they stimulate, suggest, and guide without controlling and dominating.

Leaders in Individual Schools

Their proximity to teachers and pupils makes school principals the firstline gatekeepers of curriculum improvement. They serve as interpreters of the culture, professional leaders on the educational frontier, supervisors of instruction, stimulators of local community enlightenment, and managers of important educational enterprises. More specifically, they recommend able teachers for employment, arrange reasonable teacher loads, orient new staff members, encourage teachers to evaluate their own performance, support changes in the school program, stimulate teachers to inservice growth, help their staffs understand school goals, and facilitate the improvement process in other practical ways. These listings of roles and responsibilities assume more understanding and ability than many principals now possess. The heavy instructional responsibilities that superintendents and community members place on principals call for thoroughness of preparation in curriculum and instruction.

A survey of the studies of principals' actions and behaviors indicates that, though their contributions are many, principals apparently do not have a direct effect on the school achievement of pupils.[33] A major way in which principals contribute is by serving as chief protagonists in maintaining desirable curriculum change. Principals who are willing and able to interact with teachers about curriculum matters seek the help of their central offices and of outside agencies in providing incentives for creating and maintaining change.[34] Interaction between principals and teachers should take the form of a collaborative relationship in which the exercise of raw power by principals and resistance by teachers are put aside.[35]

What the principal accomplishes in the planning process depends significantly on his or her perspective, which can affect the setting of goals and directions.[36] Constructive, helpful attitudes on the part of the principal can greatly facilitate implementation of plans. Such attitudes increase cooperation and decrease bureaucratic control.[37] Any principal may well be asked, "What is your vision of a highly efficient and effective school?" and "How do you think that vision compares with the real situation here in your own school?"

Principals' effectiveness can be damaged by feelings of insecurity about their knowledge and skill in matters of curriculum and instruction. Alvy and Coladarci reported that the first- and second-year principals whose feelings they explored said that curriculum, instruction, and personnel relations caused them more anxiety than any other aspects of their work.[38] The real curriculum leaders in individual schools are often supervisors, coordinators, and chairpersons rather than principals. The proximity of these persons to classroom teachers often pays dividends.

Leaders in the Central Offices

In the forefront of administrators and supervisors is, of course, the superintendent, who must simultaneously keep things going and inspire change. He or she provides opportunities for participation in curriculum planning, lends active support to curriculum projects, aids communication among personnel, and values efficient problem solving. Specifically, the superintendent must establish organization for improvement; interpret the revisions in program to the board of education; seek funds, personnel, and materials; and facilitate lay participation. If improvement programs are to work, superintendents must give them personal attention. When superintendents see themselves almost exclusively as business administrators, trouble tends to develop in their instructional programs.

General supervisors and curriculum coordinators have been assuming roles as superintendents' delegates in curriculum matters. They have sometimes been considered the most active and important agents of curriculum change. Frequently, they surpass superintendents and principals in their alertness to trends and developments in the curriculum field. Generally, they have more time and opportunity to think and take action about the curriculum. The most knowledgeable supervisors and coordinators find new ideas and resources, assist with staff development, and do the encouraging and troubleshooting that are so important to success.

Williams, Moffett, and Newlin summarized the generic activities of central office administrators in encouraging school renewal. Two of the activities have to do with staff, and two with organization. They are (1) developing needed skills in staff members; (2) building closer relationships among staff members; (3) specifying the goals of the school district; and (4) securing commitment, especially by classroom teachers, to the system's goals.[39] Table 9-1 suggests the kinds of specific activities that fit into these general categories.

TABLE 9-1 How Curriculum Leaders in Central Offices Typically Spend Their Time

Activity	Estimated percentage of time spent
Working with curriculum planning and other groups	17
Conferring with classroom teachers and other persons, individually	12
Working with principals and their immediate staffs	11
Working with parent groups	9
Organizing and conducting programs in staff development	7
Performing public relations functions	6
Writing memoranda, newsnotes, articles, etc.	5
Helping make organizational changes	4
Reading and evaluating curriculum materials	4
Assuming out-of-system professional responsibilities (at conventions, annual meetings, etc.)	3
Locating educational resources	3
Working with the superintendent	3
Visiting teachers' classrooms	3
Helping employ new personnel	3
Investigating new curriculum content	2
Determining and adjusting people's roles	2
Working and cooperating with school board members	2
Helping to set goals	2
Organizing networks of personnel within and beyond the system	1
Advising with regard to evaluation procedures	1
	100

Source: Author's survey

SITUATION 9-1

Achieving Balance in Participation

Monegan High School has just been evaluated by its regional association of colleges and secondary schools. Its school plant has undergone serious criticism, as have its teaching staff and its library. Among the subjects taught at Monegan, social studies has been listed as being in greatest need of improvement. According to the evaluators' report,

1. Teachers are using a single antiquated textbook and are using it to excess. Supplementary reference sources are badly needed.

2. Classroom procedures need varying; the lecture method predominates.
3. The social studies program should be in reality a citizenship education program. Youth should involve themselves, under the auspices of the school, in community affairs. They should learn firsthand what active citizenship means, not merely within their school but in the community at large.

In what ways do teachers, pupils, and administrators have roles to assume with regard to the above-mentioned three curriculum needs?

Local Boards of Education

Local boards of education are legally responsible for the schools under their direction. Formed generally of lay persons, they provide responsible lay participation in legislating for and guiding the schools. With reference to the curriculum, the responsibilities of board members have often been (1) to inform themselves about the curriculum, (2) to articulate the values of the present curriculum, (3) to affirm and help to extend the goals of schooling, (4) to inquire about and propose new curriculum content, (5) to enact general curriculum policies, and (6) to vote funds to put curriculum policies into effect. A more limited view of what boards should do about the curriculum has them monitoring the outcomes of the instructional program and subsequently taking action if the outcomes prove to be adverse.[40]

Boards of education are subject to three dangers in particular as they help to implement curriculum planning. One danger lies in making extreme decisions, either reactionary or revolutionary in nature. Another danger is in making decisions into which they have been pressured by special interest groups. A third danger is in casually, even carelessly, approving proposed curriculum changes without studying them or having anyone else study them.[41]

Intelligent board members soon learn how complex teaching and learning really are. If they are to make wise decisions, they must learn from members of the staff (in addition to superintendents and principals) by attending teachers' meetings, inservice courses, and informal discussions of school problems, and by browsing in professional libraries. At the least, they need to comprehend matters of legislation and finance as they affect the curriculum. School personnel who are knowledgeable about curriculum matters have a special obligation to help board members resolve puzzling issues. Such issues have increased in number since board members were first pressured vigorously from both the "top" and the "bottom." At the top, the federal government and the state governments have applied new pressures, while the maladies of society at large have caused schooling to become a "different game." At the bottom—the level of the local community—adverse and often unreliable publicity about schools in general, together with the down and dirty facts about what happens in some schools, gives school boards more than enough to keep them busy.

When boards of education use definite, sensible criteria for making curriculum decisions, they serve their communities and states well by resisting the pressure and avoiding the capricious decision making that have caused many boards to blunder into unwise judgments. Beyond simple blundering, some boards of education have been known to take unto themselves authority and responsibility for basic work in curriculum planning, ignoring the functions of superintendents and other staff professionals.

An interesting finding is that women who serve on boards of education are usually more concerned about curriculum matters than are their male counterparts. Also, women board members may have a greater desire to be involved in the decision making that occurs within the school systems they serve. Men, on the other hand, are apparently more likely to concern themselves with finance.[43]

During recent years, being a board of education member has become an especially onerous, thankless task. When communities are in ferment, board members are sometimes subjected to insults and even physical abuse. Service on a board of education should be a dignified responsibility, with curriculum matters receiving preeminent attention. Unfortunately, local boards have often been cast in the role of reactors rather than of initiators.[44] Board members who make the most favorable impact on life in schools learn the wiles of politicians, learn how and when to say no, learn how to contradict those in authority when they talk nonsense, and learn more and more about what is happening in their schools.

Parents and Parent Associations

Lay individuals other than members of boards of education have been assuming increasing roles in guiding the destinies of schools in the United States. Most practitioners in the public schools would agree that the feasibility of lay participation is no longer a debatable issue. Community sharing in the making of major curriculum decisions is desirable because changes prove more durable if they are understood and supported by the public, and because those who are to be affected by policies should share in their development.

Chief among lay persons who help with planning are parents. The question, then, is not *whether* lay persons other than board members should participate but *how* and *to what extent* they should participate. Certainly, no group of parents or other lay persons "without portfolio" should constitute itself a rival board of education. In their relationships with the board, parents can serve as aides, resource persons, and advisers. The generalization has been made that parent associations and other parent groups should work on real problems affecting their children, be sponsored by boards of education or school administrators, elect able officers, maintain a supply of resource personnel, agree on their own recommendations, and submit their findings to the board or to sponsoring administrators.

Carl Marburger has summarized the ways in which parents can involve themselves intimately in the affairs of the particular schools their children attend. He suggests that parents can serve in five ways: (1) routinely as limited partners in the educational development of their own children; (2) more significantly as collaborators in their children's further development; (3) in common with other parents in attending their children's school concerts, plays, and other events; (4) within school-based organizations as providers of volunteer help; and (5) in groups that give advice and that help make policy decisions.[45] None of these ways is startling or unusual, but each represents a good beginning point.

One way to assess parents' potential for helping the schools is to think of learning sites at which they could be helpful, of the particular parents who might be most helpful at these sites, and of the capacities in which they might serve. For example, consider the great outdoors as a learning site. The parents who might be most helpful are perhaps foresters, botanists, zoologists, and farmers, to name a few. They might be helpful in conducting field trips, assembling and explaining exhibits, and demonstrating procedures in plant and animal culture.

Numbers of other sites might be suggested, including ethnic neighborhoods, service agencies in the community, offices of practitioners in a variety of professional fields, construction projects, historical centers, political and governmental offices, and other work sites. School administrators generally agree that individual parent helpers cause little trouble; however, parent associations sometimes need special handling.

The importance of parental involvement has been supported by research data supplied by the National Committee for Citizens in Education, the Metropolitan Life Insurance Company, and other organizations. In this era of high dropout rates, involvement by parents is proving especially critical. Getting low-income parents interested in having continuing contact with schools is a challenging task, however. Though parents may realize that their children can drop out of school psychologically long before they are permitted to drop out physically and that their education can be endangered in other ways, the parents' own economic and personal problems, as well as memories of unfortunate experiences with the schools of their day, may cause them to avoid contact with schools and teachers.[46]

In the cities, contact between parents and schools has become a special need. When parents will not go to school as members of an organization that presumably helps their children, they will sometimes feel free to join a community organization that has contact with the individual school. Ways of profiting from the efforts of these organizations are now being discussed in the literature.[47]

As the empowerment of teachers continues, opportunities for a higher level of involvement by selected parents increase. In a number of countries, parent representatives have been chosen to serve as consultants and policy makers in the governance of schools. In the United States, Massachusetts has its School Improvement Councils; England and Wales have their Boards of Governors; France, its Conseils d'établissement; Italy, its Consigli di Instituto; and Germany, its Elternbeirate.[48] Obviously, formal organizations like councils and boards are a primary place for lay persons to become involved. In the United States, a new avenue that will interest selected lay persons is working with state officials who are bent on planning curriculum on a statewide basis. At present, school board members and other citizens who feel the threat of "state takeover" are expressing their fears in letters to newspapers and in speeches at conventions, where they refer to "serving with sinking hearts," "the strong arm of the state," and "the invalidity of decisions reached at remote places."

Other Community Members

Many of the current difficulties with lay participation result from failure to think about the extent and manner of participation. Much lay participation has occurred on too broad a front, with inadequate definition of both the nature and the duration of committee assignments. Furthermore, school officials have too often involved lay members merely to defend present practices. When these same members have suggested possible improvements, the officials have resisted mightily and the lay persons have gone away saying, "Educators are too hard-headed; we can't work with them."

School personnel working with lay persons should keep in mind the public relations aspect of this work. Public relations specialists continue to urge that the people operating schools earn the public's confidence by what they do rather than by what they say. At the same time, the public needs and deserves full information about the schools it supports. In the thrust toward good public relations, every school employee can play an important part in forming and modifying attitudes. The mystery of attitude formation makes inservice education of school personnel in public relations very important.[49]

In his classic statements about citizen involvement, M. Chester Nolte has told how boards and administrators can keep their prerogatives intact by organizing citizen advisory committees more meticulously. He has recommended that cross-sectional committees be selected, that only the board itself appoint committees officially, that the advisory nature of committees be emphasized, that the board and school personnel cooperate with committees, that these personnel remain open-minded about committee actions until the actions are completed, and that committees be disbanded when their work is done.[50]

The lore associated with forming and working with advisory committees and other lay groups has compounded during recent years. The Illinois State Office of Education has pointed out how important careful selection of committee members is, indicating that specialist members are more often needed than generalist members and that a selection committee may well be organized to select members of other committees.[51] Notice has been taken also of how difficult it is to recruit interested and helpful lower-income parents, a search group often being needed for the hunt.[52] Frequently, advisory committees should be given inservice education before they undertake their assignments.[53] According to a rather common view, it generally pays to have a lay person rather than a school person chair meetings of lay groups. The schools, however, have a clear obligation to serve lay groups faithfully by providing meeting places and amenities, by offering secretarial help, by preparing materials and making duplicating arrangements, and by sending out notices as requested.[54] The success of school personnel in finding and using the services of lay group members often depends on skillful recruitment, the making of specific assignments, and proper orientation.

Of course, school personnel do not always behave as they should in their dealings with lay groups. For example, Jenkins reported a tendency on the part of principals to try to create definite, favorable impressions of themselves in the minds of advisory committee members. Called "impression management," this ploy does not seem to fool most lay group members.[55] Without question, many school people resent the presence of lay persons during deliberations about some curriculum matters. Sometimes they show it.

Most of the references in this discussion date from the 1970s, suggesting that citizen participation in the work of school system committees has long since come of age. Much of the current writing and speaking about this matter recalls what has already been said many times. Meanwhile, of course, the search continues for more appropriate roles for lay members of committees. School personnel who have worked at length with lay persons of varying abilities say that the most competent of them perceive the levels at which they should be involved. Thus they avoid preempting the authority, either intellectual or legal, of persons who have made the study of the curriculum their life work. Occasionally, of course, one encounters lay people who have been reading unrealistic books and articles about education, who have learned somewhere to dislike teachers, who think educators are plotting against the welfare of children, or who oppose on general principles what the schools are trying to do. Special patience and skill are needed in working with these persons.

SITUATION 9-2

How Much Involvement for Lay Persons?

The new curriculum improvement program in Terrytown had been under way for nearly a year. Ned Stanley, the curriculum coordinator, had recently told the curriculum steering committee that he felt the need for lay participation but that he didn't know quite how to get it.

"Let's begin by informing our PTAs about the five study groups we've organized," one of the members of the steering committee had suggested. After some discussion, the other members of the committee had concurred. Accordingly, a "package program" containing a common message to the PTAs had been prepared. For twenty minutes, three or four members of the steering committee were to tell each association what the teachers and administrators had been doing to improve the curriculum in the Terrytown Public Schools.

Tonight was the third time Ned had spoken to a PTA. As usual, Ned told about several interesting study projects, about the released time that teachers were receiving for doing their curriculum study, and about the favorable attitudes of participants. Then he asked the same question he'd asked twice before: "What do you parents think of what we're doing to improve our schools?" Result: two or three harmless and noncommittal replies. Then the vice-president of the Terrytown Trust Company responded: "I don't think we know whether you're doing anything worthwhile or not. Why don't you professionals decide things like this for yourselves?"

What kinds of curriculum projects could the banker legitimately say belong exclusively to professionals?

What kinds of projects naturally call for the participation of parents? Think of situations in curriculum planning in which parents should be involved continuously, others in which parents should have absolutely no part at any time, and still others in which parents should be involved to a certain point.

SITUATION 9-3

Competency in Role Determination

In an era of competency-based and performance-based education, curriculum coordinators are called upon to state specifically the roles of participants in curriculum planning.

In the course of being interviewed for the position of assistant superintendent in charge of instruction, a curriculum coordinator is asked to identify four functions in the following list that are commonly considered to be "out of bounds" for lay persons. How should the coordinator respond?

1. Planning with teachers and administrators an accountability system for teachers, parents, and others in school and community
2. Participating as an elected member of the parent council on a committee that reviews goals for the school system
3. Sitting in a child's classroom during the school day without permission from the teacher and the principal
4. Raising questions about the appropriateness of the curriculum for a given group of children
5. Specifying the methods of teaching reading that should be used in School X
6. Organizing to oppose a program in sex education
7. Refusing to send one's child to school because the school is not "satisfactory"
8. Joining a school board–appointed committee on one's own initiative
9. Operating as members of a taxpayers' association to keep school costs down
10. Suggesting a list of goals and requirements for the school that one's child attends

Beyond the four "out of bounds" functions, which functions may be considered marginal?

ACTIVITY 9-1

Looking to the Future of Lay Participation

Participation in curriculum planning by lay persons needs improving. With an eye to the future of the schools with which you are familiar, answer these questions:

1. What are the constructive, forward-looking ways of working with lay persons that your experience has taught you?
2. Think especially of lay persons who, for a variety of reasons, are not likely to participate in education programs either within or outside the schools. What are some constructive, forward-looking ways of relating to them?
3. In the future, how can lay persons make constructive contributions to the cause of elementary and secondary education beyond anything they have done in this direction heretofore?

Consider saving a summary of your discussion contributions for future reference.

ROLES OF PERSONS AND ORGANIZATIONS OUTSIDE LOCAL SCHOOL DISTRICTS

As we have seen, the literature of curriculum improvement ascribes roles to several categories of planners within school districts and local communities. It tells less about the roles being assumed by other persons with an impact on education. So much has happened to shift roles and to create new ones that recent history and the current scene provide the best sources of information about who is making curriculum decisions.

Among the out-of-district role takers, those that appear to be in ascendancy are state boards of education, state commissioners of education and their departments, governors, state legislatures, federal officials and their agencies, and business personnel.

State Boards of Education

Beginning a few decades ago, the interest of state governments in accountability, performance-based teacher education programs, revision of tenure laws, and statewide testing put state boards of education and departments of education at the forefront of contemporary educational movements. The revived and newly heralded philosophy that management of education truly belongs to the state, together with a decrease in the funds available from the federal government, has further augmented the state's role.

State boards of education, which customarily guide the major actions of state commissioners (superintendents) of education, have played an important role in making policy with respect to financial assistance to school districts, accreditation of schools, certification of school personnel, determination of graduation standards, and enforcement of acts of legislatures affecting education. Recently, they have had more to say about the content of school curriculum, about selection of tests for gauging content mastery, and about certification of school personnel.[56] They attend also to criteria for evaluating teacher conformity to the values and procedures upheld by state officials. Gone is the era in which they merely or mainly approved the actions of professionals in the department of education.

Many a superintendent or principal arrives at work to find a state-made test or curriculum guide on his or her doorstep. The arrival of such a test or guide suggests that, months previously, the state board established a policy about comprehensive testing or about a segment of the curriculum that has required the functionaries in the state department of education to practice their test-making or guide-making talents.

State Commissioners of Education and Their Departments

In addition to making their own rules and regulations, commissioners and the departments they head enforce decisions made elsewhere. If a commissioner grows tall in influence, the reason may be his or her personality, ability to influence others, or harmonious relationships with politicians. The competence and professional knowledge of commissioners are too little known and remarked. Recently, commissioners and their departments have seen their responsibilities, and consequently their influence, increase as they have been called upon to implement new requirements set by their legislatures. Commissioners and their departments got a head start in administering well-endowed programs when the federal government was pouring funds into the education coffers of the states. The federal government did the departments another favor: Title V of the Elementary and Secondary Education Act of 1965 strengthened them by providing help with problems of administration and operation. The departments have now become more visible than before, and their ability to employ competent specialists has improved.[57]

Commissioners and their departments have sometimes been hearing the voices of their education-minded governors and also the voices of key state legislators. At times, commissioners have been tempted to "tighten up" in three ways: by urging that standardized tests be used as a partial means of setting curriculum objectives, by trying to make certain that teachers cover a test-related curriculum, and by finding additional ways of evaluating teacher performance. In the worst of situations, commissioners and departments have consciously or unconsciously limited pupils' experiences in schools and have increased teachers' guilt and uncertainty about what to do in their classrooms.[58]

Governors

Governors have recently been given credit by many people for leading school reform movements in their respective states. They have met on a number of occasions to participate in well-planned conferences. The governors' recommendations that more state money be spent for education have been tainted only by their decisions to support certain projects that have proved controversial. The governors of states such as Arkansas, Colorado, Delaware, Florida, Indiana, Minnesota, New Jersey, North Carolina, South Carolina, Tennessee, and Virginia have shown unusual interest in the curriculum field, at least superficially.[59] In general, chief executives of the states have been bent on reforming schools from the top down, in accordance with their perceptions of management practice.[60] Most of them have wanted to minister to local districts so that graduates of the schools would be better prepared to compete in this era of high technology and confused foreign trade. A small group of governors has taken the initiative in planning implementation of the broadly stated goals for the nation's schools, adopted in 1990 by the National Governors' Association with the encouragement of President Bush. Ex-governors from such diverse states as South Carolina, Vermont, Tennessee, and, of course, Arkansas have been active in education affairs at the federal level.

State Legislatures

In 1983, the Education Commission of the States determined that states' curriculum input should be concentrated in seven areas: staff development, statewide curriculum guides, new accreditation standards, improvement of whole schools, dissemination of technical assistance and information, new pupil tests, and parent and community involvement. Agencies such as state boards and departments of education were expected to provide the necessary planning and services.

Behind such agencies is always the power of legislatures charged with the ultimate responsibility for education within the state. Ewald B. Nyquist, former Commissioner of Education in New York State, argued convincingly in 1979 that state legislatures were largely determining the curriculum. Noting that pupils were busy learning subject matter that had been legislated for them at a remote center—that is, the state capital—Nyquist cataloged some of the legislated requirements state by state:

- In Florida, the metric system
- In California, guidelines for programs for preventing genetic diseases
- In Louisiana, the free enterprise system
- In Oregon, the contributions of organized labor
- In Washington, manners, honesty, honor, and industry; kindness to all living creatures
- In Michigan, kindness and justice to animals
- In New York, nature and effects of alcoholic beverages (within courses in physiology and hygiene)
- In Connecticut, humane treatment of animals and birds[61]

New requirements, differing state by state, have obviously increased since Nyquist wrote his article. AIDS, drugs, alcohol, and other threats to life and health have provided some of the subject matter noted in curriculum plans.

Legislatures are unlikely to do as well in legislating quality of schooling as they have done in mandating equality of educational opportunity. In the view of many local school personnel, legislatures have been saying, "We'll standardize your curriculum content, your methods (via the personnel evaluation procedures we require), and the tests that will show us whether you've done your job."[62] As a way out of the dilemma of legislated learning, Luther Kiser proposed two methods of enhancing local control of the curriculum. First, local personnel must develop curriculum ideas that appear so essential and so well supported that state officials will not want to oppose them. Second, local personnel must become better organized and more politically aware so that they can make contact with and influence legislators.[63] Which legislators to influence has become more uncertain as the functions of education committees have been reexamined in light of recurring power struggles.[64]

Federal Officials and Their Agencies

Limited participation of federal agencies, bureaucrats, and other staff members has had a long history in the United States. During the late 1980s and the early 1990s, the federal budget for education came on evil days, especially with respect to the well-publicized projects it supported during the 1960s and 1970s. At about the time the federal government became especially interested in funding projects for improving the lot of minority children, the number of projects carefully earmarked for given purposes decreased. With budget restrictions having limited the total number of dollars available from federal sources, the federal funds not specifically earmarked were used more widely and generally to help local school districts. Because the tax dollar is still considered to have "gone to Washington," the issue of how federal revenues are shared with states and municipalities remains prominent.

The roles that have been ascribed to the federal government in the past have included projecting issues, promoting research, suggesting applications of knowledge, and proposing guidelines of several kinds. As secretaries of education and their earlier counterparts have come and gone, interests and emphases in federal participation have changed. The concern of the White House and of state governors with skill development, the setting of educational goals, the implementation of goals, and the need to improve the economic status of the nation has taken public attention away from many emphases that wise, experienced educators might have proposed.[65]

Within the 1990s, repeated calls have gone out for formulation of a national curriculum. Two questions have plagued persons who support the idea of a national curriculum: "Just what subject matter would the curriculum contain?" and "How can we be sure that the curriculum would be accepted and used in states and localities throughout the nation?"

At the end of the twentieth century, public schools are drawing closer to a uniform curriculum than they have ever been. Steps en route include setting goals, specifying instruction in the three Rs, and recommending affective learnings in the attitudes/values/ethics category. Presumably, essential learning experiences can be unified best when they are advocated by one strong voice that is federal. Some of this thinking is evident in the Goals 2000: Educate America Act that has gone into effect. Two agencies have been designated to administer the act: the National Education Standards and Improvement Council and the National Goals Panel. The former is intended to be a national school board. The latter is to nominate members of the council and also to approve or disapprove actions taken by the council. Schools are expected to conform to federal regulations called "opportunity to learn standards." In return, they will have access to federal monies. Inasmuch as the end of federal regulation and control is not yet, one should be alert to coming events.

Business Personnel

Business personnel, as producers of educational materials and as individual idea developers, have influenced curriculum planning to an unanticipated degree. We should note that equipment and materials for use in school have become more numerous and varied, thanks to business and industry and the new technology. Although the textbook continues to hold its place as the chief learning tool in schools, the future of monolithic commercial texts is being threatened by in-school publishing ventures involving use of computers and word processors. Because textbooks and related materials express the values and ideals of their producers—whoever the producers may be—they will continue to help determine the curriculum.

With schooling beginning in the nursery and continuing through adulthood, and with a large percentage of the population falling into an age bracket in which schooling is most likely to occur, the market for educational materials and devices has become one of the major markets in the U.S. economy. Unlikely and unexpected mergers are occurring between producers of materials and companies entirely outside the educational materials business. The self-teaching materials, including computers, that business organizations produce are sure to have a continuing impact on life and learning in schools, homes, and communities. Educational television continues to hold promise, and devices for simulation and gaming are proving their worth.

Corporation executives continue to speak out concerning what they would like schools to be. Their influence has spread in three major ways: the ideas they suggest in speeches and news releases, their sponsorship of teaching aids, and their control of the content of corporate education programs. Some of the programs emphasize basic and remedial education in the three Rs and social behavior. A few are planned cooperatively with public and private schools.[66]

Designers and publishers of tests have long had an influence on some aspects of elementary and secondary education. Particularly, they have influenced what has been taught and have helped to determine college admission practices. It is too early to say just what will be done with the results of nationally administered and state-administered tests, but larger-scale teaching to the tests seems assured, and private test makers will receive profitable contracts.

Other Influential Individuals and Groups

A variety of individuals and groups continue to influence the curriculum in their respective ways: individual authors; colleges and universities, with their admission standards, extension programs, and consultant service by professors; pressure groups and producers interested in promoting teaching aids that contain particular propagandistic or public relations messages; and subject matter specialists. As groups bearing influence, they have maintained a steady impact, though the messages they have conveyed have varied from time to time.

National and state teachers' organizations, including unions, have lost some of the power and influence they had during earlier years, though they are showing political strength on the national front. In the past, both the National Education Association, with its affiliated subject and topical organizations, and the American Federation of Teachers have sought to strengthen teachers' impact on decision making about the curriculum. Union and association groups have sometimes made the curriculum a negotiable element in the drive for new contracts. Teachers often argue that if the curriculum is the heart of the school's life and thus a central concern to teachers who spend their time implementing it, then, time being money, their organizations should negotiate ways of using instructional time. Persons outside teaching argue that the curriculum, important as it is to so many people's destiny, should not be made a pawn of any special interest group, including teachers.

Foundations have had their place in assisting worthy causes. The foundations concerned with education recognize that they have made mistakes. In the past, many of them have eschewed research and experimentation in favor of large-scale, expensive demonstrations. Some of their fondest projects have come to naught. Still a potential source of help to education, the foundations are now seeking to use their learnings from experience to place their funds where they can do more good. Many helpful foundations and other donor sources are so obscure that school personnel do not apply to them for grants. In the future, foundations that make a real impression will probably fund projects at the heart of schooling rather than projects on its periphery.[67]

ACTIVITY 9-2

Developing a Perspective Concerning Outside Agencies

Agencies operating in differing times and places assume varied roles. For instance, this year in your community the three agencies with greatest power to remake the curriculum may be a regional accrediting association, a powerful industry, and the state board of education. Analyze your community situation by methods of inquiry and reflection. Then respond to the following questions:

1. Which three of the agencies discussed in this chapter have the most powerful influence in remaking the curriculum in your community?

2. Which two or three have changed most in role and function during the past five years? What are the directions of these changes?
3. Which two or three agencies would you like to see strengthen their roles during the next few years? Why?

Compare your responses with those of others.

ACTIVITY 9-3

Identifying New Agencies and Combinations of Agencies

It is possible that in your community additional agencies or combinations of agencies are forming to participate in curriculum planning. If so, discuss the nature and status of these independent or combined agencies. If not, are there additional or combined agencies you would like to see formed? Why? How, at this point, do you view the contributions and the dangers coming from the actions of persons and groups outside local school districts?

PRINCIPLES TO BE OBSERVED IN ASSIGNING ROLES

Human beings are so individualistic that they need principles to guide living within organizations. No chapter on roles would be complete without enunciation of a few principles to be observed in making role assignments. As the reader's experience in curriculum planning proceeds, he or she may identify additional principles that seem to be sine qua non of intelligent practice.

The four principles discussed in this section tell of accountability, planned role coverage, unity and clarity of roles, and convergent role perception.

The Principle of Accountability

A dictionary definition of accountability is "the circumstance of being answerable or liable to being called upon to render an account." People are accountable for aspects of educational programs according to their role assignments. Determining accountability becomes more complex for the persons who are trying to assign it when they realize that expectations of an incumbent's role differ among his or her constituents. Thus the curriculum coordinator in a school district is expected by the superintendent to say the "right" things to board of education members about the great progress that is being made in curriculum planning within the district; by principals to supply teachers with ideas that are "solid," acceptable to the teachers, and not too upsetting of school routines; and by the teachers to provide materials and ideas that are usable in classrooms and in term papers for graduate courses—and to provide them quickly. Of course, the expectations do not stop here. When administrators and teachers become members of the central curriculum committee, they generally expect the curriculum coordinator to "make things move," eliminate troublesome committee members, and specify the agenda for each meeting. Because the role assignments of administrators and teachers are both varied and variable, the behaviors they expect of the curriculum coordinator are compound. Meanwhile, other people have their own expectations of the coordinator. These people include parents as parents; as PTA officers; as fellow members of the coordinator's church, synagogue, or social club; and as taxpayers who are having a hard time with their family finances. Think, too, of the expectations developed as the coordinator associates from time to time with pupils, supervisors, board members, politicians, and peers in neighboring school districts. The list does not include, to this point, the coordinator's spouse, children, intimate friends, or in-laws.

Here we have the concept of role family or "role set," as Katz and Kahn called it.[68] Warren Bennis illustrated role set with a school principal as center of interest, or Pivotal Role Player. The role occupants who hold expectations concerning Bennis's principal are the Superintendent, the Board of Education, the Department of Secondary Education, Principal #3, the PTA President, Parents, the Student Council President, Teachers, Department Chairman #2, Department Chairman #1, Principal #2, and the Assistant Superintendent.[69] The number of persons could obviously have been increased. In these terms, is it hard to see why assigning accountability definitely and in detail causes problems?

Conflicts further compound the problem. Role conflict, or "mutually contradictory expectations,"[70] easily develops. Any role-defining group, such as teachers, is sure to have within it people who have differing expectations concerning what the coordinator should do. The result is what is known as intra-role conflict. The coordinator says, "Whatever I do, I can't please them."

Then there is inter-role conflict, which occurs when the coordinator occupies two or more roles, the expectations concerning which are mutually contradictory. Consider the teachers again. In curriculum work, the coordinator is expected to function with the teachers on a strictly cooperative basis. He or she is a leader who does not force or compel. Part of the coordinator's function, however, is to report teachers to the business office when they fail to appear for work for which they are to be paid. The coordinator is, in the eyes of the teachers, a monitor. Someone, it would seem, has to serve as monitor, so most of the teachers are not offended by this subrole of the coordinator. Now comes a budget crunch during which the coordinator is required by the superintendent to serve temporarily as an evaluator of the classroom work of teachers. In this subrole, the coordinator is no longer seen as a familiar cooperator or as a benign monitor, but as a role taker with potential for depriving more or less worthy teachers of their bread and butter. This kind of role conflict causes a great deal of trouble within school systems, not the least of which is in the area of determining accountability and balancing its aspects.

School personnel have long been said to be generally *responsible* for the learning accomplished by children in schools. Responsibility, with the accompanying sense or feeling it engenders in human beings, has always been considered commendable. But responsibility has remained voluntary, vague, and unassessed. In an age of systems and technology, it would seem logical that sooner or later a system of accountability would be proposed that would include an independent, unbiased, reportable assessment of the effectiveness of people and of the evidence of value received for dollars spent.

Some of the critics of accountability believe that "personal responsibility is to fiscal accountability as lovemaking is to gynecological examination."[71] Thus they criticize the relatively unfeeling, mechanistic nature of some of the evolving schemes for holding people accountable for their behavior in schools. The author of the preceding description remarked further:

> If I'm to be held accountable for my students' performance, then I must be granted powers far exceeding any ever accorded teachers heretofore—to control the materials purchased, the methods permitted, learning sites, scheduling, grouping and mixing, style and atmosphere, and to abolish censorship, centralized adoption and curriculum determination, grammar teaching (though it cost the superintendent his job), and grades and testing (though it render accountability itself difficult to implement).[72]

Most of those who object to accountability quarrel not with the importance of the concept itself but with certain ways in which it is being applied.

Pressure to establish accountability systems has been increasing for several reasons. First, the factory model of the school persists in people's thinking. According to this model, schools (like factories) turn out "products," which can be planned for, produced, and then measured for quantity and quality when they come off the assembly line. Furthermore, educators have encouraged people in this kind of thinking by talking too little about pupils as individuals (for we do not really know them well enough) and talking too much about the importance to school quality of input in dollars and material things as opposed to output in the form of accomplished, genuinely educated human beings. Also, the costs of public education have been escalating wildly. This cost increase has occurred during a period of permissiveness, when people have been unsure of the values they hold and the voices raised have been respected just because they were voices. Today, many parents and other lay persons are themselves irresponsible in a culture in which limited accountability has become commonplace.

Thoughtful educators find themselves able to accept several features of the argument for accountability. They like its proposed emphasis on individualization, with objectives thought of as being individualized and evaluation centered on the individual's progress toward his or her own objectives. They like its forward look, its emphasis on progress rather than on failure, and its recognition of gains yet to be made. They like the wide variety of pupil experiences it can foster. They like its increased attention to the outcomes of schooling, in particular the planned feedback of data about pupils that teachers and their aides can use.

On the other hand, many educators object to talk of "management," systemization, and assured consequences of schooling because they believe the education of individuals is too complex to be managed, systematized, or assured. They wonder how systemization will really take human differences into account. They are uncertain as to how generalized goals can be converted into specific objectives. Above all, they resent having measured pupil progress become the criterion of their own and other people's success in educating children because it is usually uncertain just where in their total environment children have learned given content. The school, they say, should not be held accountable for what pupils learn, except perhaps within limited areas of content that are specifically and even exclusively taught in school; but the school should be held accountable for the processes by which learning proceeds, in consideration of the limitations that individual pupils bring to learning tasks.

Attempts to make educators accountable have assumed several forms. They include the voucher plan, according to which parents are given vouchers representing quantities of education for their children, to be used at the schools the parents choose. They also include performance contracting, a scheme by which contracting firms or organizations agree to produce a fixed amount of education for a fixed number of dollars.[73] Both plans seek to assign responsibility for results.

Arthur Combs, who recognizes the worth of accountability as an essential idea in education, criticizes the methods by which persons both outside and inside professional education are attempting to make educators accountable. He points out that since one's behavior is probably never the result of any one stimulus or set of stimuli prepared by another person (because human behavior is more complex than that), no one can be held responsible for the behavior of another person except under three unusual conditions. The first of these conditions occurs when the other person is too ill or too weak to be responsible for himself or herself. The second condition exists when the other person becomes dependent on his or her mentor. The third is when the mentor's peculiar role demands responsibility, as in the instance of a prison guard's being responsible for a prisoner. Since the proper role of a teacher is to help and facilitate rather than to direct and control, these three conditions do not apply primarily to teaching. But teachers may be held accountable for five things: knowledge of the subject matter, concern for the welfare of their pupils, understanding of human behavior, the purposes they seek to carry out, and the methods they use in carrying out their own and society's purposes.[74] If, as teachers' associations and unions say, it is unfair to assess a teacher's work in terms of what pupils learn, inasmuch as the universe of their learning encompasses so much more time and space than mere schooling can occupy, then the five factors of professional competence listed by Combs become significant centers of attention.

The presence of Combs's five factors in teachers' behavior is not easy to determine, but since when has evaluation of teachers' effectiveness been easy? With carefully devised systems of observation, it is possible to sample teachers' knowledge of subject matter, to infer their purposes, to judge their methods, and to gauge their concern for the welfare of their pupils and their own understanding of human behavior. When the implications of the five factors are considered, they are readily seen to be sufficient for assessing teachers' accountability.

The accountability of teachers may rightly be based in what teachers are required and officially expected to do within the bounds of their prescribed role. In the last analysis, parents apparently want to know "What does this teacher do to stimulate and help our sons and daughters so that they show new and additional evidences of intelligent behavior?" It is obviously unjust of state agencies or boards of education to demand of teachers behaviors that are clearly outside their role, as when boards send "accountability experts" into schools to gauge teachers' competence according to inappropriate, mysterious criteria. Like all major attacks on morale, this kind of action damages the curriculum improvement process.

Another aspect of accountability that few persons have considered is interrelationships among the "accountables" in performing tasks for which several categories of role takers are to be held accountable in part. That is, some of the major tasks in school systems require the efforts of teachers, several categories of administrators, parents, other community citizens, librarians, secretaries, and consultants from colleges and universities. These efforts are made on a part-time basis by numbers of people who are expected to cooperate in attaining a common ultimate goal. Some of the efforts are distinctly those of given categories of personnel or of individual persons, who should then be held directly accountable for them. Other efforts are cooperative ones, across the categories. Only the group as a whole should be held accountable for these. For example, consider a plan that was designed for preparing California school district personnel in career education. The plan involved forming a "cadre" of personnel to lead inservice education. The cadre devised a transportable package of learning materials and proposed organizational procedures for an inservice program.[75] The cadre should be made accountable for the worth of these two products. Individual members of the cadre or teams of individuals should be held accountable only for any individual, significant contributions to which they had the right to sign their names.

Near the end of the century we have come to a "pretty pass." The specter of failing schools is causing a tightening of requirements and an elevation of standards. Having been reared in an atmosphere of low expectations and thus lacking the acumen and the preparation necessary to master the kinds of tasks that are put before them, many pupils simply give up. These youngsters gain little from hearing political figures and others in authority say, "Master what we have for you—or go!" When youngsters go, we say that they have dropped out and that the fault is essentially their own.

A rational view of accountability indicates that some of these pupils have indeed dropped out, but that others have simply been dropped. The former are often victims of what Andrew Hahn called "a host of messy problems." The latter are usually victims of institutions with hardened hearts and monolithic programs. Where school leaving—whatever the causes—has been reduced, it has been through program changes, close work with individuals, and long-term follow up.[76]

Our knowledge of accountability tells us that it reaches into many quarters and that it holds in its tentacles people who wish they were not there and who never thought that they would be held accountable. In the case of youngsters who have given up, the persons accountable include at least the following: the youngsters themselves, their parents, their peers, their teachers, the administrators and curriculum personnel in their schools, the people at state and federal levels who set standards and otherwise make provisions for education, the professional associations that speak or remain silent, the politicians and other people of influence who drop words of wisdom or despair.

ACTIVITY 9-4

When People Are Held Accountable

State the terms of an "accountability contract" you would be willing to sign because you believe you could—as a responsible professional—conform to it. Mention only those aspects of your performance or behavior you think should be included in an evaluation of your work.

Discuss your contract with others who have prepared contracts for themselves.

The Principle of Planned Role Coverage

A second principle to be respected in making role assignments is the principle of planned coverage. If a program is to succeed, all its elements must be made the responsibilities of designated personnel. For discharging this assignment function, the leaders of the program are generally made accountable. Their objective is placement of able personnel at every significant post and juncture.

Planned coverage of roles is complicated by confusion about the purposes of programs within the master purposes of the entire school. Because U.S. schools commonly need reexamination of their purposes, some school districts have followed the work of the "little White House conferences" with careful replotting of purposes in their communities. Only when purposes are known can roles be listed.

When the author was employed as director of guidance for a new program in the West Orange, New Jersey Public Schools, the superintendent worked with interested staff members to delineate the purposes of the given program and to specify who would perform necessary tasks. As a consequence, roles were assigned to classroom teachers, counselors, librarians, nurses, principals, assistant principals, and the guidance director himself. For each group, two levels of responsibility were assigned—primary responsibility, which was exclusive to persons in that group, and cooperative responsibility, which was to be shared with persons in other groups. Allocations of responsibility were stated in writing and were altered as changing conditions required.

The 1976 Yearbook of the National Society for the Study of Education contains another example of dividing large-scale responsibility for curriculum planning among a number of role takers. In this instance, the Curriculum Coordinator has responsibilities that are distinct from the responsibilities of the Professional Team Leader, of the Lay Participant in Planning, of the Classroom Aide, and of the Pupil Representative. (The selection of these five role takers for purposes of illustration is not intended to imply exclusion of other important role takers such as classroom teachers and building administrators.)[77]

Don Davies mentioned three phrases that characterize the main difficulties with role coverage: lack of ownership of a role, role overload, and role confusion.[78] Fortunately, some of the new provisions for employing teachers (as in Dade County, Florida and Rochester, New York) include increased and clarified responsibility and decision-making power for classroom teachers, with corresponding increases in financial rewards.[79]

The Principle of Unity with Clarity

No matter how carefully conceived the plan for allocation of roles, differences are likely to arise among staff members who have different temperaments and differing perceptions of their roles. One of the major disputes among curriculum personnel has now become almost classic—the dispute between new curriculum coordinators and veteran principals. Whenever a new position is created, conflicts about roles are likely to arise. Differences must be recognized and accepted and a reasonable plan of action developed.

> An example of this is to be found in the case of a newly appointed helping teacher who came into conflict with a veteran reading consultant because the helping teacher had begun to assist elementary school teachers with grouping and materials in reading. The director of instruction met with the two specialists involved in the conflict. He asked each specialist to state her perception of her own function with respect to reading as well as her view of any other areas of present or potential conflict. As the two staff members talked about their perceptions of their distinctly different roles, they found their own grounds for agreement with little help from the director of instruction. They seemed to find satisfaction in recognizing their differences in perception and then in testing these perceptions against reality. They succeeded in citing instances in which overlapping efforts to help teachers

had confused the teachers. At their second and third meetings, they agreed on specific actions concerning instruction in reading which each would take, and they then role-played the methods they would use in referring teachers from specialist to specialist for assistance.[80]

Not all stories of this sort end so happily. In this situation, there was no hidden agenda of smoldering dislike since the specialists had not known each other very long.

Reduction of both conflict and duplication can be achieved only by giving the warring parties enough opportunity to talk about their differences. Sometimes, they can settle the differences alone; at other times, they may need the intervention of a third or a fourth party or even of a policy committee. It is often the duty of administrators to mediate disputes of this kind. One should realize that conflict about roles is not necessarily unfortunate; it often serves to clear the air and results in a more definite and happy clarification of roles. By troubleshooting in cases of conflict, curriculum leaders can achieve greater balance and harmony among roles.

Unity can be achieved in both process and effect. Unity in process is suggested by the expression "Whatever we do (different as we are), let's direct our actions toward a common, agreed-upon goal." Unity, in effect, can be inferred from the words "We've achieved commendable results that represent what we all wanted to do from the beginning."

Clarity must go hand in hand with unity. Clarity owes its origin to careful thinking by role participants. When a participant can say, "Here's the way I see our problem" and find that other participants agree, intellectual clarity has been attained, at least as shown by the common agreement. Although clarity does not equal or assure correctness, it erects a barrier against role confusion, especially when persons from outside the schools register their own versions of roles. Surely, it gives the lonely participant who is new to curriculum work an opportunity to say, "I know what I am to do because the people around me agree about it and are clear in their thinking about it."

The Principle of Convergence in Role Perception

The present chapter has referred at intervals to varying perceptions of a given role. Each occupant of a role, if he or she becomes sensitive to problems of role perception, asks interrelated questions: "How do I see my own role?" "How do others see my role?" "How do I think others come to their conclusions about my role?"

The difficulty in getting perceptions to converge is demonstrated by the confusions that pervade complex organizations. These confusions result from such factors as changed and changing situations, differing personality patterns and self-concepts, inadequate preparation of role occupants, the tendency to assign several roles to one person, and the presence of subgroups within organizations.[81]

To make perceptions converge, there needs to be an official, current statement of the role that has been designated. The statement should be prepared before people begin to present their perceptions of the possible or presumed role. Until the statement is changed, it serves as the guide that contributes to the narrowing or convergence of people's views about how occupants of the prescribed role should behave. Certainly, the statement should be put in writing for distribution to all of the discussants. Discussion of differences in perception can begin with completion by each dicussant of this sentence: "I have thought that..." Individual discussants will differ in what they have thought about the role. When, as a next step, direct attention is given to areas of difference, some of the areas tend to diminish and other areas tend to disappear. At this juncture, hearing the direct testimony of current role occupants can help. So, too, can case studies developed by observers. In the heat of discussion, sociodramas can be used to develop common feelings about the nature of a given role. As a result of the whole experience, the official statement may be changed.

ACTIVITY 9-5

The Conflict Between Principals and Curriculum Coordinators

"I thought curriculum planning was *my* job!"

This statement is frequently made simultaneously by principals and curriculum coordinators in the same school district. Interview one or more principals and one or more curriculum coordinators to learn their respective perceptions of ways in which this conflict has arisen.

When you have assessed the situation, state what you believe might have been done to avoid conflict. Also state what actions should be taken in the future to prevent further conflict.

SUMMARY

Many individuals and organizations play roles in improving the curriculum. In Chapter 9, these role takers are categorized in two groupings: those who operate within local school districts and those who operate outside them. The people who usually make an impact within districts include teachers and their aides, pupils, administrators and supervisors, community boards of education, parents and parent associations, and other community members. Role takers outside school districts exert varying and shifting influence on what happens in practical ways to the curricula of elementary and secondary schools. The role takers in this category who have become more influential during recent years are state boards of education, state commissioners of education and their departments, governors, state legislatures, federal agencies and individual federal personnel, and business leaders, some of whom are involved in making school equipment, materials, and tests. A number of other groups, like national and state teachers' organizations, have had their input recognized. Principles that should help to determine role assignments are presented under the headings of accountability, planned role coverage, unity with clarity, and convergence in role perception.

ENDNOTES

1. From Long Beach, California curriculum records.

2. Mary P. Tubbs and James A. Beane, "Decision Making in Today's Schools: Who Is Involved?" *Bulletin of the National Association of Secondary School Principals* 66, no. 456 (October 1982): 49–52; see also Richard D. Kimpston and Douglas H. Anderson, "A Study to Analyze Curriculum Decision Making in School Districts," *Educational Leadership* 40, no. 2 (November 1982): 63–66.

3. An edited version of the list presented by Marilyn Winters and Babette Keeler Amirkhan at the national convention of the Association for Supervision and Curriculum Development, New York City, March 10–13, 1984.

4. Pat L. Cox, "Complementary Roles in Successful Change," *Educational Leadership* 41, no. 3 (November 1983): 10–13.

5. See the description of a 1988 study of teachers in action by Eva Weisz, in her "Curriculum Planning and Enactment of Beginning Teachers—Is There a Fit or a Gap between the Two?" Reported in ERIC # ED 299 693.

6. Dennis L. Clark and Terry A. Astuto, "Redirecting Reform: Challenges to Popular Assumptions about Teachers and Students," *Phi Delta Kappan* 75, no. 7 (March 1994): 513–520.

7. F. Michael Connelly and Barbara Dienes, "The Teacher as Choice Maker in Curriculum Development: A Case Study" (Toronto: Ontario Institute for Studies in Education, 1973). Reported in ERIC # ED 083 241.

8. Leslee J. Bishop, *Staff Development and Instructional Improvement: Plans and Procedures* (Boston: Allyn and Bacon, 1976): 138, 139.

9. David Crandall, "The Teacher's Role in School Improvement," *Educational Leadership* 41, no. 3 (November 1983): 6–9; see also Michelle Pahl Monson and Robert J. Monson, "Who Creates Curriculum? New Roles for Teachers," *Educational Leadership* 51, no. 2 (October 1993): 19–21.

10. Jere E. Brophy, "How Teachers Influence What Is Taught and Learned in Classrooms," *Elementary School Journal* 85, no. 1 (September 1982): 1–13.

11. Kerry J. Kennedy, "Creating a Context for Curriculum Deliberation by Teachers," a paper presented at the annual meeting of the American Educational Research Association, New Orleans, April 1988.

12. Rolland Callaway, "A Study of Teachers' Planning," conducted in the state of Wisconsin, 1988. Reported in ERIC # ED 292 795.

13. F. Michael Connelly and Jean D. Clendenin, *Teachers as Curriculum Planners: Narratives of Experience* (New York: Teachers College Press, 1988).

14. John Elliott, "Teachers as Researchers: Implications for Supervision and Teacher Education," a paper presented at the annual meeting of the American Educational Research Association, New Orleans, April 1988. Reported in ERIC # ED 293 831.

15. See Virginia Chaimbalero, "Developing Original Curriculum: What One Teacher Can Do," *Clearing House* 55, no. 4 (December 1981): 165–168.

16. Diane L. Common, "Who Has the Power to Change Schools?" *Clearing House* 55, no. 2 (October 1981): 80–83.

17. Diane Wells Kyle, "Curriculum Decisions: Who Decides What?" *Elementary School Journal* 81, no. 2 (November 1980): 77–86.

18. John Schwille, Andrew Porter, and Michael Gant, "Content Decision Making and the Politics of Education," *Educational Administration Quarterly* 16, no. 2 (Spring 1980): 21–40,

19. Sheldon F. Katz, "Curriculum Innovation: Teacher Commitment, Training, and Support," a paper presented at the annual conference of the American Educational Research Association, Los Angeles, April 1981. Reported in ERIC # ED 200 546.

20. R. E. Floden et al., "Responses to Curriculum Pressures: A Policy-Capturing Study of Teacher Decisions About Content," *Journal of Educational Psychology* 73, no. 2 (April 1981): 129–141.

21. Paul D. Hood and Laird R. Blackwell, "The Role of Teachers and Other School Practitioners in Decision Making and Innovation," report of the Far West Laboratory for Educational Research and Development, San Francisco, 1980.

22. William M. Bridgeland, Edward A. Dunne, and Mark E. Stern, "Teacher Sense of Curriculum Power in a Suburban School District," *Education* 102, no. 2 (Winter 1981): 138–144.

23. Bruce Thompson, "The Instructional Strategy Decisions of Teachers," *Education* 101, no. 2 (Winter 1980): 150–157.

24. The National Center for Effective Schools, *Focus in Change,* Winter 1992, no. 9, 1.

25. Larry Cuban, "The Lure of Curricular Reform and Its Pitiful History," *Phi Delta Kappan* 75, no. 2 (October 1993): 182–185.

26. Compare Samuel B. Bacharach, "Education Reform: All Together," in Samuel B. Bacharach, ed., *Education Reform: Making Sense of It All* (Boston: Allyn and Bacon, 1990).

27. Joseph P. McDonald, "The Emergence of the Teacher's Voice: Implications for the New Reform," *Teachers College Record* 89, no. 4 (Summer 1988): 471–486.

28. John Duval, "Dedication/Commitment: A Study of Their Relationship to Teaching Excellence," a paper presented at the annual meeting of the New England Educational Research Organization, Portsmouth, NH, April 1989.

29. See, for example, William Brock, "Student Participation on Curriculum Committees in a School System in Alabama," *Education* 106, no. 4 (Summer 1986): 442–443.

30. Robert L. Loar, "Curriculum Committees—Can Students Be Involved?" a paper presented at the annual convention of the National Association of Secondary School Principals, Dallas, February 1973. Reported in ERIC # ED 089 450.

31. Frank Riessman, "A School-Change Paradigm," *Social Policy* 19 (Summer 1988): 2–4.

32. Alfie Kohn, "Choices for Children: Why and How to Let Students Decide," *Phi Delta Kappan* 75, no. 1 (September 1993): 8–20.

33. Joan Shoemaker and Hugh W. Fraser, "What Principals Can Do: Some Implications from Studies of Effective Schooling," *Phi Delta Kappan* 63, no. 3 (November 1981): 178–182.

34. H. Dickson Corbett, "Principals' Contributions to Maintaining Change," *Phi Delta Kappan* 64, no. 3 (November 1982): 190–192.

35. Paul V. Bredeson, "Redefining Leadership and the Role of School Principals: Responses to Changes in the Worklife of Teachers," 1989. Reported in ERIC # ED 304 782.

36. Veronica S. Lacey et al., "The Role of In-School Administrators in Bringing about Curricular Change: The Principal's Perspective," a paper presented at the annual meeting of the American Educational Research Association, San Francisco, April 1986.

37. Linda M. McNeil, "Contradictions of Control, Part I: Administrators and Teachers," *Phi Delta Kappan* 69, no. 5 (January 1988): 333–339,

38. Harvey B. Alvy and Theodore Coladarci, "Problems of the Novice Principal," *Research in Rural Education* 3, no. 1 (Summer 1985): 39–47.

39. Richard C. Williams, Kenneth L. Moffett, and Bruce Newlin, "The District Role in School Renewal," in John I. Goodlad, ed., *The Ecology of School Renewal,* National Society for the Study of Education, Eighty-Sixth Yearbook, Part I (Chicago: University of Chicago Press, 1987), 127–129.

40. Davis W. Campbell and Diane Greene, "Defining the Leadership Role of School Boards in the 21st Century," *Phi Delta Kappan* 75, no. 5 (January 1994): 394.

41. Harold V. Webb, "School Boards and the Curriculum: A Case of Accountability," *Educational Leadership* 35, no. 3 (December 1977): 178–182.

42. Michael W. Kirst, "A Changing Context Means School Board Reform," *Phi Delta Kappan* 75, no. 5 (January 1994): 378–381.

43. Rebecca Luckett et al., "Men and Women Make Discernibly Different Contributions to Their Boards," *American School Board Journal* 173, no. 1 (January 1987): 21–27.

44. Jacqueline P. Dansberger et al., "School Boards: The Forgotten Players on the Educational Team," *Phi Delta Kappan* 69, no. 1 (September 1987): 53–59.

45. Carl L. Marburger, "The School Site Level: Involving Parents in Reform," in Samuel B. Bacharach, ed., *Education Reform: Making Sense of It All* (Boston: Allyn and Bacon, 1990).

46. Amy Stuart Wells, "The Parents' Place: Right in the School," *New York Times*, January 3, 1988.

47. See, for example, Michael R. Williams, *Neighborhoods Organizing for Urban School Reform* (Wolfeboro, NH: Teachers College Press, 1989).

48. Nicholas Beattie, "Parents as a New Found Land: Reflections on Formal Parent Participation in Five Polities," a paper presented at the annual meeting of the American Educational Research Association, San Francisco, March 1989.

49. John H. Wherry, "Building Public Confidence in Education," *Educational Leadership* 36, no. 8 (May 1979): 533; see also the entire issue of *Educational Leadership* 51, no. 2 (October 1993) for a discussion of new roles and relationships.

50. M. Chester Nolte, "Citizen Power over Schools: How Much Is Too Much?" *American School Board Journal* 163, no. 4 (April 1976): 34–36.

51. Illinois State Office of Education, *A Guide for Planning, Organizing, and Utilizing Advisory Councils* (Springfield, IL: Division of Vocational and Technical Education, 1975).

52. Gordon E. Greenwood et al., "Citizen Advisory Committees," *Theory into Practice* 16, no. 1 (February 1977): 12–16.

53. Angelo C. Gilli, *Improving Vocational Education through Utilization of Advisory Committees* (Houston: Texas Southern University, 1978).

54. Joseph T. Nerden, "Advisory Committees in Vocational Education: A Powerful Incentive to Program Improvement," *American Vocational Journal* 52, no. 1 (January 1977): 27–30.

55. Jeanne Kohl Jenkins, "Impression Management: Responses of Public School Principals to School-Community Advisory Councils," a paper presented at the convention of the American Educational Research Association, Chicago, April 1974.

56. See Michael Cohen, "State Boards in an Era of Reform," *Phi Delta Kappan* 69, no. 1 (September 1987): 60–64.

57. Calvin M. Frazier, "The 1980s: States Assume Educational Leadership," in John I. Goodlad, ed., *The Ecology of School Renewal*, National Society for the Study of Education, Eighty-Sixth Yearbook, Part I (Chicago: University of Chicago Press, 1987), 105, 106.

58. See the writings of Arthur E. Wise, beginning with his *Legislated Learning: The Bureaucratization of the American Classroom* (Berkeley, CA: University of California Press, 1979). Bureaucratization deprives people other than teachers and parents—for example, secretaries and custodians who know what is happening in their schools—of opportunities to provide useful information to curriculum planners; see also Sally Henry and Jeanne Vilz, "School Improvement: Together We Can Make a Difference," *Educational Leadership* 47, no. 8 (May 1990): 78, 79.

59. Frazier, "The 1980s: States Assume Educational Leadership."

60. See Denis P. Doyle and Terry W. Hartle, "Leadership in Education: Governors, Legislators, and Teachers," *Phi Delta Kappan* 67, no. 1 (September 1985): 21–27.

61. Ewald B. Nyquist, "So You Think Schools Make the Curriculum!" *New York Times*, November 11, 1979, 37.

62. Arthur E. Wise, "Legislated Learning Revisited," *Phi Delta Kappan* 69, no. 5 (January 1988): 328–333.

63. Luther L. Kiser, "When Mandated Courses, Mandated Programs Control the Curriculum," *Educational Leadership* 35, no. 3 (December 1977): 187–190.

64. National Center on Education and the Economy, "To Secure Our Future: The Federal Role in Education," The Center, Rochester, NY, 1989.

65. The governors and their associates are called "restorationists" by Jane Martin, whereas some of our wiser educators deserve to be called "transformationists." See Jane Roland Martin, "A Philosophy of Education for the Year 2000," *Phi Delta Kappan* 76, no. 5 (January 1995): 355–359.

66. Magazines for business executives often feature articles on the participation of businesses and industries.

67. M. Hayes Mizell, "Private Foundations: What Is Their Role in Improving the Education of Disadvantaged Youth?" a lecture delivered at the University of Cincinnati, Cincinnati, Ohio, April 28, 1989.

68. Daniel Katz and Robert L. Kahn, *The Social Psychology of Organizations* (New York: McGraw-Hill, 1966).

69. Warren Bennis, *Changing Organizations* (New York: McGraw-Hill, 1966).

70. See Thomas J. Sergiovanni and Fred D. Carver, *The New School Executive: A Theory of Administration* (New York: Harper & Row, 1980), 210–218.

71. From a paper by James Moffett presented to a discussion group at the annual conference of the National Council of the Teachers of English, Las Vegas, November 1971.

72. Ibid; see also Hannelore Wass, "Educational Accountability Here and Abroad," *Educational Leadership* 29, no. 7 (April 1972): 618–620.

73. A critic has facetiously reported the history of performance contracting in reverse chronology from the contract made for the St. Valentine's Day Massacre in 1929 to Judas's contract to betray Jesus Christ. See H. G. Vonk, "Performance Contracting from Chicago to Calvary," *Clearing House* 48, no. 6 (February 1974): 365.

74. Arthur W. Combs, *Educational Accountability: Beyond Behavioral Objectives* (Washington, DC: Association for Supervision and Curriculum Development, 1972), 33–40.

75. Charles C. Healy and James Quinn, *Project Cadre: A Cadre Approach to Career Education Infusion* (Los Angeles: University of California, 1977). Reported in ERIC # ED 170 479.

76. Andrew Hahn, "Reaching Out to America's Dropouts: What to Do?" *Phi Delta Kappan* 69, no. 4 (December 1987): 256–263.

77. Ronald C. Doll, "How Can Learning Be Fostered?" in William Van Til, ed., *Issues in Secondary Education,* National Society for the Study of Education, Seventy-Fifth Yearbook, Part II (Chicago: University of Chicago Press, 1976), 283.

78. Don Davies, "School Administrators and Advisory Councils: Partnership or Shotgun Marriage?" *Bulletin of the National Association of Secondary School Principals* 64, no. 432 (January 1980): 62–66.

79. The *Newark* (NJ) *Star-Ledger,* August 25, 1988, 60.

80. From material supplied by the author for use in the 1960 Yearbook of the Association for Supervision and Curriculum Development. See Association for Supervision and Curriculum Development, *Leadership for Improving Instruction* (Washington, DC: The Association, 1960), 84, 85.

81. See J. W. Getzels and E. G. Guba, "Structure of Roles and Role Conflicts in the Teaching Situation," *Journal of Educational Sociology* 29 (September 1955): 30–40.

SELECTED BIBLIOGRAPHY

Connelly, F. Michael, and Clendenin, Jean D. *Teachers as Curriculum Planners: Narratives of Experience.* New York: Teachers College Press, 1988.

DeNovellis, Richard L., and Lewis, Arthur J. *Schools Become Accountable; A PACT Approach.* Washington, DC: Association for Supervision and Curriculum Development, 1974.

Dickson, George E., and Saxe, Richard W. *Partners for Educational Reform and Renewal.* Berkeley, CA: McCutchan, 1974.

Doll, Ronald C. *Supervision for Staff Development: Ideas and Application.* Boston: Allyn and Bacon, 1983.

Elmore, Richard F., and Fuhrman, Susan H., eds. *The Governance of Curriculum.* Association for Supervision and Curriculum Development, 1994 Yearbook. Alexandria, VA: The Association, 1994.

Goodlad, John I., ed. *The Ecology of School Renewal.* National Society for the Study of Education, Eighty-Sixth Yearbook, Part I. Chicago: University of Chicago Press, 1987.

Gross, Neal; Mason, Ward S.; and McEachern, Alexander W. *Explorations in Role Analysis.* New York: Wiley, 1958.

Hargreaves, Andy. *Changing Teachers, Changing Times.* New York: Teachers College Press, 1994.

Howe, Harold, II. *Thinking about Our Kids.* New York: The Free Press, 1993.

Leithwood, Kenneth A., ed. *Studies in Curriculum Decision Making.* Toronto: The Ontario Institute for Studies in Education Press, 1982.

Mallery, David. *A Community School Venture: Top Professionals Work with School Students.* Boston: National Association of Independent Schools, 1963.

McCloskey, Gary N.; Provenzo, Eugene F., Jr.; Cohn, Marilyn M.; and Kottkamp, Robert B. *A Profession at Risk: Legislated Learning as a Disincentive to Teaching.* Washington, DC: Office of Educational Research and Improvement, 1987.

Storen, Helen F. *Laymen Help Plan the Curriculum.* Washington, DC: Association for Supervision and Curriculum Development, 1946.

Tanner, Laurel N., ed. *Critical Issues in Curriculum.* National Society for the Study of Education, Eighty-Seventh Yearbook, Part I. Chicago: University of Chicago Press, 1988.

Van Til, William, ed. *Curriculum: Quest for Relevance,* 2nd ed. Boston: Houghton Mifflin, 1974.

10

THE MASSIVE PROBLEM
OF COMMUNICATION

"We worked a whole year, but no one knew about it."

"How can I convey to the other teachers in my school what I've learned in recent months?"

"All that we do in Ramsey Elementary School seems to involve very few people."

The preceding comments are typical of many remarks one hears about lack of communication among staff members of U.S. schools. It is true that many years may be required for an educational idea to move from its source to common practice, but it is also true that many promising ideas are lost annually because they are never launched into communication channels of any sort. How can ideas move freely within schools and school systems and then move out into the educational world at large? How can countering ideas be fed back to the sources of the original ideas to modify, correct, and improve them? In brief, how can the news about developments in education be distributed quickly and easily so that practice will evolve with the speed that befits a thriving profession? Providing appropriate answers to these questions could materially aid the process of curriculum improvement.

COMMUNICATION: A COMPLEX ENTERPRISE

Human communication, which has been defined as transmission of facts, ideas, values, feelings, and attitudes from one person or group to another, has been called the number one problem of school administration. It may also be the greatest problem of curriculum improvement. Merely transmitting the simplest information from sender to receiver without undue loss or confusion becomes a major task. The complexity of messages about the curriculum, the intertwining of networks through which messages move, and the uncertain readiness of receivers to accept the messages all increase the problem.

The process of human communication has been described as conforming to the model in Figure 10-1. The model suggests something of the complexity of communication. Like many of the complex problems involved in curriculum improvement, human communication has been oversimplified by lay individuals. "The prevailing thought is that all the sender has to do now is transfer his ideas from his mind to the receiver's mind. He bundles his ideas into a neat package and sends them off on an unperilous journey to be opened and digested whole."[1] Actually, the model reminds one of Harold Lasswell's pithy question "Who says what to whom via what channel with what effect?"[2] The question suggests the agents of and elements in communication: *who,* the sender; *what,* the message; *whom,* the receiver; *what channel,* the communication medium and the structure of human relationships through which the message is transmitted; and *what effect,* the evaluation of results. The first four of these agents or elements can either facilitate or impede communication.

Several barriers to effective communication in schools have been identified. All of them relate to the three kinds or levels of communication problems noted by Shannon and Weaver in an early study. First, there are technical problems that affect the accuracy with which symbols are transmitted. Then, there are semantic problems, affecting the precision with which meaning is

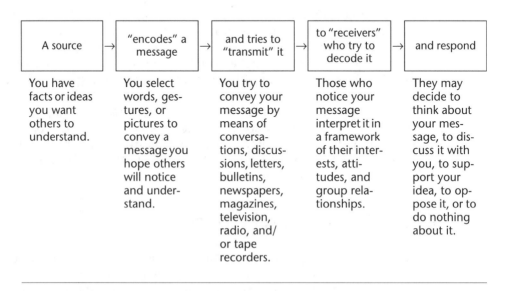

A source	→	"encodes" a message	→	and tries to "transmit" it	→	to "receivers" who try to decode it	→	and respond
You have facts or ideas you want others to understand.		You select words, gestures, or pictures to convey a message you hope others will notice and understand.		You try to convey your message by means of conversations, discussions, letters, bulletins, newspapers, magazines, television, radio, and/or tape recorders.		Those who notice your message interpret it in a framework of their interests, attitudes, and group relationships.		They may decide to think about your message, to discuss it with you, to support your idea, to oppose it, or to do nothing about it.

From Gordon McCloskey, "Principles of Communication for Principals," *Bulletin of the National Association of Secondary School Principals* 44, no. 257 (September 1960): 17–23.

FIGURE 10-1

conveyed by the symbols. Third, there are effectiveness problems, or problems involved in getting perceived meaning to influence human conduct desirably.[3] On top of these three basic problems are other barriers or difficulties. People are different, so they have differing values. They also have their own vested interests and prejudices. Accordingly, they perceive the very same situation differently. Sometimes, because of lack of intellectual capacity or because of a physical, mental, or emotional blockage, the meaning of a situation or a statement about it does not "get through" to them. Then, personal insecurities will not let people receive certain communications. Often, people do not hear the whole message because they start evaluating the first part of the message content while the remainder is being communicated. Sometimes potential receivers of messages just feel too negative in general to receive almost anything. Finally, the words and other symbols people receive mean different things to them as individuals.

Difficulties like these have caused students of communication to define what behaviors make for easier transfer of thought from communicators to receivers of messages, and back again. Their major suggestions include speaking clearly and succinctly, listening carefully, expressing ideas openly, accepting criticism in good spirit, and giving timely feedback. To these ends, good communicators master the skills of asking questions, agreeing and disagreeing, paraphrasing, checking people's perceptions, and describing feelings and actions.[4]

Research in human communication within the fields of political science, psychology, semantics, and sociology provides additional ideas about the nature, importance, and complexity of communication in schools:

- Much communication occurs informally, outside the neat, formal channels we prepare.[5] We should expect such informal communication as a plain fact of human behavior.
- True communication occurs only when we provide ample opportunity for feedback of ideas from communicatee to communicator. Research on feedback has shown, for instance, that "as the exchange of ideas, or feedback, increases, speed, accuracy, and morale of the communicators also increase."[6]
- Communication does not automatically teach. Sometimes long-term efforts to acquaint the public with vital information results in little new learning. The process of curriculum improvement (Chapter 7) requires teaching of the highest order. Thus, if communication for curriculum improvement is to occur easily and be productive, it must rely on effective teaching.

The contents of communications can express more than the words say. Analysis of contents by groups of language specialists can identify the tone of what is being communicated. From the tone, a group can infer the values being expressed. The ideology of any organization readily shows through what is communicated.[7]

People have particular trouble finding intended meaning in that which goes into the hopper of communication. The problem is not simple ignorance of what, in general, is being said; it centers in the symbolism used by the communicator. For example, to the Inuit the rose is not likely to symbolize love.

Semanticists differentiate between extensional and intensional meaning. The former derives from what words presently stand for or connote. The latter is meaning one suggests to oneself "inside one's head." Communication is easily blocked by mistaking intensional meanings for extensional ones—what a word or phrase denotes (extensional meaning) may easily be different from what it connotes to the receiver of the communication (intensional meaning). The more a word or phrase's connotation varies from its denotation, or current familiar meaning, the more confusing or misleading it is likely to be.

The problem of meaning is encountered almost daily by the classroom teacher. What is in the pupil's head, lodged there by his or her experience within the culture, tends to determine what the pupil hears and absorbs. When the author was teaching English to high school pupils, he used excerpts from Sir Walter Scott's *Lady of the Lake* to determine whether the pupils in a class were getting what Scott had said. One excerpt read

> The stag at eve had drunk his fill,
> Where danced the moon on Monan's rill, ...

One pupil's background led him to this interpretation: "It was evening when an unmarried man who had drunk too much noticed the reflection of moonlight on the side of Monan's Grill" (and presumably went there for additional refreshment).

If there is trouble with words and phrases, trouble with ideas and sets of values is assured. For one thing, ideas and sets of values seem to be conveyed faster and more accurately in "settled" professions like medicine and law than in education. Several reasons might be advanced for this phenomenon: A vast body of respectable learnings, against which new ideas must be evaluated, has been accumulated; sources such as the leading professional journals command great respect; practitioners, who usually work alone, work cooperatively on occasion; and practitioners tend to be less secretive about professional lore. Teachers "talk shop" almost unremittingly, but they talk much more about problems than about reliable solutions to problems. In a new profession, especially one that involves the uncertainties of the social sciences, respect for what is communicated comes slowly. This is a fact with which communicators in education will have to reckon for a long time to come.

Several causes of communication breakdown have been identified. One is message competition. When a message to be communicated has to compete with other messages—a common phenomenon in these complex times—the intended message is almost certain to suffer from the competition. A second cause of communication breakdown originates in the ego or the status of the communicatee (receiver of the communication). A message that threatens the communicatee's ego or status in any way is not likely to be appreciated or even understood. A third difficulty is called erroneous expectation. People often "listen past" what a communicator has to say because they expect a message different from the one they are receiving. Finally, organizations are inclined to arrange complex communication systems in which so many links or separate communicators are placed in each communication chain that both the accuracy and the impact of messages are damaged.

Gregory Bateson's discussion of his theory of communication indicates how complicated the communication process really is. Bateson said that the meaning of a message depends on its context, that messages function at different logical levels in the thinking of communicatees, and that the subtleties found in playful discussion and in artistic and religious symbolism can make meaning uncertain. The communicatee may well say to the communicator, "In what code are you communicating this time?" Beneath this question are two other questions: "What does your remark really say or denote?" and "In what kind of social relationship are we operating just now?"[8]

Jerry L. Pulley suggested that there are five interference points in the communication process. The first point is the source—for example, individuals and groups with information to report. (Is the source trustworthy and authentic?) The second point is the message, encoded in words, graphics, body language, and other symbols. The third is the delivery system—print, electronic devices, conversations, or gestures. The receiver of the message constitutes the fourth point, where the message is beclouded by varying perceptions of individuals and groups. Reaction to the message is the fifth interference point. The receivers' reactions, which result in acceptance or rejection of the message, are naturally as variable as the people who do the receiving.[9]

Research data developed in schools, businesses, and industries indicate that people who communicate best understand that real communication starts with what other people need. Of course, effective communicators also concern themselves with presenting their own ideas clearly and with whether communicatees can take in what has been said. They know that, because communication is a form of exchange, they must have feedback from communicatees by whatever means seem promising.

The Particular Case of Schools

These general comments lead to discussion of the school as a particular site of and case in human communication. In schools, people communicate with one another to inform, to teach, to change attitudes, to get recognition, to urge participation, and to tap each other's ideas and creative energies. Schools rely a great deal on printed materials to convey their messages. When administrators and teachers encounter one another face to face, they may easily threaten one another by force of personality, status, or behavior. They may seem impatient, gruff, or harsh and may engage in duplicity or attempt to manipulate others. Receivers of communications are affected by fatigue, conflicting demands on their time, varying backgrounds of experience, and specific anxieties. Considering the formidable nature of these barriers, it is remarkable that communication, whether attempted in writing or attempted in person, proceeds as well as it does.

The length or extent of communication can be viewed in at least two ways: Some communicatees desire messages that are thorough and complete, whereas other communicatees want messages that are superficial and only generally informative. Messages of the former sort are for persons who are deeply involved in the task with which the message deals. Messages of the latter kind are for persons who merely want to hear about what is happening without becoming directly involved.

It is possible to concentrate on spreading facts that most people want to know, or to go into depth by conveying assumptions, values, and points of view. Thus a message may differ not only in the nature of its content but also in its depth. Facts may be communicated by means of letters, books, bulletins, or speakers. Assumptions, values, and points of view, which are much more difficult to convey, require interactive media like workshops, meetings, role playing, and demonstrations. Multiple interactive media provide reinforcement through direct contacts among human beings. Either a simple or a complex message may be subject to differences in perspective. These differences develop not only with reference to the differing roles of communicator and communicatee but also according to the position each occupies in the organizational hierarchy.[10]

If teachers are to understand the importance of communication within their schools, they first need to examine the role of communication within their own classrooms. Alert teachers have discovered that learning and communication can scarcely be separated, that language has great significance in revealing pupils' thinking processes, and that pupils' interaction and activity help them find meaning in what they are expected to do. Applied to the work of curriculum planners, these discoveries suggest that adults, like juveniles, learn as they communicate, use language revealingly, and become meaningfully involved as they strive to improve the curriculum.[11]

Teachers have opportunities to learn the difficulty of communicating when they try to convey school happenings to parents whose contact with formal education seems like ancient history. Basic communication skills, ethical and legal considerations, and regard for the feelings of parents come into play as teachers try to turn potentially disastrous conference sessions into rewarding ones.[12]

COMMUNICATION VIA PERSONAL CONTACT

Much evidence indicates that, where geography, time, and facilities permit, the most effective communication occurs through personal, face-to-face contact. This oldest form of communication is unlikely ever to be displaced by the other media. As a matter of fact, the mass media are usually most helpful when they reinforce communication by word of mouth. Many persons believe that nothing should be put in writing or otherwise widely publicized until it has been discussed, analyzed, and, if possible, experimented with. Discussion, with feedback to further discussion, greatly facilitates communication. Philip H. Phenix referred to communication as a "personal transaction"; thus "the real barriers to communication are not technical, but personal."[13] Interpersonal communication between two individuals conferring alone is subject to fewer hazards than communication between the same two individuals in a group setting.

Personal decision making is influenced mostly by what the members of one's intimate group are saying and doing.[14] People communicate most readily with individuals they like and trust.[15] Each person tends to find within his or her own group one or more friends with whom he or she can communicate easily. Also, people who share common interests often communicate effectively about matters relating to their interests. They feel an "emotional kinship" with and are usually geographically close to the persons with whom they communicate. All of this seems to make eminently good sense and is supported by findings in sociology and social psychology.

These realities underlie the efforts of the best business and industrial organizations to create networks of informal, or face-to-face, communication. People who communicate informally and are on a first-name basis tend to be better able to work together to share information, make decisions, and then take action. In the best of organizations, informal contact among people who need to work together is encouraged, management personnel are expected to seek interpersonal relationships with employees, and furniture and writing materials that invite small-group planning are provided. To a degree, these organizations *force* communication when it does not occur naturally.[16]

The introduction of the Internet, a massive computer network, has increased contacts among individuals near and far. The Internet had reached nearly 150 countries by the mid 1990s.[17]

Toward Depth in Interpersonal Communication

The depths of communication through personal contact have been too little explored. Decades ago, Carl Rogers presented a paper that has remained a classic in the field of interpersonal communication. Rogers argued that the basic difficulty with human communication is our tendency to judge and evaluate—promptly and recklessly—the comments made by other people. The result is that people "miss each other in psychological space," failing to understand each other because each person is busy evaluating what the other person has said. Rogers suggested that real communication occurs only when people pause to listen to each other with an attempt at understanding. To achieve ability to listen, he suggested the following experiment:

The next time you get into an argument with your wife, or your friend, or with a small group of friends, just stop the discussion for a moment, and for an experiment, institute this rule. "Each person can speak up for himself only *after* he has first restated the ideas and feelings of the previous speaker accurately, and to that speaker's satisfaction." You see what this would mean. It would simply mean that before presenting your own point of view, it would be necessary for you to really achieve the other speaker's frame of reference—to understand his thoughts and feelings so well that you could summarize them for him. Sounds simple, doesn't it? But if you try it, you will discover it one of the most difficult things you have ever tried to do. However, once you have been able to see the other's point of view, your own comments will have to be drastically revised. You will also find the emotion going out of the discussion, the differences being reduced, and those differences which remain being of a rational and understandable sort.[18]

The listener needs both a sensitive ear and the ability to observe carefully. He or she should concentrate not only on the meanings of words but also on the meanings of behaviors. What does body posture tell? What are the hands of the conferee saying? What emotional tone does the voice quality communicate? Are there silent symbols in eye contacts, pauses, and hesitations? Does the behavior of the speaker suggest that he or she is relaxed, or tense, or threatened? What would the speaker say if he or she sincerely expressed what he or she is feeling and thinking? Are there clues about subconscious motivation?

From the world of business comes reinforcement of the conclusion that oral communication between individuals is influenced most by three factors: the quality of listening, the nature of the message, and the emotional behavior of either person.[19] As to the significance of emotional behavior, investigations of the meanings of people's body language have revealed patterns of their use of hands, eyes, eyebrows, facial expressions, and postures to communicate ideas. One psychologist estimates that the emotional impact of a message may be 7 percent verbal, 38 percent vocal, and 55 percent facial. Clothes and hairstyles are thought to tell more than we once realized about people's viewpoints and values. Experimenters have played back recorded voices with the sound filtered in order to study voice tone independently. Some observers report that Americans tend to "dim their lights" (shift their gaze) when they walk along crowded streets; that the English customarily stare and blink when conversing; and that Oriental conversationalists scarcely look at each other. A keen observer comments about a friend, "You think Sam is calm until you watch his left foot." The examples above are classified as *proximics* when they refer to the personal space individuals need when they associate with each other, and as *kinesics* when they refer to body language.

In listening to what other people say, the curriculum worker needs to avoid six bad habits described in a pioneering and classic book on listening:

1. Faking attention, or pretending to listen
2. Listening for facts without considering broader meanings
3. Overconcentrating on physical appearance and delivery at the expense of attending to verbal content
4. Yielding to distraction
5. Dismissing content as uninteresting
6. Ceasing to listen because the content is hard to comprehend[20]

Both in conversations in the teachers' rooms of school buildings and in formally organized meetings for reporting progress, effective listening can contribute greatly to staff development.

Role playing is an important means by which communication on a person-to-person basis can be facilitated. There is often a real advantage in reversing the roles to which two individuals are accustomed so that the participants may begin to perceive a situation from each other's viewpoint. For instance, a teacher who has participated in and supported an experimental project may defend it blindly, while a nonparticipant who has had absolutely no contact with the project may attack it bitterly. If the two agree to reverse their roles in a discussion of the project, each may be led to modify his or her extreme point of view, and they may then be able to talk together more cogently.[21]

The principal of a school is in a unique position to help create a climate in which people can communicate, as well as to take a personal interest in problems that have implications for larger groups. The subtleties of communication within the individual school remain, in part, a mystery. The story is told of a principal, who thought he was on the best of terms with his staff, saying "Good morning" to a teacher, only to overhear her ask a co-worker, "Now what did he mean by that?" Recent research on the nature of effective schools has shown that the need to improve communication pervades lists of principals' duties.[22]

Face-to-face communication with persons who are either above or distant from oneself in the hierarchy is even more difficult than most other communication because distance increases psychological static. Teachers often imagine strange things about other teachers and administrators whom they seldom see. A common if secret question is "I wonder how I stand with my colleagues and my bosses?" Social science research has shown that communication is improved by knowing how one is viewed by others, especially by persons in authority. It is improved also by knowing which actions are permissible and which are taboo. One of life's most frustrating experiences is to find, belatedly, that a decision that an individual or a group has laboriously reached is beyond the authority and responsibility of that individual or group.

Ernest R. House listed several propositions concerning influence that leads to innovation in schools and, consequently, to curriculum change. The first two state that diffusion of innovations depends on face-to-face personal contact and that "transportation routes," or channels of communication, as well as the ways schools are organized, help to condition face-to-face personal contact. Another of his propositions suggests that innovation can be increased or decreased by interpersonal contact.[23] Certainly, in a world in which people mingle freely with each other, face-to-face communication will remain without equal as a medium for transmitting subtle cognitive and affective content. The quality of face-to-face communication must, however, be improved radically in times like these, when ideas and values are undergoing rapid change. If a leader has a vision, he or she usually has an opportunity to communicate it to the school staff. When the communication has occurred, the leader needs to work toward the vision's realization and implementation. Failure to do so puts the leader in the category of the boy who cried "Wolf, wolf!" when there was no wolf.[24]

It is important for curriculum leaders to know how they appear to others during interpersonal contacts. Five possibilities were identified by the developers of the Administrator Empathy Discrimination Index. The leader may appear evaluative, behaving as a commander-in-chief; instructive, behaving as a know-it-all; placating, being a consoler; probing, serving as an interrogator; or understanding, thereby appearing to level himself or herself to the position or status of the other person.

The effectiveness of contact between individuals depends a great deal on the interdependence they develop. Interdependence comes from sharing, which can be brought about by teaming people, providing for their frequent and regular interaction, and assigning responsibilities to them commonly or jointly.[25] Constructive group work has proved helpful in the pairing of individuals who have similar interests and abilities.

Face-to-face communication sometimes begins with one-to-one conferences. From there, it may move to group conferences, presentation of ideas with subsequent comparison of notes, and group work of the kinds described in Chapter 11. Schools in New Haven, Connecticut used four media for achieving face-to-face communication among staff and parents: city-wide curriculum forums, curriculum advisory councils, a parents' center, and Curriculum Monday. The first two media are being utilized in a number of school systems; the other two are almost unique. The Parents' Center, housed in an old building near Yale University, was opened to increase communication among parents, teachers, and supervisors, who did what they could to make it a nonthreatening environment. The third Monday of each month was declared Curriculum Monday, a day on which subject matter supervisors visited the schools to talk about curriculum matters with staff members.[26]

A research study in British Columbia revealed the modes that parents prefer for communicating with school personnel about mastery of the curriculum by their children. The three most preferred modes were direct contact by telephone or in person, parent-teacher conferencing, and service by parents as school volunteers. Of the remaining seven preferred modes, four were clearly of an interpersonal kind.[27] Information about what parents and other community members think of the school curriculum has been acquired in several ways: by using specially prepared survey forms; by interviewing "key communicators," who are presumably the most knowledgeable people; by placing reaction cards in public places; by making random telephone calls; and by establishing hotline telephone systems.

Generally, the modes or media are less important than the accuracy of the message. After years of experience in using euphemisms in written and oral communication, educators are being asked today whether they are telling the truth about test results, incompetence hidden (or sometimes very evident) in teaching staffs, flagrant waste of pupil and teacher time, and unwise expenditure of scarce funds. Unkind and unjustified comments we will have with us always, but it is foolish to draw additional fire from people who could be sterling friends of the schools.[28]

SITUATION 10-1

The Storms at Stoneham Center

The April faculty meeting at Stoneham Center Elementary School was about to get under way. At least the clock said it should. But Ed Ringo, the new young principal, had not yet arrived.

"He must have had a flat tire again," remarked Elsie Kingsland, the oldest member of the group.

"Always excusing Mr. Ringo's actions, aren't you?" retorted Mr. Kermit.

Mr. Kermit's remark proved to be the gun that opened another battle. When Ed Ringo arrived breathlessly thirty-five minutes later, he found a donnybrook in progress. Ed had already learned that there were two or three troublemakers in the faculty of twenty-four, and Mr. Kermit was one of them. Originally, Ed had hoped to team the teachers in groups of three or four so that they could exchange ideas, engage in some simple experimentation, and ease the problem of continuity among grade levels. Abstractly, the idea was excellent, but it apparently could not work at Stoneham Center—not right now, anyway.

Next, Ed thought of organizing informal grade-level meetings simply to share ideas about good teaching. Miss Perry, who seemed to be a ringleader for evil causes, had sabotaged that idea by remarking at the February faculty meeting, "I wouldn't be caught giving my best ideas to anyone. Let other people learn for themselves. I always erase my blackboard as promptly as I can so no one will have a chance to borrow what I do."

"Face-to-face communication!" thought Ed. "Only twenty-four teachers and I can't get most of them to have anything to do with one another. What can I do?"

Discuss the Stoneham Center problem as you see it.

Ed asked the question "What can I do?" How should he behave just to keep the situation from growing worse?

What other question or questions might Ed have asked?

If you were in Ed's place, what long-range plans would you make for improving interpersonal communication among the twenty-four teachers and the principal?

ACTIVITY 10-1

Interpersonal Effects of Some Interpersonal Communications

Indicate orally or in writing the responses you think a supervisor might expect and deserve from teachers to whom she has written the following individual communications:

> Perhaps you and I could confer about ways children can spend their time in classrooms so they stay out of trouble. I'm convinced the real curriculum of the classroom genuinely affects discipline. Do you want to talk with me about some ideas you and other teachers have used in selecting what children are to learn?
>
> Beginning Tuesday at 9 A. M., please send your plan book to me through your grade leader. Every other Monday thereafter, your plans will be due. For information, see your copy of our "General Rules for Planning and Use of Plan Books."
>
> Teach something new today! Innovation will make a big difference to your pupils, believe me! We are all being paid to innovate.

COMMUNICATION WITHIN SCHOOLS AS ORGANIZATIONS

If communication between and among individuals is complex, we may conclude that whenever the phenomena of communication and miscommunication appear within an organization, the complexity increases. In elementary and secondary education, the organization is usually identified as a department, an entire school, or a school system. Inasmuch as good communication does not occur automatically, it needs to be planned. Its object is to spread the word in all necessary respects about curriculum improvement events wherever they occur within the system.

Most communication activities within school systems are hit or miss. Occasionally, however, a school system or an individual school organizes a committee on communication that plans and coordinates a series of communication activities. In general, the planning should take into account criteria like these:

• *The media of communication used to disseminate information about curriculum projects should depend on the special purposes to be served.* Brief written reports may be used for one purpose, tape recordings for another, individual contacts with staff members for another, news bulletins for another, and meetings for still another. As Louis Forsdale said, "Appropriate communication behavior in one situation, with one audience, for one kind of purpose, is not necessarily appropriate in another setting with another audience for another purpose."[29]

• *Communication units should be kept small.* This criterion applies in both large and small school organizations. Groups with a membership of over forty persons tend to have problems with communication. Seven to ten persons may constitute optimum size for a group. However, some different viewpoints and talents should be sought in groups, because they enrich feedback, which in turn produces further improvement in communication.

• *Messages should usually be brief, direct, and pointed.* There is no sense in using more words than necessary. Several brief messages are often more effective than a single comprehensive one. The nature of the message definitely affects the degree of cooperation or compliance.[30]

• *Ample time for communication is decidedly necessary.* Face-to-face contacts, the preparation of written messages, and the use of electronic devices all require time.

• *Both formal and informal communication channels should be employed.* An example of the former is the prearranged faculty meeting for sharing understandings and insights; an example of the latter is permitting teachers to assemble where they wish, in groups of differing sizes and constituent personnel, to discuss curriculum problems that concern them.

• *Lines of communication should be kept short.* This criterion applies especially to vertical communication, which is aided by decreasing the number of hierarchical levels through which the message must pass from bottom to top and from top to bottom in the organization. For example, what happens in a faculty meeting in School X could easily be reported to the Curriculum Steering Committee without being told and retold to numerous intermediaries.

• *Some persons or groups should watch over communication activities in the school or school system.* Without supervision and perspective, planning and coordination are likely to go awry. Perhaps the best answer is formation of a central committee on communication. However, much care should be exercised to ensure that members of such a committee are not merely unwilling representatives of faculties or departments.

• *Emergent communicators should be sought among members of the staff.* Experience indicates that certain personnel do very well as communicators. They need only an invitation to serve an ongoing organization whose purpose is improved communication.

• *Invention is needed in developing new communication practices.* So little has been reported during recent years concerning communication practices in school systems that persons responsible for communication are finding it increasingly necessary to develop new practices of their own.

In the West Orange, New Jersey curriculum improvement program of the early 1950s, a committee on communication reported that the following methods of communication were in use:

• Brief written reports are issued at intervals to persons who request them. Frequently, these are summaries of the recent work of action groups.
• Teacher members of the Central Curriculum Committee confer with teachers and principals in the schools they represent. Often, the

conferences are in the nature of informal conversations held wherever people meet. Sometimes, there are small groups meeting in lunchrooms. At other times, they are more formally organized portions of faculty meetings. One of the advantages of conferences in the local school is that they capitalize on face-to-face, two-way communication.

- Members of the CCC are instrumental in maintaining curriculum bulletin boards in local schools and in displaying curriculum materials on office counters, in school libraries, and in teachers' restrooms.
- Leaders and other key persons in action groups are sometimes invited to attend meetings of the Central Curriculum Committee to report for their groups and receive advice and promises of assistance. Hearing the reports and the discussions of reports of action by group members is helpful to communication between groups, between groups and the CCC, and between CCC members and the staffs of local schools.
- Other agents of communication include status persons who discuss curriculum projects in meetings and in less formal situations. The supervisor of elementary education, for example, attends many action group meetings and subsequently, in supervisory meetings which she herself calls, encourages participants in curriculum activities to share information and insights with nonparticipants.
- Action group recorders have been given limited training. Reports of meetings prepared by recorders are sent to the central curriculum office where they are duplicated and forwarded to CCC members, Institute [Horace Mann-Lincoln Institute of School Experimentation] personnel, and action group members who are directly concerned with the matter being reported.
- Tape recordings are sometimes made of summaries of group decisions, curriculum proposals, or teacher-made units. Recordings which might be of interest to large groups of staff members are then transferred to discs for playback in local schools. An example is a disc reporting the development of a social studies unit.
- An informal news bulletin is issued irregularly to all staff members. This bulletin would have more attention if communication committee members felt that written materials had a great deal of value for communication purposes, but the tendency has been to distrust the written word as a communication medium.
- One work conference has been tried, partly as a communication device. The evaluation of the work conference on reading held in February 1951 showed that it was valuable enough to be worth repeating. Similar conferences, and even more elaborate ones, are tentatively scheduled for the future.[31]

The methods just described seem to have been suitable in the West Orange situation; variations on these communication procedures may prove useful in other school systems. Research has revealed additional ideas that may affect organization for communication:

- Theoretical communication structures are not necessarily the actual ones. Considerable study is needed to determine just how communication is occurring.[32]
- Big schools and school systems do not necessarily suffer from malcommunication because of their size. In a study of school administration, "communication problems were reported somewhat less frequently in the larger schools than in the smaller schools."[33] This is true because larger schools may be better organized.
- Curriculum planners should become acquainted with the teaching situations of the members of planning groups so that they may know the experiential backgrounds that influence the members' words and actions.[34]
- Status affects communication. Information and ideas initiated by top-level administrators move into channels of communication more readily than information and ideas initiated by teachers.[35]
- Of the means of communication, individual school faculty meetings are primary.[36]
- If communication is to proceed upward, downward, and horizontally, the organizational structure of the school may have to be adjusted to permit a wide-ranging flow of messages.[37]
- Several key actions need to be taken initially in planning communication systems. They include making clear statements of goals to be achieved, assessing specific needs for communication, designating responsibility for communication activities, striving to build credibility, determining staff members' communication rights, and opening the most suitable communication channels.[38]

The state of Texas has tried to organize a communication system to benefit both the state's Education Agency and local school districts. Convinced that these clients needed information about curriculum planning and "decision support," the State Board of Education organized the Public Education Information Management System.[39]

Wedemeyer and Bossert took a future view of the designing of communication systems. Defining *transportation* as moving people to experience and *telecommunication* as moving experience to people, they said that the basic physical and psychological welfare of people should be the first consideration in developing a communication system. Other, more specific considerations are giving attention to personal or private threats, providing facilitation via telecommunication, arranging for data storage and retrieval, keeping information current, and putting the receiver in definite control of the media. When the receiver (recipient) is in control, he or she is operating within a "demand-pull" rather than a "supply-push" system.[40]

There are several practical steps that creators of communication systems may take in opening a school to free communication. The first is to observe what channels of communication presently exist. Some channels are natural and obvious, others are hidden. One of the usual channels is a pattern of relationships among teachers who have known and trusted one another a long time. Computer networks are proving useful in disseminating information among personnel.[41] With the passage of time, the projected information super highway will contribute to communication with and among schools.

When a promising communication channel has been identified, a way of entering it must be found. Frequently, the medium of entry is a faculty member who is experienced, knowledgeable, and respected. Next, the channel must be put to use. Much of the use is necessarily vertical, with messages coming from the top of the organization down or going from the bottom up. Thus the person serving as the medium for the communication of a message may receive that message from the principal or other top administrator, or he or she may receive it from new faculty members whose uncertain status puts them at the bottom of the hierarchy. The message can easily be blocked by the malfeasance or misfeasance of persons anywhere in the channel. Hypersensitivity to disturbing messages on the part of the top administrator is especially likely to bring about blocking. Finally, as a means of assessing the quantity and quality of communication, a system of evaluation needs to be established.

Experience in curriculum work suggests the following summary guidelines for organizing improved communication arrangements:

1. Emphasize good human relations. This is fundamental.
2. Make exchange of ideas the major goal of the system.
3. Communicate with people at the levels of their interest and understanding.
4. Be as sure as possible that a message that is sent is received.
5. Use varied communication media.
6. Decide whether a message should be talked about or put in writing.
7. Provide needed facilities, materials, and services.
8. Schedule time for communication.
9. Make every message clear.
10. Make the materials that convey each message attractive.

SITUATION 10-2

Influencing the Eighty-Nine, Less Seven

As a school leader, you have worked with a committee in your school to achieve ungrading (nongrading). You and the committee hope that next year the pupils in your school will be grouped three ways: in large groups to receive mass instruction, in small groups to explore meaning, and in two- to three-person teams to complete projects. The former school grades will be ignored to permit newly created organized groups of learners to include pupils of widely differing ages.

You and the committee need to influence the other members of your school faculty to accept this proposal and to cooperate in making the necessary changes. The total teacher population of the school, including aides, numbers eighty-nine. How can you and the committee members, consisting of seven teachers, communicate with the remaining eighty-two so that they are constructively influenced?

SITUATION 10-3

A Plan for Banksdale

Banksdale Central School District had two high schools, five junior high schools, sixteen elementary schools, and a pupil population of about 15,750. Under the guidance of an assistant superintendent in charge of curriculum and instruction, thirteen recognized curriculum projects were under way. "Recognition" of the projects was the responsibility of a central curriculum committee. The members of the committee knew that, in addition to the thirteen acknowledged projects, there must be numerous other more informal ones, chiefly at the individual school level. Like many central steering committees, the Banksdale committee discovered that not only were they and other school personnel ignorant of such curriculum improvement activity in schools other than their own, but few school faculty members were even acquainted with faculty members of other schools in the district.

Some of the discussion in a central committee meeting went as follows:

Member A: How is it I'm just hearing of the work the teachers in Pleasant Valley School are doing in science? Science is my field.

Member B: The bigger the system becomes, the worse off we'll be. Imagine trying to keep track of all the things happening in the different schools. I guess we'll just sit here and talk to ourselves without knowing what's going on.

Member C: Stewartsville has solved the whole problem. They have a staff publication that tells what's happening. I recommend that we get someone to serve as editor of a publication of our own. Each of us could be a news representative.

Member A: I have a better idea. People don't want to read. Let's tape reports of what's going on and mail the tapes each month to every school for playback in faculty meetings.

Member D: But the teachers in our schools don't even know one another! Hadn't we better begin by introducing ourselves to one another?

Indicate which of the comments made by the committee members seem to you to make sense.

What other ideas can you think of? Simply list them without any effort to organize them into a communication complex.

In a school system the size of Banksdale, what steps do you consider absolutely essential in organizing a program to improve communication about instructional matters? If your proposals can be expressed in chart form, make a chart of your organization for communication.

HOW MESSAGES ARE COMMUNICATED

To this point, the present chapter has dealt with two topics—who sends messages and who receives them. We turn now to the ways messages are sent and received.

How do people in the society at large communicate with one another? The means that come to mind include words, both oral and printed; diagrams, drawings, tables, and charts; symbols, such as highway signs and punctuation marks; gestures, such as pointing; photographs, pictures, and displays; colors, such as the green, yellow, and red of a traffic signal; sounds, such as laughter, groans, music, and whistles; personal appearance or dress; insignia and regalia; facial expressions; and overt behavior.

The most common medium is, of course, face-to-face conversation. After that, the list includes speeches, telephone calls, radio and television programs, letters, telegrams, cablegrams, memoranda, newspapers, computer printouts, motion pictures and other audiovisual aids, bulletins, brochures, pamphlets, monographs, books, and magazines. These stock means and media have now been supplemented with additional devices of a new era—the information age. Television transmission by way of satellite, wide-ranging uses of computers, and the new features associated with the information superhighway have appeared in our era of sophisticated technology. The face that information can now be had by masses of people everywhere places new demands on communicators to sort information, to plot its use, and to monitor its effects.[42]

In schools and school systems throughout the United States, communication of facts, ideas, values, feelings, and attitudes occurs commonly through literary and electronic media. Discussion of the usual curriculum documents and other written materials, the oldest medium, appears below. Discussion of electronic and other technological aids will follow and will be succeeded in turn by a listing and identification of less well-known literary materials.

Customary Literary Materials

In the early days of organized curriculum improvement programs, the chief method of formal communication was the writing and "installation" of courses of study, which were conceived as detailed and prescriptive statements of the required activities of teachers and pupils in classrooms and, occasionally, in other sites in and about the school. The customary procedure was to "have a committee of representative teachers . . . meet with one or more of the assistant superintendents and with the director of the subject, if there [was] a director. The course thus prepared [was] submitted to the board of superintendents for approval and this [went] to the school committee (board of education) for authority to print as a school document."[43] The course of study was then "installed" by transmitting to school staffs a mandate from a highly placed school official and sometimes by conducting meetings to emphasize the importance of the document.

The real problem with courses of study has been that they have too often found their way into the bottom drawers of teachers' desks rather than into their nervous systems and thus into the ongoing activities of teachers and pupils. Despite this, prescriptive courses of study continue to be produced in a sizable number of U.S. school systems both large and small. Theoretically, at least, curriculum workers now believe it is as foolish to legislate educational experiences for a large group of children simultaneously as it is to prescribe physical treatment aimlessly for numbers of children who are suffering from malnutrition. They recognize that courses of study tend to be repetitious of other courses of study, matching the tables of contents of leading textbooks. Scissors and pots of paste are too often the chief tools with which unthinking, uncreative "curriculum builders" borrow ideas formulated by other people. Rigid courses of study are still being perpetuated partly because administrators find them useful in achieving uniformity (or alleged uniformity) in educational experiences, in facilitating the orientation of new teachers, and in pacifying critical lay groups who want to be certain about "what our children are learning." The wise administrator knows that, after a limited period of taking instruction, teachers are likely to do what they want to do when the classroom door is closed. There is no such thing as idea-tight, uniform administration of the curriculum.

The need in any era is for curriculum documents that truly communicate. Armstrong and Shutes prepared the Curriculum Document Assessment Instrument, which they invite curriculum workers to use freely; it is not copyrighted or otherwise legally protected. The instrument consists of twelve criteria that should prove helpful in assessing the quality of documents:

1. Legitimacy of the document
2. Credibility of the developers
3. Specification of intended learners
4. Specification of intended users
5. Specification of document purpose
6. Scope of document coverage
7. Labeling of contents
8. Consistency with other curriculum documents
9. Clarity and usability of format and organization
10. Maintenance of internal consistency
11. Specification of intended document use
12. Evidence of professional editing and reproduction

The meanings of these criteria are expounded in the article in which they appear.[44]

The documents that communicate curriculum ideas include curriculum guides; statements of philosophy, aims, and objectives; policy statements; resource units; research reports; lists of teaching materials; newsletters; and booklets and brochures. Of this long list, curriculum guides have attracted the most interest and effort.

Curriculum guides, which are intended to be less prescriptive than courses of study, enunciate principles, guidelines, and suggested actions. They contain hints and aids of all sorts, such as lists of books, brochures, articles, and audio-visual materials. Students of curriculum planning should examine several guides and several courses of study to see the distinction between the two kinds of documents. Neither guides nor courses of study are in themselves capable of providing curriculum sequence, and their contents are not usually based on research findings. Special education, early childhood education, drug abuse education, and alcohol education are content elements for which numbers of guides have been produced during recent years. In an era of heavier emphasis on science, mathematics, and other academic subjects, large numbers of guides have resulted from idea development in financially supported instructional projects.

A redeeming feature of guide making is that teachers are being increasingly involved in generating and trying out ideas. In fact, the keynote of guide making is involvement of staff. Because it is difficult to communicate to others either the substance or the spirit of an experience, staff members of school systems should be involved at different levels of operation and in different ways in experiencing the development and communication of ideas. Schools should search for methods of involving staff members freely and vitally. The staffs should be helped to suggest ideas, try them, and describe them in writing, in addition to participating in meetings for planning, preparing, and evaluating innovative guides, and feeding back suggestions for improving the guides. Most curriculum guides should contain blank pages on which teachers can write their reactions and suggestions, which can then be communicated to the persons mainly responsible for guide making.

The tendency of teachers to ignore guides has caused curriculum planners to give greater attention than they did originally to the quality of the guides being produced. Guides can be improved through meticulous need determination, careful selection of writers, early communication with potential recipients, and tryout of finished documents.[45] Many guides contain the following features: introductory explanations, overviews of content, indications of content sequence, generalizations and concepts to be taught, possible instructional approaches, and proposed evaluation procedures.[46]

Fenwick English condemned curriculum guides as a waste, accusing them of being "unfriendly" to users, poor in quality, little used by even the people who prepare them, expensive of time and money, and based on what English terms "the myth of local control." Instead of guides, he proposed using curriculum alignment materials designed to relate content and testing closely so that administrators can be more certain that teachers are doing what curriculum planners expect them to do.[47]

Given such criticisms, planners are attempting to prepare guides that are genuinely useful and acceptable. The most useful guides are usually planned in great detail before pen is put to paper. The kind of guide to be prepared, what is to be included in it, how acceptance of the guide can be encouraged, and how its real worth can be gauged are important consider-ations.[48] The ideal curriculum guide places emphasis on freeing teachers to think, on extending their range of operation, on developing their teaching skills, and on challenging them to try ideas that are new to them and then to report results.

Other literary media that have become commonplace in enlightened school systems include statements of philosophy, of goals, and of objectives. Beliefs about the role and purpose of the system or the school appear in these statements. The beliefs need to be restated occasionally in revised form to help prevent the system or the school from stumbling along without direction under changing social conditions.

Philosophy, in this instance, reflects the general beliefs held by people (especially local people) concerning what schools ought to be. Goals indicate the direction or directions in which persons responsible for a school or a school system are seeking to go. More specific than philosophy, goals are less specific than objectives, which should be formulated where learning occurs. The most logical creators of objectives are practicing teachers and their aides, assisted, of course, by pupils.

Media Provided by Technology

A century ago, it would have been impossible for media of a mechanical sort to rival written materials. In our century, audiovisual materials have been used increasingly to supplement literary ones in attempts to communicate curriculum data and ideas. Marshall McLuhan referred to our electronic age as being dominated by auditory forms rather than by the centuries-old linear and pictorial forms.

The way communication has been changing is exemplified by evolution of learning centers. Learning centers in schools have become much more than libraries housing books and magazines. They are, in fact, centers where all sorts of instructional materials, including computers, can be found. The computer is appealing increasingly to those who want to gain statistical information or summaries of information quickly.

When they are interviewed, curriculum leaders say they need the best and the latest in technology to improve communication among schools and school systems. They express four specific needs:

1. The need for "distance learning," through which curriculum committees can see and hear about bright, relevant ideas developed in other school districts in the region and the nation
2. The need for closer contact with centers of knowledge (e.g., university institutes, government data banks, resource and materials centers, and research data repositories)
3. The need for conference-by-telephone arrangements that permit the participants to see one another and to see displays of data

4. The need for interactive communication with other nations in which productive curriculum study and planning are under way

Technology is moving rapidly to satisfy needs like these. In an era in which there is simply too much printed material, improved transmission of both the human voice and nonvocal messages, together with greatly improved storage capabilities of new generations of computers, has become a priority of communication technology. Three of the most promising of recent developments are the advent of digital transmission, fiber optics, and more powerful and adaptable computers.[49]

Digital Transmission

The genesis of digital transmission was the introduction of pulse code modulation in radio communication between Dover, England and Calais, France during the invasion of Europe in World War II. Commercialization of digital transmission was delayed until the late 1950s, when the American Telephone and Telegraph Company used metallic conductors for the purpose. Use of digital transmission has increased; probably by the end of the 1990s, all major telephone interconnection networks in the United States will have been converted to the digital mode.

Fiber Optics

To provide the conductive medium for high-speed digital transmission, Corning Glass Company developed a replacement for copper wire: namely, fiber glass drawn so fine that each fiber is not much thicker than a human hair. By transmitting modulated light, fiber glass is capable of carrying thousands of messages along each individual fiber. With the cost of this medium declining rapidly, President Bush urged, in late 1989, the development of high-speed fiber optic networks to link university, corporate, and government research centers. As new networks become more sophisticated, new techniques will be needed to facilitate access. Access is predicated on a block distribution system bearing the colorful name "fiber-to-the-curb." The long-term effect of universal use of this medium will be a stable arrangement characterized by accuracy of transmission, economy, and freedom from environmental interference. The prospect for computer use is much enhanced. In their desire to increase fiber-based transmission, the British are using former water troughs along railroad tracks to carry fiber cables between major cities.

More Powerful and Adaptable Computers

New generations of large computers will use laser-beam interconnections to provide centers with immense memory and multiple access. At the same time, personal computers are becoming more powerful and adaptable. These advances will permit economy of operation, reduction of time spent, and easy retrieval of information. Time-sharing, or "renting" time, on large computers will become a common means of storing and distributing data. The massive memory and storage capabilities of today's computers make the procedures used in many huge projects—such as manufacture of the 747 jet—largely outdated. Gone are the days when designing and producing a plane like the 747 required a quantity of paper weighing more than the completed aircraft.

The implications of these developments for the transfer of curriculum data and cooperation of personnel are impressive. Purchase or "rental" of time on mainframe computers will permit clients to receive selected information on demand in any quantity they desire. Both raw data and abstracts of finished documents will be available. Panels of specialists, widely scattered throughout the nation, can be "assembled" to respond to curriculum proposals and to answer questions; conversations can occur in traditional form or in computer language. When curriculum leaders communicate internationally, they will be able to rely on machines to convert and interpret different languages. Cooperative planning on an international scale will become genuinely feasible because of the speed with which ideas can be transmitted and then altered after consultation. The quantity of paperwork will be reduced significantly. In summary, the information age will give curriculum planners easy access to previously undiscovered data, to experts in subject and other fields, to curriculum specialists elsewhere, to groups of curriculum workers simultaneously, to ways of sorting and combining data, and to facilities for transmitting visual images.

The future of the newer technology holds some startling possibilities. Advances will probably occur in computer chip and fiber optic technologies. Soon, desktop computers will gain the power of the modern supercomputer. Data will be transmitted at lightning speed and will consist of printed materials, images, and sounds. The much-touted information superhighway will permit teachers and pupils to "travel to London," "browse" through the Library of Congress, "attend" an art show, or "go to" a conference in Geneva without leaving their classrooms. Meanwhile, computer users in educational institutions will communicate with one another by way of the Internet. The ease with which curriculum theory and practice will be able to be communicated at a number of levels is striking. Pupils will contribute to curriculum planning by creating "living experiences," as opposed to the predigested ones found in textbooks. More and more, the challenge is not lack of information but wise decision making as to what information to use in planning.[50]

SITUATION 10-4

How Can They Present It Most Effectively?

The kindergarten-through-twelfth-grade Language Arts Committee of the Eberville Consolidated Schools has been conducting experiments in the teaching of linguistics. Individual members of the committee have found that pupils in the fifth, eighth, and tenth grades—the grades in which experiments have been tried—are making unusual progress in understanding and interpreting the structure of English. On a Tuesday afternoon in January, they meet in the office of Mrs. James, the language coordinator, to plan means of attracting the interest and enthusiasm of other teachers on the Eberville staff.

"We can't possibly describe what we've done," says a tenth-grade teacher.

"No, we can't," replies an eighth-grade teacher. "The method we've used is strange enough to make analysis of English look like analysis of a strange language. Just the vocabulary we use presents a problem: *determiners, verb signals, patterns of writing,* and so on. Maybe we should buy copies of the books by Paul Roberts, Henry Lee Smith, and Charles Fries and ask the teachers to read them so they'll understand what we're talking about. I'm convinced that the linguistic approach to teaching the structure of English is just what we need, but I've almost given up trying to convince other people who are entirely new to it."

After some discussion, Mrs. James suggests that the committee think about its communication problem between now and the next week. "Concentrate on written and pictorial ways of communicating with our teachers," Mrs. James says as the meeting concludes.

What is the first step you would take in helping people who have used a formal grammatical approach for many years to become acquainted with a new method of language analysis?

What written or pictorial material would you hope to see prepared to give teachers an opportunity for careful study of the new method?

What additional long-term learning opportunities would you need to provide?

Relatively Less Familiar Literary Media

Though less familiar to personnel in school systems than are courses of study, curriculum guides, statements of philosophy, and lists of goals and objectives, some other literary media have proved useful in systems in which thorough, careful communication is prized. Descriptions of several of them follow.

Policy Statements

Policy statements are frequently enunciated by committees or task forces that compile instructional and other policies from school system records and from the expectations of school and community personnel. Today, an abbreviated kind of policy statement, a summary of important committee decisions, is being produced. The more open the system under which teachers and others do their curriculum planning, the shorter and less stringent policy statements are likely to be. General agreements, which can be altered without major difficulty, usually suffice in guiding curriculum development. Teachers' unions sometimes add to "official" policy statements their own statements highlighting particular terms of contracts they have negotiated.

Recommendations concerning policy can sometimes be found in reports to the community and other groups. Cases in point are a manual prepared in Manitoba and a survey report about bilingual education written in Texas.[51]

Resource Units

Resource units are "master" units designed to be used by teachers as resources in preparing units for classroom use. Individual teachers and groups of teachers write resource units that contain descriptions of the nature of the unit problem, purposes of the unit in developing understandings, skills, and attitudes, sequence of the subject matter content, nature of pupil experiences within the unit, methods of teaching the unit, resources (written and other) for learning, and ways of evaluating the learning experiences. State departments of education and the education departments of industries prepare resource units that form valuable starting points in developing more precise and usable teaching units.

Statements of learning rationale help to make resource units more realistic by identifying worthwhile instructional tasks. These statements clarify what learners are to do to master subject matter content. Furthermore, they set a level of quality that is to be achieved in the teaching-learning process, and they point to needed changes in curriculum plans.[52] For example, a resource guide for programs to challenge the gifted and talented originated in Hawaii, and resource manuals on the education of exceptional children came from Georgia.[53]

Research and Survey Reports

Reports of research activities assume varied forms: articles in journals, photocopied statements for staff distribution, and survey reports, to mention a few. For a number of years, grants from foundations and the federal government spurred issuance of printed reports on subjects such as team teaching and educational television. Obviously, most school system research reports originate in systems that can afford the time, energy, and money required to conduct research.

Some of the best information on research and surveys of practice is contained in state-sponsored reports, such as that of the New York State Education Department concerning English composition. Some reports use previously collected evidence to support an extension of educational services. An example is a West Virginia report entitled *Beyond Special Education Compliance*.[54]

Lists of Teaching Materials

Teaching materials lists are often formulated in a materials center in a school or school system for use throughout the organization. Names of books, magazines, films, filmstrips, still pictures, tape recordings, and other learning aids are presented to teachers on annotated master lists. Nationally, the Association for Supervision and Curriculum Development has periodically distributed lists of the newer teaching and learning materials of interest to curriculum specialists.

Newsletters

Newsletters have become more common as communication has become more informal. They contain items of interest, briefly stated. Sometimes they are humorous; sometimes they achieve a personal tone by referring to staff members by their first names. One advocate of newsletters as a communication device recommended that they approach discussion topics positively, be printed or duplicated on paper of an appropriate color, and begin with a superior first issue.[55]

Booklets and Brochures

Booklets and brochures serve numerous purposes, from orientation of new teachers to development of lay understanding of instructional programs. They are time consuming and costly to prepare and therefore should be written only when the expenditure of considerable time and money can be justified. Wide distribution is usually considered valid justification, as in the case of Minnesota's booklet of guidelines for gifted and talented education and Kentucky's *The Path to a Larger Life: Creating Kentucky's Educational Future.*[56]

Booklets and brochures need to be "brightened" to make them more attractive to readers. The Iowa Department of Public Instruction has prepared a handbook of ideas for curriculum improvement that is attractively presented and that includes headings designed to invite readership: "Where Does One Begin—And How Much at Once?" and "Good News—Change Can Be Planned."[57]

Guides to Planning

Because planning procedures are sometimes considered to be a mystery, a number of planning guides have been issued by planners in state departments of education. They include steps in planning, matters to be dealt with, and cautions against pitfalls. In New York, the State Department of Education produced a guide to planning the curriculum in elementary school social studies and to organizing classrooms for more effective instruction.[58] From Wisconsin has come *A Guide to Curriculum Planning in Foreign Language, A Guide to Curriculum Planning in Science,* a guide to planning processes in health education, and also a more general guide to the purposes and procedures of curriculum planning.[59] California has issued *Program Guidelines for Severely Orthopedically Impaired Individuals* and also a framework for developing a curriculum in physical education; Iowa has distributed *A Tool for Assessing and Designing Comprehensive School Health Education in Iowa Schools.*[60]

Other Literary Media

Still other media of a less well-known nature have included manuals supporting training programs, "packages" devised by consultants, and special guides for implementation and field testing of ideas.

One may rightly wonder what constitutes a really effective communication medium, literary or other. To be effective, media must be in conformity with the roles of their recipients. For example, the new importance of parents in planning makes well-worded messages to lay persons unusually essential. Written materials should emphasize the informal wherever possible and should sometimes be spiced with touches of humor. For instance, consider a memorandum to teachers written by an unusually popular and effective administrator to convey that, because of certain recent events, inconvenience was about to affect all of them. The message began, "News flash! Sit down, please, and prepare to stifle small screams of anguish. Ready? Good." The administrator concluded her message with two quotations: "'The unexamined life is not worth living,' says Socrates; 'Sigh,' says Snoopy."

Certainly, a communication should be absolutely accurate in presenting bad news with the good. The messsage may be short or lengthy, simple or complex, according to the requirements of the particular communicatees. In every case, it should give the impression of brightness and attractiveness.

WHAT CAN AFFECT COMMUNICATION?

Of a number of influences affecting communication of curriculum ideas and matters, perhaps three are most significant: one affirmative and helpful, two negative and destructive. The first is diffusion of ideas and lore. The second is the impact of rumor; the third, a phenomenon known as filtering.

The Process of Diffusion

The term *diffusion* suggests distribution or spread that is intentional and planned. Sometimes diffusion occurs in depth, as when the ideas that are diffused seem especially complicated. More often, the distribution or spread is wide, covering many people with showers of information. Sometimes people who are the targets of deep diffusion are heard to say, "They told us more than we wanted to know."

Some people have tried to make diffusion equivalent to instructional change. Charles B. Myers pointed out that mixing the two has prevented both diffusion and instructional change from succeeding. As a remedy, he recommended cooperative planning by teachers and supervisors, school system personnel, change agents from outside the district, and specially designated diffusers.[61] Similarly, Gerald W. Marker said that role specialization that distinguishes designers and testers of innovations from diffusers who demonstrate and disseminate the innovations is possible. Marker also suggested three other ways of achieving diffusion. One of these is a social interaction model that emphasizes the informal social channels through which ideas move, such as in small discussion groups and conversations. The second way, called the problem-solver model, focuses on the problems of the client using the ideas to develop local commitment to the ideas. The third way is termed the linkage process because it emphasizes the openness of channels between idea creators and users. Back-and-forth flow of information between the two may make this the most usable method of all.[62]

An interesting study of diffusion by a variety of means was made by Arnold Grobman. The diffusion Grobman discussed is international in scope. He reported that diffusion of educational ideas occurs most rapidly among heavily populated countries that spend the most money on public education. Diffusion is discouraged, however, when the goals of a receiving, participating school district are different from the goals specified in the model materials. Other discouraging influences are barriers to open information exchange, limited publishing technology, and domination of educational proposals by government officials and entrepreneurs.[63] One of the great diffusion efforts has been that of the Nuffield Science Teaching Projects in Great Britain. P. J. Kelly reported a follow-up study of the Nuffield effort that took into account who adopts ideas and how the ideas come to the attention of these people in the first place.[64]

The Damage Done by Rumor

On the negative side of the ledger, one finds rumor—a report without foundation or basis in fact. Indeed, it may be a fabrication out of whole cloth, an educated guess about an impending event, a "leaked" preannouncement of a circumstance that later becomes a reality, or a product of wishful thinking. A famous general, retired from the United States Marines, is alleged to have said, "Dame Rumor is the biggest liar in the world."

A rumor does the most damage when the situation in which it originates is unsettled, as when a former curriculum leader leaves and a new one is just beginning his or her tenure, when important information has been concealed from curriculum personnel who should have received it, or when insecurity and distrust have run rampant in the school or school system.[65] Politicians and others have been known to spread rumors purposely as "trial balloons" and then to turn the rumored circumstances into reality. A rumor may become more pointed or brief as it spreads, since the communicators usually focus on a detail that suits them, and the content they decide to emphasize depends both on their interests or motives and on what they think their hearers want to hear.

Countering rumors in schools and elsewhere is never easy. First, the curriculum leader in a school or school system must form a pattern of attending to all interpersonal and group relations that he or she has the power to affect. This action is, of course, more easily talked about than done. It means keeping fellow workers informed and involved, analyzing rumors to see what they really suggest concerning ways of helping the organization, and contradicting rumors with accurate information. Merely quelling rumors will not eliminate the effects they have already created. The ideal solution is to prevent rumors from starting and spreading in the first place. At best, this solution can be achieved only in part.

The Problem of Filtering

Filtering, another barrier to communication, is the process of eliminating or screening out important information that should be passed along a given communication chain. Filtering occurs in upward, downward, and horizontal communication among school personnel. Frequently, it is most troublesome in large organizations, such as large school systems. Subordinates are sure their superiors do not welcome certain ideas, responses, and criticisms, so they filter them out of their communications to them. Superiors soon learn they are not hearing the whole truth from subordinates. Meanwhile, they in turn withhold information from their subordinates. Superiors may adopt open-door policies to encourage their subordinates to talk with them, and sometimes they call for written suggestions from subordinates, being reasonably sure that all suggestions will be discreetly given. If the suggestions are seldom considered, however, sources will soon dry up. People tend to filter out reports of their failures (data that would make hearers react unfavorably to their pet projects), favorable information about their enemies, and unfavorable information about their friends.

A study of the importance of trust as it relates to the accuracy, direction, and completeness of information flow was conducted in elementary schools. The findings indicated that the greater the degree of trust among personnel in an elementary school, the greater the accuracy of the communicated information. Accuracy was positively related to trust regardless of whether the flow was upward, downward, or lateral. Interestingly, in high-trust situations, more upward than downward communication occurred, and the information communicated was more complete. Obviously, more filtering occurred when the degree of trust was low.[66]

How can curriculum leaders reduce filtering? Perhaps by employing the most moral, ethical, and psychologically secure persons they can find. Perhaps by keeping the working environment of the school open so that teachers and others can admit their failures and state their problems. Perhaps by making it very clear that not all available information can be distributed to school staffs freely and indiscriminately at any one time.

Suppose a popular middle management curriculum leader is discovered altering achievement test scores to favor certain pupils. Interviews conducted by the superintendent and an assistant superintendent reveal that he has altered school records repeatedly during the preceding five years. A discussion among the three results in the offender's volunteering to resign and leave the school system immediately. What, if anything, should be said publicly about the reason for the sudden departure? The ethical questions involved are complex. Curriculum workers who discuss questions of this kind can understand that information may sometimes be filtered with perfect justification, and that at other times filtering should be absolutely taboo.

The Overall Effect of Communication About the Curriculum

Harold Lasswell was wise in asking people to watch for the overall effect of their communication efforts.[67] Initially, one can be trapped into thinking that a message sent is a message received, considered, and accepted in full. In fact, the level of final effect depends much on the abilities and attitudes of communicatees.

There exist no pencil-and-paper tests for determining whether messages have really "gotten through" to the point of making a difference in the lives of people. Nevertheless, what people say and do as a consequence of internalizing communications they have received proves genuinely telling. Most of us have no time to await the appearance of long-term consequences, so we have to settle for short-term revelations.

SUMMARY

Communication of curriculum ideas and changes is complex mainly because human beings and their interactions are so complex. In the past, communication related to the curriculum has proceeded clumsily, but many attempts have been made to effect it. School personnel have communicated through documents like curriculum guides; statements of points of view, intentions, and policies; and written aids to teaching and curriculum planning. The current limited use of audiovisual materials as replacements for written ones will burgeon in the near future into startling applications of new communication technology.

The communication that has proved most satisfactory thus far has been achieved by personal, direct contact between and among persons. Though in practice interpersonal communication is often imperfect, we do have at our disposal enough knowledge to make it more effective. In relationships among people, communication both wide and deep is aided by a process called diffusion. It is seriously injured by the presence of rumor and by the filtering of information. Fortunately, there are ways of organizing to improve communication within schools and school systems. This fact gives us hope for the future.

ENDNOTES

1. Fred R. Dowling, "The Teacher and Communication Theory," *Education* 81, no. 3 (November 1960): 182.

2. Quoted in Gordon McCloskey, "Principles of Communication for Principals," *Bulletin of the National Association of Secondary School Principals* 44, no. 257 (September 1960): 17–23.

3. Claude E. Shannon and Warren Weaver, *The Mathematical Theory of Communication* (Urbana: University of Illinois Press, 1949), 96.

4. David Coursen and John Thomas, *Communicating* (Washington, DC: Office of Educa-

tional Research and Improvement, Department of Education, 1989).

5. Wilbur Schramm, "Educators and Communication Research," *Educational Leadership* 13, no. 8 (May 1956): 503–509; see also Stanley Elam, "Attitude Formation: Direct Experience Best," *Bulletin of the National Association of Secondary School Principals* 58 (January 1974): 38–40.

6. Dowling, "The Teacher and Communication Theory," 148.

7. Kathryn T. Theus, "Organizational Ideology, Structure and Communication Efficacy:

A Causal Analysis," a paper presented at the annual meeting of the Association for Education in Journalism and Mass Communication, Washington, DC, August 1989.

8. Gregory Bateson, *Steps to an Ecology of Mind* (New York: Ballantine Books, 1972); see also Eric Bredo, "Bateson's Hierarchical Theory of Learning and Communication," *Educational Theory* 39, no. 1 (Winter 1989): 27–38.

9. Jerry L. Pulley, "The Principal and Communication: Some Points of Interference," *Bulletin of the National Association of Secondary School Principals* 59, no. 387 (January 1975): 50–54.

10. J. J. Richards, "People Problems: The Human Component in PPBS," *Bulletin of the National Association of Secondary School Principals* 56 (October 1972): 50–59.

11. See Iowa State Department of Education, *A Guide to Developing Communication Across the Curriculum* (Des Moines: The Department, 1989).

12. Joseph C. Rotter et al., *Parent-Teacher Conferencing: What Research Says to the Teacher,* 2nd ed. (Washington, DC: National Education Association, 1987); see also Joan Brady, "Smooth Talk," *Currents* 16, no. 1 (January 1990): 38–43.

13. Philip H. Phenix, "Barriers to Academic Communication," *Teachers College Record* 59, no. 2 (November 1957): 88.

14. Elmo Roper, in Elihu Katz and Paul F. Lazarsfeld, eds., *Personal Influence* (New York: Free Press of Glencoe, 1955), xv.

15. George C. Homans, *The Human Group* (New York: Harcourt, Brace and World, 1950).

16. See Thomas J. Peters and Robert H. Waterman, Jr., *In Search of Excellence* (New York: Harper and Row, 1982), 121–124.

16. Bob Pawloski, "How I Found Out about the Internet," *Educational Leadership* 51, no. 7 (April 1994): 69–73.

18. Carl R. Rogers, "Communication—Its Blocking and Its Facilitation," a paper presented at the Centennial Conference on Communication, Northwestern University, October 11, 1951.

19. S. Clay Willmington, "Oral Communication for a Career in Business," *Bulletin of the Association for Business Communication* 52, no. 2 (June 1989): 8–12.

20. Ralph Nichols and Leonard Stevens, *Are You Listening?* (New York: McGraw Hill, 1957).

21. For further development of this idea, see Kenneth D. Benne and Bozidar Muntyan, *Human Relations in Curriculum Change* (New York: Dryden, 1951), 272–282.

22. Philip Hallinger and Joseph Murphy, "Instructional Leadership in Effective Schools." Reported in ERIC # ED 309 535.

23. Ernest R. House, "The Micropolitics of Innovation: Nine Propositions," *Phi Delta Kappan* 57, no. 5 (January 1976): 337–340.

24. Sharon J. Bolster, "Vision: Communicating It to the Staff," a paper presented at the annual meeting of the American Educational Research Association, San Francisco, March 1989.

25. H. Dickson Corbett, "To Make an Omelette You Have to Break the Egg Crate," *Educational Leadership* 40, no. 2 (November 1982): 34, 35.

26. Nicholas P. Criscuolo, "Communicating with the Staff and Public about Curriculum," *Educational Leadership* 40, no. 2 (November 1982): 25.

27. Juleen Cattermole and Norman Robinson, "Effective Home/School Communication—From the Parents' Perspective," *Phi Delta Kappan* 67, no. 1 (September 1985): 48–50.

28. Joanne Jacobs, "Stop Lying about What Our Children Are Learning," *Asbury Park* (NJ) *Press,* April 26, 1990.

29. Louis Forsdale, "Helping Students Observe Processes of Communication," *Teachers College Record* 57, no. 2 (November 1955): 128.

30. "Overcoming Obstacles to Interpersonal Compliance: A Principle of Message Construction," *Human Communication Research* 16, no. 1 (Fall 1989): 33–61.

31. Ronald C. Doll, A. Harry Passow, and Stephen M. Corey, *Organizing for Curriculum Improvement* (New York: Teachers College Press, 1953), 63, 64. Used with permission.

32. George E. Ross, "A Study of Informal Communication Patterns in Two Elementary Schools," doctoral dissertation, University of Illinois, 1960.

33. F. H. Knower and P. H. Wagner, *Communication in Educational Administration* (Columbus, OH: Center for Educational Administration, Ohio State University, 1959). Communication in larger schools is now being aided by the presence of carefully organized schools-within-schools.

34. Marcella R. Lawler, *Curriculum Consultants at Work* (New York: Teachers College Press, 1958), 107.

35. Ralph M. Peters, "The Effectiveness of Internal Communication in Selected School Systems in East Tennessee," doctoral dissertation, University of Tennessee, 1960.

36. Ibid.

37. Patricia S. Kusimo and David A. Erlandson, "Instructional Communications in a Large High School," *Bulletin of the National Association of Secondary School Principals* 67, no. 466 (November 1983): 18–24.

38. Walter St. John, "How to Plan an Effective School Communications Program," *Bulletin of the National Association of Secondary School Principals* 67, no. 459 (January 1983): 21–27.

39. Texas Education Agency, *Long Range Plan for Information Systems from the State Board of Education* (Austin: The Agency, 1989).

40. Dan J. Wedemeyer and Philip Bossert, *Communication, Earth 2020 Workshop* (Honolulu: University of Hawaii, 1974).

41. Richard F. Elmore and Susan H. Fuhrman, writing in the 1994 Yearbook of the Association for Supervision and Curriculum Development, *The Governance of Curriculum*, 214.

42. See Margaret B. Balentine and Kenneth T. Henson, "Back to Basics: Skills Needed for the Information Age," *Contemporary Education* 56, no. 4 (Summer 1985): 213–216.

43. National Society for the Study of Education, *The Foundations and Technique of Curriculum Construction*—Part II: "The Foundations of Curriculum Making" (Bloomington, IL: Public School Publishing, 1926), 121.

44. David G. Armstrong and Robert E. Shutes, "Quality in Curriculum Documents: Some Basic Criteria," *Educational Leadership* 39, no. 3 (December 1981): 200–202.

45. Bill Lamperes, "Is There Life After the Curriculum Guide?" *Curriculum Review* 21 (May 1982): 133–137.

46. David G. Armstrong, *Developing and Documenting the Curriculum* (Boston: Allyn and Bacon, 1989).

47. Fenwick W. English, "It's Time to Abolish Conventional Curriculum Guides," *Educational Leadership* 44, no. 4 (December 1986–January 1987): 50–52.

48. See J. Harvey Littrell and Gerald Douglass Bailey, "Administrators, Teachers: Stop Writing Curriculum Guides That Won't Be Used!" *Bulletin of the National Association of Secondary School Principals* 65, no. 443 (March 1981): 29–32.

49. Dr. William C. Hedge provided publications describing the information age.

50. See *ASCD Update* 35, no. 8 (October 1993): 1, 4, 5; see also Andrew Kupfer's article, "The Race to Rewire America," in *Fortune,* April 19, 1993, 42–61; and Stratford Sherman's "The New Computer Revolution," in *Fortune,* June 14, 1993, 56–80.

51. D. Bruce Sealey and J. Anthony Riffel, *The Development of Education in Fairford: A Community Manual* (Ashern, Manitoba: Interlake Tribal Division for Schools, 1986); and Texas Education Agency, *Bilingual Education Pilot Programs Interim Study Report* (Austin: The Agency, 1985).

52. Lowell E. Johnson and Carolyn P. Casteel, "The Learning Rationale Statement as a Component of Instructional Materials: A Generic Model for Development," *Educational Technology* 23, no. 4 (April 1983): 22–25.

53. Pearl Ching and Vivian Hee, *Resource Guide for Gifted and Talented Programs* (Honolulu: Hawaii State Department of Education, 1985); and Georgia State Department of Education, *Deaf/Blind: Resource Manuals for Programs for Exceptional Children* (Atlanta: Office of Instructional Services, The Department, 1986).

54. Marta A. Roth, ed., *Beyond Special Education Compliance: Administrative Challenges for Reaching Educational Excellence. Final Report and Training Manual* (Morgantown: College of Human Resources and Education, West Virginia University, 1986).

55. Barry S. Sigmon, "Informal Newsletter Improves Communication, Staff Meetings," *Bulletin of the National Association of Secondary School Principals* 63, no. 429 (October 1979): 122, 123.

56. Minnesota Curriculum Services Center, *Minnesota Guidelines for Gifted and Talented Education* (St. Paul: Minnesota State Department of Education, 1986); and Prichard Committee for Academic Excellence, *The Path to a Larger Life: Creating Kentucky's Educational Future* (Lexington: The Committee, 1985).

57. Iowa State Department of Public Instruction, *A Handbook of Ideas for Curriculum Improvement* (Des Moines: The Department, 1981).

58. New York State Education Department, *Planning for Social Studies in Elementary Education* (Albany: Bureau of Elementary Curriculum Development, 1974).

59. Foreign Language Curriculum Task Force, *A Guide to Curriculum Planning in Foreign Language* (Madison: Wisconsin State Department of Public Instruction, 1985); Kenneth W. Dowling et al., *A Guide to Curriculum Planning in Science. Bulletin No. 6270* (Madison: Wisconsin State Department of Public Instruction, 1986); Chet E. Bradley, ed., *Health Education: A Planning Resource for Wisconsin Schools* (Madison: Wisconsin State Department of Public Instruction, 1977); and Eunice Bethke, *A Guide to Curriculum Planning: Purpose and Procedures. Bulletin No. 6095* (Madison: Wisconsin State Department of Public Instruction, 1985).

60. Winnie Bachman, *Program Guidelines for Severely Orthopedically Impaired Individuals* (Sacramento: California State Department of Education, 1985); California State Department of Education, *Handbook for Physical Education: Framework for Developing a Curriculum for California Public Schools, Kindergarten through Grade Twelve* (Sacramento: The Department, 1986); and Iowa State Department of Public Instruction, *A Tool for Assessing and Designing Comprehensive School Health Education in Iowa Schools* (Des Moines: The Department, 1986).

61. Charles B. Myers, "'Diffusion' Does Not Equal 'Instructional Change,'" a paper presented at the annual conference of the National Council for the Social Studies, Cincinnati, Ohio, November 1977.

62. Gerald W. Marker, "Spreading the Word: Implementing Alternative Approaches in the Diffusion of Instructional Materials," a paper presented at the annual conference of the National Council for the Social Studies, Cincinnati, Ohio, November 1977.

63. Arnold B. Grobman, "Factors Influencing International Curricular Diffusion," *Studies in International Evaluation* 2, no. 3 (Winter 1976): 227–232.

64. P. J. Kelly, *Outline Report: Curriculum Diffusion Research Project* (London: Chelsea College of Science and Technology, 1975).

65. See Bernard M. Bass, *Organizational Psychology* (Boston: Allyn and Bacon, 1965).

66. Gayle A. Hurst and Daniel U. Levine, "Trust as It Relates to Information Flow Variables in Elementary Schools," a paper presented at the annual meeting of the American Educational Research Association, San Francisco, March 1989.

67. See Wilber Schramm, "Educators and Communication Research," *Educational Leadership* 13, no. 8 (May 1956): 503–509.

SELECTED BIBLIOGRAPHY

Bereday, George Z. F., and Lauwerys, Joseph A., eds. *Communication Media and the School.* The Yearbook of Education, 1960. Tarrytown-on-Hudson, NY: World, 1960.

Berlo, David. *The Process of Communication.* New York: Holt, Rinehart and Winston, 1960.

Didsbury, Howard F., Jr., ed. *Communications and the Future.* Bethesda, MD: World Future Society, 1982.

Doll, Ronald C. *Leadership to Improve Schools.* Worthington, OH: Charles A. Jones, 1972, Chapter 10.

Eisenson, Jon; Auer, J. Jeffery; and Irwin, John V. *The Psychology of Communication.* New York: Appleton-Century-Crofts, 1963.

Harms, L. S. *Human Communication, the New Fundamentals.* New York: Harper and Row, 1974.

Kelly, P. J. *Outline Report: Curriculum Diffusion Research Project.* London: Chelsea College of Science and Technology, 1975.

Maidment, Robert. *Straight Talk: A Communication Primer.* Reston, VA: National Association of Secondary School Principals, 1980.

McCloskey, Gordon. *Education and Public Understanding.* New York: Harper and Row, 1972.

McLuhan, Marshall. *Understanding Media.* New York: McGraw-Hill, 1964.

National School Public Relations Association. *Communication Ideas in Action.* Washington, DC: The Association, 1970.

Nichols, Ralph, and Stevens, Leonard. *Are You Listening?* New York: McGraw-Hill, 1957.

Nostrand, Peter F., and Shelly, Richard W. "An Educational Leadership Listening Model." Privately published, 1973. Reported in ERIC # ED 087 100.

Pearce, W. Barnett. "Trust in Interpersonal Communication." A paper presented at the annual meeting of the International Communication Association, Montreal, 1973. Reported in ERIC # ED 087 069.

Peters, Thomas J., and Waterman, Robert H., Jr. *In Search of Excellence.* New York: Harper and Row, 1982.

Schramm, Wilbur, ed. *The Process and Effects of Mass Communication.* Urbana, IL: University of Illinois Press, 1954.

Sereno, K. K., and Mortensen, C. D., eds. *Foundations of Communication Theory.* New York: Harper and Row, 1970.

Winters, Marilyn. *Preparing Your Curriculum Guide.* Alexandria, VA: Association for Supervision and Curriculum Development, 1980.

11

CURRICULUM LEADERSHIP:
ITS NATURE AND STRATEGIES

How can one describe leadership that facilitates the curriculum improvement process? What are some of the important actions curriculum leaders take to make curriculum planning effective? These are the questions this final chapter is designed to answer. Having seen how decisions about the curriculum are made and what process is used in effectuating them, we come to the place at which we need to think about how to lead other people in planning.

People who have worked in schools are sure to have seen both effective and ineffective leaders, but they are often hard put to explain just what has made their favorite leaders effective. Actually, superstitions and fallacies about the nature of competent leadership continue to abound in schools as elsewhere. Among the common ones are the following:

- Leaders are *born;* we cannot hope to develop them, only to embellish their innate abilities.
- Conformity and uniformity in thinking should be stimulated by competent leaders.
- Leaders should be so far ahead of their followers in quantity and quality of ideas that few followers can hope to catch up.
- Leaders should always be found in the act of "leading"; quiescence is for followers.
- Leaders should not tolerate conflict, even when it "clears the air."

Historically, the leader's role has been thought to resemble the role of the cue ball in billiards: Nothing happens until the cue ball goes into action.[1] Such a conception pleases a Hitler or a Mussolini. Other conceptions have included those of transactional leadership and transforming leadership. In the former, transactions are considered to occur between leaders and their followers. In the latter, leaders and followers seek to attain mutual goals, which they expect will become higher and more demanding.[2]

Perhaps the epitome of what leaders do in democratic organizations is to help their co-workers identify worthwhile goals, and then help the co-workers achieve these goals. As helpers, leaders provide service. As models of appropriate speech and behavior, they teach. *What* they do is important, and *how* they do it is just as important. Some of the what and much of the how are, in fact, invisible and are therefore beyond description.

Dwight Eisenhower, in what he called his first teaching enterprise after his retirement from the military, headed Columbia University. One day he demonstrated, simply and graphically, a fundamental of effective leadership. He pulled a string across a table. Then he tried pushing it across. An easy, orderly operation became a difficult, muddled one. The lesson was clear.

What leadership *ought* to be, according to our best understanding, differs from what many people will accept it as being. People have both culturally based and individual notions of what desirable leadership is. Furthermore, the theories that have been propounded have often failed to stand the test of careful investigation in varied situations. Leadership as an area of inquiry has thus been plagued with "theory trouble." In fact, even defining leadership accurately causes difficulty. The author of a yearbook chapter called educational leadership "that action or behavior among individuals and groups which causes both the individual and the groups to move toward educational goals that are increasingly mutually acceptable to them."[3] Then he said that "leadership action is more than words can describe—it is a quality of interaction which takes on added meaning for people as they live and study its significance."[4]

Some leaders occupy positions of authority and responsibility because they have forced their way into them. Other leaders have been put there, sometimes by doting parents or loyal friends. For a long time, top administrators have tried to identify potential leaders—persons termed *emergent leaders*. Appointing emergent leaders to important positions has seemed humane, democratic, and usually sensible, but it has not always produced the best results. Luvern Cunningham, a long-time student of leadership theory and practice, pointed to the need for another stratagem: that of consciously *developing* new leaders. This can be done, he said, if the novices are taught to focus on present and future at the same time, to reconcile the different interest groups around them, to observe events carefully, to appraise what they see, to use their intuition in managing the symbols or signs they present to other people, and to serve freely as teachers of others.[5] In the schools, a key means of developing leaders is empowering teachers to assume leadership roles to which they have seldom been accustomed.

In looking forward to the 1990s and beyond, Cunningham identified several challenges to educational leadership. One of these challenges has been mentioned frequently in this book: the decline of the school, particularly the public school, as a viable institution. Within decrepit buildings, lax educational practices, bureaucratic behavior by leaders, "raw" pupil behavior, discouragement and low morale affecting teachers and pupils, and an increase in the number of underachieving learners have characterized recent schooling.

A second challenge has claimed the attention of many political leaders. It is the drive for equity in schooling. Inequities appear essentially in two forms: the fiscal and the personal. School districts are unequally supported by tax monies and thus become unequal environments in which to attend school. On a personal level, minorities, the poor, and females do not always receive the same attention and help as their opposite numbers in the population.

A third challenge originates in new technology. School leaders have more to do than ever before as they reckon with both the advantages and the handicaps of the electronic equipment and other technological aids now at hand. They are only beginning to comprehend the meaning of the communication explosion and to take advantage of the gains that are possible when computers are used to the fullest.

A fourth challenge involves the cooperation of schools with other community agencies and institutions. Input by parents is increasing. Thinking in sophisticated school districts is turning to consortia, compacts, networks, and organizational patterns that will prevent the school of the future from remaining an island. Also, school leaders are recognizing the need to talk the language of people of other occupations whose work has an impact on schools.[6]

WISDOM THAT EDUCATIONAL LEADERS CAN PROFITABLY HEED

Years of experience have produced wisdom that school leaders can profitably heed. Common sense dictates that leaders should strive for physical stamina, ability to make judgments "in the heat of combat," skill in interpersonal relations, courage and dependability, competence in doing what they are assigned to do, and understanding of the needs of their followers. Furthermore, leaders should recognize that one of their prime obligations is to help members of their organizations feel confident and capable as they become motivated.

Because only some of the characteristics of an effective leader are innate, certain characteristics or attributes must be cultivated over the long term. A primary area for development is communication; therefore the cultivation of clear, judicious speaking and writing becomes an immediate, primary objective. In filling leadership positions, employers look for statesmanlike individuals who are willing to work hard for important causes, who work well with other people, and who exhibit steadiness and good sense in crises. In education, as in any other important field, only those persons who *know* the field should be employed in leadership capacities. This comment would be unnecessary if important people in government and business had not suggested that competent educational leaders can be recruited from anywhere outside the field of education as long as they have had leadership responsibility or preparation somewhere.

For several reasons, it is now more necessary than ever before that we have educational leaders who are knowledgeable about education:

1. In our disunited world, many school systems are fragmented as institutions.
2. Much of the fragmentation in the United States results from diversity of populations. Each differing population or culture naturally has its own needs and requirements.
3. To unite people and to reorient institutions, current and potential leaders must possess skills that previous leaders have seldom had to exercise. A primary skill involves "seeing the big picture" and so grasping the place and meaning of one's own institution within a large societal complex. Another skill consists of achieving and nourishing agreement when differing, even warring, parties must be induced to work toward the same goals. A third skill is the ability to exercise power in ways that go beyond simply making judgments: by publicizing, by creating ideas, by persuading, by securing cooperation. This skill makes possible the development of networks enrolling persons and organizations that have a real prospect of working together. Finally, a much-needed skill is the capacity to accept and promote desirable changes within organizations that are evolving with remarkable speed. This skill proves especially useful to leaders who are charged with improving the curriculum.

Let us now consider more precisely the nature of *curriculum* leadership.

THE NATURE OF CURRICULUM LEADERSHIP

Curriculum leadership performs a particular function within the general realm of educational leadership. Effective curriculum leadership is characterized by the ability of leaders to hold to clear and viable curriculum principles, and by their willingness to make long-term commitments affecting the curriculum, unswayed by the politics of the moment. Such leadership is found too seldom among middle management personnel, not only in education but also in business and industry. Too many leaders are afraid to make commitments according to principles in which they really believe, lest they be blamed for failure or be left "holding the bag" and so lose status. Effective leaders have ideas of their own—and the courage to advance them.

Taken alone, these statements might suggest that curriculum leaders should operate dictatorships, a notion that runs counter to the ideas about democratic curriculum leadership that have been advanced for decades. Mackenzie and Corey, writing in the early 1950s, spoke of four ways of exercising leadership: by force, by bargaining, by paternalism, and by determination of mutually acceptable goals and means. Of the four, they opted for the last.[7]

More recently, Karolyn Snyder has suggested a school improvement procedure highlighting cooperative planning, specific development of teachers and programs, and careful assessment of results. With this procedure, leaders emphasize cooperative envisioning of what is possible and then proceed to thinking and acting with school staffs.[8] Those who would achieve increased productivity in schools by applying the much-heralded Theory Z recognize that trust and participative decision making are essential.

Years ago, Douglas McGregor spoke of two fundamentally antithetical views leaders have of their followers. One of them he called Theory X; the other, Theory Y. Leaders who subscribe to Theory X, said McGregor, take the position that most people (including teachers) dislike work and the responsibility associated with it and must therefore be controlled, directed, or threatened. Leaders who subscribe to Theory Y, on the other hand, hold that most people consider work to be a natural function and will control themselves and seek responsibility as they pursue worthy objectives.[9] Then came Theory Z. James O'Hanlon listed four characteristics of leaders who subscribe to Theory Z, which he called a model rather than a theory: acceptance of a clear philosophy, concentration on long-term development, trust based on belief in common goals, and cooperative decision making.[10] Two years earlier, William Ouchi had reported the existence in Japan of Z-type business and industrial firms.[11] The effects that application of Theory Z is supposed to bring about include decision making by common consent, commitment to working together, concern for other people, open communication, a sense of equality, and high expectations of results. Ultimately, however, decision making rests with one responsible person. Some students of curriculum leadership have seen real possibilities in careful application of Theory Z during the planning process. Its essential features have already been put to use in some of the wise curriculum planning accomplished in earlier decades.

In the world generally, leadership is still thought of as being concentrated in official leaders, persons who symbolically wear the big "L" on their outer garments. An interesting feature of truly democratic curriculum leadership, however, is wide distribution of leadership functions among many planners. These varied, differently talented individuals operate when and where their abilities are needed. For example, in a total assemblage of eight, while five are serving as leaders of discussion groups, two may be treating research data needed by the groups and still another may be writing a memorandum to communicate what the respective groups are doing. In this way, each of the eight persons is exercising a leadership function. These activities represent in a minimal way the spread of functions that will be referred to in this chapter.

Some Theories of Curriculum Leadership

Three other major leadership theories have influenced planners' views of curriculum leadership: the traits theory, the group theory, and the situational theory.

More than a hundred studies have been made of leaders' traits. In the findings, only a few traits appear again and again. They are (1) empathy, or identification with the emotional needs of others; (2) surgency, or enthusiasm, geniality, alertness, expressiveness, cheerfulness; (3) group recognition, or obvious ability to fit the norms of the group without seeming different or odd; (4) helpfulness, or ability to give practical, direct assistance; (5) emotional control, or ability to give the appearance of serenity or poise; (6) intelligence, including verbal and social adeptness as well as academic brightness; and (7) interest in leading, or full-heartedness in assuming leadership responsibilities.

There is little agreement as to which of these traits are most important to the success of curriculum leaders. Often the traits that strengthen a leader's position in one situation may damage his or her position in another. Also, leadership traits usually admired by Americans are not always the traits admired by people of other nations and cultures, or even by Americans who belong to certain of our subcultures. We are becoming more certain of something else, however—that in our era of decline in moral and ethical values, leaders need to exhibit and stand for virtues that contribute to constructive change in the lives of teachers, pupils, parents, and others.[12]

A second theory, the group theory, emphasizes achievement of the goals accepted by staff groups and accordingly downplays the characteristics and actions of individual leaders. According to this theory, leadership in a group is shared by members of the group for the sake of reaching commonly determined goals in a cooperative manner. An experiment reported by Kimball Wiles illustrates diffusion of leadership within a group:

> We did a study of our students in P. K. Yonge High School at the University of Florida. There were 240 students in it at the time. We asked them questions like these: Suppose all the football equipment had burned up—which person would you choose to head a campaign to buy new equipment? Suppose we were going on the radio to explain our school program to the public—which people would you choose to be on the panel? There were seven types of activities like this in which a person's leadership could be identified. We guessed that 25 to 50 students would be selected. Over 200 out of the 240 were identified by their fellows as the persons they would choose.[13]

Some leaders are appointed by their groups for at least temporary action, whereas other leaders emerge, or rise to the occasion. Apparently, assertive leaders are tolerated best by large groups; leader behavior varies according to the nature of the task; and emergent leaders can succeed more readily than status leaders by being forceful and individualistic. Always, however, the ultimate emphasis should be on working *with* people, not over them.[14] This emphasis has become prominent in the theory and practice of transformational leadership.

According to the third theory, the situational theory, a given situation calls for leadership of a given kind. Out of the situation and the need it engenders there arises a demand for leadership that can deal effectively with that situation. Therefore the leadership considered competent in one circumstance may not be considered competent in another, and the image of the monolithic leader is thus inappropriate. The ingredients or factors in a given situation include the structure of interpersonal relations within the organization, the nature of the culture in which the organization exists, and the physical conditions and tasks with which the organization must reckon.[15]

Both task performance and human relations are present in the situational theory. Numbers of studies have been made in an effort to relate these two leadership dimensions. Within the situational theory, there has also been included a third dimension: the maturity level that followers achieve in performing a given task. Maturity is exhibited by setting high but attainable goals, by showing willingness and ability to take responsibility, and by demonstrating the effects of relevant education and experience. When followers show increased maturity, the leader should presumably reduce the number of his or her behaviors designed to get the task done and should increase the number of his or her behaviors designed to secure better relationships with the followers. When a follower shows decreased maturity—for example, after having been shifted to an unfamiliar job assignment—the leader should probably offer additional emotional support and then involve other group members in helping the individual with his or her task performance.[16]

As the curriculum leader moves from school to school and from group to group within the school system's organization, different situational ingredients operate. According to the situational theory, no single status leader can hope to perform effectively and with maximum initiative in all the groups with which he or she meets. In this sense, the release of leadership potential in others is forced upon the status leader.

If the nature of leadership could be explained adequately by forming a happy combination of the three theories, much time could be saved in future study. However, other factors with which the three theories do not reckon enter the scene. These factors include the nature of the social organization within which leadership is to be established, the value systems that exist within organizations, and differing expectations of leadership behavior and role.

An updated description of the interaction of the three theories would probably include the following statements:

1. Although all educational leaders cannot be said to have the same traits or characteristics, they do have traits or characteristics that make a difference in the quality of their performance.
2. It is true that leadership in any democratic group or institution is, in fact, widely distributed. Thus leadership that emerges has its place.
3. Of course, the situation, defined in such terms as *nature of environment, kinds of tasks, distribution of power,* and *priority of goals,* makes a vast difference.[17]

The three theories just discussed provide background for answering the question "What makes leaders effective?" but they have been unable to offer a direct answer. Of the three, the situational theory has been extended most in studying the effectiveness of educational leaders. The situation or setting in which educational leaders exercise their skills with greatest effect appears to be one that supplies trust, caring, mutual respect, cohesiveness, high morale, effort at improvement, use of people's input, and continuing academic and social gains.

A specific theory of leadership effectiveness is needed. Fred Fiedler, who developed the Contingency Theory of Leadership Effectiveness, found that three factors determine how favorable work situations are for leaders: the quality of leader-member relations, the degree to which tasks are structured, and the amount of formal power the leader has. Fiedler discovered, however, that there is no simple relationship between the favorableness of leadership situations and the effectiveness of leaders. Task-oriented leaders seem to be most effective in situations that are either very favorable or very unfavorable. Human relations–oriented leaders are apparently at their best in moderately favorable situations.[18] The contingency theory is based on four propositions, all having to do with competency. The first proposition says that people want to be competent; the second, that they satisfy the terms of competence in different ways; the third, that people's competence depends on the fit between task and organization; and the fourth, that higher goals stimulate people to additional competence.

Underlying a leader's effectiveness are the culture of his or her school and the tactics being used there in attempts to achieve educational excellence. The leader can make a contribution to the formation of both. What Fiedler found about the effectiveness of school leaders in general needs to be modified to satisfy the requirements of the curriculum leadership role in particular.

What people say about school leaders and their work tends to reflect statements made by leadership theorists of the past. Today, the tug is stronger than ever before between two hardly formulated theories of curriculum leadership. The first theory is an ancient and "common sense" one that can be summarized in the idea that the boss, often a father or mother figure, is best prepared and qualified to determine tasks, to gauge performance, to distribute incentives and rewards, and to judge quality of production. This boss accepts and demonstrates the factory model of schooling. With one eye on production and the other on responses of employees in performing assigned tasks, this leader honors suggestions that come from politicians and corporation executives concerning mandated curriculum, tight supervision, and national testing. After all, should not schools be operated like manufacturing concerns that concentrate on turning out products? And, by the way, there is nothing soft or unethical about jollying teachers, parents, and others into accepting decrees originating high in the education hierarchy.[19] This theory will predictably have a long life because of the amount of current practice and popular support behind it. It is called *transactional leadership*.

At the other end of the tug rope, there exists *transformational leadership*. Years ago, the statesman James McGregor Burns spoke of leadership representing two kinds of culture: (1) culture that emphasizes incentives and (2) culture that seeks to work with the goals and aspirations of members.[20] The latter culture cherishes transformational leadership. This kind of leadership makes of the school environment a hospital environment rather than a factory environment. In this "hospital," the "patients" (pupils and teachers) stay together a long time. In staying together, they form a community as opposed to a rigorous organization. Thomas J. Sergiovanni has defined transformational leadership by emphasizing the idea of community, at the heart of which are commonly held values, sentiments, and beliefs. Because teachers think similarly about crucial matters, they tend to work hard for "the team," to help others become successful, and to keep abreast of new ideas, which they are willing to communicate. By working with parents and others, teachers acquire ability to state goals and objectives that fit the situation. What Sergiovanni calls "professional virtue" pervades teachers' actions, finding its basis in the values of hard work, responsibility, honesty, fairness, and caring. When teachers view the school as a community, they live together in such a way that what they find rewarding and obligatory gets accomplished.

Meanwhile, where is the official leader? He or she is in the midst of the action, urging but not telling, saying *we* more often than *I*, and striving with others to transform the situation in desirable ways.[21]

Here are some useful rules for transformational leaders:

- Spend time, with others, in redefining educational goals.
- Think of talented classroom teachers as creative artists.
- Strive for cohesiveness and coordination.
- Keep before you the needs and interests of pupils, teachers, parents, and other stakeholders.
- Don't be shocked at the thought of restructuring the school.

From Theory to Practice

Where do we go from here? Superbly built theories do not lead to practice on their own strength. We need to use sensible theories in making sensible, practical applications. For instance, the traits theory tells us something about the kinds of new teachers we should employ, while the transactional theory tells us that employing new teachers is a structured operation, is not everyone's business, and is therefore mainly the function of a few responsible people in the school system. If the school in which a new teacher is to be placed subscribes to the theory of transformation, some of the teachers and the principal will need to probe the candidate's beliefs and values as well as his or her professional competency. When the candidate has finally been employed, he or she will be projected into an environment of group work and decision making, an environment that the new teacher will find comfortable and satisfying.

From the standpoint of curriculum improvement, what kind of leader—official or unofficial—do we want? In sum, we want a moral/ethical leader who can help to get the job done. Elbert Hubbard has said that the recipe for having beautiful children is to be beautiful parents. When transposed to the school, this aphorism says that if we want achieving pupils, the people in leadership positions around them must look and behave like moral/ethical achievers.

At present, the transformational (change-in-people) theory holds greatest promise of helping people become what they can and should be by providing a means of improving their accomplishments. The task of transforming people is never easy; in our time, it seems to be unusually difficult. Reform needs to begin in individual schools led by persons who themselves are committed to desirable change. State and federal officials can do no more at these sites than stand aside and give advice.

ACTIVITY 11-1

Assigning Values to Leadership Traits

In general, what traits or characteristics do you wish to see in your leaders? The following is a list of leadership traits. If you tend to like a given trait, place a plus next to it. If you tend to dislike it, put a zero next to it. If you are not certain, record a question mark. When all class members have assigned values to the traits, discuss the possible reasons for the differences among individual class members in assigning values.

Adaptive	Impulsive
Aggressive	Informal
Assertive	Laissez-faire
Autocratic	Paternal
Benevolent	Reclusive
Brave	Resistant
Democratic	Rigid
Despotic	Soft
Determined	Stimulating
Distant	Strict
Efficient	Strong
Empathic	Sympathetic
Fair-minded	Thoughtful
Firm	Tough
Friendly	Warm
Imaginative	Willful
Impersonal	

SITUATION 11-1

Leadership Without Equilibrium

Leona Riordan was new at her position as elementary school coordinator. In the view of many of her fellow teachers, she should never have been appointed coordinator, but politics had accomplished it. Today, she felt newer and more inexperienced than usual. "Something's wrong either with them or with me," said Leona. ("Them" referred to the teachers in Graves School with whom Leona had to work.)

"They tell you a lot of things in college and university that are of no practical use," Leona continued. "Here on the job, someone is always thinking up something for you to do or to avoid. Keeping it all in balance is a real problem. Yesterday, I told some of our teachers to meet this afternoon in Room 104. Fewer than half of them arrived for the meeting. In meetings, I often run into real trouble. Last week in the meeting on science, one of the fourth-grade teachers asked me what I thought of experimentation with electricity in fourth-grade classrooms. I didn't reply. The next day in a meeting on reporting to parents, the question was whether children ought to be compared with each other according to national achievement test norms. What are the teachers trying to do—test *me*? Then, of course, there's the weekly complaint that we don't know what direction we're taking in the elementary schools. And so it goes until I don't know which way I'm expected to turn."

How does Leona's conception of educational leadership compare with the theory that leadership is the property of the group? How does it compare with the conception you now hold? What does Leona seem to need to gain equilibrium and security in her position?

ACTIVITY 11-2

Finding Situational Factors That Affect Leadership

Every curriculum leader meets with numbers of groups and individuals. In doing so, he or she encounters situational differences of many sorts. Identify a responsible leader, such as the principal of a large school or the general supervisor or coordinator in a school system. Ask this leader to recall the events of his or her professional life during the past week. Make notes while he or she talks about the differences in situations that seemed to affect the quality of his or her leadership.

If others in your class or group carry out this activity, pool your findings with theirs.

ACTIVITY 11-3

Finding Applications of the Transformational Theory

By making direct contact with people in several schools, try to find applications of the transformational theory. Look especially for evidences of community feeling, of genuinely cooperative work, and of satisfaction based on the rewards of the work, enthusiasm of teachers for it, and the sense of obligation associated with it. If and when you find one or more schools that seem to represent the theory, inquire further to find out how leadership has been distributed within the school or schools.

FACTORS AFFECTING CURRICULUM LEADERS' WORK

A number of factors affect the quality of curriculum leaders' work. They include the perceptions that people have of curriculum leadership, the definitions and expectations of curriculum leaders' roles, leaders' styles, leaders' behaviors and behavioral orientations, difficulties that appear in leaders, the amount of authority that accompanies responsibility, and the attitudes and competencies of the curriculum leaders themselves.

Varied Perceptions of Curriculum Leadership

There are many gaps in our understanding of curriculum leadership. One of the greatest needs is for clarification of the precise roles of elementary and secondary school principals in instructional matters. The center of activity for improvement continues to be the individual school. Therefore everything possible must be done to build the security and competence of principals and their assistants. This observation raises the question "What can be done to increase the confidence and the competence of persons who lead staffs and programs in individual schools?"

The first question leads promptly to another. Much that has been done in directing instructional improvement programs in the past has included patterning and copying of ideas. There is a growing need for leaders who can stimulate creativity and discovery in themselves and others. The question then is "What ways of thinking and what educational experiences do leaders need if they are to be encouraged to create and inquire?"

Many leaders are uncertain about what it means to behave democratically, according to teachers' perceptions of democracy. Actually, teachers do not have a clear image of the democratic leader. They are much better at describing what a democratic leader *is not* than at describing what he or she *is*. Since they cannot identify him or her clearly, and since they have given little real thought to the advantages of democratic leadership, can it be that, at the present time, they do not really wish leaders to be democratic? At times, teachers seem to want autocratic leaders to do some of their work for them. This is not meant to suggest that teachers are perverse or lazy; their reaction is often a natural effect of being uncertain about where an unknown quantity called "democratic leadership" might place them. One may advance the thesis that a leader can be democratic only to the extent to which the staff of the school or school system is willing to assume both new and old responsibilities. These comments return us to some really basic questions:

1. What do we mean by democratic leadership?
2. What responsibilities and obligations might result from enjoying democratic leadership?
3. Is democracy in schools really somewhere between autocracy and laissez-faire, as it has often been pictured? Or is it "softened autocracy" and/or "organized laissez-faire"?

These questions need to be pondered by all persons who aspire to, or are already engaged in, curriculum leadership. To answer them, teachers and status leaders need to consider the possible effects of democratic behavior and then watch for those effects as leaders behave democratically.

Definitions and Expectations of Curriculum Leaders' Roles

Views of curriculum leaders' roles obviously differ widely. One study indicates that leaders in individual schools do not have accurate perceptions of the total concept their staffs and their superintendents have of the leader's role, that closer agreement exists between the principal and the staff than between the principal and the superintendent regarding concepts of the principal's ideal role, and that principals are seen by their staffs as overemphasizing public relations and strictly administrative functions at the expense of curriculum functions. Role definition, as it affects curriculum leaders, will need better clarification in the years to come, especially as leadership responsibilities are distributed more widely among teachers and others. Already status leaders in individual schools have much autonomy in instructional matters, but they are both unclear as to their roles and overinterested in "housekeeping" functions.

Superintendents and other persons who supervise the work of leaders in the schools should help them decide whether they should be *nomothetic* leaders, who emphasize institutional requirements and conformity to role expec-

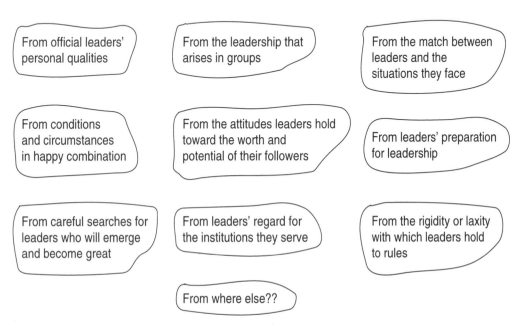

FIGURE 11-1   Whence Comes Great Curriculum Leadership?

tations, or *idiographic* leaders, who minimize role expectations in favor of the requirements of individual personalities. Idiographic leaders are likely to be much less "neat" in their leadership performance and to behave less as "good boys and girls" in the opinion of central offices.

Leaders' Styles

Every leader has a style of his or her own. An individual's style is very difficult to change. From the time of the Ohio State studies by John Hemphill and others, educational researchers have tended to think of leadership style under two headings, the task oriented and the human relations oriented, but practitioners have tried to say more definitively what they mean by style. For example, they describe particular leaders (mainly principals) as follows:

- "He acts like an executive secretary, so we form committees to make decisions."
- "Of course he behaves paternalistically. He is, after all, the father of our school family, and father knows best."
- "People call her pseudodemocratic because she solicits ideas freely, rejects most, and acts on a few to suit herself."
- "I suppose I am autocratic. The buck stops on my desk, so the decision is mine."
- "He leads by whim. Nearly every need to make a decision calls forth an unpredictable emotional reaction."
- "She leads by threat, often engaging in demeaning chastisement of those who are in disagreement with her."
- "She jawbones, explaining and explaining but never helping us decide. She's pleasant, but she gives no straightforward answers. Somehow she reminds us of too flexible, overcooked spaghetti."[22]

Fiedler's Contingency Theory emphasizes the importance of having a leader's style fit his or her situation. Inasmuch as style changes with great difficulty, it pays to change the situation to try to achieve a fit.[23] As new leaders are appointed, persons with particular styles should be designated to work in situations that suit their styles. As an elementary school teacher once said, "Good leader here is not necessarily good leader there!"

Recent considerations of style have gone beyond that teacher's situation-related comment. For instance, Gene Hall and others thought of the curriculum leader as initiator, manager, and responder. If the leader wants to achieve success in implementing ideas, he or she should be a responder to requests for help. If the leader wants to develop morale among teachers, he or she can "manage" by monitoring teachers' work, keeping close contact with teachers, supporting them, and minimizing their problems. If the leader wants to prove that he or she is "on top of the situation," the leader can serve as an initiator by anticipating needs, gathering usable information, supervising implementation of ideas, and generally knowing what is happening to learners.[24] Because purposes change, merge, and blur, consistency of style is not always to be prized.

It may be that the best evidences of a curriculum leader's style can be seen in the leader's view of other persons in his or her organization, how the leader likes to see decisions made, and how he or she helps create change.[25] Sources of style may be found in inherited traits, early childhood experiences, attitudes toward other people, and later experiences in life. Studies of biographical factors affecting the work of school leaders have brought some partial conclusions. Evidently, we should expect these leaders to be intelligent in a broad sense, exhibiting intelligence in pursuing approved goals, in sharing responsibilities, in dealing judiciously with people, in exhibiting virtues that count most, and in using their own mental powers.

Leaders' Behaviors and Behavioral Orientations

The behavior of curriculum leaders is readily noticed by teachers. John Hemphill and others at the Ohio State University, reporting in their *Situational Factors in Leadership,* discussed leadership behavior as involving both showing consideration to others and initiating structure within the organization. Through the years, showing consideration has often been highlighted at the expense of initiating structure. This emphasis has suggested to many students of leadership that school administrators, coordinators, and supervisors should give more attention to "being nice" than to getting jobs done. Recently, however, Kunz and Hoy have sought to determine effectiveness of leader behavior by isolating a single measure—the leader's success in having his or her directives followed. They identified three domains in which a leader might give orders: maintaining the organization/operation of the school, guiding (regulating?) teachers' personal behavior, and guiding teachers' professional behavior. They found that teachers would accept leaders' orders affecting organizational maintenance but would reject their mandates about personal behavior. Regarding teachers' acceptance of leaders' guidance of their professional behavior, the variation was so great that Kunz and Hoy considered teachers' professional behavior to be the zone within which leader effectiveness could really be seen. It is, of course, the zone in which curriculum leaders are greatly interested. Kunz and Hoy report that teachers are most willing to accept the professional directives of leaders who are high in *both* showing consideration and initiating structure.[26] Of the two, they found initiating structure to be more significant.

Though teachers want more in their status leaders than friendliness and congeniality, they do want to participate in decision making that affects them and the quality of their work. A number of investigators have found that groups of people who have a stake in the results of decisions make decisions of better quality than individuals can make. For example, Donald Piper found that the involvement of several people resulted in better decisions than could be made in what he called his "one man deciding alone" model.[27] Involvement by teachers is increasing to an extent that has seldom been known heretofore. *Teacher empowerment* is becoming more than a catch phrase.

The tug in almost any leadership situation is between the human relations dimension of performance and the productivity dimension. Good human relations emphasizes mutual respect, good will, faith and trust in others, and recognition of the dignity and worth of other people. One of the best-known studies of leader behavior pictures the leader who practices good human relations as finding time to listen, doing favors for others, making things pleasant, seeking to understand and to be understood, looking out for people's welfare, treating people as equals, showing willingness to make changes, making people feel at ease, and putting other people's suggestions to use.[28] The present author has found that school leaders demonstrate human relations skills—according to the perceptions of teachers and parents—in the following ways:

1. Meeting prominent psychological needs of teachers and other persons in schools
2. Guarding and guiding their behavior and words
3. Recognizing the worth of other people
4. Helping other people
5. Coordinating the work of teachers and other people.[29]

To stimulate productivity, the school leader evidently needs to do such things as make his or her viewpoints clear, help try new ideas, conscientiously criticize poor work, maintain standards of performance, develop staff role assignments, emphasize the meaning of deadlines, and try to make certain that staff members are working to capacity.[30] Rigorous as one or two of these actions may look, they are instrumental in moving commonly agreed-upon projects forward. Some actions to stimulate productivity must be unilateral on the part of the leader; more of them require cooperation between the leader and his or her associates.

From industry comes a catalog of leadership actions often labeled "best" by personnel at the middle management level. One of the first actions mentioned is making it clear to people that they are expected to have problems. There are also actions that involve improving the quality of group work so that meetings lead to results and not merely to more talk, so that group goals become clear, and so that regular time can be provided for important and worthwhile meetings. Other actions have to do with making decisions cooperatively about performance standards and with helping personnel achieve progressive growth in responsibility and independence.[31]

From the world of baseball comes a tongue-in-cheek statement attributed to Casey Stengel, former manager of the New York Yankees: "The secret of managing is to keep the guys who hate you away from the guys who are undecided."

Difficulties That Appear in Leaders

Many of the difficulties encountered by leaders are indeed in the nature of the people around them, but some of the difficulties are within the individual leader. A leader's potential personal difficulties can be expressed in the following questions: To what extent can I be liked and still do an effective job? To what extent do I fear failure? To what extent do I actually fear success? These questions imply conflicts within the person which are characteristically American. We Americans want to be liked, but as leaders we do not wish to be merely likeable or lovable. We want to produce. Consequently, we fear failure. At the same time, we may fear success because the presence of success brings us guilt feelings about displacing other people or leaving them behind.

Leaders need more wisdom than they usually possess. Many of the difficulties they encounter originate in the senseless errors they make. Plain common sense should be applied to the making of choices that affect the progress of their organizations.

Enough Authority to Accompany Responsibility

Books on school administration sometimes discuss *administrators* and their *authority.* Books on curriculum and instruction tend to discuss *leaders* and their *responsibilities.* Under an ancient concept of leadership still in evidence today, authority resides in the superintendent of schools and those staff members to whom he or she delegates it. Frequently, superintendents do not delegate authority to instructional personnel, though they do delegate it to business managers. In these instances, the business of a school district appears to be more important than the curriculum.

Major modification of this concept is needed. First, delegating authority increases "the number of levels of authority and thus results in a pyramidal rather than a flat organizational structure. This type of organization has often been authoritarian rather than democratic and has not promoted a free flow of communication."[32] *Authority,* a term used to describe institutionalized power, should sometimes be shared rather than delegated. "Shared decisions make it possible for the staff to be importantly involved...."[33] As William F. Whyte puts it, the problem is not that of eliminating authority but of weaving authority and participation together.[34] Delegation may be regarded as giving authority to another person or other persons for temporary or limited use, whereas sharing suggests continued, cooperative control of an enterprise by both a status leader and his or her co-workers. Inasmuch as, within the structure of U.S. school systems, superintendents are responsible to boards of education for total administration of the schools, superintendents are directly responsible to their boards for instructional programs. If they want the best instructional programs, however, superintendents will share their concerns, responsibilities, and authority for curriculum planning with members of their staffs.

Responsibility without authority tends not to produce results. As Hollis L. Caswell said, "It is much more effective to have the responsibility for curriculum work accompanied by authority over matters that fall within the curriculum area. This arrangement will foster cooperative and effective work in curriculum development."[35] Individuals such as directors of instruction, principals, department chairpersons, coordinators, and classroom teachers and groups such as curriculum committees should have authority to plan for and make improvements in instructional programs. The extent and nature of the responsibility and the authority that accompanies curriculum work should be made clear to those who are to perform duties in schools. Where there is any possibility of conflict of interest among groups and individuals, the conflict should be foreseen and resolved as early in the life of a project as possible.

Attitudes and Competencies of Curriculum Leaders

From beyond the walls of school buildings have come points of view about people in organizations that are shared by curriculum leaders. Here, for example, are three such points of view.

The first perspective may be termed the *utopian.* It holds that people are inherently good and that they proceed naturally toward self-actualization, but if the structure and values of an individual's work situation block him or her in the attempt to achieve self-actualization, the individual will join with his or her fellows to resist authority. The remedy is to restructure or otherwise correct the situation or system.

A second point of view about the functioning of people in organizations is *individualistic.* According to this view, people are neither good nor bad, but they do have particular needs that must be met. Preeminently, they need freedom and opportunities to make choices. They should be helped and developed within a congenial person-organization interaction. Where tension exists, some action should be taken to release the tension so satisfaction of needs can ensue.

A third position may be termed *moral-ethical.* It holds that people are inherently bad, particularly in the sense that they are self-centered. They need reorientation toward more constructive, cooperative, selfless behavior. Thus the problem is first with people and then with the organization. A chief function of the leader is to make reorientation possible; turning people toward goodness will improve the organization, and the organization will become beneficent because of the quality of the people in it.[36]

Innovative spirit, imagination, congeniality, respect for others, hard work, and follow-through are apparently features of leadership behavior that get results.

Specific competencies that curriculum leaders need include the abilities to

1. Practice good human relations
2. Adhere to principles of human growth and development

3. Know when, where, and under what conditions curriculum change occurs
4. Use group process techniques
5. Relate quickly to other people
6. Develop the creative abilities of other people
7. Invent new plans for organizing personnel and facilities
8. Know how to solve educational problems
9. See themselves as others see them

SITUATION 11-2

Choosing the Principal's Assistant

Woodhaven School District was finally going to give its high school principal an instructional assistant. Principal Matthews had just visited the superintendent, who, busy with the building program and a bond issue, had turned the problem of selecting an assistant over to the principal himself. Back at his office, Matthews shuffled through the sets of employment credentials and came up with two leading candidates.

The basic requirements of the assistantship seemed clear enough to Matthews and to five staff members whom he had consulted. They were

1. Ability to secure a state certificate in the general supervision of secondary education
2. A broad educational background
3. At least two years' experience in a similar position elsewhere
4. Special competency in leading groups and counseling individuals about instructional matters
5. Ability to coordinate warring groups and uncooperative personalities

Matthews and his consultants had been afraid to go further in listing job requirements. Like almost any other instructional position, this would be a difficult one to fill.

As he looked at the list, the principal muttered to himself, "I think I'll take a new tack. I'll look for the man or woman who has what it takes to fill the position." Accordingly, he made a list of the characteristics of his two leading candidates by inferences from their credentials and from his interviews with them.

Candidate Smathers	*Candidate Rink*
Very enthusiastic about professional advancement	Moderately enthusiastic about professional advancement
Reserved in her social contacts	Outgoing in his social contacts
Broadly experienced in supervisory work	Somewhat experienced in supervisory work
Excellent academic record	Satisfactory academic record
Fair ability to adjust to differing groups with which she works	Superior ability to adjust to differing groups with which he works
Interested in some of the facets of her past professional work	Interested in most of the facets of his past professional work

Almost icily self-controlled   Sometimes lacking in self-control
Generally well accepted by other staff   Generally well accepted by other staff
    members   members

Which candidate do you think Principal Matthews should favor?
What else should Matthews seek to know about these and other candidates?

ACTIVITY 11-4

Interrelating Human Relations and Task Performance in Curriculum Leadership

The text mentions the human-relations and task-performance aspects of leadership. These two elements of leadership should function simultaneously. That is, while educational leaders are trying to be pleasant and cooperative in their dealings with their associates, they should, at the same time, be doing important work to get educational jobs accomplished.

The following sociodramatic episodes are meant to emphasize the simultaneous interaction of human-relations and task-performance skills. Choose members of your group to act out the episodes, and then discuss them with reference to the quality of human relations and of task performance.

Sociodrama 1

Five complaining parents arrive outside the principal's office to protest the new program in drug education being offered in the high school. Their basic argument is that the program does not *prevent* drug abuse; rather, it informs youngsters about how to use drugs and therefore encourages them in drug abuse.

The principal, after inviting the parents into her office, defends the school's drug education program chiefly on the basis that the high school has a legal and moral right to provide it. Behind the principal sits her "conscience," a person who makes comments that run counter to some of the principal's public arguments. The principal is aided in making her public, official arguments by the assistant principal in charge of instruction, who knows most about the content of the drug education program.

The objects in this episode are (1) to resolve the immediate situation tentatively and thus to "cool" it and (2) to pose possibilities for permanent resolution of this and similar conflicts.

Total number of actors: 8.

Sociodrama 2

Three teachers representing a majority of the total teaching staff of an elementary school meet with the principal and others to object to the workshop in reading instruction that has been conducted in the school every other Thursday afternoon since September. The main thrust of the teachers' complaint about the workshop, which was planned by the principal and an outside consultant in reading programs, is that it is largely a waste of time and, at any rate, should not have been planned without the teachers' participation.

The principal takes the position that, as principal, he knows the needs of the faculty and has both a right and an obligation to plan for the teachers' inservice education. The outside consultant defends the nature and quality of the workshop. A reading consultant from the assistant superintendent's office bewails the conflict between her point of view about reading instruction and the point of view taken by the outside consultant. The union delegate is present to determine whether the teachers can make a grievance case of this situation.

The purposes here are to highlight the importance of leaders' ways of working and to note the complications created by input from persons with differing motivations and objectives.

Some of the roles of actors may be reversed part way through this episode.

Total number of actors: 7.

SITUATION 11-3

What Shall We Do to Improve Our School?

Act out the following role-playing episode.

The Characters

1. The principal, who has just returned from an administrators' convention and now advocates a plan for teaming teachers in teams of three
2. The union steward, who automatically resists all attempts to manipulate teachers
3. The chairperson of the school's curriculum steering committee, who insists that the three curriculum projects involving teachers are already "set" for the year and should not be moved aside now in the month of March
4. The principal's stooge, currying favor for unknown reasons, who maintains that the remainder of the year should be devoted to trying the principal's idea
5. The unofficial leader of the school faculty, a popular habitué of the teachers' lounges, who wants nothing to succeed that would give the principal additional power or publicity
6. A sincere and somewhat naive teacher who wants "what is best for our children," regardless of whether the principal's plan is implemented or not
7. A bright young teacher who is bucking to become a curriculum coordinator in the administrative district and who is interested in promoting curriculum projects which the teacher can later defend

Description of the Scene

1. This is a meeting of presumably interested persons who have responded to the principal's call to the faculty to attend a voluntary session concerning a "new" idea the principal has garnered at a recent national convention.

2. The principal opens the meeting by pushing his plan, which basically consists of dividing the faculty of 66 classroom teachers into 22 teams of three teachers each, allocated wherever possible by the teachers' personal preferences, but certainly by competence in subject matter and special skills.

3. The plan would lead to alteration of teachers' schedules so that trios could plan together an hour each day, work in unison at times, and continue working in self-contained classrooms most of the time.

4. The curriculum steering committee already has scheduled three projects involving three-fourths of the teachers: one in corrective reading, another in improvement of pupils' self-esteem, and a third in consumerism.

When the roleplay is over, discuss its implications for curriculum leadership.

SITUATION 11-4

The Curriculum Leader Without Authority

The Branchville Consolidated Schools had an active, thriving curriculum improvement program. Thirteen curriculum committees and five study groups were under way in the eight schools of this rural district. The curriculum coordinator, Lillian Dinsmoor, was busier than usual. She had recently helped the superintendent make a cooperative arrangement with the state university to begin curriculum experimentation for which the school district and the university would share the costs. Mrs. Dinsmoor had many responsibilities, but the superintendent saw to it that she was strictly a staff officer, lacking line authority to make decisions.

At 3:30 on a Thursday afternoon, Mrs. Dinsmoor telephoned three of the principals of the Branchville schools to ask whether they could find substitutes for a previously selected teacher from each of their schools for a full day of meetings one week from the following Monday. The purpose, Mrs. Dinsmoor explained, was to secure teacher representation on a new committee that would help her and Dr. Campbell, of the state university staff, plan for curriculum experimentation in Branchville. The first two principals she called readily agreed to release their teachers. Mr. McKay, the third principal, refused. "What kind of school do you think I'm operating?" he asked. "We have important things for Mrs. Fineman to do here on that day." Mrs. Dinsmoor knew that she had the responsibility for organizing the committee, which was to meet partly on school time, but no one had told her what to do when principals refused to release teachers to serve during the school day. She concluded the telephone conversation with Mr. McKay as quickly and as graciously as she could.

What, if anything, should Mrs. Dinsmoor do immediately about her problem?

What should she do over the long term?

How should her own actions take into consideration the possible actions of others in the school system who might help prevent similar situations from developing in the future?

LEADERSHIP STRATEGIES FOR IMPROVING THE CURRICULUM

A strategy is a comprehensive plan or series of maneuvers for achieving a result. As curriculum leaders think of what should be done to improve the curriculum over a period of years, they attempt to find strategies. The strategies they choose should fit their particular situations.

A half-dozen strategies have found important places in curriculum planning process. They are (1) strategic, centralized planning; (2) planning within and around classrooms and individual schools; (3) improvement of people through inservice education and staff development; (4) cooperative supervision for mutual helpfulness; (5) restructuring, or reorganizing, schools to facilitate learning; and (6) experimenting with curriculum and conducting minor research. Leaders may think of other means of promoting curriculum improvement, but the means they propose will probably not have the significance of the strategies noted above. Two or more strategies may, of course, receive emphasis in a school system at a given time or for overlapping periods of time. Each strategy has its own contribution to make, and each differs so much from the others that danger of duplication among them is minimal.

Strategy 1: Strategic, Centralized Planning

What was once called master planning or long-term planning now bears a different name and a different emphasis. The name is *strategic planning,* and the emphasis is on *probable futures.* This strategic, centralized planning for a whole school system or an administrative district of a large city or county involves, among other things, establishing purposes, policies, and criteria to guide improvement. The work is accomplished in places of central authority, with selected personnel being brought in from the field. We have seen in earlier chapters that most of the work accomplished in planning during the 1920s and 1930s was done in central offices of school systems. Although the site of planning has moved increasingly to the individual school, the central office has retained its functions of initiating, leading, and guiding major actions for curriculum change. Several arguments have been advanced for giving the central office a maximum of authority. One is that a system-wide approach brings the schools close to the community as a whole, with the result that citizens appreciate where the entire teaching staff stands on important educational issues. Another argument is that "across-the-board activity" is administratively neater and easier to manage. A third is that communication is improved because there are fewer conflicting actions and procedures. Other arguments are these:

1. People who "know" are usually housed in the central office.
2. Time is saved by avoiding detailed analysis of the needs and problems of individual schools.

3. There is maximum assurance that a given project or product has received the blessing of the powerful central office.
4. Coordination and comprehensiveness can be made keynotes of system-wide activity; hence, things can run smoothly and handsomely on a large scale.
5. A major result of system-wide activity is continuity—the presence of a common thread in the curriculum.

In the past, much of the planning done in the central offices of school districts was unsystematic. Currently, there is a stronger emphasis on system, order, and series of sequential steps in making major plans, and an occasional use of the systems approach to planning. With or without this approach, however, central offices are exercising increased care in planning, partly because of the demand for stricter accountability.

Actions taken by central office personnel to achieve long-range planning on behalf of entire school systems or major divisions of large systems include conducting large staff meetings, issuing directives and memoranda, preparing policy statements, organizing major projects for study and research, preparing course guides and unit plans, considering and announcing school system aims and general objectives, collating annotated lists of materials, producing booklets, pamphlets, and brochures on numerous topics, and preparing packages of learning materials. Modern strategic, centralized planning can repeat any of these actions that seem useful in looking forward from a "control tower" perspective. As issues of central importance are discussed, questions like the following should be asked: "If we take this proposed step, what's the most favorable probable scenario?" "What's the worst thing that could happen?" The emphasis in departing from failing tradition should be on futures. Michael Fullan has listed four questions that are instrumental in top-down analysis:

- What are the standards the central offices expect all pupils to meet?
- What are the goals that all schools in our district should try to attain?
- What can we do to keep the whole from becoming greater than the sum of its parts?
- What is our common belief system that needs to be shared throughout the school system?[37]

As P. Senge has said, to think that curriculum can be controlled from the top is an illusion.[38] Years ago, Doll, Passow, and Corey maintained that a centrally coordinated approach involving cooperation among central office and individual schools was needed.[39] By means of such an approach, individual schools would be encouraged to develop their own action groups. Similarly, Fullan has stated more recently that both centralized and decentralized strategies are essential.[40]

Strategic, centralized planning should accomplish those tasks that do not rightfully belong to the individual school. These tasks should be undertaken chiefly for three reasons: coordination, desirable uniformity, and economy of time and effort. The case for coordination needs no pleading. The expression *desirable uniformity* says clearly that much uniformity now found in school systems is *not* desirable. Therefore those who would encourage uniformity should assess whether it is really needed. *Economy of time and effort* refers to the importance of having certain tasks performed by one agency so as to bypass unnecessary duplication by several agencies. Duplication of effort is one of the great ills of organizations, and it needs to be rooted out of school systems that have existed for years without analysis of roles or even the most elementary time study.

Strategic planning can be made effective by (1) designating someone to have the responsibility and necessary authority to lead system-wide planning, (2) organizing a central steering committee to guide planning, (3) working closely with lay advisory committees and other groups of citizens, and (4) forming special interest committees or task forces to assume the responsibility for particular system-wide assignments. An added function of our era is "catching the curriculum baseballs" that are thrown toward the school system by state and federal agencies.

There are, of course, certain dangers in strategic, centralized planning, no matter where or by whom it is conducted. One is failure to involve enough professional personnel and lay persons in the decision-making process. Another is the well-known tendency of central offices and state agencies to overemphasize paper work. A third is the unfortunate temptation to make system-wide comparisons of teachers and children. A fourth is the compulsion to issue military-like directives. These dangers are theoretically reduced by bringing the planners and the planned-for together in individual schools. In practice, some school systems that are alleged to be most forward looking have in charge superintendents and other top-echelon personnel who seem to believe that improving the curriculum depends solely on accepting the wisdom dispensed by leaders of national and state curriculum projects and the status leaders of school systems. This limited view of the process of curriculum improvement can in the long run lead to impoverishment of the curriculum and to the rise of insurgent movements among teachers who have learned that participation on a system-wide basis is both possible and productive.

ACTIVITY 11-5

Finding Evidence of Centralized Planning in a School System

Identify a school system or a district of a medium to large city system in which you will be permitted to inquire about the curriculum planning that is conducted centrally. Keep in mind the examples of planning given above, but do not limit your inquiry to these. Ask one or more responsible persons in the central offices what phases of the curriculum are determined centrally. Inquire about the ways in which decisions relating to the curriculum are communicated to the schools, and ask to see documents that are used in the communication process. If you compare your findings with those of another inquirer, you will both learn much about centralized planning.

Strategy 2: Planning Within and Around Classrooms and Individual Schools

When the teacher closes the classroom door, much of the *real* curriculum of the school goes into operation. Most of the best curriculum improvement that occurs anywhere is accomplished in classrooms of the individual school, where teachers and pupils live together for five or six hours each school day. Here, the differences among children are revealed. Here, the teachers, no matter how stringent the supervisory authority of the school, are free to try some of their own ideas and ways of working and to put into practice what they have learned elsewhere. Here is the "cutting edge," the real frontier of education.

In the individual school, teachers of similar children or teachers with like professional problems can meet most readily. In faculty meetings or in small, informal groups, these teachers can discuss their problems, share information about possible methods of solving them, and design investigations in an attempt to find new solutions. Unless a domineering principal, an equally domineering central office, or the community itself ignores the concerns of the faculty, the problems selected for consideration are likely to be the real and immediate ones of the faculty itself. The real problems might be what to do with certain troublesome discipline cases, how to talk with parents during parent-teacher conferences, and what supplementary books to order with the dollars allocated for this purpose. Some of the real problems of teachers—such as the fatigue of children who watch television too late at night—originate in the community and require that teachers cooperate with parents and other school patrons. Other problems, such as those on the frontier of teaching and learning, often require lengthy, well-led consideration of what to do in the future.

One of the special advantages of the individual school as a curriculum planning unit lies in the fact that faculty groups are usually small. Small faculties have much face-to-face contact and can easily get together. In large high schools, teachers often meet in departmental groups, with occasional interdepartmental meetings. In large elementary schools, teachers assemble according to grade level and according to location in the school.

Four features of individual schools make them loci for the spread of leadership:

1. The individual school can become the site of productive meetings.
2. It is the place where teachers are usually freest to plan.
3. It can coordinate its work voluntarily with the work of other schools.
4. It can open curriculum study to people other than teachers, broadening participation and providing practice in leadership.

Experience with meetings in schools has caused specialists in group process to suggest ground rules that teachers and principals should know and observe:

1. Call meetings for times when teachers and other participants are alert.
2. Arrange for social contacts and refreshments before or after meetings.
3. Devote a continuing series of meetings to one or more important topics rather than staging "one-shot performances" in single meetings.
4. Encourage faculty participation in planning the meetings.
5. Seek out subject matter of real concern to the persons who participate.
6. Keep the meetings "on the beam."
7. Apply what has been learned about effective group procedures—for example, arrange for clarification of the problem or situation under discussion, encourage requests for information, urge a search for facts rather than mere opinion, and plan frequent summaries of progress made during the meeting.
8. Evaluate meetings by means of discussion or prepared evaluation forms; then use the data in planning subsequent meetings.

The customary role of individual schools makes one wonder whether the emphasis placed on them in curriculum planning implies that every school should develop its own exclusive and different curriculum. To expect the individual school to stand alone in planning would be foolhardy. There are at least two important reasons for this. First, similarities as well as differences exist among schools in the same system, and these similarities should be capitalized on through central or system-wide planning. Second, improving the curriculum from the ground up in each building would prove wasteful of time and funds. Whatever can be done legitimately in a central place should be done there. What is left to be done will be sufficient to keep the staffs of individual schools more than amply occupied. Today, the central place may be either school system offices or planning centers established by state government.

School staff and parents often worry about differences among the curricula of schools within the same system. What happens, they wonder, when a fifth-grade child moves from School D to School A and finds that fifth graders in the new school are learning something quite different in the social studies? Worries of this kind have doubtless been exaggerated. The pace and content of learning in Schools D and A may correctly vary, as they may indeed among several fifth-grade classrooms within a large individual building. Furthermore, a given experience in the social studies or in any other subject may, within limits, be as valuable as another experience.

The most important question is whether the diverse experiences contribute directly to educational goals that have been set for the system and for the individual school. The question then is "What experiences best serve *definite* purposes?" If concepts, major ideas, and varied points of view are learned, the details of the subject matter through which they are studied may safely differ from classroom to classroom and from school to school. Coordination, then, can be achieved best by focusing attention on big matters rather than a collection of little ones.

As community concern about schools increases, more community members will assume roles at the local level. In the future, leadership by community adults will be seriously needed in helping to determine the destiny of public schools, especially as more and more parents remove their children from public schools to be home schooled and/or educated in private schools.

ACTIVITY 11-6

Some Practical Problems in Local Planning

In planning educational experiences, there are several alternatives to developing units of instruction. One alternative is to follow a topically or chronologically organized textbook. Another is to use a "grasshopper approach," hopping from topic to topic without any long-range plan. Can you think of other, more constructive alternatives? Are there situations in which unit planning should not be used? If so, describe such a situation.

Now think how you would proceed to help a teacher who exhibited the following symptoms of poor planning: (1) a tendency to skip from subject matter item to subject matter item without regard to sequence and (2) a failure to identify and follow cues from pupils that indicate the pupils are confused by the subject matter and are losing interest in it.

Strategy 3: Improvement of People Through Inservice Education and Staff Development

Curriculum leaders of all sorts and levels have clear responsibility for directing activities that belong under the headings of inservice education and staff development. If the curriculum is to be improved, teachers must have the necessary insights, skills, and attitudes for planning and implementing curriculum change. They gain these insights, skills, and attitudes by being educated or reeducated on the job. If the education tends to be formal, stringent, and mandated, it is usually called *inservice education*. If it is informal, free in nature, and guided by teachers toward their own need satisfaction, it is usually called *staff development*. The justification for engaging in both inservice education and staff development activities rests on the assumption that learners' lives will not be changed very much unless the professional and personal lives of their teachers are made ever richer with fruitful experience.

Teachers have professional problems that well-conducted inservice and staff development programs can help them solve, although, naturally, these problems do not fall neatly into premade categories. The problems in their original formulation are crude; they need reformulation and explication. They cover a broad spectrum and require limitation of content to what can appropriately be discussed in inservice situations.

It is possible to reeducate teachers using a variety of means and media. For instance, it is possible to reeducate them by a behavior modification process—for example, by giving a teacher special privileges in return for increasing the number and variety of his or her teaching procedures or by penalizing a teacher for refusing to increase the number and variety of procedures used. Or teachers may be asked to observe and criticize their own teaching behavior after it has been videotaped and also observe and criticize the work of a versatile teacher. The author believes that, by using procedures of behavior modification, we tend to keep teachers in bondage, and by using a system of observation and criticism—especially self-criticism—we help to liberate them, though we are uncertain of the precise direction they will take in their liberated state.

If we want teachers to possess a broad repertory of teaching procedures—evidence now indicates that having such a repertory aids teachers in helping pupils learn—we should similarly have a broad repertory to use in the reeducation of teachers. If we want teachers to behave differently, we must reeducate them to believe differently. One route to helping teachers believe differently is to convince them that what they are being reeducated to do is indeed practical and useful.

Such reeducation must also be *practiced.* On this point, Louis J. Rubin says,

> New modes of behavior develop when particular actions are rehearsed again and again until they become an organic part of the individual. Accordingly, in-service education must begin with perception, kindle the freedom and the lust to change, then provide a method and support, and end in the confirmation of newborn habits. In this form, professional growth becomes self-transcendence.
>
> Where the desired change is a matter of ritual, the difficulties are minor. Where it is a matter of value, or belief, or master craftsmanship, there is no easy way....[41]

Studies of inservice and staff development programs show need for across-the-board involvement in planning and operating programs, need for careful scheduling of program activities, need for sequencing of events, need for consultant help, need for display of simulations and real performances, and need for adequate funding.

Many ways of reeducating principals, teachers, and parents with leadership responsibilities have become commonplace. Examples are courses, seminars, directed reading, intervisitation, attendance at conventions, and participation in retreats. Other less well-known means of reeducation come into use as the meanings of commonly agreed-upon beliefs and skills in the competence/performance category need reinforcing again and again. Both official and unofficial leaders sometimes need microcounseling, increased independent study, skill practice, analysis of recorded teaching episodes, participation in study groups, and experience in action research. These means are discussed in recent books on inservice education and staff development.

A comprehensive means of reeducation, the workshop, is particularly worth describing at length. The term *workshop* recalls the words of a spiritual, "Everybody talkin' 'bout heaven ain't agoin' there." The term has been much misused. The workshop in its bona fide state has been described by Earl C. Kelley as differing from meetings, classes, and other gatherings by including planning sessions, work sessions, and sessions for summarizing and evaluating.[42] This definition implies that the workshop is a democratically organized and rather lengthy medium of inservice education. It permits varied activities, which may include listening to consultants, discussing common problems, reading professional literature, assembling materials, watching film presentations, playing roles, filling evaluation forms, and picnicking with other participants. Not the least important of the workshop's features is the social proximity and the good feelings that can be developed among participants. Another feature is the devotion to solving problems that seem most significant to the participants.

Workshop sessions may be held on consecutive days for several weeks, as during the summer months. Sometimes sessions are conducted at intervals ranging from a few days to a week. In any event, time is scheduled so that programs like the following can operate:

- *First hour:* General session (singing, whole-group planning, listening to consultants, viewing films)
- *One-and-a-half hours:* Special interest groups (discussion by each group of a subject of special interest to it)
- *One-half hour:* Informal conferences (with staff and other workshop participants)
- *One hour or more:* Study and planning period (study, research, planning, trips, and tours)
- *One hour or more:* Activities (social events and sports)

A program of this kind may stretch to fill a full day or it may be condensed to occupy a shorter period. Workshop participants should be given responsibility for helping to plan their own programs.

Organized programs of inservice education and staff development may be said to serve as one of the two or three major direct stimuli to curriculum improvement. By organizing the programs, teachers and administrators consciously set aside time for activities that promote curriculum change. The blocks of time they reserve pay off in great or slight progress depending largely on two factors: (1) the concern staff members feel for the idea or subject being dealt with and (2) the cooperativeness and good feeling engendered by the program. The twin sparkplugs of concern and cooperativeness can fire the whole curriculum program in a school system. Cooperative study helps to reveal hidden problems, and organizers of the best programs encourage staff members to work on those problems that, after due consideration, prove to be most significant to the members' own thinking. Then they watch for ways of working together to encourage good human relationships. Programs based on the viewpoint mentioned above are an excellent takeoff point for further curriculum study and planning because effective programs contribute what a thriving curriculum improvement program needs: a cadre of interested, motivated teachers and insightful, prepared leaders.

ACTIVITY 11-7

Themes and Procedures for Planning Inservice and Staff Development Projects

Inservice projects organized in various school systems in the past have had the following themes:

- In Baltimore, Maryland: "How can we develop leadership among our staff members?"
- In Aberdeen, South Dakota: "Let's find out what our goals should be and then make them visible through concrete action."
- In Nyack, New York: "We need wide involvement of the people who should become fully aware of our more pressing problems."
- In Van Dyke, Michigan: "We must plan a variety of helpful, coordinated activities designed to meet teachers' needs."

Who should determine the theme of a project or a program? What should be the deciding factors in determining the theme?

When the theme has been determined, how would you help decide which inservice media (institutes, workshops, and so forth) to use?

Strategy 4: Cooperative Supervision for Mutual Helpfulness

Experience has indicated that the term *supervisor* can have two primary meanings: (1) the person designated by superintendent and board to supervise certain employees of the school district and (2) the administrative officer or teacher who helps others within the school organization, who then help others in return. The second meaning suggests that any competent member of a faculty is eligible to help one or more other members. These unofficial supervisors thus become mutually helping teachers.

Either kind of supervisor faces a formidable array of tasks. These tasks originate in needs like the following:

- The need to improve long-term and day-to-day planning with reference to objectives, pupil motivation, homework, and ongoing curriculum projects within the school system

- The need to improve use of pupils' time by achieving variety in classroom activities, relating learning theories to activities, adopting appropriate teaching procedures, relating classroom activities to school-wide activities, and reassessing homework policy
- The need to improve understanding of the dynamics of classroom groups with respect to ways of grouping, what really happens in group situations, classroom control, and humanization of the classroom
- The need to give attention to individuals, with reference to actions and materials that assist personalization, and to ways in which creativity can be fostered
- The need to use available resources wisely, including facilities and materials, the organization of the classroom for learning, and human talent
- The need to improve the quality of evaluation, with reference to objectives, comprehensiveness in the evaluation process, development of test items, and the planning of marking and reporting practices

Leaders who serve as supervisors need conceptual skills that permit them to help plan; to organize people, time, and resources; to lead by stimulating, communicating, and making suggestions for moving ahead; and to monitor what is happening. Of course, they need interpersonal skills also so that their own and others' relationships may become smooth enough to facilitate progress.

At one time, school personnel seemed to think of supervision as being distinct and vastly different from curriculum improvement. Supervisors were originally employed to inspect teaching and to build programs of instruction that teachers would closely follow. With the advent of curriculum specialists, supervisors were assigned to "supervise," and curriculum coordinators were designated to direct curriculum planning. Experience has shown, however, that the duties of supervisors and curriculum coordinators inevitably overlap and that people who carry these titles should constitute a service team for better teaching and learning.

Traditionally, teachers have disliked what some of them call "snoopervision." Old-style supervision has emphasized inspection and rating of teachers' work. (Many people believe we have returned to many of the abuses perpetrated by old-style supervisors.) According to the perceptions of most of those supervised, inadequate effort has been expended in helping teachers with the problems that concern them. The day the supervisor comes to visit the classroom is still regarded in some schools as a black day of fear and distrust. Adverse feelings about supervision have caused teachers to devise all sorts of artful dodges, such as changing suddenly to a specially prepared lesson or passing a red book from classroom to classroom to alert other teachers to the supervisor's arrival in the building. Fortunately, in some school systems, the supervisor's function has shifted to that of helping teacher or consultant. Teachers and supervisors *should* work cooperatively to improve the quality of pupils' school experiences.

School systems that can afford them often develop unusually strong supervisory programs. These programs depend significantly for their success on the quantity and quality of the supervisors and on the functions they serve. In some states, county offices of education provide supervisory services through specially staffed service centers.

Perhaps the most natural and productive situations calling for the teamwork of supervisors and teachers grow out of ongoing curriculum study. For example, development of a course guide in the social studies may require classroom experimentation with content, methods, and materials. Two or three central office supervisors, several principals, and a score of teachers may involve themselves in the project, working in classrooms, meetings, and conferences and planning both the experimentation and the course guide. In situations of this kind, the fear and artificiality that have often characterized supervision tend to disappear.

Alert supervisors recognize that they must work differently in different situations—with experienced teachers, with first-year teachers, with parent groups, with fellow supervisors and administrators, and with varied groups of teachers in a kaleidoscope of settings. Supervisors are regularly involved in curriculum improvement activities so diversified as to challenge their adaptability and ingenuity. In general, however, supervisors are concerned with three giant tasks: (1) helping to determine purposes of education and helping to see that these purposes are adhered to in daily practice, (2) giving democratic instructional leadership, and (3) keeping channels of communication in school organizations open. If they are not careful, supervisors fall into the habit of manipulating teachers to achieve the ends that the supervisors themselves consider desirable. Patience and willingness to see the other person's point of view are among the fundamental qualities that supervisors should possess.

Of the numerous procedures that supervisors have developed, a few have become very common. These include classroom observation, supervisor-teacher conferences, group work, and demonstration teaching. Other supervisory procedures, some of which are similar or akin to procedures used in organized inservice education, are intervisitation; directed reading, in which professional reading is planned both for and with teachers; preparation of written bulletins, exhibits, and bulletin displays; courses; professional conventions; and selection and development of teaching materials.

Teachers seem to consider supervision effective when it supplies stimulation, encouragement, ideas, materials, and skill in troubleshooting. As a strategy of curriculum improvement, supervision has the advantage of dealing with down-to-earth situations, building consciousness of highly specific needs for improvement, and keeping close to the feelings of teachers.

Supervision is sometimes considered a likely prospect for application of the systems approach. A systems model in supervision usually has three phases: input, process, and output. Input involves determination of needs, setting of goals, and identification of strategies for meeting the needs. Process consists of implementing and monitoring the strategies. Output is determined by evaluating the effectiveness of the strategies in light of the goals. The output phase may involve suggesting modifications in the system. Feyereisen, Fiorino, and Nowak have developed a supervisory system that includes designing curriculum, providing teachers with advice, and helping an instructional staff with problems of teaching and learning. These authors recommend the systems approach because it integrates elements of supervisory strategy into a single plan.[43]

Another development of promise is *human resources supervision,* which is not to be confused with human relations supervision. The human resources supervisor places first emphasis on important and meaningful work. In accomplishing this work, teachers gain the kinds of satisfaction that the advocates of human relations supervision desire and to which they assign top priority. The emphasis on the work involved in improving the curriculum (at a time when the work ethic is again looming larger) makes human resources supervision a potential asset.[44]

Both human relations supervision and human resources supervision are concerned with teacher satisfaction. The former calls for action that will increase teacher satisfaction so that teachers are easier to work with and to lead and so that, in the long run, schooling becomes more efficient and effective. Human resources supervision, on the other hand, sees satisfaction as an end toward which teachers aspire if they have important and meaningful work to do. The accomplishment of worthwhile work is the way to efficient and effective schooling.[45]

During the late 1970s and the 1980s, many leaders with responsibility for supervision were influenced by state departments of education and presumed public opinion to emphasize evaluating and monitoring teachers' work. As the pendulum swung in this direction, there was a flurry of interest in evaluation devices, merit pay plans, alternative routes to entry into teaching, and other means of compulsion and extrinsic reward. A countermovement emphasizes a longer view of the improvement process, with supervision focusing on careful and thorough development of current staff who, under existing tenure laws, are likely to serve in the schools for years to come.[46]

ACTIVITY 11-8

Surveying Teachers' Needs for Supervisory Help

The late J. Minor Gwynn, an authority in the field of supervision, surveyed teachers along the Atlantic coast to learn ways in which they believed their supervisors could help them best. The top five needs for help that these teachers identified were associated with (1) planning, (2) finding teaching materials, (3) evaluating pupil progress, (4) establishing discipline or control, and (5) solving professional, community, and social problems.

Conduct a similar survey of your own, even though your sample of teachers will necessarily be smaller. Combine your findings with those of your fellow students.

How do your combined findings compare with those of Dr. Gwynn? What implications do your findings have for the organization and nature of supervisory programs?

ACTIVITY 11-9

Getting to Know Teachers' Strengths

Considering that attempts to study teachers' work have often ended in conflict, perhaps we should try *describing* teaching episodes we see, emphasizing not only how teachers currently perform but also what their teaching can become. The following questions may be pertinent:

1. What can this teacher do well in his or her teaching? What strengths do you recognize?
2. How do you describe the nature and degree of control this teacher has over what he or she can do?
3. What is your description of the fit this teacher achieves between what he or she does and his or her objectives?
4. What is your description, based on your experience with this teacher, of the teacher's ability to learn from work in the classroom so that he or she may have special competence in helping with an aspect of curriculum development?

If you are in a position to do so, study the work of a teacher in these terms as a means of determining the particular strengths of the teacher and the teacher's probable potential for helping to improve the curriculum and instruction in your school.

Strategy 5: Restructuring, or Reorganizing, Schools

The assumption has been widely made in the past that the curriculum can be improved to a marked degree by reorganizing the school. Reorganizing a school can affect its personnel, its buildings, its facilities and materials, and its entire way of operating. For some time, educational planners outside local school systems have been asking, "What will happen if pupils' and teachers' time is used differently because the school has been reorganized? What will occur if teachers have altered responsibilities and novel kinds of help? What about changing the basic organizational structures within which people work?"

Reorganizing schools is now often called *restructuring*. Restructuring requires making changes in factors like the duration of time teachers spend with given groups of pupils, kinds and sizes of instructional groups, teaching by individuals versus teaching in teams, amount of aid by paraprofessionals and other persons on the "career ladder," and close grading versus nongrading of pupils. Some of the means that have already been used to create varied effects through reorganization are team teaching, teacher aides, large- and small-group instruction, nongraded elementary and secondary schools, and departmentalized elementary schools.[47]

Some of the ways in which leaders may propose to reorganize, or restructure, their schools are specified in the following paragraphs.

Team teaching has now been accepted as a fundamentally sound idea. Implementing it has proved to be the real problem. Committed teachers, appropriate space, and the necessary facilities are all requisites. Team teaching permits pupils to gather information in large groups, to explore meaning in small groups, and to pursue their individual interests. To make team teaching work, the people involved must believe in the importance of individualization, be willing to work together and to plan extensively, and cherish flexibility and creativity. The more cynical supervisors maintain that the crucial factor is whether or not team members can endure associating with one another.

The present is a time of increased *differentiated staffing*. At first, aides in the classroom tended to perform routine chores for teachers and pupils. Currently, on the levels of the "career ladder" are paraprofessionals, cadet teachers, teachers in charge of research, and teachers in charge of curriculum development. Both educators and the lay public are at least partially convinced that staff differentiation can increase efficiency in classrooms. However, the roles of all interrelated personnel need further defining, standards need to be established for choosing personnel within categories, and improved programs for preparing categories of personnel must be established.

In a limited sense, *nongrading* is as old as the one-room school. Modern nongrading is intended to remove the labeling that has accompanied assigning pupils to grades, and to permit children to achieve mastery of subject matter before they move to another level in the educational hierarchy. Nongrading is meant to enhance our recognition of children as individuals and thus to improve their self-concept. Naturally, effective nongrading requires committed, skilled teachers who realize that the individual child has such varied potential in performing the different tasks the school sets before him or her that "grading" each individual becomes a practical impossibility. As Bernard McKenna said, grading is "a survivor of an agrarian society." He suggested that groups of 100 pupils each might profitably be kept together for a period of two to four years and taught by an assigned team of teachers and support staff.[48]

The *middle school,* originally adopted in many communities as an expedient for accommodating a rapidly increasing school population, has its own purposes and programs. This level of schooling between primary and secondary often bears the name *intermediate.* The search is continuing for relevant content, with the thought that the middle school could, without due care, go the way of the junior high school, becoming a miniature high school. Presumably, if the middle school provides appropriate experiences for children, it can meet the needs of early-developing adolescents, whose physical maturation and peer interaction patterns are those formerly associated with pupils higher on the age scale. Programs emphasizing individualization, varied group activities, inquiry, helpful guidance, and subject matter that permits pupil action give promise of helping the middle school succeed.

Flexible scheduling permits a loosening of school organization so that pupils can use their time in more varied ways. Dividing the school day into more blocks of time and altering time allocations assigned to given school experiences are means of increasing flexibility.

Open space schooling permits pupils to have varied experiences throughout the school building and beyond.

New building designs depart from the traditional by providing areas and rooms for activities constituting additions to the curriculum. At best, the new designs are created specifically to accommodate new and carefully planned reorganizations of the curriculum.

New learning facilities and materials, ranging from recorders to computers, make implementation of curriculum ideas easier. The general learning center occupies a crucial place in schools where the newer facilities and materials are prized.

These innovations are only examples of means for reorganizing schools as institutions. Prospects for improving pupils' learning within reorganized schools seem to depend on this significant condition: If teachers are given more time away from the routine duties or away from duties they lack competence to perform, they should spend this time productively in performing professional tasks. These tasks might include becoming better acquainted with individual pupils, working closely and more insightfully with alienated or disadvantaged learners, and helping pupils improve the quality of their thinking and the clarity of their values. Much depends, after all, on how profitably pupils and teachers spend their time *within* the restructured institution with its new arrangements. Where these considerations are taken into account, restructuring schools as workplaces seems to increase the fruitfulness of staff development activities and the general effectiveness of teaching and learning.[49]

Among the acceptable goals of reorganizing, or restructuring, schools are (1) achieving quality with equality for all pupils, (2) arranging more educative environments for both pupils and teachers, (3) building partnerships and networks of personnel, and (4) involving parents and other community members. If these goals are to be achieved, both principals and teachers must serve as leaders. The willingness of both groups to cooperate in solving common problems is essential.[50]

ACTIVITY 11-10

An Investigation of Local Trends and Tendencies in Reorganizing, or Restructuring

Note the numerous ways of reorganizing, or restructuring, schools that have been previously mentioned. Learn what is being done under the heading of reorganization in a school or school system you know well. What advantages and what deficiencies do you see in the plans for reorganization that are now in operation and in those that are projected? Compare your findings with those of other investigators.

Watson and others have described the ground-level leadership and decision making in a restructured school. Characteristics of the school might now include

- Organization of teams of teachers functioning semi-autonomously
- Curriculum planning by advocacy groups involving teachers and administrators
- Unit planning, purchase of materials, and coordination effected by teacher advocates
- Cross-school advocacy groups for conceptualizing and evaluating programs
- Released time for advocates (three to seven days a year)
- Summertime preparation of curriculum units
- Service by administrators as facilitators, monitors, advocates on behalf of children, co-planners with teachers, and continuing holders of school-wide authority
- Annual retreats to enhance staff unity

Experience with restructuring will produce additional characteristics.[51]

SITUATION 11-5

Improve Curriculum Design or Change the Organization of the School?

The superintendent and the principals of the Bellevue Public Schools had spent nearly a year studying plans for altering the allocation and use of pupils' and teachers' time. In the process, they had considered core-type programs, plans for team teaching, the employment of teacher aides, and part-time use of programmed learning. It was time now to decide what should be done both to improve the curriculum and to impress the community. Sometimes the latter objective seemed to take precedence over the former. At a crucial meeting, Principal Anna Jones said: "We can talk about improving the organization of the curriculum or about improving the organization of the school, but the two actions are not necessarily the same. Manipulating external things is often popular and sometimes easy; improving the experiences of children may be difficult and even unpopular. I hope we're concerned about experiences and that we'll ignore gadgetry and moving people around."

To what extent do you agree with Principal Jones's point of view? Suppose you made organizational changes in the school itself. How could you tell whether these changes had improved the quality of children's learning experiences? Be specific as to the change or changes you have in mind and as to methods of determining their effect.

Strategy 6: Curriculum Experimentation and Minor Research

Curriculum experimentation is an important means of moving educational practice out on the frontier. It is a medium for trying new content and procedures and for testing ideas in action. It does not, in the manner of research, provide definitive data on which one can rely, but it does offer many cues to improved practice.

Research, on the other hand, is systematic inquiry that helps solve instructional problems. It consists of conjecturing intelligently about steps to be taken in solving a given problem, taking one or more actions in line with the conjecture, and then observing whether the actions have brought the results that were predicted or anticipated in the conjecture,

Research comes less naturally to teachers than experimentation does. So little research has been conducted in U.S. classrooms that data about even the most important facets of education—the learning process, the learners, and methods of teaching—are fragmentary. Occasionally, teachers are involved cooperatively in broad-scale research in the teaching of reading, spelling, and other school subjects. In the past, this research has been sponsored by university groups and by individual professors, or else by research bureaus in the larger school systems. Actually, the quantity of well-directed research involving classroom teachers has been small.

Though few teachers have had opportunities to engage in formal research, they do experiment informally. At a low level of experimentation, they often move pupils from seat to seat to quell disruptive behavior. At a higher level, they may experiment with the four classic elements of effective classroom practice: (1) seeing what the goals of their schools mean with respect to establishing the directions of their efforts, (2) gauging the worth of varied teaching materials that accord with the goals, (3) experiencing staff development activities that are expected to help with attainment of the goals, and (4) allocating time variously in attempts to attain the goals.[52] The teacher who wishes to be more certain of what is happening when he or she makes changes uses procedures of operational research—or *action research,* as it is usually called. Action research has been described by Stephen M. Corey as research conducted "in the heat of combat." Others have defined it as controlled experimentation by means of which practitioners study their problems to guide and correct their decisions and actions. The elements of the overall action research design are

1. Identification of a problem area about which an individual or a group feels enough concern to take action
2. Selection of a specific problem and formulation of an "educated guess" (hypothesis or prediction) that states a goal and a way of reaching it
3. Careful taking of action, recording of action, and collection of evidence to determine the degree to which the goal has been reached

4. Drawing conclusions or making generalizations from the evidence as to the worth of the actions in reaching the desired goal
5. Continuous retesting of the generalizations in practical school situations[53]

Consider an example of the use of this process.

Example

A teacher became disturbed about the disinterest and poor performance of her eighth-grade pupils in written composition. She made the hypothesis that if writing were more closely related to the real-life experiences of children, both the children's interest in writing and the quality of their writing would improve. She learned from her pupils by interview, by a specially prepared inventory form, and by observation what they thought of their present composition projects. She also analyzed, from the viewpoint of fluency of expression and technical quality, two or three samples of each pupil's written work. She then arranged excursions to an airport, a construction project, and the United Nations center in New York. Subsequently, she encouraged the children to write about one or more of these excursions, inquired by the methods indicated above about their interest in describing the excursions, and analyzed the new compositions for fluency and technique. The evidence showed improvement in both interest and performance, with interest showing more improvement than performance. The teacher generalized that a writing project originating in real-life experience resulted, at least for her group of pupils, in improved interest and performance in writing. She realized that this was a tentative conclusion that merited additional testing in her own and other classroom situations.

The procedures in research or experimentation of this kind have been attacked as lacking the tightness and neatness of more careful research, but they may be defended as providing the classroom teacher with some evidence on which to base decisions. Perhaps the greatest handicap to performing action research is a lack of the understanding and skill required—an experimental outlook, understanding of the research process, and skill in formulating testable hypotheses. In the immediate environment, the leader-researcher should have a supportive administrative staff, favorable community climate, adequate resources, and open lines of communication. The classroom teacher should become familiar with at least the better-known references concerning research—*Encyclopedia of Educational Research; Review of Educational Research; Education Index,* which does for education what *Readers' Guide to Periodical Literature* does for general literature; *Bibliography of Research Studies in Education;* compilations of research studies by Phi Delta Kappa, an honorary fraternity-sorority in education; and the ERIC materials.

The problems that research and experimentation help to solve usually come from one or more of the following sources: the teacher's own feelings of need, criticisms by lay people of the program of the school, and evidence of shortcomings revealed by evaluation. The teacher who feels dissatisfaction with conditions as they are is ready—psychologically, at least—to undertake reasoned inquiry.

The teacher's self-evaluation of his or her own work offers one of the most promising ways of improving schools. Teachers need help in studying the differences between the nature of their intent and the outcomes they are achieving. Their objectives may need changing or amending; their methods may be faulty. To know that such circumstances exist, teachers need to observe carefully and to record data carefully.

Attention has been directed recently to a way to identify problems that need further study—the "quality circle" idea created by Japanese industrialists to improve the postwar output of their industries. The quality circle consists of ten to fifteen volunteers who meet weekly for one hour to identify problems that block high-quality work and to discover sources of information about them. A circle in the school or the school system could also prove useful in formulating hypotheses leading to further inquiry and eventual problem solution.[54] Quality circles, which have been tried in industrial firms such as Honeywell and General Motors, usually go through a four-step process. First, participants brainstorm possible problems and choose one for attention. Second, they discuss and select the essential cause of the problem. Third, they brainstorm three possible solutions and choose one. Fourth, they submit to administrators a description of the problem and their proposal for solving it.[55]

Research and experimentation can surely open the door to curriculum improvement. Their ultimate usefulness, however, depends on the extent to which the evidence they turn up is employed to advance improvement. Much depends, then, on the willingness of school personnel to respect and use data for functional purposes in the improvement process. The key to success in practical use of research and experimentation is the teacher. When teachers are permitted to participate from the beginning to the end of a project, they are most likely to accept the idea of researching and experimenting. Functional research methodology can and should be determined by professional researchers, but the presence of desirable staff attitudes depends on building participation and support from the bottom of a school system upward.[56]

Research by teachers and other staff members can produce the kind of leadership (cultural, as opposed to technical/managerial) that directly assists curriculum development. Here, the principal becomes a cultural leader who encourages teacher initiative and inquiry. Subsequently, teachers lead the way by questioning present policy and practices, making observations, collecting data, keeping records, thinking about tentative results, and drawing conclusions. Meanwhile, the principal shares knowledge and authority in a work environment of checks and balances.[57]

SITUATION 11-6

A Guide to Research by Classroom Teachers

John B. Barnes, writing in *Educational Research for Classroom Teachers,* suggested nine questions to be asked by school leaders before they encourage teachers to undertake projects in research and experimentation:

1. Does the school problem which you have in mind definitely limit the operation of your school or decrease the value of your educational program?
2. Can your educational program be improved by concerted study, reflection, and research on this problem?
3. Are the various school publics—students, teachers, school board members, parents, and general public—aware of this educational problem?
4. Have teachers and parents discussed the problem and failed to solve it?
5. Has the school board discussed this problem at a regular board meeting?
6. Is this educational problem one that seems perennially to cause concern?
7. Have you carefully identified, described, and analyzed the problem?
8. Do you see its parts, its ramifications, its possible causes?
9. Can you list on paper the effect that this school problem has on the educational program?

Which of these questions seem most important in the evaluation, research, and experimentation projects you have in mind?

What are these projects? Make a written plan for conducting the evaluation, research, or experimentation in one of the projects.

IMPLEMENTING THE STRATEGIES

Leaders need to act specifically and precisely in implementing the six strategies that have been discussed. What they do necessarily conforms to the powers and constraints that go with their positions. Among the prominent status leaders with particular assignments of duty are system-wide curriculum directors or coordinators, principals of schools, and local school coordinators and chairpersons. Other status leaders, such as superintendents and supervisors, have particular assignments also, but most of the responsibility for overseeing curriculum planning and implementation falls to the three kinds of functionaries just mentioned, whose cases can be used as prototypes. The detailed work in planning and implementation then devolves upon teacher-leaders.

Some general leadership tasks are, however, distributed among numbers of status leaders and other persons:

Task 1: To help the people of the school community define their educational goals and objectives. In the early days of activity for curriculum improvement, defining goals and objectives was a frequent first step. Because many school systems did not get beyond this step, goal definition fell into some disrepute. The attention of curriculum workers turned to the problem census, the isolated experiment, the demonstration project, and other steps as a means of starting improvement. The result has been an absence of purpose-centered education and an eventual realization in some quarters that, without vision, the ideas of the people in schools, as elsewhere, perish. When they fail to set goals and objectives, curriculum workers do not know what educational values they stand for, where they are going, or how to evaluate what they have accomplished. Definition of goals, then, is a fundamental task in curriculum improvement; this task is to be shared with lay persons.

Task 2: To facilitate the teaching-learning process; to develop greater effectiveness in teaching. Task 2, which formerly resided chiefly in the central offices of school systems, now belongs more and more in individual schools under the status leadership of building principals. It is accomplished by whatever means the staff decides to emphasize from year to year—programs of supervision, the newer studies of subject matter, projects in in-service education and staff development, experimentation and research, testing programs, and curriculum planning activities of many kinds. We are in danger of seeing this task, in its full meaning, obscured by easy panaceas and nostrums, the use of which impedes serious study of teaching and learning and supervisory assistance to individual teachers.

Task 3: To build a productive organizational unit. The importance of building organizational structure should be self-evident. An appropriate organizational unit has as its essentials cooperative planning and group deliberation. It releases people to examine their own and one another's roles, and to decide calmly who has the power and qualifications to assume particular responsibilities. In addition, this organizational unit keeps the channels of communication clear and makes it possible to find out how well pupils are attaining the goals set for them and for the schools.

Task 4: To create a climate for growth and emergence of leadership. Much of the previous discussion has stressed the importance of freeing teachers and other personnel to express themselves and to ask for help. This task highlights the importance of providing opportunities for staff members to accept and discharge various leadership responsibilities. It calls for emergent leaders to enrich the work of the school by their contributions and to free status leaders for assignments they could not undertake without help from emergent leaders. For heavy responsibilities, teachers who emerge as leaders need released time. However, when problems of the school are seen as *our* (the whole staff's) problems rather than *his* or *her* (the administrator's) problems, teachers are more willing to share freely in the detailed tasks of planning and operating the instructional program.

Task 5: To provide adequate resources for effective teaching. Teachers have more resources at their disposal than they realize, including personnel in the school and the community. Other resources are material in nature—homemade, commercially produced, or borrowed. Leadership must keep alert to lapses in the utilization of presently available resources and also must continually search for new resources that make teaching lively and practical.[58]

These tasks are broad and general enough to fit any situation, and they are shared by many persons. Narrower leadership tasks are assumed to belong to specific persons who have strong leadership roles. One of the common expectations concerning democratic leaders is that, although they should share many responsibilities with others, certain responsibilities should be affixed to them as individuals of special competence and with special license to act.

Accordingly, the whole range of responsibilities divides into three categories. Some responsibilities for curriculum planning are shared freely by all who have any stake in the planning. Others are shared cooperatively by status leaders and certain selected or representative staff members, as in curriculum steering committees. Still other responsibilities belong strictly to status leaders—with such titles as superintendent, assistant superintendent in charge of instruction, director of instruction, curriculum coordinator, or some other title that suggests comprehensive curriculum leadership—and to other leaders with narrower but more concentrated responsibilities—principals, special subject supervisors, coordinators under whose aegis a portion of the instructional program falls, and department heads in secondary schools.

What Curriculum Leaders with System-Wide Assignments Do to Lead

The general leadership of curriculum programs falls to persons in the central offices of school systems who bear such titles as assistant superintendent in charge of curriculum and instruction, director of curriculum, director of instruction, and curriculum coordinator. Inasmuch as they are often regarded as surrogates for the superintendent of schools, these persons usually do in the area of curriculum and instruction what the superintendent would presumably do if he or she had the necessary time, inclination, and expertise. Many times, they make their positions what they want them to be, subject to the will of one or more higher administrative officers. They have varying degrees of authority, so their positions range from powerful line assignments to weak staff or advisory posts. At any rate, they must share many of their responsibilities with other personnel. Which responsibilities are shared and which are retained by general curriculum leaders depends so much on organizational patterns in school systems and the personal preferences of the leaders themselves that one cannot distinguish, by general rules, between responsibilities that should be shared and responsibilities that should be retained. No one but the curriculum leader with system-wide responsibilities is likely, however, to accept leadership in achieving curriculum balance, in seeking the elimination of contradictions in the total curriculum, in trying to improve curriculum design and organization, in urging continual evaluation, in serving as a curriculum change specialist, and in retaining a total view of all curriculum matters.

The preceding list of large responsibilities does not, of course, represent what most curriculum leaders do day by day. Curriculum leaders are found more often meeting with supervisors and faculty groups about other matters, serving as consultants to principals and teachers, helping make policies of all sorts, arranging for exhibits and demonstrations, representing the superintendent at ceremonial functions, working with community groups, and helping interview candidates for positions. Important as these tasks may be, they do not tax the abilities of most curriculum leaders. It is not uncommon for the superintendent to assign his or her front-line curriculum leader responsibilities that are less than worthy of the person's abilities while important curriculum tasks are left untouched.

Using the strategies discussed earlier in this chapter, the leader with system-wide responsibilities finds much to do in guiding centralized planning, in helping coordinate local planning, in establishing and presiding over programs of inservice education and staff development, in supervising the supervisors, in helping plan school reorganization, and in giving general direction to research activities. International scholars in the curriculum field honor system-wide leaders for their demonstrated abilities in developing ideas, in alerting their school systems to needs and trends, and in making accurate predictions of things to come. In brief, a well-prepared generalist in curriculum study not only has a promising career ahead but also occupies the role of prime curriculum expert in his or her community. The effort to design university programs to better prepare leaders for system-wide responsibility continues.[59]

Edward Pajak sees the leadership roles of central office directors and coordinators to be pulling things together in the instructional arena, presiding over the development of desirable attitudes in situations filled with real or potential conflict, and arranging for effective communication within systems. He uses terms like *order and sense, understandings and agreements, trust, reciprocity, cooperation,* and *information.*[60] Pajak makes two remarks that get at the core of the director/coordinator's leadership responsibilities. The first is that the director/coordinator needs to have basic concern for children's welfare and for the quality of their schooling. The second is that he or she finds that meaning and purpose come from conducting dialogues with other people.[61]

SITUATION 11-7

The Responsibilities of a New Curriculum Leader

The president of the Wasson Board of Education turned to Superintendent Rogers at the conclusion of the board's regular monthly meeting. "What are your specifications for the new position of director of instruction?" she asked.

Rogers was caught flat-footed. "We haven't really determined the specifications," he had to admit.

"Don't you think you ought to—right away?" the president asked.

Early the next morning, Rogers assembled several of his aides to help him establish a set of responsibilities for the directorship. Within an hour or two, they had the basic responsibilities listed to their satisfaction. The trouble came in trying to assign approximate percentages of the director's time to the responsibilities. "Maybe we can't do it very accurately," Superintendent Rogers said, "but I'd like to see each of you put on paper a percentage figure to indicate the amount of time the director should spend on each responsibility." When the proposed allocations of time had been assembled by the superintendent's secretary, they looked like this:

	Time allocations (in percent)				
Activities	**Aide #1**	**Aide #2**	**Aide #3**	**Aide #4**	**Aide #5**
1. Attending curriculum meetings	30	20	0	50	10
2. Visiting individual classrooms	10	2	40	8	60
3. Conferring with individual teachers	10	15	10	10	2
4. Employing new teachers	20	10	30	5	10
5. Attending teachers' social functions	3	2	0	10	0
6. Reviewing lesson plans	2	5	15	0	10
7. Conducting meetings, workshops, and other inservice activities	25	45	2	15	3
8. Ordering and assembling materials and supplies for teachers	0	1	3	2	5

What can you observe about the aides' perceptions of the curriculum director's role?

If, as the new director of instruction, you felt obligated to accept the list of activities as constituting your basic responsibilities, how would you want to allocate your time among them? Tell why you would favor your plan of allocation.

What School Principals Do to Lead

The pivotal, firing-line position on the curriculum scene is often said to be the school principalship. Principals have the advantage of serving at a middle management level where they can make certain that proper attention is given to both goals and people. Principals who want to be influential in curriculum planning and implementation proceed by helping provide teachers with intrinsic rewards, by influencing teachers' beliefs about curriculum matters, and by making certain that teachers are involved in crucial decision making.[62] Effective principals help set instructional norms, maintain orderly environments for learning, and do whatever else is necessary to emphasize pupil achievement.[63]

The role of principals as improvers of teaching and learning is of such classic, historic importance that it has, until recent years, remained unquestioned.

Lately, some critics have been raising their voices against the principalship as an instructional leadership position; they would relegate it to institutional management. The justification for perpetuating the principalship as a significant position in the administrative hierarchy, however, depends on continuing to place it at the center of the instructional leadership system and on improving the education of both new and experienced principals. If we did not have principals who understood schools, pupils, and learning, we would have to invent them. This statement can be made with confidence—though a modern school of innovators would let unprepared people into the principalship. For example, state officials in New Jersey have, in the recent past, proposed nearly eliminating from principals' preparation formal professional education and replacing it with requirements with respect to achievement on a standardized test of educational leadership, a residency carried out under the supervision of a mentor, and an assessment of management and teaching skills. But most curriculum people doubt that a distant, nonspecific approach to preparation of candidates who enter school administration from other occupational fields will do. As Effective Schools research indicates, principals who do their jobs well are close physically and psychologically to classrooms and schools. They feel comfortable in talking with their staffs, monitoring teachers' work, visiting classrooms informally and often, and helping to improve the curriculum.[64]

Years of experience have shown that the familiarity of principals with details of schooling makes a great deal of difference in their effectiveness. One reason is that their goals and values complement those of their staffs and of members of the communities in which they serve.[65] Evidence from both experience and research suggests that, to influence other people in valid directions, principals need to be personally secure, tolerant, analytical in their approach, and willing to involve others in worthwhile activities. But these personal qualities are not enough, for they may be found in ill-prepared people. The principal needs to *know,* and he or she needs to have a vision of ways of increasing pupils' achievement. Knowing theory and practice and possessing both a vision and the ability to communicate it to others are essentials in an era in which more and more youngsters are in danger of failure and of leaving school.[66]

Principals who are truly effective leaders in curriculum planning know the bases that support curriculum decisions. They understand curriculum design, and they function well as organizers and coordinators. They know how people are helped to change their behavior and what they themselves can do to encourage worthwhile change in others. As persons who keep activities in perspective and balance, they lead people both within their schools and in their communities. They are close to the needs and concerns of teachers and pupils, and they are able to translate ideals into day-to-day realities. In short, they epitomize the best in leadership by manifesting executive ability and maintaining desirable human relations. Significantly, they accomplish their work in the most important place in the school system—the individual school. They adapt master plans to fit their schools, guide and coordinate local planning, tailor inservice education and staff development to the needs of their own teachers, supervise teaching, suggest and implement evaluation plans, and help with experimentation and research. William Rutherford prepared still another summary of what effective principals do as curriculum leaders: (1) They have visions about the destinies of their schools, (2) they translate these visions into goals and expectations, (3) they establish helpful school climates, (4) they monitor educational progress, and (5) when necessary, they intervene to support and correct.[67]

To know and do all the things that have been noted in the preceding paragraphs, incumbent principals and candidates for the principalship need both "book learning" and experiential study and practice. To this end, a number of academies and special programs have been organized to emphasize the experiential approach. They include Indiana's Principal Leadership Academy, the Utah Principals' Academy, the Danforth Program for the Preparation of School Principals, the Performance-Based Preparation Program for Principals, and the Leaders' Preparation Program at Brigham Young University.[68]

In the past, principals were not noted for having exceptionally strong preparation in the curriculum field. In years to come, however, internal problems with principals may be less common than threats to principals' roles and functions coming from outside schools. A study distributed by the Education Commission of the States shows that policy makers at the state level are unfamiliar with and possibly unconcerned about the demands being placed on principals.[69]

Other barriers to effective performance by principals originate inside schools and school systems. As long as principals are expected to be jacks of all kinds of managerial trades, their idealized destiny as curriculum leaders cannot be fully realized. As Allen C. Ornstein says, leaking roofs, shrinking budgets, and personnel squabbles simply consume too much of principals' time.[70]

ACTIVITY 11-11

What the Best Principals Do to Lead

Identify by professional reputation two or three principals who are believed to have done a great deal to help improve the curricula of their schools. Inquire as deeply as you can into the reasons for their reputations. Do this by asking persons who know them professionally what the principals have done to merit recognition as curriculum improvers. Then talk with the principals directly about their accomplishments.

What do you conclude that these principals have done to assist with curriculum planning?

As you compare your findings with those of classmates who have inquired about other principals, what do you discover the best principals do to make curriculum improvement possible and effective?

What Local School Coordinators and Chairpersons Do to Lead

Coordinators in elementary and secondary schools and department or division chairpersons in secondary schools are closest to the sites at which curriculum is implemented. They are close to curriculum needs as expressed by teachers and others in immediate learning environments. Thus their input is essential to careful, thorough curriculum planning.

Local coordinators and chairpersons need to know all they can about the details of curriculum. They should know the subject matter both within the range of their supervisory responsibility and beyond. In addition, they should make themselves as expert as possible in the process of curriculum change, in techniques of teaching varied kinds of learning content, in organizing instruction, and in dealing with great varieties of instructional problems. No one in the local school environment should be expected to know more about available instructional materials, their selection, and their use. Increasingly, the emphasis in school operation has fallen on coordination. Therefore coordinators and chairpersons are relied on heavily for assisting people and interrelating subject matter to the end of coordinating elements of the curriculum.

Characteristically, local coordinators and chairpersons assume leadership in the following areas of responsibility:

1. Setting instructional goals pertinent to the work of their instructional units
2. Designing units of instruction
3. Adapting to local use selected curriculum plans devised elsewhere
4. Developing new curriculum proposals and plans for their departments and divisions
5. Evaluating and selecting learning materials
6. Producing new learning materials specific to local needs
7. Evaluating the long-term effectiveness of learning materials
8. Reassessing goals and objectives
9. Preparing change strategies.[71]

The weekly log of a coordinator serving two elementary schools within a given school district listed the following tasks relative to curriculum matters, excerpted from the total range of tasks performed by the coordinator during a week in April: recommended textbooks for adoption following a series of staff meetings on textbook needs; sent away for sample curriculum materials in elementary school science; conferred with other coordinators about curriculum proposals affecting the work of all of them; and advised a school librarian about purchases of children's books and other materials.[72] Although not all the weeks in a school year are filled with many significant tasks, this example highlights some of the major responsibilities that fall to coordinators.

Most coordinators and chairpersons participate in implementing at least four of the six leadership strategies discussed previously: coordinated local planning, inservice education and staff development, planned programs of supervision, and educational experimentation and research. Essential to implementation of the strategies are the ideas of collaboration and collegiality. Efforts to further social health and educational progress through collaboration and collegiality can readily begin where coordinators and chairpersons work. Most of the literature describes coordinators' and chairpersons' work with teachers in individual schools as a prelude to further work in curriculum councils, local professional associations, regional study groups, counterpart arrangements with other school districts, and national and state organizations.[73]

SITUATION 11-8

How Far Does Competency in Leadership Extend?

When the Blankton Valley Schools employed Dana Jenkins as general supervisor, they found the best supervisor in the whole state. Dana seemed to have all the personal qualities, skills, and understandings anyone could ask for in an instructional leader. Members of the Board of Education were impressed with her knowledge of curriculum problems, as was Superintendent Roush. Roush had always had one reservation about Dana, however. "How," he'd asked several people, "can someone know about instruction from kindergarten all the way through the twelfth grade?"

Superintendent Roush found his reservation borne out when the "Adams case" developed at the high school. Miss Adams, a second-year teacher, was, in the words of the high school principal, "doing only fairly well." The principal asked Dana to visit Miss Adams's French classes, and she did so on three separate occasions. Dana concluded that Miss Adams was not doing at all well. Miss Adams was almost sadistic in her treatment of the pupils, ridiculing and embarrassing them and assigning them unreasonable loads of work. In addition, she was using antiquated and questionable methods of teaching. Accordingly, Dana wrote an adverse report and conferred with Miss Adams and the principal about it.

Miss Adams, who was the daughter of the town's most influential and wealthy merchant, prided herself on her knowledge of French. Having been in France on nine separate occasions and having secured a masters degree in the teaching of French, she knew that she was, technically, an excellent French teacher. When she faced Dana in the presence of the principal and the superintendent and later in a Board of Education dismissal hearing, which was attended by her father's two lawyers, she forced Dana to admit that she knew no French. The superintendent, the board members, and nearly everyone else in the Board of Education room began to question Dana's competency to judge Miss Adams's teaching.

What should Dana have said to the Blankton Valley Board of Education about her qualifications for judging Miss Adams's work? What rather typical lay points of view about teaching and learning was she encountering?

To make a well-rounded estimate of Miss Adams's performance in the classroom, what help should Dana have had? Where might she have secured this help?

What, apparently, was Superintendent Roush's viewpoint about the qualifications a curriculum leader should have? What, then, was probably his view of curriculum leadership?

Our Hope for the Future

Books on curriculum planning may properly conclude with a forward-looking statement. When people lead other people, sometimes continuously, sometimes intermittently, and sometimes interchangeably, hope of improving a complexity like the curriculum is magnified. By experiencing leadership patterns and situations in varied schools, students of curriculum leadership have formulated ideas that can guide action during coming years.

People who have important work to do want to be led. Depending on the nature of the work, they need to be helped by either status leaders or emergent leaders. The emergent leaders usually appear *entre nous;* therefore nearly any member of a faculty or other group may be expected to lead temporarily.[74]

The hope for exercise of constructive, distributed leadership rests on several premises:

- We must emphasize the psychic rewards one gains by helping other people learn.
- We must identify and pursue goals that take into account present deficiencies in both the competency and moral/ethical domains.
- We must find and reward new teachers who will accord with these goals.
- We must give teachers, parents, and others numerous opportunities for collaboration.
- We must be ready for changes in the structure of what we now call schooling, to the end that our goals may actually be met. Can we imagine, for example, that the traditional schoolhouse may give way to centers of education beginning with the home and utilizing counseling and coaching centers, centers for library and media service, centers for laboratory experience, and places for group activities of all kinds?

Surely, the challenges to alert leadership are many!

SUMMARY

Curriculum leadership, like leadership generally, has in it elements of mystery. We know, however, that the words *principle, commitment, cooperation,* and *skill* figure prominently in any definition of curriculum leadership. Several theories of leadership have appeared in the literature during recent years. Obviously, a number of factors influence the quality of curriculum leaders' work. They include, for instance, the leaders' roles, styles, and behaviors, and also the outside factor of people's perception of leaders and leadership.

A half-dozen strategies for improving the curriculum have become the obligation and responsibility of curriculum leaders. They are strategic, centralized planning; coordinated local planning; inservice education and staff development; supervision of personnel; the reorganization, or restructuring, of schools; and curriculum experimentation and elementary research. With the help of unofficial or emergent leaders, three groups of status leaders find ample work to do: leaders with system-wide assignments, principals of schools, and local coordinators and chairpersons.

ENDNOTES

1. Edward Pajak, *The Central Office Supervisor of Curriculum and Instruction: Setting the Stage for Success* (Boston: Allyn and Bacon, 1989), 153–156.

2. Ibid., 156–158.

3. Association for Supervision and Curriculum Development, *Leadership for Improving Instruction,* 1960 Yearbook (Washington, DC: The Association, 1960), 27.

4. Ibid.

5. Luvern L. Cunningham, "Leaders and Leadership: 1985 and Beyond," *Phi Delta Kappan* 67, no. 1 (September 1985): 17–20.

6. Luvern L. Cunningham, "Educational Leadership and Administration: Retrospective and Prospective Views," in Brad Mitchell and Luvern L. Cunningham, eds., *Educational Leadership and Changing Contexts of Families, Communities, and Schools,* National Society for the Study of Education, Eighty-Ninth Yearbook, Part II (Chicago: University of Chicago Press, 1990), 12–16.

7. Gordon N. Mackenzie and Stephen M. Corey, *Instructional Leadership* (New York: Bureau of Publications, Teachers College, 1954), 23–30.

8. Karolyn J. Snyder, "Instructional Leadership for Productive Schools," *Educational Leadership* 40, no. 5 (February 1983): 32–37; see also Floretta Dukes McKenzie's discussion of leadership in an "information society" entitled "Leadership: The Critical Variable," a paper presented at the annual meeting of the Florida Association of School Administrators, Orlando, June 1985.

9. Douglas McGregor, *The Human Side of Enterprise* (New York: McGraw-Hill, 1960).

10. See James O'Hanlon, "Theory Z in School Administration?" *Educational Leadership* 40, no. 5 (February 1983): 16–18.

11. William Ouchi, *Theory Z* (Reading, MA: Addison-Wesley, 1981).

12. Some of the most helpful and interesting references concerning the traits theory are as follows: Graham B. Bell and Harry E. Hall, Jr., "The Relationship Between Leadership and Empathy," *Journal of Abnormal and Social Psychology* 49 (January 1954); Raymond B. Cattell and Glen F. Stice, *The Psychodynamics of Small Groups* (Urbana: University of Illinois, 1953); and F. Loyal Greer, Eugene H. Galanter, and Peter G. Nordlie, "Interpersonal Knowledge and Group Effectiveness," *Journal of Abnormal and Social Psychology* 49 (July 1954); see also William E. Martin, Neal Gross, and John G. Darley, "Studies of Group Behavior: Leaders, Followers, and Isolates in Small Organized Groups," *Journal of Abnormal and Social Psychology* 41, no. 4 (October 1952), 842; Launor F. Carter, "Some Research on Leadership in Small Groups," in Harold Guetzkow, ed., *Groups, Leadership and Men* (Pittsburgh: Carnegie Press, 1951), 151; and Fillmore H. Sanford, "Leadership Identification and Acceptance," in Guetzkow, *Groups, Leadership and Men,* 174.

13. Kimball Wiles, "Human Relations Approach to Supervision," address to Baltimore supervisors, *Baltimore Bulletin of Education* 37, no. 1 (November 1959): 19.

14. Valued references concerning group theory include John K. Hemphill, *Situational Factors in Leadership* (Columbus, OH: Bureau of Educational Research, Ohio State University, 1949); Gordon Lippitt and Warren H. Schmidt, *My Group and I* (Washington, DC: Arthur C. Croft, 1952); and Muzafer Sherif and M. O. Wilson, eds., *Group Relations at the Crossroads* (New York: Harper and Row, 1953).

15. Cecil A. Gibb, "Leadership," in Gardner Lindzey, ed., *Handbook of Social Psychology* (Cambridge, MA: Addison-Wesley, 1954), vol. 2, 901.

16. Philip E. Gates, Kenneth H. Blanchard, and Paul Hersey, "Diagnosing Educational Leadership Problems: A Situational Approach," *Educational Leadership* 33, no. 5 (February 1976): 348–354.

17. See Gerald R. Firth, "Theories of Leadership: Where Do We Stand?" *Educational Leadership* 33, no. 5 (February 1976): 327–331.

18. Fred E. Fiedler, "The Effects of Leadership Training and Experience: A Contingency Model Interpretation," *Administrative Science Quarterly* 17, no. 4 (December 1972): 453–470.

19. Douglas E. Mitchell and Sharon Tucker, "Leadership as a Way of Thinking," *Educational Leadership* 49, no. 5 (February 1992): 30–35.

20. James McGregor Burns, *Leadership* (New York: Harper and Row, 1978).

21. Thomas J. Sergiovanni, *Moral Leadership: Getting to the Heart of School Improvement* (San Francisco: Jossey-Bass, 1992).

22. From descriptions given by practitioners in the author's classes.

23. See Fred E. Fiedler, *A Theory of Leadership Effectiveness* (New York: McGraw-Hill, 1967).

24. Gene Hall et al., "Effects of Three Principal Styles on School Improvement," *Educational Leadership* 41, no. 5 (February 1984): 22–29.

25. Jo Ann Mazzarella and Stuart C. Smith, *School Leadership: Handbook for Excellence,* 2nd ed. (Eugene, OR: ERIC Clearinghouse on Educational Management, 1989).

26. Daniel W. Kunz and Wayne K. Hoy, "Leadership Style of Principals and the Professional Zone of Acceptance of Teachers," *Educational Administration Quarterly* 12, no. 3 (Fall 1976): 49–64.

27. Donald L. Piper, "Decisionmaking: Decisions Made by Individuals vs. Those Made by Group Consensus or Group Participation," *Educational Administration Quarterly* 10, no. 2 (Spring 1974): 82–95.

28. Andrew W. Halpin, *Theory and Research in Administration* (New York: Macmillan, 1966), 88, 89.

29. Ronald C. Doll, *Leadership to Improve Schools* (Worthington, Ohio: Charles A. Jones, 1972), 40–54.

30. Halpin, *Theory and Research in Administration,* 88, 89.

31. From an inspection of literature in industrial relations.

32. Roald F. Campbell and Russell T. Gregg, *Administrative Behavior in Education* (New York: Harper and Row, 1957), 280.

33. Ibid.

34. William F. Whyte, *Leadership and Group Participation,* Bulletin No. 24 (Ithaca: New York State School of Industrial and Labor Relations, Cornell University, May 1953), 41.

35. Hollis L. Caswell et al., *Curriculum Improvement in Public School Systems* (New York: Bureau of Publications, Teachers College, 1950), 81, 82.

36. See the treatment of the first two viewpoints by Abraham Zaleznik in *Human Dimensions of Leadership* (New York: Harper and Row, 1966). Zaleznik favors the Freudian view, which is the second viewpoint.

37. Michael Fullan, "Coordinating Top-down and Bottom-up Strategies for Educational Reform," in Richard F. Elmore and Susan H. Fuhrman, eds., *The Governance of Curriculum,* 1994 Yearbook (Alexandria, VA: Association for Supervision and Curriculum Development, 1994), 208.

38. P. Senge, *The Fifth Dimension* (New York: Doubleday, 1990), 290.

39. Ronald C. Doll, A. Harry Passow, and Stephen M. Corey, *Organizing for Curriculum Improvement* (New York: Bureau of Publications, Teachers College, 1953).

40. Fullan, "Coordinating Top-down and Bottom-up Strategies for Educational Reform," 190–193.

41. Louis J. Rubin, ed., *Improving In-service Education: Proposals and Procedures for Change* (Boston: Allyn and Bacon, 1971), 276.

42. Earl C. Kelley, *The Workshop Way of Learning* (New York: Harper and Row, 1951). This book is a classic in its field.

43. Kathryn V. Feyereisen, J. John Fiorino, and Arlene T. Nowak, *Supervision and Curriculum Renewal: A Systems Approach* (New York: Appleton-Century-Crofts, 1970).

44. Thomas J. Sergiovanni and Robert J. Starratt, *Supervision: Human Perspectives,* 2nd ed. (New York: McGraw-Hill, 1979).

45. Ibid.

46. Ronald C. Doll, *Supervision for Staff Development* (Boston: Allyn and Bacon, 1983). Used with the permission of the publisher.

47. See Charles E. Moore, "12 Secrets of Restructured Schools," *Education Digest* 39, no. 4 (December 1993): 23–26.

48. Bernard McKenna, "Policy Implications of Research on Class Size: View from the National Education Association," in Gene V. Glass et al., eds., *School Class Size: Research and Policy* (Beverly Hills, CA: Sage, 1984), 93–102.

49. Judith Warren Little, "The Power of Organizational Setting: School Norms and Staff Development," a paper presented at the annual meeting of the American Educational Research Association, Los Angeles, April 1981.

50. See Ann Lieberman and Lynne Miller, "Restructuring Schools: What Matters and What Works," *Phi Delta Kappan* 71, no. 10 (June 1990): 759–764.

51. Anne Watson et al., "A Lab School Explores Self-Governance," *Educational Leadership* 49, no. 5 (February 1992): 57–60.

52. These four elements are distinguished by their unswerving focus on goals.

53. Stephen M. Corey, *Action Research to Improve School Practices* (New York: Teachers College Press, 1953), 40, 41.

54. Thomas O'Neill Dunne and Rick Maurer, "Improving Your School Through Quality Circles," *Bulletin of the National Association of Secondary School Principals* 66, no. 457 (November 1982): 87–90.

55. The Association for Supervision and Curriculum Development has produced a videotape that demonstrates use of the four steps.

56. Center on Evaluation, Development and Research, "Research Bulletin," Phi Delta Kappa, March 1986.

57. Ann Lieberman and Lynne Miller, "Problems and Possibilities of Institutionalizing Teacher Research," in Sandra Hollingsworth and Hugh Sockett, eds., *Teacher Research and Educational Reform,* National Society for the Study of Education, Ninety-Third Yearbook, Part I (Chicago: University of Chicago Press, 1994).

58. For further discussion of these tasks, see Association for Supervision and Curriculum Development, *Leadership for Improving Instruction,* 1960 Yearbook (Washington, DC: The Association, 1960); see also Doll, *Leadership to Improve Schools,* 130–328.

59. See, for example, Ann M. Little et al., "Developmental Needs Data as Determinants for Professional Development Offerings in University Settings," a paper presented at the annual meeting of the Southern Regional Council on Educational Administration, Atlanta, November 1986.

60. Pajak, *The Central Office Supervisor of Curriculum and Instruction,* 229–234.

61. Ibid., 180.

62. See John A. Ross, "Strategies for Curriculum Leadership," *The Australian Administrator* 2, no. 5 (October 1981).

63. ERIC Clearinghouse on Educational Management, *Research Action Brief* 23 (February 1984).

64. Greg K. Gibbs, "Effective Schools Research: The Principal as Instructional Leader," a personal statement 1989; see also Marilyn L. Grady et al., "A Review of Effective Schools Research as It Relates to Effective Principals," a monograph prepared for the University Council for Educational Administration, Tempe, Arizona, 1989.

65. Roslyn Moorhead and William Nediger, "Behaviours of Effective Principals," a paper

presented at the annual meeting of the Canadian Society for the Study of Education, Quebec, Canada, June 1989.

66. Barnett Berry and Rick Ginsberg, "Effective Schools, Teachers, and Principals: Today's Evidence, Tomorrow's Prospects," in Mitchell and Cunningham, eds., *Educational Leadership and Changing Contexts of Families, Communities, and Schools*, 155–178.

67. William L. Rutherford, "School Principals as Effective Leaders," *Phi Delta Kappan* 67, no. 1 (September 1985): 31–34.

68. Jerry Rodriguez, "Growing towards Excellence: An Experiential Approach to the Professional Development of School Leaders," a paper presented at the International Conference on Educational Leadership, Cologne, Germany, July 1989.

69. "Study Notes Lack of Policy Activity on Principalship," *Education Week* 9, no. 32 (May 2, 1990): 5.

70. Allan C. Ornstein, "Leaders and Losers: How Principals Succeed," *The Executive Educator* 15 (August 1993): 28–30.

71. Thomas J. Sergiovanni, *Handbook for Effective Department Leadership: Concepts and Practices in Today's Secondary Schools* (Boston: Allyn and Bacon, 1977), 283–320; see also the second edition of this handbook, dated 1984.

72. Contributed by Eleanor Noyes, former supervisor/coordinator in the West Orange, New Jersey elementary schools.

73. See Roger Niemeyer and Robert Hatfield, "Using the Curriculum Process as the Basis for Supervision/Leadership within a Collegial Environment," a paper presented at the annual conference of the Association for Supervision and Curriculum Development, Orlando, Florida, March 1989; see also Peter P. Grimmett and E. Patricia Crehan, "Teacher Development, Collegiality, and Instructional Supervision: The Cases of Audrey and Barry," a paper presented at the International Conference on Teacher Development, Toronto, Canada, February 1989.

74. See the writings of Luverne L. Cunningham about the significance of homes and communities in achieving wider distribution of leadership.

SELECTED BIBLIOGRAPHY

Barnes, John B. *Educational Research for Classroom Teachers.* New York: G.P. Putnam's Sons, 1960.

Bennis, Warren, and Nanus, Bert. *Leaders.* New York: Harper & Row, 1985.

Berry, Barnett, and Cunningham, Luvern L. *Educational Leadership and Changing Contexts of Families, Communities, and Schools.* National Society for the Study of Education, Eighty-Ninth Yearbook, Part II. Chicago: University of Chicago Press, 1990.

Combs, Arthur W., et al. *Helping Relationships: Basic Concepts for the Helping Professions,* 2nd ed. Boston; Allyn and Bacon, 1978.

Corey, Stephen M. *Action Research to Improve School Practices.* New York: Bureau of Publications, Teachers College, 1953.

Cunningham, Luvern L., and Gephart, William J. *Leadership: The Science and the Art Today.* Twelfth Annual Phi Delta Kappa Symposium on Educational Research. Itasca, IL: Peacock, 1973.

Doll, Ronald C. *Leadership to Improve Schools.* Worthington, OH: Charles A. Jones, 1972.

———. *Supervision for Staff Development: Ideas and Application.* Boston: Allyn and Bacon, 1983.

Duke, Daniel L. *School Leadership and Instructional Improvement.* New York; Random House, 1987.

Elmore, Richard F., and Fuhrman, Susan H. *The Governance of Curriculum.* Association for Supervision and Curriculum Development, 1994 Yearbook. Alexandria, VA: The Association, 1994.

Glatthorn, Allan A. *Curriculum Leadership.* Glenview, IL: Scott, Foresman, 1987.

Glickman, Carl D., ed. *Supervision in Transition.* Association for Supervision and Curriculum Development, 1992 Yearbook. Alexandria, VA: The Association, 1992.

Griffiths, Daniel E.; Stout, Robert T.; and Forsyth, Patrick. *Better Leaders, Better Schools: Perspectives on School Administration.* National Society for the Study of Education. Chicago: University of Chicago Press, 1988.

Gwynn, J. Minor, and Chase, John B., Jr. *Curriculum Principles and Social Trends.* New York: The Macmillan Company, 1969.

Hollingsworth, Sandra, and Sockett, Hugh. *Teacher Research and Educational Reform.* National Society for the Study of Education, Ninety-Third Yearbook, Part I. Chicago: University of Chicago Press, 1994.

Holmes, Mark, and Wynne, Edward A. *Making the School an Effective Community: Belief, Practice, and Theory in School Administration.* Philadelphia: Taylor and Francis, 1989.

Hoyle, John R., et al. *Skills for Successful School Leaders.* Arlington, VA: American Association of School Administrators, 1985.

Martin, David S., et al. *Curriculum Leadership: Case Studies for Program Practitioners.* Alexandria, VA: Association for Supervision and Curriculum Development, 1989.

Pajak, Edward. *The Central Office Supervisor of Curriculum and Instruction: Setting the Stage for Success.* Boston: Allyn and Bacon, 1989.

Ross, Murray G., and Hendry, Charles E. *New Understandings of Leadership.* New York: Association Press, 1957.

Rubin, Louis J., ed. *Frontiers in School Leadership.* Chicago: Rand McNally, 1970.

———, ed. *Improving In-service Education: Proposals and Procedures for Change.* Boston: Allyn and Bacon, 1971.

Sergiovanni, Thomas J., and Starrett, Robert J. *Supervision: Human Perspectives.* New York: McGraw-Hill, 1979.

Tanner, Laurel, ed. *Critical Issues in Curriculum.* National Society for the Study of Education, Eighty-Seventh Yearbook. Chicago: University of Chicago Press, 1988.

Zaleznik, Abraham. *Human Dilemmas of Leadership.* New York: Harper and Row, 1966.

EPILOGUE

What Preparation Do Curriculum Practitioners Need?

Anyone who has read this book and other current literature knows that we are in the midst of an era of presumed school reform. In recent years, the reform movement has "progressed" from debates about ways of teaching the three Rs to deploration of the evident underachievement of pupils who now attend our schools to indictments of teachers for their alleged laxity. Eventually, the question has arisen, "How well qualified are the people in charge of our schools?" Naturally, fingers have been pointed first at school principals. During the 1980s, sixteen reports were issued concerning the performance of elementary and secondary school principals. The preparation of principals was criticized in these reports for its focus on a social science model, for its failure to help incumbents and candidates understand "the core technology of education," and for its disregard for the hard realities of the classroom. As time passed, the lay public was informed that principals simply were not leading their schools and that the education children were receiving was therefore inferior.

It occurred to political leaders in a few states that the supply of school administrators and supervisors who could be called genuinely competent was limited. These political leaders believed that a new supply of school leaders needed to be tapped. Perhaps new, able candidates could be attracted from other fields. This idea has been pursued in several places. It is likely to be extended elsewhere, despite the disillusionment that the new incumbents often feel with their lack of preparation.

The elimination of formal professional preparation from programs for principals (and earlier from programs for new classroom teachers) could spread to the education and state certification of curriculum specialists. When unqualified curriculum "mechanics" are turned loose in the schools, the current curriculum morass will deepen.

Consider the following hypothetical report of a curriculum coordinator who transferred into education from a position in business management. What happened to him is likely to happen to many an eager, able person who lacks preparation in the field of education.

I've always liked children. At one time, I thought I'd like to be an elementary school principal, but I knew that if I wanted to work in a public school, I'd have to be a teacher for perhaps three years first. I couldn't endure that much waiting. I wanted to be at the top of the heap somewhere, so I went to a good college of business administration and eventually came out with an M.B.A.

The big corporation that employed me put me into a frustrating job. After a couple of years, I was sick of the whole thing. Then I heard of what seemed to be a wonderful plan. I could actually become a curriculum coordinator in a public elementary school in less than a half-year!

Need I tell you I soon quit my job and moved to where the action was? Things moved fast, and they moved fine for a while. I landed in the fourth grade with a cooperating teacher I thought was pretty good. Before long, my 300 hours of teaching experience were over. (The experience actually consisted mostly of watching.) I passed the examination of knowledge of teaching and then had a short seminar in what they said were school situations. Within four and a half months, I was ready to coordinate!

I was placed in a kindergarten-through-sixth-grade school where most of the kids came from broken homes. I was unprepared for children who seemed unable to achieve in school and for children who didn't seem to care whether they succeeded or not. Many of the parents couldn't understand what I said to them, and I wasn't sure I understood all of it myself. The quality of the teachers, as I'd expected, seemed to vary, but no one had taught me how to tell the poor teachers from the good ones. What bothered me most, though, was the presence on the staff of three or four teachers who delighted in asking me hard questions. I began noting questions that these teachers—not to mention board of education members and PTA officials—were asking me:

"How do you school people teach arithmetic now? Is the 'new math' I was exposed to still in vogue?"

"Where do you stand on the matter of teaching phonics in an elementary school reading program?"

"Assuming that you believe in sex education, how early in the elementary school program should it be started?"

"Can you give us board members three or four criteria of high-quality teaching?"

"What's the best original science project you've seen prepared by an elementary school child?"

"If we Americans are really as illiterate as people say we are, what are some of the things you'll do to help increase literacy here?"

"What can we teachers do to help plan the curriculum? Do we have to have parents crawling all over us as we plan?"

"What children with problems would you mainstream, and what children would you put in special groups?"

"Elementary school children today are said to know more than children of the same age knew thirty or forty years ago. What do they know that's different?"

"Do you think there are central or universal values that all children should be taught? What, for instance?"

When I found that I couldn't answer questions like these, I decided to leave my shiny coordinatorship and go away to learn something. I wanted to know all I could about children, how they learn, how their homes and communities influence them, and so on. I thought the children I had met deserved no less. But my biggest shortcoming was my ignorance of curriculum matters of all sorts. That, I had discovered, was a deficiency I shared with a lot of practicing principals. The moral: Don't let yourself be thrown into water that's so deep it soon drowns you!

To be an effective curriculum practitioner, what do you need to know and what should you be able to do? On the following pages you will find an inventory of needs and requirements that ought to be addressed in the preparation of curriculum practitioners. The fifty-item inventory is divided into two parts. The first part, labeled Knowledge/Understanding, lists cognitive learnings that constitute the underpinnings of further preparation. This further preparation involves education and practice in an arena we'll call Skill/Competence—the arena in which one masters those learnings that cannot be derived from education directed toward knowledge and understanding.

Cognitive learnings can be acquired in the courses and seminars available to you in your college or university. Skill learnings to make you competent on the job can be gained through internships sponsored by colleges and universities, as well as under the auspices of regional, association, and university institutes.

An Inventory of Preparation Needs

In the arena of knowledge/understanding, curriculum practitioners need

1. To understand children and youth, especially children and youth as learners in school
2. To know the community environments from which youngsters come to school
3. To know the demands that society at large places on schools
4. To understand the cultures represented by the pupils in our schools
5. To understand psychological principles (e.g., concerning motivation to achieve) that affect pupils' ability and desire to learn
6. To know subject content that is pertinent to teaching and learning in schools
7. To know how subject matter can be taught effectively
8. To be aware of new developments and trends in individual subjects
9. To know how the process of curriculum change and improvement can work
10. To be aware of actions that can be taken to improve, rather than merely change, the curriculum
11. To know how to fit curriculum to learners, as opposed to fitting learners to curriculum
12. To be aware of current and possible systems of school organization and administration
13. To know how to direct enterprises in curriculum planning
14. To know functional methods of instructional supervision
15. To know how to conduct simple educational research
16. To understand the historical foundations of and events in movements toward curriculum improvement
17. To understand possible uses of computers and other machines for curriculum planning
18. To know alternative ways of making curriculum plans
19. To understand ways of restructuring schools to achieve educational improvement
20. To be familiar with the ideas of differing schools of educational philosophy
21. To know what curriculum plans to propose for youngsters of differing levels of ability and for youngsters with special handicaps
22. To be able to recognize the presence or absence of sequence, balance, and other features of a suitable curriculum
23. To know one's philosophical beliefs about human potential and schooling
24. To be able to recognize valid research data and conclusions
25. To know where to find help with difficult curriculum problems

In the arena of skill/competence, curriculum practitioners need

1. To be competent in reading and understanding the literature on teaching, learning, and the curriculum
2. To be competent in writing cogently and at length about curriculum matters
3. To be able to state clearly worthy aims, goals, and objectives of schooling
4. To be able to answer the questions of teachers and other people about details of the curriculum
5. To be skilled in working with parents and other community members of differing backgrounds, abilities, and cultures
6. To be skilled in conferring with teachers and curriculum specialists about difficult aspects of the curriculum
7. To demonstrate competence in proposing and developing original curriculum designs
8. To exhibit skill in directing and bringing to completion varied planning enterprises
9. To be competent in teaching other professionals and lay people to plan
10. To be skilled in leading differing groups
11. To demonstrate skill in practicing methods of instructional supervision
12. To be able to speak convincingly to the public about curriculum proposals
13. To demonstrate skill in counseling co-workers and assistants
14. To show competence in planning and implementing inservice and staff development programs
15. To show familiarity with available instructional materials
16. To be capable of helping teachers and others devise new and different instructional materials
17. To be competent in creating criterion-referenced tests
18. To be skilled in scheduling and coordinating curriculum improvement activities
19. To demonstrate skill in reconciling the conflicting viewpoints of fellow planners and in identifying and overcoming barriers to planning
20. To be able to work with officials of state or national educational agencies in the interest of curriculum improvement
21. To demonstrate skill in facilitating regional and state evaluations of the curriculum and of the improvement program
22. To be able to guide curriculum planners to significant sources of evidence
23. To be skilled in representing their school system at professional conventions and meetings of lay persons
24. To demonstrate skill in working with learners in classrooms to show the worth of new curriculum plans
25. To demonstrate grace and ease at social and professional functions where the reputation of the school counts

You may use this inventory as you wish, adding to it or subtracting from it at will. Unlike the preceding material in this book, the inventory may be reproduced freely. It may prove useful for self-analysis, or it may form a basis for group discussion.

To face the years ahead, you simply cannot be too well prepared. Sufficient preparation will help you advocate valid curriculum plans and proposals and thereby make lasting contributions to a significant field of endeavor.

NAME INDEX

SUBJECT INDEX